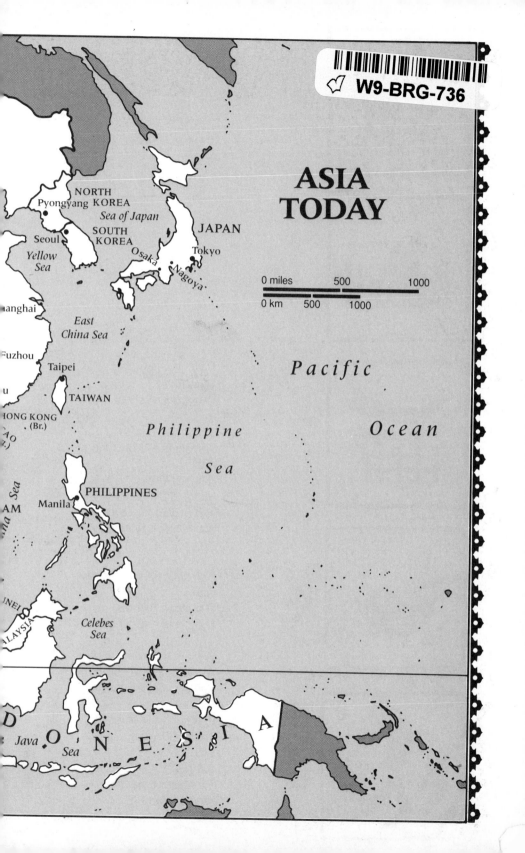

ASIA TODAY

NORTH KOREA
Pyongyang

Sea of Japan

JAPAN

SOUTH KOREA

Seoul

Osaka

Tokyo

Yellow Sea

Nagoya

anghai

East China Sea

Fuzhou

Taipei

Pacific

u

TAIWAN

HONG KONG
(Br.)

Philippine

AO
(.)

Ocean

Sea

PHILIPPINES

a Sea

Manila

AM

NEI

Celebes Sea

ALAYSIA

D O N E S I A

Java O
Sea

0 miles	500	1000
0 km	500	1000

Akira Iriye,
Harvard University

Edward J. Lazzerini,
University of New Orleans
with
Richard Yang,
*National Sun Yat-sen University
and Professor Emeritus,
Washington University*

David S. Kopf,
University of Minnesota
with
C. James Bishop,
Manchester College

William J. Miller,
*Associate Professor Emeritus,
Saint Louis University*

J. Norman Parmer,
Trinity College
with
John Cady,
*Professor Emeritus,
Ohio University*

THE
WORLD
OF
ASIA

Second Edition

Harlan Davidson, Inc.
Wheeling, Illinois 60090-6000

Library of Congress Cataloging in Publication Data
The world of Asia / Akira Iriye . . . [et.al.]. — 2nd ed.
    p. cm.
  Includes bibliographical references and index.
  ISBN 0-88295-921-2
  1. Asia—History.   I. Iriye, Akira.
DS33.W67   1995
950—dc20   95-13349
                                                     CIP

Cover design: Jay Bensen

Contents

The World of Korea
by William J. Miller

The World of Southeast Asia
by J. Norman Parmer with John Cady

Indexes

Maps

Acknowledgments

I wish to express my sincere and enthusiastic grati- tude to the staff of Harlan Davidson, Inc., espe- cially Maureen Hewitt, Vice President and Editor- in-Chief, for inspiring this revision and for all her splendid counsel and patience during its prepa- ration. Andrew J. Davidson devoted much of his valuable time to the project, especially in the final stages of publication, and Lucy Herz copyedited the chapter on Chinese history and designed the book with care and skill.

Also, I would like to thank my patient wife, Irene, who proofread so capably much of my preliminary writing and made so many valuable suggestions.

My coauthors, Edward J. Lazzerini, F. James Bishop, Richard H. Yang, J. Norman Parmer, and David Kopf deserve much praise for their hard work on the project. Finally, I would like to thank Professor Akira Iriye of Harvard University for writing the excellent and appropriate introduction for this second edition of *The World of Asia*.

William J. Miller
Editor

Introduction
Asia and America

Asian traditions are worth studying in part because, to paraphrase Sir Edmund Hillary, "they are there." They are not only there; they have been in existence for several thousand years. To study them, therefore, is to learn something about endurance, continuity, and survival. For Americans, with a much shorter history of their national society, this should be an illuminating experience.

Societies, however, are not quite the same thing as mountains. Human beings, to be sure, are part of nature; they are born, live, create their offspring, and eventually die just like plants and animals. They respond and adapt themselves to changing climatic and ecological conditions in order to survive, and they are governed by certain biological needs to perpetuate their species. However, for humanity "survival" or "existence" is not merely a physical act. It is also a cultural phenomenon, for men and women, young and old, live and survive as members of a community, and in order to have a group life it is necessary for them to have common codes and symbols. They serve as principles for organization and maintenance of society. They are the means through which people establish their identity and ascribe meaning to their collective and individual existence. As Clifford Geertz, the anthropologist, has written, "The imposition of meaning on life is the major end and primary condition of human existence." All societies develop cultural patterns which help organize personal and group experiences in meaningful fashion. Without such patterns there will be no society, and without society there will be no "human" existence. All people are alike in that they are cultural beings, but they are also different in defining their respective historical patterns. To study other societies and cultures, therefore, is to learn about the unity and diversity of humankind.

By studying how other societies have survived, we learn something about the ways in which various peoples have sought to define and maintain themselves; their belief systems, institutional setups, and interactions with other societies. We learn about one of the central questions of history: how does a society preserve order and stability amidst forces of change? All societies seek to maintain systemic equilibrium to ensure cohesion without which they will disintegrate; but at the time there are always pressures from within and without for change, such as technological advances, rebellions, and invasions. Sometimes these pressures are so intense that a society is transformed beyond recognition, and it may even cease to exist. There are also cases where, despite cataclysmic changes, people's habits and ideas remain stable. Regardless of such differences, they all tell a story of humanity as cultural beings. Americans interested in the question of their survival or of the direction in which their society seems to be moving would be well advised to turn to that story, for others have gone before them grappling with the same problems. Since a seemingly identical problem has more than one answer—in fact it has an infinite number of possible answers—we will gain a sense of perspective by studying the examples of others who have come up with their own solutions.

Americans tend to think of survival first and foremost in physical, material terms. Their national history is a story of heroic battles with forces of nature; the American drama is that of frontiersmen and women turning wilderness into a habitable land. Old settlers and new immigrants alike had to struggle to find food, shelter, and additional material comfort. Collectively, their existence and survival till the end of the nineteenth century necessitated the arduous task of fighting against the Indian tribes; but national security was relatively easy to maintain because of the country's physical separation from Europe and Asia. Protected from serious external threats, the American people built their nation from scratch. Every generation found its life an improvement over the preceding generation's; constant motion, mobility, and change characterized national history. With their society in perpetual motion, Americans often looked at other societies with disdain; other societies seemed to be moving ever so slowly or not at all. They appeared to be so preoccupied with maintaining the status quo that no innovation seemed to be possible nor improvement in living conditions; consequently, Americans expected, life in such societies would go on without a trace of progress.

And yet, if one looks more closely, one finds that Americans, no less than others, have been concerned with order and stability. Because of the very fact that the country underwent rapid material changes, there were always those even in the eighteenth century, and more in the nineteenth, who worried about the maintenance of some sense of national cohesion and identity. Rapid agricultural growth in the South before the Civil War tended to turn the region into a semi-autonomous region, while industrialization in the postbellum North created problems of unemployment, labor unrest, and anarchism. As life in America became increasingly more complex, ways had to be found to ensure social peace amid turmoil, organization out of chaos. Even as individualism and competitive spirit were singled out as unique American values and virtues, people spoke of the need for discipline and regulation in order to control social disruption and preserve stability. Thus even in a society changing as rapidly as America, concern with order was always present. This became even clearer at the beginning of the twentieth century, when government leaders, business people, and publicists grew alarmed that the nation's social and political institutions had not kept pace with the quick tempo of industrialization and urbanization. The economic transformation was accompanied by cultural change, as technological innovations such as the radio, the automobile, and the cinema were creating a mass society characterized by what some called "conspicuous consumption." The survival of American democracy amidst economic and cultural change became a key theme of national politics, and in many ways it has remained a major challenge confronting the country. Today, more than ever before, Americans are interested in social order and political stability. They recognize the necessity for some stable framework of social relations because of their awareness that the country's resources are not unlimited, and that in order to accommodate the [redifine] various cultures they have created, they must redefine the basis of national and [politics] local politics. [to acc, culture]

Another reason for the increasing concern with stability has to do with America's external relations. So long as the country was secure from attack, it had little reason to be concerned with foreign affairs. With a few notable exceptions, issues of foreign policy did not affect domestic politics or social relations. This ceased to be the case after Japan's attack on Pearl Harbor in 1941. Victory in the Second World War did not ensure security as the Cold War presented a new challenge, in circumstances in which nuclear weapons threatened to destroy the whole planet. Even the Cold War's end has not brought about a sense of equanimity in America's external relations, for such global issues as population explosion and migration, terrorism, and environmental degradation affect all nations, above all the United States because of its economic power and its relatively open immigration and refugee policies. In the meantime, the development of multinational enterprises has blurred boundaries among states, making it extremely difficult to distinguish national and international affairs. Thus we can no longer dissociate problems of internal order and stability from those of external order and stability. Americans, wondering how their country may survive constant pressures of foreign events, may turn with profit to the examples of other peoples who have had to face the same question. Many other nations have had to cope with foreign invasions and economic penetrations far worse than those that have plagued the United States, and yet they have managed to maintain a sense of national organization and cohesion. How have they done it?

These observations clearly indicate the value and relevance of studying other societies and their traditions. They help put contemporary issues in a broader, comparative perspective. But for Americans there is something particularly valuable about the study of Asia. This is because of certain historical circumstances that have made America's relations with Asia unique.

First, the United States was created out of European antecedents; although its population has always included people of non-European origin, its language, arts, political organization, and economic activities have been predominantly derived from the European tradition. America, in a word, has been a Western society. Its evolution has been part of the drama of modern Western history. That drama, at one level, has been a story of "the rise of the West" in the modern world. America became a nation just at a time when the modern West was being created, with its expansive energies overflowing distant lands. The major receptacle of that influence has been Asia, ranging from India to Japan. Although

colonialism

India, Southeast Asia, China, Korea, and Japan are so different as to make it impossible to talk of them as one civilization, nevertheless the world of Asia as a whole became an object of Western political, economic, and cultural penetration. By examining the repercussions the Western impact brought about in these countries, we can better understand a central phenomenon of modern history, often summed up by the phrase "meeting of East and West." American history, whether the people are aware of it or not, has been one part of that drama. Its part in it is inseparable from its own history, and conversely, its history cannot be fully understood without realizing what it has meant in the development of modern Asia.

Second, although the United States is by and large oriented toward the European world, it has also been a country astride two oceans. Americans may not consider themselves Asians, but they would not hesitate to call their country a Pacific power. It has been no less an Asian nation than Russia. American merchants, business people, educators, and missionaries have been involved in the lives of Asians just as extensively as their European counterparts. It is well known that American economic development—such as the growth of the Southern cotton textile industry and the development of New England shipping—has been bound up, to a considerable extent, with Asia. Equally familiar is the fact that the United States has been involved in Asian wars—in the Philippines in 1898, against Japan in 1941, in the civil wars of Korea and Vietnam more recently—on more occasions than in European conflicts. Less obvious but equally significant has been the transformation of American culture and politics brought about by the contact with Asian immigrants, visitors, and various artifacts. Today it does not seem peculiar to find, even in a small rural community in New England or the Midwest, a Chinese restaurant side by side with a gasoline service station and a post office. In Hawaii and California, Asian Americans have become a major force in politics. In large cities throughout the country one encounters immigrants from nearly all Asian countries, and the sense that they are quaint or "non-American" has dissipated over the years as the country has become more deeply involved in Asian military, political, and economic affairs.

Third, in recent years the destinies of the United States and the Asian countries have become more closely interwoven than ever before because of fast economic changes in the Asian-Pacific region. First Japan, then the "four little dragons" (South Korea, Taiwan, Hong Kong, Singapore), then the countries comprising the Association of Southeast Asian Nations, and now China and India—these countries have undertaken economic growth with unprecedented speed. The "Asian economic miracle" has transformed the region into the fastest growing area in the world, now producing more than a quarter of global industrial output and accounting for over 20 percent of international trade. The whole area, which only a few decades ago seemed to contain teeming millions with inadequate food and shelter, is literally bursting at the seams with productive energy—and with higher and higher living standards. Per capita incomes in some Asian countries even exceed those of many European nations.

The United States has been very much part of this story. It supplied large portions of the initial funds for Asian industrialization through foreign aid, loans, investment, and technology transfer; it absorbed huge quantities of Asian exports, enabling trans-Pacific trade to surpass trans-Atlantic trade in 1982 for the first time in history; and some Asian countries, in their turn, began building factories in the United States, employing tens of thousands of American workers. Not only American business but also the national government borrowed money from Asian sources. In the meantime, the United States provided for regional security first through the strategy of containment and then through a detente with the People's Republic of China. The containment strategy often created American-Asian tensions, as seen most notably during the Vietnam war, and the U.S.-Chinese rapprochement did not lead to the creation of a regional security apparatus comparable to the Conference on European Security and Cooperation, established in Europe in 1972. Still, America's military presence did enable Asian countries to devote more and more of their resources to economic objectives.

[handwritten margin note: A relaxing as of strained relations btwn. Nations]

To learn about Asia, then, is to come to a fuller understanding of American history, society, and culture. It is to study the roles the United States has played in modern Asian history, and the roles Asians have played in America's own development. Through such an inquiry we learn how human societies have interacted with one another to the point where today their politics, economic activities, and aesthetic tastes are more interdependent than ever before. We will then be able to view international affairs as intercultural relations, and to appreciate the rich cultural contexts in which American foreign policy operates. Most important, in their own contemporary search for order and meaning in social and individual life, the American people will find much that is suggestive in the ways that Asians have for centuries sought to establish a stable relationship between individuals, nature, and society.

It may be argued that most Americans are so convinced of their superiority that they will find little that is instructive or usable in other peoples' traditions. It is to be hoped that the readers of this volume will be disabused of such cultural arrogance. At the very least, they should realize that the sense of superiority is itself a product of intercultural relations. It dates from the economic and cultural transformation of Europe in the eighteenth century. It is well to recall that by about 1700, which coincided with the period of gestation for what would become the American nation, Asian societies had produced mature civilizations. China, the most developed society in Asia at that time, had been able to maintain relative political and cultural stability for nearly two thousand years. First united as one empire at the time of the Roman republic's wars against the Carthaginians (around 220 B.C.), the country developed political institutions and cultural patterns which remained more or less immutable through the centuries. While Europe went through successive stages of cataclysmic change, from the rise and fall of the Roman empire to the emergence of feudalism, from medieval Christian unity to the Protestant Reformation, and from Arabic science to Newtonian physics, China remained one civilization, and, generally speaking, one political entity. It was a system in which power and culture sustained each other; the state was ruled by the emperor and his servants, the bureaucrats, both of whom were supposed to act in accordance with the canon of Confucianism. There was a harmony of nature, people, and society, not an alienation between nature and people or between society and the individual. All embodied certain principles of concord; everything and every person complemented one another; and a person's position in society determined his or her existence, just as all natural bodies had their proper places in the cosmic universe. Poetry, art, and music echoed this sense of harmony. There were, of course, changes. They were caused by natural disasters such as floods and drought, by human conduct such as an incompetent emperor, and by invasions of nomadic "barbarians." Periods of instability, however, were almost always followed by the reestablishment of Confucian order, as though nothing had really changed. Actually, much had changed, but the Chinese on the whole preferred to believe that their fundamental system of politics and culture had remained strong. Even barbarian invaders such as the Mongols and Manchus made use of Confucian scholars as officials, and they were just as eager as all others to proclaim themselves to be Sons of Heaven. Intellectually, centuries of accumulated wisdom consisted mostly of commentaries on, and compendia of, the classics. They had all the answers; if a question did not have an answer, something was wrong with the question itself. Common people, no less than scholars, argued among themselves, but most disputes were settled through personal intercession, not by resorting to an impartial court of justice.

This was a society characterized by systemic durability and conceptual harmony. It was not unlike eighteenth-century Europe, in the Age of Enlightenment. European civilization, too, had reached a maturation point, a plateau, around 1700. Much had happened, of course, during the religious wars of the seventeenth century and the emergence of modern nation-states which accompanied it. But as a reaction against such change and disunity, people of the new era stressed rationalism, moderation, and balance, as against conflict, emotion, and extremism. The new sense of stability and cosmic harmony which had been generated by the writings of Isaac Newton and John Locke was not, to be sure, the same thing as Confucian rationalism. The point is, however, that both were autonomous systems of thought with practical implications, and that both provided intellectual underpinnings for a smooth functioning of society. Equally important, there was no frontal collision or violent confrontation between the two. They kept their distance as two centers of civilization, each going its own, predictable way. Although the situation was not exactly identical with regard to other countries of Asia, these other countries shared some of the same orientations toward political and cultural stability. This was certainly the case in Japan where the early eighteenth century saw the apogee of samurai-and-merchant civilization, and in Korea where the prestige of Confucian scholars was reaching its zenith. The countries of India and Southeast Asia were politically more complex, but they, too, developed more or less on their own cultural momentum, attaining a level of sophistication and elegance rivaling those of China or Japan.

In a world such as this, it made relatively little difference where one lived; so long as a person belonged to an historical tradition, he or she had a fairly predictable view of life and society. To go from a point in Europe to a point in Asia was to leave one civilization for another, neither of which was considered unquestionably superior to, or dominant over, the other. If you were a European around 1700, you might have been curious about Indian architecture or Chinese philosophy or Japanese art, but you would not have "learned" much from Asian culture any more than an Asian might have learned from Europe. You would have been content with what your society and culture offered to you. Neither would you have felt that your well-being was dependent on what went on in distant lands.

The picture would never again be the same after the middle of the eighteenth century. The physical distance between Europe and Asia would be shortened, thanks to technological innovations brought about by the introduction of steam and, later, electrical power in the West; at the same time, these innovations would bring about a sharper differentiation than ever between the two civilizations. While Europe and the United States made use of the new sources of power and revolutionized productive activities, creating a new class of factory workers, urban dwellers, consumers, and capitalists, the countries of Asia carried on their affairs much as their ancestors had for centuries. The Industrial Revolution, moreover, was accompanied in the West by various social movements assaulting existing institutions, by the concept of "the rights of man," by popular participation in politics and culture, and by a much stronger sense of national pride and prejudice than had ever existed. Monarchies fell, new nations were created, the authority of established religion was undermined, mass armies marched across national boundaries, and traditional customs were abandoned. These changes within the West were matched by a transformation of Western relations with other countries in the world. Western goods, ships, and merchants began pouring out of Europe and America. The rest of the world became a huge market for products of the Industrial Revolution. This economic expansion was sustained by a sense of military and, ultimately, cultural superiority of the West. Gunboats supported merchants, who began speaking of the universal law of mankind to open up all ports to foreign commerce. Commercial dealings now required the observance of European international law by other societies. These merchants were no longer servants of the crown but represented private interests, pursuing their own trade profits and opportunities. Still, they were "extraterritorial" people, not subject to the control of the local governments but enjoying the protection of their own countries' political and military power.

They were not only Westerners arriving in Asia. They were joined by missionaries, educators, travelers, and adventurers who found it relatively easy to travel to distant lands, physically as well as mentally. Few of them now would have to undergo the kinds of hardship a Francis Xavier had experienced in an earlier century. In the aftermath of the American, French, and Industrial Revolutions, Europeans and Americans developed a vision of history as one tending toward greater material comfort and liberal values. When they went to Asia they inevitably asked if Asians lived more comfortably than the people they had left behind, and if political rights and individual liberty flourished as much in Asia as in the West. The answer to all these questions was, predictably, in the negative. Still, they went to Asia, not because they enjoyed relative poverty and oppression, but because they were richer and more enlightened, and also, though not always, because they believed they could change the traditional societies and bring them closer to the fulfillment of their potentials as defined by Western conceptions of liberty, rights, and opportunity. Asia was to be "developed" just as the West had been, so that in time its millions would be "awakened" and join the march of progress.

sounds like he's questioning this vision of history

The result of this wave of Westerners going to Asia was the accelerated diffusion of Western ideas, knowledge, goods, funds, customs, and life-styles to Asian societies. A changing and expanding West was intruding upon a traditional and stable Asia, both of which had boasted their own unique cultural heritages. But it would be too simplistic to say that Asia was automatically transformed as an inevitable result of this diffusion. Rather, the important fact was that the whole region became a laboratory to determine how its different parts appropriated and, consciously or unconsciously, became affected by various aspects of Western civilization. How would the social and cultural system of a country change as a result of the infusion of foreign influences? How could one measure change? How, amidst drastic transformation, could societies maintain stability? These were among the most intriguing questions of the nineteenth century. Asia was a fascinating region for exploring them because its various regions offered differing solutions. Japan managed to subject itself to a great deal of cultural change without losing national independence; China changed relatively little culturally but underwent one serious political crisis after another; Indochina became colonized by Western powers, as did India and Burma. And yet, throughout Asia there remained a great deal of social stability underneath such a drama. Life in the villages went on very much as it had for centuries; the landed gentry retained prestige and power; and the mass of people was not incorporated into national politics. Even when, toward the end of the century, Asian countries began to industrialize, it was far from clear that they would generate a class-conscious labor force as in the West, or that industrialization would transform the social and cultural outlooks of Asians.

It was the political implication of this question of change versus stability which particularly fascinated Western observers in the first half of the twentieth century. They still retained a liberal vision of changing Asia along Western lines. But they were less and less certain whether such a transformation was really possible; some of them doubted that even if it were possible it would necessarily be a good thing either for Asians or for Westerners. Much was written about the conflict between East and West. It reflected a concern with the persistence of premodern traits in the face of the physical transformation of traditional societies. It also expressed misgivings about Asia's political, economic, and military strengthening without the underpinnings of social and cultural values. If Asia should transform itself materially but not spiritually, would it not pose a serious threat to Western supremacy in the world, if not to Western civilization itself? It is interesting to note that while Asia as a whole seemed to represent a monolithic cultural system, quite often it was viewed in terms of alternative paths of modernization. Japan was one extreme. It emerged as one of the three or four greatest military powers, and its economic development made it a formidable competitor in international trade. Would such a country be joining other advanced industrial countries of the West to carry on their task of modernization and, presumably, progress, or would it become a serious antagonist, an Asian country with as much power and wealth as a Western nation but without the latter's spiritual values and emotional ties? The 1920s seemed to indicate the first alternative, and the 1930s the second. China, in the meantime, never developed as a Westernized nation, going its own way to break away from the past and organize a new society. The Chinese were fiercely nationalistic, but the fulfillment of their national aspirations did not lead them along the path of Western democracy, capitalism, or liberalism. When the masses were eventually mobilized to create a new united nation, in the middle of the century, they and their leaders derived their inspiration from those strains in the Chinese and European past that had stressed such things as mass consciousness and community organization, combined with personal sacrifice and will power. India, another alternative, went through decades of colonial administration looking to an ultimate independence, and despite the absence of national unity and sovereignty, many observers argued that British rule would prepare the people for democracy and modernization better than the examples of either Japan or China could demonstrate.

In a fascinating twist of history, in the recent decades it has been Asia that changed rapidly, more rapidly indeed than the West. While it took a country like Britain two hundred years to go through various stages of industrialization, from the introduction of steam to that of iron and steel, from electrification to the spread of telecommunications technology, some countries in Asia have done all this in one generation. Industrial production, trade, national income, and just about every economic indicator has doubled, tripled, and quadrupled faster than anywhere else. Some in the West even began talking of learning from the Asian model of development, with its emphasis on governmental guidance ("industrial policy"), state-business cooperation, and high saving rates. Foreign observers have noted that despite their phenomenal economic growth, Asian countries on the whole have managed to retain social cohesiveness and political stability, although it is likely that forces for fundamental change, for instance in the protection of individual human rights, will assert themselves with increasing vigor and may in time bring about reformulation of social relations and political practice.

How the Japanese, Chinese, Indians, and other Asians have tried to preserve order and stability amidst forces of change is thus an extremely important problem of modern history. The days are past when American ways of life automatically spelled universality and superiority, or when Western culture and Western power were synonymous. Such achievements as the elimination of hunger in China, or the attainment of an extremely low crime rate in Japan, should be taken seriously by those who are troubled by similar problems in America. The Chinese and Japanese have developed drastically different ways of organizing their respective societies, the former stressing self-discipline and loyalty to the state, while the latter would make use of the psychology of interpersonal dependence for maximizing productivity and reducing waste. Neither of these examples will be immediately applicable to a society like America which is at once more individualistic and "corporatist" (that is, characterized by a strong sense of identifiable economic interests). Nevertheless, some of the problems faced by contemporary Asian societies are quite similar to those in the West, and their attempts at solving them should no longer be lightly dismissed as efforts by underdeveloped peoples or inscrutable Oriental minds. They are, after all, fellow human beings who share the planet with Americans and all others. There is nothing unnatural about asking, "How do they do it in China?" any more than it was strange for a Japanese to ask, "How do they do it in America?" All countries of the world will be richer the more they are eager to exchange information and join forces in a common quest for survival and welfare.

The key issue today, as it has always been, is self-preservation. Not only in the passive sense that the countries of Asia have managed to exist for centuries, but also in the more positive sense that they are, in their various ways, succeeding in transforming themselves without losing much of their unity and cohesiveness, there is much that Americans can learn from them. All of us have a stake in the survival of ourselves, our society, and our world. But preoccupation with one's welfare alone without an eagerness to benefit from the examples of others is a sure way to self-destruction in a world that is intimately interwoven and interdependent. Whatever America does affects Asian countries, and vice versa. Changes in such things as rates of exchange, levels of domestic saving, labor wages, or literacy in one country have immediate implications for others. Likewise, technological innovations, medical discoveries, fashions in food and clothing, or scholarly and artistic trends take little time to cross national boundaries. It is time, therefore to stop thinking of America and Asia as two separate entities. They cohabit the same universe. They are members of the Asian-Pacific region, and whether there will in time develop an Asian-Pacific community is a major question Americans and Asians are bequeathing to the twenty-first century. Above all, they are fellow humans concerned with similar problems. Their ends and their means may not be identical, but their quest for finding the right means for their respective ends is. In this quest, mutual learning is far more preferable to complacent isolation. And this, essentially, is what this book is about. Asia has learned many lessons from the West since the eighteenth century. It is time Asia gave something in return. But such reverse lessons would not mean much unless Europeans and Americans were willing to look for them. I hope they are.

Akira Iriye

The
World
of

CHINA

Introduction

1.3

China today, with about 1.2 billion people, is the world's most populated nation. In fact, one out of every four persons in the world at present speaks some dialect of Chinese. Stretching over 3.7 million square miles—from the Amur River in the north to Southeast Asia and the South China Sea, and from the Pamir Mountains in the west to the Pacific Ocean in the east—China ranks second behind Canada in land area. Only somewhat larger than the United States and located within that country's approximate latitudes, it experiences much the same climatic range and variety.

Russia.

Despite being endowed with a topography that has historically encouraged regional separatism, China owes much to geographic factors for its remarkable cultural unity. The country's location at one extremity of Eurasia and the existence of formidable natural barriers (mountains, deserts, wastelands, and oceans) along its periphery have traditionally isolated it from the rest of the world and militated against easy and extensive contacts with the other great centers of civilization. Such geographic isolation, confining though it may have been, has nevertheless stimulated the Chinese to cultivate a rich and, for the most part, indigenous culture that has never lost contact with its point of origin.

The country comprises two general areas: China Proper (the historic homeland of the Chinese) and the outlying territories of Manchuria, Mongolia, Xinjiang, and Tibet (all situated along China's frontiers and never settled by significant numbers of Chinese). China Proper has three main divisions, each centered in a river valley. In the north the Yellow River flows for 2,700 miles through an area often called "brown China." Because of irregular rainfall, this semiarid region yields only one crop a year (usually wheat, millet, or soy beans) from its wind-blown loess soil. Frequent flooding by the Yellow River has enriched the land but has often caused great destruction. Rightfully it has earned the epithet "China's Sorrow." Farther south, the Yangzi, China's longest river at 3,100 miles, dominates a second area of China Proper. Called "green China," this region enjoys

3

forty inches of rainfall a year and produces tea, rice, and silk. The lower Yangzi valley became in time the population center and heart of the country. Its largest city, Shanghai, lies near the river's mouth. Finally, the mountainous south and the adjacent West River valley make up the third area of China Proper, which for some time also included the Tonkin Delta of northern Vietnam. Canton (Guangzhou), China's second largest port city, overlooks the mouth of the West River. This area became the country's greatest rice-growing region.

Manchuria, the richest of the four outlying territories of China, lies to the north of the capital city of Beijing beyond the Great Wall. The region produces timber and wheat on its fertile plains, as well as some coal and iron. To the west of Manchuria is Mongolia, a land of desert and grassy steppe and the home of historically nomadic tribes that often invaded the Yellow River valley. Beyond Mongolia, in distant Central Asia, one finds Xinjiang, an area of high mountains and deserts, through which pass the only significant overland routes leading westward. Tibet, lying adjacent to the forbidding Himalayas (bordering India to the south), is a land whose remoteness, intense cold, and aridity have proved enormous obstacles to economic development.

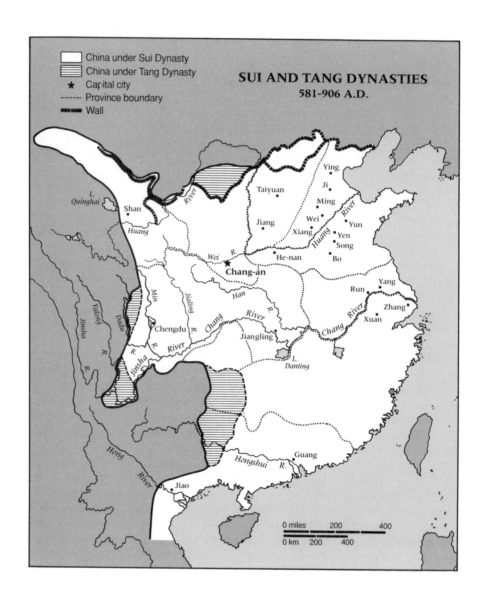

China under Sui Dynasty
China under Tang Dynasty
★ Capital city
Province boundary
Wall

SUI AND TANG DYNASTIES
581-906 A.D.

Ying

Ji

Taiyuan

Ming

L. Quinghai

Shan

Jiang

Wei

Yun

Huang River

Xiang

Huang River

Yen

Song

Wei R.

He-nan

Bo

Chang-an

Run

Yang

Min R.

Jiating R.

Han

Zhang

Yalong R.

Dadu R.

Chengdu

Chang River

River R.

Chang River

Xuan

Jinsha R.

Jinsha River

Jiangling

L. Danting

Hong River

Hongshui R.

Guang

Jiao

0 miles   200   400

0 km   200   400

Formative Age

to the Later Empire, Prehistory to 1800

1

The earliest evidence of settled life in China dates from around 4000 B.C. in the area of the northern bend of the Yellow River. From that time until the beginning of the second millennium B.C., the process leading to the birth of Chinese civilization developed slowly. While archaeologists have striven to understand precisely what took place during the late prehistoric period, the Chinese have long possessed a mythical explanation for the origins of their first societies. The myth rests upon the claim that civilized life was taught them by a number of "culture heroes" who showed them how to farm and domesticate animals, instituted family life, and created a rudimentary central government, as well as introduced the bow and arrow, the calendar, silk cloth, ceramics, and, above all, writing. The last of these "culture heroes," named Yu, is supposed to have built dams for flood control and established China's first recorded dynasty, the Xia, around 2205 B.C. The dynasty may indeed have been legendary, yet its place in Chinese mythology is strong indication that the tradition of unified government has roots deep in China's past.

Chinese recorded history begins about 1766 B.C., when an aggressive tribe of Mongolians, brandishing weapons of bronze, conquered the central portion of the Yellow River area and established the Shang dynasty. Excavations in the region have verified the existence of such a dynasty and the society it ruled. However, as with all ancient peoples, our knowledge of Shang China remains sketchy. We do know that the Shang cultivated both wheat and millet and may have introduced a system of irrigation for growing rice as well. Furthermore, it would appear that they ate dog flesh and pork and domesticated the goat, sheep, ox, horse, and chicken. Although pit dwellers at first, the Shang eventually built houses set on foundations of the closely packed loess soil of the region, with thatched roofs raised by wooden walls.

Two of the more characteristic features of Shang culture were its mastery of advanced techniques for working bronze and its development of writing. While bronze was used for a wide range of products, the most extraordinary pieces included drinking cups, chalices, libation bowls, and vases or urns of diverse sizes and shapes whose purposes may have been largely religious or ceremonial. Since the form of many Shang bronze vessels was obviously derived from the pottery styles of earlier cultures in the area, scholars have been at a loss to explain their astonishingly high level of artistry and technique in the absence of evidence of a more primitive (earlier) local bronze technology. This has fueled speculation that a considerable influence from the Near East may have contributed to this Shang capability.

Even more significant are the written records that have come down from this first period of Chinese history. Composed on animal bone, horn, or tortoise shells, numerous inscriptions have survived, providing the oldest known form of Chinese writing and most of our knowledge of Shang society. The Shang utilized these bones for divination, with the inscriptions addressed to deities or to deceased relatives, often on matters of family concern, thereby reflecting an early stage in the development of Chinese ancestor veneration. As for the script, specialists agree that the basic features and principles that characterize the present-day Chinese writing system were in place by the end of Shang.

In addition, the Shang were consummate warriors. They effectively walled in their chief settlements and took advantage of a superiority in military hardware provided by horsedrawn chariots to subdue their neighbors. Prisoners-of-war provided a major source of slaves and also hapless victims for the human sacrifices performed in religious ceremonies, including elite burials.

The Age of Zhou and Quasifeudalism

Around the year 1122 B.C., a western tribe subject to the Shang, the Zhou, defeated the forces of its overlord and established a new dynasty in China. The Zhou leadership took much from the Shang elite, especially its writing system, and intermarried with it in order to consolidate the new administration. Declaring that the last Shang ruler had been guilty of terrible crimes—and hence had forfeited the right to govern—the Zhou sought to legitimize their power by claiming that they had come to the throne by means of the rebellious actions of the people and with the "Mandate of Heaven" (*Tian-ming*). In so doing, the new dynasts introduced the concept that the people had a right granted by heaven to challenge a corrupt and unjust ruler. As the Zhou proclaimed: "Heaven sees and hears through the eyes and ears of the people." Therefore, the new leader assumed the title "Son of Heaven" (*Tian-zi*). This political theory subsequently justified every dynastic change in China until the abolition of the monarchy in 1912.

Historians divide the Zhou period into two principal eras: Western Zhou (from ca. 1122–771 B.C.), with its capital located at Hao, and Eastern Zhou (771–256 B.C.), during which the royal family and court resided in Loyang. Throughout most of the first period, the Zhou managed generally to maintain order in North China and to expand the frontiers of their realm. But even then, owing to the practice of decentralizing authority by allowing members of the royal family, favorites, and even descendants of the former Shang elite to exercise autonomy in parceled-out regions, the Zhou experienced difficulty in preserving the unity of their state. As time went on the kings were less and less successful in commanding the loyalty of subordinates as the latter slowly began to identify their own interests more with their allotted territories than with the central government. According to historian Charles O. Hucker, by the time the Zhou were forced to transfer their capital in order to escape the threat of barbarian attack, the foundation of a feudal society, with fiefs, vassalage, and protocontractual arrangements, was already in place.

After the move to Loyang, the central government ceased to wield any real power. Instead, the various regional states that emerged in increasing numbers like the cells of a beehive exercised whatever authority there was in China. Some of the local lords even presumed during the later stages of the period to call themselves "king" (*wang*), a title previously reserved for the Zhou ruler. And so it went for some four hundred years more, with the Zhou powerless to reign with authority and no single lord strong enough to win out over all others. At first, conflicts among the various states were more diplomatic than military, a matter of adroit maneuvering rather than actual fighting. But by the fifth century B.C., a change had come over those who now participated in Chinese politics: interstate conflicts became deadly wars of annexation. As strife intensified, only the strong could survive, and with time the number of independent states decreased. Driven by the ambition to capture the Mandate by military action, each of the lords exhausted himself and his domain in the protracted struggle. The ensuing chaos and destruction would not end until the third century B.C., when the western kingdom of Qin overran the other states. Not surprisingly, however, all the fundamental and confusing changes that long afflicted China now called forth an unprecedented effort by Chinese thinkers to reexamine the traditions and institutions of their society and to seek a path to a more normal and harmonious existence. Two thousand years of struggle under Zhou, B.C.

Life in Zhou Times

Before turning to a discussion of the intellectual ferment of the later Zhou period, it is useful to survey some of the other developments down to the third century B.C. that contributed to the formation of so much of what has come to be identified as traditionally Chinese.

In the realm of politics and administrative practice the concept of the Mandate of Heaven has already been noted, but to this must be added a number of other principles that became firmly established: that a single ruler (the Son of Heaven) should reign with effective centralized control over all of China; that to govern well a ruler must heed the advice of counselors and officials; that the government had the right and obligation to exert its authority in all areas of life; and that it should show a genuine concern for the welfare of the people. Beyond these principles, the political leaders of the Zhou period took steps to improve and rationalize their administrations by instituting regular taxation and substituting appointive offices for hereditary ones.

The Zhou era also witnessed the formation of two fundamental features of Chinese social organization, the family and class differentiation. The family had served as China's basic social unit at least since Shang times, but with the growth of population, the clan, based on blood kinship, extended the family's significance and added a new dimension to the country's social development that has persisted to this day. At the same time, the Chinese were proceeding to develop a society in which class distinctions were paramount. The traditional division into four classes—scholar-officials, peasants, artisans, and merchants, ranked in that order—rested on several criteria, but the most important was occupation. To the Chinese, some occupations (those demanding intellectual rather than manual labor, for example), made greater contributions to society and were therefore more important and more worthy than others.

Finally, important developments occurred in Chinese economic activity. The use of money, largely copper coins, expanded, particularly for interregional trade. New implements such as the hoe and ox-drawn plow were introduced into agriculture, as was the so-called "well-field system" of land distribution, whereby eight families lived on a central plot (with a well), worked it in communal fashion for the local lord, and labored individually on one of eight surrounding plots for their own welfare. Despite the difficulty of maintaining this system in normal, let alone, hard, times, and against land speculators, it became the traditional, ideal method of Chinese landholding.

The "Hundred Schools of Thought"
Confucianism

Amidst the social and political chaos of the later Zhou period, a small group, mostly from aristocratic families, began to devote themselves to study and contemplation. Out of their dissatisfaction with contemporary Chinese life emerged such broad and sophisticated criticism of the established conventions and institutions that the parameters of Chinese philosophy were essentially defined for all but the most recent periods of Chinese history. The analyses of and prescriptions for current ills were numerous enough for later Chinese to talk of this philosophical flowering as the "Hundred Schools of Thought." Of the various schools, five proved to have the most lasting significance for Chinese culture: Confucianism, Daoism, Moism, Naturalism, and Legalism.

In its essential points, the first was the intellectual product of Kongzi (hereafter, Confucius), who was born in 551 B.C. to a lower-ranking, possibly impoverished aristocratic family. Information concerning his life is sketchy and of doubtful authenticity, but it is reasonably certain that his early years were spent in difficult and humble circumstances. Except for about a decade in midlife when he wandered about North China trying to convince the region's rulers to apply his principles, Confucius devoted his mature years to teaching.

Confucius viewed politics as an ethical problem and social improvement as a matter of individual morality. Order and good government would return to society only when the ruler and administrators reformed themselves and set moral standards for the rest of the population. As grass bends with the wind, to paraphrase a Confucian aphorism, so society is influenced by the ruler. Because Confucius believed that knowledge led to virtue, he emphasized the major role that education should play to ensure proper leadership.

The great sage also upheld what the Chinese call *ren*, a virtue that encompasses benevolence, love, compassion, and sympathy toward fellow human beings. The stress on *ren* reveals the central humanism (or man-centered orientation) of his philosophy. Cultivation of this virtue produces the "gentleman" (*jun-zi*), the person who is "as concerned about what is right as the petty man is about what is profitable." Any man, regardless of birth or wealth, could aspire to the perfection that should characterize the *jun-zi*, and achievement of it should

3 Greats of Confucianism - Confucius, Mengzi and Xunzi
Humanity, simplicity, and appeal to noble instincts —
reverence, virtue, respect for learning and devotion to family

Formative Age to the Later Empire   ■   11

be most highly honored. Because such ideals challenged the established aristocratic order, some historians have regarded Confucius as a revolutionary of sorts.

There is, however, another side to Confucianism which is explicitly conservative. He proclaimed the writings of the ancients to be the most important guides to virtuous behavior and extolled the Duke of Zhou (twelfth–eleventh century B.C.) as the ideal ruler. Likewise, he taught respect for authority and deference to superiors as expressed in the term *li* (social and moral propriety) and in the five basic human relationships: ruler to subject, father to son, elder brother to younger brother, husband to wife, and friend to friend, the first four of which were relationships between superiors and inferiors. These also stressed the preeminence of the family, the fundamental social unit for Confucius. He clearly viewed himself not as an innovator, but merely as a transmitter of the old ways.

Throughout the *Analects,* that collection of pithy Confucian "sayings" that provides us with our single reliable source for his thought, we find the sage attempting to deal with the everyday world of social problems and individual relationships. There is a noticeable lack of interest in religion and theology except in a negative sense, as when he says, "Being unable yet to serve men, how can one serve the spirits," or "Not yet understanding life, how can one understand death?" Instead, Confucius emphasized that it is better for people to focus their attention on immediate human problems, leaving the spirits to themselves.

One of Confucius' most important disciples was Mengzi (Mencius, ca. 372–289 B.C.), popularly known as the Second Sage. Like his mentor, Mengzi emphasized the equation between knowledge and virtue, especially for the ruler, who should cultivate "sageliness within and kingliness without." More significantly, he stressed that the virtue of a ruler must be measured by benevolence to the people. Thus the first duty of a government was to ensure the material well-being of the populace; failure to do so provided grounds for popular rebellion. If successful, the revolt would clearly signify the withdrawal of the Mandate of Heaven.

While historians regard Mengzi as a sentimentalist and idealist, they tend to see Xunzi (Hsün Tzu, ca. 300–235 B.C.), another Confucian of great stature, as a harsh, unsentimental rationalist. Unlike Mengzi, whose humanistic emphasis rested on the belief that people were by nature good, Xunzi regarded human nature as innately evil. He certainly acknowledged that education could correct personal faults and lead to virtue, but he also insisted that law, coercion, and discipline were required to control the natural human inclination to wickedness. While this last point bore some resemblance to the basic argument of the Legalists, it would be unfair and misleading to draw the parallel too closely. Xunzi, despite his assessment of the basic human character, remained a humanist.

Over the centuries the basic doctrines of Confucius would be reinterpreted time and again by his followers, at times as part of a simple evolutionary process, at other times in response to ideological challenges. Through it all, however, Confucianism survived because of its practicality devoid of mysticism, its humanity, its simplicity, and its appeal to the nobler instincts through reverence for virtue, respect for learning, and devotion to family.

Daoism

Obscurity clouds the roots of Daoism even more than those of Confucianism. One tradition holds that a certain Laozi (Old Master) served for many years as keeper of the imperial archives at Loyang before giving up his post to head west into Central Asia. Along the way, as he passed through the Great Wall, the gatekeeper admonished him by saying: "Old Man, you have lived a long time and know a great deal. Why don't you write it down before you die?" In response Laozi composed the 5,000-character text of the *Dao de Jing* (Classic of the Way and of Virtue) and thereby provided the basic source of Daoist teaching.

In opposition to the humanistic thrust of Confucianism, Daoism emphasized nature and achievement of harmony with it. Whereas Confucius advocated the pursuit of knowledge to attain virtue and hence the path (*dao*) to happiness, the philosophy of Laozi suggested something quite different: relaxed conformity to nature. Because civilization had corrupted humankind, forcing people to act contrary to nature, they should withdraw from society with its formalities and ceremonials and fit themselves into the great natural pattern. To oppose nature could only bring misery.

The ideal society for the Daoists had existed in primitive times before people needed conventions; by the same token the unborn child represented the perfect person. As the way to happiness, the *dao* defies precise definition; it is "nameless," "formless," and "fathomless." The individual must become accommodated to the impersonal natural order, actually realizing and attaining everything by doing nothing. As water overcomes obstacles in its path by flowing around them, so the *dao* triumphs by adjusting and yielding. Thus, while the Confucians had urged the ruler to direct society by moral example, the Daoists preferred that authority be discreet, governing without appearing to govern.

Although in most ways contradictory, Confucianism and Daoism complemented each other in molding the Chinese mind. Like two great rivers, they flowed through Chinese philosophy, art, and literature, appealing simultaneously to opposite sides of the Chinese character. While Confucianism taught the Chinese to be sober, moralistic, and hardworking, Daoism urged them to relax, enjoy life a little more, and cultivate their individuality. In both philosophies the Chinese found principles of enormous value that served some part of their social and personal needs. As a popular saying suggested: when in power an official followed Confucianism, but after leaving office he preferred the tranquility which Daoism offered.

Moism, Naturalism, and Legalism

Mozi (ca. 470–391 B.C.) seems to have begun his intellectual odyssey as a Confucian but to have ended it by formulating a philosophy that directly challenged revered tenets of Confucianism. For example, he regarded Confucian concern for ritual and ceremony as not only foolish and worthless but also wasteful. He thought that people should devote their attention to what is useful in promoting the material welfare of society; in fact, happiness for Mozi more than for any of the other leading philosophers was defined in material terms.

In addition to his materialism and utilitarianism, Mozi is noted for his emphasis on religion (being the only important Chinese philosopher to view religion as a means to promote proper human behavior), his concern for the middle and lower classes, and his demand for "universal love," which included a call for the abandonment of war. The latter proved especially disturbing to Confucians, because in advocating the idea of "love for all men equally," Mozi scorned the family's place of honor.

Although Mozi presented his philosophy in a more systematic and logical manner than did most of the other sages, it proved impossible to implement. As a result, despite affirming some rather profound truths, his writings received little attention in later centuries.

For its part, the Naturalist school taught that two balancing cosmic forces—the *yin* (female, passive, cold, and dark) and the *yang* (male, active, warm, and light)—governed reality. This pair, later complemented by the "five agents" theory, which argued that wood, metal, fire, water, and earth determined all natural events, represented the endless alternation of opposites throughout all nature. The symbol of this mode of thinking was a disc divided into two equal parts by a curved line, with each part shaded differently yet containing an element of the other's color to illustrate their distinction as well as their harmonious interplay. Although Naturalism failed to develop into a true school of thought, its concepts influenced later Chinese views concerning the physical universe and probably encouraged the Chinese proclivity to synthesize diverse philosophies.

The last of the major "hundred schools," Legalism, belongs in the same category as Confucianism and Daoism in terms of importance for the development of Chinese culture. Yet it stands out from these two schools by its emphasis on law, its single-minded concern for the prosperity and survival of the state, its negative attitude toward human nature and the latter's potential for improvement, and its cynicism and amorality. The Legalists found both the Confucian emphasis on *li* and the Daoist encouragement of "nonaction" to be impractical and ineffectual as means for ensuring good government. Instead they argued for a system of elaborately defined laws and regulations, replete with explicit, even exaggerated, rewards and punishments, in order to compel people to be good. A regimented population ruled over by an authoritarian monarch was the ideal for which the Legalists strove. What mattered to them in the final analysis was power, not virtue, wisdom, or talent as proclaimed by others.

Out of the era of the late Zhou dynasty there thus emerged a number of contending philosophies providing analyses of China's problems and visions of its future. Despite the success of several of them in dominating Chinese culture at different times, that domination was never complete. Except for the brief period of the Qin dynasty discussed below, the Chinese never chose one philosophy to the exclusion of the others, but rather tended to accept principles from at least the five treated here in order to create a philosophical synthesis. In the long run eclecticism rather than exclusivity came to characterize the intellectual underpinnings of Chinese society and culture.

China Unified

The Qin Dynasty, 221–207 B.C.

Qin emerged as a small state located in a valley of the Wei River west of the Zhou domain. Constantly threatened by barbarian attacks, the Qin rulers gradually organized their state along authoritarian, military lines, subordinating everything and everyone to the will of the monarch. Shang Yang, a fourth-century B.C. prime minister and one of the initial practitioners of Legalism, built perhaps the first totalitarian state in history. His policies, which included organized forced labor, military training, and secret police surveillance, fully regimented Qin society. To ensure law and order, the state held people responsible not only for their own acts but for those of relatives as well. As a political tactic, the Qin condoned any action that might prove beneficial to the state, including assassination and deception. For example, when Shang Yang arranged a conference with a neighboring ruler in order to discuss a border dispute, the prime minister ambushed him, scattering his army and seizing his territory.

A well-prepared Qin campaign led to the conquest of the Zhou in 256 B.C. Within the ensuing thirty years, six more states were overrun as easily "as a silkworm devours a mulberry leaf." Northern and central China fell under Qin domination by 221 B.C., and with the completion of military action the new rulers of China launched policies designed to obliterate the feudal system and unify the country.

King Zheng, who proclaimed himself "First Emperor" (*Shi Huangdi*), successfully completed this task. He extended the central administration of the Qin to the whole country, abolished the old semifeudal states, divided the now unified empire into administrative districts and subdistricts, and brought an end to nepotism in government employment. To contribute further to the unification of China, the First Emperor standardized the laws, customs, written language, weights and measures, agricultural tools, and even the length of cart axles so that their wheels would fit set grooves in the roadways. He also inaugurated tremendous public works projects to improve and expand China's irrigation system and construct highways (often two hundred and fifty feet wide) to link various parts of the country. Perhaps his most famous and impressive project was the extension of a fifteen-hundred-mile fortified wall to protect China's northeastern frontier from invading "barbarians." Known as the Great Wall, this structure averages twenty-five feet in elevation with towers from thirty-five to forty feet high situated every two hundred to three hundred yards. Its width of twenty-five feet at the base tapers to about fifteen feet at the top—wide enough for four horseback riders to ride or eight soldiers to walk. Like some enormous grey serpent, the wall follows a winding course over mountains and valleys equal to the distance from New York City to Omaha.

To accompany his other policies and projects, the First Emperor took concrete steps to ensure intellectual uniformity and suppress dissent by banning philosophical debate, prohibiting glorification of the past or criticism of the present, and proscribing all writings other than official Qin chronicles and practical manuals relating to agriculture, medicine, or divination. Since no one was allowed to possess any other texts, all copies were ordered collected and burned except for those that would be preserved in the imperial library for use by government officials.

Although the emperor boasted of establishing a dynasty on Legalistic principles that would endure for "ten thousand generations," his oppressive policies inspired only terror and enmity in the hearts of his subjects. When the inevitable revolt began in 207 B.C., the Qin quickly lost all popular support. A new leader, Liu Bang, emerged from the ranks of the peasantry to overthrow the dynasty and claim the Mandate of Heaven which the Qin had forfeited. Though ruling only briefly, the Qin, nevertheless, bequeathed to China a defeudalized political system which, despite later events, would remain a feature of Chinese life until the end of the imperial system in 1911–12.

Stone figures in the Forest of Confucius, near the birthplace of the philosopher.

Fang Lei vessel of cast bronze. Early Western Zhou (1122–771 B.C.). The Saint Louis Art Museum Purchase.

The Han and the Institutionalization of Confucianism, 202 B.C.–220 A.D.

Emerging from the chaos which followed the collapse of the Qin, a new dynasty styling itself Han assumed power in 202 B.C. and proceeded to build a new state. Because Qin harshness and brutality had caused its overthrow, the Han leaders carefully avoided imitating the extreme methods of their predecessors. To despise Qin excesses, however, did not mean abandoning those institutions and practices which had proved so successful in unifying the country and reestablishing order and centralized government. Some aspects of Legalism may have been distasteful to the new regime (the early leaders of which were inclined more toward Daoism), but there was no denying that as far as the daily practice of politics was concerned, Legalism more than any of the other major philosophies seemed more realistic.

On the one hand, then, the organizational structure and administrative practices of the new regime remained rooted in Legalistic thinking. Not long after taking power, however, the Han leadership realized that Legalism could not by itself, unless implemented in the Qin manner, be the ideological basis of society. As a result, the government quickly invited Confucian scholars into official service. After that, Confucianism (not unaffected by the other major schools of thought) gradually rose to such prominence that it was finally declared the state ideology in 124 B.C. With the introduction of a Confucian curriculum into the national university founded in that same year and with the somewhat later (6 A.D.) establishment of a competitive civil service examination system based on Confucian writings, the Confucianization of Chinese culture and politics was well under way.

The Han dynasty reigned continually for a little over four hundred years except for a brief period between 9 and 23 A.D., when Wang Mang, the highly popular chief minister, usurped the throne. As emperor, Wang proclaimed a new dynasty (Xin), but even more importantly inaugurated a series of reforms that if fully implemented would have revolutionized Chinese society. By the time of Wang's rule, much of the general prosperity of the earlier Han period had waned, because of a large increase in the peasant population and the appropriation of more and more land by the small elite class. Together the two phenomena had the effect not only of creating within the peasant class a substantial number of landless families, but also of reducing tax revenues for the state. In order to reverse these trends, Wang Mang proposed a program that included nationalization of all land, its equitable redistribution, price fixing, government loans to poor farmers at low interest rates, and the abolition of slavery.

The written records do not reveal clearly the reasons for the failure of Wang's reforms. Right from the beginning all sorts of natural disasters and freakish events cast an ominous shadow over his reign and may have diminished the popularity he had once enjoyed. Possibly certain groups in society, particularly the wealthy landowners who stood to lose the most by the proposed changes, obstructed his efforts. In any event, Wang's reform program barely got underway before it began to experience difficulties. The outbreak of rebellion sparked by drought, famine, and numerous breakdowns of the levee system, coupled with declining support from the great families of China, led to Wang's death and the end of his short-lived dynasty. After some further conflict among the various pretenders to the throne, the future Emperor Guangwu defeated his rivals and proclaimed the restoration of the Han dynasty in 25 A.D.

The four centuries of Han rule are noteworthy for major developments in literature. First, along with the recognition of Confucianism as the official state ideology, a number of texts transmitted from pre-Qin times were thought to embody truths of such significance that they came to be esteemed as the *Five Classics*. These texts of often-disputed date and authorship included the *I Jing* (Classic of Changes), the *Shu Jing* (Classic of Writings), the *Shi Jing* (Classic of Songs), the *Jun Ju* (Spring and Autumn Annals), and the *Li Jing* (Classic of Rituals). Together the five texts were regarded as essential for the maintenance of Chinese civilization and along with later additions to the list served as the sources upon which the government based the civil service examinations.

Second, historiography experienced an upsurge of activity, stimulated by the invention of paper, that produced two impressive achievements. One was the *Shi Ji* (Records of the Historian), begun by Sima Tan (d. 110 B.C.) and completed by his son Sima Qian (145–87 B.C.?). Although this work is largely a compilation of excerpts from original sources, it is more than a mere chronicle. In it the authors explore the interrelationships among events, display a keen interest in the personalities of important people, and show an awareness of the changing nature of institutions and social practices over time. The second major historical writing was the *Han Shu* (Book of Han) by Pan Gu (32–92 A.D.). The author imitated Sima Qian in his organization of the *Han Shu*, but he surpassed his predecessor by introducing a bibliography and several new subjects into his text, including justice and administrative geography.

Before leaving the Han it should be mentioned that the dynasty fulfilled the concept of China as the "Middle Kingdom" (or *Zhongguo*—China as the center of the universe), by pacifying the barbarian tribes on all its frontiers. Imperial forces defeated the Xiong-nu (Huns) in the north and extended dominion in the south into coastal Annam and Tonkin, present-day Vietnam. Late in the dynasty's history, the Han imperium reached westward to the Caspian Sea and, in so doing, stimulated trade with Europe via Xinjiang and Central Asia along what became known as the "silk route."

The Era of Disunity, 220–581 A.D., and the Advent of Buddhism

The Empire of the Han disintegrated in the early third century A.D. in ways comparable to the experience of Rome in a slightly later period. In both instances, causal factors included an imbalance of wealth, a decline of loyalty to the empire, and a shortage of arable land. When the end came, fragmentation and decentralization were some of the immediate results; in China several kingdoms made their appearance, none particularly significant. At the same time internal division invited "barbarian" incursions across China's northern frontiers into the

Yellow River valley, but the Chinese managed to hold at the line of the Yangzi. At this time, however, the center of Chinese culture began a move to the south that would be completed centuries later.

The ensuing era of political disunity, which saw northern China controlled by various nomadic groups of non-Chinese, continued until 581, when a northern dynasty, Sui, reunified the country and restored effective central government. In times of crisis like the third through sixth centuries A.D., people frequently seek the consolation of religion. Just as Christianity penetrated the Roman Empire in its period of collapse, so Buddhism gained prominence in the era of disunity that followed the Han. This religion first arrived in China around the beginning of the common era, and by 65 A.D. the country already had a Buddhist community. Only in the fourth century, however, did this alien faith begin its dynamic growth on Chinese soil.

The basic tenets of Buddhism are contained in the Four Noble Truths: (1) all life is suffering; (2) suffering originates in desire; (3) suffering can be escaped only by a complete suppression of desire; and (4) desire can be overcome only by following the Noble Eight-Fold Path consisting of right views, right intentions, right speech, right conduct, right livelihood, right effort, right mindfulness, and right concentration. Success in conquering desire leads to the attainment of Nirvana, a state of perfect peace and bliss. In a sense, then, Buddhism offered to the Chinese a promise of an afterlife hitherto lacking in their philosophies and religions.

In many respects Buddhism challenged basic Chinese beliefs and attitudes. For example, monastic celibacy contradicted the Chinese respect for family life and the whole notion of filial piety; asceticism ran counter to Chinese humanism; while mendicancy collided with the Chinese disdain for beggars. Yet its spiritual qualities attracted many discouraged people previously more concerned with the worldliness of Confucianism. (For much the same reason Daoism enjoyed a resurgence of popularity during this same period.) In keeping with the Chinese habit of intellectual syncretism and tolerance of diverse views—and despite two serious official efforts to repress the religion—Buddhism soon found a permanent place in Chinese culture.

The Restoration of Political Unity and the Tang, 581–906 A.D.

Despite the collapse of the Han dynasty and with it all remnants of central administration in China, the idea of empire survived (particularly in the south) to be resuscitated in the late sixth century by a non-Chinese, but Sinicized, northern state, the Sui. The effort to reunite the country, however, so exhausted the new dynasty that it was unable to retain the throne for more than a generation. Like the Qin before it, though, the Sui prepared the way for the establishment of a much more powerful and long-lived dynasty, the Tang (618–906 A.D.), which led China to new heights of cultural, economic, military, and administrative achievements.

The Tang extended the empire's frontiers to their greatest limits yet attained. Successful campaigns brought Korea, parts of Manchuria, Tonkin, and the areas of present-day Xinjiang and Tibet under China's sway, as imperial armies everywhere subdued barbarian neighbors and forced them to acknowledge the Chinese emperor as their overlord. The pattern of diplomatic relations that developed between these peoples and China became institutionalized as the "tributary system." Originated by the Han, this system allowed foreign peoples to retain their native leaders yet secure Chinese protection in return for periodic tribute in the form of native products (largely symbolic) and homage rendered to the emperor at the imperial capital in recognition of the superiority of the ruler of the Middle Kingdom.

Owing to the expansion of international trade, stimulated in large part by a growing demand for silk and Chinese porcelain, foreign cultures in the Tang era affected Chinese life to a greater degree than in any previous dynasty. Contacts with the West were renewed, and trading ships from India and Arabia exchanged wares at southern Chinese ports, bringing tea from Southeast Asia for the first time. The impact of foreign religions deepened during these centuries. Indian Buddhist priests and Nestorian Christian missionaries, as well as adherents of Zoroastrianism and Islam, made their way to China and added new dimensions to Chinese culture.

More significantly, Sinicized forms of Buddhism flourished, converting many among the aristocratic Chinese. New sects appeared, notably the *Tian Tai* and the *Zhan* schools. The latter preached meditation as the path to knowledge and became the forerunner of Zen, a significant form of Buddhism in Japan. Buddhist monasteries acquired title to vast tracts of land in the Chinese countryside over which they enjoyed an extraordinary autonomy. In time, monastic wealth became a problem for the imperial administration and a target for persecution by some rulers. Nevertheless, Buddhism reached its zenith in China during the Tang period, and from China the religion passed to the Koreans and Japanese.

The government sought to deal with the age-old problem of land hunger by reviving the ancient well-field system and distributing public lands among the vastly increased number of taxpaying peasants as soon as each reached adult status. Government subsidies further assisted China's farmers. The Tang made no effort, however, to break up the estates of large landowners. Despite providing some relief for small cultivators, the well-field system in the long run could not cope with the continued rise in population, and collapsed after the fall of the Tang.

Several significant innovations were launched in the spheres of administration and governmental operations. First, although the Tang drew upon patterns and institutions established under the Han, they did improve organization by the creation of new offices to handle imperial affairs. Secondly, the regime published a code of laws that served as a model not only for later Chinese codes but also for those drawn up in Japan and Annam. Finally, it encouraged a major change in the method of recruitment for state service. While the bureaucracy continued to be staffed largely on the basis of family and other connections, the trend during Tang times was clearly for men increasingly to enter the government through an elaborate system of state-run examinations. Candidates competed in four sessions, the last of which they took in the imperial palace itself. The *jin shi* degree ("advanced scholar worthy of government appointment") represented the highest possible attainment. By the end of the dynasty, not only were the majority of high officials in the land products of this system, but enormous honor and prestige had come to be attached to passing the various tests successfully.

The military, political, and economic achievements of the Tang era inspired a flowering of Chinese culture characterized by the haunting poetry of Li Bo and Du Fu and Buddhist themes in both painting and sculpture. The perfection of block printing produced the first books probably by the seventh century (although the oldest printed text from China dates from 868 A.D.), almost seven centuries before a similar development in Western Europe. Perhaps the rebuilding of Chang'an, the imperial capital, represented the most dramatic symbol of Tang accomplishment. A city of 2 million inhabitants and almost as large as modern-day Paris, Chang'an was laid out as a rectangle, with streets running at right angles in a gridiron pattern. Foreign visitors marveled at its cosmopolitan character and splendor; the Japanese, in fact, copied its basic lines for their first permanent capitals at Nara and Kyoto.

The Tang dynasty weakened in the final century and a half of its existence when population growth, having overtaxed the well-field system, created unbearable rural problems and inordinate wealth corrupted the court, the scholars, and the imperial army. Also, frontier defenses decayed and allowed tribes from beyond the Great Wall to invade China once again. The Tang finally succumbed in the opening years of the tenth century.

The Rise of the Song, 960–1270

With the collapse of the Tang dynasty, China found itself once again without effective central government. In the north, which soon would fall behind the south in population, cultural attainment, productivity, and wealth, several states known as the Five Dynasties stole the political spotlight from one another in rapid succession over the next fifty years. In the south the situation was worse in one respect yet better in another: there were twice as many states (the so-called Ten Kingdoms), yet their longer histories provided a greater degree of stability to politics and society at large.

Ironically, however, it was a northern regime, the Song, that restored centralized government to the whole of China in the third quarter of the tenth century. Taking advantage of the achievements of one of the preceding short-lived dynasties in the region (Later Zhou), the Song gradually incorporated the formerly independent states of northern and southern China into their empire. With the aid of a bureaucracy more intricate than that of any previous dynasty, whose members now were drawn predominantly from examination candidates chosen after intense competition, the Song could provide more uniform, capable, and effective leadership both on the local and national levels. While some criticism was leveled at the examination system for encouraging impracticality and pedantry in successful candidates, the admittedly scanty statistical evidence shows that the system did provide a channel for upward social mobility without producing a self-perpetuating elite. Perhaps 30 percent of all who passed became the first of their families to do so.

In spite of the prosperity that an expanding economy soon brought to Song China, social problems remained the most pressing domestic concern of the rulers. A monotonously recurrent feature of Chinese life, however, worsened the plight of the peasant. The small farmer could not compete with a growing number of large landowners whose capital resources allowed them not only to acquire more and more land but, through investment in reclamation and irrigation projects and new implements, to derive greater productivity from their estates.

As pressure on the domestic scene increased, so too did threats from belligerent neighboring states. In the northeast, the Khitan tribes of Manchuria united to form the state of Liao in 907. Taking advantage of the political disunity of northern China during the period of the Five Dynasties, the Liao carved out a kingdom for themselves that included some territory on the Chinese side of the Great Wall. Conflict between the Liao and the Song continued intermittently until 1004, when both sides negotiated a treaty that called for the frequent exchange of envoys, development of trade, and respect for the current borders between their respective territories. In addition, the Song agreed to pay an annual tribute to the Liao—a reversal of traditional Chinese practice. This method of appeasement was used again in 1044 to deal with the Tanguts of the northwest.

The burden of these substantial tribute payments, along with the enormous expense of the military forces necessary to protect the northern frontiers, proved so onerous that the government sought to extract more taxes. The population, however, failed to respond in the way the regime wanted. The peasants could not help, because they had nothing to give; the merchants and landowners would not cooperate, because they jealously guarded their wealth. As a result, revenues fell, black marketeering grew, and society verged on rebellion.

At this point, in 1069, the emperor appointed an official by the name of Wang Anshi to become prime minister and carry out needed reforms. Wang enacted measures that effectively procured supplies for the court (a money-saving effort), offered loans to small farmers at interest rates lower than those of the moneylenders, and established a neighborhood militia system (the *bao-jia*) that improved rural security. He also reformed the bureaucracy, which, as a good Confucian, he knew to be essential to effective authority. In this area he stressed the Imperial University as the best place for training bureaucrats and revised the examinations so that they would test the candidate's practical knowledge of government and problems of administration. On the lower levels, Wang instituted salaries and corporal punishments for nondegree-holding personnel in order to keep them on the virtuous path.

The outcry against Wang led to his resignation after seven years in office. His reforms remained in effect until the death of the emperor who had supported him, but the new government repealed his entire program. Whether Wang's ideas would have worked is difficult to determine, but because they were never effectively implemented, China made little progress toward solving its fundamental problems. The outbreak of peasant rebellion in several provinces and the failure to beat back the Jurchids (a new power in the northeast who invaded in 1125) are ample proof of this. As a result, Song control collapsed in the northern half of China. Withdrawing to the Huai and Yangzi valleys, the Song set up their new capital in Hangzhou and maintained the dynasty until 1279. The rest of China, however, would remain subject to alien domination for more than two centuries.

Faced with an ever-present threat from tribes to the north, the Southern Song (as the dynasty was now called) became increasingly self-centered and less receptive to alien elements in their society and culture. One example of this changed mood was the rejection of Buddhism as a foreign religion by intellectuals who turned once again to their native Confucianism for inspiration. But Song thinkers soon discovered that Confucianism had changed substantially over the previous centuries. As a result, they undertook to reexamine the basic texts and reinterpret their contents. The product of their effort was a synthesis known as Neo-Confucianism, with Zhu Xi as its most notable exponent. By incorporating both Daoist and even some Buddhist elements into his philosophy, he broadened and enriched Confucian concepts to explain humankind's relationship to the universe. While creating a new orthodoxy, however, Zhu Xi continued to emphasize virtuous behavior and subservience to superiors, two ideas which provided ideological justification for the increasing authoritarianism of Song politics.

While many people have criticized the Song dynasty for its failure to preserve the empire's territorial integrity, it is important to note that in many respects Chinese civilization reached its apogee during the Song centuries. Art, literature, and technology (including the priceless invention of printing) all reached a peak of development. This was an age when artisans produced some of China's finest porcelain; when writers like Su Dongbo praised wine, women, and song in exquisite poetic style; when painters drew some of the most beautiful landscapes; and when Sima Guang wrote his monumental *History as a Mirror* to chronicle thirteen centuries of China's past.

Under the Song, China also almost achieved significant sea power. Thanks to a marked increase in the productivity of the country's economy and to improvements in maritime technology (especially the invention of the compass), the volume of foreign trade rose beyond anything experienced before. For the first time seaports rather than inland cities, which connected the overland trade routes, became the centers for China's contact with the outside world. In many respects, the Chinese seemed on the verge of an experience similar to the Commercial Revolution in Western Europe in a slightly later period. But the potential for the empire to become a world power, to carry its culture across the seas and in turn be influenced by distant cultures, was never realized.

China Under the Mongols, 1279–1368

During the period of Southern Song rule, which proved to be an exceptionally peaceful and prosperous time, the northern half of China continued to live under foreign occupation. As has been shown, first the Khitans of the Liao dynasty and then the Jurchids of the Jin dynasty succeeded in controlling all or part of that region. Finally, the Mongols swept out of the steppe to engulf northern China and spread untold death, suffering, and destruction. Since these occupations weighed most heavily on that region and because the plains area had suffered terribly from the flooding of the Yellow River at the end of the twelfth century, North China lay in ruins for nearly a hundred years.

The Chinese in the south might have continued to live undisturbed had their rulers not become involved in the problems of the north. Around 1215, the Jurchids appealed for Song assistance against the Mongols who had already driven them out of Beijing. The Song emperor dispatched infantry in response. Later, after the Mongols had overwhelmed the Jurchids in 1234, the Song foolishly attempted to reconquer North China. Kublai Khan, who would succeed to the Mongol throne in 1256, promptly launched an invasion of the south. The fighting dragged on for decades before the relentless steppe warriors finally subdued the region in 1279. For the first time the whole of China was ruled by nomads who had not been previously Sinicized and who, despite adopting Chinese institutions and techniques and using Chinese to help administer the country, always remained totally alien.

As the new rulers of China, the Mongols faced the task of administering not only a vast and heavily populated country but also one with cultural and institutional features at total variance with their own. Accustomed to ruling from the saddle over a tribally organized society, what were the Mongols to do with China? At first there was some support for destroying Chinese society, annihilating most of the population, and turning the land into a gigantic pasturage more suited to the nomadic Mongol lifestyle. But the conquerors soon accepted the advisability of leaving the Chinese and their system basically intact to exploit the country more effectively. Thus, the Mongols established an administrative apparatus essentially similar to that which the Chinese had developed. While filling lower-level posts largely with Chinese, the Mongols nevertheless kept all high offices and other important positions for themselves. Furthermore, they tended to make greater use of nondegree-holding personnel and foreigners (recall the career of Marco Polo, the Venetian traveler) rather than members of the Chinese elite whom they trusted very little.

The ruling Mongol minority sought to avoid assimilation by clearly relegating the Chinese to secondary social positions. Yet, Kublai Khan himself, greatly influenced by Chinese advisers, ruled as much like a Chinese emperor as a traditional Mongol chieftain. He dutifully performed the Confucian imperial rites, took a Chinese name for his dynasty (Yuan), and even reinstituted the examination system, although examinations were held only once until late in the dynasty.

Because of its exploitive, alien character and relatively short duration, Mongol rule in China did not leave any lasting imprint on the country; yet, the conquest was not entirely without positive results. For one thing, the choice of Beijing as the new capital of China made that city one of the country's most important administrative, economic, and military centers, which it has remained to this day. Secondly, the *pax mongolica* (Mongol Peace), which stretched at its peak very nearly from the Mediterranean to the Pacific Ocean, enormously stimulated and facilitated overland travel and trade between China and the West. Furthermore, the West received a great flow of Chinese technical and scientific inventions, including printing and gunpowder, which would enormously affect European society.

The first two emperors of the Yuan dynasty, Kublai Khan and his grandson, Timur, proved capable and effective rulers, but their successors were incompetent and too much given to a debauched life at court. Misrule, fratricidal conflict that saw seven emperors on the throne during the last twenty-two years of the dynasty, mismanagement of the country's finances, a series of military defeats, and widespread famine in North China caused by the frequent flooding of the Yellow River contributed to the outbreak of popular revolts in the 1360s all across the country. In 1368, unable any longer to hold on to their conquest, the Mongols withdrew swiftly to the steppe. With their ouster, the Ming, a new *Chinese* dynasty, succeeded in uniting the whole of China under native rule for the first time in four hundred years.

The Restoration of Chinese Rule Over China

The Ming, 1368–1644

Zhu Yuanzhang, the leader of the successful revolt against the Mongols, grew up from humble origins. In fact, he was the first peasant to establish a dynasty (the Ming) in a millennium and a half. His education was informal, which perhaps contributed to his lifelong scorn for intellectuals, yet he had enormous organizational skills and proved astute enough to see the value of recruiting some learned men to assist in administering the territories that he conquered and the state that he would ultimately rule. A man who knew how to handle others, his harsh and autocratic character had an indelible effect on the dynasty which he founded.

Despotism, in fact, became one of the hallmarks of Ming rule. It resulted in part from new institutional arrangements inaugurated at the very beginning of the dynasty by which emperors exercised enormous and direct responsibility for everyday decisions. It also resulted from the tradition of terrorism, surveillance, and frequent purges that the first emperor established.

As a consequence of the increased authority of the emperors and, later on, their closest advisers and eunuchs, the bureaucracy suffered an erosion of its influence at the upper levels. The early establishment of Neo-Confucianism as the officially sanctioned ideology further encouraged this tendency. Ordering the publication of a new edition of the Confucian *Classics* with the commentaries of Zhu Xi, the government declared these writings to be the corpus of orthodox thought. When one recalls that the *Classics* formed the basis of the examination system that provided the bureaucracy with its membership, the full impact of this action becomes clear. Furthermore, the government revised the examinations themselves in a way that encouraged conformity through what was called the "Eight-Legged Essay." Originally designed to assist candidates to organize their thoughts, before long the essay's format severely stifled originality on the examinations and placed a premium on rote memorization and stylistics. All in all, these measures not only harnessed the bureaucracy but also, considering the increased insecurity of official life, helped transform it into a closed, privileged institution whose members were more interested in self-preservation than in the betterment of society.

Zhu Yuanzhang and his successors, consciously trying to recapture the glories of Tang times, created a stable, prosperous, and militarily strong China that once again dominated East Asia. Less threatened from the outside than at any time since the early Tang period, the Ming sent tribute-seeking fleets of gigantic size as far as Java, the coasts of India, the Persian Gulf, and even the east coast of Africa in the early 1400s. At the same time, some of the empire's neighbors, like Korea, became loyal tributary states, or like Japan, sought trading opportunities with this majestic power.

The Great Wall of China dates from the third century B.C. It extends for 1,500 miles from the coast to the frontier of Outer Mongolia.

Interior of the Forbidden City.

The early Ming period represented a time of feverish activity and forward movement. The new dynasty reopened and enlarged the long-neglected Grand Canal connecting Beijing with the Yangzi valley, rebuilt a portion of the Great Wall, and planned and constructed the city of Beijing in its modern form. That city became the capital of China in 1421, when the Yonglo Emperor ordered three great walls constructed to protect it. A huge outer fortification enclosed the imperial palace wall, which in turn surrounded the red wall of the "Forbidden City." The emperor's palace lay within, its two thousand rooms and spacious grounds staffed by ten thousand servants. All structures faced southward, away from threatened frontiers. Skillful use of space separating the various buildings created the illusion of ascension to Heaven itself as one approached the abode of the ruler of the "Celestial Empire."

Culturally the Ming period witnessed a substantial effort to produce variations largely on traditional themes and forms, but at the same time one can detect the birth of what John T. Meskill, the American historian, calls a "modern temper." Whether it was the interest of Wang Yangming in the workings of the human mind, the proliferation of academies in the sixteenth century, the challenge to tradition and convention by the likes of the eccentric Li Zhi, the introduction of spontaneity, action, and sensuality in literature (particularly in novels and dramas), or the favorable treatment accorded Christian missionaries who began to arrive shortly after the Portuguese first appeared off the south China coast, one can see in the Ming Chinese a vitality, dissatisfaction, anticonventionalism, and even individualism that might have led to many of the same kinds of changes in China that had occurred in Western Europe during the late Middle Ages and the Renaissance. Why this "modern temper" failed to take root and blossom is a question with an enormously complex answer, but one that is probably tied intimately to the fate of the Ming dynasty itself. Suffice it to suggest that in the sixteenth century the Chinese seemed to have a chance to throw off at least some of the constraints of tradition and strike out in new directions. Their failure to sustain what seemed so promising may go a long way toward explaining their traumatic experience with the West in the nineteenth century.

For two centuries Ming China thrived. Then by the early part of the 1600s a number of developments began to disrupt the normal workings of government and society. First, there was a growing failure of leadership. Factionalism and intense bureaucratic partisanship, the enormous expansion of eunuch power, and the indifference of many of the emperors made misgovernment almost inevitable. Second, China lost both Annam and Burma as a result of uprisings in these tributary states, while two Japanese invasions of Korea, although repulsed by Chinese troops, placed a heavy burden on the imperial treasury. So too did attacks from the north by Mongols and raids all along the China coast by Japanese pirates and Chinese outlaws. Third, the perennial problem of creeping landlordism, particularly in the Yangzi area and the south, led to a considerable number of peasant revolts. Fourth, a doubling of the population caused pressure on the empire's land resources that could not be eased by the repopulation of the formerly devastated northern regions. Finally, increasing governmental incompetence, corruption, arbitrariness, and insensitivity served to alienate most

Chinese intellectuals. The growing power of the eunuchs, whose number reached about one hundred thousand, was especially abhorrent to the bureaucratic class.

Imperial China at Its Peak

The Manchus, 1644–ca. 1800

For several generations during the late sixteenth and early seventeenth centuries, a tribe known as the Manchus was quietly becoming a unified military power in the southern part of Manchuria. Through diplomacy and conquest a young Manchu chieftain named Nurhaci slowly brought the clans together under his leadership. By the time he was ready to challenge Ming rule over China, Nurhaci's Manchus were already imbued with Chinese culture, had developed Chinese-inspired administrative practices and institutions, and enjoyed the support of large numbers of Chinese farmers who had settled beyond the Great Wall and Chinese officials who had defected from the Ming.

Ever since 1616, when Nurhaci adopted the title of emperor and founded his own dynasty (at that time called the Latter Jin, the same name taken by the Jurchids who had earlier driven the Song out of North China), the Manchus had been planning to attack the Ming. Nurhaci died before fulfilling his dream, but his successors continued to work toward the day when a Manchu would sit on the "Dragon Throne." In the 1640s, with the Ming beset by massive internal rebellion, the opportunity came for which the Manchus had waited patiently. In the face of little opposition, they took Beijing in 1644 and then swept through the rest of the country. Ming loyalists continued to hold out in remoter areas of the south (especially Taiwan), but eventually they too were destroyed.

Paradoxically, imperial China reached the zenith and the nadir of its development while ruled by the Manchus, who adopted the dynastic title of Qing. Under three emperors (Kangxi, Yongzheng, and Qianlong), who must rank with the greatest ever to hold that position during China's extensive history, the empire enjoyed extraordinarily long (1661–1796) and dynamic leadership. The results were impressive. On the domestic scene, peace and stability provided the background for such prosperity that under the Qianlong Emperor taxes were canceled on more than one occasion. Trade continued to expand throughout the period and handicraft industries proved enormously productive in both quantity and range of commodities. Internationally, the Manchus were especially successful. Brilliant military campaigns extended the empire to Mongolia, much of Central Asia, and Tibet. In the south, Burma, Annam, and Nepal fell under Chinese domination as well.

To ensure the success of their dynasty, the Manchus sought to become "more Chinese than the Chinese." They made few changes in the Ming administrative system (except to balance Chinese officials with Manchus as a controlling mechanism) and, perhaps more importantly, passed themselves off as protectors of Chinese civilization. The examination system, with its Neo-Confucian basis, remained an integral part of the political and social setting. The emperors, particularly Kangxi and Qianlong, patronized scholarly endeavors, which included some of the most monumental projects ever undertaken anywhere (such as the *Com-*

plete Library in Four Branches of Literature in thirty-six thousand manuscript volumes). They also attempted to become ideal Confucian rulers by assiduously practicing the proper rites and writing and painting in the manner of the scholar-bureaucratic elite. Nevertheless, the Manchus remained conscious of their non-Chinese origins and strove to retain their identity by forbidding intermarriage with Chinese, banning Chinese settlement in Manchuria, and prohibiting the adoption of certain Chinese customs (such as footbinding), while preserving the Manchu language.

By the end of the eighteenth century, in spite of outward signs of continuing stability and prosperity, much was beginning to change for the worse in China. Many of the problems that surfaced in the new century were the same ones that had plagued dynasties throughout China's long history. But to those perennial problems would be added a new factor—the intrusion of the West—which eventually proved so disruptive that it would contribute more than anything else to the end not merely of the Qing dynasty but of the entire imperial system itself and practically all of the traditions and values that gave it meaning.

China's Collision

with the West, 1800 to 1912

2

At the beginning of the nineteenth century, many non-Chinese regarded China as the mightiest empire in the world. Asian neighbors eagerly sent tribute, while countless Western intellectuals lauded China for being a society run by those best able to govern and guided by a natural morality. Such adulation, however, reflected a distorted sense of Chinese reality that resulted from misunderstanding or, worse, willful selfdeception. In truth, fearful of assimilation and increasingly on the defensive, the Manchus were fast losing their hold on Chinese society. Population pressure and land hunger, China's perennial problems, were once again threatening to disrupt domestic harmony. Already the portents were ominous, and rebellion was in the wind. Furthermore, the bureaucratic elite had become a haven for the privileged and ambitious. Too much corruption and too little dedication among its members undercut the efficiency and effectiveness of local administration and would contribute enormously to the outbreak of rural discontent. When the Europeans finally kicked in the doors of old China, they would be amazed to perceive so much decay, and the empire, hitherto greatly admired, would reveal itself to be weak and moribund. *in a dying state*

In the Western European nations China found itself face to face with a civilization whose values, attitudes, institutions, and general world view were totally different from its own. What is more, China was confronted by people who refused to play its game, who not only wanted to ignore the old rules but arrogantly sought to draw up the new ones unilaterally. Thinking these "barbarians" to be similar to all the others who had crossed its threshold over the centuries, China expected them to recognize it as the Middle Kingdom, while acknowledging the emperor as the Son of Heaven and paying him homage, and to absorb Chinese ways. But these barbarian "ocean devils" came by way of the sea-going and coming as they wished, making assimilation difficult—instead of overland as heretofore. The total inability of China to make the Europeans heed its traditions and the humiliation that resulted from its attempts to do so, proved so traumatic that traditional Chinese selfconfidence was irrevocably shattered. The

European influences on China

collapse of the Manchu dynasty, the end of the imperial system, and the emergence of Chinese nationalism all developed as direct results of this tragic experience.

The Violent Opening of China

By an imperial decree issued in 1757, the Western presence in China at the beginning of the nineteenth century was limited to merchants permitted to ply their trade solely in the port of Canton. Required to live within special compounds, or factories, the British, French, Dutch, and later American traders conducted their business through a committee of thirteen Chinese merchants known as the *Cohong*. Residing in Canton was not easy for the Westerners. They labored under all sorts of restrictions that affected not only their business dealings but also their private affairs. Thus, they were prohibited from employing Chinese servants, rowing on the Pearl River that flowed past the city, and bringing their wives to China. All in all, the Chinese treated them as was to be expected; moreover, the Westerners were merchants and foreigners trying to peddle goods for which the Chinese really had no need. Their confinement to Canton, then, amounted to dispensing charity to beggars at the back door.

In 1834 an event occurring in faroff Britain set in motion an effort to change the Canton system. The House of Commons in that year voted to cancel the commercial monopoly hitherto held by the East India Company in China. With passage of the bill, any English businessman with goods and capital could now participate in the China trade. Yet, without substantial change in the way the Chinese were willing to do business with the West, there was little chance that private traders would be able to take advantage of what had been granted to them by their own government. With this in mind, a newly appointed British superintendent of trade, Sir Charles Napier, tried to negotiate a commercial treaty with the Chinese viceroy of Canton. His effort was in vain largely because the viceroy saw no reason to alter an arrangement that was rooted in the traditional Chinese tributary system and that profited many of his subordinates personally.

Soon, however, another factor contributed to increasing tensions between the Westerners and the Chinese: the opium trade. As an import, opium had been arriving in coastal ports of the empire from India long before any Westerners had become involved in the China trade. The dubious honor of being the first European shippers of the drug belonged to the Portuguese, but during the last quarter of the eighteenth century, despite repeated imperial decrees prohibiting the importation of opium, British agents had taken over the trade. By 1800 the volume of opium being sold in China was substantial; in the 1830s it increased markedly to over 5 million pounds annually. Consequently, Napier tried to convince the Chinese to legalize the drug traffic, but the government refused his request, denouncing the use of opium as a menace to public health and a drain on China's reserves of precious metals (coin). On both counts the throne's concern was well-founded. In the first instance, the drug was having a deleterious effect on China's elite; in the second, from 1831 to 1836 opium imports had produced an estimated loss of 30 million taels of silver to the royal treasury.

The issue finally reached the crisis stage at the end of the decade. In 1839, after having called for and received opinions from various officials, the emperor

Sir Charles Napier, Superintendant of Trade

appointed a ranking bureaucrat, Lin Zexu, as commissioner at Canton and ordered him to put an end to the trade in "foreign mud," as the Chinese sarcastically called opium. Taking a hard line against continuation of the drug traffic, Lin forced the foreigners to surrender the approximately twenty thousand chests stored in the Canton factories; thereupon, with great public display, he had it all destroyed. The British superintendent of trade, Sir Charles Elliot, condemned this action as unjustified confiscation of property and helped to convince the authorities in England that what Lin had done constituted an attack against the British crown. Hostilities between the two countries commenced almost immediately.

For the first time "barbarians" assaulted China from the sea. The British fleet, supplied from Singapore, bombarded Canton and then proceeded northward along the coast, easily destroying or dispersing the Chinese war junks sent against it. Unable to match Western arms and apparently unwilling to mobilize the forces at their disposal, the Manchus sued for peace in 1842. The Treaty of Nanjing, signed in that year, called for the opening to commerce of five ports—Canton, Amoy (Xiamen), Fuzhou, Ningbo, and Shanghai—and implicitly recognized the legal equality of foreign states with China by permitting consuls to reside in those same cities. The Chinese also ceded the island of Hong Kong, agreed to regulate tariffs (set later at 5 percent), and gave in to the demand for an indemnity equal to 21 million pounds sterling. New agreements forced upon the Chinese in 1843–44 by the British and Americans added two more features to the new relationship between China and the West soon known as the treaty system: a "most-favored nation" clause, which stipulated that further concessions made to any one country would be shared by all, and "extraterritoriality," which granted to Westerners the right to be governed by their own nations' laws while residing in China.

For the long-term development of Sino-Western relations, these early treaties were ominous signs of future trouble for China. Tragically, the Chinese failed generally to comprehend the full implication of these documents. Rather than learn from the bitter experience of defeat, they preferred to pretend not only that little had changed but that in fact what had changed should be viewed as a Chinese victory of sorts. This thinking is clearly illustrated by the interpretation that the Chinese applied to the two most important concessions granted to the Westerners: most-favored nation treatment and extraterritoriality. Very simply stated, they viewed both as reformulations of traditional Chinese practices for handling non-Chinese. The former, it was argued, would permit the government to play off foreigner against foreigner ("barbarians against barbarians") to China's ultimate benefit; the latter would appease the foreigners and perhaps dissuade them from making any further demands. Even taking all of the concessions into consideration, the Chinese convinced themselves that they had managed to confine the foreigners to China's periphery and thereby keep them from interfering in the country's internal affairs.

Yet, if most Chinese understood the treaties of the early 1840s to be the end to concessions, the Westerners saw them as merely the first steps toward the goal of opening the interior of China to Western diplomatic, business, and cultural interests. Such conflicting views ensured the probability of future military clashes. After slightly more than a decade of peace, the inevitable occurred with the outbreak in 1856 of the Second Opium War, or Arrow War as it is often called. At the end of four years of sporadic fighting the Europeans triumphed again and vengefully burned the Summer Palace of the emperor. The signing of the Treaty of Beijing in 1860 opened the interior of China to Western merchants and missionaries, required the Chinese to accept permanent diplomatic representation in the capital, and granted certain additional territorial concessions to both the British and Russians.

Many Chinese blamed the Manchus for their problems with the Europeans, arguing that military defeats and humiliating concessions were all signs that the dynasty had lost its right to rule. As far as the imperial court was concerned, however, the barbarians represented less of a threat to its survival than the shattering explosions of domestic rebellion at midcentury.

Domestic Rebellion and the Taiping Movement

Since Western penetration of China largely disturbed only the coastal areas of the empire, its effect on the Chinese people living in the interior remained minimal. Of greater concern to most Chinese were a number of domestic developments that, taken together, were producing intolerable living conditions in several major regions. Causes of distress included inflation, unemployment, famine, natural disasters, and corruption and inefficiency in the bureaucracy. By the middle of the nineteenth century the country was ripe for a major eruption of popular unrest. As it turned out, three sizable rebellions would rock the empire from the 1850s to the 1870s: the Nian (1853–68) in the region between the Huai and Yellow Rivers; the Muslim (1855–78) in the southwest and northwest provinces; and above all, the Taiping (1850–64), engulfing much of south and central China. The Taiping, a threat to the very survival of the dynasty, deserves closer scrutiny.

Hong Xiuquan, the son of a peasant couple living in wretched conditions outside of Canton, was the future leader of the Taiping movement. His family descended from a group known as the Hakkas, a minority people who had fled to southern China to escape the Manchus at the time of their invasion. As the brightest of his family, Hong was given the opportunity to prepare for the civil service examinations. His first three attempts to pass the licentiate's degree, however, resulted in failures, and following the third (1837) the strain produced a high fever and delirium that lasted, according to later Taiping tradition, for forty days. During that time he reportedly dreamed that he had seen God and Christ (although at the time he did not know them as such) and that the latter, addressing him as a younger brother, ordered him to rid the world of demons. Nothing came of this experience until a few years later when, after failing to pass the examination a fourth time, he read a collection of Christian tracts which he had received from missionaries in Canton in 1836. There he found the meaning of his dream: God had called upon him to purge China of the alien Manchu dynasty and of the baneful teachings of Confucius and to establish a theocracy called the Heavenly Kingdom of Great Peace in their stead. Hong's ideology, as it developed over several years, presented an odd mixture of native Chinese and grossly distorted Christian concepts. While much of what he proclaimed sought to conserve some aspects of traditional Confucian thought, his program of land reform, abolition of private property, and equality of the sexes, if fully imple-mented, would have helped revolutionize Chinese society.

The enormous popular support accorded to Hong and his movement, in ad-dition to the initial ineptitude of the imperial armies sent out against him, helps to explain the early successes of the Taiping Rebellion. But internal squabbles among the rebel leaders, strategic blunders during later military campaigns, ideo-logical fanaticism that alienated many possible supporters (especially the elite of China), discrepancies between the theory and practice of Taiping life, and the failure to take advantage of early Western sympathy, all contributed to the movement's ultimate collapse. So too did the extraordinary efforts of a number of Chinese officials like Zeng Guofan and Li Hongzhang to revitalize the de-fenses of the dynasty and rally new, better equipped and organized provincial armies to its cause.

Despite its failure, the Taiping Rebellion became an inspiration to later gen-erations of Chinese rebels and revolutionaries. In addition, it led to several major developments in imperial politics: an increase in the appointment of Chinese as opposed to Manchu officials to decision-making positions; a greater indepen-dence of action and input into imperial affairs on the part of provincial officials; and the first tentative efforts to reform and modernize Chinese society. All three would have important bearing on the fate of the Qing dynasty and the imperial system itself.

The Restoration of the Dynasty and "Selfstrengthening," 1861-1895

The ascension to the throne of a new emperor in 1861 inaugurated an era of high spirits and energetic activity at the imperial court. As the Taiping Rebellion subsided and the threat to the dynasty diminished, both Manchu and Chinese leaders turned their attention to the task of rehabilitating the nation. Confucian idealism, with its emphasis on good government through properly trained and virtuous leaders, enjoyed a resurgence as the regime sought to attract the best it could find to fill the top posts in the bureaucracy. This idealism made the reign of the Tongzhi Emperor (1861-74) a period of restoration and revival.

Feng Guifen, a scholar-official well-read in many areas other than the Confu-cian Classics, best personified the spirit of this period. In a series of essays written in 1860, Feng noted that the West was not only superior in technological and scientific capability but also ahead of China in its utilization of human and material resources. Furthermore, governments in that part of the world skillfully utilized more effective communication between themselves and their subjects. Feng regarded China's defeat at the hands of the West as the "greatest outrage since creation, which should infuriate every red-blooded person." He argued, however, against both the blind impulse to expel the Westerners and the strata-gem of "using the barbarians against the barbarians." Instead, he urged that the Chinese recognize with shame their country's inferiority. "When we are ashamed," Feng wrote, "the best thing to do is strengthen ourselves." "Selfstrengthening"— a phrase that he coined and that came to describe the reform era which spanned the rest of the century—could be achieved, however, only by improving upon existing Chinese institutions, making greater use of China's own human talents and economic resources, increasing the links between monarch and people, and making practice conform to ideals. These improvements would serve, it was expected, to restore the vitality of the Confucian system. Nevertheless, Feng made it clear that China needed to learn from the West on matters concerning technology and science. In this respect his argument anticipated Zhang Zhidong's enunciation in the 1890s of the so-called "*ti-yong* dichotomy" in his famous slogan, "Chinese learning for substance [ti], Western learning for function [yong]." This dichotomy suggests using Western means for Chinese ends, retaining Confucian values while utilizing Western tools, supporting Chinese traditional civilization while importing Western technology.

The "Tongzhi Restoration" was, as the American historian, Mary C. Wright, argued in her study of this period, the "last stand of Chinese conservatism." The story of the restoration attempt represented the search for Confucian stability on the one hand and for modernization on the other. It concerned the efforts of an often brilliant group of conservative officials both at the imperial court (Prince Kong) and in the provinces (Zeng Guofan, Li Hongzhang, and Zuo Zongtang) to bring about some radical innovation within the old order, when in the long run what China required was a radical change of the old order itself. Faced with defects in the traditional Chinese system that should have been obvious, these conservatives set to work shoring up the nation's Confucian foundation by initiating a series of broad reforms. Aimed at a true restoration of all that was inherently useful and beneficial in the Confucian system, the reform projects unfortunately failed because they were based upon misconceptions. Adhering to the Chinese conservative tradition, the restoration leaders directed their attention largely toward administrative improvement. Preoccupation with the symptomatic abuses of the system rather than with its substantive defects produced the inevitable result.

If the restoration attempt came to an end when the emperor died in 1875, the ideas that justified it continued to influence Chinese reformism for another decade and a half. The selfstrengthening movement managed to introduce a number of reforms, but its total achievement was negligible and its ultimate objective unattained. The failure cannot be blamed exclusively on the few leaders of the movement, although they deserve some criticism for their shortsightedness. More significant in the long run was the unsurprising inertia of the bureaucracy as a whole. Too many officials simply refused to accept even that which the self-strengtheners realized: that the Chinese system did not function as it should. The overwhelming number of officials distrusted and opposed every innovation. Even the reformers themselves accepted change only if it was clearly advantageous and did not undermine any bulwark essential to the preservation of the old order. In the end, the selfstrengtheners could not resolve the contradiction in their goals. On the one hand, they desired to transform China into a modern state able to compete effectively with the Western powers; on the other, they sought to maintain the Confucian system virtually unchanged. Unfortunately for China, the requirements of the one ran counter to those of the other.

Foreign Expansionism in China
When the selfstrengthening movement got underway in the 1860s, it was aided by the decision of the Western powers to pursue a policy of cooperation with the Chinese government and allow it a chance to recover from the chaos and de-

struction which domestic rebellion had caused. Apparently satisfied with the concessions that they had already wrung from China, the Westerners sought now to ensure that nothing would endanger their treaty rights. This thinking led not only to a cessation of hostilities toward the empire but also to a conscious effort to help the Chinese revive and modernize their system.

Within less than a decade, however, a rash of anti-Christian acts in the countryside in 1869–70 and the almost immediate renewal of Western demands on China had succeeded in undermining the cooperative policy in short order. The massacre of missionaries at Tianjin (1870), the revival of a longstanding Western request for audiences with the emperor (1873), and the murder by guerrillas of a British vice-consul near the Chinese-Burmese border (1875) launched a new period of intensified foreign imperialism. The Russian occupation of Ili in Xinjiang (1871–81), the Japanese attack on Formosa (1874) and seizure of the Liuqiu Islands (1879), the British attempt to open Yunnan province (1875), and the French seizure of Annam and the war of 1884–85, all served to further weaken China and set the stage for the Sino-Japanese War of 1894–95.

That conflict began as a result of a longstanding dispute between China and Japan over control of Korea, for centuries a Chinese dependency. In 1894, when a nationalist revolt known as the Tonghak Rebellion broke out in the peninsula, both the Chinese and the Japanese landed troops to restore order, fearing Russian action. In August, a Japanese fleet attacked a Chinese troopship without a declaration of war. From that moment on Japanese naval and land forces achieved one easy victory after another over their Chinese counterparts. Had Japan not feared the total collapse of China and the loss of gains it had already made, it could have occupied Beijing itself. Instead, negotiations commenced leading to the signing of the Treaty of Shimonoseki in April, 1895.

According to the treaty, China had to surrender Formosa, the Pescadores Islands, and Port Arthur, and pay an indemnity to the Japanese. In addition, Korea would become independent. Before the terms of the agreement could be carried out, however, Russia, Germany, and France (the Triple Intervention) presented separate notes to the Japanese foreign minister, demanding that Port Arthur remain in Chinese hands. Each of the three powers had its own reasons for making an issue of this strategic facility: Russia feared Japanese encroachment in northern China which it regarded as its own preserve; Germany sought a port on the Chinese coast to develop a sphere of influence; and France wished to cement its recently concluded Dual Alliance with Russia. Faced with this opposition, Japan had no choice but to return Port Arthur.

Japan's defeat of China revealed the latter's military impotence, despite decades of selfstrengthening measures, and triggered a scramble by the powers for shares of the Chinese pie before the empire might collapse. In 1897, Germany seized the Shandong port of Qingdao, which lay at the entrance to the Yellow River valley. Russia countered by taking a lease on nearby Port Arthur. For its part, France negotiated a lease for the southern port of Guangzhou, while the British moved into Weihaiwei. One year later, Britain also claimed the entire Yangzi valley as its exclusive commercial sphere. All parties seemed resigned to the inevitability of China's wholesale partition.

At this point the United States intervened in an effort to stabilize the situation. In 1899, Secretary of State John Hay (with British encouragement) proclaimed the doctrine of the "open door." In a letter circulated among all the nations concerned, Hay called for equal commercial access throughout China and an end to spheres of influence. Although not one of the major powers committed itself to supporting the idea, Hay announced that everyone had wholeheartedly accepted it. Only Japan took issue with the American conclusion. Surprisingly enough, while the open-door principle probably had no effect on the imperialists, their moves to slice up the "Chinese melon" slowed noticeably after its pronouncement. Probably fear of conflict with one another inspired their separate decisions to consolidate gains already made rather than continue to seek new spoils.

The Reform Movement of 1898

China's humiliating defeat at the hands of Japan and its impending dismemberment by the imperialists gave final impetus to a new method of reform that had been first broached by certain intellectuals outside the emperor's court. Their writings discussed the usual range of possible measures for improving the economic condition of the nation, but more significantly they called for radical reforms, including the abolition of the civil service examination system and the introduction of representative government. In brief, these reformers demanded basic institutional changes in contrast to the cosmetic touchups that had characterized the thinking of the selfstrengtheners.

Spurred on by the growing mood of crisis that began sweeping the country after the mid-1890s, a handful of knowledgeable men, under the leadership of an unorthodox scholar named Kang Youwei, began an allout campaign to plead the cause of radical reformism. Making effective use of all of the traditional channels (memorials and audiences) as well as more modern means of communication (newspapers and magazines), they soon attracted the attention of the Guangxu Emperor himself. The climax of their effort came during a one-hundred-and-three-day period in 1898 when the emperor invited Kang and his associates to court to institute their reform program.

In spite of Kang's argument that there was really nothing unusual in the idea of radically changing the Chinese system (with the then provocative thesis that Confucius himself had been an innovator and had intended his philosophy to promote institutional change), he had gone too far too fast. The forces of opposition within the bureaucracy and especially at court gathered around the powerful figure of the Empress Dowager Cixi. The personification of the old order and bitterly antiforeign once she had witnessed the burning of the Summer Palace in 1860, she may have poisoned her own son, the Tongzhi Emperor, in 1874 and then been responsible for selecting her nephew as his successor. Although not completely averse to adopting Western methods in the selfstrengthening tradition, she decided to oppose the radical reformers both because of their extremism and because her own influence over the throne seemed threatened. Once she had determined to call a halt to the reforms, she moved quickly with the support of the most powerful warlord general, Yuan Shikai, and his army. Kang Youwei fled for his life, but six of his colleagues were caught and put to death. The emperor, who had given the reformers so much support, was virtually deposed and spent the rest of his life in confinement. Perhaps only Western interest in his survival kept Cixi from having him eliminated altogether. Thus, the "Hundred Days of Reform" were dramatically terminated.

The 'Boxer 'Rebellion, 1900

During the 1890s, in many areas of China, secret societies arose as centers of opposition to the alien Manchus. Toward the end of the century, however, these organizations underwent a significant change: their enmity shifted from the dynasty to the foreigners who for the past fifty years had heaped humiliation and misfortune on their country. With the encouragement of local officials, who saw in the popular mood a weapon of potential value against the imperialists, many of the secret societies began to engage in anti-Western activities. One of the most significant groups, known as the "Righteous and Harmonious Fists" ("Boxers" to the Europeans) ignited the fuse for the furious antiforeign rebellion that erupted in 1900.

In June of that year, fearing the imperialists might restore the emperor to power, the Empress Dowager ordered provincial authorities to organize the Boxers to fight an expected foreign invasion. In the countryside fanatical bands of Boxers committed all sorts of violent acts against Westerners and their property. In Beijing itself, after seeking safety in the embassy compound, the foreign community came under Boxer siege. The defenders had to hold out for fifty-five days until the arrival of an international relief force. Driving the Boxers from the capital, an allied army under the command of a German general then proceeded to smash the rebellion in the provinces.

Shattered by the Boxer catastrophe, the old Empress Dowager fled to Xi'an in a donkey cart, but not before ordering Li Hongzhang (one of the heroes of the anti-Taiping campaigns) to negotiate with the allies as his final official act. As revenge for the Boxer "outrage," the imperialists mercilessly imposed an indemnity of almost $334 million, fixed the tariff at 5 percent, ordered the immediate execution of specified Chinese officials, and permanently stationed troops in the capital. In the aftermath of the episode, China lay prostrate before its enemies, the Manchus hopelessly discredited.

Historians today view the Boxer Rebellion as one aspect of early Chinese nationalism, heralding a trend, not just in China but worldwide, that would intensify as the twentieth century progressed. Writing at the turn of the century, Sir Robert Hart, the British official who had so effectively reformed the imperial customs administration, predicted that in fifty years' time "twenty million Boxers" would terminate the unequal treaties and repay China's humiliations with interest.

Toward the First Chinese 'Revolution

In the aftermath of the Boxer Rebellion, there were fewer thinking Chinese who questioned the need for change. Reformers and revolutionaries argued strenuously over innovations to be pursued. Returning to the capital in 1901, the aging Empress Dowager immediately solicited advice on reform from her officials. As a consequence of the deliberations that followed, the government announced the initiation of a series of institutional changes closely resembling those proposed in 1898 by Kang Youwei. This time, however, these efforts (1901–1905) would produce lasting results. The more important features of the emerging program included abolition of the civil service examinations, introduction of Western-type schools based on modern educational concepts, and the sending of students abroad. A deafening clamor for constitutional government in China, especially from students attending foreign schools, followed hard upon these events. The pressure became so great that the regime had to acquiesce. In 1908 it proposed a constitution to become effective after nine years of tutelage, culminating in a system very close to democracy. In spite of last-gasp efforts by the Manchus to preserve the government's traditional power, the mood in society was so anti-Manchu that the transition to constitutionalism seemed inevitable.

Meanwhile, for some, reform no longer held the answer to China's problems. Rooted in the tradition of China's secret societies, revolutionary organizations began to form in various locales. They attracted many of those same young people who had studied abroad only to return home to find few official jobs awaiting them and incompetent reactionaries still in charge of the government. After numerous false starts and failures, the revolution began on October 10, 1911, when a student munitions storehouse at Hankou exploded. Today the Chinese still celebrate the anniversary of this "Double Tenth" (the tenth day of the tenth month). The fall of the centuries-old imperial system followed rapidly. A newly elected parliament meeting in Nanjing chose Dr. Sun Yat-sen, a generally unsuccessful but well-known revolutionary, to be the first provisional president of the Chinese Republic.

Sun was born of a poor peasant family in 1866 in a village near Canton. At the age of thirteen he went to live with his brother, a successful merchant-farmer in Hawaii. There Sun attended a local missionary school and later graduated from Oahu College in 1883. Frequent travel between China and the islands over the next few years helped develop his revolutionary attitudes. During the late 1880s and early 1890s, he studied medicine in Canton and then Hong Kong, and upon earning his degree began to practice in Macao. All the while he was planning for the day when he would help to overthrow the Manchu dynasty. In 1895 his revolutionary activity began in earnest with travels abroad to raise money among the overseas Chinese.

As a constitutionalist, Sun Yat-sen admired the French Third Republic but looked upon Japan as the most logical model for the Chinese revolution. Japan intrigued him because it had borrowed the institutions and culture of China yet had managed successfully to modernize itself and rise to great-power status. Beyond his commitment to constitutionalism, Sun based his revolutionary thought on what he called the "Three Principles of the People:" the people's nationalism, the people's democracy, and the people's livelihood. The revolution itself, he argued, would progress through three stages: military government, political tutelage, and constitutional democracy.

When the revolution actually broke out in 1911, Sun was in the United States on one of his many fundraising trips. Upon his return to China, the provisional assembly named him president, but a formidable rival stood in his way. Yuan Shikai, the treacherous warlord who had aided the deceased Empress Dowager in her elimination of the radical reformers in 1898, now commanded China's most powerful and disciplined army and controlled Beijing. Yuan had already overthrown the Manchu dynasty, but his forces now threatened the country with civil war. Everyone feared that another outbreak of violence would enable the Westerners to impose new and more burdensome treaties upon China. Seeking to eliminate that possibility, Sun resigned his presidency in exchange for Yuan's promise to govern the republic according to the new constitution and with the national assembly. Sun's selfless act, together with Western loans and promises of future support, strengthened Yuan's position. His commitment to constitutionalism, however, soon revealed itself to be completely insincere.

Nationalist

3

to Communist Revolution, 1912 to 1949

Its violent collision with the West in the nineteenth century had proved humiliating and traumatic for China. Mired in complacency and committed to preserving the traditional system, too many Chinese and Manchus had failed to grasp the significance of mounting Western triumphs at China's expense. Convinced that the problems either would disappear in time or could be solved by the application of centuries-old practices in barbarian relations, government leaders unwittingly signed the death warrant of both the Qing dynasty and the imperial system. Reluctantly they responded to calls for change, but their efforts proved disappointingly superficial. As the twentieth century opened, growing numbers of Chinese who had lost faith in the possibility of saving their country through reform were turning to a more radical solution: revolution. But what kind of revolution? The decades after 1911 would see this question debated over and over again; and to this day it is a subject of controversy among the Chinese.

Yuan Shikai's Regime, 1912–1916

Yuan Shikai, destined to serve as China's first president, was born in Hunan Province in 1859. Hoping to rise out of his poor peasant environment, he prepared for the civil service examination but was unsuccessful. With the bureaucracy thus closed to him, he entered the military and eventually gained favor with the Empress Dowager. In 1898, contrary to his pledge to support the emperor's program, he helped Cixi to reassert her authority and bring an end to the Hundred Days of Reform. Well aware of Yuan's penchant for trickery, the Manchu regent dismissed him after the Empress Dowager's death in 1908, but during the revolution of 1911, the government solicited his services in defense of the dynasty. At first he gave his patrons cause for hope by suppressing disorder in Hankou, but then he refused to proceed further unless appointed premier.

Dictating his own terms, he treacherously forced the Manchus to abdicate and deceptively "persuaded" Sun Yat-sen to step aside as provisional president of the new republic. After he obtained loans from the great powers in return for a guarantee of their treaty rights, his position seemed unassailable. The Chinese revolution had apparently come to an end with a capable "strong man" to ensure stability.

Yuan, however, nurtured greater aspirations than the presidency of a liberal republic. Remaining in Beijing on the pretext of keeping order in the capital, he refused to cooperate in 1913 with the national assembly in Nanjing, where Sun Yat-sen's party, the Guomindang (Kuomintang, hence KMT), or Nationalists, held the majority. When the assembly delegates protested, Yuan attacked Nanjing and dispersed them. Sun departed for Japan where he would remain in exile until after Yuan's death in 1916. With his opposition out of the way, Yuan scrapped the constitution and proclaimed himself president for life. China now found itself ruled by a virtual military dictatorship as Yuan edged closer to his ultimate ambition—the ascension to the Dragon Throne.

Yuan had powerful enemies, however, in the increasingly aggressive Japanese. Since 1905 Japan had dominated East Asia, partitioning Manchuria and Mongolia with the Russians and annexing Korea. As an ally of the British at the outbreak of World War I in August, 1914, Japan easily took the German concessions in Shandong and several islands in the southwest Pacific. Many Japanese, who had supported the more malleable Sun, regarded Yuan Shikai's capture of the Chinese Revolution as a threat to Japan's interests. In January, 1915, with China at its mercy, Japan presented Yuan with the infamous "Twenty-One Demands," intending to reduce the young republic to satellite status. Among other terms, the document called for extension of Japanese leases on Chinese railways and mines, exclusive rights in the Yangzi valley, and installation of Japanese advisers in the Chinese government. Despite a flood of Chinese popular protest, Yuan accepted (with U.S. support) an altered version of the original stipulations in a treaty signed with Japan toward the end of May.

With the Japanese temporarily appeased, Yuan moved towards his intended goal—the founding of a new imperial dynasty. After months of public preparation, he announced that his reign as emperor would commence in 1916. Protest arose from all quarters. Students, businesspeople, and peasants voiced their hatred of the perennially opportunistic Yuan and his betrayal of the republic. Even army officers now sought to oust him. The storm of opposition finally drove Yuan to renounce the throne and withdraw from politics. He died within six months, an embittered man. Yet, far from improving China's political situation, Yuan's ouster left a vacuum in national politics which no successor could adequately fill. In the absence of strong central government in Beijing (where the fiction of republicanism was preserved), local warlords with private armies emerged in numbers too large to count. Their separatist ambitions as well as lack of commitment to republicanism and nationalism kept China politically fragmented and internationally weak for well over three decades. For his part, Sun Yat-sen would struggle in vain over the next few years to establish a workable government in Canton as a base from which to lead the struggle for national unification.

Japan / Russia / Britain vs. Germany ?

US / china

The Intellectual Revolution and New Culture Movement, 1917-1923

The twentieth century has witnessed the collapse of traditional China. The first blow was struck when revolutionaries not only overthrew the Qing dynasty but also signaled the death of the imperial institution itself with the establishment of the republic. Even though the new political order failed to survive the machinations of Yuan Shikai and the disruptive acts of the warlords, there was little sentiment among thinking Chinese for a restoration of traditional politics. As their enthusiasm carried them further to the left, many withdrew support even from the republic, thus eliminating any possible return to monarchy.

The reason for this attitude is not hard to find. A new generation of intellectuals, Western-educated or at least Western-influenced, had emerged to challenge not merely the old politics but also the whole philosophical basis of traditional China. As yet politically impotent, the progressives nevertheless wielded enormous influence over a growing reading public, which was increasingly willing to ponder radical solutions to China's problems. Western standards became the yardstick by which the "new" men and women judged China, and Western political institutions, culture, scientific knowledge, and technology promised the means by which they sought to forge a modern nation.

To achieve the complete transformation of national life, men like Chen Duxiu, Cai Yuanpei, and Hu Shi (products of American education) called upon their countrymen to abolish all vestiges of the past. Unlike previous reformers, they had no desire to purify or revitalize Confucianism; rather, they strove to discredit it as a reactionary, obscurant philosophy whose continued domination of Chinese society would only further impede the country's progress. To replace Confucian ideas, the new people published magazines (*New Youth, New Tide*, and *Weekly Critic*) in which they offered a tantalizing array of Western substitutes, including the philosophies of Kant, Nietzsche, Dewey, Bergson, and Marx. In the short space of a few years, Chinese were introduced to ideas and systems of thought which had taken Europeans more than a century to develop and digest. For the time being, few people made a personal commitment to any particular philosophy. Most merely dabbled in the vast reservoir of Western wisdom available for the first time. To be sure, there was much foolishness, as the glorification of science exemplifies, but finally the debates and controversies that flourished in those years had two major consequences: they enormously stimulated the thinking public in China and strengthened nationalist sentiment, and they popularized such notions as progress, democracy, freedom, and individualism, particularly through the new magazines whose editors and writers abandoned classical Chinese in favor of the vernacular (*bai hua*).

The Search for National Unification, 1916-1926

Together with the intellectual revolution which was sweeping China, developments at the Paris Peace Conference (convened in 1919 to conclude the post-World War I settlements) contributed to the growing activism of many Chinese in the early 1920s. The Chinese had hoped to obtain some revision of the unequal treaties by their participation in the war on the side of the victorious allies. If nothing else, they felt certain that Germany's concessions would be returned to

China and, if the slogans "territorial integrity" and "national self-determination" as proclaimed by many of the world's statesmen had any substance, perhaps one could expect even more. However, because of a secret agreement signed in early 1917 by England, France, and the warlord government in Beijing to turn over Germany's Shandong holdings to Japan, Chinese hopes were frustrated. The revelation of allied duplicity released a torrent of protest among incredulous Chinese of all classes that culminated in a major eruption on May 4, 1919. While this public outcry had little effect on China's relations with the outside world, it represented a significant step forward in the growth of Chinese nationalism. Many people received their initial taste of political activity by participating in the strikes, demonstrations, and boycotts that swept the country (particularly its urban centers) as part of what became known as the "May Fourth Movement."

Perhaps more than anything else, party politics in China benefited from the spirit of activism which now pervaded society. Hundreds flocked to Sun Yat-sen and his Guomindang (KMT), revitalizing it after years of precarious existence, while a select few also joined the newly formed (1921) Chinese Communist Party (CCP). While increased membership would provide the KMT with the broad popular support it sorely needed, the infusion of new blood only exacerbated a problem that had long plagued Sun—the matter of discipline and organization.

To overcome these weaknesses, Sun gradually turned to the Soviet Union and its Bolshevik leadership for assistance. Once again the West had angered him by refusing any substantial adjustment in the unequal treaty system at the Washington Conference (1921–22). Inspired by Lenin's success in forging a new state system in Russia (a feat that owed much to the kind of party he had created), impressed by the Soviet offer of assistance to China's revolution, and concerned with the growing influence of the Chinese Communist Party, Sun finally contacted the Soviet Union. In early 1923, after months of negotiations, he agreed to cooperate in the establishment of a United Front with the CCP in return for guidance from Soviet political and military advisers and financial backing. Making it clear that the Communists were entering the KMT and not vice versa, he took steps to ensure that his new allies would not use the United Front to subvert the Nationalists or thoroughly communize their organization.

Still, Sun paid a price for the advisers, money, and weapons which now assisted his movement. On the one hand, they compelled him to modify the "Three Principles of the People," which underlay the Nationalist program, to stress antiimperialism, the need for strong government, and anticapitalism, thereby bringing his previous pronouncements on nationalism, democracy, and the public welfare more in line with Soviet ideology. On the other hand, Sun created dissension within the ranks of the KMT because some of his followers refused to accept the party's reorientation. Despite his best efforts, many conservatives persisted in their disapproval of the United Front. When they came to dominate the party in 1927, they moved quickly to destroy the alliance.

The Rise of Chiang Kai-shek and the Northern Campaign, 1926-1928

Political reorganization along Bolshevik lines invigorated the KMT. Under the direction of Comintern agent Michael Borodin, Soviet advisers helped to centralize the party's administration, regularize its finances, and coordinate its propaganda. With Sun and his associates assuming effective leadership, Canton became the center of a small but enterprising government by 1925, a microcosm of Nationalist aspirations. Although recognized by neither warlords nor foreign powers, the Canton government rapidly consolidated itself and created its own "new model" army, which would provide the main force for the military effort to reunify China.

Following Sun Yat-sen's sudden death in March, 1925, in the midst of negotiations with the warlord faction at Beijing, a struggle for control of the KMT ensued. One of the claimants was Chiang Kai-shek, a young military officer and director of the Whampoa Military Academy near Canton. Born in 1887 to a poor merchant family in Zhejiang province, Chiang had met Sun in Japan and later participated in the revolutionary events of 1911–12. For the next ten years, however, he generally remained aloof from politics. Not until 1923 did he emerge again as a devoted and active follower of Sun's cause. Nevertheless, within four years, he would become the leader of the KMT.

By 1926, the Canton government had grown strong enough to begin the longawaited campaign against the northern warlords. Under Chiang's command, Nationalist forces swept into the Yangzi valley, overran half of China's provinces and "liberated" scores of important cities, often with the assistance of local Communist party cells. In the midst of the campaign, however, an open break occurred between conservative and radical wings of the KMT, fomented by Communist-inspired riots among the peasant and working classes and the killing of numerous foreigners. Both actions frightened the wealthier and more conservative members of the Guomindang, the very people who were Chiang's principal supporters.

Suddenly, Chiang attacked all Communist cells, following the capture of Shanghai. For a brief period, the political purge raged furiously, but by late March, 1927, the conservatives had triumphed with their resolve to sever the alliance with the Communists. By mid-April, they liquidated the Chinese radicals and dismissed the Russian advisers of the KMT, while survivors fled underground or to the safety of the countryside. Mao Zedong and Zhu De, youthful leaders of the CCP, led two shattered contingents to the frontiers of Jiangxi, a southeastern province. Protected by its mountains and forests, they kept alive the Communist movement, regrouped its forces, and turned to guerrilla action against Chiang and his party, resolving to repay their "blood debt" to him for his betrayal of the alliance.

Meanwhile, his opposition crushed, Chiang resumed the Northern Campaign. By the end of 1928, his armies had occupied Beijing and achieved at least nominal control over most of China. While many warlords continued to ignore his authority, the foreign powers recognized the new government which he established at Nanjing. Financial assistance from abroad bolstered Chiang's regime, and tentative steps were taken toward a revision of the unequal treaties. Following the lead of the United States, the great powers agreed to relinquish control of the country's customs and tariffs, and over the next couple of years they abolished a number of foreign-held concessions. In such circumstances, there was every reason to expect that the victorious Guomindang could now undertake

Nationalist leader Chiang Kai-shek toasts Mao Zedong in Chongqing (fall of 1945) in one of the failed attempts to create a coalition government with the Communists.

Rural village.

the reconstruction of the country. Japanese aggression and the persistent opposition of the Communists, however, distracted Chiang's attention from this critical task.

The Japanese Invasion of Manchuria, 1931-1933

For Japan, the 1920s were a decade of growing crisis and disillusionment. All of the uncertainties engendered by modernization, coupled with population pressure and a weakening economy, worked together to create domestic tensions that ultimately would find release in foreign adventurism. Military leaders, alarmed by the worsening circumstances of Japanese rural life and resentful of their own lack of influence in determining their country's policies, began to maneuver for political power and to advocate a program of expansionism (beginning with China) as a cure for Japan's problems. They especially coveted the rich province of Manchuria. Convinced that Japan must directly control the region's raw materials vital to its industrial machine and great-power status, local officers in charge of the Japanese Guangdong Army pressured for immediate action. On September 18, 1931, a minor explosion on the South Manchurian Railway near Mukden (Shenyang), set off by the Japanese but blamed on the Chinese, provided the pretext for a full-scale invasion of Manchuria. Meeting little resistance, the Japanese overran the entire region within five months. In so doing, they launched the long series of events that would add a Pacific theater to the Second World War.

At that time, Chiang Kai-shek chose not to fight because of China's weaknesses. In the southeast, his armies were still clashing with the Communists, whom he regarded as the more dangerous enemy. "The Japanese are a disease of the skin," he reportedly observed, "whereas the Communists are a disease of the heart." Resolved to avoid an armed clash with Japan and certain defeat, Chiang instead appealed to the League of Nations. He undoubtedly knew that this would be a vain effort, but he was seeking time to strengthen his hand. The League took up the issue, called for a cessation of hostilities, and sent an investigatory mission to the scene. Beyond this, however, it did nothing except express its moral disapproval of the Japanese, who by May, 1933, had successfully occupied China's four northeastern provinces. A truce signed at that time brought a temporary halt to Japanese expansion in China and acknowledged their acquisitions. Chiang felt justified in making concessions to avoid military disaster against the Japanese. As a result, the policy of "internal pacification before resistance to external aggression" continued to guide his actions. The decision to adopt this tactic, however, proved a costly miscalculation in the long run. Refusal to resist the Japanese eroded Chinese nationalism's support of Chiang, and his failure to capitalize on Japan's aggression cost him a major opportunity to mobilize the Chinese people.

The Nationalists and the Communists, 1927-1937

When the remnants of the Communist movement fled to Jiangxi following Chiang Kai-shek's attempt to liquidate it in 1927, the future looked bleak. Yet, by taking advantage of popular discontent to broaden its base of support, the Communists created a professional military force (the Red Army) which refined the technique of guerrilla warfare into an effective strategy. Thus, the Communists were able to resist Chiang's armies successfully. While organizing a network of local cells, they established a Chinese Soviet Republic in the southeast by 1931 with Mao Zedong as the key figure.

Born in 1893, the son of a relatively well-to-do peasant family, Mao rebelled against landlordism and the tyranny of paternal authority at an early age. Like many youths during the first decades of the twentieth century, Mao was caught up in the groundswell of change and became a revolutionary activist. One of a handful responsible for founding the CCP in 1921, he assumed the task of organizing the peasants during the period of the first United Front. His experiences in the countryside strengthened his conviction that the success of the Communist cause in China depended upon the mobilization of the peasantry. For years he argued this theoretical position long and hard against both Chinese and Russian Communist leaders, whose interpretation of Marxism-Leninism and infatuation with the Russian revolutionary experience led them to concentrate on the Chinese urban proletariat. But in the end he managed to convince the world of the validity of his assertion that whoever won over the peasants would gain China.

Before that day arrived, however, Mao successfully parried Chiang Kai-shek's efforts to crush the Communist movement. Had Chiang been entirely free, he probably would have hounded the CCP remnants to extermination immediately following his 1927 purge. But other matters distracted him, thereby providing his archenemies a much-needed respite. Not until late in 1930 was he able to launch the first two "bandit annihilation offensives" designed to encircle the Communist stronghold in the Jiangxi-Hunan region. A rude surprise, however, awaited him. Rather than encountering a ragtag force of disorganized rabble, Chiang's troops confronted well-trained, aggressive, and highly mobile Red Army units who fought skillfully against a more numerous foe. The KMT suffered serious setbacks. In 1931, Chiang tried again, this time leading the attack himself. Success seemed imminent, but news of the Manchurian Incident forced a Nationalist withdrawal. Throughout the rest of the year and into 1932, Japanese aggression required most of Chiang's attention. After the situation in North China had stabilized somewhat, he conducted a fourth campaign against the Communists in late 1932 and 1933, but this ended in a stalemate. Advised by volunteer German officers, Chiang next constructed a series of blockhouses along the perimeter of the Communist-held territory. This relentlessly tightening blockade would set the stage for the fifth KMT campaign, which by spring of 1934 was ready to deliver the final blow.

With the Nationalists closing in, the Communist leaders decided to abandon their base. In October, 1934, the main force of some one hundred thousand men, women, and children slipped through the battlelines, headed west as far as the border of Tibet and then turned northward. Carrying all of their possessions, they crossed twenty-four rivers, eighteen mountain ranges, twelve separate provinces, and ten hostile warlord-held territories before completing what history would know as the "Long March." After three hundred and sixty-eight days of flight over more than five thousand torturous miles, walking mostly at night to escape Chiang's aircraft, only twenty thousand arrived at the final destination. Mao, who during the flight had succeeded in wresting leadership of the party from Stalin's agents or "returned students" (he was now chairman of the Politburo since the Zunyi Conference of January, 1935), settled his force around

Yan'an, which would remain the Communists' headquarters until 1947, shortly before their final victory over the Nationalists.

The Long March, for all of its drama, had decimated the Communist ranks and thoroughly exhausted the survivors. Under those conditions, it seemed unlikely that they would be able to withstand the expected KMT attack on their new base. Chiang counted on Manchurian troops under the command of the "Young Marshal," Zhang Xueliang, in his final battle with the Communists, but their commitment to an anti-Communist offensive took second place to a desire to liberate their homeland from Japanese occupation. When Zhang Xueliang failed to move against Mao's forces as ordered, Chiang Kai-shek flew to Zhang's headquarters at Xi'an in December, 1936. There he was confronted by rebellious officers who, encouraged by the Communists, demanded an end to the civil war and the formation of a united front against the Japanese. Arrested and detained for two weeks, Chiang finally had to agree. As a result of the new alliance, following this Xi'an Incident, the Red Army was nominally placed under KMT command. In view of the fiasco of the first KMT-CCP cooperation in 1927, neither Mao nor Chiang had any illusions about the long-term success of the Second United Front. Nevertheless, for a short time most of China rallied behind Chiang in an outpouring of Nationalist sentiment that reflected a desire for allout resistance to the Japanese.

China During the Sino-Japanese War, 1937-1945

Well before the Japanese launched their full-scale invasion of China in 1937, they had been making serious inroads into the country's northeastern sector and had engaged in extensive smuggling. Yet, when Chinese and Japanese troops clashed at the Marco Polo Bridge near Beijing on July 7, 1937, the Japanese did not expect or desire the incident to lead to allout war. By this time, the Japanese military was headed by more responsible leaders than had been the case in the late 1920s, and Japan's goals were limited to consolidating its control over northern China so as to protect its interests from Russian interference. Had Chiang Kai-shek followed his longstanding policy of negotiating with the Japanese and avoiding war, the events following the Marco Polo Bridge Incident might have taken a different course. But the Xi'an Incident and public objection to any further concessions or collaboration severely limited Chiang's options. While some negotiations were undertaken, growing hostility on both sides made accommodation impossible. The Japanese hoped to persuade Chiang to accede to their wishes by massing troops in the Beijing area and dispatching naval and military forces to take up positions off Shanghai. These moves, however, served only to deepen Japan's involvement in China and led to the outbreak of major hostilities at Shanghai on August 13, 1937. Although the belligerents did not make a legal declaration before December, 1941, the second Sino-Japanese War had begun.

The long years of fighting that would merge into World War II had ensued, despite the Japanese command's promise to the emperor that a mere two months' campaign would conquer northeastern China and terminate the conflict. Even though the Japanese eventually overran the great coastal cities and almost all of eastern China, thereby forcing the Nationalist government to transfer its capital far inland to Chongqing, they had never planned to absorb the entire country. Safe behind the protective barriers of the upper Yangzi and the mountains of Sichuan, Chiang refused all peace offers while pressing for American entry into the conflict, tying down sizable Japanese forces during World War II. Avoiding costly operations against the Japanese because of Chinese military weaknesses, Chiang apparently reserved his resources for the day when he would resume action against the Communists, despite the counsel of American advisers.

But Chiang's prolonged refuge in his inland capital, in the end, did much to separate him from important segments of his people. Settled in Chongqing, cut off from the industrial and banking resources of the coastal urban industrial centers, Chiang had to rely more and more on the conservative landlord class whose main goal was to preserve the old agrarian social system. In time the interests of this landlord group prevailed over the more progressive urban intellectual and business elements who had fled with the Nationalist government and who were more inclined to support necessary social and agrarian reform, antagonizing many of the latter elements from the KMT cause. In addition, evacuation of the eastern areas abandoned millions of peasants to brutal Japanese occupation, forcing many to turn away from the Nationalists and toward Communist guerrilla units for protection. Thus the Communists commenced their conquest of Chinese nationalism. Had Chiang proclaimed a future land reform program at the peak of his popularity (1938), he might have cemented peasant loyalty more effectively to his leadership.

Meanwhile, in Shanxi province, the Communists were working to rebuild their shattered movement. Thanks to the declaration of the Second United Front and the Japanese invasion of China, they were relieved of serious military pressure throughout the years of the Sino-Japanese War. During that period, which began what is commonly called the "Yan'an" stage of CCP history (from the fact that Yan'an became the movement's northwest capital in January, 1937), a new revolutionary technique was born that would contribute to a remarkable reversal in the fortunes of the CCP and that continues to have political and psychological significance for Chinese Communists today. Lasting over a decade until 1947, the Yan'an era also witnessed the consolidation of Mao's power within the party. Perhaps most important, it was the period when Mao took up the study of Marxist-Leninist theory in earnest for the first time, evaluated it in the light of Chinese conditions, the experiences of the CCP over the previous two decades, and his own intellectual predispositions, and formulated a distinct variant of it known as "Maoism."

Maoism, of course, is first of all a method of political and social analysis. But it is also a set of concepts, an ideology, which provides the underlying motive for action. Complex and diffuse, the "thoughts of Mao Zedong" can be defined, however, by a few basic precepts. First, Maoism promoted the idea that human consciousness is the decisive factor in history and that people's wills and actions can not only change objective reality but also accomplish the seemingly impossible. Second, Maoism emphasizes the development and maintenance of "correct" thought in order to be able to analyze properly current situations and conditions so as to be prepared to take advantage of immediate opportunities for revolutionary action. As a result, Maoists have refused to be restricted by the rigid formulas of Marxism-Leninism as proclaimed by Moscow, and instead have granted more importance to "subjective factors" in the determination of strategy and tactics. Third, Maoism argues for the distinctiveness of the Chinese revolution and, conversely, for the limited applicability of the Russian experience as a model for China. "Although we must value Soviet experience," Mao wrote in 1936, "and even value it somewhat more than experiences in other countries throughout history, . . . we must value even more the experience of China's revolutionary war, because there are a great number of conditions special to the Chinese revolution and the Chinese Red Army." What determined China's uniqueness in Mao's opinion were three characteristics: (1) it was a semicolonial country; (2) it was controlled not by one but by several imperialist powers; and (3) it was "unevenly" developed economically and politically. From these observations Mao drew two conclusions: first, that the very uniqueness of China's situation made the likelihood of a successful revolution there even greater; and second, that the revolution would spread from the rural areas to engulf the semimodern and nonrevolutionary cities.

The Yan'an experience entailed, however, more than just the development of the ideology which would lead the CCP and its supporters to victory by 1949. On the practical side, it was characterized by the abandonment of the United Front with the Nationalists in early 1942 and its replacement by a commitment to build a unified party on Maoist foundations. The "rectification" (*zheng feng*) movement of 1942–44 sought to bring an end to party heterodoxy and to instill in cadres common ideology and goals. Through intense criticism and self-criticism and the study of selected documents clearly in line with Mao's views, thousands of party members (many of them recent recruits) were introduced to "correct" thought and made more amenable to accept the radical shift in policy which the party was about to initiate.

By 1941, the failure of the United Front strategy and severe losses to the Japanese had revealed shortcomings in prevailing CCP policies and tactics. As a consequence, the party leadership, headed by Mao, devised a new strategy to sustain the movement, prevent further erosion of support, and ultimately to strengthen the whole Communist cause and prepare it for the next round of action. The rectification campaign was an essential step in that direction, but it was accompanied by a number of other campaigns, moderate in spirit, yet designed to indoctrinate the people, exclude as few as possible from the revolutionary process, unleash the energies of the masses, and direct them toward the task of solving social problems in the Communist-held base areas. Among the many programs inaugurated in those years were: (1) the "to the village" campaign (1941 and 1942), which helped to break down the isolation of many communities by sending cadres into their midst and shifting the focus of government work to the lower levels of society; (2) the campaign for the reduction of rents and interest (1942–44), which served to awaken apathetic peasants by rallying them around an issue that had great appeal; (3) the cooperative movement (1942–44), which, by stressing the concept of mutual aid, worked to increase production and develop new relationships among peasants; and (4) the education movement of 1944, which spread literacy and indoctrinated the masses in Communist ideology. It is instructive that the party's emphasis was on adult education rather than that of children during this campaign.

Through programs such as these, the party sought to mobilize the masses, involve them actively in resolving the many problems which beset them, and gain their commitment to the Communist cause seemingly by equating its goals with theirs. The success of the campaigns, however, depended on the effectiveness of mobilization. To encourage and increase popular involvement, the party developed a propaganda technique known as the "mass line." Simple and not very original in concept, the technique comprised a three-stage process. First, cadres would go to the people to determine what kind of program appealed to them. Once the determination had been made, the second step was to square popular desires with party ideology and goals. This was often the most difficult task because in the third stage the cadres had to persuade the masses that to support the program was in their best interests. Even more than that, the key to the success of the mass line technique was in arousing the people to believe in the program and to act upon it with true commitment. The mass line opened up leadership possibilities for peasants through its promotion of quasidemocratic debate; it also provided the needed link between the party and the masses to involve every individual in the effort to resist the Japanese and to reconstruct the economy and restructure the political and social order within the base areas. As a leadership technique, the mass line has become a permanent feature of the Chinese Communist scene.

The campaigns of the early 1940s and use of the mass line technique had scored well by the end of the Sino-Japanese War in 1945. Communist propaganda reached millions of people, party membership had risen to 1.2 million (compared with forty thousand in 1937), and the Red Army numbered about 1 million. What had been a movement on the verge of extinction only ten years before was now capable of challenging the KMT for the leadership of China. It had not only developed the material resources, the organizational ability, and the military tactics to succeed, but more importantly had the support of millions indoctrinated with Communist ideals and a feeling of confidence in the struggle's outcome.

U.S. Assistance and the Stilwell Controversy, 1940–1944

As Nationalist allegiance in the provinces steadily weakened, Chiang's regime at Chongqing grew increasingly isolated, unable to take much part in the war against Japan after Pearl Harbor. In 1940, the Japanese established a puppet government at Nanjing under his old enemy, Wang Jingwei. Chiang's coalition with the Communists collapsed after a Communist-Nationalist clash on the lower Yangzi in January, 1941, and from then on, his army clamped a tight blockade (excluding all trade) on the Communist areas. The Chinese civil war resumed from that point.

In addition, Chiang's relations with his foreign allies came under considerable stress as they found it increasingly difficult to assist him. American and British aid dated from 1931, the Russian from 1937. But the Japanese conquest of Southeast Asia (1941–42) isolated Chongqing. Flights over the Himalayas ("the Hump") brought some U.S. help just as Russian arms shipments through

Xinjiang came to a halt. In the words of General George C. Marshall, the U.S. Army Chief of Staff, China was "at the end of the thinnest supply line of all." The "Europe First" strategy of the allied powers also put China far down on the priority list—"like feeding an elephant with an eye dropper." President Franklin D. Roosevelt, however, wanted Nationalist China to participate actively in the war in order to replace Japan in the future East Asian power balance. Washington projected an invasion of Burma to secure access to Chongqing, and the president appointed General Joseph W. Stilwell as Chiang's chief of staff for the newly created China-Burma-India theater. Born in 1883, Stilwell graduated from West Point and saw extensive duty in the Far East where he became fluent in Mandarin Chinese. In the early 1920s he headed a language school in Beijing under General Marshall. Although Stilwell personally trained a Chinese army for the campaign, the Japanese disastrously defeated his first Burma invasion in 1942.

Stilwell proposed drastic reforms for the Nationalist army: reduction to a smaller, more efficient size, elimination of the warlord element, and full cooperation with the Communists. Mao Zedong's mobile guerrilla warfare against the Japanese dominated the countryside in many occupied regions. Communist leaders offered to place their forces under Stilwell's command when the general journeyed to Yan'an for talks. Stilwell then tried to persuade Chiang to reach an agreement with Mao and to withdraw his blockade of Communist areas.

Chiang procrastinated, as he secretly did not share these views. He could not directly oppose Stilwell's reform program, however, lest this jeopardize American aid. Yet he realized that reduction of the army would eliminate his landlord support, while a modernized force might defect to the Communists. Moreover, Chiang deeply distrusted the Yan'an proposal since two agreements already had been shattered. Gradually, Stilwell discerned Chiang's attitude. Despite a successful Burma campaign in 1943, the American quarreled constantly with the Chinese leader. When President Roosevelt proposed Stilwell for commander-in-chief of the Nationalist forces in 1944, Chiang resented this intrusion on his authority and demanded Stilwell's recall. When the general returned to the United States, he expressed his bitterness to the news media. Stilwell's subsequent discussions with General Marshall undoubtedly dimmed the latter's view of the China situation prior to the Marshall Mission in 1945–47.

Stilwell's criticism of Chiang's regime exposed much of its so-called "corruption" to the American people, who hitherto had regarded Chiang as a heroic figure. The erosion of American support for the Generalissimo began from that point.

Final Stage of the Civil War, 1945–1949

The Far Eastern extension of the Second World War came to an end in August, 1945, but in its wake peace did not come to China. No sooner had the Japanese capitulation been announced than both Communist and Nationalist forces rushed to fill the vacuum created by their departing enemy and secure control of as much of China as possible. In the scramble for territory, the advantage seemed to lie with the Nationalists. For one thing, the Japanese had been ordered to surrender only to Chiang Kai-shek's forces; for another, American ships and planes facilitated the movement of Nationalist troops from their inland positions to the coastal areas and northern China. At this point, however, Chiang made two major tactical blunders that significantly affected the outcome of the civil war. The first was his decision to concentrate on the occupation of the principal cities. While not a surprising move on his part, in view of the KMT's longstanding reliance on China's urban economy and population, it was militarily disastrous because it allowed the Communists to gain firm control of the countryside. The second error resulted from Chiang's decision to commit some of his best divisions to Manchuria, trying to prevent division of the country north and south. He hoped to seize this industrial region and strike a crippling blow against the Communists; instead, he found out very quickly that his lines of communication and supply were stretched dangerously thin, extremely vulnerable to the guerrilla tactics used so effectively by the Red Army. Also the Russians had thoroughly looted the province and then presented stored Japanese arms to the Chinese Communists as they entered Manchuria.

Meanwhile, American efforts to mediate KMT-CCP differences in the hopes of avoiding a full scale civil war continued. In December, 1945, President Harry S Truman sent General Marshall to China to negotiate with Communists and Nationalists alike. As a result of a Political Consultative Conference attended by delegates from both camps, Marshall was able to announce several agreements that held out promise for a peaceful resolution of China's potentially explosive political troubles. The Conference called for a military truce to begin immediately, established procedures for moving China in the direction of a political settlement that would be democratic in nature, and envisioned the eventual integration of Communist and Nationalist armies into a nonpoliticized national military force.

The spirit of compromise proved ephemeral. Almost immediately, disputes over the political control of certain areas, notably Manchuria, led to military clashes. The violations of the truce reported by American officers mounted through the remainder of 1946. Communist complaints were directed not only at the refusal of some Nationalist commanders to honor the truce but also at the KMT government for its clear lack of commitment to the proposed establishment of a constitutional order in China. Moreover, as mediator, Marshall found his neutral position compromised because the United States openly supported one of the belligerents. By the beginning of 1947, his last effort to reconcile the country's contending forces proved an obvious failure, and both KMT and CCP leaders prepared their supporters for allout civil war to determine the future leadership of China.

The outcome of the struggle still could not be determined as late as 1947. In that year the Nationalists launched a major offensive that resulted in some dramatic victories (such as the capture of Yan'an, the Communist capital); yet, such triumphs as were claimed by Chiang Kai-shek had very little substance and did nothing to either strengthen his position or to weaken that of the Communists. By the spring of 1948, in fact, Red Army tactics of avoiding major clashes with KMT troops in favor of harassing supply lines and encircling Nationalist-held cities had begun to tip the balance in its favor. A major Communist success was achieved in Manchuria where Chiang's forces had isolated themselves and had taken up defensive positions in and around the major urban centers. Denied the opportunity to either attack or withdraw, KMT troops found themselves caught in numerous traps, surrounded, and cut off. By the summer of 1948, Red Army units had succeeded in completely severing overland supply lines to Manchuria, with the result that Nationalist troops had to be provisioned by air. From summer through late autumn, the KMT military situation deteriorated rapidly. Heavy troop losses following the evacuation of several Manchurian cities and the surrender of the army at Mukden (Shenyang) were accompanied by the abandonment of huge amounts of American supplies and armaments which then fell into the eager hands of the Communists. By December, China north of the Yangzi was under Red Army control and Nationalist resistance had been all but shattered. James E. Sheridan, the American historian, offered a graphic illustration of the victorious Communist guerrilla strategy. He compared the Chinese landscape to a checkerboard, wherein Mao's forces in the rural areas occupied the spaces, while his Japanese and Nationalist opponents controlled the lines (the roads, railways, and communications), and especially the intersecting points, where the cities were located. Thus, Mao utilized domination of the countryside to surround and strangle the enemy.

Defeated on the field of battle, hamstrung by economic collapse, panicked by runaway inflation (the yuan-to-dollar exchange rate had risen from one thousand to 1 in 1945 to forty-five thousand to 1 in mid-1947) and cancerous fiscal corruption, unable to maintain the morale of its supporters, and abandoned by millions who felt that their interests had been too long ignored, the Nationalist government faced a situation that few would have thought possible even five years before. In one last desperate ploy to salvage at least something of KMT influence in Chinese affairs, Chiang resigned the presidency and sought a negotiated settlement with his adversary. The time for such maneuvers, however, was long past. Flushed with their victories in the north, the Communists used the negotiations to consolidate their hold over territory already acquired and prepare for the anticipated campaign to "liberate" China south of the Yangzi. In 1949, the final push commenced, meeting only token resistance as one after another of the great cities—Nanjing, Shanghai, and Canton—fell. Meanwhile, with most of his government, some fifty thousand troops, and 2.5 million civilians, Chiang Kai-shek withdrew to the island of Taiwan. The civil war was over, but many aspects of the China problem remained.

Epilogue: The Nationalists on Taiwan, 1949-1994

The evacuation from the mainland of the Nationalist leadership and many of its followers brought millions of refugees to the island of Taiwan. These recent arrivals soon controlled the central government, while native Taiwanese, who were descendants of seventeenth-century Chinese immigrants, continued to run the local administration. For nearly forty years thereafter, Taiwan (officially the Republic of China on Taiwan) remained under martial law (declared in May, 1949) and was dominated by the KMT party (the only party legally allowed to function); in effect, the island's political life was shaped by conditions of political authoritarianism, however "soft," or limited. By the mid-1980s, however, socio-economic modernization and the growing strength and maturity of the political opposition had created conditions favorable to political liberalization. Under presidents Chiang Ching-kuo (1978–88) and Lee Teng-hui (1988–), major steps along the road to democratization have been taken, beginning in July 1987 with the lifting of martial law and the removal of the ban on organizing new political parties. In January 1989 Lee promulgated the Civil Organizations law setting rules for the formation of new parties, with laws enacted the following month that lifted many restrictions on campaign activities. In the aftermath of a political crisis resulting from factionalism within the KMT over the forthcoming presidential election, as well as the rising temper of opposition and student activism, the KMT leadership encouraged the National Assembly to pass constitutional amendments in April 1991 providing for a total renewal of the three parliamentary bodies composing the central government (the National Assembly itself, the Legislative Yuan, and the Control Yuan). Over the next three years elections for each of these bodies were scheduled; in 1994, mayoral elections for the island's largest cities (Taipei and Kaohsiung) were likewise held, the first since 1967, with Taipei's voters putting the opposition candidate into office. All in all, the transition from authoritarianism to democracy, though still incomplete, has made remarkable headway.

Much of the impetus for this political trend comes from a second major development in Taiwan over the past fifty years: the island's own version of an economic miracle. As a result of consistently high rates of growth in GNP and foreign trade since the 1950s, Taiwan found itself in 1994 second only to Japan among East Asian nations in terms of industrialization, foreign currency reserves, and quality of life. By 1988, per capita income had risen to $6,053, nearly triple what it was in 1980; even with modest growth, that figure should at least double again by the end of the century. Although small and resource-poor, Taiwan has benefited from its leaders' sound economic strategy that until the 1970s gave priority to agriculture and light industry, in sharp contrast to the approach taken by the Chinese Communists in Beijing, under the influence of the U.S.S.R. For two decades, land reform and agricultural diversification, along with labor-intensive and export-oriented consumer industries, stabilized and improved the domestic economy while allowing Taiwan's products to penetrate foreign markets and create larger and larger currency reserves. Beginning in 1973 with the announcement of the Ten Major Projects (including a north-south freeway, an international airport, a modern steel mill, a petrochemical complex, and a giant shipbuilding corporation), development emphasis shifted to more sophisticated and heavier industry. The trend was maintained into the 1990s by the launching of other large-scale, high-tech, and capital-intensive industrial projects during the past decade.

Forty years of economic development and growth, accelerated by American, European, and especially Japanese investments, has meant the transformation of the Republic of China from a predominantly agricultural society to a major industrial power, one with increasingly democratic practices and institutions. As such, it has become something of a model, or at least an alternative to the socioeconomic and political system that has developed not far away in the People's Republic of China. The ROC's evolution and achievements, coupled with the

PRC's own policy shifts since the death in 1976 of Mao Zedong, have also contributed to a diminishment of hostility between the two countries and a significant improvement in interstate relations as well as rapidly increasing economic interaction, tourism, sports and cultural exchanges, and people-to-people contact. While the issue of reunification of the two Chinas, left over from the long and bitter civil war, is still far from resolved, the two sides are now dealing with one another at many levels.

The Communist Revolution, 1949 to 1995

4

Mao Zedong proclaimed the People's Republic of China (PRC) on October 1, 1949, before cheering millions in Beijing's famous Tiananmen Square. This was one of the great turning points in recent world history, for it inaugurated an attempt to transform China and its people that has continued ever since. If the goal of constructing a new China has gone virtually unchallenged since 1949, the means for its achievement have not been so easily agreed upon. Much of the history of the People's Republic over the past quarter century has been determined by shifts in policy that have derived from an ongoing dispute over one fundamental question: Is the "revolution" over? That is, is it necessary to continue the effort to transform the character of the Chinese people, or can the elite and society turn to the task of developing the material base of the country? This question, despite its apparent simplicity, in fact encompasses others which have defined the main parameters of factionalism in Chinese politics: What role should ideology play in China's development? What should be the nature and goals of policy? By what means should policy be implemented? To understand the internal and external developments of the People's Republic since 1949 requires that one focus upon these issues and the tensions and conflicts which they have fostered. In doing so, it will become clear that the path from 1949 to the present has been neither straight nor smooth for China.

Like all revolutionaries, who spend years in the struggle to win power, the Chinese Communists before 1949 devoted little attention to specific policies that they would pursue after attaining victory. Concerned more with the survival and expansion of the revolutionary movement, Mao and his colleagues gave little consideration to the future. As a result, when the "future" arrived at midcentury, the CCP was suddenly faced with all of the responsibilities that come with wielding power as well as the pressing need to undertake two major tasks: the reintegration of political authority after nearly four decades of ineffective central control over all of China; and the reconstruction of an economy shattered by years of civil and international strife.

Recovery and Consolidation, 1949-1952

In spite of the mood of optimism which permeated the ranks of the CCP in 1949, the wide popular support that the party enjoyed, and the dedication and discipline that the rank-and-file would bring to the tasks at hand, the new regime had to proceed slowly and with moderation over the next several years. Mao understood this well and pointed out repeatedly that China was not yet prepared for the "second revolution" intended to transform it thoroughly. Socialist construction, the first stage in this process, would have to await the political and economic stabilization of the country.

Given the limited numbers and inadequate training of party cadres, success in achieving the goals of rehabilitating the country and consolidating the new regime came to depend in part on the party's ability to approach China's problems with ideological flexibility and moderation. The conscious decision to de-emphasize theoretical considerations for more pragmatic goals enabled the party to mobilize all available human resources, accept temporary solutions, and retain many of the old Nationalist administrators. Along with ideological temporizing, the party worked to organize the population, much as it had done on a lesser scale during the Yan'an period, in order to achieve major political and/or social change with full mass participation. Between 1950 and 1953 party cadres launched several movements which left hardly any of China's millions untouched: (1) the land reform movement (1950–52), conducted to involve the rural masses in peasant associations and "people's courts" for the purposes of completing the process of breaking up large landholdings, equalizing the distribution of land among farmowners and laborers, and undercutting the traditional power of the landlord class; (2) the campaign for "implementation of the marriage law" (beginning in 1950), designed to end the inequality of Chinese women (epitomized and maintained by the traditional marriage system) and involve them in public activity of all kinds; (3) the "Resist America–Aid Korea" campaign (1950–53), begun to intensify patriotic sentiment and recruit volunteers for the army in support of Chinese participation in the Korean War; (4) the "thought reform" campaigns (1950 and after), organized to attack traditional and "bourgeois" ideas and values through programs of self-evaluation, mutual criticism, and indoctrination; (5) the "bandit suppression" campaigns (1951), inaugurated to root out remnants of active Nationalist resistance and persons suspected of inadequate loyalty to the new regime; (6) the "three-anti" campaign (1951–52), initiated to rectify the behavior of party cadres and government officials who were accused of corruption, waste, and bureaucratism; and (7) the "five-anti" campaign (1951–52), directed largely at urban middle-class businesspeople for their alleged "bribery, tax evasion, theft of state assets, cheating on government contracts, and stealing of state economic secrets."

The success of these separate campaigns varied, as did their impact on individual Chinese. But from the standpoint of the CCP, the gains acquired through these efforts at mass mobilization (and through adoption of conciliatory policies) were significant. By 1953, not only was the economy revived, state control over it increased, and the political system strengthened, but society was also

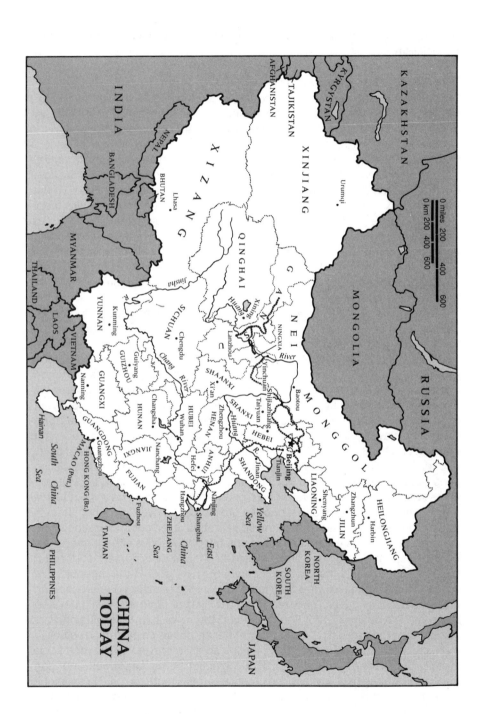

CHINA TODAY

organized to a degree that seemed to prove China's readiness for the transition to socialism.

The First Five Year Plan, 1953-1957

In late 1952, the Chinese leadership announced the First Five Year Plan (FFYP) for the following year, although it was not put into full practice until February, 1955. Designed to move the country rapidly forward economically, it had all the earmarks of Soviet Russian influence: emphasis on industry rather than agriculture, heavy industry rather than light, large enterprises rather than small, centralized planning, and full exploitation of the peasantry through collectivization in order to finance development. To accompany the plan and assist its fulfillment, technical and monetary aid flowed from the U.S.S.R., the population was mobilized to increase production, moderation prevailed in political life (as did institutionalization), and a policy of "peaceful coexistence" and renewed contact with the outside world characterized China's foreign relations. In sum, at least until 1956, the general thrust of party policies was in the direction of minimizing social and political tensions so as to avoid disrupting production and proceed with the task of nationbuilding.

The successes of the First Five Year Plan were reward enough for the immense commitment of resources. Agriculture, although underfunded, seemed to be thriving—the summer of 1955 provided the best crop since 1949—and practically all peasant households had been collectivized (although not without growing peasant objection). As for industrial development, gains were even more impressive. For some within the Chinese leadership, however, there were disturbing aspects of the FFYP. As a result, an intense debate within the party ensued in 1956–57 over the implications of FFYP results and trends. The opponents, who have been called pragmatists or conservatives on the one side, and idealists or radicals on the other, found themselves at odds over issues of policy and ideology. (It should be emphasized, however, that at this time the distinctions between positions were not yet hard and fast.) Specifically, several concerns sparked the debate. First, should priority continue to be given to industrial development (that is, should economic growth be "uneven" between industry and agriculture)? Second, should the socialization, even communization, of the countryside continue regardless of the potentially disruptive effect it might have on the economy? In other words, should economic development continue to receive higher priority than social revolution? Third, should the bureaucratization of Chinese administrative practice and planning be allowed to proceed unchecked because it was "necessary" for the kind of rapid economic development implied by the FFYP? Fourth, should the revolution be institutionalized instead of perpetuated (that is, should greater emphasis be placed on establishment of regular procedures and institutions so as to provide the needed social stability for orderly national growth, or on the notions of social struggle and "contradictions among peoples" and the practice of mass mobilization)? Fifth, should the party continue to rule unopposed? Regardless of one's position on these issues, the FFYP offered ammunition which could be used against one's opponents. The conservatives could point to solid evidence of growth and the potential for continued growth if only realism would prevail among China's decisionmakers; as for the radicals, they could point to the threat to the revolution posed by bureaucratization, institutionalization, centralization, and excessive pragmatism.

As the leader in the latter "camp," Mao felt compelled to intervene directly and use his enormous prestige to challenge the thinking of the pragmatists, modify the FFYP, and "correct" some of the worst tendencies emerging from it. He was driven to this course of action not only by domestic Chinese concerns but by events within the Soviet Union and Eastern Europe: specifically, Premier Nikita S. Khrushchev's denunciation in February 1956 of Stalinism and the uprising in Hungary from late October to early November of the same year.

At first Mao appears to have been unsuccessful, since it now seems clear that his opponents, led by Liu Shaoqi, a revolutionary comrade of Mao since 1921, had enough support in the party and governmental apparatus to temper and control the radicals and their policies. This was certainly the case with regard to the countryside, where the collectivization process continued but was slowed, steps were taken to make it less disruptive of traditional rural village organization, and the peasants were restored the right to maintain private plots and livestock. Pragmatist domination of the ruling organs was also reflected in the public assertion of collective leadership within the party, a concept which, inspired by Khrushchev's critique of Stalin's "cult of personality," directly challenged Mao's authority. Mao continued to defend his positions in private and public, with articles in the press and speeches (notably his "On the Correct Handling of Contradictions among the People," delivered in February, 1957), and most dramatically by means of the "Hundred Flowers" campaign (May-June, 1957), which invited people in and out of the party to speak their minds about the state of the country and the CCP leadership. The volume and range of criticism, however, surprised all of China's leaders, including Mao. The party's response was to close the door immediately and launch "anti-rightist" and rectification campaigns to root out erroneous and counterrevolutionary tendencies among elite groups and expand socialist education (ideological training) among the masses. In addition, party leaders, only recently opposing one another, agreed to seek accommodation, gloss over their differences, and present a united front against a society which was obviously not yet imbued with the revolutionary spirit needed to build Communism in China. Maintaining the party's political hegemony was unquestioned, not only in light of the "weeds" that had sprouted during the "Hundred Flowers" campaign but also the counterrevolutionary character of the Hungarian uprising some months earlier.

The temporary healing of party wounds seems to have benefited Mao the most. He had been losing ground to his opponents, but now had managed not only to save face but to rally sufficient support to enable him to impress his views on the economic and political decisions that would affect China for the next couple of years. The set of policies that began to emerge with the convening of the Third Plenum of the Central Committee in September-October, 1957, were to acquire the designation of "Great Leap Forward."

The Great Leap Forward. 1957-1960

The Great Leap Forward (GLF), which coincided roughly with the inauguration of the Second Five Year Plan but gradually subsumed it, was less a program of specific measures (although these were issued), than a set of ideological assumptions. These aimed to establish a frame of mind that would make possible a frantic drive to harness the total energies of the Chinese people for the task of propelling the country into the future. The assumptions, not necessarily novel but certainly expressed with extraordinary vigor and fanaticism, were three in number. One was a commitment to the concept of voluntarism; that is, to the idea that the human will can accomplish the impossible and can be a decisive factor in history. Another was contained in the slogan "Politics takes command," which implied that China's problems and its very backwardness were less matters of economics than politics. Ultimately, "correct" politics and "proper" thinking would be more important than investment capital, fertilizer, or technical expertise, and one's political reliability ("redness") would count for more than one's specialized skills. The third cornerstone of the GLF was the belief in the possibility and necessity of simultaneously developing all areas of Chinese life. To give priority to some spheres would only delay the arrival of full Communism as other aspects lagged behind.

The reasons for fostering the GLF mentality were probably numerous, but they all come back to a basic dilemma facing the CCP leadership. During the First Five Year Plan, investment in heavy industry consumed roughly one-half of Chinese capital with perhaps another 10 percent going to light industry. Total industrial production grew by about 140 percent as a result, thereby justifying the large investment. Agriculture, however, which was to help finance further industrial growth through surplus production, was able to increase output during the same period only enough to provide for China's expanding population. Failure to raise agricultural production in 1956 and 1957 only added to the problem, as did declining peasant willingness to continue making the sacrifices demanded of them. As a result, the party found itself faced with a major dilemma: how to win over the masses to the effort of increasing agricultural production while at the same time continuing the rapid industrialization of China without adequate investment resources.

The solution was to exploit to the fullest China's massive population, to do with people what was otherwise impossible. Hence the Great Leap Forward (GLF) began, with its emphasis on mass line and mass mobilization, socialist education, economic decentralization (epitomized by the backyard furnaces that sprang up by the thousands to produce steel), competition and quotas rising to extraordinary heights, a foreign policy that encouraged belief in China as a beleaguered nation, and especially the reorganization of rural life into communes. All of these facets of the GLF phenomenon were viewed as means for turning liabilities into assets and weaknesses into strengths. Above all, it was thought that they would lead not only to economic progress but also to the creation of a new society by breaking down traditional barriers between city and countryside, industry and agriculture, intellectual and physical labor.

Begun in late 1957, the GLF was in trouble well before the end of 1958. To be sure there were positive results that could be counted (or at least official reports of such). Production of many commodities probably did increase, even dramatically in some cases, as a consequence of mobilizing the country's labor force as never before and encouraging the kind of feverish labor reminiscent of Stalin's Five Year Plans in Soviet Russia during the middle and late 1930s. The positive results, however, were easily overshadowed by the failures and the damage done to agriculture and industry. The GLF simply did not work, whether owing to adverse weather conditions and party cadre failings, as claimed by Mao, or the irrationality of the Great Leap concept itself and the resistance of the peasantry to communization and regimentation, as argued by many Western specialists (and since Mao's death, by many Chinese themselves). Rather than advancing the economy, the GLF nearly wrecked it; and rather than leading China to some golden age, it only engendered crisis. Moreover, the unity that had character- ized the party leadership in the autumn of 1957 was now dissipated, and the differences of opinion over policy now reemerged to coalesce into several fac- tions which would engage in a power struggle for most of the next decade. The announcement of Mao's replacement by Liu Shaoqi as head of state in April, 1959, given little attention at the time, was in fact one of the first signs of the political crisis underway.

As criticism of the GLF grew, numerous conferences were held in 1958 and early 1959, during which Great Leap policies came under increased attack. To- ward the summer of 1959, Mao attempted to counter his opponents and salvage the GLF. He succeeded temporarily when the Eighth Plenum of the Central Com- mittee (July-August) called for a campaign against rightists (that is, Mao's oppo- nents), reasserted the correctness of GLF policies, and forced the dismissal of Defense Minister Peng Dehuai, the critics' leading spokesperson. Mao's victory, however, was shortlived. By the end of 1960 his influence had once again de- clined as more discouraging and negative news concerning the economy poured in. By the time the Ninth Plenum of the Central Committee met in January, 1961, the pragmatists had succeeded in wresting control of the party and rejecting the Great Leap approach.

From Recovery and Retrenchment to Cultural Revolution, 1961-1969

Concerning domestic matters, the years from 1961 to 1965 witnessed two con- current developments. On the one hand, with the reins of party and government firmly in their grasp, the pragmatists under Liu Shaoqi devoted their attention to economic restoration and political retrenchment. In order to revive the economy, measures were taken to centralize planning once again, increase the produc- tion of consumer goods, establish incentives for the peasants (including permis- sion to use private plots and organize free markets), emphasize expertise rather than "redness," and deradicalize the communes by reorganizing them and lim- iting their size. In the political sphere, along with efforts to play down mass mo- bilization and socialist education, the Liuists purged the middle and lower level party organs and replaced Maoist cadres with their own supporters and "ex- perts." Veiled attacks against the Great Leap and Mao's leadership multiplied, including that contained in a soon-to-be-famous play produced in 1961 entitled Hai Rui Dismissed From Office. Taken together, the economic and political poli- cies of Liu and his colleagues provided the means for recovering from the ex- treme disruption of the Great Leap period and represented a desire to give prior- ity to economic over political matters.

Meanwhile, those same years witnessed a persistent, initially lowkeyed effort by Mao to win back his former influence over the CCP. Unhappy with his own political demise and the current "line" of the pragmatists, and convinced that the

Great Leap was a sound approach to solving China's problems, he campaigned to win new supporters and lay the foundation of yet another attempt both to rectify the party and change the thought and behavior of the Chinese people. Finding himself without a sufficient audience in the central organs of the party and government, Mao turned to local and provincial cadres (notably in Shanghai) for allies. He also engaged the services of the army through his protégé Lin Biao, named Defense Minister after Peng Dehuai's dismissal in 1958. Finally, as the struggle for power came increasingly into the open, Mao appealed to China's youth to rally to his cause. With these allies, he launched a nationwide campaign known as the Great Proletarian Cultural Revolution (GPCR) in 1966. The battle was joined—"Red vs. Expert."

What was the GPCR? It probably defies full explanation, although one thing is now certain: it was the result of longstanding conflicts among party leaders over power, ideology, and policy, which until the mid-1960s had remained largely hidden from the outside world. One of the most surprising features of a phenomenon filled with startling and bizarre events was Mao's apparent willingness to risk the destruction of the very party which he had spent so many years nurturing and trying to shape. In his view, the CCP had become a haven for rightists and "capitalist-roaders," who, having lost touch with the masses, had betrayed the revolution as a result. Since the party was dominated by those who would not accept Mao's views, he had no choice but to strike out at the country's leading institution. His weapons were propaganda against his opponents and in favor of his own positions (hence the enormous emphasis on the "Little Red Book" and the "thoughts of Mao"), and a politicized army and youth. The army, in fact, was increasingly portrayed as a model for society, and students and other young people were formed into units of Red Guards. As the GPCR unfolded, demands for rectification of the party were accompanied by an extraordinary effort to change the content of literature, art, and the theater (in this work Mao's wife, Jiang Qing, was prominent), reform the educational system, and reject the values and attitudes of traditional China, all in the name of some vague "proletarian" virtues and orientation. Mao's goal was to preserve for and transmit to the rising generation the revolutionary spirit which it had never experienced.

The course of the Cultural Revolution is too complex to be dealt with here in any detail. It should be noted, however, that one of Mao's chief tactics was to isolate his major enemies and tarnish their names by turning on their subordinates and/or persons known to be associated with them. This he did successfully early on with Peng Zhen, Beijing's mayor, later with Deng Xiaoping, the party secretary-general, and ultimately with Liu Shaoqi himself. At the Eleventh Plenum of the Central Committee (August 1–12, 1966), Mao's forces succeeded in winning control of that body and issuing in its name a "Sixteen-Point Decision" which officially sanctioned the Cultural Revolution. Thereafter the GPCR escalated and spread throughout the country, bringing with it a tidal wave of unrest, economic and political disruption, and near civil war. By the time that revolutionary committees had been set up nationwide in September, 1968, Mao, probably under the calming influence of Premier Zhou Enlai, had begun the process of restoring order, phasing out the activities of the Red Guards, and consolidating the changes that had occurred in Chinese life. His victory seemingly won, his enemies purged from positions of authority, and his vision of the new China in everyone's mind, Mao could now pause in his race to the future to rebuild the party and the economy which lay in rubble about him.

Foreign Relations

Since 1949 China's foreign relations have undergone a series of bewildering changes that have seen détente (relaxation of tensions) with "imperialistic" America, considerable accommodation with the former Japanese enemy, and virtually total alienation from its revolutionary ally, the Soviet Union.

The United States' support of Nationalist China antagonized Mao towards Americans despite efforts by their consular officials (remaining behind in the larger cities in 1949) to open negotiations with the victorious Communists. Ambassador John Leighton Stuart talked with the Communist representative, Huang Hua (a former student), with no success. During the Korean War (1950–53), the commitment of the U.S. Seventh Fleet to the protection of Taiwan and China's eventual intrusion into the conflict finally created an implacable enmity towards the United States for the next two decades.

Despite occasional talks in Warsaw with Chinese Communists, the United States agreed to defend the Nationalists on Taiwan by the Treaty of 1954 and thereafter successfully maneuvered to prevent admission of the People's Republic to the United Nations. When Beijing attempted to seize the offshore islands in the Taiwan Strait (1958–59), President Dwight D. Eisenhower threatened retaliation. The "running sore" of Vietnam brought war close by, as this former Tang outlying dependency had served as a buffer, protecting China's southeastern frontier. Following the Communist victory over the French in Indo-China, the Geneva Treaty of 1954 had divided Vietnam into northern and southern zones, the latter with a U.S.-sponsored government. When Communist North Vietnam infiltrated southward, the United States sent military advisers to Saigon's forces. In 1964, President John F. Kennedy introduced combat units and commenced restricted air strikes the following year. Despite a U.S. pledge not to invade North Vietnam, China felt endangered, recalling its experiences with "foreign devils" in the nineteenth century.

The United States struggled in quicksand, unable to advance or withdraw, as "protracted war" bled its forces in Vietnam. The fighting soon spread to Laos and Cambodia, engulfing all of Indo-China. Skillfully exploiting the Sino-Soviet split, however, U.S. Secretary of State Henry A. Kissinger negotiated a treaty facilitating American withdrawal in February, 1973—part of the new détente policy with both China and the U.S.S.R. The United Nations' admission of the People's Republic to full membership in October, 1971, and President Richard M. Nixon's trip to Beijing the following year had provided effective diplomatic preparation.

Some American difficulties with China remained, however. The Chinese government still insisted on the return of Taiwan and maintained a deep concern for Washington's commitments to the U.S.S.R. These differences made for a rather cool reception of President Gerald R. Ford and Secretary Kissinger on the occasion of their visit in December, 1975. Despite this momentary downturn in relations, however, China still sought an American presence in East Asia as a force

US SOUTH VIETNAM

Laos, CAMBODIA & VIETNAM — INDOCHINA

for stability—especially to balance Soviet power and prevent Japanese rearmament. At the time of Richard Nixon's second visit to China (February, 1976), it
encouraged U.S. forces to remain in Japan, South Korea, the Philippines, and
Thailand in reduced capacity. Despite the death of Zhou Enlai (January, 1976),
who had piloted China's foreign policy toward the United States, it kept to this
course. Stalemate resulted, however, when American public opinion forced
Washington to delay implementation of Beijing's three demands for "normalization" (full diplomatic recognition): troop withdrawal, severance of relations, and
abrogation of the 1954 treaty with Taiwan. Thus, once again U.S.-Chinese détente
encountered its principal obstacle. More recently, human rights issues have
proved an additional sticking point, with debate in the United States over most-
favored nation status for China a near-annual event.

China's relations with Japan improved very slowly because of their conflicting policies toward the United States after 1949. The American-Japanese Security Treaty of 1952, which provided for the presence of American troops in Japan, combined with Chinese fears of renewed "Japanese militarism" to prevent a
final peace treaty. In the late 1950s some commerce opened between China
and Japan, equal to barely 4 percent of Japan's trade. Japanese economic expansion into Southeast Asia—commerce, factory relocation, and some foreign
aid—disturbed the Chinese, whose Marxist views interpreted this as preparation
for imperialist conquest. Indeed, Japan's "economic miracle" since the 1960s
appeared to China as a capitalist "Great Leap Forward" into that area.

Still, both powers desired more contacts—China to procure Japanese technology, Japan to obtain coal, iron, and oil from northeastern China. Yet, because
of American considerations, neither could act unilaterally. When the United States
requested Chinese assistance to evacuate Vietnam, a breakthrough occurred.
The new U.S.-China policy permitted Japanese recognition of the People's Republic in September, 1972. Over the next three years commerce between the
two nations tripled. China then enticed Japan with the prospect of lucrative oil
exploration off the Chinese east coast. A proposed final peace treaty, however,
stumbled over Japan's objection to an "antihegemony" clause that seemed aimed
too obviously at the Soviet Union. Japan desisted, lest it be drawn into the quarrel between the two powers. Hence, Chinese-Japanese accommodation proceeded slowly.

Sino-Russian relations since 1949 have stormed from revolutionary partnership to outright hostility, although ties have improved especially since the collapse of the Soviet Union. Mao's policy of "lean to one side" resulted in the
alliance treaty of February, 1950, but the conclusion of the Korean War intensified their differences. Truthfully, both countries had little more than ideology and
common enemies to unite them. The Communist Chinese considered Soviet
Premier Khrushchev's denunciation of Stalin's "cult of personality" in 1956 an
indirect attack on Mao, provoking the Sino-Soviet split. A number of factors fed
the conflict: the historical experience from which the Russians recalled the Mongol
invasion of the thirteenth century, and subsequent depradations, while the Chinese remembered the perennial "barbarian" threat on China's northern frontiers, capped by nineteenth-century Tsarist imperialism; the territorial issue, in
which China demanded that Russia admit the illegality of its occupation of the

[margin handwritten note: leadership: preponderant influence or authority esp. of a government or state]

trans-Amur region, the Maritime Province, Outer Mongolia, and part of Chinese Turkestan, forced from the Manchus after the Opium Wars; the doctrinal dispute, emerging from the late 1920s, when Stalin regarded the proletariat as the "vanguard of revolution," while Mao favored the peasantry; the struggle for hegemony within the Communist family, wherein China claimed leadership of the Third World (or underdeveloped nations)—the historic Middle Kingdom updated—while rejecting the U.S.S.R. as a "social imperialist" and asserting Mao's superiority over contemporary Russian leaders, fully equal to Marx and Lenin as a founding father of Communism; and the debate over strategy and the pace of revolution, which became evident in the late 1950s. China wanted to move rapidly—even to risk atomic war—calculating that its agricultural society could salvage more from that conflict than urban-centered America or the Soviet Union. Russia preferred a more devious route, utilizing infiltration and temporary accommodation with the West. Such divergence of views stemmed largely from differing environmental factors in addition to the generation gap of the two revolutions.

Border clashes occurred in the 1960s along China's northern and western frontiers. During the Cultural Revolution, the Soviets mobilized their huge army along the boundaries of Mongolia and Manchuria. Recalling the thrust of Russian troops into China on three occasions since 1900 (during the Boxer Rebellion, the Northern Campaign, and World War II), the Chinese dug air raid shelters, stockpiled arms, developed the atomic bomb (October, 1964), and trained the masses in hand-to-hand combat. Faced with Russia's overwhelming military assistance to North Vietnam and naval domination of the Indian Ocean, the Soviet-Indian treaty of 1969, and finally Soviet-Japanese economic cooperation, China struggled to avert containment. The danger of a "surgical strike" by the Soviet army against Xinjiang nuclear installations reached a climax in the spring of that year in an actual clash over an island in the Ussuri River. Mao Zedong's death in September, 1976, failed to improve relations despite the efforts of Moscow's special emissary. A year later, restored First Vice-Premier Deng Xiaoping announced that China would not renew the old Soviet alliance treaty at its expiration in February, 1980. Thus, the split widened further.

The opportunity to restore more fruitful relations depended greatly on both the death of Mao and Deng Xiaoping's advocacy of openness. While Chinese leaders considered the Soviet intervention in Afghanistan and Moscow's ongoing alliance with Vietnam important obstacles to reconciliation, negotiations between China and the U.S.S.R. began in 1982 and led to expanded trade and cultural exchanges. As the Soviet Union experienced economic and political disruption in the late 1980s and then ceased to exist in 1991, Chinese leaders could afford to temper their alarm about their northern neighbor and begin reassessing the new realities of Europe and Asia.

Mao's Last Years

The meeting of the Ninth Congress of the CCP in April, 1969, marked the conclusion of the Cultural Revolution and the seeming culmination of Mao's struggle with his opponents. But the coalition of factions that controlled the ruling organs of party, state, and army were hardly of one mind. As reconstruction and consolidation became primary goals in the immediate aftermath of the GPCR, Zhou Enlai began to play an increasingly prominent role in managing affairs of state, all the more so as Mao once again withdrew from public life and Lin Biao (his heir apparent) was killed in a plane crash (September, 1971) while reportedly trying to flee China following a failed coup against Mao. Factional relationships in the early 1970s are especially intricate and resistant to easy analysis on the part of outsiders. Despite this, it has become clear that already in this period moderate and pragmatic leaders were beginning to return to positions of influence, and that Deng Xiaoping, with support from Zhou, was being groomed to succeed his benefactor as premier.

Even in his semiretirement, Mao was quick to react. Working to resist this latest phase of a seemingly perpetual problem (the waning of revolutionary fervor, bureaucratism, capitalist backsliding, careerism, and other "evils"), he gave his blessing to two major campaigns: the "anti-Lin Biao, anti-Confucius" campaign of 1973–74 (aimed, through allusion, at Zhou Enlai), and the "beat back the right deviationist wind" campaign of late 1975 (targeted at Deng). Leading the way were Mao's wife, Jiang Qing, and three of her associates—Wang Hongwen, Zhang Chunqiao, and Yao Wenyuan—who had all been promoted to leadership positions during the Tenth Party Congress in 1973 and were clearly favored, and protected, by Mao. Aided by the secret police, and taking advantage of Mao's increasing debility, this "Gang of Four" tyrannized the country for the next several years and plotted its own succession to the mantle of the "Great Helmsman," as Mao was popularly called.

The year 1976 would prove to be a major turning point in China's post-1949 history. Within the space of nine months, three of the country's preeminent revolutionary leaders passed away: Zhou Enlai in January, Marshall Chu De in July, and Mao himself in September. The inevitable political instability that resulted was accompanied by a series of natural disasters, including earthquakes and numerous floodings of the Yellow River, the combination of which had a disquieting effect on large segments of the population. In the midst of these events, political maneuvering intensified. Deng Xiaoping offered a stirring eulogy to Zhou Enlai at a memorial service on January 15 but then disappeared from public view without explanation. Mao made known his choice for premier: Hua Guofeng, the sixth-ranking vice-premier. Under the circumstances, Hua was a clear compromise between radicals and pragmatists, but his nomination as acting premier had the added purposes of giving the Gang of Four time to expand its base of support while preventing Deng from moving into the position himself. While Mao remained alive, Hua proceeded cautiously, making allies among senior cadres and military leaders but angering Jiang Qing and her friends. Meanwhile, public sympathies for Deng were revealed on April 5 by a spontaneous demonstration of one hundred thousand people in Tiananmen Square, ostensibly protesting removal of wreaths in tribute to Zhou but also chanting anti-Mao slogans and hoisting pro-Zhou and Deng banners. As the Gang of Four proceeded confidently and brashly toward what it thought would be a successful seizure of power, Hua completed his own plans for a preemptive strike made possible by solid support from the military. Under the guise of an emergency meeting of the Politburo in the early hours of October 6, the Gang of Four and its chief allies were arrested and placed in solitary confinement by sunrise. The following day,

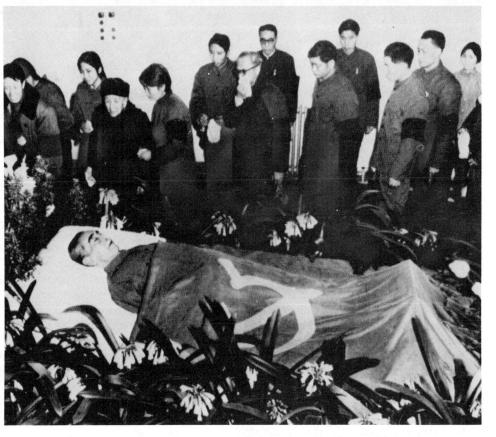

Mourners file past the flag-draped body of Zhou Enlai, Premier of the People's Republic of China, at the time of his death in January, 1976. Wide World Photos.

Student demonstrators marching in Beijing, 1989. Gregory A. Levitt.

the Politburo heard three reports, two from Hua Guofeng, outlining charges against Jiang Qing and company; Hua was rewarded with the additional chairmanships: those of the Central Committee and the Military Commission. On October 24 an enormous rally filled Tiananmen Square to celebrate the Gang's smashing and recognize the triumph of Hua as Mao's successor.

China Since Mao: The Four Modernizations

Meanwhile Deng Xiaoping, hiding in the south since February, was plotting his own political comeback. With the invaluable protection and support of General Xu Shiyou, the military governor of Guangdong and former military chief of the Nanjing region (comprising the wealthy provinces of Jiangsu, Anhui, and Zhejiang), as well as the backing of the first party secretary of Guangdong, Deng's case for rehabilitation was pushed in the CCP's Central Committee. The pressure worked: Deng was reappointed to a vice-premiership, to the Politburo, and to the Military Affairs Commission (MAC) in July 1977, albeit over the objections of Hua Guofeng and other party and army (PLA) officials. Throughout the remainder of that year and most of 1978, the unfolding of China's domestic and foreign policies reflected the ambiguous relationship between Hua and Deng. Supposedly Hua was still in control; in reality, however, by the Third Plenum of the Eleventh Central Committee in December, 1978, Deng and his allies had succeeded in neutralizing Hua's influence and capturing control over main party organs. For a time Hua retained his official titles, but these too he gradually was forced to relinquish to Deng and two protégés: in September, 1980, the post of premier was passed to Zhao Ziyang; and in June, 1981, the chairmanship of the party went to Hu Yaobang and of the Military Affairs Committee to Deng himself.

With protégés in key positions and the powers of party vice-chairman, vice-premier, and PLA chief-of-staff in his own hands, Deng completed his comeback, remaining until late 1994, when advanced age and medical problems effectively forced him out of the center of active power, China's paramount leader, the arbiter of unresolved political rivalries, and the architect of the country's remarkable domestic and foreign policies. Those policies have been consistently intertwined in an overriding effort to ensure China's entrance into the world of economically advanced countries by the early twenty-first century, to achieve what have become known as the "four modernizations" in agriculture, industry, national defense, and the linked areas of science and technology. First proposed by Zhou Enlai and subscribed to by virtually all of China's leaders since the mid-1970s, pursuit of the "four modernizations" has nevertheless produced unending and often vitriolic debate over questions of scope, timetable, and implementation. Deng's position derives from his understanding of the consequences of the Cultural Revolution and the underlying "leftist" (Maoist) assumptions that produced the phenomenon. To him the Cultural Revolution nearly ruined the country, setting it back economically in incalculable ways and simultaneously undermining the legitimacy of the CCP in many minds. In fact, unless a way could be found to correct China's economic weaknesses and deficiencies rapidly, the very survival of the party, he believed, would be in doubt.

The problem was ideology: not its central role in Chinese experience, but its emphases. If Mao insisted on the priority of class struggle over economic productivity, Deng argued for the availability of more and more consumer goods; if Mao preferred ideological rectitude to technical expertise, Deng valued the technicians; if Mao looked askance at and punished individual enterprise, Deng wanted to stimulate the search for profit; and if Mao proclaimed the virtues of selfsufficiency, Deng advocated looking to workable models wherever they might be found. In a classic example of the Chinese penchant to reduce policy to number-based slogans, Deng's approach has been aptly proclaimed as comprising "one central task, and two fundamental points." The central task is economic development, the achievement of which will, Deng believes, not only move the country forward into the ranks of the most highly productive societies but ensure the loyalty of the people to the basic system inaugurated in 1949. Of the two fundamental points, one focuses on persevering in the policy of economic reform and openness to the outside world, meaning, among other things, maintaining the system of privatized agriculture that replaced collective farms, closing or eventually privatizing much unprofitable state industry, dismantling central planning generally in favor of private entrepreneurship and the market, and fully integrating China into the global economy. The second fundamental point concerns domestic politics and the need to ensure political stability by fostering the "four cardinal principles" (first enunciated in 1979): socialism, the dictatorship of the proletariat, Communist Party leadership, and Marxism-Leninism Mao Zedong Thought. These principles are not to be challenged publicly, a fact requiring the removal from the Chinese constitution of the so-called "four great freedoms" (speaking out freely, airing views freely, holding great debates, and writing big-character posters).

The work of redirecting China so as to encourage development was officially launched at the Third Plenary Session of the 11th Central Committee of the CCP in December 1978, when delegates agreed to Deng's proposals to reform the economy and bring China back into the global mainstream. Since that time, China has made extraordinary strides economically. Though not yet one of Asia's "tigers," the country is clearly ahead of many other developing nations and enjoys a standard of living overall that is dramatically improved for many of its citizens. The GNP has grown by an average of 9 percent a year since 1978, contributing to a quadrupling of the economy, significantly higher levels of consumption (whether of food or televisions, refrigerators, and washing machines), a drastic decline in the number of those living in severe poverty, and a steady rise in life expectancy. Learning from its East Asian neighbors, China under Deng Xiaoping began by pursuing a two-stage reform process that focused first on agriculture and foreign trade and then on industry.

From the late 1970s through the early 1980s the goal was to create a market economy in food that meant freeing most prices (grain being the notable exception). Once the mechanism of supply and demand was reintroduced, the next step was to abolish the communes as units of production and replace them with family farms. In this Deng not only reversed a major feature of Maoism but rejected the experience of the Soviet Union under Stalin; and in the process, significantly eased the policy of "milking the peasants" to help pay for development. At the same time the government's monopoly of foreign trade was eliminated, opening up opportunities not only for domestic entrepreneurial activity but for foreign capital and expertise as well. To affirm the government's commitment to an emergent private business sector, four experimental "special economic zones" were set up in 1979 (three in Guangdong and one in Fujian), all close to Hong Kong and Taiwan with their large ethnic Chinese populations. From 1984 to 1987 attention turned to industry, where, as in agriculture, prices were allowed to reflect relative scarcities rather than the dictates of a plan, competition was encouraged, and efficiency declared a major goal. Between the beginning and end of the 1980s, the number of people in private business rose from 2.3 million to 23 million and the volume of retail trade in free markets increased by a factor of 14.

Despite the unmistakable progress from an economic standpoint, some within the CCP grew concerned over the negative consequences of the reforms. Urban inflation that seemed to be careening out of control; official corruption that took advantage of the tiered marketing system, the partial nature of deregulation, and the economy's growing decentralization; profiteering and tax evasion; and the tensions resulting from uneven economic development, rising economic inequality, and confusion over the rules of upward social mobility—all these combined with fear about the subtle impact of foreign influences. Deng Xiaoping's argument that "Time is money, efficiency is life" seemed increasingly to miss the most important point: the preservation of CCP control over China under conditions of fundamental change that were breeding public restiveness, widespread concern for narrow selfinterest at the expense of social goals, and rampant cynicism about politics (and political leaders) generally. When public opinion research revealed what many had suspected, the conservatives were able, in late summer and early fall of 1988, to force a retreat from economic reform so as to cool the overheated economy and rein in the private sector.

These measures were accompanied by a resurgence of political tensions in the second half of the 1980s and complaints from intellectuals and students about limits to democratic practices. Demonstrations in late 1985 in Tiananmen Square spread to other urban centers, as did such actions a year later that began in Hefei but quickly involved students in Shanghai and sixteen other cities. While these events were easily suppressed by the authorities, they managed to further confuse the political situation at the top of party and government. Hardliners, of course, railed against the protests, complaining about the spreading tide of "bourgeois liberalization" and excessive "rightism"; more moderate leaders, such as Hu Yaobang, advocated conciliation. When Deng Xiaoping sided with the hardliners, Hu's fate was sealed: he resigned as general secretary on January 16, 1987, and with his departure, reprisals against students, intellectuals, and academic officials ensued.

But the campaign against "bourgeois liberalization" and the effort to bring more conservative party cadres into leadership positions, as with Li Peng, did not succeed in turning the tide of reform. Dissatisfaction persisted and pressure on the regime found daring and imaginative ways to express itself. Students continued to request permission to demonstrate, but typically had their petitions denied; some newspapers risked retaliation for their bolder reporting; Chinese Central Television broadcast a startling series entitled "River Elegy" that, using the metaphor of the Yellow River, pointedly lamented the albatross of oppressive "old" ways that stood in the path of progress; and early in 1989 prominent intellectuals urged the party to release political prisoners, including Wei Jingsheng, who had a decade before called for a "fifth modernization": that of political democracy.

In the midst of inflation and an overheated economy, faced with a growing list of popular grievances, and confronted by increasingly bolder intellectual challenges to fundamental features of the communist system, the party seemed able to do little to lead the country and command society's respect. Rent by its own ongoing political infighting and further weakened by the emergence of multiple centers of power in the provinces, it seemed locked into a cycle of unimaginative responses that reflected above all the unresolved tension between conflicting desires: economic development and maintenance of dictatorial rule. Commencing on the night of April 17–18, 1989, the world began to witness seven extraordinary weeks of unprecedented behavior on the part of students, many ordinary citizens, and the authorities themselves. What started as a heartfelt response by students to the sudden death of the popular Hu Yaobang mushroomed into a mesmerizing drama that played itself out principally on the stage of Tiananmen Square. Marches, demonstrations, class boycotts, sit-down strikes, encampments, and a hunger strike, much in full view of the world, thanks to television, propelled students into a confrontation with the party. Young leaders appeared, such as Wu'er Kaishi, Wang Dan, and Chai Ling, to upstage the country's leaders and force them through one humiliation after another.

Restrained initially by its own lack of resolve, by the visits of several foreign delegations and Mikhail Gorbachev, the Soviet General Secretary, and by the surprising maneuvers of the protesters, the party waited until May 18 to impose martial law. Troops began to filter into Beijing, although they were frequently stymied by the outpouring of support for the protesters from ordinary citizens who put up makeshift roadblocks and swarmed around soldiers to remind them that they were part of the *people's* army. Patience grew increasingly thin as the regime pursued what amounted to a war of attrition against the students. As incidents of violence multiplied on June 2 and 3, the stage was being set for a final showdown. It began to unfold toward midnight on the 3rd, quickly turning the capital into a battle zone. The number of casualties remains unknown, though it was probably higher than the official figure of around 300 dead eventually released. Once launched, repression was swift, the party reasserted its traditional preeminence, and the elder leaders—principally Deng Xiaoping, Chen Yun, Peng Zhen, and Yang Shangkun—once more ruled the roost. Some subordinates had to be replaced, as was the case with Zhao Ziyang who had served as General Secretary of the Central Committee but was ousted for being too conciliatory toward the demonstrators. His successor would be Jiang Zemin, a one-time mayor and party secretary of Shanghai. Jiang's appointment as well as the formation of a new Standing Committee not surprisingly reflected a compromise between the competing factions in the party.

Repression and party housecleaning were only part of the leadership response to the tragedy of Tiananmen. Quelling what was officially described as a "counterrevolutionary rebellion" launched by hooligans was only the first step in getting the country back to a normalcy and orthodoxy as defined by the regime. Pursuit of appropriate reform and openness to the outside world were restated as basic policies, but they were to be accompanied by renewed ideological work and a push to reinstill patriotism especially in the schools, and by a variety of measures to improve the party's standing in the public's eyes. Largely because the economy perked up toward the end of 1989 and through 1990, the conservatives, with Li Peng in the forefront, were able to sustain their political viewpoint. But a downturn in 1991 and the global demise of communism seem to have prompted Deng Xiaoping to push more aggressively for economic development and allow more liberated thinking. In a major speech delivered in January, 1992, during a tour of Shenzhen and Zhuhai, the two special economic zones near Hong Kong, Deng set the party once more in the direction of reform.

We cannot tell how successful the current policies will prove to be over the longer haul. China clearly has been more successful since the late 1970s in transforming its political economy than any of the other communist regimes, especially the Soviet Union, has been. For the most part China's leaders have managed to avoid rampant inflation and maintain financial stability, even as they have pursued flexible and incremental institutional reform; moreover, their policies have been rewarded with significant economic growth and higher rates of accumulation, and the dismal prospects that have overtaken Russia and Eastern Europe are not visible in China.

Still the People's Republic faces enormous problems as it approaches the twenty-first century. Many derive from the presence of a huge and ever-growing population (despite implementation of the one-child policy in 1979), but others result from the fact of China's prolonged transition from a centralized economic, social, and political system to one more open, variegated, and free. The legacy of Marxism in its Maoist variant has cost the country dearly and will continue to weigh heavily on any efforts to escape the past and build a different and better society. Defining that better society will itself consume Chinese attention, especially since the quest for egalitarianism (social and economic justice) pursued as a fundamental goal over the past four decades will likely find fewer and fewer advocates. The attractions of marketization, mobility, and cultural freedom are everywhere, and apparently, difficult to resist. In addition, economic development will continue to create regional disparities that may well breed resentments and ultimately political tensions; some of these will likely have ethnic aspects to them. Moreover, the countryside, despite making a relatively easy transition from collectivized farms to household contracts, is still the China of most people and is beset by widespread poverty, inadequate services, an outflow of capital, deep underemployment, and environmental degradation on a massive scale. Finally, however much the party may desire to speak of "socialism with Chinese characteristics," the discrepancy between proclamations and the reality of economic, social, and political behavior will likely weaken the rulers' legitimacy further, unless Deng's hopes for real economic achievement across the country is on the horizon by the end of the century. In the end, the willingness of Deng's successors, now maneuvering to replace the ailing leader, to pursue political reforms and institutional democratization will certainly figure prominently in the success or failure of so much else.

Suggestions for Further Reading

Anderson, E.N., *The Food of China* (1988).

Barnett, A. Doak, *China on the Eve of the Communist Takeover* (1963).

Bianco, Lucien, *Origins of the Chinese Revolution, 1915–1949* (1971).

Bodde, Derk, *China's Cultural Tradition* (1957).

Chesneaux, Jean, *Peasant Revolts in China, 1840–1949* (1973).

Chow, Tse-tsung, *The May Fourth Movement: Intellectual Revolution in Modern China* (1960).

Creel, Herrlee G., *Chinese Thought from Confucius to Mao Zedong* (1953).

DeBary, William T., et al. (eds.), *Sources of Chinese Tradition* (1960).

Eastman, Lloyd E., *Family, Fields, and Ancestors: Constancy and Changes in China's Social and Economic History, 1550–1949* (1988).

Ebrey, Patricia Buckley (ed.), *Chinese Civilization and Society: A Sourcebook* (1981).

Elvin, Mark, *The Pattern of the Chinese Past* (1973).

Fairbank, John K., and Edwin O. Reischauer, *China: Tradition and Transformation* (1978).

———. *The United States and China* (Fourth revised edition, 1979).

Fay, Peter Ward, *The Opium War, 1840–1842* (1975).

Gasster, Michael, *China's Struggle to Modernize* (Second edition, 1983).

Goldman, Merle, *China's Intellectuals: Advise and Dissent* (1981).

Hinton, William, *Fanshen: A Documentary of Revolution in a Chinese Village* (1966).

Hsiao, Kung-ch'uan, *Rural China: Imperial Control in the Nineteenth Century* (1960).

Hsu, Immanuel C. Y., *The Rise of Modern China* (1975).

Huang, Ray, *China: A Macro History* (1988).

Hucker, Charles O., *China's Imperial Past* (1975).

Kuhn, Phillip A., *Rebellion and Its Enemies in Late Imperial China* (1970).

Levenson, Joseph R., *Confucian China and Its Modern Fate* (1968).

Leys, Simon, *Chinese Shadows* (1977).

Liang, Heng, and Judith Shapiro, *Son of the Revolution* (1983).

Meisner, Maurice. *Mao's China and After: A History of the People's Republic* (1985).

Meskill, John T. *An Introduction to Chinese Civilization* (1973).

Mote, Frederick W., *Intellectual Foundations of China* (1971).

Needham, Joseph, *Science and Civilization in China* (1954).

Ropp, Paul S. (ed.), *Heritage of China: Contemporary Perspectives on Chinese Civilization* (1990).

Schiffrin, Harold Z., *Sun Yat-sen and the Origins of the Chinese Revolution* (1970).

Schoppa, R. Keith, *Xiang Lake—Nine Centuries of Chinese Life* (1989).

Schram, Stuart R., *Mao Zedong* (1966).

Schurmann, Herbert Franz, *Ideology and Organization in Communist China* (1968).

Sheridan, James E., *China in Disintegration* (1975).

———, *Chinese Warlord: The Career of Feng Yu-hsiang* (1966).

Sih, Paul K. T., *Nationalist China During the Sino-Japanese War, 1937–1945* (1977).

———, *The Strenuous Decade, 1927–1937* (1974).

Snow, Edgar, *Red Star Over China* (1938).

Spence, Jonathan D., *The Search for Modern China* (1990).

Teng, Ssu-yu, and John K. Fairbank, *China's Response to the West* (1954).

Terrill, Ross, *China in Our Time: The Epic Saga of the People's Republic, from the Communist Victory to Tiananmen Square and Beyond* (1992).

Wakeman, Frederic, Jr., *The Fall of Imperial China* (1975).

Watson, W., *Early Civilization in China* (1966).

Wright, Mary C., (ed.), *China in Revolution: The First Phase, 1900–1913* (1968).

———. *The Last Stand of Chinese Conservatism* (1966).

Xinxin, Zhang, and Sang Ye. *Chinese Lives: An Oral History of Contemporary China* (1987).

Glossary

Analects: Collection of "sayings" attributed to Confucius.

Bao jia: Mechanism for local control through neighborhood selfpolicing. Inaugurated during the Song dynasty (960–1279 A.D.).

Chiang Kai-shek: Chinese Nationalist leader, successor to Sun Yat-sen after 1925. Movement defeated on the mainland and driven to island of Taiwan in 1949. President of the Republic of China there until his death in 1975.

Dao: "The Way" or path to personal and societal happiness and harmony. Each of China's great philosophies prescribed its own *dao*.

Dao de Jing: Basic text of Daoist teaching.

Deng Xiaoping: A long-time party leader who survived several purgings to become the PRC's preeminent leader in the post-Mao years. Most responsible for reversing China's economic policies to encourage development and an openness to the outside world.

Eight-Legged Essay: Rigid format for the civil service examinations. Developed during the Ming Dynasty (1368–1644 A.D.).

Great Leap Forward: Campaign launched late in 1957 to raise China's economic production rapidly and create a new society. A significant failure for Mao.

Great Proletarian Cultural Revolution (GPCR): Campaign by Mao Zedong (1966–69) against the moderate policies of Communist Party pragmatists and the values and attitudes of traditional China.

Guomindang: The official ruling party of the Republic of China (presently on Taiwan), the KMT. Also known as the Chinese Nationalist Party. Originally founded in 1905 by Sun Yat-sen, who established the Chinese republic following the anti-Manchu revolution (1911–12).

Hundred Schools of Thought: General name for the extraordinary flowering of philosophy along with political and social thought during the Eastern Zhou period (771–256 B.C.).

Jun zi: "Gentleman." The properly cultivated person; the ideal of Confucianists.

Khrushchev, Nikita S.: Soviet premier whose policies of "de-Stalinization" and "co-existence" with the West were regarded as dangerously "revisionist" by Mao Zedong. Vital issues in the Sino-Soviet split after 1956.

Kongzi: The "Great Sage" (551–479 B.C.). Philosopher and teacher whose ideals gave China its fundamental character. Known in Western writings as Confucius.

Laozi: Purported author (604?–531 B.C.) of the *Dao De Jing* and founder of Daoism.

Li: Confucian virtue denoting social and moral propriety.

Long March: The trek of some one hundred thousand supporters of the Chinese Communist Party to escape the forces of Chiang Kai-shek in 1934–35. Covered five thousand miles from southeastern to northern China. Confirmed Mao Zedong's leadership.

Mandate of Heaven: Ancient political concept which claims that dynasties come to power with Heaven's consent and remain as long as they provide proper leadership through moral example. If not, the people may rise in revolt.

Mao Zedong: Undisputed leader of the Chinese Communist Party after 1934–35. Concept of guerrilla warfare and mobilization of the peasantry captured the countryside of China for the Communists against the Nationalists by 1949. Then Chairman of the Central People's Administrative Council of the People's Republic of China.

Marshall Mission: Unsuccessful attempt by the American General George C. Marshall to mediate a peace between the Chinese Communists and the Nationalists from 1945 to 1947. Its failure resulted in a steady erosion of American support to Chiang Kai-shek from that point.

Mass line: Technique developed by the Chinese Communist Party during the Yan'an Period (1935–47) to facilitate mass mobilization by providing a link between the party and the masses.

May Fourth Movement: A cultural and political campaign launched by Chinese students and intellectuals on May 4, 1919, first precipitated by the resentment against the weak warlord government in Beijing as well as the cession of the Shantung (Shandong) concessions to Japan by the Versailles Conference. Subsequently evolved into a modern literary revolutionary movement.

Middle Kingdom: *Zhongguo*. China perceived as the center of the universe with outside barbarians in a tributary status. The key expression of Chinese cultural superiority.

Ren: Confucian virtue encompassing benevolence, love, compassion, and sympathy toward one's fellow human beings.

Sino-Soviet split: Dispute between the Soviet Union and the People's Republic of China, emanating from Premier Khrushchev's denunciation of Stalin's "cult of personality" in 1956. Quarrel raged over historical, doctrinal, territorial, hegemonic, and strategic issues.

Tael: Chinese coin valued at approximately U.S. $1.63 in the early nineteenth century; at least half of that by 1900.

Ti/yong: "Substance/Function": from the slogan "Chinese learning for substance, Western learning for function." The approach to reform characteristic of the selfstrengtheners of the late nineteenth century.

Tributary system: Traditional Chinese systematic approach to dealing with barbarians based on the tradition of the Middle Kingdom. China was the center of all things, the foundation of culture, to which non-Chinese brought tribute in return for protection from the emperor and access, through trade, to the immense wealth of China. A familial concept, founded on Confucian principles. Originated by the Han, it reached its zenith in the period of the Tang (618–906 A.D.).

Wang: "king." Title originally reserved for Zhou rulers, but increasingly used by feudal lords during the Eastern Zhou period (771–256 B.C.).

Well-field system: Utopian system of land distribution and agricultural practice whereby eight families shared nine equal plots: one for each family's needs, and one worked communally for the local lord, or to pay taxes.

Yin/yang: A unique Chinese cosmological theory based on two contending, complementary, and interacting cosmic forces governing the universe and its dynamics. Yang is the masculine, positive, and active element, while yin is the feminine, negative, and passive.

Zhou Enlai: Long a party associate of Mao Zedong. Premier of the People's Republic from 1949 to his death in 1976. Foreign Minister, 1949–59.

The
World
of

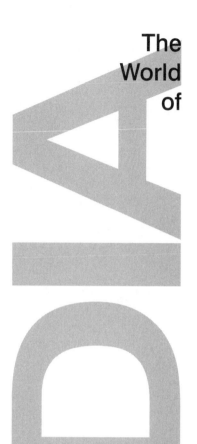
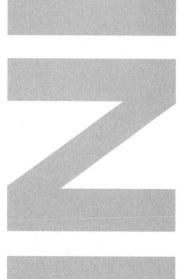

Introduction

 Like Europe, India is more than a nation; India is a subcontinent, rich in tradition and diversity. Few, if any, modern states contain within their borders the cultural and linguistic pluralism that to India has been a way of life for thousands of years. The slogan adopted by the Republic of India, "Unity in Diversity," is a living testament to this phenomenon. But diversity to the contemporary Indian has been both a blessing and a curse. It has encouraged tolerance but made planning difficult; it has deepened the religious experience but frustrated education, and it has enriched the cultural legacy while retarding technology. Many observers, especially those from the West, have attempted to develop an appreciation for and an understanding of this diversity by comparing it to a yet unborn United States of Europe. They argue that within the proposed state, united under one hegemony from Dublin to Vienna and Oslo to Rome, there might be found (within one political framework) an equivalent of the cultural pluralism and ethnic diversity that seems to have long existed within the confines of traditional India. While the Europe-India comparison could probably be duplicated by artificially creating states in other global areas, the fact remains that more than a little historical understanding can be gained through thinking of India as a geographical or cultural entity rather than as a nation per se.

India, like Europe or the Middle East, is a region through which many different peoples have passed and left behind a legacy that survives in the present. It is a land where people speak at least fourteen major languages and more than one hundred major dialects. The current Census of India enumerated well over one thousand mother tongues present in the republic. This type of pluralism staggers the minds of inhabitants from states whose nationalism is based, at least in part, on linguistic homogeneity; and it is not uncommon for people to question whether a system composed of what appears to be an endless variety of parts can in fact endure. Some, particularly Westerners, have written volumes arguing that it cannot. But time has proved the prognosis wrong. India can survive as a free and independent state. Why? How? The answers are to be found in its history.

The Making of
Traditional India

1

India is a subcontinent of Asia. The Indian Ocean, which borders nearly half of India, has provided effective insularity from people living to the south of the subcontinent. Although Romans and Arabs interacted with Indians by sea, migrations, military excursions, and even cultural influences did not generally come to India via waterways. The only exception to this general rule occurred after the arrival of the Europeans in India. The Europeans destroyed India's relative maritime isolation by converting the Arabian Sea and the Bay of Bengal into vehicles of change in both a military and a cultural sense. However, this development came long after the arrival of the Portuguese, the Europeans who arrived first, in 1498. Generally speaking, the water that surrounds much of India has served as a protective shield rather than an avenue of entrance. Likewise the mighty Himalaya Mountains on the northeast border of India have served as a nearly impregnable barrier, as have the jungle lands on the Burmese (Myanmar) side, though the jungle appears to have been far less formidable a shield than the mountains.

Geographic Factors

Peoples, ideas, religions, and other significant influences have come to India by one main route: over the northwest passes of the Hindu-Kush Mountains. These and other lesser mountain ranges, which today comprise the Afghan-Pakistani border, extend along the northwest rim of the subcontinent on approximately a forty-five-degree angle; they run from the Arabian Sea to Kashmir, where they join with the Himalayas. Though the ranges of the northwest form a clearly discernible border, they are unlike the formidable Himalayas, which average well over twenty thousand feet in height. The mountains of the northwest are fairly easily scaled in some places, for they contain three or four major passes through which migratory peoples, including many of the subcontinent's conquerors, have passed since the beginnings of recorded history. The most famous of these passes, the Khyber, has facilitated the passage of large numbers of nomadic tribes, mostly from Central Asia, who have come, settled, and been rapidly assimilated into the social structure of the indigenous population on the Indian plains below. A case in point would be the Rajputs, a group of tribes who are believed to have migrated from Central Asia to the area north of Bombay over twelve hundred years ago. Once in India these migrants came to be considered the vanguard of Hindu militancy and were afforded a high rank for a millennium or more.

Seldom have incursions through the passes caused cataclysmic confrontations or destruction. But occasionally conquerors with superior organization and weaponry have poured down through the mountain passes leaving death, destruction, and change in their wake. In the last four thousand years this has happened at least twice: once around 1500 B.C., when an Indo-European nomadic and pastoral people known as the "Aryans" imposed their sway (and their civilization) and again around A.D. 1200, when Turkish-speaking armies professing the Muslim faith established an Islamic state in North India. But these invaders, both of whom appear to have originated beyond the Hindu-Kush Mountains, never obliterated the existing civilization, no matter how they tried. The conquerors simply added another level of diversity or enrichment to that which already existed. Thus waves of intruders found their place in Hindustan (place of the Hindu) much as waves of conquerors found their places and identities in Europe after centuries of acculturation and adjustment. India and Europe share a common history of migration, conquest, and assimilation, though India probably never experienced conquests as destructive as those of Eastern and Central Europe in the thirteenth century, when hordes of Mongols swept across half of the European continent.

The sea and the great mountain ranges of the north are not the only topographical features that have helped shape contemporary India. Equally important are the two great rivers of the subcontinent, the Indus and the Ganges, for it is on the plains through which these rivers flow that most of India's history has been written. It would be difficult to overestimate the importance, particularly to the Aryan north, of these two river systems. Their water and silt have played a major role in the agriculture, transportation, and industry of the region. On their plains have flourished all of India's major empires, and the bulk of the population's socio-religious patterns have been clearly tied to these rivers and their tributaries. The River Ganges, which flows parallel to the Himalayas, is the most sacred as well as the most productive of India's rivers. Varanasi (Banaras), the Jerusalem of India, is located on its banks; and the adjacent plains can be compared to those of the Egyptian Nile in terms of fertility and productivity. Furthermore the long stretches of monotonously flat plains through which the Ganges and the Indus flow facilitated the cultural unity of the people in the north. On the other hand, the short rivers of South India, which flow through rocky terrain, discouraged formal settlement. Therefore, all of the great dynasties of India were North Indian in origin, and their expansion always followed the paths carved by these two river systems.

No discussion of the historical importance of topographical formations would be complete without reference to the Deccan Plateau. The Deccan exists in the form of a triangular table, bounded on the north by the Vindhya Mountains and on the southeast and southwest by the Eastern and Western Ghats, ranges small in height but large in importance. Between the Ghats and the sea are narrow stretches of land, nearly five hundred miles in length, that have harbored self-contained city-states whose identities developed quite apart from one another, as well as apart from India as a whole. And, finally, between the lower end of the Deccan Plateau and the southern tip of the subcontinent lies a large, beautiful, and productive area known as Tamilnad. Here in the land of the Tamil many a civilization has flourished, and it may well be that the precivilized culture of the inhabitants predates the cultures of the north. The Deccan itself has played a significant role historically. This large plateau, which rises three thousand to five thousand feet above the plains below, frequently helped its indigenous people to resist invasion. The Deccan, then, separates the Aryan north from the Dravidian south, and its rough terrain has fostered a lifestyle that, while very Hindu, is quite different from those which thrive at the lower sea levels.

Regionalism as a Factor in Polity

Historically the Indian subcontinent has been united administratively but not culturally. India's first universal state dates back to the third century B.C. with the rise of the Maurya dynasty. India, like Europe, has seldom known true cultural unity. The great difference is that most of India is today one political entity, whose leaders are attempting to rule and coordinate all regions within one centralized framework, while Europe has remained a patchwork of relatively small states. The stumbling block to unity is often geographical, not cultural. As C. Collin Davies has argued, "One of the most important lessons of Indian history is that a united India was impossible until the development of communication after 1857 facilitated centralization." Before the development of railroads and the telegraph, a few northern rulers like Muhammad bin Tughluq, Asoka, and Aurangzeb did conquer the Deccan and add it to their Gangetic-based empires, but their rules over this area represented little more than temporary military decisions. Armies from the north could penetrate the Deccan, but the logistics of communication taxed the northern empires beyond their abilities. Thus the Vindhya range, which virtually cuts India into two parts, traditionally served as a dividing line—politically, culturally, and linguistically.

India north of the Vindhya is popularly termed Aryan India, while the area south of the range is known as Dravidian India. This classification is not entirely accurate, but it is useful as a guideline. Regionally speaking, there has existed in the subcontinent for three thousand years a northern region, the culture and language of which are closely tied to Sanskrit, the tongue spoken by the Aryans who conquered India in the second millennium B.C., while in the south there has existed for at least that long a civilization or culture known as Dravidian. Hence the Aryan north and the Dravidian south for thousands of years have existed as great cultural and linguistic blocs, separated by the mountainous, impoverished, and underdeveloped Deccan hinterland.

India is, however, not divided simply into the threefold division of Aryan, Deccan, and Dravidian, as is often purported in older textbooks. Within each of the three great divisions are to be found strong regional identities that may have greater call on the allegiance of inhabitants than do the larger divisions. None of the three classic divisions has ever really enjoyed unity, except perhaps the northern one. Still, none has experienced political unity often or for long durations; what unity has existed is more a product of language and culture than of political structures. Also most of the regional identifications of South Asia developed in a pretechnical age when even small political aggregates were difficult to sustain. As a result, most regionalism in South Asia is tied to language and ethnic groups.

If one keeps in mind that most of what is described as "nationalism" in the West is built around ethnic or linguistic groups, then "regionalism" in India becomes more easily understood. If Europe (or at least most of it) were united under one or two governments, what is now termed German nationalism would become German regionalism. If India were to break up into fifteen or twenty sovereign states, what is today termed regionalism would tomorrow have to be called nationalism. The borders of most of the twenty states that today comprise the Republic of India coincide with linguistic patterns, and over the past two or three decades, much of the political energy of India has been directed at nothing more than making state boundaries coincide with linguistic ones. And though the Centre (meaning national) government has opposed movements designed to bring the two in line, it has time and again acquiesced rather than risk the threat of civil strife and dismemberment.

The Culture of the Gupta Period, 320–ca. 500

After the Mauryan Empire, the second great era of political unification occurred under the dynasty of the Gupta, the classical age of Hindu India, although the ancient religions of Buddhism and Jainism continued to contribute to the culture. At a time of unmatched cultural splendor as well as imperial grandeur, the heart of the new empire lay in northern India around the Ganges Valley. The zenith of its glory was attained in the reign of Chandragupta II (375–415). The Guptas gave India a magnificent period of civilization, comparable to the Periclean Age in Greek history, but the fruits of the Gupta culture were enjoyed only by the privileged classes.

The Gupta patronized the flowering of literature in what became the golden age of Sanskrit, the sacred language of the Brahmins. For instance, under the Gupta the epic poem the *Mahabharata* was recast and put into its present form. The court encouraged gifted writers, who developed a significant secular literature—undoubtedly the eminent poet and playwright Kalidasa best personified this era. His poetry portrayed love, nature, and legends of the gods and their consorts, while ignoring the dreary side of life, since poets were forbidden to mingle with those of lower caste. Usually recited at court, Indian poetry of this period emphasized the beauty of language. Cultural historians have long regarded Kalidasa also as the Shakespeare of Sanskrit drama. The aristocratic classes enjoyed plays such as those by Kalidasa, which were known as *nataka*. These were performed at court, local temples, or for private groups, and were often presented in conjunction with religious functions, much like the miracle plays of medieval Europe. Stages utilized little scenery and few props, and dance themes and hand gestures (*mudras*) were important elements of the productions. Stories concerned love affairs, humorous romantic mixups, and improb-

Gometeshwara, Sravanabelgola. Consulate General of India, Chicago.

able social blunders, with happy endings to conclude the frolics. *Sakuntala*, Kalidasa's most popular play, has been long admired in the West. A veritable storehouse of children's stories—fairy tales and animal fables (especially the *Panchatantra*)—flourished in India before making their way to the Mideast and Europe.

Art reached its classical period inspired by religious themes, both Buddhist and Hindu. The Buddha images found at Sarnath, near Banaras, constitute some of the finest sculpture still found in India. Buddhist sculpture sought somewhat to dehumanize the Buddha and strip away individuality in line with his teachings. This trend resulted in the creation of figures bearing a rigid, mask-like face, with chiseled eyes, mouth, and eyelids. Artists consider the most-famous Gupta paintings to be the frescoes adorning the walls and ceilings of the Ajanta caves (about two hundred miles northeast of Bombay), which represented Indian court life and episodes in the life of the Buddha. Many scholars regard these works to be the climax of the achievement of Indian art. As for Gupta architecture, there remains nothing comparable to the foregoing, although a few rock-cut Hindu temples have survived the ravages of later Muslim and Hun invaders. Artists and craftsmen, however, proved their skill in metallurgy. The pillar at Delhi, made of wrought iron, is a marvel of artistic achievement in this field. Casting copper figures of the Buddha climaxed with one statue eighty feet in height created at Nalanda.

Classical Hindu music and dance, currently of great interest in the West, flourished under Guptan patronage. The mastery of King Samudragupta (ca. 330–ca. 375) in music and song was commemorated by the coins and medals of the period, which depict him seated on a couch playing the Indian lute or *vina*. Again religion (Buddhist and Hindu) helped to spur artistic genius. The traditional Indian musical scale was heptatonic (seven-toned), and the improvisational character of Indian classical music, following a complicated set of formulas called *ragas*, is surprisingly modern by Western standards. Musicians could, by improvisation, set the emotional mood and philosophic interpretation of theatrical performances. Dance forms appeared in a new Sanskrit textbook, which explained the symbolic significance of each of the hand gestures and movements of the classical school of Hindu dance.

Under the Gupta, great advances in science and technology led to breakthroughs in the fields of medicine, mathematics, chemistry, and astronomy, which was influenced to some degree by early Greek contacts. The outstanding university of Nalanda (with its eight colleges and three libraries) attracted students from all over Asia. Indian physicians understood the structure and function of the spinal cord and the complexities of the nervous system, combining this knowledge with consummate skill in bone-setting, plastic surgery, caesarian delivery, and other medical techniques. Objection to dissection, however, prevented further advances in medicine. Mathematicians introduced so-called "Arabic numerals," the zero, and the decimal system, later adopted by the Islamic world and transmitted to Europe. The techniques for using square and cube roots as well as the formulation of the relation of the diameter to the circumference of a circle (pi=3.1416) were marvelous products of Indian knowledge. Chemistry and metallurgy advanced the tempering of steel and iron and the processing of dyes for exotic fabrics. The Arabs named one Indian fabric *quittan*, hence the word "cotton." *Calico* comes from Calicut, the Indian city, while the terms *chintz*, *cashmere*, *madras*, and *bandanna* are also Indian.

The wealth of the Gupta attracted many traders and visitors from abroad. Especially attractive to them were the silk textile industries of Bengal and Banaras and the cotton cloth of Mathuria. Contacts with the West and East increased rapidly. Land routes through Persia carried Indian goods to the West. Roman gold paid for Indian pepper, indigo, jewels, and spices to such an extent that the successors of Emperor Nero, fearing a drain on precious metal by others, took measures to monopolize the Indian trade.

The intensity of overseas exchange made the city of Ujjain a bustling commercial center, situated as it was at the convergence of many principal trade routes. Seeking further commercial advantage, numerous Indian colonists sailed eastward to Burma, Malaya, Borneo, Java, Indochina, and Ceylon to establish settlements. Kambuja (Cambodia) represented one of the most significant areas of colonization, where there were several successive Hindu dynasties. Among these were the Khmer kings, who around the year 1100 erected the magnificent temple of Angkor Wat. Built to honor the Hindu deity Shiva, its galleries are adorned with scenes from Hindu epics—certainly one of the most resplendent religious monuments ever created by man and a tribute to Gupta traditions.

China and India maintained close relations during the Guptan period for one of the rare times in their histories, for their cultures have developed largely isolated from one another. When the Han Emperor Ming-ti encouraged Buddhist monks to bring their faith to China (A.D. 64), the secularistic-minded Chinese sought the religious comfort of an afterlife in the Buddha's promise of deliverance to Nirvana—something Chinese philosophies had left void. The Chinese sent streams of devout Buddhist pilgrims to India's monasteries and to seats of learning like Nalanda for centuries afterward. Such an enthusiast as the Chinese pilgrim Fa-hsien regarded India as the "Holy Land of Buddhism." During the years 399–414 he traveled to seek the authentic texts of the *Vinaya-pitaka*, or Buddhist books on monastic discipline. His journal, one of the authentic sources of the period, described the Gupta as an empire religiously tolerant, peaceful, prosperous, and well governed.

The known world justifiably envied the achievements of the Gupta, which granted northern India political unity and peace for almost two centuries. But decline set in as the covetous eyes of central Asian barbarians awaited the decay of the Gupta's unified power. The Huns' attack in 455, although repulsed, so exhausted Guptan armies that the empire virtually collapsed in 480. Two hundred years later, long after the splendor of Guptan culture had passed into history, the Islamic tidal wave found northern India practically defenseless, an inviting political vacuum.

Linguistic Unity and Diversity

Sanskrit, the language of the Aryans, served as did Latin in the West as the *lingua franca* for most of South Asia (meaning India, Pakistan, Bangladesh and Ceylon (Sri Lanka)). There were times when other languages challenged the supremacy of Sanskrit, as in the case of the Buddhist period when Pali became the language of the learned; but usually Sanskrit was the medium for the exchange of ideas and culture. This is particularly true in North India, where most of the languages prevalent today are derivatives of Sanskrit. Even Urdu, a language written in a Persian script, is not very different from Hindi, the modern tongue most directly akin to Sanskrit. Hindi is written in the Devanagri (Sanskrit) script, but one who speaks Urdu can clearly understand one who speaks Hindi, though the two may not be able to correspond.

Most of the citizenry of South Asian nations have been multilingual historically, especially the learned. The Aryan conquest established the supremacy of Sanskrit among the rulers by ca. 1000 B.C. The Muslims who conquered most of South Asia in the late medieval period (ca. A.D. 1200 to 1500) favored Persian or Urdu, and much of the populace learned it. This was also true during the British era, though the English language was restricted to a much smaller number. Far less than one-half of 1 percent in India lay claim to English as their mother tongue, while fully 5 percent claim Urdu. The Aryan conquest also created a bloc of Sanskritized languages in North India, where nearly a dozen languages derived from Sanskrit are today spoken as mother tongues by over two-thirds of the population. An even greater percentage understands what is termed Hindustani, a *bazaar* language understood perhaps by 80 percent or more of the populace.

Sanskrit was the dominant force as much because of culture as conquest. Sanskrit, as mentioned, was the language of the Brahmins, the Aryan priests. Through the Brahmins a Sanskritized culture was imposed in most of South Asia. When in the post-classical period (A.D. 600–1200) Hindu culture emerged as the dominant socio-religious ethic, Sanskrit became a pan–South Asian tongue. As the so-called "great tradition" of Hinduism spread, it made accommodations for "small" or regional traditions. Most of the region south of the Vindhya range resisted the linguistic expansion of the Aryans but accepted their cultural legacy. Thus the major Dravidian tongues of the south continued to flourish. Tamil, Telegu, and Kannada (the major Dravidian tongues) served as the basis of regional identification and literature, but all incorporated Aryan concepts, ideals, and words into their indigenous literary outpourings.

Hinduism: The Religion of Most of the People

Well over 80 percent of the population of India is and has been Hindu from the seventh century A.D. Hinduism resembles more a confederation of religions than it does a single, integrated faith. It is thus not like Christianity or Islam, which historically were puritanical and tightly organized. Hinduism, a tolerant faith, encompasses a wide range of beliefs that seem to many to be virtually contradictory. The diversity that exists in Hindu society as a whole understandably extends to Hindu religion. Thus one can find philosophical justification and religious sanction for almost any ethical norm or structure. Few Westerners have been able to view Hinduism as a historical religion with a pattern of continuity and change like those of other universal religions.

The scriptural bases of Hinduism are to be found in the *Vedas*, a collection of literature passed on from the Aryan tribes of antiquity. The Vedas are four in number, and many devout Hindus consider them to be the final authority. But Vedic literature was developed to meet the needs of a nomadic society; and much of the Vedas, particularly the *Rig Veda,* was probably composed outside of India itself. As the Aryans developed a more settled existence on the plains of North India, a new body of literature, which was primarily antithetical to the Vedas, was developed. The most famous and perhaps most significant of the new literature, the *Upanishads* (dialogues between the teachers and the taught), represented a reaction against Brahmanical ritualism and blind orthodoxy.

The bulk of the Upanishads was composed between 900 and 600 B.C. They are deep probings in dialogue form into questions of unity and diversity, reality and illusion, self and nature. Contrary to the teaching of Brahmins, the Upanishads repudiated sacrifice, magic, and mechanical rituals as paths to salvation. The most important idea to come out of the Upanishads perhaps was that *Atman,* or self, was identical with *Brahma,* or the ultimate nature of reality. The philosophy of the Upanishads has been called monism because of its nontheistic view of overriding unity.

After the Aryans conquered North India (ca. 1500 B.C.), there slowly evolved a settled civilization centering on the Gangetic Plains, and the distinction between the conquering Aryans and the defeated *dasyu* slowly diminished. As they became less nomadic, the Aryans came to call the region Aryavarta (land of the Aryans). Pataliputra (modern day Patna), in the eastern Gangetic region, evolved as the center of this new civilization. It was in this new civilization in the ancient state of Magadha that Buddha emerged and preached his anti-Brahmanical ideology of salvation. Buddhism, with its stress on non-violence (*ahimsa*) and ethical strengthening, became the moral basis of the Maurya universal state under Asoka (third century B.C.).

The Varna System
The Aryans, long after their conquest, appear to have retained a feeling of racial superiority in regard to the conquered *dasyu* or dark-skinned. The fair-skinned victors devised elaborate rationales and rituals to keep their subjects in place. One of these rationales came to be termed the Varna System. *Varna* literally meant color, and it is quite possible that color was the decisive criterion used, at least in the beginning, in deciding where one should be placed on the social scale. But whatever the original purpose, it appears to have been lost sometime in the Buddhist Age, for the Buddhists revolted against the rigidity and exclusiveness of the Brahmins. What did remain to become peculiarly Indian was an idealized, socio-religious structure that argued that society (or those that count in it) was divided into four *varnas* or groups.

The four varna groupings in descending order of their importance came to be Brahmin (priests), Kshatriya (warriors and administrators), Vaishya (cultivators and merchants), and Sudra (peasants and menial laborers). The dasyu were, however, mostly considered to be below the pale of what came to be Aryan society, and this proletariat group came to be termed "untouchable." As a consequence, ancient India, like other classical civilizations, developed a system of social stratification on the basis of class function. The varna structure grew more rigid over the centuries, and by the Gupta period elaborate ceremonies and legal codes were developed to ensure that the Sudra and the untouchables would never challenge the authority of the Brahmin or others higher on the social ladder. The famous Law Code of Manu, which dates from two thousand years ago but was probably altered later on, prescribed that those of low origin who heard the sacred teachings being discussed should have their tongues cut out and their ears filled with molten wax so as to ensure that they would neither repeat what they had heard nor listen again to that which they might pollute.

Dharma, or duty, virtue, law, was the core concept of the social system. A number of dharmas were developed in ancient legal texts (*smritis*) as modes of conduct for rulers, soldiers, priests, merchants, and cultivators. Each code contained guidelines for achieving the ultimate good within a given occupational group. Thus the *rajdharma*, or king's code, offered guidance on how to govern most effectively. Dharma encouraged mobility and perfection within one's own occupational grouping but discouraged mobility between the groups. It was believed that social corruption would occur when kings became merchants or when intellectuals became politicians or soldiers. The ideal was for each person to become the best possible priest, politician, merchant or cultivator and accept his ranking.

The Jati System

Though the origins of the jati system are obscure, they appear to be tied to more settled times than those of early Aryan society. Therefore, the jati system probably did not develop fully until the era of the Gupta. During the Gupta period the jati evolved possibly from hereditary guilds or organizations based on a specialization of labor associated with a settled economy. There is little doubt that labor specialization played a significant role in jati formations, but over the centuries many jatis changed their specialties while members did not change their jati. Hence in the contemporary period it is not uncommon to find all the barbers of one area belonging to the same jati, while still another jati in a nearby city may be tied together by nothing more than kinship. *Jati* then can be defined either as extended kinship groupings or as groups that now share or at some time in the past appear to have shared job specialty. However, jati cannot easily be termed what it often has been termed, a subcaste system. Jati was apparently never a workable subdivision of varna, even though there are well over three thousand different jati in India, and the tendency to classify the larger number as divisions of the four-fold varna classifications has proved nearly irresistible.

The jati, far more than the varna, has served as India's basic societal unit. The strong pollution prohibitions such as those associated with intermarriage and interdining are tied primarily to jati. So also is pollution tied to job specialization. Untouchables who remove night soil (human waste) or the dead carcasses of animals are considered highly polluted because of the nature of their work. Yet many untouchables have never undertaken unclean work; they are polluted because of their lineage. One jati will not eat meat, another will, while still others will eat fish but not fowl. There exist fish-eating Brahmins along with Brahmins who are strict vegetarians. Untouchables in some areas of India have been considered so polluting that they have been required to remain far distant from others and were required to make loud noises when approaching people of higher station, while untouchables living in a different region have never experienced such treatment.

Each jati usually has a group of elders who regulate the behavior of its members, and these elders often exercise their prerogatives by ostracizing those who refuse to abide by the rules. Many Indians live in fear of being "outcaste," especially those who inhabit the rural areas. Being an outcaste means being denied the right to dine or marry within one's own group, and this ostracism can even be extended to one's family and siblings. Therefore the importance of the jati as the societal unit which most claims the loyalty of a Hindu can easily be understood. It is this kinship group that has been the policing agent for the average Hindu for all of the modern era. Bold indeed has been the individual who challenged the elders of his jati.

Every jati has its own dharma that its members are expected to follow, and this is what contributes greatly to India's diversity. Since, as mentioned, there are over three thousand jatis, there are well over three thousand different sets of rules, or dharma. Also there exists more than one level of dharma. For everyone there is a general Hindu dharma, as there is a general Christian ethic. The general dharma argues, for instance, that one should not eat beef, and the overwhelming majority of Hindus do not. But dharma is also a philosophical abstraction that argues that each group has its own rights, duties, and responsibilities, even though many of these are absolutely contradictory to others. Thus one jati may require its members to be vegetarian, to abstain from taking life, and never to cross the ocean, while another jati may encourage the opposite. It has, therefore, proved difficult for governments to encourage similar actions on the part of its citizens when society not only condones but encourages each unit of the jati system to follow its own dharma.

Since the jati has been a basic unit in society from the Hindu Middle Ages through the eighteenth century, it is the unit to which many other socio-religious concepts are tied. An orthodox Hindu believes that his quest for immortality centers on his realizing the true nature of the relationship between brahman (universal soul) and atman (the individual's soul). He feels if he follows his dharma he will build up pure *karma* (result of action) and be reincarnated at a higher plane of existence. The orthodox Hindu views hell as existing here on earth and hopes to escape *samsara* (the cycle of rebirths) by doing what is correct, or following his dharma. If a Hindu builds up enough good karma, he will eventually reach *moksha* (release from rebirths), and the atman will be reunited with the universal creative essence, brahman. Rebirth to the Hindu is punishment, for it condemns him to repeat an earthly existence, either as man or beast, fish or fowl, and so on, as the atman migrates from one existence to another based on past karma. Every existence is based on a former life. Therefore, an untouchable, who presumably led a poor life in an earlier existence, is simply being punished for past action (karma). The only way an untouchable can improve his position is through the practice of correct dharma and rebirth.

It must not be overemphasized that the above describes the orthodox ideal of Hinduism, for modern Hinduism has changed as much as have Christianity, Islam, and Buddhism. It would be as absurd to depict the modern West in terms of orthodox Christianity as it would to depict modern India in terms of orthodox Hinduism. It is thus important that these comments on the ideal of the Hindu tradition be weighed against later references in this text to social change in modern India.

The Islamic Community: A Vocal Minority

Today 12 percent of the population of India is Muslim. Prior to the 1947 Partition of India and Pakistan the percentage was around 25 percent. Thus the role of Muslims in the subcontinent and in the Republic of India has historically been larger than their small percentage of the population might otherwise indicate. And though Muslims, as the followers of the prophet Muhammad term themselves, are latecomers to civilization in India, their role there has been significant and their contribution large. Muhammad (570–632) is the inspiration for Muslim thought and culture; and the *Quran* (Koran), a book completed shortly after his death, is the source of all authority according to his followers. For centuries observers have admired the success of Islam, attributing it to the simplicity of its doctrine or the success of its armed forces. Many have viewed it as a medieval storm that overwhelmed most opposition in its attempt at world dominion. Others have marveled at the strength of the Islamic organization that swept out of the Arabian desert, united by the creed; "There is but one God, Allah, and Muhammad is his prophet." Others, still, have viewed Islam as a retarding or intolerant ethic, for a fear and distrust of Islam has been long ingrained in the minds of Hindus, Christians, and Hebrews alike. Islam was born at the crossroads of empire. Within easy reach of Arabia are to be found most of the regions that gave birth to the ancient civilizations of the world. Nearby are the lands where Christ first lectured to his disciples, where the Jews came to know captivity, where the Pharaohs sat amid theocratic splendor, and where for centuries the Zoroastrian Persians, the Hellenistic Greeks, and the conquering Romans mingled ideals and concepts. It seems ridiculous to explain Islam's spread as a result of its being a simple religion born in desert wastes among people of a militant and aggressive tradition. Southwest Asia was anything but primitive at the time of the rise and triumph of Islam. Something else accounts for the fact that every seventh person in the world today is Muslim. Perhaps the explanation lies in doctrine.

In many respects Islam resembles other religions. It is monotheistic and shares much of the cosmology of the Judeo-Christian tradition. It claims Muhammad as the last or "seal" of the prophets but respects most of the important figures in the Judeo-Christian tradition. It does not accept Christ as God but as a prophet. Likewise, Muhammad is a prophet, not a god. Members of the faith should not be called Muhammadans, for he is not worshipped by followers of Islam. The correct name is Muslim or Moslem. A Muslim (one who submits to Allah) distrusts those who, he feels, do not practice monotheism, including those who believe in the Christian trinity, which is held to be a belief in polytheism. Also strong is the conviction that idolatry is evil and that human representations ought not grace the *masjid* (mosque or building of worship).

Islam favors charity, particularly toward those within the Islamic brotherhood, and frowns on usury. It asks its adherents not to wrong others and promises that they, in turn, will not be wronged. It argues that "Allah Knows All Things" and that contracts, particularly those written, should not be broken. What then has made Islam unique? Why have Europe and South Asia opposed it? Perhaps simply because its domain borders each area, politically and culturally, now and in the past. Still, there seem to be other reasons. Both the Hindu and the Christian have reacted bitterly to the Muslim concept of *jihad* (holy war), which promises salvation to all who die on the battlefield attempting to spread Islam to the nonbelievers. Muslims on the other hand find it difficult to understand why non-believers condemn the jihad, for to them a jihad is simply a group of believers attempting to carry out the will of God.

Muslims also fail to comprehend why the application of *jizya* has elicited violent response from non-Muslims, especially in India. *Jizya* is a tax imposed on non-Muslims when a government is dominated by Muslims (as has often been the case in certain of India's regions). Islam holds that the world is composed of two spheres, the abode of peace and that of war. The peaceful sphere is the area over which Islam presides. A non-believer may live within this sphere, especially if he belongs to a tradition that has a holy book, so long as he pays a tax for the privilege. Muslims feel that they are being tolerant when they permit nonbelievers to exist within a Muslim state. Next to the jihad, the jizya has been the most hotly contested issue in India historically. Those Muslim leaders termed great by the Hindu majority are those like Akbar, ruler of the late sixteenth century, who chose not to implement the tax. Other Muslim rulers brought on war by imposing the jizya, like the Emperor Aurangzeb (1658–1707), who in the process destroyed Islamic paramountcy in India and opened the doors for British penetration. To a Hindu, Aurangzeb was a great bigot, but to a Muslim he was a religious zealot, only implementing what was expected of him.

Many differences between Muslims and Hindus that exist on the popular level often lead to mutual antagonism. Muslims eat beef; Hindus do not. Muslims do not eat pork; Hindus are permitted to do so. Unlike the Hindus, Muslims have no special priestly class. Muslims worship together on Friday while the Hindus have no special day for prayer. Islam forbids dancing and music during worship while Hinduism encourages the use of music. Islam disparages visual depictions of God; Hinduism relishes them as much as any religion on the globe. Muslims pray publicly five times daily; Hindus usually confine their daily devotion to a private room. A Muslim is expected, if possible, to make a pilgrimage to Mecca; the Hindu makes his pilgrimage to holy places within India. The Hindu (at least philosophically) admires asceticism; the Muslim does not. Only during Ramadan, when Muslims are expected not to partake of food or drink from sunrise to sundown for one month, do they even come close to an ascetic tradition. And, finally, the Muslim abhors the jati or caste system, while the Hindu sees little to admire in the Muslim promise of equality within the brotherhood of Islam because the provision is tied to a religious exclusiveness that postulates one path to salvation.

Islamic Conquest

In the early eighth century, the first wave of Islamic expansion carried Muslim banners across North Africa to Europe. India, on the opposite flank of Islam, was virtually ignored, though an Arabian general in 711 entered the Indus Valley. Islam did not appear in South Asia in force until a second wave of conquest carried Islamic culture to Central Asia and Afghanistan. Islam did penetrate many of the port cities along India's west coast, but Muslim merchants in these settlements seem to have created no challenge to Hindu hegemony, and peaceful trade relations developed between the Arab and Indian worlds. The mutual antagonism, hatred, and hostility that have come to characterize Hindu-Muslim relations in the last millennium seem to be a direct result of the assaults on the Hindu world launched by Central Asian peoples who had been themselves converted to Islam only shortly before their forays. The first and perhaps most famous of these intruders was Mahmud of Ghazni. Between A.D. 1000 and 1026, from his fortress city of Ghazni, he led about twenty expeditions down from the mountain citadel, carrying back to the hills of Afghanistan great wealth that had been looted from Hindu homes and temples. Waves of Turks, Afghans, Mongols, and other peoples followed his lead in the centuries that followed.

The Hindus who inhabited the plains seemed incapable of sustaining a system of united defense against these onslaughts, and around 1200 the Muslims succeeded in establishing a Muslim state in North India known as the Delhi Sultanate. Sultan literally means "one who wields authority," authority bestowed by the Caliph, the theocratic head of the Islamic state and successor of the Prophet Muhammad. From 1206 to 1526 the Delhi sultans, supposedly as the agents of the Caliphs, spread religious tyranny among all the peoples of South Asia. Hindu temples were destroyed, Buddhist monasteries were looted, and icons and statues were defaced with impunity. The sultans looked upon India as a region where jihad should be applied, and for centuries the fury of the Muslim zealots knew few bounds. Also the Muslim hierarchy, which distrusted the indigenous people of the lands it acquired, reinforced its position by importing foreigners from Central Asia, mostly as slaves. Once under the sultanate, some slaves were castrated as young boys and were raised to be rulers. It was felt that eunuchs, not able to create their own families, would give all their loyalty to the conquering minority, and the thirteenth century is usually termed the era of the Slave or Eunuch Kings. The slave system could not endure, and in the early fourteenth century Muhammad bin Tughluq succeeded in establishing a state that encompassed the largest amount of territory ruled by any Indian dynasty since the reign of Asoka in the third century B.C. Tughluq was a ferocious ruler. He made an art of torture, and the Tughluq state did not long survive his death in 1351, for by 1400 the Tughluq Sultanate had ceased to be an important kingdom. Regional rulers appeared who resisted the attempts of various succeeding sultans to return the unity of the past. And as decline set in, Delhi rulers lost contact with the Afghan areas that in past centuries had provided the manpower and stimulus necessary for conquest. Contact was, however, re-established forcefully in 1526 by Babar, a Mongol king from Kabul, Afghanistan, who again swept onto the Indian plains to found a new dynasty in the Delhi area.

The Mughal Dynasty

Babar defeated the last of the sultans near Delhi on the plains of Panipat and thus established the Mughal Dynasty. "Mughal" is a corruption of "Mongol," for Babar was a Mongol who traced his lineage to Genghis Khan and the famous Timur, who on a destructive foray in 1398–1399 dealt a blow to the Delhi Sultanate from which it never recovered. Babar actually claimed he had the right to rule in Delhi based on Timur's conquest, though he preferred to reside in Kabul. Babar disliked the Indian plains, and he remained with his courts in the mountains most of the time; but he followed an enlightened policy in regard to his Hindu subjects, and most of the forced conversions and bloody destruction of the Sultanate era ceased. Akbar, his grandson, who ruled India from 1556 to 1605, followed the lead of his famous ancestor, and from 1556 to 1605 relations between the Muslim and the Hindu improved rapidly.

Traditional India reached its zenith under the Mughal administration. Four able men whose reigns span the period from 1556 to 1707 provided the stability necessary for the Indian subcontinent to flourish as it never has since. Akbar, the first of the great Mughals, provided good government and unity, in part, through an enlightened religious policy. Akbar also fostered the arts and encouraged religious debate to be held publicly at his court in Fatehpur Sikri, his capital that still stands near the modern city of Agra as a silent testament to the skill of the artisans who built it. The successors of Akbar were also builders, and South Asia from Agra to Lahore is full of monuments that testify to the magnificence of the era. The son and successor of Akbar, Jahangir (1605–1627), continued his father's policy of building monumental structures, but it was under Shah Jahan (1628–1658) that Mughal construction reached its fulfillment. Shah Jahan, however, virtually bankrupted the nation with his extensive building program. The Taj Mahal, which he built as a final resting place for his favorite wife, Mumtaz Mahal, is considered to be the world's most beautiful building; but it was built at a tremendous cost. For nearly twenty years, seven days a week, over twenty thousand workmen labored to build the colossal Taj. Aurangzeb (1659–1707), who was the last of the great Mughals, was more austere than his predecessors; and he, preferring to live in the buildings of his ancestors, built no monuments of note.

The empire so ably presided over by Akbar is thought by many historians to have been the best-managed state of its day. Akbar was a tolerant ruler and an able administrator. He took as brides two Rajput princesses, and these marriages to Hindu females of high-caste ranking helped quiet opposition and ensure loyalty, especially among the militant Rajputs. But it was his repeal of the hated jizya that endeared him to Hindus for all time and helped encourage peace and prosperity throughout the kingdom. Without the able rule of Akbar, it is to be doubted if his successors, Jahangir and Shah Jahan, would ever have been able to build the colossal structures for which they are justly famous. It is perhaps also to be regretted that Shah Jahan was the man who reinstituted a policy of destruction in regard to Hindu temples. It was this policy coupled with that of Aurangzeb, his son and successor, that caused India once again to erupt into war. Aurangzeb not only destroyed temples; he brought back the jizya. The result was war on a scale not seen in centuries. A Hindu leader named Shivaji rallied his people, the Marathas, and challenged the Mughals at every turn. Before long the Maratha people themselves were the dominant power in much of the subcontinent, and the once proud Mughals saw their empire quickly eclipsed. Even before Aurangzeb died, while fighting the Marathas in 1707, it was clear that his policy had failed. He had weakened the state beyond repair.

Other Religious Minorities

Next to the Hindu and Muslim communities today, as in the past, all others are insignificant numerically. About 2.5 percent of the population of the Republic of

*Above:
Sun Temple
Konarak,
Orissa State.*

*Right:
The Taj Mahal in
Agra. Both photos,
Consulate General
of India, Chicago.*

India is Christian, .5 percent is Jain, nearly 2 percent is Sikh, and less than one-half of 1 percent are Parsi. Christians are congregated primarily in the state of Kerala, a province that appears to have been Christian for fifteen hundred years or more. The Kerala Christians, also known as Syrian Christians, claim that the apostle Thomas brought the word of Christ to India and that he is buried there. Until the early nineteenth century there were few other Christians in India, except the Roman Catholics who inhabited enclaves like Portuguese Goa or French Pondicherry. British administrators reluctantly opened India to Christian proselytism in 1813, and, though missionary activity increased rapidly after that time, the number of converts was never large.

The Jains are another minority that has never enjoyed a large following, though they date their founding to the time of the Buddha or earlier. But again their numbers are not indicative of their legacy historically. The Jain concern for the sanctity of life strongly affected Buddhist and Hindu thought. The Jains are famous in India for their contribution of *ahimsa*, an ancient doctrine later borrowed by Hindus and Buddhists, which is usually explained as meaning non-injury to all living things. It is not uncommon to see a Jain wear what looks like a surgical mask, least any living thing enter his mouth; sometimes they also are seen with feather dusters, which they use to sweep the path before them as they walk.

The Jains are, however, not the smallest important minority; the two hundred thousand Parsi claim that distinction. The Parsis, like the Jains, are important in the mercantile realm, and they exert influence far beyond their numbers. The Parsi community claims to be Zoroastrian or Persian in origin and to have migrated to India around the eighth century in order to escape Muslim expansion in West Asia. They have always gotten on well with the Europeans, in part because they closely resemble each other, and this helps explain their importance as a community in recent centuries.

The last significant minority group is the Sikh. Sikhism is an eclectic religion that has borrowed heavily from Hindu and Muslim thought. Though Sikhs are today identified as militant, they were initially a very pacifistic community. Their religion dates to early Mughal years and particularly to Guru Nanak (1469–1539), the founder, whose followers called themselves Sikhs (disciples). Nine spiritual leaders also called guru (teacher) followed Nanak, and it was the Ten Gurus collectively that formalized the religion. The Punjab is the province in which most Sikhs reside, though they have spread over most of North India. Sometimes their distinct appearance gives the impression that Sikhs number more than they do, for they stand out wherever they appear. Because of the persecution and even execution of gurus by Mughal emperors after Akbar, a Sikh Khalsa (pure fraternity), appeared. Govind Singh, the tenth guru, required that all Sikhs: wear a particular type of undergarment and a steel bracelet; carry a dagger or sword, and a comb; and never cut their hair, which has necessitated the wearing of a turban to protect the long, tightly wrapped hair. Also all Sikhs have as their last name Singh (lion). These five requirements, or five K's as they are called, helped develop a distinctive character among Sikhs and helped to turn them into a militant community. Govind Singh, was horrified by the decapitation of his predecessor by Aurangzeb, and he turned the Sikhs away from pacifism in self-defense.

India: Rural and Urban

Many people like to speak of two Indias—one urban and sophisticated, the other rural and technologically backward. There is no doubt that many nations have this type of gulf, but it is equally true that the gulf seems to be greater in India. A large part of rural India, particularly in the northeast, is peopled by tribal aboriginals who have always lived outside the pale of Hindu society. One of these groups, the Nagas, have given up the practice of head-hunting only in this century. Most of rural India is, however, not aboriginal or animistic; most of it is Hindu and Muslim. Most of it is also poor and has been so for centuries. Technology did not begin to penetrate the traditional countryside until recently, and poverty and hunger have long marred life in the rural areas. This is partly due to the startling increase in population during the last century. Economic development under the British was slow, but the population grew rapidly. The disparity in incomes between the rural and urban people seemed to grow in proportion to the length of British rule. In the eighteenth century the British conquered a relatively prosperous South Asia; in 1947 they left it a torn, tattered, poor, and overpopulated land. While British rule was on the whole humane, the colonial exploitation helped destroy rural India. British industrial products flooded the hinterlands and destroyed the livelihood of many skilled artisans, and rural or traditional India paid the price for the development of the great urban centers built by the British—Calcutta, Madras, and Bombay.

While urban India grew (and perhaps flourished) under the British aegis, rural India remained tied to the weather and the ancient agricultural techniques. Rural India even to the present day is virtually dependent on the monsoon rains. Because there has not been any exclusive production of agricultural products for many a decade, there are no granary stores to fall back on. India, which was a grain exporter until half a century ago, exists without a commodity surplus. And when the rains fail, as they did in 1966 and 1967, India, with its teeming millions, faces famine on a magnitude unknown in the Western world, partly because the communication network essential to a famine relief program simply does not exist in rural areas, where 80 percent of the nation's population lives.

The Making of
British India

2

As they commenced their "Age of Exploration," which reflected the insufficiency of their homelands, Europeans first came to India to trade, not to conquer. To many of the early European adventurers, however, the difference between the two motives was small. The Portuguese, who, as mentioned, were the first Europeans to arrive in India (1498), quickly succeeded in establishing fortified settlements at strategic locations near the coastline of the Indian Ocean. The Portuguese, lacking the necessary manpower for territorial expansion inland, never managed to get beyond these "enclaves," and their mercantile empire was built on the sea, not on the land. Mercantilism, the prevailing European economic practice, sought to accumulate gold and silver by an excess of exports over imports. The prosperous Portuguese enclave system saw fortified settlements at Goa, Ormuz, Diu, Malacca, and later Macao in the South China Sea. Each enclave was under the charge of a factor, and the collection of buildings used for trade was termed a factory.

Up until this time, the Venetians and the Arabs had prospered because of their roles as middlemen in the trade between Europe and Asia. The Portuguese ended this monopoly, and the center of East-West trade began to shift to the Atlantic periphery of Europe and away from the Adriatic and Mediterranean seas. Spices, silks, and luxury items such as jewels, porcelain, and artisanware flowed to Europe in Portuguese ships. Naturally, the Portuguese were looked upon with envy by other merchants who also enjoyed a favorable location on Europe's western seaboard, and before long the ships of many European nations came to be common sights in the Indian Ocean.

The Trading Companies

Unfortunately for the Portuguese merchants, just at the time when Dutch and British merchants began to aggressively horn in on their Indian trade, domestic affairs on the Iberian Peninsula seriously curtailed Portugal's ability to meet its challengers. When the Portuguese throne fell vacant in 1580, Philip II of Spain forcibly united the Iberian Peninsula by annexing Portugal. Philip then proceeded to ignore the needs of Portuguese merchants, particularly if they conflicted with those of Spain. The obvious sentiment of the ruling house encouraged another part of the Spanish Empire to attempt to destroy the monopoly enjoyed by the Portuguese in Asian seas throughout the sixteenth century. The Low Countries, as that portion of the Spanish Empire dominated by Dutch mercantile interest was then termed, had long been attempting to share in the profits of Eastern trade. Dutch ships completed their first round-trip via the Cape of Good Hope in 1597. It took them that long to overcome Philip's adamant refusal to grant the Dutch permission to use Iberian ports and to obtain from the Catholic Iberians the maps and knowledge necessary to get there. Following the first success, Dutch merchants outfitted many more ships and in 1602 founded the famous Dutch East India Company in order to better facilitate trade.

The Dutch, however, were never really involved in India, but for a short time their interest in South Asia focused on Ceylon. Though they did not entirely confine their trade to Indonesia, they centered it there after nearly eliminating Portuguese influence in Southeast Asia with the capture of Malacca in 1641. Britain, a working partner of the Dutch, replaced the Portuguese as the European power in India.

The British, throughout the period from 1560 to 1660, sided with the Dutch because of a mutual Protestant antagonism toward Catholic Spain. When Portugal was annexed in 1580 the British and the Dutch took advantage of the situation to weaken the Portuguese in the East. A series of religious wars in Holland, which saw Spanish troops decimate the Protestant population, resulted in open reprisals and warfare on the high seas against the Portuguese, who were viewed by all but the Portuguese themselves as citizens of Philip II of Spain.

The British were actually the last Europeans to enter Asian trade in force because of their preoccupation with their American empire between 1620 and 1780. Also the British had many religious questions and a civil war to settle at home. But as the 1600s came to a close and their religious problems seemed to fade, the British, who had chartered the British East India Company in 1600, now began to push a more active trade policy in India. Britain's Glorious Revolution of 1688 witnessed the triumph of influential commercial interests in Parliament over certain political prerogatives of the Crown. The time of Britain's new policy coincided with the loss of vitality of the Mughal Empire under the Emperor Aurangzeb, and, as mentioned, the long war in India brought about by opposition to Aurangzeb's policies left the Mughal dynasty prostrate by the time of his death in 1707.

Anglo-French Rivalry

The power vacuum created by a dying Mughal regime invited others to vie for supremacy in India. For twenty-five years most of the attempts to replace the mighty Mughals came from the indigenous Marathas or the Afghans, who had again begun to pressure Delhi. But this changed in the 1740s when Joseph Dupleix, the Governor of Pondicherry, began to commit European soldiers to fight in the interior of South India. Dupleix was employed by the French East India Company, an organization which never played a significant role in Indian affairs directly. Dupleix, however, did have an enormous impact. He learned early that the fragmentation of the Mughal state made it easy to apply the European "balance of power" policy to India. He would provide well-trained Europeans, who possessed superior fire power, to the various princely claimants in the Karnatic, the plains between Madras and the Deccan Plateau. When a prince whom he supported emerged victorious, he would then make known the demands of the French Government, the owners of the French Company. The British, noting how successful this policy was, rapidly followed suit. Robert Clive, an employee of the British East India Company in Madras, rallied British Company loyalists and routed the French, climaxing the Anglo-French "World War," which encompassed the American French and Indian War and Europe's Seven Years' War. Dupleix was recalled in disgrace, and Clive came to be regarded as one of the founders of British India.

British Conquest

Anglo-French machinations frightened Indian leaders. Siraj-ud-daula, the Nawab or Governor of Bengal, decided to end foreign intervention in territory under his jurisdiction. The Nawab was, in theory, the underling of the Great Mughal in Delhi. But since the death of Aurangzeb in 1707, governors had virtually ignored the Great Mughal and had ruled as independent sovereigns. Acting hastily, the Nawab ordered the British to leave Calcutta, one of their three major bases in India. When the British refused to leave, the Nawab had them arrested and interred in a small cell that came to be known to the world as the "Black Hole of Calcutta," because nearly all of those imprisoned therein allegedly smothered to death within hours. Though many doubt the Black Hole story, there is no doubt that the Nawab's actions again brought Clive back into the picture. Clive moved from Madras to Calcutta and quickly chastised the Nawab at the Battle of Plassey (1757), a contest won more through cunning than through superior weaponry. Clive bribed certain supporters of the Nawab not to fight for the Indian during the battle. However, Plassey proved inconclusive, for local princes were not yet ready to concede defeat. Another round seemed inevitable. Clive, who had been resting on his laurels in Britain, returned to India. In 1764, while Clive was en route, British arms at Buxar decisively defeated the Nawab of Oudh, the territory adjacent to Bengal. When Clive arrived in 1765, the British had only to decide where the borders of their new-found empire should be drawn. Nothing lay ahead of them in North India for a thousand miles except the vast Gangetic Plains and a Mughal emperor in Delhi whose day had long since passed. Clive chose to accept this defeated monarch as his political superior and in 1765 had the East India Company appointed by the Great Mughal to the office of Diwan (revenue collector) of Bengal, Bihar, and Orissa. This agreement had two consequences: it kept the Mughal emperor alive as a legal fiction, and it made the British East India Company a functionary of the Great Mughal, making its legality beyond question, or so the Company argued.

Consolidation of Company Rule

Merchants founded the British Raj (rule) in India, but it was the bureaucrats who ruled India during most of the British period. The transition from Company to Crown rule was not simple, nor was it carried out as expeditiously as it might have been. The British East India Company claimed the right to rule until 1858, as did the Great Mughal, for whom it continued, supposedly, to administer. Parliament was not happy about the peculiar system that had been devised by Clive and others, but it was reluctant to end the Company's prerogatives through the legislative process. While it was true that the Crown had helped the Company establish suzerainty in India, it was equally true that conquest was primarily a result of Company policy, funding, personnel, and arms. Parliament was reluctant to claim what others had built.

Following the victory at Buxar, British merchants expanded their sway through a series of wars and agreements concluded in India with local princes, as often as not against the expressed desires of the Company's directors in London. In the process, many "servants" of the Company amassed enormous wealth, including Robert Clive, while the Company, in whose name all lands were conquered, was threatened with bankruptcy. Criticism of Company servants grew, as did the demand for control of Company activities, and when Clive returned to Britain, he was faced with a parliamentary inquiry into the sources of his wealth. Though cleared of wrongdoing, he committed suicide in 1774. Clive's successor, Warren Hastings, fared little better; he was recalled from India in disgrace and brought before the House of Lords for a great public trial that lasted six years. Though Hastings was acquitted, the British government gained the ascendancy, and Parliament asserted its right to supervise the Company it had chartered.

Actually, Hastings himself represented the first real attempt to control the Company. He was appointed governor-general in 1774 as a result of provisions imposed by the Regulating Act of 1773, an act prompted by the threatened bankruptcy of the Company. But because the 1773 act was ambiguous in regard to the exercise of power in India, the Pitt India Act, which provided for joint Crown and Company participation or jurisdiction, was passed in 1784. By the terms of the Pitt Act, suzerainty passed to a newly created Board of Control and out of the hands of the proprietors of the Company, who retained sole control over commercial transactions. The Board of Control was very much concerned about the public image that had been created by the trial of Hastings, which through the late 1780s seemed as though it would never end. With attention focused on scandal and the need for reform, the Company's charter came up for renewal once more.

The charter renewal of 1793 started a tradition. Henceforth the Company received its renewal every twenty years; and every time the year for renewal grew near, the demand for change swept across Britain. Thus the charter renewals of 1813, 1833, and 1853 are important landmarks in Indian history. In 1813 the Company lost its monopoly of the Indian trade to the free-trade advocates and was forced as well to open the doors of India to Christian missionaries. In 1833 the Company lost its commercial rights altogether and became simply the legal agent of the Crown, vested solely with the political administration of the land. In 1853 the Company lost control over patronage when open competition became mandatory for all appointed to the Indian Civil Service.

The Cornwallis Legacy

As part of the plan to renovate the Company's image and administration, Lord Charles Cornwallis, who had commanded the British Army in the last decisive battle of the American Revolution, was appointed governor-general of India. Cornwallis, who knew little or nothing about India, was considered a paragon of virtue, and his years in power, 1786–1793, were identified with reform—though strongly Anglicized. He consolidated the higher company offices into an organization subsequently known as the Indian Civil Service (I.C.S.). Members of the I.C.S., in return for higher salaries, promised not to engage in personal trade nor to accept gifts. The major British criticism of Company servants was thus muted, and men of questionable integrity or doubtful morality began to seek their fortunes elsewhere. The I.C.S. was proud of its high salary, its prestige, and its Anglicized character. The organization became known as the "Steel Framework," the structure which because of its loyal, honest, frugal, and intelligent membership, held together the entire structure of British India. The I.C.S., however, was racist to its very core, and it offered no apology; in fact, pride was its most distinguishing characteristic throughout its long existence.

Another perplexing problem that Cornwallis solved centered on what has often been termed the "search for the landlord." Cornwallis, like many of his British peers, felt someone must own the land. He did not seem to appreciate that the Mughal concept of a *zamindar* (tax collector) differed from that of a landowner in the west. The zamindar, because of meritorious service, was assigned land from which to collect taxes and as a reward kept a portion of the revenue. The Mughal emperor owned the land; the zamindar was his steward. The difference in point of view was significant, for under the terms of the Permanent Settlement of 1793, Cornwallis ceded the land to the zamindars in return for fixed annual payments to the Company. Consequently the zamindars became owners or landlords at the expense of others, particularly the cultivators. The peasantry paid a heavy price for the creation of this landed nobility, and the zamindars comprised a class of parasitic, absentee landlords that every Indian government ever since has attempted with little success to eliminate. The Permanent Settlement was recognized as a blunder almost immediately, and as the British Raj spread beyond Bengal, Bihar, and Orissa, land in other areas was often ceded to the *raiyats* (peasant cultivators) rather than on the tax collectors.

As the eighteenth century drew to a close, the Company appeared to have worked out a system whereby many could prosper. Parliament was pleased by the Cornwallis policy; he had raised the image of the Company and, perhaps more important, had refused to continue the policy of aggressive and expensive expansion so disliked and feared by many in Britain. The Company, as master of Bengal, Bihar, and Orissa, already ruled an area with a population larger than that of Britain. But Lord Richard Wellesley Mornington, the governor-general who arrived in 1797, had other ideas. He followed an aggressive expansionist policy for the next seven years under the guise of defense against a possible attack by the Egyptian-based troops of Napoleon Bonaparte. Finally in 1805 he was recalled, but not before he had managed to involve the British in a series of wars with the Marathas. After a brief respite of nearly eight years (which the Company used to replenish its treasury), the Maratha resistance was crushed, and by 1818 the British were the paramount power on the subcontinent. From 1818 to 1947 the British ruled India with a firm hand and from a position of unquestioned military supremacy. Virtually hundreds of princely states remained outside British India, but all had to conclude subsidiary alliances that made them recognize

British paramountcy and accept a resident European to serve as an "advisor" in their respective states.

Westernizing of the Governmental Structure

Though some Westernizing of the political and social structure occurred in the eighteenth century, it did not become policy until 1828, the year in which William Bentinck became governor-general. The elder bureaucrats in the administration, known as the Orientalists, argued that the Company should conform when possible to Mughal ways. The Orientalists, many of whom helped found the empire in the subcontinent, were not all opposed to Westernization or essential change; many simply feared it might lead to social demoralization and chaos, especially if change were directed at social and religious rather than political structures. It was one thing to set up a political superstructure; it was another to force alien-inspired social and religious ideas, values, and attitudes, as many of the younger bureaucrats, known as the Anglicists, planned to do. Also, many Orientalists actually saw much to admire in India culturally and religiously, while the Anglicists saw little that was not to them reprehensible.

The Bentinck era (1828–1835), perhaps more than any other, came to be identified with the Anglicists. Though the European nature of the bureaucracy had always made it sensitive to demands for change emanating from London, this was a period during which those demanding change were in the ascendancy. The Anglicists had grown in strength as the Company grew and by the 1830s were gaining support from new quarters. In Britain, Evangelical reformers, foremost of whom was a group known as the Clapham Sect, agitated publicly for reform from the top by pressuring Parliament, while the Utilitarians, foremost of whom was Jeremy Bentham, attempted to institute reform from within the Company itself. Bentham taught at Haileybury, an institution set up in Britain by the Company to train young men for service in India, and his friend James Mill shared a similar influence within the Company, especially after the publication in 1817 of his monumental *History of India*. Bentinck, an avowed Utilitarian, and other Evangelicals like William Wilberforce felt that they had a duty to help remake India, though their motives differed. The Utilitarians thought many Indian customs were based on useless and expensive traditions, not on utility, while the Evangelicals viewed Indians as heathens or idolaters who needed to be reformed.

Under Bentinck, as mentioned, the Anglicists had their way. Bentinck forbade the practice of *sati*, the immolation of widows on the funeral pyres of their husbands. He also launched an aggressive campaign against the *thugi*, groups of thieves and murderers who claimed such action was a part of their dharma. Similarly, infanticide was prohibited, as were other practices long accepted by the Hindus but which Bentinck argued were counter to all moral and ethical systems. Bentinck and the Anglicists ran roughshod over the Orientalists, and they swelled their ranks as a result of the Charter Act of 1833. Under its terms, Thomas Babington Macaulay, the famed essayist and historian, joined the Bentinck administration. Quickly, Macaulay became a driving force for Westernization through education. Because of his influence and his position as Law Member on the Council of the Governor-General, Macaulay was given the opportunity to spread his often-quoted belief that the best way to educate or reform was by creating a class "Indian in blood and color, but English in taste, opinions, morals, and intellect." Macaulay, though he lacked facility in any South Asian tongue, argued in his famous "Minute" or Memorial to Bentinck in 1835 that he had "never found one among them [Indians] who could deny that a single shelf of a good European library was worth the whole native literature of India and Arabia."

Macaulay and Bentinck, like most of the Anglicist bureaucrats who followed in their steps, actually came to feel that they alone knew what was best for India. They continued to argue that India needed British ideals, institutions, and administrators. In 1835, English replaced Persian as the language of the Indian courts, and before long future Indian barristers were flocking to the European schools to receive an education. Even though the Westernization of India continued unabated, the pace was slower than many Anglicists had hoped it would be. In part, this was because the new education never got beyond the confines of the new elite that Macaulay had predicted would arise. English ideals did not "trickle down" to the masses; they remained the property of the select few who prepared for future roles in the administration, primarily as barristers.

Company Relations with the Princely States

Bentinck and others encountered little Indian opposition to their enforced reforms, probably because of the peaceful nature of administrative efforts between 1818 and 1839. Only a fairly small and indecisive police effort in Burma in the 1820s disrupted the quiet consolidation of the British Raj in this period. Governors-general constantly interfered in the affairs of the princely states, usually through the "advisors" who had been forced on local rulers through some three hundred separate treaties, all of which included recognition of the Company as the "paramount" power in the subcontinent. The claim of paramountcy enabled the British to appoint, recognize, and replace native rulers with impunity. Of course, the British always rationalized such involvement in the internal affairs of the "Native States" as actions necessary for the good of "their" people. Though over five hundred native states survived and remained outside British India, their independence was more nominal than real. The one real exception to this in the first half of the nineteenth century was the Lahore-based state of Ranjit Singh. Singh ruled over an ably administered state in the Punjab (land of the five rivers) until his death in 1839.

Many Europeans had long been interested in Ranjit Singh's Sikh state because of its strategic importance. It was felt to be an area whose acquisition would help round out the natural boundaries of the Company, for its territory included all the land in the northwest from the plains to the foothills of the great mountain ranges of the north. Lucrative trade there also seemed possible, for the state sat astride the Indus and its major tributaries. Like many of the other states' rulers, Ranjit Singh had accepted a resident advisor as a result of a treaty (negotiated in 1832), but he was able to resist further encroachments, primarily because the British respected his ability and that of his regular army of seventy-five thousand men. The Sikh state was, however, too dependent on the personality of Ranjit Singh, and his death in the summer of 1839 unleashed the forces of disruption and disintegration. Ranjit Singh's son and successor was assassinated in 1840, as was his successor in 1843. Sikh factionalism threatened to bring total chaos, for no leader appeared who had the charisma necessary to restore order. The invitation was more than Company officials could resist, and between 1845 and 1848 the Lahore state of Ranjit Singh vanished as a result of military operations brought to conclusion under Lord Dalhousie.

The Dalhousie Years, 1848-1856

Lord Dalhousie, the new governor-general, annexed not only the Punjab; he actually made Britain master of India from Burma to Afghanistan. Dalhousie could rightly claim to be the ruler of India, and in 1852 he added lower Burma to the Company's domains. In fact, between 1839 and 1857 the only area that the Company wanted to add to its territory but failed to was Afghanistan. They tried in the first Afghan War of 1839–1842, but they failed miserably when their invading army of nearly sixteen thousand soldiers was annihilated to a man by either the weather or the ferocity of the Afghan warriors.

Dalhousie's success in the Punjab, however, seemed to increase his hostility towards all that was Indian, and he pushed Westernization there, imposing new civil and criminal codes and undertaking large public projects in road building and irrigation, which eventually made the Punjab one of the most prosperous provinces of British India. A testament to the success of Dalhousie in the Punjab occurred in 1857, when the Sikhs of that region remained loyal to their British overlords while most of the rest of North India rose in armed rebellion.

To subvert the power of the princely states, Dalhousie virtually invented a policy termed the "Doctrine of Lapse." He considered all princely states less efficient, more corrupt, less democratic, and less susceptible to reform than the area under his direct rule, and he was determined to consolidate all under his sway. Dalhousie argued that Britain, as the paramount power, had the right to recognize succession in the various states, so if an heir were deemed by the Raj to be lacking, it could annex that state. Dalhousie insisted that if a natural son were not available to replace one of the current princes, only the Company had the right to decide if an adopted son could succeed the father. If recognition were withheld, then the princely line had "lapsed" and the state passed directly to the Company as the paramount power. He forcibly applied this doctrine to a number of princely states, arousing a wave of protest and apprehension. Dalhousie was further accused of attempting to destroy Hindu states when he also annexed other principalities whose rulers he accused of misgovernment. Together the various annexations looked like an attempt to destroy the remnants of traditional India. Still, Dalhousie made the Company and himself the unquestioned arbiter of all within his purview. He even attempted to abolish the old Mughal line by decree, though he was ultimately prohibited from doing so by London.

Dalhousie's legacy was not, however, entirely negative. He built the Grand Trunk highway from Calcutta to Peshawar as well as many other less-ambitious road networks. He introduced telegraphic communications, organized an efficient postal department, and instituted large-scale irrigation projects. But the railway system represents the project for which he has been justly remembered.

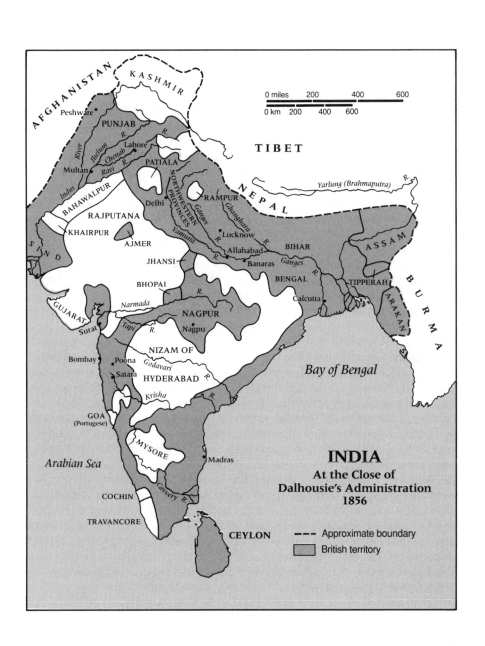

INDIA
At the Close of
Dalhousie's Administration
1856

AFGHANISTAN

KASHMIR

Peshware

PUNJAB

TIBET

Lahore

Multan

River

Jhelum

Chenab R.

Ravi R.

Indus

PATIALA

BAHAWALPUR

RAMPUR

Delhi

NORTHWESTERN PROVINCES

Ganges

Ghanghara R.

NEPAL

Yarlung (Brahmaputra) R.

RAJPUTANA

KHAIRPUR

AJMER

Yamuna

Lucknow

BIHAR

ASSAM

SIND

JHANSI

Allahabad

Banaras

Ganges R.

BENGAL

BURMA

BHOPAI

Narmada

R.

Calcutta

TIPPERAH

ARAKAN

GUJARAT

Surat

Tapi

R.

NAGPUR

Nagpu

NIZAM OF

Bombay

Poona

Satara

Godavari

HYDERABAD

R.

Krisha

R.

Bay of Bengal

GOA
(Portugese)

MYSORE

Madras

Arabian Sea

COCHIN

Canvery R.

TRAVANCORE

CEYLON

0 miles   200   400   600

0 km   200   400   600

- - - Approximate boundary

British territory

For years railway construction in India was delayed because London felt that it might not be a profitable venture. Dalhousie did not succeed in convincing London otherwise until 1853, and when he left in 1856, only two hundred miles of railway had been completed. Still, transport by rail had begun and developed unabated in the years that followed. Railway construction was, however, not entirely a blessing. Railways helped destroy handicraft industry in the interior, for they placed inland markets within easy reach of the machine-made products of the West. Also, railways and the crews that built them became agents for the spread of diseases that took heavy tolls in villages in which resistance to world diseases was virtually nonexistent due to their long-standing isolation. The development of railways, coupled with Dalhousie's push for Western education, and for roads, telegraphs, and consolidation, helped spawn what the British called the Mutiny of 1857, what many Indians term the First War of Indian Independence. By the time Dalhousie departed India, there was little doubt left in the minds of the inhabitants—India was ruled by Europeans for *European* interests.

The administrative edifice was European and would continue to become more European for a decade or two. By 1856 the Company was no longer simply one of many states in India; it was virtually the only one. All others were mere shadows of their former selves. Dalhousie made it clear to all that native princes were living anachronisms. As governor-general he had added 150,000 square miles of territory to the Company's domain through consolidation or liquidation of native states.

1857 and Its Aftermath

When Dalhousie left India in February 1856, he left behind an empire that seemed quiescent. Yet within a year much of India was ablaze, and the empire itself apparently teetered on the brink of dissolution. Why the sudden reversal? Perhaps no one will ever explain it to the satisfaction of all, but the Sepoy Mutiny represented only one of many nineteenth-century resistance movements by subject peoples against Western imperialism. The Sepoy troops, a native army trained and administered by the British, became enraged over the British practice of lubricating cartridges with animal fat. This inflamed the religious sensibilities of Muslims and Hindus who composed the Sepoy troops. Muslims, who considered the pig unclean, and Hindus, who considered the cow sacred, understandably refused to handle the ammunition. The first such refusal occurred in January 1857, near Calcutta, and was rapidly followed by others. By the end of the spring, troops stationed in northern India rose in mutiny, seizing control of great inland cities like Delhi. The British responded quickly, treating the protesters as the worst type of traitors, while refusing to admit that too great an involvement in the daily life of the inhabitants had started the conflagration.

When electrifying news of the massacre of European officers by the Sepoy troops in the northern hinterland began filtering into Calcutta, the British, in righteous indignation, responded with a vehemence unmatched during their rule. Administrators viewed it as a struggle between East and West, civilization and barbarity, Christian and heathen. British troops stormed the old Mughal cities and forts that the insurgents had occupied in the land of the upper Ganges, capturing Delhi, the rebel capital, in September 1857. Before another year had passed, they had pacified all of India. By mid-1858 British rule had been restored, but at a great cost in lives and money; and the cruel excesses on both sides during the war left an intense feeling of hate and fear in the hearts of all, native or foreign, for a generation and more.

The Hindu Widows' Remarriage Act of 1856 was a good example of how the Company felt it had the right to change customs in accordance with Europeanized Indian views against the traditional Hindu majority. This act gave Hindu widows the right to remarry by law, thus ignoring the orthodox religious leaders who opposed the act. Also the manner in which Hindu College (at Calcutta) was changed into Presidency College in 1854 was another example of the British attitude that argued that European views and practices were dominant over Indian concerns and interests. Dalhousie knew his policies threatened to remove decision making from the hands of the elders and to give it to the courts and bureaucracy, which were becoming more Anglicist in outlook with each passing day. Why did he persist when reaction was bound to come? With their way of life threatened, it is no wonder the indigenous responded violently in 1857. The ranks of the rebels were swelled with the rajas, who had been treated poorly, with the former landed aristocracy, who were being replaced by English-speaking barristers, and with Muslim and Hindu spiritual leaders, who feared the influence of the Western Christian—both missionary and bureaucrat. The widespread uprising was the strongest in places like Oudh, a princely state annexed by the Company only months before the mutiny broke out. The War of 1857 was an exercise grown out of desperation.

To many the mutiny was simply the last attempt by the old regime, the remnants of the Mughals, to reassert themselves. Undeniably the old order fought to reassert itself and to reclaim lost prerogatives and dignity. But there was another dimension that cannot be ignored; the mutiny was supported by a large segment of the population that had little to gain from a return to the old order. Many Indians were stirred perhaps by nothing more than frustration. The pace of British-mandated reform had been too rapid for many. For instance, a requirement issued in 1856 that made it obligatory for all military personnel to serve wherever sent struck a raw nerve. For many a Hindu, a trip across the ocean meant pollution, a loss of caste, or social ostracism. The British too often refused to consider the effects of their actions. They found it easier to attribute opposition and even uprising to mindless traditionalists, particularly Muslims, who because of their "inferior nature" simply could not comprehend the blessings of European rule, than to evolve a system in which all participated in the decision-making process. Paternal despotism was to the British in India as much a statement of lack of faith in the ability of the indigenous to rule as it was a political system designed to bestow wealth and glory on its inheritors, if not its founders.

The uprising of 1857 caused British officialdom to turn to imperialism; administrators now were convinced that it was dangerous to attempt reform of social and religious customs. The government therefore became far less innovative and far more conservative for the remainder of the nineteenth century. The attitude that permeated every level of the I.C.S. was one of *noblesse oblige*, and it clearly intensified as the century wore on. Thus, during the zenith of British rule, 1858–1905, the governmental administration became unabashedly exclusive.

Indians were advised to be patient, to watch, to learn; and one day in the distant future the indigenous would be brought into the administration. But it was their mentors who would, of course, judge when Indians were fit to participate more fully in their own government. Thus the Crown, which assumed direct rule in 1858, found it necessary to prove to Indians why the British Raj was beneficial as well as moral, stable, and Christian. The British came to believe their own myth—the myth that they and they alone could provide the unity and the stability necessary for all in India to prosper.

Rise of the Middle Classes

Since the Crown and its agent, the I.C.S., forsook innovation in favor of maintaining the status quo, the initiative and driving force behind change fell to a new class that appeared in strength on the Indian scene in the latter part of the nineteenth century. This group arose and existed on the fringes of British society. For want of a better term its members are often called the Indian Middle Classes. They were native agents by virtue of their broker relationship to the English, but they were not middle class in the European sense of the term; they resembled more a professional intelligentsia. Most of the members of this new group were from the lower echelon clerks needed by British administrators as functionaries. This group had remained loyal to the British in 1857, for they had felt that the British in the long run stood for more enlightened government than did the princes, whom they equated with a return to a feudal age.

The Hindu Renaissance

In the first half of the nineteenth century, when the middle classes were numerically small, there appeared a group of native intelligentsia who pushed reform of Indian customs and mores every bit as hard as had Bentinck. One of the most significant of these was Rammohun Roy, a man often termed the "Father of Modern India." Roy was a social reformer who in the 1820s founded the Brahmo Sabha (Society of God), later known as the Brahmo Samaj, in his native Bengal. Roy reinterpreted Hinduism to his followers. He denounced caste restriction, opposed idolatry, favored women's rights, and stressed monotheism. He also rejected Christianity and the claim by missionaries of the superiority of the Christian ethic. He depicted Christianity as superstitious and stressed the Asian rather than the Western origins of the faith of Jesus. He launched what has been called the Hindu Renaissance.

Roy, who died in 1833, was followed by other notable reformers such as Debendranath Tagore and Keshub Chandra Sen. The most important reformer outside of Bengal was probably Dayananda Saravati (1824–1883). Dayananda founded the Arya Samaj (Society of the Aryans), demanded that all ritual from the past millennia be discarded, and called upon Hindus to return to the Vedas as their source of religious and social thought. Though himself a Brahmin, he attacked ritual as stifling and as post-Vedic in origin. He argued that there was no sanction in the ancient Vedas for untouchability, child marriage, or the subjugation of women. He ceaselessly attacked idolatry as well as Islam and Christianity, which he viewed as foreign imports, and frequently debated theological points with Muslims and Christians in large public assemblies. Dayananda, like Vivekananda, another zealous reformer of the latter half of the century, urged his followers to take technical knowledge from the West while dismissing Western religion as inferior to that of the indigenous.

The spiritual reformers of the Hindu Renaissance gave a sense of pride to those long on the defensive. They made many indigenous people believe that they could reform India better than their British overlords and helped lay the basis for a feeling of religious identity in which Indians could take pride. They could study Western culture in order to better defend their own. Still, the commonality of the rising middle classes was derived as much from exposure to the West as it was from the burning demands for reform that emanated from the religious reformers of the Renaissance. In fact, the English language alone was a cohesive bond for the middle classes. Its use permitted those from distinct linguistic regions to speak, write, and communicate with one another on a level never possible in pre-British days.

The Role of the Middle Classes

The British, whose numbers were small, always resented the aspiring middle classes that they had created, possibly because they were as dependent upon them as the new classes were upon their political masters. Indians were, after all, needed to administer the empire, and as the British took on more and more responsibilities, a greater shortage of European manpower developed. In the 1880s there were fewer than 90,000 Europeans in all of India, and thousands of these were planters, missionaries, and businessmen, while well over 55,000 were army personnel. Administrative manpower was largely drawn from the great urban centers like Calcutta and Madras where schools, anxious to educate their pupils in English, abounded. The Hindus flocked to these schools in order to prepare themselves for administrative positions, while Muslims, on whom the uprising of 1857 was blamed, were slow to respond to the educational opportunities that became readily available even in the *mofussil* (back country).

The Indian Middle Classes were by the 1880s a new elite, and like elites of any time they were interested in expanding their role in the decision-making process. They began to form organizations to agitate legally for greater participation in government. Caste organizations designed to help educate caste brethren and schools owned and run by the indigenous began to dot the Indian landscape. This new elite was far different from the old. They were seeking positions in government in order to increase their upward mobility and wealth, and for some time many were little interested in obtaining the religious sanction or stamp of approval traditionally necessary for acceptance. Their position depended more on marketable skills than on acceptance by princes. Though the middle classes eventually found their upward mobility blocked by both prince and bureaucrat, they considered the British as the lesser of the two evils standing in their path. Thus they found themselves alienated from the old elite and not trusted by the British.

Political and Cultural Response among the New Elite

By now the British were aliens in the empire they had created. They could or would not easily adopt or adapt to a relationship similar to that which evolved in Canada after the British Parliament passed the North American Act of 1867. The implementation of this act offered hope to the rising Indian Middle Classes, for they rightly viewed the act as the germinal legislation around which a dominion type of government would grow. Indian reformers looked to a future date when a British Empire based on mutually beneficial cooperation between its Indian and English components would exist. Most of the new elite accepted for a time the fact that they were not yet ready for full participation; they had remained loyal to the British during 1857 for that reason. But the good faith exhibited by the rising class was not reciprocated, and by the 1870s some of the new elite were hoping to prod the British government into change. Surendranath Banerjea began demanding that the administration open its ranks more fully to Indians. In 1876 Banerjea formed the Indian Association as a pressure group designed to gain for its members greater access to the coveted positions in the I.C.S. Banerjea and others hoped to convince their British overlords through legal means to accept cooperation with the aspiring educated classes. The British, however, had turned away from innovation. Their attitude remained imperialist, in the sense that they still felt militarily, technologically, politically, and culturally superior to the non-Western world.

British Policy in the Princely States

After 1857 the Crown actually attempted to make an ally of the old elite. Past mistakes were blamed on the Company and its overly ambitious and hasty policy. In very rapid succession the Crown abolished the Company, renounced the doctrine of lapse, and accepted princely successors based on traditional law and custom, including adoption. Once emasculated, the old elite now were looked on as allies—to be used in the name of the Crown to stifle criticism from the middle classes. After Queen Victoria was officially declared Empress of India in 1877, her governors-general, now called viceroys, began to accept the various states' princes as the "spokesmen" for India. This infuriated the new elite, who claimed that right, mostly on the basis of their education, for themselves. The "educated and thoughtful" classes now came to resent the princes more than they did the British, and this made it easy for the British to pose as the objective arbiter between two self-seeking and self-interested classes. Thus the British openly favored in the last half of the century the very group it had labored so hard to destroy, and the class the British had created was the class to which it refused political participation. This change in attitude helped create a class of parasitic princely pensioners, who became more interested in their own survival than in the survival of others, helping to sow the seeds for the destruction of this princely class.

Reform Sponsored by the Educated

Though the British were not successful in restoring the princes to their traditional role, they persisted in the 1890s and thereafter to make membership in newly constituted councils of the viceroy more readily available to princes than to the educated middle classes. Europeans knew before the end of the century that political activism, if it were to develop, would not emanate from the princes. It would surely arise from the ranks of the newly educated. Men like Banerjea and Mahadev G. Ranade began espousing social and political change in the 1870s in forceful terms. Banerjea, on the east coast in Bengal, and Ranade, in

Maharashtra on the west coast, demanded reform of bureaucratic abuses. Both organized societies, which, along with less-well-known groups, had as their focus two distinct goals: 1) to educate Indians in the Western style, hopefully in Europe, without being opposed by traditionalists who would stigmatize such persons upon their return; and 2) to convince the British to continue to expand openings in the administration for qualified Indians, at the expense of Europeans if need be.

No small amount of time was devoted to reform of traditional structures in Indian society in the period 1885–1914. The educated elite were convinced that social reform had to precede political reform. They felt their requests for greater participation would fall on deaf ears unless they purged themselves of what they considered the disabilities of the past. Many of the educated risked ostracism by marrying outside their caste, by dining with members of other castes, by marrying widows, and by journeying across the ocean to Britain for training. The strictures of the past were most pronounced in the mofussil, where orthodox members of the communities declared outcaste all those who broke the traditional rules. But by the time World War I broke out, the reformers had won the day. The orthodox fell before the onslaught of modernity, but the battle for reform left many scars.

The Beginnings of Political Activism

In the 1880s B. G. Tilak, the noted traditionalist agitator, was one of many who came to resent the haughty, pretentious, racist attitude of the post-Mutiny administrators. Another was Dadabhai Naoroji, a Parsi businessman, termed the Grand Old Man of the National Movement. Naoroji (1824–1917) provided the rationale for why the British should accept Indians as full participants in the administration of their land. His famous "economic drain theory" held very simply that Britain had grown wealthy and prosperous due to the wealth it drained from South Asia, and that Britain had a moral obligation to help those who had paid and were continuing to pay for its prosperity. The proof of the theory, it was argued, was undeniable. Clive had won the Battle of Plassey in 1757, and the first phase of the Industrial Revolution in Britain commenced in 1760. Indian wealth in incalculable amounts had been "drained" from India to finance British industrialization, it was argued, particularly by youthful Indian barristers who fell under the spell of the Grand Old Man. The younger educated knew the work of the historian Arnold Toynbee; many had heard him lecture on the origins of the Industrial Revolution, and they had no trouble coupling the teaching of Toynbee with that of Naoroji. The economic drain theory became a solid basis for the philosophical underpinning of the nationalist movement launched by the new elites. It took little imagination to justify demands for participation in the decision-making process once one felt the process was being subverted by requiring Indians to support a system that existed to serve the interests of Liverpool and Manchester industrialists rather than the native peoples.

The Founding of the Indian National Congress

Among the many organizations founded by the educated classes to vocalize their claims in the closing decades of the nineteenth century, the Indian National

Congress (the Congress) stands out as their singular achievement. The Congress, organized in 1885, quickly emerged as the major voice of the hopes of the educated classes. It became the vehicle of the independence movement, and no discussion of modern India is complete without some analysis of the importance of its creation and composition. At the time of its founding, India was seething with discontent prompted by an outcry of protests from the European community in India. Europeans were aroused over a piece of legislation known as the Ilbert Bill. The bill would have permitted Indian judges to preside in cases in which Europeans were to be tried; and its introduction, in 1883, during the last months of the administration of Lord Ripon (1880–1884), was the last straw for the European community in India. Ripon had repealed a number of laws hated by Indians, including the Vernacular Press Act, which made it nearly impossible to publish a critical newspaper, and the Arms Act, which required non-Europeans to have a license for arms. The Europeans organized such an outcry over being tried before Indian judges that the Ilbert Bill was withdrawn. The educated Indians, perceiving the advantage in organized opposition, formed the Congress in December 1885.

For the first ten or fifteen years of its existence, the Congress was little more than a part-time debating society. It met only in December, during the Christmas holidays, when government offices were closed, and passed a seemingly endless round of resolutions designed to prod the government towards acceptance of more participation on the part of those Indians in the higher echelons of administration. Also, for most of its early career, the Congress was essentially a rich-man's club. Membership fees were high (about the price of a good tailored suit), and there appears to have been little attempt to bring into the membership people who were nonprofessionals. Membership was limited almost solely to the Western-educated, and they labored hard to present a united front in regard to British policy on all the major issues of the day. But close below the surface of the unity and amity theme that the Congress so publicly projected lay deep cleavages that were both cultural and political.

Nationalists versus the Reformers

A split in the Congress became obvious in the 1890s with Tilak's emergence as a national leader. Tilak was the first to bridge the gap between "arm chair" politicians and the masses. Tilak was not a liberal; he viewed the British in his nation as aliens who had no right to interfere in socio-religious customs and traditions of the people. Tilak was not willing to see his customs purged or modernized in order to make them more acceptable to those who wielded political power. He wanted a grass-roots alternative to British policy, not a willing acquiescence to it. Tilak's weapons were tradition and emotion. Armed with these, he started newspapers in Marathi, his native language, and launched one editorial crusade after another designed to arouse among his readers a desire to protect their way of life against the onslaught of the British and his opponents, the reformers. His aggressive attacks helped split the Congress into two factions, the Moderates (reformers) and the Extremists (nationalists). Just as the Moderates (who had founded the Congress) used meetings as a forum for educating, via long Victorian speeches on the virtue of reform, Tilak came to use Hindu festivals as opportunities to present speeches and dramas that eulogized the Hindu accomplishments of the past. Tilak supported associations designed to prohibit the killing of cows, opposed state-administered inoculations against smallpox, and argued that the British had no right to impose an age restriction for marriage.

Tilak sincerely believed that the British had no right to raise the minimum age at which females could marry to twelve from the traditional ten. It was not that he truly felt that the age should not be raised; rather he objected to its being raised by the alien British. Though losing the battle over the marital age limit, in 1891 Tilak won the war. He quickly became one of India's best-known heroes, rapidly expanding his base by organizing festivals commemorating Maratha deities and heroes. Every year celebrations with week-long festivals were held in honor of Ganesh, the Elephant God, or Shivaji, the Maratha warrior who had helped destroy the mighty Mughal Empire. Understandably, Muslims were incensed by Tilak, and they regularly rioted at the Hindu festivals. Tilak was not sensitive to the Muslim protests, however, for the Muslim was almost as great an object of his hostility as was the Christian Englishman.

Hindu opposition to Tilak came primarily from G. K. Gokhale, an accomplished debater and leader of the Congress from the 1890s until his death in 1915. Gokhale and his Moderates were horrified by the violent tone of Tilak's rhetoric. They viewed him as something reborn from the distant past—a symbol of the possible return to the dark days of the medieval world. Tilak, they felt, would not take India forward, for he opposed social reform. Many of the Moderates were Social Darwinists. They felt Indians must prepare themselves first through education, purge themselves of deficiencies in social and political organizations, and only then demand full participation or independence. The Moderates wanted change and participation, but they fully expected it to come slowly. Otherwise, they rationalized, India would become free only to be conquered by another foe, foreign or indigenous. The Moderates believed that the British were not their only enemies. The princes and the Extremists were in many respects much greater foes. The road to modernity was, to the Moderates, a British road, which they must travel or else perish. Tilak, they feared, would destroy all the progress made in the last several generations; he was a communalist (a person interested only in his community's well being). Moderates felt that Tilak as the major spokesman of Hindu Communalism would tear the nation asunder. They viewed the future in terms of separation of church and state; in fact, they argued that a secular state was the only possible way to keep India together—with or without the British. Legal separation of church and state was to the Moderates one of the truly positive features of British rule. They wanted to continue it, to extend it; they wished never to risk a confrontation between the Hindu and Muslim peoples.

The Muslim Response

Muslims were slow to agitate against the British Raj. At first they were bitter; they were the rulers who had lost an empire. They still held positions in the nineteenth century in proportion to their percentage of the population, but they had lost the prestige of old. Also the Muslims, for some reason, seemed to withdraw from the world the British were building, at least for the first half of the century. Historical antagonism between Muslims and Christians may account for some of the withdrawal. By midcentury it became clear to many Muslims that the new Hindu elite were entering the new British world willingly. Muslims knew that many of the Hindus actually favored a British over a Muslim government, and a fear of being overwhelmed by Christian/Hindu administrators began to dawn in the consciousness of the Islamic community. Something needed to be done to protect their economic interests. This was not easy in the 1860s and 1870s, for the British believed the 1857 uprising to have been primarily the work of Muslims and, accordingly, since that time had followed a discriminatory policy towards them.

It was not until the 1880s that official policy began to change. Part of the explanation for this may be due to the publications of W. W. Hunter, a bureaucrat turned historian, who argued that Muslims would become a desperate community if the government did not change its attitude toward them. But it must be remembered that changes in the treatment of Muslims by British overlords seem to be concurrent with the stepped-up pressure by the Hindu middle classes for change through the founding of organizations like the Congress. The change in the British attitude towards Muslims might also have been due in large measure to the Aligarh Movement, which was spearheaded by Sayyid Ahmad Khan (1817–1898), a man who helped solve for Muslims the problem of how to obtain a Western education without attending the European missionary schools.

Khan was in the service of the Company during the upheaval of 1857. He remained loyal and became a trusted servant of the Raj. In 1875 he founded Aligarh College in order to provide Muslim youth with a Western education transmitted in an Islamic milieu. His movement helped revitalize his community, and his advice soon became synonymous with action. Khan convinced his Islamic brothers that British rule would not soon pass away and that they must therefore cooperate with the Raj. He also advised Muslim youth to remain aloof from politics, to study the West, to keep the faith, and to remain outside the Congress. He argued against helping to democratize the government, for a representative republic would be a government that the Hindus would dominate. Therefore, he openly advocated the retention of British paternalism. Khan advised all Muslims to prove their loyalty to Britain, to be above suspicion, to be apolitical, and to avoid any and all types of agitation. He saw the Muslims as a dominant force only if they tied their destiny to that of the European minority, and he thought one could borrow Western technology while rejecting Western ethics. More important, he convinced other Muslim leaders of the wisdom of his way, and the new elite of the Islamic minority entered the twentieth century as a group virtually determined to remain consciously apolitical but bureaucratically influential.

Problems of Identity

The cultural response to the upheavals of the nineteenth century helped lay the basis for the clear Hindu/Muslim split of the twentieth. The British, who have often been charged with a policy of divide and conquer, used the identity crisis to their own advantage. The British did not create the regional, communal, and linguistic divisions in India; but they encouraged their widening, in part because neither the Hindus nor the Muslims seemed to have understood the identification problem of the other. But communalism was only one of many manifestations at the root of India's identity crisis, for in most respects the cultural response to the Raj had been political as well as religious, social as well as economic, and regional as well as national. Tilak had a Hindu as well as a regional appeal. Shivaji was more a regional symbol than a national one. Still Tilak had a national appeal in that he stressed direct action to rid all of South Asia of British influence, though his means alienated the Moderate nationalists, who were devoted to constitutional means.

British India suffered as few states have from diversity of almost every type—linguistic, ethnic, religious, political, and social. It was difficult for many individuals to decide what was the first claim on their loyalty. Was a person a Hindu, or was he or she a Bengali, an Indian, a prince or princess, a Westernizer, a reformer, an urban dweller, a believer in caste—or was he or she simply confused? What was to tie an Indian's identity together? Was it to be traditional history? Tilak had tried that, but his symbols were exclusively Hindu; how then did a non-Hindu follow Tilak without rejecting his or her own culture? Then there was confusion over how to best combat the British assertion that they alone could provide India with peace, unity, and good government: wouldn't cooperating with the existing government be emulating the hated foreign power? Finally, how could one overcome the regional animosity that existed in regard to the Bengali or Madrasi administrators who had pushed into the hinterland (and into good positions) with the British expansion at the expense of the natives of the various regions? Long before the end of the century, citizens of the Punjab and Bihar were launching movements designed to rid their provinces not of Europeans but of people of Bengali lineage.

The administrative unity of Britain and its overlords seems to have provided most Indians with little except a channel for their negative feelings. What remained to be done by 1900 was to find a way to direct the negative feeling of being non-European into a positive feeling of being Indian. British policy, however, never really attempted to foster cooperation between themselves and the majority in the subcontinent. In fact, the British fostered division because it suited their needs. They had won India through cunning and the sword, and now they held it by playing off one group against the other. It can be said that cooperation was never a conscious British aim after 1857, perhaps never after 1837, and the British must accept no small share of the blame for many of the problems that exist in South Asia to this day.

The Making of
Independent India

 As the nineteenth century drew to a close, indigenous India clearly seemed headed for a confrontation with its alien masters. Many Hindu and Muslim leaders of the 1890s were clearly aware that such a clash was inevitable, though, as explained, they differed widely as to the best policy to be pursued. Some national leaders favored violence, but the overwhelming majority were more inclined to support pressure tactics and agitation of a "constitutional" or legal nature. The latter group (Moderates) felt education must precede freedom, and with this in mind wealthy Indians began founding newspapers and colleges. However, the confrontation came long before anyone expected it would, in part because of the nature of the administration of the last of the true imperialist viceroys, Lord George Nathaniel Curzon, a Conservative party leader, who assumed that post in 1899.

The Curzon Years

The administration of Lord Curzon, from 1899 to 1905, marked both the zenith and the decline of the Raj. He was arrogant, aristocratic, and contemptuous of the Congress and the middle classes and all that they symbolized. His administration was a climax to the era inaugurated by Dalhousie. Curzon believed in paternal despotism, and his despotism and his high-handed treatment of Indian subordinates became legend. He was responsible for the first mass demonstrations organized in opposition to viceregal policy, and he helped create the environment in which the first rumblings of Indian nationalism were heard.

Percival Spear, the British historian, has argued that Curzon was guilty of a common mistake among post-Mutiny administrators. Spear has contended that "the average administrator erred, because he was still looking for Western reform in aristocratic places and did not perceive the significance of the new rising middle class." Curzon, who "shared in this fallacy," foolishly "provoked by his action a rude awakening." Of course, one can argue with this assessment by pointing out that Curzon was not an average administrator, that he should have recognized the importance of the new elite, and that the rising middle classes were headed for a confrontation with or without him. Still, Curzon was the catalyst, for he was so easy to dislike. All nationalists could agree on one thing—their intense hatred of the viceroy. Curzon represented all things they disliked about British rule. He was to them a repudiation of progress. Many Britons agreed, and Curzon often found himself at odds with London politicians. Throughout his years in office, however, Curzon insisted that he had to be free of interference, either British or Indian.

After his appointment, Curzon was not long in revealing his sentiments toward the educated middle classes. In his first year in office, he changed the composition of the municipal boards that administered the urban centers, a system that dated from the Ripon era. Ripon, who had wanted to introduce some measure of self-government, had inaugurated the boards as a training ground for Indians. Two-thirds of the board members were elected indirectly, by organizations like chambers of commerce, but fully one-third of the members were appointed by the viceroy. Curzon claimed that the boards were corrupt and that he could increase their efficiency as well as reform them by reducing elected representation to 50 percent. The middle classes realized the enormous advantage this would give the government, for now the middle classes' only forum for opposition would be seriously curtailed. Curzon's policy was viewed as an attempt to deny the new elite a role in the governance of their land—and more important, an attempt to return the Indian administrative structure to undisguised despotism.

Curzon had a free hand for the whole of his first administration. The educated suffered what they considered to be affront heaped upon affront. In 1903–1904 Curzon threatened the Bengali educated by introducing the Universities Act, which, like his other "reforms," was designed to enhance efficiency at the expense of autonomy. Curzon argued, not unjustly, that Calcutta University, with its myriads of affiliated colleges, was in need of corporate restructuring. His proposal was to improve the administration as well as the nature of the instruction by increasing again the number of appointed members on the governing bodies, while reducing the number of members elected by the faculties. Educated Bengalis knew their positions and wealth were a result of the training that they had received at Calcutta University. They wanted to see the curriculum expanded to produce more educated Indians. So when persons of lessor ability were brought in to replace the educated Bengalis already on the university's board, the Bengalis rose in protest. Their movement found support across India, for others felt that such a policy could be used in other schools to thwart the aspirations of all. Therefore, the Universities Act of 1904 opened completely the chasm between the educated and the administrators, and it was never again to close.

The 1905 Partition of Bengal

After completing one five-year term, Curzon was reappointed to a second. Following a summer's rest in Europe, he returned to India in 1904 determined to destroy the Congress and the middle class elite who had dared challenge him. Curzon had written in 1900 that "[the] Congress is tottering to its fall, and one of my great ambitions while in India is to assist it to a peaceful demise." Shortly after returning, with revenge in mind, he announced that the province of Bengal was too large an administrative unit and would be split or "partitioned" into two parts. The immediate reaction to this announcement of administrative restructuring was the organization of "monster petitions" and "monster meetings" to demonstrate displeasure. Curzon was, however, not to be defeated by "native rabble." He effected the partition of Bengal in 1905; but he won the battle and lost the war. The Curzon partition hastened his end and probably the end of the Raj as well. As a result of Curzon's decree, Bengal was ablaze with political activity such as it had not witnessed in its entire existence. Even the conservative Surendranath Banerjea, now an old man, came forward to lead what became known as the Swadeshi Movement.

Swadeshi was a term used to describe the policy of purchasing only those goods produced in India by Indians. Its leaders asked all Indians to boycott foreign goods and picket foreign shops. The European business community became alarmed, but the Congress leaders used the agitation to demonstrate for the first time an active and virulent opposition to Curzon. Bengali leaders depicted their "nation" as split—bleeding—for the partition created two provinces out of the previous one. A poetry of revolt appeared in which the authors called on the Congress to agitate from the Himalayas to Cape Comorin to help rescind the measure. One ethnic group should have, the Bengalis argued, one province. If partition was necessary, draw the boundary so as to keep most Bengalis in the same province. Curzon, however, remained adamant; he would not be pressured by what he dismissed as the tactics of the street. But the waves of antagonism did not subside as the viceroy felt they would, and finally, in 1912, the Raj rescinded Curzon's action in favor of a new partition that was based on ethnic divisions rather than administrative efficiency.

Unquestionably, British officials had underestimated the impact of the Swadeshi Movement, and they were surprised when the movement turned violent. The defeat of Russia by Japan in 1905 (the Russo-Japanese War) had added fuel to activist fires, for the Japanese had proved that Asians were not inferior to Europeans. Violence began to appeal to a wider spectrum. Revolutionaries like Aurobindo Ghose appeared, demanding that the educated youth give themselves to the task at hand—to free India so that its people could at long last regain their rightful place among the great civilizations of the globe. Aurobindo challenged his fellow nationals to prepare themselves for India's rising, to train themselves for service to a new India, and to master violence if need be so that India might live again as a society free of European domination. Secret organizations began to multiply, even in the remote areas, where political activity such as that led by Aurobindo had been unknown previously. A new day had dawned.

The Indian National Congress Split

Curzon resigned in 1905, partly as a result of the outcry generated by the Swadeshi Movement, but this was unimportant to many activists. What was important was the failure of the demonstrators to force Curzon to rescind immediately the partition of Bengal. The Congress Extremists held the Moderates responsible for the failure, for they depicted the Moderates' caution as cowardice. The Extremists, still led by Tilak, demanded activism on the violent anarchist model then prevalent in the West. They now accused the Moderates of actually helping to prop up the system that had drained India of its wealth and dignity. The proof of one's true sentiments, they argued, was in action, not rhetoric. The Moderates controlled the Congress, but they refused to support even a resolution requesting self-rule, though the Extremists pushed for it regularly at every sitting of that august body.

The Moderates argued that violence was stupid. The best political tactic was constitutional agitation. They thought that breaking the law, even for good reasons, would lead to a widespread chaos similar to that which had initially enabled the British to gain control of India. Also the Moderates pointed out that Lord Minto, the new viceroy (1905–1910), had the support of John Morley, a leading Liberal, who was placed in charge of the India Office in 1906. Both Morley and Minto promised reform and a complete reversal of the Curzon policy. Hoping to reduce the appeal of the Extremists, the Moderates began to support, though not too warmly, the twin ideals of Swadeshi and Swaraj. The term *Swaraj* had several connotations; it could be translated as self-rule, independence, or dominion status. Gokhale interpreted it to mean participation within the empire, but Tilak's rhetoric gave it an entirely different coloring. Tilak argued that Swaraj was his "birthright" and that he "would have it."

Confrontation between the Moderates and the Extremists was inevitable; it blossomed at the Congress's meeting at Surat in 1907. At this meeting Tilak's Extremists were told to adhere to a testament of loyalty and constitutional agitation or face expulsion. They chose expulsion, and the Moderates remained in control of the organization for the next twelve years. This was made easier than it might have been by the removal of Aurobindo and Tilak from the ranks of open opposition. Aurobindo was accused of complicity in a terrorist bombing incident in 1906. He was found innocent in the trial that followed, but shortly thereafter he retired from politics in favor of a life of religious contemplation in Pondicherry, a French enclave, where he lived until his death in 1950. Tilak himself was charged with encouraging sedition in 1908 and sentenced to exile in Mandalay, Burma, where he remained for the next six years. With their leadership in jail or retirement, the Extremists quickly sank into obscurity, while the Moderates successfully regained their following.

Communalism and the Founding of the Muslim League

One of the unexpected results of the Curzon partition was the founding of the Muslim League. Obviously, the Congress had been overwhelmingly Hindu from its founding, and part of the protest over partition had centered on the fact that the province of Eastern Bengal had a clear Muslim majority. Muslims resented this protest by the Congress and accused it of being thoroughly communalist (interested only in their own community's well being); their fears were confirmed when communal riots swept across much of Bengal, East and West, in the 1905 partition's wake. Many Muslim leaders felt the Congress could never serve as their spokesman, though the Congress claimed to be the secular spokesman of all native Indians. In 1906, a number of leading Muslims gathered to found a league that could vocalize the interests of what they declared to be "a distinct community of our own with additional interests of our own" which, as they clearly argued, were "not shared by other communities."

Moderates in the Congress strongly resented the formation of the Muslim League and argued that the Muslims were playing into the hands of the British by once again making "divide and rule" an easy task. Of course, this is why the Moderates claimed that they had opposed the formation of East Bengal in 1905; they argued that Curzon was using the Muslims. The Congress wanted only one spokesman for India, *the Congress*, and the founding of other political organizations weakened its role. However, the new viceroy, Lord Minto, did not share the opinions of the Moderates. He became convinced that Muslims needed legal safeguards to protect them from the overwhelming Hindu majority, and he helped write safeguards into the first major reform scheme, introduced in 1909.

The Morley-Minto Reforms

The Morley-Minto Reforms were of momentous importance, though they contained a little for everyone but not much for anyone. The Congress's Moderates were granted a concession they had long desired—a greater role in government policy making. An Imperial Legislative Council was established, and Indians were included in the Executive Council of the Viceroy. Also the Moderates gained their cherished ideal of election as the criterion for membership, and half of the representatives on the Imperial Legislative Council were to be elected. The electorate was not large, for the franchise was limited to interest groups like those of the planters and the chambers of commerce. Furthermore, the reforms relied on a complicated system of indirect elections in order to present a façade of representative government. The Moderates would probably have been highly pleased by the new scheme if provisions had not been made for the introduction of separate and weighted electorates for Muslims. That was the issue that nearly made the Moderates reject the reforms altogether and that helped drive the wedge between Hindus and Muslims even deeper.

Weighted and separate electorates ensured that seats were set aside in the imperial and provincial councils to be held only by Muslims. Also the number of such seats was weighted in order to give Muslims numerical representation greater than their actual percentage of the total population. It should be pointed out that these practices were similar to those used in Britain, where seats in the House of Commons were set aside for the academic community, the church, Scots, Irish, and others. British voting patterns as well as representation was tied to the practice of ensuring interest-group representation in the councils of government. Most people in Britain had one vote in 1910, but many could vote also as businessmen, landowners, churchmen, university graduates, and so forth. Britons in India therefore felt they were applying their time-proven techniques to guarantee that Muslim opinion would be heard in the councils, thus avoiding the possibility of tyranny of the majority.

The Moderates of the Congress were not willing to accept the contention that circumstances in India and Britain were similar. They protested vehemently, arguing that the Raj was once again attempting to divide and rule. The Congress accused the British of attempting to institutionalize an ancient tactic. Moderates argued that this was not the reform they had been led to expect in 1907 when

they had helped quiet the Extremists, and they flirted with the idea of not participating in the elections planned for 1910. Gokhale, however, finally convinced his
fellow Moderates that democratic government proceeded to grow from precedent to precedent and that they should get into the councils and labor for more
extensive change. Thus the Moderates accepted the reforms, though they continued to be rankled by the provision that all Muslims (who could meet the property qualification) could vote for Muslim representatives, while the Hindus enjoyed no such provision. Also the fact that Muslims could stand for election to
seats on the council besides those set aside for them disturbed Hindus, for this
meant that Muslims could actually win seats, as they did, *far* in excess of their
proportion of the population.

Thinking that something was better than nothing, the Moderates labored to
make the Morley-Minto Reforms work. The first councils sat for three years. In
this time Gokhale and the Congress pushed hard their old theme of Muslim-
Hindu unity and amity, while the British began to withdraw from the support they
had so recently given to the Indian Muslims, in part because of trouble brewing
in the Balkans and the Middle East, where European Christians and Turkish
Muslims were waging the Balkan Wars of 1912–1913. Dwindling British support
made many Muslims more willing to join actively with their Hindu counterparts in
an effort to make the reforms work. Also, both Muslims and Hindus decided
separate electorates might be meaningless, so long as Muslims and Hindus
worked together to improve their nation. Still the idea that religion could serve
as the basis for designating representation was never popular, especially with
the Hindu-dominated Congress, and separate electorates remained a burning
issue.

World War I

World War I was an important turning point in South Asian politics. The Moderates, in hope of gaining new reforms, fully supported the British, and the Congress leaders stumped South Asia helping to sell war bonds and encouraging
men to enlist in service of the British Empire. Indian industry supported the war
effort wholeheartedly and willingly supplied much of the materiel needed to pursue the war successfully, while hundreds of thousands voluntarily served on the
war fronts. Indians fully expected that their aid would be rewarded once the war
was successfully concluded, and there were vague promises as to a new round
of reforms once the Germans were defeated. As a result, the Moderates were
little inclined to press for much during the war, putting their faith in British goodwill. Even the Extremist Tilak, who was released from Mandalay in 1914, now
followed a fairly conciliatory policy. Six years in prison seemed to have taken its
toll on his health, though he quickly re-emerged as a leading politician. His old
opponent Gokhale died in 1915; but the void he left was filled in part by Annie
Besant, an Englishwoman who had first come to India thirty years earlier as a
missionary for Theosophy, a religion that quickly won adherents among the educated. During the war Besant and Tilak organized the Home Rule League with
the active support of Moderates.

The spirit of cooperation that manifested itself in the early years of the war
even spilled over into Hindu-Muslim relations. The entrance of the Muslim Turks

Above: Street market in Goa.

Right: Mohandas K. (Mahatma) Gandhi (1869–1948). Both pictures, Embassy of India, Washington, D.C.

on the side of Germany was probably a factor in the improved relations between the Hindu and Muslim communities. Many of India's Muslims had feared British policy in regard to Turkey before the war; now they feared for their religious brothers and the *Khalif* (Caliph) even more. In the closing days of 1916, the Congress and the League held their yearly meetings jointly in the city of Lucknow. At the Lucknow Conference the two organizations worked out an accord that came to be known as the Lucknow Pact. By its terms, the League accepted the principle of representative government, while the Congress gave up its opposition to separate electorates in return for a Muslim promise not to contest any seats designated as part of the general electorate. Both organizations also pledged to work together for self-rule.

The Lucknow Conference occurred at a time when the contending factions seemed devoted to participation and cooperation. But as the tide of the war began to turn in favor of the Allies, the British seemed to pull back from the vague promises it had made earlier to the native Indians. It was not until late in August 1917, that the British announced that they would soon introduce a new reform scheme that would help India move closer to "responsible government." The announcement pleased Indians, for they interpreted it as something they justly deserved. The problem was that when the new Montagu-Chelmsford Reforms were finally implemented in 1919, they fell far short of what had been expected, and the Indians wasted no time in making their dismay and disappointment known.

Dyarchy and Gandhi
The reforms introduced by Viceroy Chelmsford, 1916–1921, and Edwin Montagu, Secretary of State for India, helped crush the Moderates as a force in Indian life. Long before the reform scheme, which provided for limited self-government, became law in December 1919, Indians of all political persuasions expressed a fear of the actual British intentions. S. Sinha, a leading Moderate from Bihar, in a speech before the provincial legislature remarked that he was "sick" of the "very essence of the bureaucratic government" which in its "own infallibility" argued that it did "for the people not what they want, but what they ought to or are supposed to want." In the minds of Indians, the reform scheme was too little, too late. In 1905, Indians would probably have heralded its implementation as a giant step forward. But 1919 was not 1905, and many felt Sinha was correct when he argued that the quality of Indian life would improve only if Indian citizens "agitate, agitate, agitate . . . and inform the British people of the rights of the Indian people and why they should grant them."

The problem was not what Indians wanted in 1919; the argument was over how best to obtain it. Constitutionalists like Sinha wanted "to agitate and agitate on constitutional lines till our people . . . become permeated with one uniform idea." Others claimed the time for education was over; it was time for action. The British, most Indian politicians felt, would never willingly hand over the reins of government, even though the reforms promised to consider such a proposal in the future—after the British decided how well the reforms had worked. The reforms were liberal in the sense that they provided for the organization of various councils and assemblies at the national and provincial level in which two-thirds or better of the members would be elected through a widely increased franchise. A principle, dubbed "dyarchy," was written into the reforms, but it was viewed with skepticism. Dyarchy meant Indians could help administer and could legislate, but they still could not have authority over crucial governmental departments such as police, revenue, and finance. Ultimate authority in these areas, as in foreign affairs, rested with the administration. In other words, Indians were to continue as second-class citizens behind a façade of representative government. Also, the principle of weighted and separate electorates was preserved, though it was watered down by setting aside additional seats for members of the Christian, Parsi, Sikh, and Anglo-Indian communities. But the most telling reason why the 1919 reforms were unacceptable centered on the hostile atmosphere that existed after March 1919, when the government passed the famous Rowlatt Acts.

The Rowlatt Acts and the Mahatma

The Rowlatt Acts armed officials with the power of preventive detention. Anyone considered dangerous could be imprisoned, without being charged, purely on the basis of suspicion of sedition or disruptive activities. These acts now made even the best British proposals suspect, and probably no other single piece of legislation so antagonized Indians. Mohandas K. Gandhi, a gifted London law graduate, rightly termed the Rowlatt legislation "unjust, subversive of the principle of liberty, and destructive of the elementary rights of the individual." The Moderates could not have expressed the view any better; they did, however, disagree with Gandhi over the tactics that should be employed to dissuade the British from carrying out the acts. Gandhi, who had developed the basic tactics of non-violent resistance while defending Indian workers' rights in South Africa, called for what he termed a "hartal" as a viable demonstration of displeasure at the government's reversion to paternal despotism. The hartal, or the suspension of all economic activity, was no idle threat. Gandhi had gained worldwide fame by the application of the hartal (in South Africa), and his naming of April 6, 1919, as the day for a total general strike marked his entry into the Indian political arena.

Gandhi had returned to India in 1915. At the time he was admired and respected by Europeans and Indians. He announced that he would remain aloof from politics for a year in order to ease back into the nation, and he was slow to respond to overtures and entreaties asking him to take up the struggle for Indian rights in India. But Gandhi was drawn into politics quickly as a result of the Lucknow Conference. At Lucknow, a Bihari peasant had asked Gandhi to come to the Champaran District of Bihar to help alleviate the suffering of the peasants who, much against their will, were being terrorized into submission by a landlord class of planters, who were mostly European. When Gandhi appeared in Champaran, officials there attempted to intimidate him with the threat of imprisonment; but he refused to leave the province, announcing that he was perfectly willing to be imprisoned for what he considered to be right. The provincial administration did not know how to handle the man who by now was openly called the *Mahatma* (great soul), so they forced the planters to accept new laws and rules that favored the peasants. The planters viewed the actions of the government as cowardice and said so often and vehemently. Gandhi's success in Champaran inspired fear in the bureaucrats, hatred in the planters, and love and adulation in the hearts of the peasants. Gandhi had long commanded respect; now respect turned to adoration in the hearts of many. Gandhi became *the* Mahatma, and the masses traveled far and wide for a *darshan* (glimpse) of him. In the tradition of old he began to hold *darbars* (audiences) in order to hear the grievances of the oppressed.

Gandhi's decision in 1919 to oppose the Rowlatt Acts by breaking unjust laws frightened many, both Indians and Europeans. While these people may have admired his work in Africa, they feared its consequences in India. The Moderates wanted to wage war against the Rowlatt Acts in the councils and the courts. Gandhi wanted to confront the government on his terms, not on theirs. Though Gandhi was an activist, he always claimed that Gokhale was his guru. On the other hand, he was not like Tilak, for he did not believe that the end justified the means. In fact, Gandhi did not wish to win a victory if the means used were morally questionable. Nonetheless, Gandhi managed to remove politics from the parlors of the elite and present it to the masses in the streets and villages of India, where his movement had far greater results than any elite movement previously had dared dream.

Gandhi's called-for hartal, however, left violent clashes in its wake. Tension grew especially intense in Amritsar, the capital of the Punjab. There, meetings and demonstrations were held in direct defiance of the forbiddance by the provincial government, which had responded to the violent protests by placing the province under martial law. After riots broke out in protest to the "preventive detention" and deportation of two politicians, General Reginald Dyer was called upon to restore "law and order." On April 13, 1919, General Dyer learned of a meeting being held in Jallianwallah Bagh, a garden enclosed on three sides by small walls and houses. The general hurried to the entrance to the garden and blocked it with his most trusted soldiers. Without any advance warning, he then ordered his fifty armed men to pour into the garden and open fire on those congregated. Dyer's obedient soldiers fired until their ammunition was entirely consumed: it took about ten minutes. Dyer then ordered his men to leave. Behind lay nearly 400 dead and 1,200 wounded. The soldiers had been remarkably accurate. With 1,650 rounds of ammunition at their disposal, they had managed to wound or kill nearly 1,600 people.

Gandhi was horrified, as were many others. He had been accustomed to launching hartals in Africa with trained men who knew better than to resort to violence, such as that which had triggered the imposition of martial law in Amritsar. Gandhi, admitting that he had committed a "Himalayan [sized] Blunder," called off all hartal activity, and began to cooperate with the government, for he needed peace in order to effectively train his followers. Also he wanted to give the government every opportunity to discipline General Dyer. Instead, Dyer was knighted, and a committee of inquiry exonerated him of any wrongdoing. This was the last straw; Gandhi became convinced that the Raj was not capable of being fair, and his faith in British justice all but evaporated. Indians who had long respected Gandhi were now drawn to follow him loyally. The Amritsar Massacre had given birth to Indian nationalism. The quest for an independent India was now more than a hope or aspiration; it was a reality—four hundred martyrs had made it so.

Congress and Non-Cooperation

The Amritsar Massacre turned Congress permanently away from cooperation with the British and catapulted Gandhi into the role of the leader of the Nationalist Movement. By mid-1920 Gandhi called for total resistance and was promising "Swaraj within the year" if everyone cooperated. By the end of that year the Congress had voted to accept non-cooperation as the policy, and *satyagraha* (the force of truth), the name Gandhi gave to his movement, quickly swept aside the opposition.

Gandhi ignited the fires of resistance as no Indian has before or since, partly because his talents extended far beyond those of the simple utopian dreamer that some of the old politicians saw in him. He was an organizer, and he quickly set about restructuring the Congress into an effective tool of nationalism. He based the new organization on a format not far different from Lenin's democratic centralism. He organized local committees at the lowest levels, which in turn elected state groups, which finally chose the All-India Working Committee. A part of that organization formed the small Executive Committee, which acted as coordinator when the Congress was not meeting. Gandhi thus organized a well-integrated Congress on the remains of the old.

His followers were asked to become full-time revolutionaries for the cause of freedom. Lawyers heeded the call to boycott the courts, students left their colleges, and politicians spurned the councils newly organized by the 1919 reforms. Famous men like Rabindranath Tagore, India's literary genius and Nobel Prize winner, renounced their titles, honors, and awards and returned pensions and decorations to the government that had bestowed them. Total anarchy seemed to threaten. Yet the British Raj weathered the storm, even after many Muslims began to join the man Winston Churchill once dubbed a "naked Fakir."

It was clear that Gandhi had seized the initiative from the British. He and the Congress represented India, not the British and their reform schemes. Gandhi had turned the Congress into a party with a mass following, lowering the membership fee to four annas, from the previous (high) fee of forty rupees. Now, for a few cents one could claim membership in the organization of the mighty, even if one was not inclined to join in the satyagraha campaigns themselves. Gandhi was able to create among the masses a sense of identity with the Congress leaders, enabling that body to rely on popular support rather than on the benevolent attitude of the government. Not to join the government became a source of pride and accomplishment, and an expectation of ultimate success inspired the members of the Congress. A euphoric optimism developed that was not shattered until 1922, when Gandhi called off the first great non-cooperation campaign because some village followers in Chauri Chaura had killed twenty-two Indian policemen during a tax boycott. In calling off the movement, Gandhi admitted to having committed another Himalayan Blunder by encouraging peasants who were not fully trained in non-violence to take part in his movement. But in so doing, the Congress and Gandhi lost political momentum, which in the years ahead was difficult to regain.

Gandhi's followers, thousands of whom were by now in prison, could not believe that he had called off the movement just when it appeared that they might be successful. Avid supporters called on him to reverse his decision, but Gandhi refused to budge. The people, he reasoned, were not ready, and he was not about to plunge his nation into uncontrolled violence, lest the carnage of Chauri Chaura be re-enacted. Gandhi announced that the time had come for "constructive programs." Though badly confused, the Congress accepted Gandhi's decision and helped launch a program of reform. The Congress committees now began to teach people how to weave their own homespun cloth, called *khadi*, the wearing of which became more than a symbol of revolt. Gandhi, however, seemed to take little interest in the new Congress he had created. He announced his retirement from politics and devoted the next few years of his life to improving the lot of the Untouchables, whom he had renamed *Harijans* (God's children).

The Simon Commission and the Demand for Independence

With Gandhi in retirement, the Congress split over policy. Some were alarmed by the fact that members of the newly formed Liberal party were beginning to monopolize the bureaucratic positions that the Congress, in solidarity with Gandhi, had rejected. Some leaders decided to organize a new party within the Congress; it was named the Swaraj party. The Swarajists contested elections, while others who kept true to the boycott by remaining aloof from government came to be termed the "no-changers." The quiet that crept over India in the next several years was deceiving. The British came to feel that they had persevered; the reforms of 1919 seemed to be working. In 1927–1928 Britain sent the Simon Commission to India to study how well dyarchy was functioning. By the terms of the 1919 reforms a commission was not to make such a study until 1929, but the British were so pleased with themselves that they decided to send one early; it was a mistake from the start, primarily because the committee had no Indian members.

When the Simon Commission arrived in India, it found itself heavily embroiled in a boycott. The Congress openly disdained the hearings of the Simon Commission so as to demonstrate its displeasure at its all-European composition. This was viewed as yet another affront to all the indigenous people and a reassertion of the age-old racism of the past. The Congress's action angered the British, and following the report of the Simon Commission the government announced its intention to convene a Round Table Conference in London in 1929 to decide how best to introduce Dominion status for India. The Congress at its 1929 meeting, under the leadership of Jawaharlal Nehru, rejected the plan and instead called for complete and total independence. A resolution empowering the Congress's Central Committee to launch a second great campaign of civil disobedience was passed. Before long, the battle lines were redrawn, and the Congress declared January 26, 1930, to be Independence Day. All India also was electrified when it learned the Mahatma himself had been induced to return from his retirement to lead the campaign.

The Dandi Salt March

Gandhi, back from his hiatus, was eager to provoke the government. He knew he needed a symbol around which to rally the masses. He found the answer to his needs in salt. The British Raj not only forbade anyone to produce salt, as it was a government monopoly, it also required all to pay a salt tax. The law fell hard on all, particularly the poor, who could least afford to pay much for a necessity of life. Gandhi proposed a 240-mile march from his *ashram* (commune) to Dandi, a city near the sea, where he proposed to break the law by producing salt from sea water. He commenced with a few fellow walkers, but the enormous publicity that surrounded the twenty-four-day march encouraged thousands to join the trek. By the time Gandhi reached the sea he was again the uncontested head of the Congress. Before long thousands were again in prison, including Gandhi, where many remained for the better part of the next two years, martyrs to the cause of freedom. This Second Civil Disobedience campaign virtually robbed the British of any goodwill they had hoped to gain from the First Round Table Conference. The current viceroy, Lord Irwin, decided that Gandhi would have to participate in another such conference and ordered his release. Therefore, Gandhi attended the Second Round Table Conference (also in London) as the sole Congress representative. The second conference, like the first, ended in dismal failure, mostly because the British refused to accept the claim that the Congress represented India rather than the Liberals, princes, and others (also invited to attend the conference). Gandhi returned to India and to prison.

The Politics of Communalism

As mentioned, no man ever stirred India as did Gandhi; satyagraha gave meaning to millions. Students found purpose in life, men rediscovered a lost dignity, and bored women discovered a sense of meaningful participation in street politics and in the constructive works of the movement. The masses were finally exposed to the mainstream of political life. The elites sensed their mission was drawing to a successful conclusion. Non-cooperation became a way of life to millions, and it significantly revolutionized India politically. British intransigence became the object around which a sense of Indian identity developed and flowered between World War I and World War II. The elites of Gandhi's youth may have sown the seed of nationalism, but they were incapable of the harvest. In the 1930s Gandhi became the living representative of a resurgent India, nationally and internationally. His fame resembled a clear lake in which millions could bathe and bask in reflected if not participated glory. Muslims, however, were alienated by the success of Gandhi; they saw little to admire in the Hindu ascetic. His Sanskritized vocabulary was foreign to them, and *ahimsa* (non-violence to living things), the source of his philosophy, they viewed as Hindu or Jain, and the Muslims could not identify with it.

Thus Gandhi, in finding the key to a mass identification, had also unleashed Muslim fears. The more Gandhi succeeded in his purposes, the greater the Muslim apprehension became. No Muslim could accept the Gandhi proclamation that the *Bhagavad Gita* and the Sermon on the Mount were the great pieces of didactic literature. Nor could a Muslim identify with the image of poverty that Gandhi so consciously cultivated. Terms like Swaraj, Swadeshi, and satyagraha had a very non-Muslim ring to them. Gandhi's symbols were primarily Hindu symbols, and they naturally evoked primarily a Hindu response. Gandhi knew this, and he searched for symbols that might invite Muslims into his movement. The treaty settlements of World War I that dismembered the Turkish Empire conceivably might provide a common anti-British ground. Muslims feared the British might not treat the Khalif with kindness; victors seldom exhibit such a quality to the vanquished. The dismemberment of the Turkish state looked like the first step in such a policy, and for a time it appeared that Gandhi had found the symbol in the Khalifat (Caliphate) Movement, which the Congress vigorously supported. The movement, however, fell apart when the Turkish President Kemal Attaturk abolished the Khalifat in 1924, after having let the office fall vacant two years earlier.

The failure of the Khilafat Movement resulted in a revitalization of the Muslim League. Once again many Muslims felt that the famous "inner voice" Gandhi followed was a Hindu voice. The future founder of Pakistan, Muhammad Ali Jinnah, expressed it clearly when he said, "Inner voice be damned." By the mid-1920s the Hindu-Muslim split was complete. Some Muslim leaders remained loyal to the Congress, Gandhi, and secularism, but most clearly supported the Muslim League. Some like Jinnah, who was an old Moderate and once a leading spokesman of amity and unity, forsook both groups. Jinnah even spurned India and took up residence in Britain, where he practiced law for some years. While in Britain, Jinnah came under the spell of Muhammad Iqbal, a poet who had a dream of a separate nation, a land of the "pure," where Indian Muslims could live peacefully under an administration of their own. Jinnah was reluctant to join Iqbal at first because he felt, as did most old Moderates, that politics should not be based on religion. That, he had always argued, was one of the failings of Gandhi. When he returned to India, however, Jinnah returned to a region dominated by Hindu symbols that he detested. Everywhere he looked there were pictures of spinning wheels, people clothed in khadi, and politicians wearing the famous Gandhi caps. And in the months it took to re-establish Jinnah's ascendancy over the Muslim League, communalism was everywhere on the rise. Jinnah and his people were never able to accept the Nehru argument that communal antagonisms were simply economic in origin. Before long Jinnah became an outspoken advocate of Pakistan, a separate Indian Muslim nation.

The Government of India Act of 1935

Rising communalism poisoned the climate for change, yet it was in this milieu that Britain introduced the most far-reaching legislation in the history of Congress-Raj relations. The expense of administration, not to mention the world image of Gandhi, led to a willingness to grant the substantial changes included in the 1935 act, which provided for the introduction of responsible or ministerial government in the provinces. The act also envisaged the creation of a federation in which the princely states could participate, though this never came about due to a failure of the princes to support it. Also the voting franchise was extended to include the participation of well over 25 percent of Indian adults. The Congress was forced to admit this act had substance, though it was critical of the continuation of special electorates and the federation principle, which gave new political life to the princes. The Congress stood for unitary government along secular lines. Gandhi himself had in 1932 renewed his commitment to this through a "fast until death," which caused the British to revoke the special electorates planned for the untouchables.

Though its reservations were large, the Congress decided to participate in the elections for the newly organized provincial legislatures. As expected, the Congress overwhelmed the opposition, especially the Muslim League. When ministries were organized to run the provinces, the Congress stuck to the principle innate in the 1935 Act and argued that the new ministers must be drawn entirely from the party of the majority. Jinnah's request that some Muslims be included in Congress provincial governments when they took office in 1937 was abruptly rejected. The Congress was not interested in coalition, especially with the Muslim League. The election, they argued, had represented a rejection of the League's divisive communalism; the Congress spoke for all—Hindu, Muslim, Parsi, Jain, Sikh, and Christian. This attitude made the break complete; Jinnah was now convinced that a separate nation was the only solution to the Muslims' discontent.

Last Days of the Raj

The Congress ministries labored for two years to prove that they could run the provincial administrations as well as had the British. Then, in 1939, World War II broke out, and the imperial government, via the viceroy's statement, declared India to be at war with Germany without even consulting Indian leaders. The Congress viewed this as a deliberate insult, especially since the viceroy had promised prior consultation on all major decisions when the Congress took charge of the provincial administrations. The Indian National Congress decided the time for independence was at hand. It offered to support the war effort fully in return for a promise of complete independence upon the successful conclusion of the war. When the British refused, the Congress ministries resigned en masse, an act that Britain's Prime Minister Churchill viewed as nearly treasonable. There matters stood until 1941.

The Japanese attack on Pearl Harbor on December 7, 1941, helped bring India into the war and into the last major confrontation with the Raj. Both the United States and China needed India as a base for operations against the Japanese. They felt that Congress's support in this matter was essential, and both nations began pressuring Churchill for a conciliatory move. After Chiang Kaishek, the Chinese Nationalist leader, visited India in February 1942, Churchill decided to send Sir Stafford Cripps to offer the olive branch. The Cripps mission was a disaster, for he was empowered only to promise dominion status upon conclusion of the war. The Congress's leaders realized that Britain had its back to the wall; the war in Europe was going poorly. The Congress wanted independence now and not on the terms offered by Cripps. The Congress wanted to inherit a united state, but Cripps insisted that any province that did not want to be a part of a future Dominion of India must have the right to remain apart from it. Cripps was especially concerned that the princely states should not be forced into an Indian Republic against the will of their rulers. But the Cripps proposal was viewed as a concession to the ideal of Pakistan, which the League had fully endorsed and made a part of their program in 1940. In 1942 the Congress absolutely opposed the formation of a Muslim state. When discussions with Cripps failed, the Congress launched its last great civil disobedience, the Quit India Movement. The movement had as its slogan "Do or Die," and Gandhi, the practitioner of non-violence, observed that India might actually profit from the death of a million in the cause of freedom. Gandhi, now an old man, had given India nationalism; now he wanted to give it freedom. Instead, he and most of the Congress were imprisoned for the rest of the war. Some militant nationalists like Subbas Chandra Bose left the country and allied themselves with the Japanese in an attempt to liberate India through invasion. But India remained chained to an outdated imperialism while Britain waged a war in Europe in the name of freedom. The incarceration of Congress's leaders meant the end of passive resistance as a viable force in India. By the end of World War II, India, it became clear, could only be held by force, and by the war's end, the British were exhausted, spiritually and financially. Also Britain's Conservative party lost the election in 1945, and the Labour Ministry of Clement Attlee was willing and almost eager to get out of India. In 1946 the British sent a delegation known as the Cabinet Mission to negotiate a transfer of power.

The Cabinet Mission proposed the creation of an Indian union rather than a unitary state. In the union the central government's jurisdiction would correspond to that of the Raj, while the provinces were to be grouped into three regional entities, one of which closely resembled the region Muslims demanded for Pakistan. The Congress disliked the proposal but accepted it, as did the League. Nehru, who was by now the president of the Congress, realistically announced his support with the observation that it made little difference, because once the British were gone Indians would determine their own destiny. The Nehru line stirred Muslim fear afresh, and the Muslim League abrogated its previous acceptance in favor of the partition of the Indian subcontinent. Communal riots and massacres began to flare up, but the British insisted that independence was at hand. Lord Louis Mountbatten, former commander of the wartime China-Burma-India Theater, was appointed viceroy in early 1947 to preside over the transition. The Congress reluctantly agreed to a partition based on a plebiscite; citizens of British India were to vote for union with Pakistan or union with India. The rulers of the princely states were to decide whether they would join one of the new nations or remain independent. On August 15, 1947, power was formally transferred to native rule, and the long chapter in British Indian history came to a close.

The Nehru Years

Partition aroused hopes and fears seldom matched in history. Millions of people began to migrate to the new states. Waves of anarchy snuffed out the lives of tens of thousands, including that of Gandhi himself, who was felled by the bullet of a Hindu fanatic on January 30, 1948. The uncontrolled violence long feared had come, and "the old India hands" claimed they knew it all along—South Asians could not rule the subcontinent. Churchill seemed to have been correct when he termed the leaders "men of straw." Between twelve and fifteen million are estimated to have migrated after partition, with about 60 to 65 percent coming to India and 35 to 40 percent going to Pakistan. For years great migrant camps dotted the landscape of the big urban centers like Delhi. Nehru, who as prime minister of India and the president of the Congress had acquiesced and accepted partition in order to prevent violence, was visibly shaken. But he and his most trusted ally, Sardar Patel, were determined to build a strong and free India, despite the passion and destruction of the hour.

Patel was a master at negotiation and pressure tactics; he had proved this often during the satyagraha campaigns. He now called upon all his skills to help integrate the princely states into independent India. This was difficult because the agreements made in 1947, as mentioned, specifically allowed for the princes to remain independent, to join Pakistan, or to join India. Paramountcy lapsed with the end of the Raj, through the legal and mutual consent of all; Mountbatten had declared it could not be transferred. Most of the princes were pressured into signing an "Instrument of Succession," the terms of which joined their territory to that of India. Only a few joined Pakistan. The prominent princes were not easily intimidated, and by the time freedom came they had not yet decided whether or not to "accede." The largest of the princely states was Hyderabad; there a "spontaneous" rebellion, actually sponsored by the Congress, erupted, demanding accession to India. The Indian army was "forced" to intercede in the name of peace. Some Pakistani leaders protested, but there was little that they could do. Hyderabad had an overwhelming Hindu population, and it was located in the middle of India. The fact that its Muslim Nizam (prince) refused to yield to "popular" desire was depicted in India as a simple case of intransigence; but another of the princely states whose ruler refused to accede posed a much more difficult problem.

The ruler of Kashmir was a Maharaja (Hindu prince), but his people were overwhelmingly Muslim. Also Kashmir bordered both of the subcontinent's new nations. In the hysteria of late 1947, Pakistani tribes invaded Kashmir. The Maharaja decided to accede to India and sent word to Nehru. Indian and then Pakistani troops poured into the area, and a full-scale war erupted. Finally, in 1949, a cease-fire line was established with the help of the United Nations (U.N.). This line, which provided India with the lion's share of Kashmir, has changed little in the intervening years, but war has raged over the region intermittently ever since. The nation that holds Kashmir has a grip on much of Pakistan, which lies to its south, and India has never retreated from the claim that the Maharaja's accession has given it the legal and moral rights of sovereignty of the region. India has refused to consider a plebiscite in Kashmir, though it has been proposed by many who argue that Kashmir is an integral part of the nation. After having settled most of the pressing questions with Pakistan to his advantage, Nehru moved to remake India. Among other things he was a Fabian Socialist and quite unlike Gandhi. Gandhi loved, understood, and typified traditional India. Nehru did not. Nehru represented the best of both worlds, but possibly felt comfortable in neither. He had been reared in Britain, schooled in Cambridge, and trained in jail. He was a universalist who felt all men could be brothers, and his philosophy is clearly imbued in the Constitution of India that took effect on January 26, 1950. By its terms universal suffrage came to India, untouchability was legally abolished, and ministerial government on a European model was institutionalized.

Still the years in which Nehru dominated India (1947–1964) were years of economic growth. He introduced economic planning and, through various Five-

Top Left: Jawarharlal Nehru, Prime Minister of India (1947–1964). Embassy of India, Washington, D.C. Top right: Mrs. Indira Gandhi, daughter of Nehru, and Prime Minister of India, (1966–1977 and 1980–1984). Bottom: Mr. Rajiv Gandhi, son of Indira Gandhi and Prime Minister of India (1984–1989) addressing a public rally in rural India. Last two pictures, Consulate General of India.

Year Plans, managed to develop much of the infrastructure necessary for the vitality of an industrial state. Nehru poured funds into dams, railroads, power plants, and irrigation projects. As a result, India is today one of the major industrial states in the world.

Tragically, however, Nehru's very successes contributed to India's decline through the 1960s. In his early years he posed as the leader of the Afro-Asian Bloc and could call for new nations to follow his policy of non-alignment. The crushing poverty India experienced in 1947 could, with no small justification, be blamed on the British; but as the years passed and poverty continued to spread, Nehru had to share responsibility.

Nehru spent a good deal of the nation's money on education, electrification, and hygienic reforms while allocating virtually nothing for military hardware. His international reputation was based on the fame India gained as the workshop of non-violent resistance, not on international realities, and every success seemed only to add to the nation's spiraling population. Social and hygienic reforms lowered the death rate dramatically, while the nation's birth rate fell only slightly. The eradication of malaria, one of the major accomplishments of the Nehru years, amounted, ironically, to a curse; more living bodies meant more poverty. At the time of Nehru's death, in 1964, India was not as well off economically in terms of real per capita income as it had been at the time of his birth. India was free and democratic, the nation had industry, the people lived longer, and illiteracy was in retreat, but India was still a long way from economic self-sufficiency. And freedom from want is still a cherished goal of all of India's people.

India Under Indira Gandhi, 1966–1977 & 1980–1984

From January 1966 through March 1977, Indira Gandhi, the daughter of Jawaharlal Nehru, was India's prime minister. Like her father, she seemed most skilled in foreign policy and found Pakistan to be her most difficult problem. However, Indira moved India away from a low military profile and a non-alignment policy. In her era, India's detonation of an atomic bomb signaled the nation's arrival as a great power, at least in Asia. And Indira successfully played a major international role. In 1971–1972 she intervened in a war between East and West Pakistan, which helped free East Pakistan from the latter's domination. Her effort brought on war with West Pakistan; but India won easily, creating the independent nation of Bangladesh from the conquered Muslim state. But her most significant commitment in foreign affairs came in 1971, when she negotiated a treaty of non-aggression and mutual aid with the Soviet Union. This action made the Bangladesh intervention possible, gained Russian support for Indian hegemony in South Asia, and secured protection from China, a state deeply distrusted by both India and the Soviet Union.

Domestically, Indira Gandhi was not as successful. She had to contend with opposition in the Congress, with linguistic politics that threatened dissolution, and with new movements like those of the Naxalbari. The Naxalbari revolutionaries, dedicated to class warfare, utilized political assassination to spread fear and violence throughout the land. Indira did, however, rigorously attack the most basic of India's problems, the population explosion. Her immediate predecessor, Lal Bahudur Shastri, like her father before him, had placed too much faith in economic planning and industrial development, at the expense of agriculture and family planning. Mrs. Gandhi reversed these priorities. She hoped to stabilize India's population and improve agricultural production to the point where India would be self-sufficient in foodstuffs.

Indira, however, attempted to deal with India's problems in part by strengthening her political position at the expense of the constitution and, especially, the legislative branch. With the support of her party she suspended basic civil rights, largely to stifle criticism of her administration. Though she successfully attacked inflation, she also assaulted her critics by temporarily silencing, intimidating, or, in many cases, even imprisoning them. Publishers of newspapers and periodicals as well as radio and television broadcasters were systematically censored. Even prominent elder statesmen like J. P. Narayan were forcibly detained for months without trial. Though the direction and substance of her policy remained unclear, there is little doubt that Indira refused any longer to tolerate the free exchange and public criticism suffered by her father for nearly two decades.

Indira felt confident that the nation approved of her forceful actions. Therefore, following a two-year period in which her ministry ruled under extra-constitutional powers granted by a series of emergency decrees, Indira in mid-January 1977 announced that general elections would be held two months hence. At the time her position seemed secure. But once she eased press censorship, Indira saw that her standing with the electorate had waned considerably since 1972, when the victory over Pakistan had climaxed her popularity. Her ministers, denied of accurate press, had failed to perceive that confidence in the regime had eroded steadily. The government had felt emboldened by its efforts to redistribute the land, abolish bonded labor, and reduce rural indebtedness. In fact, Indira's ministry had ameliorated a number of acute problems, inflation being foremost among those addressed most successfully. However, Indira and her government did not survive the elections of March 1977.

Had she not silenced her political opponents and stifled the press, Indira might have been informed that confidence in the regime was steadily eroding. For instance, her opponents clearly saw the increasing animosity generated through her aggressive birth-control program. Within a few days of the announcement of the forthcoming elections, leading opposition parties met and merged into a political coalition called the Janata party. Morarji Desai, a former member of the government who had been purged from the Congress party ranks by Indira a couple of years earlier, led the new coalition. Though Mrs. Gandhi provided only six weeks for the campaign, the Janata effectively closed ranks against her. Politicians who formerly opposed Desai merged under his leadership into one united front. The success of the Janata union stemmed largely from the popular fear that the elections offered the last opportunity to save democracy in India.

The "do or die" determination generated by the Janata soon brought results. Jayaprakash Narayan, a politician with a saintly image and one long critical of Congress corruption, joined Desai and added considerably to the prestige of the Janata party. Also, Jagjivan Ram, a Congress leader and one of Indira's own ministers, resigned from the government and joined the opposition. During the campaign, Indira's critics directly accused her of faulty administration during her tyrannical rule. The Janata concentrated their attacks on Indira's son, Sanjay, and his connection with a government project to produce an inexpensive auto-mobile, a "people's car." When the scheme failed, it did so amid charges of corruption and incompetence. Also, Sanjay had been identified with the government program of population control, now immensely unpopular throughout the subcontinent. Desai's coalition campaign for a restoration of democracy paid large dividends. Sanjay was successfully depicted as the symbol of Indira's reign, as a wayward son, and as a blundering incompetent at best and a worthlessly ambitious sibling at worst. The good harvests of recent years, the decline in prices, the new legislation, and success in foreign affairs did not provide Indira with the favorable image she had expected.

Most of the voters believed the Janata; they feared Indira would institutional-ize an authoritarian regime. Mrs. Gandhi herself helped create this impression, for she made martyrs of many of her opponents. Rural India, in particular, viewed Narayan as the embodiment of the saintly tradition of Gandhi. His arrest and imprisonment by Indira Gandhi's administration had been deeply resented. When the tabulations were completed, Janata and its allies had 328 of the 542 seats in the Lok Sabha (the lower house of parliament). The Congress, the party of Indira, could claim only 153 places. Indira Gandhi herself lost her seat. The Congress party supremacy, enjoyed for thirty years, had ended.

The Congress (INC) dominance was displaced after 1977 by the splintered political union, the Janata or Peoples' party, held together by its opposition to Indira Gandhi. Desai was an ascetic Hindu of questionable judgment who was frequently depicted in the foreign press as the Indian prime minister who drank his own urine as part of his daily yoga routine. A devoted follower of Mahatma Gandhi, he lived largely on dried fruit and cow's milk and was a known vegetar-ian and teetotaler. Many soon questioned his ability to lead in a political arena that was increasingly seen as violent. Indira Gandhi was in agreement with this view and blamed her defeat to a considerable extent on her aunt Vijiya Lakshmi, a former speaker in the U.N. General Assembly and ambassador to the United States and the Soviet Union, who had rigorously campaigned against her. For this Indira never forgave her aunt. The new Janata government, however, could not hold back the corruption that swept over the country as a consequence of lifting Indira's emergency decrees. Prices of basic food goods rose dramatically, while inflation, previously under control, resumed its sharp climb. Food reserves, so carefully built up under other administrations, were severely diminished, while the foreign surplus, also previously abundant, was wiped out. Both domestic and foreign media now felt their fears had been realized. In 1979, Desai, who had unsuccessfully tried to impose prohibition, lost most of his able followers on both the left and the right. Therefore, in India's seventh general elections (Janu-ary 1980), Indira Gandhi was again triumphant. One newspaper enthusiastically welcomed back ". . . a government that works." In her first address Indira asked for an end to "mutual recrimination and vindictiveness." But this time her most serious problem was national unity and diversity. India's leading families, like its provinces, suffered from internecine infighting. This was true in Pakistan as well. The Nehru and Bhutto families that dominated most of the politics of the sub-continent were famous for their family squabbles, which were essentially politi-

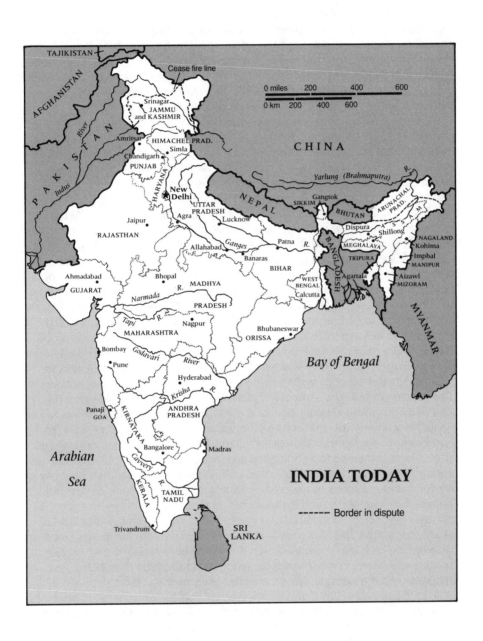

INDIA TODAY

------ Border in dispute

cal. India's provinces, like Pakistan's, were not homogeneous states in a federal union but distinct linguistic and cultural regions, each with the potential of launching another separatist movement (i.e. Bangladesh). In the northeast, a series of escalating revolutionary movements proliferated in the so-called tribal or indigenous states of Assam, Nagaland, Manipur, Mizeram, and Tripura. The trouble started when indigenous peoples of the area resisted Bengali intrusion, which they did both violently and non-violently. But ultimately, radical wings arose in the various states, which demanded independence for their peoples.

In the northeast, there was always troublesome Kashmir—at least since the Partition of 1947—a disputed territory between India and Pakistan. The problem became more complex when a Kashmiri element demanded freedom for the Kashmiris, without manipulation from Indian and Pakistani forces. But for Mrs. Gandhi, the most serious problem of the time was the emergence of radical nationalist elements in the Punjab, which happened to be the province with the highest agricultural productivity and standard of living in the nation. At the very center of the conflict was a community of Sikhs, among the most progressive of India's ethnic groups and the most technologically advanced. Though only 2 percent of India's population, Sikhs constituted 10 percent of the officers in the nation's military forces. In fact, a prominent Sikh, Zail Singh, was elected president of India in 1982, succeeding N. Sarjiva Reddy. The Sikhs demanded autonomy in a deepening crisis. They came to be radically represented politically by the *Akali Dal* or Eternal party. In 1983 this group launched a "morcha," a campaign in defiance of the law. The Sikhs originally were championed by Guru Nanak (1469–1539) within the Hindu religion, and later became militant under Govind Singh (1666–1708). Amritsar became the religious capital of Sikhism.

The Punjab had originally been composed of Hindus, Muslims, and Sikhs. The Partition of 1947 drove most Punjabi Muslims into Pakistan, whereas Hindus and Sikhs from the western part of the Punjab moved across into India. The Akali Dal gradually transformed its ambiguous desire for Khalistan (Land of the Pure) into an ambitious nationalist demand for a unified autonomous Punjabi state. They threatened to withhold the area's food supply, which the nation desperately needed. Then, in 1984, Akali extremists entered the Sikh holy city of Amritsar and captured the sacred precincts of the Harmandir or the Golden Temple. Mrs. Gandhi viewed the event not as an heroic act of national liberation, but as a vile act of terrorism. On June 6, 1984, she ordered Indian troops to attack the temple, the Sikh's most revered shrine, with the full force of modern artillery. The Sikh leader Jarnail Singh Shindranwale was killed. Sikh civilian casualties numbered in the thousands, along with hundreds of soldiers. Also, invaluable Sikh manuscripts were lost in the general destruction.

In perspective, Indira Gandhi's method of dealing with the Sikh "militants" was disastrous, not only for the Punjab, but for herself. Sikh terrorism escalated, and Mrs. Gandhi, while walking to her office, was murdered by her Sikh guards, who riddled her body with thirty bullets. While Sikh expatriates in the United States, Canada, and elsewhere celebrated the act with champagne, Sikhs in India were hunted down and butchered in retribution for the assassination. Likely, a thousand Sikhs were murdered by Hindus.

India since Indira Gandhi

Indira Gandhi's only surviving son, Rajiv Gandhi, became the new prime minister of India, being sworn in on the evening of October 31, 1984. He was the third member of his family to serve as prime minister—his grandfather was, of course, Jawaharlal Nehru, the first to hold that office (1947–1964). Rajiv Gandhi's dignified demeanor and reputation for honesty, as well as his position in the prominent Nehru-Gandhi family, raised expectations. One of his first official acts was, sadly, to ignite the fire under the funeral pyre of his own mother on the banks of the Jumna River in New Delhi. He made a moving appeal for peace: "Nothing would hurt the soul of our beloved Indira Gandhi more than the occurrence of violence in any part of the country." Immediately, he called for elections to be held on December 24, in which he was elected by a landslide greater than either his mother or grandfather had ever enjoyed. Rajiv had studied engineering at Cambridge University, married Sonia Mainu in 1968, and had become a commercial pilot for Indian Airlines. For many years his mother had groomed her elder son, Sanjay, to succeed her, but Sanjay was killed in a plane crash in 1980. Indira then persuaded Rajiv to quit his position and take his brother's place. He won election to parliament in 1981, then became the Congress Party's secretary in 1983. His firm and unruffled bearing in the wake of his mother's assassination earned him many admirers, and he soon became known as the ". . . Mr. Clean of Indian politics."

At the age of forty, Rajiv was India's youngest prime minister; thus he largely lacked political experience. Nevertheless, only one day after the twelve-day mourning period, he was also named president of the Congress Party. Evidently, the people were so attracted to his youthful manner and effortless charm that they gave his party 395 seats out of the 508 in the Lok Sabha—truly a smashing victory at the polls. People also were drawn to support Rajiv in part because he appeared to be the last of a family that had paid dearly for its devotion to India. The parallels to the Kennedy family in the United States would continue to be held up in the media for a decade or more.

Domestically, Rajiv departed from his mother's and grandfather's policies most decisively in inaugurating a new era of free-enterprise economics. In doing so, he anticipated a dramatic shift globally from faith in government-controlled economics to greater entrepreneurial freedom as the basis for industrial and economic well-being. With Rajiv, in fact, earlier blueprints of various sorts for India's future, such as Mahatma Gandhi's program of indigenous modernization or Nehru's faith in scientism and Fabian socialism, were totally disavowed in favor of consumerism and other facets of the old Congress dream. Too many of the Congress's leaders had just assumed that once the British were gone and once they themselves were in charge, the future would be full of products long desired by India's people. Now these leaders had to face the reality of life. A spiraling population had eaten up much of the fruits of independence. Civil strife and war had taken a heavy toll as well.

As for India's persistent problem of trying to unify a diversified land, Rajiv was, in the final analysis, no better able to resolve it than was his mother. Rajiv's well-intentioned efforts to negotiate settlements or accords with "militants" who considered themselves "nationalists" only accentuated the crucial question as to whether India, heir to the regionally and religiously Mughal and British empires was, in modern terms, a unified nation-state.

For example, the Punjab Accord of July 1985, which granted considerable concessions to Sikhs there, was a failure even though it was an act of statesmanship by Rajiv. Written in tragedy, this agreement was concluded, unfortunately, with Sant Harchand Singh Longowal, a moderate Sikh leader, who thereby received his release from jail by the government. He signed a document that granted most of the Sikh demands, leaving the issue of an autonomous Sikh state in the Punjab to a future commission. The agreement called for the expansion of the Punjab's boundaries to increase the Sikh population of the province, lenient treatment of those arrested, and compensation to the victims of the 1984 anti-Sikh riots. Nevertheless, Sikh extremists fumed in anger, and they continued to carry out violent activity in order to warn the government that all Sikhs were not ready to accept the olive branch. While he was addressing a gathering in the summer of 1986, Sikh extremists assassinated Longowal for his efforts. Indeed, many Sikh extremists continued through that year to press a program of selective assassination; most notably this was seen in the murder of General Arun Kumar Vaidya on August 10, 1986. As army chief of staff, he had commanded the dramatic Golden Temple raid two years before.

Not only did the problem of national unity and diversity plague Rajiv as it had Indira; it destroyed the son as it had the mother. As fate would have it, the events that would engulf Rajiv and make him a victim of the most grotesque of tragedies unfolded not in India, but in Sri Lanka (Ceylon), the independent island south of Indian Tamil Nadu, which has long witnessed violent communal strife based partly on ethnicity and partly on religion.

When the British left Ceylon in 1948, the dominant Buddhist community there (the Sinhalese) gradually began to assert itself politically and culturally. When in 1956 the government sought to legislate the Sinhal's language as the "one" national language of Sri Lanka, the Tamil minority, long favored by the British colonial administration, exploded in violent opposition. By the late 1970s, the most prominent Tamil protest group was called the Liberation Tigers of Tamil Eelam, portions of the territory of Sri Lanka where the Tamil population was concentrated. Similar demands for autonomy were made in the Punjab, where a famous Sikh leader was permitted by Nehru to fast "until death," while attempting to make use of one of the Mahatma's favorite political tactics.

The Tamil war of liberation that started in 1983 intensified throughout the decade and so did the genocidal acts committed by both sides. After Rajiv had a conference with President J. R. Jayawardene of Sri Lanka in November 1986, the Indian prime minister decided to intercede by offering to bring both sides to the peace table at his city of Bangalore. After all, India had sixty million Tamil within its own borders. There had been an agreement in July 1986 for limited Tamil autonomy, but this was rejected by them and the majority of Sinhalese. The Tamils, who had made up 18 percent of Sri Lanka's population of 17.5 million, were Hindu, while the Sinhalese were Buddhist. The Tamils reorganized resistance as the "Tamil Tigers," while the Sinhalese organized as "The People's

Liberation Front." Possibly with the Punjab Accord fresh in his mind, Rajiv had come to believe in his Jimmy Carter-like facility of convincing terroristic nationalists to surrender their aspirations and their arms for concessions that actually did make for greater autonomy, if falling short of true independence. Unfortunately, in this case, his efforts fell apart far more quickly than they had in the Punjab. In 1987, Sri Lanka authorized Rajiv to send Indian troops into the Tamil city of Jaffna as a 10,000-man "Peacekeeping Force," whose primary purpose was to disarm all the Tamil warring groups, including the Tigers. Meanwhile, the Sri Lankan troops were ordered to withdraw from their positions and desist from any military operations. So began India's own "Vietnam War" (July 1987–April 1990), which nurtured only more bloodshed. Indian forces reached 50,000 troops by the time of their departure three years later. By that time Rajiv was out of office, because of the revelation of a munitions contract scandal, and though the government of V. P. Singh ordered the evacuation of the Indian troops, the Tamils, who lived in the North and East of Sri Lanka, remained a festering problem.

Rajiv's peacekeeping efforts failed to accomplish a single objective against the Tigers, and it ultimately led to that fateful day of May 21, 1991, when he was blown up by a LTTE assassin, while on a campaign tour in Tamil Nadu. He was about to address an election meeting when a woman in the reception line detonated a bomb that shattered the upper body of the former prime minister. Some fourteen persons in all were killed. Rajiv was forty-six years old at the time. His funeral took place three days later. In the final analysis, despite an appealing public image, he was largely deemed to be an ineffectual leader.

The Congress chose as their new leader the elder statesman P. V. Narasimha Rao, a secularist in the Nehru school with experience in the foreign service. He was a respected scholar and politician with some thirty-four years of government experience. He had held numerous cabinet posts including foreign affairs (1980–1984) and defense (1985). Rao, who was at the time of his appointment as India's new prime minister (1991) seventy years old, already had a history of heart trouble, but he proved to be far healthier, shrewder, and creative than his enemies had predicted. Committed to Rajiv's economic program, Rao appointed as his finance minister Monomohan Singh, an economist who favored true capitalism for India. This meant, in effect, a sharp cut in deficit spending, privatization of industry, and a total reversal of India's xenophobic policy against foreign investment in the nation. Since July 1991, Singh's reforms have had a tremendous impact on all facets of the economy: exports are up dramatically; India is no longer dependent on the International Monetary Fund (IMF) for loans; consumer prices have come down; the trade deficit has fallen; and foreign investment, which averaged $100 million (U.S.) in the 1980s has risen to $3 billion in 1993.

The "Ayodhya incident" of December 1992 proved once again how volatile was the problem of national unity and diversity. This time, the crisis was not one of regional loyalty versus the center, but of the far greater problem of the Hindu-Muslim conflict on an all-India scale. Hindu fundamentalists, organized behind the façade of the Bharatiyer Janata party (BJP) or All-India party, had long threatened to destroy the 464-year-old mosque built by the Mughal Emperor Babar, which had defiled Rama's birthplace in Ayodhya. They then planned to erect a temple dedicated to Vishnu, a Hindu deity. Party leaders announced they would start "kar seva" or "manual service" on December 6 with thousands of volunteers, who demolished the mosque on that date. Rao arrested BJP leaders on December 8 and BJP governments were dissolved on December 15. This sparked religious riots in several cities, in which over 1,100 people died. Rao, a Hindu, maintained the supremacy of constitutional law over communal loyalty or sectarian animosity.

Terrorism in the Punjab appears to have been brought under control during Rao's administration. The Kashmiri problem has not disappeared, partly because of covert Pakistani help to "freedom fighters" and partly because of internal conditions that favored the demand for independence. To Rao's government, as to previous governments, Kashmiri separatists are seen as "terrorists" or "militants." Whatever the case may be, India has evidently sent 500,000 troops to crush the movement in Kashmir and to protect Kashmiri Hindus against a rising tide of communal feeling.

The Kashmiri situation is only part of the most explosive problem India under Rao faces, namely, the chronic state of confrontation on several levels between India and Pakistan since the Partition. A serious border clash in the region of Siachen in the Karakoram Range took place in 1987. There 150 Pakistani troops were killed. Reportedly, New Delhi accused Pakistan of aiding militants in the Punjab, Jammu, and Kashmir, especially with a Muslim separatist campaign in Kashmir in 1990. Since that year, the struggle between these two South Asian powers has become exceedingly dangerous because of the atomic factor. It is now fairly well-established that by early 1990, Pakistan had developed the first "Islamic bomb" and, given the right circumstances, that Pakistani officials would have used nuclear weapons in a war against India. Much atomic technology came by way of the People's Republic of China (PRC) and the Middle East, largely Iran and Iraq. A crisis of this kind actually occurred in May 1990, when Indian troops entered Rajasthan, ostensibly to back up an operation in Kashmir. According to U.S. sources, the danger arose when Pakistan decided to launch a nuclear first strike against India rather than to risk experiencing a repetition of the disgraceful defeat that it suffered against the Indian army during the Bangladesh war of 1971. Fortunately, the nuclear strike never happened nor did a new war break out between the two belligerents. To deal with the Chinese factor, Prime Minister Gandhi visited the PRC in December 1988, while in 1991 Li Peng of the PRC traveled to India and thus became the first Chinese official to come to India in the thirty years since the border wars of the early 1960s. India charged two years later that Kashmir "militants" received direct armed support from the Inter-Services Intelligence of Pakistan. Parallel to this, the United States charged that Pakistan was smuggling narcotics, especially heroin, into America. Likewise, Washington criticized that country in 1991 and again in 1992 for its possession of the nuclear bomb. Most probably, Pakistan developed that very weapon because of its vulnerability to India's nuclear weapon, achieved in 1977. In addition, the United States accused China of sending missile technology to Pakistan in 1993. At long last, Rao traveled to Beijing that year, probably to discuss all of these problems. Nevertheless, neither has the Kashmiri problem been solved nor has peace been declared between India and Pakistan.

Both the republics of India and Pakistan continue in the 1990s to be plagued by the problems of ethnic, communal, religious, and territorial identity. Both states have large factions, who argue that each country must realize its future and present by accepting the fact that India must be a "Hindu state" and Pakistan a "Muslim state." This growing demand consistently has erupted in violent clashes, in which thousands have died (as recently as 1991). Even before the British had turned over the levers of power to the Indians, politics rather quickly began to evolve primarily around crises of identity, whether these sprang from linguistic, ethnic, or communal concerns. Sometimes of course, these disparate grievances blend into one. But whatever the source, conflicts continue, and the prospect for peace and nation building within a non-violent framework continue to be bleak. Much of this is compounded by a crisis of overpopulation that has grown out of control. India's current population stands at around 900 million people.

A clear ray of hope lies, however, in India's decision to open its markets to a freer world trade, while inviting increased international investment, which is, of course, attracted to India's inexpensive labor. If indeed this will help the nation, only the future will decide, but it seems to be a positive step.

Suggestions for Further Reading

Ahmad, Aziz, *Studies in Islamic Culture in the Indian Environment* (1964).
Basham, L. S., *The Wonder That Was India* (1963).
Bolitho, Hector, *Jinnah: Creator of Pakistan* (1964).
Bondurant, Joan, *Conquest of Violence: The Gandhian Philosophy of Conflict* (1961).
Brecher, Michael, *Nehru: A Political Biography* (1962).
Broomfield, J. H., *Elite Conflict in a Plural Society: Twentieth-Century Bengal* (1968).
Brown, W. Norman, *The United States and India, Pakistan, Bangladesh* (1972).
Cannon, Garland, *The Life And Mind of Oriental Jones* (1990).
Chandra, Bipan, *The Rise and Growth of Economic Nationalism in India* (1966).
Chaudhuri, Nirad, *Autobiography of an Unknown Indian* (1951).
Collet, Sophia Dobson, *The Life and Letters of Raja Rammohun Roy* (1962).
Davies, C. Collin, *An Historical Atlas of the Indian Subcontinent* (1963).
de Bary, Wm. Theodore (ed.)., *Sources of Indian Tradition (1958).*
Desai, Morarji, *The Story of My Life* (1974).
Embree, Ainslie T., *Charles Grant and British Rule in India* (1958).
————, *India in 1857: Mutiny or War of Independence?* (1963).
————, *India's Search for National Identity* (1972).
Fischer, Louis, *The Essential Gandhi: His Life, Work, and Ideas* (1962).
Gandhi, Mohandas K., *An Autobiography: The Story of My Experiments With Truth* (1957).
Gordon, Leonard A., *Bengal: The Nationalist Movement: 1876–1940* (1974).
Greenberger, Allen J., *The British Image of India* (1969).
Gunaratna, Rohan, *Indian Intervention In Sri Lanka* (1993).
Gupte, Pranay, *Mother India: A Political Biography of Indira Gandhi* (1992).
Harrison, Selig S., *India: The Most Dangerous Decades* (1960).
Hay, Stephen, *Asian Ideas of East and West: Tagore and His Critics* (1970).
Hazarika, Sanjay, *Strangers Of The Mist* (1994).
Heimsath, Charles H., *Indian Nationalism and Hindu Social Reform* (1964).
Irshick, Eugene F., *Politics and Social Conflict in South India* (1969).
Jain, Girilal, *The Hindu Phenomenon* (1994).
Jones, Kenneth W., *Arya Dharm: Hindu Consciousness in 19th-Century Punjab* (1976).
Kapur, Rajiv, *Sikh Separatism The Politics of Faith* (1986).
Karve, D. D., (ed.)., *The New Brahmans: Five Maharashtrian Families* (1963).

Kejariwal, O. P., *The Asiatic Society Of Bengal And The Discovery Of India's Past* (1988).

Kopf, David, *British Orientalism and the Bengal Renaissance: The Dynamics of Indian Modernization, 1773–1835* (1969).

——, *The Brahmo Samaj and the Shaping of the Modern Indian Mind* (1979).

Majumdar, R. C., *History of the Freedom Movement in India,* 3 vols. (1962–1963).

Menon, V. P., *Transfer of Power in India* (1957).

Metcalf, Thomas R., *The Aftermath of Revolt: India 1857–1870* (1965).

Moraes, Dom, *Never at Home* (1992).

Naipaul, V. S., *A Million Mutinies Now* (1990).

Nehru, Jawaharlal, *The Discovery of India,* R. I. Crane (ed.). (1960).

——, *Toward Freedom* (1958).

Panikkar, K. M., *Asia and Western Dominance* (1959).

Philips, C. H. (ed.)., *The Evolution of India and Pakistan, 1858–1947: Select Documents* (1962).

Rosselli, John, *Lord William Bentinck: Making of a Liberal Imperialist* (1974).

Rudolph, Lloyd I., and Rudolph, Suzanne H., *The Modernity of Tradition: Political Development in India* (1967).

Singh, Khushwant, *Train to Pakistan* (1956).

Smith, Donald E., *India as a Secular State* (1963).

Smith, Vincent A., *The Oxford History of India,* Percival Spear (ed.). (1967).

Srinivas, M. N., *Social Change in Modern India* (1967).

Stokes, Eric., *The English Utilitarians and India* (1959).

Wolpert, Stanley A., *Tilak and Gokhale: Revolution and Reform in the Making of Modern India* (1962).

——, *India* (1965).

Glossary

ahimsa: Ancient doctrine of not injuring living things.

Akila Dal: Sikh nationalist party.

Amritsar: Holy city of the Sikhs.

Aryan: Ambiguous term for branch of Indo-European peoples who invaded India in 1700 B.C.

Ayodhya: Birthplace of Vishnu's avatar (reincarnation), Rama, upon which the Muslims had erected a mosque. The mosque was destroyed by Hindu fundamentalists in December 1992.

bazaar: Market place in Urdu language.

Bentinck Era: Period of 1828–35, when Anglicist socio-cultural policies prevailed.

Bharatiyer Janata (BJP): Fundamentalist Hindu political party.

Brahmo Samaj: An important movement within the modern Hindu world which pioneered a new and dynamic Hinduism.

British East India Company: Controlled and ruled much of India from 1772–1857. Company originally chartered in England in 1600 by Queen Elizabeth I.

Buddhism: Reformation ideology attributed to the Buddha (6th century B.C.) and aimed at ridding Aryan religion of its violent, orthodox, and unethical abuses.

Calcutta: Capital of British India from 1772–1911.

Clive, Robert (Baron Clive of Plassey): In the military service of the British East India Company, he won a series of battles against the French, culminating in Plassey (1757). As the first governor of Bengal he was the true founder of the Empire of British India.

Communalist: Term used to designate one who seems interested solely in the welfare of his community, be it Hindu or Muslim.

Cornwallis, Lord Charles: Former British general in the American Revolution, who was Governor General of India, 1786–1793, and known for his westernized solutions to problems of Indian administration.

dasyu: Most likely, the Aryan term of disrepute for original Indian inhabitants.

Delhi: Capital of India (1206–1529). New Delhi, a 20th-century city built adjacent to the old, has been the capital for the past half century.

dharma: Core concept of classical Indian ethics based on duty to the occupational grouping to which one belongs. Later reinterpreted to mean religion.

Dravidian Languages: The indigenous languages of South India.

Harijans: Name Mohandas K. Gandhi liked to use for the untouchables, or scheduled classes. Means the "Children of God." The term is today widely used in India.

hartal: Political technique popularized by Mohandas K. Gandhi which attempts to force suspension of all economic activity.

Hastings, Warren: First Company Governor General in 1772, who tried to establish order out of chaos by compelling company servants to study Indian languages and become responsive to the people whom they ruled.

Hindi: The modern tongue or language more directly related to ancient Sanskrit. Hindi is the mother-tongue of nearly one-third of the population.

Hindu Renaissance: Hindu response to intrusive impact of British colonialism and imperialism. A Hindu intelligentsia appears which seeks ways of reforming existing abuses in Hinduism and finding a new identity for a revitalized India in the modern world.

Islam: Religion of second largest community in India. Based on the scriptural source known as Koran and first articulated by the prophet Muhammad.

Janata Dal: Party of diverse elements which united to defeat Indira Gandhi.

Jati System: Basic social unit among Hindus founded on specialized occupational activities and/or kinship groups.

jizya: Special tax on non-Muslim-governed country.

Khalistan: Territorial goal of Sikh nationalists.

karma: Good and bad deeds which determine rebirth.

Liberation Tigers of Tamil Eelam (LTTE): Most effective Tamil nationalist guerrillas in Sri Lanka who strive for independence.

mandir: The Hindu temple or place of worship.

masjid: Mosque or place of worship for Muslims.

moksha: One of several Hindu concepts denoting the ultimate goal of salvation.

Mughal Dynasty: Rulers of India from early 16th century to the rise of the British raj in the late 18th century. Akbar is considered the eclectic architect of the empire, while Aurangzeb, who died in 1707, is looked upon as the bigoted emperor who hastened its decline.

Muslim: A believer in Islam.

nirvana: Buddhist equivalent of moksha.

Orientalist-Anglicist controversy: Conflict between values and attitudes by British officials in India on how best to improve Indian institutions, traditions, and beliefs. Orientalists favored policies which were based on Indian linguistic and cultural models, whereas Anglicists chose the westernized models.

Pali: The language of the Buddhists.

Parsi: Indian word for Persian. Minority community in India which professes Zoroastrianism, the pre-Islamic faith of Iran.

Plassey, battle of: In perspective, battle between Clive and Nawab of Bengal in 1757 which was won by the English and initiated the British conquest of India.

Rajputs: Feudal-like warrior dynasties of western India.

Sanskrit: Classical language of north India. Modern languages of north India are derived from Sanskrit as many modern European languages are derived from Latin.

satyagraha: Name Mohandas K. Gandhi gave to his movement. Means literally the force of truth.

Sikhism: New religion based on fusion of components of Hinduism and Islam. Adherents located mostly in the Punjab.

Sultan: A Muslim (Moslem) title used by medieval conquerors and rulers whose headquarters were in or near Delhi.

Swaraj: What many Indian leaders, including Mohandas K. Gandhi, promised to followers. Can be and was variously interpreted to mean freedom, self-government, status within the empire.

Taj Mahal: Magnificent marble tomb built by Shah Jahan, a Mughal ruler, for his favorite wife, who died in childbirth.

Upanishads: One of the six classical schools of Indian philosophy which constituted a reaction against Brahmanical orthodoxy between 900–600 B.C.

Urdu: Lingua franca of Mughal India and official language of Pakistan.

Varna System: Fourfold stratification of Aryan society into warriors, priests, merchants, and cultivators.

Vedas: Earliest scriptural sources of the Aryans, later appropriated by the Hindus.

Zamindari System: The introduction into Bengal (1793) of the private property principle by which former tax collectors or zamindars became land owners.

The
World
of

JAPAN

Introduction

The amazing Japanese were the first non-European peoples to master modern industrialization completely. The words "Made in Japan" have long identified their manufactures throughout the world. Japanese VCRs, high definition televisions (HDTVs), automobiles, cameras, watches, computers, and textiles, compete in virtually every international market.

Long regarded as a poor, small, and insignificant country, Japan over time has presented various images to the outside world. At the dawn of history, Chinese traders called Japan "The Land of the Rising Sun" because, since it was east of every "known" country, there the sun rose earliest. In the sixteenth century, the first Portuguese merchants beheld Japan merely as a quaint, picturesque, and remote land. Since 1868, following almost two and a quarter centuries of seclusion, however, the world has seen Japan as the prize student of modernization because of its rapid absorption of modern technology. Trained effectively in armaments, in the twentieth century Japan became a military expansionist that invaded China, attacked the United States (at Pearl Harbor), and quickly overran the Southwest Pacific in World War II.

Following its disastrous defeat, Japan remained supine and cooperative under U.S. occupation after World War II. From that time on, Japan made an astounding recovery, climaxed by its "economic miracle," which began in the 1960s and in which Japan eventually surged to second place among the world's great industrial powers. Although the rest of the world has beheld Japan in various guises throughout history, the Japanese have always been "tremendous achievers," in the words of historian and former U.S. ambassador to Japan Edwin O. Reischauer—a tribute to their individual initiative, strong sense of social responsibility, dedication to family, and patriotism in the name of the emperor.

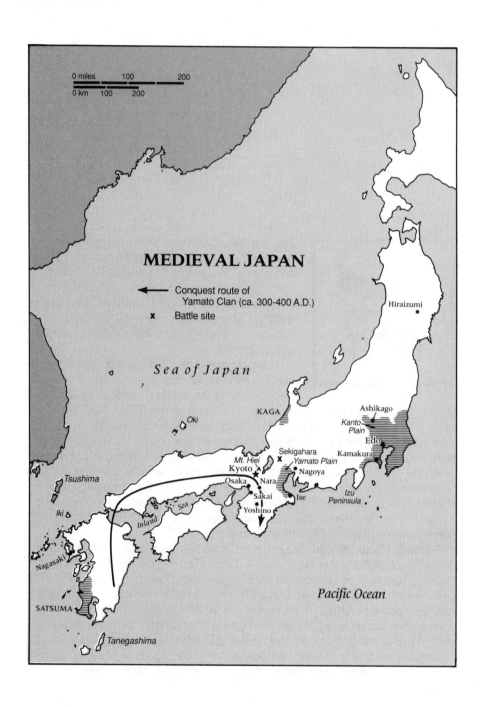

MEDIEVAL JAPAN

⟵ Conquest route of
   Yamato Clan (ca. 300-400 A.D.)
x Battle site

0 miles   100   200

0 km   100   200

Sea of Japan

Hiraizumi

Oki

KAGA

Ashikago

Kanto
Plain

Edo

Sekigahara

Yamato Plain

Kamakura

Mt. Hiei

Kyoto

Nara

Nagoya

Tsushima

Osaka

Sakai

Ise

Izu
Peninsula

Yoshino

Iki

Inland *Sea*

Nagasaki

Pacific Ocean

SATSUMA

Tanegashima

Early History 1

to the Opening of Japan, 660 B.C. to A.D. 1854

Four main islands in a mountainous, volcanic chain of four thousand, stretching southwesterly along the east coast of Asia, constitute the heart of Japan. Honshu, the main island and the site of the most important cities, stands in the middle, with Hokkaido to the north, and Shikoku and Kyushu to the south. About the area of the state of California—larger than the British Isles—Japan lies in the same latitudes as the United States and enjoys a climate with plentiful rainfall, similar to that of the U.S. East Coast.

Even though the predominantly mountainous land is unsuitable for extensive agriculture, intensive though sometimes simple cultivation of its arable land, about 16 percent, produces the highest yield per acre in the world and makes the country self-sufficient in some foodstuffs such as rice. Japan lacks natural resources, except for extensive forests, and must import 98 percent of its oil and coal. A restless area geologically, Japan records about sixteen hundred earthquakes a year.

Japan's island location, with seventeen thousand miles of coastline, has made it a proud maritime power that leads the world in ship building, scientific research in the extraction of food from the sea, and in the consumption of seafood. Japan's insularity, like Great Britain's off the coast of Europe, has left it free to accept or reject the ideas and institutions of its neighbors. Only twice in its history has foreign influence dominated Japan's life: when the Chinese did so, from the seventh to the tenth centuries, and when Westerners imposed themselves, in the nineteenth and twentieth centuries. At all other times in its history Japan has been isolationist, most notably during the two centuries before 1853.

Origins and Early Society

Japanese society developed later than Western or Chinese civilizations. The Japanese race stemmed from a combination of proto-Caucasian peoples (the Ainu),

155

immigrants from Southeast Asia, and Mongoloid invaders from northern China, most of whom streamed into Japan in various periods before the onset of the Christian epoch. Ancient Chinese merchants referred to the Japanese in derision as "dwarfs." The original Japanese tribal structure and religious views were unsophisticated. The people venerated the objects of nature, ascending in a hierarchical order to the sun. This nature worship—later called *Shinto*, "The Way of the Gods"—possessed no creed, scripture, or concept of right and wrong, but stressed a childlike gratitude for the bounty of nature and emphasized personal purity and cleanliness.

The Mongoloid invaders introduced rice cultivation, which created a demand for land. Scattered tribes then consolidated and organized into clans or *uji* (a kind of family unit) ruled by priest-chieftains with religious and secular functions. From these clans the Japanese derived their first military heritage. Each group had its own guardian or deity, regarded as the common ancestor of all members. As nature itself was a hierarchy, so also was early Japanese society, and the prestige of the protecting god determined the eminence of the clan. Professions shaped the social classes. Workers toiled in occupational groups, hereditary subunits of the uji, called *be*. In these, farmers, fishermen, weavers, and potters were ranked according to their usefulness in society. The Japanese early developed a sense of personal obligation and group responsibility, so evident in their society and business organization today.

Life in Early Japan

These early Japanese dwelt in wooden, straw-thatched houses usually of rectangular or oval shape. Household articles included mallets, bowls, spoons, and ladles made of wood or clay. They mastered the craft of pottery making quite early. Rice was the most popular food, but the Japanese also raised peaches, melons, walnuts, and soy beans, cultivating with spades, rakes, and wooden hoes tipped with iron. Hunters made bows of wooden strips bound together by bark, and arrowheads of iron, bronze, or stone. The seafarers fished with nets of hemp. Their clothing also came from hemp fiber woven on primitive looms. The early Japanese oftentimes adorned their clothes with jewelry. They drank *sake*, a fermented alcoholic drink made of rice, and buried their dead in various ways, principally in pottery jars. Settled communities lived in small groups along coastal areas or streams.

About A.D. 300, one of the uji from northern Kyushu launched a series of military campaigns into Honshu. Following the northern shoreline of the Inland Sea into the center of the island, they settled in the plain of Yamato and assumed its name. This Yamato clan honored the Sun Goddess, the highest ranking of the deities, and they soon dominated central Japan. As rulers over central and southern Honshu, as well as northern Kyushu, the Yamato incorporated other uji cults into an official mythology recognizing the supremacy of the Sun Goddess, the protectress of the country. Japanese recognized her shrine at Ise as the most sacred in the entire land. In the words of historian J. Edward Kidder: "Ise is Japanese to the core." Japan's present dynasty is directly descended from the Yamato clan.

Japanese Assimilation of Chinese Culture, 552–710

To build a system of central government, the Yamato turned to the greatest model of their day—the mighty T'ang Empire (618–907) of China. The peoples of East and Southeast Asia looked on China as the great "Middle Kingdom," to which they paid tribute, and regarded this "Celestial Empire" as the center of the universe, beneath only Heaven itself. The philosophy of Confucius formed the ideological basis of China's relations with its East and Southeast Asian neighbors. Stressing respect for the family, Confucianism fostered harmony in human relations along with a deep reverence for virtue and knowledge. In this Confucian relationship, a family concept, China acted as the great teacher to the "student" nations on its frontiers—such as Japan, Korea, the Ryukyu Islands, and Vietnam. The Chinese emperor was "the father and mother" to his own and neighboring peoples and generously dispensed the knowledge, institutions, and material goods of his bountiful realm to those less fortunate. Members of this East Asian family voluntarily approached his "Dragon Throne" by offering tribute through the ceremonial *kowtow* ("head-knocking")—the three kneelings and nine prostrations. Thus, Chinese foreign relations stressed harmony, the patronage of the Chinese emperor, and recognition of Chinese "superiority" over the rest of the world. What the Roman Empire was to Europe, China represented simultaneously to its neighboring countries of East Asia.

Since the beginning of the fifth century, Chinese scholars, fleeing barbarian invaders from the north, had reached Japan by way of Korea. At first, the Chinese language and Confucian ideals affected only a narrow segment of Japanese officials. In 552, the ruler of a Korean kingdom sent an image of the Buddha to the leader of the Yamato clan, recommending Buddhism as a new religion. This faith, developed in India about 500 B.C., had spread to East and Southeast Asia. It taught that only the suppression of material desires—riches, fame, sex, etc.—would enable one to attain Nirvana, or the release from care and pain after death. The promise of an afterlife filled a notable gap in the old faith, and Buddhism gave a strong impulse to the spread of Chinese learning throughout Japan. Prince Shotoku, chief minister for the Japanese empress, personified the Chinese reform movement by championing Buddhism. Later, the Taika Reforms of 646 introduced many Chinese institutions into government and made Buddhism the religion of the aristocracy. Shinto, the unsophisticated nature cult, remained relatively undisturbed among the common people.

In what was probably the first organized program for study abroad, Japanese students regularly traveled to China to observe the great T'ang governmental system in operation and returned to assume official positions in Japan. Japan became virtually "a miniature T'ang" and cultural satellite of China. The head of state assumed the Chinese title of emperor with the designation "Son of Heaven." Central authority functioned through eight ministries, and local administration passed into the hands of an intellectual class on the model of the Chinese "scholar bureaucracy." This Japanese elite formed a kind of civil service of government administrators, who gained their positions by competitive examinations. This system was based upon the Confucian precept that only the most knowledgeable and virtuous should rule. Meanwhile, Chinese Buddhist monks established temple schools in Japan to train this new class. Japan's emperors also attempted to follow a Chinese pattern by periodically redistributing the lands belonging to the clans, dividing portions of them among the peasants who worked the soil. Twelve distinct ranks separated those in attendance at the imperial court, and the T'ang governing city in China became the model for Japan's first permanent capital, at the present site of Nara. This terminated the Shinto tradition whereby a revulsion to death prompted the removal of the capital at the passing of an emperor. Thus, Japan "is culturally a daughter of Chinese civilization" in Professor Reischauer's words.

The Capitals at Nara and Kyoto, 710–794

Nara remained the imperial capital from 710 to 784 and with its seven great temples was a center of Buddhism. One of the most famous today is Todaiji Temple, the largest wooden structure in the world, which houses the beloved *Daibutsu*—the fifty-three-foot Great Buddha of Nara—cast in 745. Reflecting the complete benevolence of the all-powerful Buddha, the Buddha of Nara's hands signify "Fear not, you may approach," and "I grant your petition." This magnificent figure personifies the Nara period as the apex of the Chinese cultural influence on Japan.

A new system of writing represented another manifestation of this Chinese impact. Using abbreviated forms of Chinese characters, Japanese scholars developed three alphabets or syllabaries. One system retained individual Chinese characters but gave them Japanese pronunciations and meanings. This cumbersome writing system has burdened the Japanese to the present day; nevertheless, the syllabaries made possible the new literature of the later Heian period.

The intellectual classes of Japan continued to use the Chinese language and script. Chinese enjoyed a prestige similar to that of classical Latin in medieval Europe. It even played a part in strengthening central authority. New emperors claimed divine origin by means of two histories written in the eighth century in Chinese script. The *Kojiki* (Record of Ancient Things) and the *Nihongi* (Chronicles of Japan) recount the mythical creation of the Japanese islands and the emperor's direct descent from the Sun Goddess, the special protectress of Japan.

These histories tell us that two deities—a brother and sister, standing on the bridge spanning heaven and earth—created the Japanese islands. The god probed the waters below with his spear, and as he withdrew it the droplets formed the islands. Other deities were born of the first two, including Amaterasu, the Sun Goddess. Ascending to the heavens, she sent her grandson to rule Japan, bearing a mirror, a sword, and a necklace—the "Imperial Regalia." Jimmu Tenno, the mythical grandson's descendant, became Japan's first emperor in 660 B.C., almost a century and a half before Cyrus the Great established the Persian Empire. The present Emperor Akihito is the 124th successor of Emperor Jimmu.

Thus, the new Japanese emperors strengthened their dynastic claims against rival clans by adapting Chinese religion, philosophy, governmental institutions, language, and literary forms to their own needs. Overall, the Chinese heritage contributed greatly to the stability of present-day Japanese society.

In 784, the emperor, fearing the growing influence of the Buddhist monks through their control of temples, education, and extensive monastery lands, or-

Todaiji ("Great Eastern") Temple houses the Daibutsu ("Great Buddha") of Nara. The world's largest wooden structure, it dates from 745. Consulate General of Japan, Kansas City.

The Daibutsu of Nara. Japan National Tourist Organization.

dered the capital moved to the small town of Nagaoka. Ten years later it was relocated at Heian-kyo ("Capital of Peace and Tranquility") the site of the present city of Kyoto, meaning "Capital City." For the next four hundred years, the emperors remained the central authority at Heian-kyo. This era of Japanese history is now referred to as the "Heian Period."

The Culture of the Heian Period. 794-1185

Barbarian invasions of China weakened the T'ang dynasty, and China's prestige waned over the next century and a half. The Japanese ceased their tribute missions after 838, and the cultural borrowing from China dwindled in time. No longer did the Japanese copy the "Middle Kingdom" but instead attained a degree of their own cultural maturity. During the Nara period they had enthusiastically embraced Chinese learning, customs, and institutions. As the eminence of China diminished during the early Heian period, Japanese civilization matured so that the assimilation of things Chinese became more selective. The aristocracy, for example, still fancied Chinese dress but began to add distinctive Japanese touches. For some time the attempt to create a T'ang-style scholar bureaucracy, based solely on intellectual attainment, had clashed with the hereditary principle, because the ambitious landed lords often arranged the competitive examinations to ensure the success of their own sons. Moreover, the Chinese land system, which provided for peasant ownership and redistribution every six years, conflicted with the interests of the court aristocracy, who controlled the largest estates. The imperial governmental system, the philosophical ideals of Confucianism, the religion of Buddhism, and the Chinese language, however, remained with the Japanese.

Confucianism taught the Japanese the necessity of courtesy in personal relationships and respect for the family. The philosophy of Taoism, which also had entered Japan from China over the years, taught resignation to the forces of nature, thus granting a fundamental equilibrium to the individual. Buddhism promised an existence after death, giving more meaning to life. At court, Buddhism became a more distinctly Japanese religion, with new sects adding novel and esoteric rituals of Japanese origin. At the same time, Buddhism penetrated the lower classes. Combined with the practicality of the native Shinto, it lost some of its mysticism but became a vehicle of faith and hope to the common people. Buddhist monasteries steadily acquired land at a distance from the cities, and, while managing and working their great estates, the monks came to identify with the peasant classes and became increasingly independent of the central authority. Monastic armies, formed from younger priests and estate workers, began to wage war against neighboring landed lords in total disregard of the emperor at Kyoto.

The Court, Literature, and Art

The Imperial court, bound by Confucian ceremonials, dwelt in an aesthetic, superficial atmosphere of ritual and dilettantism borrowed from the T'ang. Regulations of the court—dedicated to *miyabi* (courtly refinement)—compelled all to observe meticulous formality and etiquette. Edicts fixed the color of officials' robes, the length of their swords, and the nature of their salutations. Ministers of state wore dark purple, those of a lesser rank, a lighter shade, while exact rules governed the protocol for ministers while greeting a prince of the blood—or for any encounter with a person of superior station.

Increasingly absorbed by this atmosphere, even the most able rulers found it steadily more difficult to cope with urgent problems of government. More and more, the court lost effective power outside the capital city. Imperial tax collectors weakened the taxation system in outlying areas when they pocketed the revenue for themselves. The remote emperor thus became dependent on his own lands for income. Because of attacks on the frontier by the Ainu, a proto-Caucasian people dwelling in northern Honshu and Hokkaido, even military commanders were absent from the capital, so that the preoccupied emperor became quite isolated from both sources of power and his people.

During this time, however, the imperial court and its aristocratic women gave rise to the beginning of a truly Japanese literature. While the traditional literary scholars continued their struggle to master the Chinese classics, the ladies-in-waiting attending the empress recounted their experiences at court in their diaries. In poetic Japanese, the women gave free play to their own intimate emotions, instincts, and fancies.

The Heian period achieved its crowning literary accomplishment with the massive work, *The Tale of Genji*, by Murasaki Shikibu, a lady-in-waiting. Perhaps she created the first psychological novel, so insightfully did she sketch her characters. This lengthy literary creation tells the story of an emperor's son who devoted himself to the pursuit of love, becoming involved in endless romantic entanglements. As the personification of Heian virtues, this "shining prince" excelled also as a poet, calligrapher, musician, and dancer; hence, someone of exquisite taste in a society dominated by the aesthetic. Another lady-in-waiting, Sei Shonagon, composed the light, gay, and witty *The Pillow Book,* which gives only a faint hint of life outside the little world preoccupied with arts and letters.

In art also the Chinese model gradually yielded to Japanese refinements. Sculpture and painting now reflected the esoteric tastes of the new Buddhist sects, especially in the architecture of the new monasteries. Landscape gardening became an art in itself. The garden reflected nature in miniature and the traditional Japanese respect for it, with the *torii* (gateway) gracing the entrance. Picture scrolls, which unfolded to tell a continuous story, were called *Yamato-e* or Yamato Pictures and often portrayed historical events. Although borrowing much from China, the Japanese remained true to themselves, retaining "a clear sense of their own identity" to achieve "a new synthesis," as Reischauer observed.

Japan absorbed and in many ways changed Chinese institutions. As the Japanese developed their own cultural identity, however, they grew increasingly confident—so much so that the ruler of China fumed when Japan's Prince Shotoku, who earlier had presided over Japanese reforms on the Chinese model, addressed the Chinese emperor as the ruler of "the land where the sun sets" while extending greetings from the sovereign of "the land where the sun rises."

Social and Political Change in the Countryside

In the countryside, political and social changes took place which would eventually transfer effective political power into the hands of one of the great landed lords. The Chinese land distribution system proved unsuccessful in Japan largely because the peasants were unable to make a living by farming their small plots. They also bore a crushing tax burden. In desperation many peasants commended themselves and their lands to the nearest lord in order to escape imperial taxes as well as the endemic warfare. With their increased holdings, the lords of these *shoen*, or privately owned estates, became independent of the imperial court. At the same time, Buddhist monasteries, established centuries earlier, had acquired extensive estates by private bequest and government grants, while enjoying the favor of a tax-free status. Moreover, the emperors often gave land to their sons who could not be employed at court, granting these new landed lords tax exemption because of their exalted rank.

The growing independence in the provinces, as well as the ostentatious life at court, set the stage for the decline of imperial power. Emperors found that presiding over the court with its Confucian ceremonials took most of their time—especially in combination with their religious duties as Shinto priests. Consequently, many of them retired at an early age to seek peace in a Buddhist monastery, leaving their thrones to infant sons. At such times, a distinguished court family, the Fujiwara, stepped forward to act as regents and administrators for the young emperor. The Fujiwara ensured their positions by intermarriage with the imperial line, yet made no attempt to usurp the throne for themselves. These "prime ministers" to the emperors present the first example of "government from behind the scenes"—a time-honored Japanese political practice. The emperor became a figurehead, a national symbol, while a powerful personage behind him performed the duties of administration.

The Shogun and "Decentralized Feudalism," 1185–1333

In the provinces, administrators, who also acted as fighting men, managed the lords' shoen. These *samurai* ("one who serves") were destined to become the great military class of Japan. While they sometimes held land, more often they helped oversee the lorded estates in peacetime and fought as mounted warriors in times of strife, receiving a lord's protection and patronage in return. The samurai became a privileged class and the traditional defenders of society. Like the medieval European knight, they had a traditional code of honor—later called *Bushido* or "The Way of the Warrior"—comparable to medieval chivalry. These horsemen fought with bows and arrows, pick axes, and the famed short and long curved swords. Persistent conflict among the landed lords and the Buddhist monasteries, as well as the frequent threat of the marauding Ainu, demanded the loyal service of these armed retainers.

For almost a century private armies of the various lords waged constant warfare. Eventually, one victorious lord, Minamoto Yoritomo, compelled the emperor to appoint him virtual commander-in-chief of the imperial armies. With this commission went the title of *shogun* ("Barbarian Subduing Generalissimo"), sometimes given to military leaders who campaigned against the troublesome Ainu. Disdaining to become involved in the intrigues of the imperial court, Yoritomo established a separate court at Kamakura in 1185, almost contemporaneous with the reign of Richard the Lion Hearted of England. In effect, Japan now had two governments, a civil authority under the emperor at Kyoto and the shogun's military regime. Like the "Mayors of the Palace" and the Merovingian kings of medieval France, this new *Bakufu* ("Camp Government") relegated the emperor to the role of a "do-nothing" ruler who merely bestowed titles of nobility and offered prayers to the deities for the protection of his people.

As the effective administrator of the realm, the shogun appointed special constables who acted as supervisors over the lords. According to historian Jeffrey P. Mass, Yoritomo here appointed "elite officers" to control the local power of the estates. Thus, Japan entered a period of "decentralized feudalism," not to become "centralized" until the seventeenth century. Though local authority dominated and every landed lord remained autonomous on his own estate, each owed ultimate allegiance to the shogun as his overlord. This arrangement proved itself in the successful defense of Japan against the invasion fleets of Kublai Khan, the Mongol emperor, who attempted to conquer the country from Korea in 1274 and again in 1281. A storm wrecked the attacking ships, and the Japanese regarded the coming of this *Kamikaze* ("Divine Wind") as a sign of the Sun Goddess's protection of their island empire.

The massive mobilization of feudal armies, however, so impoverished the Bakufu that the shogun's authority weakened and internal warfare erupted again. The constables who commanded powerful samurai armies on the great estates soon subjugated the weaker ones, consolidating them into much larger holdings, some as great as entire provinces. These commanders became a new class of landed lords, the *daimyo* ("Great Names"), who waged continuous war in a struggle for supremacy. The shogun's effective authority dissolved in feudal anarchy. After 1333, Japan plunged into bloody civil war and entered its "Dark Ages."

Culture and Economy in the "Dark Ages," 1333-1568

Within the political and social dislocation caused by feudal warfare, the weakened shogunate and imperial government barely survived; nevertheless, the era produced surprising cultural and economic advances. The prevailing uncertainty fostered religious belief, and Buddhism continued to attract many from the lower classes. New sects, especially the True Pure Land, the Lotus, the Nichirin, and Zen, took hold and enriched the native Shinto. Commoners continued to embrace Shinto as a religion for their daily lives, while Buddhism promised them life after death. Zen, the faith embraced by the rising samurai class, taught a rigid internal discipline, total disregard for pain, and meditation as the way to truth. Zen also taught the warrior to seek the sublimity and simplicity of the "tea ceremony" after the violence of the day's fighting. Gardens became sacred to the samurai because of their representations of nature, with flower arrangements symbolizing the heavens, earth, and mankind in the spirit of Zen. The silk scroll, a type of tapestry depicting scenes of nature, flourished, along with a unique form of theater known as *No* (a kind of dance drama with masked actors). At Kamakura, the shogun ordered the casting of the *Daibutsu* ("Great Buddha") in 1252 as a symbol (glorifying meditation) of the samurai's dedication to the new faith. Kyoto's Golden Pavilion, built originally in 1394 as a summer home for the shogun but soon converted to a temple, was the period's finest architectural representation of the tranquillity of Zen. This Muromachi age produced "cultural advance within political weakness," as historian John Whitney Hall explained.

Beautiful Kinkajuji Temple, or Golden Pavilion, Kyoto. Consulate General of Japan, Kansas City.

Below: Shizuoka Prefecture. Lofty Mt. Fuji in the spring. Consulate General of Japan, Kansas City.

Encouraged by the Chinese Ming emperors' increased patronage of overseas trade, enterprising Japanese engaged in an expanded commerce. Many of the powerful daimyo, coveting exotic items—silk, porcelain, jade, and tea—from the continent, participated in the trade of East and Southeast Asia. Colonies of Japanese traders settled in Thailand, Indonesia, and the Philippines, and many obsequiously performed the ceremonial kowtow before the emperor to gain commercial advantage. On the other hand, certain elements of the warrior classes turned to conducting pirate raids on the Chinese coast. The Ming emperors protested vehemently to the shogun, and when this proved useless, they placed Japanese trade under heavy restriction. In addition, one Chinese ruler decreed that his subjects dwelling along the coast must move two miles inland for their own protection against these hated pirates or *wako*.

The Three Unifiers of Japan, 1568-1603

After the consolidation of estates under the daimyo, three great military figures accomplished the political reunification of Japan and thus ended the feudal wars. In the mid-sixteenth century, Nobunaga, a powerful lord with vast estates in the vicinity of Nagoya (central Honshu), conquered the capital region, deposed the powerless shogun, and then campaigned against the Buddhist monasteries, the symbols of provincial autonomy. With his flanks protected by two able lieutenants, he subdued the main Buddhist monastery on Mount Hiei, which was the key to control of central Japan—approximately one-third of the country.

When a treacherous officer murdered Nobunaga in 1582, Toyotomi Hideyoshi seized power and conducted the remaining campaigns that eventually completed unification. Hideyoshi, who once had been Nobunaga's stable boy, had mastered the privileged military profession and trained a small group of samurai who were passionately loyal to him. Known as "the ape" because of his ugliness, this able soldier subdued Japan by vigorous campaigns against both the eastern and western clans. With the army of Tokugawa Ieyasu, a loyal ally, shielding him from counterattack, Hideyoshi seized the capital city, Kyoto. He compelled the court to appoint him imperial regent (*kampaku*), thus providing the emperor's sanction to his conquests.

Hideyoshi unified the country but could not assume the title of shogun because of his peasant origins. In 1586, he completed the mighty Osaka Castle, his center of power, and by decree froze everyone in his profession. A rigid class structure thus consisted of (1) samurai (and daimyo), (2) peasants, (3) artisans, and (4) merchants. In 1587 Hideyoshi drew a new and strict line between the privileged samurai and the other, common, classes when he conducted a "sword hunt" to disarm all but the military classes. The wearing of the two swords thus became an exclusive samurai badge of distinction. Hideyoshi had ensured the allegiance of the warrior class.

After the unification of Japan, the restless samurai probably induced Hideyoshi, the "Napoleon of Japan," to undertake the conquest of China, ostensibly in reply to an insult by the Ming emperor. An invasion of the Chinese dependency of Korea in 1592 resulted in an indecisive Japanese withdrawal. Korean ironclad warships of tortoise-like design had effectively intercepted the Japanese supply lines. Five years later a second Korean campaign unleashed a massive Chinese retaliation across the Yalu River, and a tidal wave of imperial Chinese troops almost inundated the Japanese. Hideyoshi had sworn to "roll up China like a map," but he died in 1598 before further expeditions were undertaken. Although the ventures provided action for the samurai warriors, Hideyoshi's precise motive in the whole disastrous affair remains obscure.

After Hideyoshi's death his chief lieutenant, Tokugawa Ieyasu, seized power in 1600, following a decisive victory at Sekigahara over a coalition of western clans. A cruel autocrat who murdered his wife and son, Ieyasu founded the military-political dynasty of Tokugawa, which ruled the Japanese for the next two and one-half centuries under virtual martial law. Although his dynastic regime grew less absolute under his successors, Ieyasu brought Japanese feudalism to a climax by his institution of a "centralized" feudal system, governed directly by the shogun. A tyrant, not unlike his contemporary Ivan the Terrible in Russia, Ieyasu is known as "the maker of modern Japan," in historian A. L. Sadler's words, because he inspired many of the social obligations and group disciplines that continue to direct the conduct of the Japanese today.

The Development of "Centralized Feudalism"

In 1603, Ieyasu compelled the emperor to appoint him shogun, thereby legitimizing his position, and then proceeded to redistribute the land belonging to those lords overrun in his drive to power. As indicated by historian Conrad Totman, the Tokugawa Bakufu grew directly out of the Tokugawa family's earlier private government. By awarding estates around the Kanto Plain to trusted relatives, the *Shimpan* (Related Lords), Ieyasu formed a buffer area behind his strategically located capital, Edo, to ensure against attack by land. After that he granted the most productive of the remaining estates to those lords who had served him faithfully before the decisive battle of 1600; these were the *Fudai* (Inside Lords), whose new holdings frequently controlled an important crossroad or strategic waterway from which they could keep watch on less trustworthy lords. Finally, Ieyasu parceled out the more undesirable lands to those who had not joined his forces until after 1600, the *Tozama* (Outside Lords). Though he permitted some in this latter category to retain their estates, in many cases he reduced the size of their holdings. The Outside Lords remained antagonistic to Ieyasu, and, with their estates (some of the wealthiest in the land) at a considerable distance from the capital, they constituted a formidable threat to his power.

Ieyasu required all lords to spend alternate years at Edo and to leave their wives and children behind in the capital whenever they returned to check on their estates. These "Periods of Alternate Attendance" kept many of the lords impoverished because they had to maintain two residences, one at the capital and another on their estates. Indeed, the shoguns encouraged the lords to live extravagantly and to enjoy the good life while in Edo. The lords also were liable for their own travel expenses and those of their numerous retainers and servants. Officials demanded passports at many checkpoints in the mountains surrounding the Kanto Plain and watched for "outward wives and inward guns"— signs of revolt in the capital. The lords were also required to sustain their local Shinto shrines and Buddhist temples, as well as to keep roads and bridges in repair. "The Laws of Military Houses" (1615) obliged all lords to report violations of any kind by their neighbors and to refuse protection to fugitive samurai. Always present were the *metsuke* (official informers) who acted as an efficient secret police and regularly reported the activities of all lords to the central authority. Thus, by means of these "checks and balances," Ieyasu maintained his intricate system of "centralized feudalism."

Ieyasu controlled the imperial court by prohibiting anyone to approach the emperor except by permission of the shogun, while keeping all courtiers under strict surveillance. Nijo Castle, constructed in 1603, was Ieyasu's official residence whenever he visited Kyoto, while his appointed deputy dwelt there the year around. Its ingenious "nightingale floors" (an alarm system whereby a subdued whistling sounded as one walked) gave warning of intruders and potential assassins.

The samurai represented Ieyasu's greatest threat because many from this privileged warrior class had become "masterless" when their lords were killed in feudal wars or deposed in the redistribution of estates. Since they were sworn to avenge their lords, they constituted a potentially dangerous element against the regime. Hostile bands of these masterless samurai (*ronin*) roamed the countryside. To win their loyalty, Ieyasu reaffirmed their privileged status, thus underscoring the class structure enunciated by Hideyoshi—samurai (and daimyo), peasants, artisans, and merchants. The long and short swords still distinguished the privileged samurai, who possessed the right to "cut down" a commoner for any infraction.

Since peace prevailed in Japan, the shogun and the lords encouraged all samurai to take up a life of study and become a governing class of intellectual elite on the model of the Chinese scholar bureaucracy. The samurai were urged to study Neo-Confucianism because of its emphasis on loyalty to rulers. The shogun intended this to cement samurai allegiance to his regime and to ensure harmony in society by the cultivation of knowledge and virtue. Although the great majority of masterless samurai sank humiliatingly into commoner status, a significant number did become scholars.

European Traders and Missionaries, 1543-1614

Europeans first came to Japan when Portuguese merchants engaged in the China trade landed on a southern island in 1543. Western commerce attracted the Japanese because the merchants introduced a new musket, much desired by the embattled feudal lords, and brought Chinese goods, especially silks. Since the Ming emperors of China had finally broken commercial relations with the shogun because of Japanese pirate attacks on Chinese coastal cities, Portuguese merchants took over the carrying trade between China and Japan. Jesuit missionaries from Portugal accompanied the trading ships to Japan and gained a significant number of religious converts among the influential lords. The Jesuits strove to influence primarily the aristocratic classes, because once converted, a landed lord often commanded his followers to embrace Christianity. The missionaries soon became middle men in the flourishing Portuguese trade at the port of Nagasaki, which the newly Christian lord had consigned to the exclusive use of the Jesuits. This placed them in a useful position to make contacts and thus furthered their religious efforts. By the year 1600, the Jesuits had converted about three hundred thousand Japanese of all classes.

In 1593, the Spanish intruded into the Portuguese trade, bringing the first Franciscan missionaries to Japan. The Dutch came in 1609, and the English four years later. In contrast to the Jesuits, the Franciscans worked among the common people and were critical of the Jesuits' involvement in Western trade. Increasingly, the two orders took opposite sides in feudal quarrels. Fearing Christianity would divide the country and weaken his authority, Hideyoshi officially banned the missionaries as early as 1587, but he took no direct action until ten years later when he executed seventeen Japanese Christians, six Franciscans, and three Jesuits at Nagasaki.

By 1603, when Ieyasu became shogun, there had been numerous Christian conversions among the hostile Outside Lords who controlled important ports, enabling them to trade for European arms—a practice the distant government at Edo could not stop. An alliance between these suspect Outside Lords and the foreign powers, using the Christian converts as a "fifth column," seemed to be a real danger to the regime. Ieyasu became convinced that the missionaries were the vanguard of foreign conquest and officially expelled all the religious orders in 1614.

The Closing of Japan, 1616-1639

The persecution of all Christians began in earnest in 1616 under the new shogun, Hidetada. Officials tortured many Christians, forcing them to tread upon a cross or holy picture as a denial of their faith. Crucifixion, the water torture, and suspension head-down in a sulphur pit resulted in about three thousand martyrdoms. Approximately thirty thousand Japanese Christians made a final defense of their faith in 1637–1638. Joined by a few ronin and a handful of peasants, a last remnant took refuge in Hara Castle on the Shimabara Peninsula near Nagasaki. Seeking commercial advantage by helping the ruling authority, the Dutch bombarded the castle from the sea while the shogun's forces stormed the fortress and massacred almost all of the defenders. What historian C. R. Boxer had termed "Japan's Christian century" had reached its climax in blood. A few survivors went into hiding. When their religion was finally legalized in the 1870s, their descendants, a group of Japanese "crypto-Christians" or secret Christians, emerged, having concealed their statues, relics, and holy pictures behind figures of Buddha or within Shinto altars.

Between 1635 and 1639, the shogun closed the country to virtually all foreigners. Laws prohibited construction of any ship except small boats suitable for coastal traffic and forbade the return of all Japanese living abroad. Japan entered the era of *Sakoku* (the "Closed Country Policy"), which lasted for the next 215 years. Regulations permitted the Dutch to send one ship a year to the little island of Deshima in Nagasaki harbor, where they submitted to numerous degrading restrictions in order to maintain their limited commercial foothold.

The Bakufu enforced virtual total foreign exclusion to preserve the absolutist system of Ieyasu. Mere expulsion of the missionaries or a suppression of Japanese Christianity would not have accomplished this. Insecure in their supremacy, the successive shoguns saw the seclusion of Japan as the only way to maintain their positions in an authoritarian state.

Japan in Seclusion, 1639-1854

Preparation for Modernization

For more than two centuries Japan remained virtually closed to all outside contact. Far from being a long period of stagnation, however, seclusion proved a time of preparation for eventual modernization.

Largely shut off from the rest of the world, the Japanese developed a fervid nationalism with a corresponding anti-foreign sentiment. This xenophobia, derived from Japan's bitter experiences with Christianity, was stimulated also by humiliations imposed on the subservient Dutch at Deshima. Moreover, Japan's geography was a factor in this conditioning: its physical and political boundaries were one and the same, and its people were homogeneous, making Japan a "perfect nation state." This acute sense of distinction proved a decided asset when the country began to modernize in the nineteenth century's age of nationalism.

While in seclusion Japan had no direct contact with significant European developments such as the Renaissance, the Scientific Revolution, the Enlightenment, or the American or French revolutions, whose ideals of "freedom" constituted the "liberal tradition" of the West. These movements helped to emancipate the Western mind and spirit, culminating in the Industrial Revolution and its achievement of modern technology. Japan's feudal system, however, still conditioned it for modernization in significant ways. Feudalism, founded upon the military tradition, assisted in Japan's later transition to a Western-type army and navy. It also cultivated devotion to the emperor, who symbolized Japanese nationalism; thus, the emperor could provide the leadership for modernization. The feudal system likewise fostered education, providing a relatively literate and informed populace. Finally, the system patronized the merchants' prospering internal trade, which served as the embryo of Japan's international economy.

During seclusion the disciplined dynastic state of the Tokugawa shoguns rested on the foundation of Hideyoshi's social structure and Ieyasu's system of centralized feudalism. The ideals of Neo-Confucianism, with its emphasis on loyalty to superior authority, combined with long-standing military traditions to produce a society governed by a strict code of social ethics. Like a spider web, obligations enmeshed the individual, demanding respect and obedience to lawful superiors and a dedication toward the fulfillment of one's duties. The Japanese developed their own version of the "work ethic," motivated by a cultivated sense of obligation to the group, through which the individual learned effective coordination with others. As the fundamental institution to which the individual owed his loyalty, the family continued to be the core of society. To fail in one's tasks reflected on the honor of one's entire family.

Yet over time the degree of Tokugawa absolutism gradually lessened. As new social problems developed, the shoguns relied increasingly on a burgeoning bureaucracy, tending toward some governmental decentralization. But the basic stability of society remained throughout seclusion because of the fundamental soundness of the Tokugawa governmental structure, its recognized legitimacy as military conquerors of Japan, its Neo-Confucian philosophical foundations, and its historic role as protector of the emperor. Only when the Western intrusion proved the shogun's incapacity to fulfill the last function was the Tokugawa position effectively challenged.

Society and Economy

Seclusion further solidified the class structure; yet by the seventeenth century there were significant changes within society. Merchants found themselves completely cut off from overseas markets, but they prospered due to domestic commerce. These business classes profited from the constant journeys of lords to and from the capital as they complied with the "alternate attendance" law. Because these travelling lords needed housing and food for hundreds of their attendants, the lords' resting places—frequently castle towns—grew into larger communities, especially those located on the main commercial route, the coastal Tokkaido Road from Kyoto to Edo. With growing internal trade, money replaced rice as a more convenient medium of exchange, to the immense gain of the merchants—the monied classes. Towns grew into cities. Osaka and Edo burgeoned; the latter may have been the largest city in the world by the eighteenth century. Edo's growth was conspicuous also because of the elaborate residences built there for the lords. A large merchant class, which had developed from the extensive overseas commerce before seclusion, therefore, congregated in the expanding cities. These businessmen pushed for the reopening of foreign trade to secure markets. They criticized the shogun's closing of the country and felt their new wealth to be incompatible with their social inferiority. Their hostility against the Bakufu intensified as seclusion progressed, and their wealth helped subsidize the eventual overthrow of the Tokugawa regime.

The growing urban areas also consisted of a relatively small group of artisans, who engaged in handicrafts, especially carpentry, pottery, and shoemaking. While these workers profited modestly from the stimulated economy, their restrictive guilds prevented advancement and froze them in their occupations. They, too, blamed the shogun for their plight and thus formed a significant bloc of urban support for the overturn of the Bakufu.

The peasantry, as usual, suffered most grievously. The transition to a money economy resulted in even greater autonomy for the village, putting the peasant at the mercy of his lord. This intensified the economic burden on the peasants as the daimyo crushed them with taxes. Often they could turn only to the usurious local money lender. Throughout the eighteenth century, numerous peasant revolts occurred—descriptively termed "smashings," as all were ruthlessly suppressed. Under Tokugawa martial law, any attempt to depart from the established order earned severe punishment, often death. To protest was fatal. One peasant slipped a note to an inspector, bewailing his lord's oppression. Though the offending lord was punished, the peasant and his wife had to witness the beheading of each of their six children, after which the wretched couple were crucified. For a long period of time, peasants knew only the grinding work of producing rice for the samurai. Understandably, the peasantry also deserted the shogun and eventually supported the emperor's restoration.

Even in the privileged classes many fared disastrously during seclusion. Although the new money economy gradually created some rural autonomy from central governmental control, daimyo wealth, founded on a land or a rice economy, steadily eroded. Land values declined by one-half to two-thirds as money largely replaced rice as the standard of value. Many financially ruined daimyo dismissed their retainers, increasing the number of masterless samurai who marauded the countryside. Burdened with debts, the daimyo often turned to the despised merchants for loans; some became desperate enough to marry their daughters into merchant families. Most impoverished daimyo now also blamed the shogun for their troubles.

Seclusion transformed the samurai most profoundly of all classes. Formerly, the samurai had been the feudal retainers and administrators on the great *han* (estates) and hence the traditional military class. As feudal warfare subsided under the autocratic control of the shogun, the samurai's services as mounted warriors were no longer required. A great number suffered what was regarded as an unbearable fate, sinking into a lower social level. Over time the burgeoning governmental bureaucracy absorbed a substantial number, but the poverty of many samurai drove them, too, to the despised money lenders. Since the samurai class nurtured the sharpest hatred against the administration of Edo, the shogun encouraged all of them to undertake scholarly study in order to cultivate their loyalty. The shogun hoped that the study of Chinese history would deepen samurai devotion to Confucianism, which, as mentioned, placed great emphasis on duties according to one's class, especially loyalty to superiors. The traditional samurai aesthetic interests made their transition to an intellectual class possible, as S. R. Turnbull explained. The shogun also exhorted mastery of such "Martial Arts" as Judo and Kendo, which expressed the ideals of Bushido, the military code. Ironically, the samurai who became scholars found through their studies that Chinese history and Confucianism made no mention of a shogun. Many scholars concluded, therefore, that the shogun had usurped the Japanese emperor's legitimate authority. Moreover, their reading of Japanese history revealed the origins of Shinto and represented another source of renewed reverence for the emperor. The belief in the divine origin of the imperial family through the Sun Goddess won reaffirmation as samurai intellectuals studied the old native religion.

In still another way, the shogun unwittingly undermined the Tokugawa state. After 1720 the shogun permitted samurai scholars to contact the Dutch traders at Deshima for books on Western science. A few of the samurai intellectuals studied the Dutch language and then laboriously translated these European works into Japanese. The study of Western science, especially medicine, came to be called *Rangaku* or "Dutch learning" and proved to some samurai scholars that enforced seclusion was stifling Japan.

As numbers of masterless samurai sank into the commoner classes, their old martial pride inflamed their bitterness against the shogun. Moreover, many of the samurai who became scholars were also estate administrators for the Outside Lords who were only partially reconciled to the Tokugawa government. A segment of these administrators, knowledgeable in world affairs and accustomed to exercising authority, eventually charted the course that removed the Tokugawa shogunate, restored imperial rule, and masterminded Japan's successful adaptation to the modern world. The pronounced changes taking place, however, failed to disrupt the fundamental stability of society due to the continued general recognition of Tokugawa authority. It was the intervention of Westerners in the nineteenth century that profoundly disturbed the situation.

New City Culture

Rapidly growing cities created a new culture. Weary businessmen sought diversion after hours, and places of amusement became centers of a new night life. The theater, Sumo wrestling, the Judo match, bathhouses, and elaborate parties entertained the *Chonin* (townspeople). The Ginza—today the Fifth Avenue of Tokyo—became the amusement area of Edo. The *geisha* ("art person"), a professional entertainer, adept at conversation, food preparation, serving, dancing, and party games, personified this new life. Renowned for her unique hairdo, whitened face and neck, and beautiful *obi* (sash) tied around her lovely *kimono* (robe-like dress), the Geisha was also an accomplished musician, especially on the *samisen* (an instrument similar to the banjo) and the *koto* (a stringed horizontal harp).

This new culture, called the "floating world" or *ukiyo*, was almost exclusively urban and middle class. Artists developed the woodblock print, often depicting city life—particularly its actors and beautiful women—enlivened with humor and caricature. Utilizing the combined talents of a painter, engraver, and printer, the artist made a drawing on translucent paper, pressed it onto a block of cherry wood, then carefully etched it with a knife and chisel. After color was applied with a brush, the block was impressed onto small sheets. Popular among the common people for its decorative qualities, the woodblock print represented a unique art form, known for its simple lines and delicate coloring.

A new literature, called *ukiyo-zoshi* (stories of the ukiyo), dealt mainly with entertainment and affairs of the heart. These salacious stories of amorous young businessmen pursuing a rapid succession of courtesans in places of ill-repute, as well as biographies of prominent actors and actresses, were often just one jump ahead of the shogun's censors. The ukiyo-zoshi bore such titles as *An Amorous Man* and *Twenty Examples of Unfilial Conduct in This Land*. Descriptions of merchants and their business activities, as in *The Everlasting Storehouses of Japan,* represented the more serious side of the new city life.

Of far greater value as literature was the new distinctive form of poetry known as *haiku*. Consisting of only three lines, it comprised seventeen syllables on a 5–7–5 pattern.

> Tsuki ni e o   To the moon, a handle
> sashitaraba yoki   add—a good
> uchiwa kana   fan indeed!

The haiku was up to date in both vocabulary and concept, while its brevity reflected the wit so popular with the townspeople, as well as the sudden enlightenment of Zen. The haiku eventually was used to express humor and satire and even matters of social interest.

A view of Ginza Avenue, Tokyo. Consulate General of Japan, Kansas City.

Sado or Tea Ceremony. Consulate General of Japan, Kansas City.

Popular with the common people was the puppet theater, called *Joruri*, in which small figures were manipulated and moved in rhythm to the accompaniment of a stringed instrument called a *biwa*, while an off-stage narrator told the story. The technique evolved to allow for larger figures, about two-thirds of life size, handled by puppeteers dressed in black. Known as *Bunraku*, these plays were based on tragic themes. The most eminent playwright of this art form, Chikamatsu Monzaemon, is considered the creator of the modern Japanese theater.

The *Kabuki* (derived from a word meaning "to deviate from normal manners and customs") appeared in the seventeenth century as the most significant innovation in drama. Authorities banned it at first because of its use of women and sensuous themes. Forced to use male actors exclusively, Kabuki flourished during the Genroku Era (1688–1703). The players performed upon a stage (*seri*) that revolved for scene changes. Other devices included a section of the stage floor that could be raised and lowered and the *hanamichi*, a runway that extended into the audience. Themes were invariably tragic, usually involving the conflict of *giri* (duty or social obligation) versus *ninjo* (passion or natural inclination). In the typical story line, a boy and a girl (usually a courtesan) fall in love, but their families' objections forbid them to marry. In their frustration, they decide to die together, sometimes by drowning or hanging. Most often the boy slits the throat of his beloved before turning the knife on himself, all in the suicide ritual of *Seppuku*—popularly called *Hara Kiri*.

Another favorite theme stressed the samurai code of honor. The story of the *Forty-Seven Ronin* and their loyalty to their lord became the best-known presentation of the Kabuki. In this story, Asano, a virtuous and kindly lord, drew his sword when publicly insulted by the treacherous Lord Kira, a high official of the shogun. To unsheathe one's sword in the shogun's palace warranted death, so Asano was compelled to commit Seppuku that very night. After Asano's death, his samurai automatically lost their privileged status. Some forty-seven of Asano's loyal retainers swore revenge against Lord Kira, but in order to catch him off guard, they lived dissolute public lives for two years, seemingly accepting their degradation. Then, on an agreed-upon night, they gathered, broke into the unsuspecting Kira's house, slew the wicked lord, and placed his severed head on the grave of their avenged master. After lengthy consideration, the shogun ordered the loyal "forty-seven" to commit Seppuku. This conflict between Bushido, the traditional samurai code of honor, and the law and order of the Tokugawa has thrilled and saddened Kabuki audiences for years. It taught unwavering loyalty to one's lord and, ultimately, to the emperor.

Western Intruders

For the most part, Europeans forgot Japan after 1639, regarding it as an exotic, far-away land of little importance. In the nineteenth century, however, a series of events—the Russian expansion eastward, the forcible opening of China by the British, and the United States' desire to obtain a share of the lucrative oriental trade—threatened Japanese isolation.

Between 1580 and 1640, the Russians had pushed across Siberia to reach the Sea of Okhotsk, or Sea of the Hunter, in search of furs. A commercial center on the Mongolian frontier conducted trade with China after 1727. Japan looked desirable to the Russians as a protective barrier for their Pacific flank, especially considering its strategic position near the mouth of the Ussuri River, important in the China trade. Furthermore, Russian warships, commercial vessels, and fishing boats might obtain provisions at Japanese ports. Although Russia made several attempts to open Japan after 1792, the wars of the French Revolution and Napoleon kept them occupied in Europe.

By the "No Second Thought Edicts" of 1825, the shogun at Edo, Ienari, ordered his port authorities to fire immediately on any foreign intruders. Antiquated Japanese armaments proved inferior against the Westerners, however, and after this date visits by Russian, British, and U.S. ships increased to such a degree △ that individual lords feared to enforce the edict. When the British smashed the Chinese in the First Opium War and acquired the island of Hong Kong, forcing the opening of China in 1842, the anxious shogun modified regulations to permit the provisioning of visiting ships, though the Japanese authorities advised foreigners to depart quickly. The appallingly easy defeat of China had thoroughly alarmed the Japanese. A famous woodblock print exaggeratedly pictured one hundred thousand British ships mobilized on the Thames beneath London Bridge, preparing to transport a million men overseas for the conquest of China. It seemed as if Japan's turn would be next, and its people felt helpless in face of such a threat.

Rather than Russia or Britain, it was the United States which eventually opened Japan. Americans sent their first trading ship to China in 1783 as they edged into what had been a virtual British commercial monopoly. The first American contacts with Japan were made ten years later, when the United States temporarily assumed the trade at Deshima by arrangement with the Dutch, while the Netherlands were under French occupation. The Americans soon discovered at first hand what humiliations the Dutch had endured from the Japanese for a century and a half. When the Dutch resumed their commerce at Deshima in 1815, American whalers kept interest in Japan alive as they recounted tales of the brutal treatment of sailors shipwrecked in Japan. Moreover, the desirability of Japan as a base for the China trade was undeniable. Aaron Palmer, representing New York commercial interests, saw the advantage of opening Japan and, as a friendly gesture, sent his unarmed ship, the *Morrison*, carrying Japanese who had been shipwrecked on Southwest Pacific islands to Nagasaki. His hopes of winning both a commercial agreement and a treaty to protect American whalers were dashed, however, as the Japanese fired on the *Morrison*—then humiliatingly towed it out to sea. Nine years later (1846), Commodore James Biddle entered the harbor at Edo, hoping to open talks on trade, but waiting guards rudely shoved him back into his lifeboat when he tried to come ashore. These facts were well known to the man who succeeded in opening Japan, Commodore Matthew C. Perry.

Perry 2
to the Russo–Japanese War, 1853 to 1905

U.S. naval forces, led by Commodore Matthew C. Perry, opened Japan in 1853–1854, concluding 215 years of seclusion. This foreign intrusion pervaded a fundamentally stable society but caused all internal discontent to center on the shogun, because he could not protect the emperor. As was seen, every major class in the society had its particular grievance against the shogun. Yet Ieyasu had bequeathed an efficient governmental system—especially an effective bureaucracy—to his successors, which was still intact at the time of Perry's arrival. Most likely the Tokugawa could have solved their domestic problems if the West had not intervened.

Perry Opens Japan, 1853–1854

Besides the pressing need of American whalers for reprovisioning ports, Japan had long attracted the United States as a base for East Asian trade. With the development of the steamship, the United States also looked upon Japan as a desirable coaling station on the great circle route to Asia. Commodore Matthew C. Perry sought to advance his country's commercial position in the Far East by acquiring an "American Hong Kong," equivalent to the British trading island off the southern Chinese coast. He favored the acquisition of Okinawa in the Ryukyu Islands, just south of Japan, from which the United States could control the western sea approaches to China, as Britain dominated the eastern approaches. On July 8, 1853, Perry arrived in Japan with "four black ships" (as the frightened Japanese called them) to present a letter from President Millard Fillmore to the emperor, which requested a commercial treaty and protection for American whalers seeking port. Determined on a calm, dignified approach to his "diplomacy," but with an implied threat of force, Perry announced he would return within a year for an answer. Departing from Japan, he laid U.S. claim to both the Ryukyu and Bonin islands and then recoaled in China. He subsequently heard ominous news, however, that a Russian ship had visited Nagasaki. Now there was a danger that the Russians might open Japan before the United States did so. There-fore, Perry returned to Japan early, in February 1854, with a larger fleet. Although informed of Perry's coming by the Dutch, the Japanese knew their seventeenth-century defenses were hopelessly inadequate. By European standards, Japa-nese arms were those of the Thirty Years' War in Europe—more than two hun-dred years behind the West. With his threat of force Perry secured the Treaty of Kanagawa (March 31, 1854), opening two Japanese ports to U.S. trade and promising shelter for shipwrecked American sailors. European powers demanded and received similar agreements soon after. The Americans gave the Japanese a miniature locomotive and railway cars, a telegraph line, and Colt revolvers. The Japanese never had seen these products of modern technology before, but Perry's sailors observed how quickly the Japanese grasped their significance.

Although given warning, the Japanese reacted in consternation as to what to do about the Western visitation. As historian Samuel Eliot Morison says, the American intrusion was seen virtually as a landing of "Men from Mars" to the horrified Japanese. When the shogun took the unprecedented step of asking the emperor and the great lords for advice, these "nationalists" demanded the immediate closing of the country and forcible expulsion of the foreigners. On the other hand, a few lords around the shogun favored opening the country in order to learn foreign technology, especially in armaments. Since the shogun was the traditional defender of the emperor, it was his task to expel the Americans. How-ever, most of the "nationalists" were well aware of the inadequate defenses of the country and of the shogun's inability to carry out their demands for foreign expulsion. It is obvious that the "nationalist" slogan: "Revere the emperor, expel the barbarian," was meant to discredit the Bakufu.

Amidst this confusion, Townsend Harris, the first official U.S. consul, stepped ashore at the little port of Shimoda demanding permanent residence and a full commercial treaty for the United States. For eighteen months, Harris lived in isolation as the Japanese tried to persuade him to depart. With no U.S. fleet to assist him and accompanied only by a young Dutch interpreter, Harris, never-theless, stayed on. When the initial engagements of the Second Opium War again revealed China's weakness before the European great powers, the Japa-nese realized once more how vulnerable they were. After a bitter succession dispute to the shogunate, the Bakufu's adviser contacted Harris and granted his treaty (1858), opening five ports to American trade. This also provided for an exchange of diplomatic representatives, foreign residence at Edo and Osaka, and moderate duties on imports and exports. Thus the agreement fully "opened" Japan to commerce. Within the year the Japanese concluded similar treaties with the major European powers, with Harris acting as mediator. Histo-rian Oliver Statler observed that "Perry had unlocked the door to Japan, but Harris opened it."

The Overthrow of the Shogun, 1858–1867

The Harris treaty, however, enraged many Japanese. A terrorist faction within the "nationalists" began a series of assassinations and antiforeign demonstra-tions. They murdered the shogun's adviser and Harris's young companion. Out-side Yokohama, the samurai guard of a Satsuma lord slashed to death a young

British businessman, Charles L. Richardson. Richardson and his two companions, while on horseback, had refused to yield the road to the lord's procession, which was returning from the required residence at Edo. In retaliation, a British fleet blasted the Satsuma port of Kagoshima.

The emperor now summoned the shogun to Kyoto and demanded the expulsion of the foreigners by the summer of 1863. Forts commanding the Shimonoseki Straits fired on foreign shipping as it entered the western end of the Inland Sea, and in reprisal, an international fleet bombarded Shimonoseki, the main port of the lord of Choshu. Once again modern Western armaments proved superior. The powers held Japan at their mercy, and the Europeans demanded heavy indemnities from the Bakufu and the offending lords.

The shogun was helpless. His arms could not repel the Westerners, and the "nationalists" blamed him because he was the commander-in-chief, the defender of the emperor and the country. "Nationalist" opinion rallied enthusiastically around the emperor and demanded the overthrow of the Bakufu, with Satsuma and Choshu—most prominent of the Outside Lords—leading the movement. The British bombardment of Kagoshima had prompted the Satsuma clan to dispatch several young samurai to England to study naval gunnery. Upon their return a few years later, these men assumed command of the modernized imperial navy. The Choshu clan also sent samurai abroad to gain knowledge of modern ordnance, and from this time on, the Choshu dominated the officer corps of the army.

In desperation, the Bakufu foolishly attacked the estates of the Choshu, who repulsed the shogun's forces with an efficiently trained peasant army equipped with Western arms. In 1866, the main line of the Tokugawa dynasty died out, passing the Bakufu succession to a collateral branch resigned to the emperor's restoration. When the young, well-educated Keiki became shogun, he accepted the Tosa Memorial, which demanded his own resignation, although it assured him that he would head the new imperial council. Almost all lords protested this, however, and demanded that Keiki yield most of his lands. In a brief but futile revolt, the young shogun and his defenders made their last defense of the Bakufu but saw their military and naval forces decisively defeated. A samurai coup, led by Saigo Takamori of Satsuma, captured the gates of the imperial palace in Kyoto from its Tokugawa guards on January 3, 1868. Then a proclamation announced the restoration of power to the emperor. Historian Conrad Totman points out that three groups overthrew the Bakufu: the Outside Lords; the Imperial Court Nobility; and the "Masterless Samurai," acting as terrorists.

Edo (renamed Tokyo, meaning "Eastern Capital," to designate its relation to beloved Kyoto) became the new imperial residence, and the fifteen-year-old Mutsuhito (who became emperor in 1867), assumed the reign name of Meiji—the "Era of Enlightened Rule." At Nijo Castle in Kyoto, the defeated Shogun Keiki announced the end of the Bakufu. On its main building, the imperial crest, with its sixteen-point chrysanthemum, replaced the hollyhocks, the emblem of the Tokugawa. In April 1868, the new emperor appeared in public for the first time before the assembled daimyo and read the Charter Oath, which proclaimed that "wisdom and knowledge shall be sought all over the world," while "all matters would be decided by public opinion." He sounded the theme for the period of modernization to follow.

Early Meiji Reforms

The Samurai Oligarchy

Japan now experienced its second great wave of foreign influence, this time from the West, paralleling its earlier "borrowing" from China. A select group of young samurai, mostly from Satsuma and Choshu, directed the modernization program. Abandoning the slogan "Expel the barbarian," which had brought down the Bakufu, the new regime, in a paradoxical about-face, turned to the West to achieve "a rich country and strong military."

Although definitely a revolution from above, the Meiji reforms were not the result of a class movement. Rather, it was an elite group of young samurai who propelled the reforms. They did not seek to preserve privileged positions and propertied interests. Instead, they acted primarily from national considerations—to defend the independence of their country from the foreign threat. The reformers came from lower-ranking samurai with no special attachment to the old feudal regime. In cooperation with the merchant class they established a capitalistic system because it was in Japan's best interest.

The ruthless Western exploitation of China warned the young Japanese leaders of the penalty of failure. At almost any cost, the country had to be strengthened through Western technology and institutions. Civil war must be averted, for that would invite more foreign intervention and more restrictive treaties for Japan. The young samurai strove to make Japan recognized as an equal with other nations, to rid the country of the hated "unequal treaties" with their "extraterritoriality" (right of Westerners to be tried by their own laws in Japan) and regulations of customs. In the midst of change, however, they skillfully preserved the cultural integrity of their country. As historian Sir George Sansom expressed it, Japan merely dressed its own institutions in Western clothes.

Young, progressive, and energetic, this samurai group used the emperor as the national symbol to hold Japan together on the road to modernization. This samurai oligarchy represented a new, more vigorous Bakufu by their continuance of many features of the old shogun's administration—especially the governmental bureaucracy. Later generations respectfully applied the term *genro* (elder statesmen) to this oligarchy.

Politics and Society, 1868–1877

Japan needed an effective central government and modern armed forces. In 1869, the lords of Satsuma, Choshu, Hizen, and Tosa—to avoid China's fate—voluntarily gave their estates to the emperor. Reluctantly, others followed their example out of fear of civil war and foreign intervention, and two years later, the new government decreed the abolition of feudalism, thus placing all power in the hands of the central authority. The new leaders gave preferential treatment to the disgruntled daimyo, however, appointing many of them governors of the new prefectures—seventy-seven in number—or awarding them other official positions. These prefectures conformed to the boundaries of the old estates as closely as possible; in a sense, the most important daimyo gained back their estates with new designations. Although these measures gave the daimyo only one-tenth of their former incomes as salaries, the government abolished the crushing debts they had accumulated. Overall, the daimyo fared quite well, and their privileged positions continued when new Western titles of nobility—baron, marquis, count, etc.—replaced their traditional designations of rank.

Unlike the daimyo, the samurai as a class did not fare as well from modernization. Permanently detached from their profession as warriors, they were forbidden to wear the topknot and the traditional two swords. As compensation, annual pensions were granted them, representing two-thirds of their former incomes. However, when a lump-sum payment terminated these pensions in 1876, the great majority of samurai sank into commoner status. A few entered government service and the police forces, and a few more enlisted in the army. A small number, however, wisely invested their government pensions in new business enterprises—such as textiles, iron, and steel—and became officials and administrators. This fortunate segment of former samurai came to dominate management, bringing their old feudal ideals of loyalty, service, and patronage into the new business structures. The solicitude of the employer for his employees and their attachment to him and the company, so evident in Japanese business today, is a direct heritage from the old feudal system. Mitsubishi, probably the best-known business association in modern Japan, established itself as a samurai organization. Begun as a shipping line, in later years it engaged in mining, manufacturing, marketing, and banking enterprises.

For the most part, the merchant class financially supported the imperial restoration and adapted well to Meiji reforms. The traditional commoner subservience of the merchants during the Tokugawa period, however, lingered on and discouraged their undertaking management of the new industries. The need to establish a modern economy made the merchants indispensable, but most remained in their customary commercial and financial ventures and did not enter the new industries until the samurai had taken over administration. Two exceptions were the merchant-established organizations of Mitsui and Sumitomo, both dating from the seventeenth century. These companies were involved in mining, manufacturing, banking, and shipping.

Although reforms returned much land to the peasantry, this class still suffered from the old grievances, and was saddled with a new burden. When Japan introduced universal conscription in 1872 to provide an effective armed force, the bulk of the military obligation fell on the peasants, despite the fact that the measure applied to all classes. Yamagata Aritomo, the "father of the Japanese army," became minister of war and built a national army modeled on the Prussian system. He established the right of the chief of staff to approach the emperor directly and made it clear that the ruler exercised supreme command of the army and navy, thus guaranteeing the independence of the armed forces from the civil government. A German, Major Jakob von Meckel, spent nine years instructing the Japanese army, while Captain John Ingles, a British officer, trained the imperial navy. Yamagata established six military districts, each with it own garrison, and by 1874, Japan had a standing army of about thirty-two thousand, a force considered adequate to suppress any civil disturbance.

The Final Resistance of Feudalism, 1877

The new army strengthened the government against civil war. Many samurai, however, were still bitter at their loss of privileged rank and indignant to find their pensions provided insufficient income. The ruling genro sought to allay the hostility of this former warrior class, numbering almost two million, and a proposed military expedition against Korea in 1873 seemed to offer a solution, because the Korean king had insulted Japanese representatives when they had solicited diplomatic relations. Korea was in seclusion as Japan had been before 1853. The Japanese leadership hoped that an armed invasion to punish the Koreans would unite the country in a national cause while offering the samurai an outlet for their military talents and pent-up frustration. At the same time, the expedition would thrust Japan's influence into Korea ahead of the Westerners. Saigo Takamori, a samurai from Satsuma who had led the decisive coup in 1868, favored this campaign, but a diplomatic mission returned from Europe with a warning of possible Western intervention if such a venture were undertaken. Iwakura Tomomi, the spokesman for this group, used every argument against the Korean attack and persuaded the government to abandon the plan, leaving Saigo spurned and resentful. Hoping to placate the disgruntled Saigo and his followers, the ruling group undertook some safer ventures. Feeling a need to show the exact extent of its sovereignty to foreign powers, Japan incorporated the Ryukyu Islands in 1874, thus thwarting a Chinese claim. The following year, Japan exchanged its possession of Sakhalin Island for Russia's claim to the Kuriles. Then, following the example of Perry, a small Japanese flotilla officially "opened" Korea in 1876. In retrospect the decision not to undertake the Korean invasion in 1873 proved fortunate, since it forced the Japanese to postpone expansion on the Asiatic continent in favor of internal reform and consolidation. By the 1890s, Japan's government was functioning effectively under a constitution, and industrialization moved well on its way when Japan began its imperium against China.

Disappointed over the abandonment of the Korean expedition, the angry Saigo accused the government of betraying samurai ideals and resigned. Sullenly, he withdrew to his estates. When the government attempted to seize his store of arms at Kagoshima, he raised a revolt. About forty thousand resentful samurai, furious over the abolition of the wearing of two swords and virtually impoverished by the commutation of pensions, joined his insurrection. This Satsuma Rebellion of 1877 represented the final resistance of feudalism against modernization. The government's new Prussian-trained conscript army crushed Saigo's forces, a triumph of the new order over the old. The samurai suffered their ultimate humiliation—defeat by the despised commoners. Saigo committed Seppuku in a last defense of his honor, and from this time forward, the feudal order became reconciled to the changing times.

Later Meiji Reforms

Economy and Society, 1877–1889
During the Meiji era, Japan adopted the facade of Westernization yet retained its own essential traditions. Continuity consisted in the retention of historic values (especially group orientation), contrasting with changes in cultural content and large-scale institutional and organizational forms. Although contradictory in many ways, these forces combined to hasten Japan toward modernization.

To secure Japan's agricultural base, the government paid relatively liberal cash subsidies to farmers. Combined with the abolition of feudal taxes and increased peasant ownership of land, crop yield per acre increased by 21 percent in the 1880s. Total agricultural production doubled again in the next twenty-five years. To coordinate the strategic industries on which modern military power depended, the government took over the metallurgical foundries from the great clans, which had successfully adapted Western technology to the manufacture of arms and the construction of steamships. The government established new shipyards, most notably at Nagasaki, and munitions factories at Tokyo and Osaka.

The government next began to build railroads and telegraph lines. The first railway, built in 1872, ran twenty miles from Tokyo to Yokohama, carrying four thousand tons of freight and two thousand passengers by 1880. Another railway from Kobe to Osaka, completed in 1874, was extended to Kyoto three years later. However, railway construction was difficult in mountainous Japan, and by 1881 there were only about seventy-six miles of track. Telegraph lines, important for administrative control over the nation, were cheaper to construct and spread more rapidly, connecting most of the major cities by 1880. Although foreigners advised and invested in this construction, the Japanese urged their prompt departure upon completion of their work and quickly repaid international loans. Japan did not want to be shackled like China by foreign interests.

Because of lack of private funds for investment in the new industries, the government took over a number of iron, copper, and coal mines in the 1870s, especially in northern Honshu. In Tokyo, the government managed factories for the production of machine tools, glass, and brick. Moreover, the ruling group operated the woolen and cotton mills, important to the new Japanese interest in Western clothes. Silk production did not require a large factory system, as silk reeling could be accomplished in small farm cottages where it was processed by hand. Although the government built three plants in the large cities, applying steam and water power to manufacture, most silk processing was completed in the rural areas. In the 1880s, silk represented 42 percent of Japanese exports. Because of foreign demand, silk export gave a favorable trade balance to Japan by 1885 and was a ready source of national revenue.

In order to finance modernization, the government sold a number of industries, many of which were losing money by the early 1880s, to private concerns at a fraction of their original investment. The new managers of these concerns often held government positions, which ensured continued close cooperation between government and industry, a carry-over from the Tokugawa. Since Japan was a young, struggling industrial power, it eliminated internal competition in favor of national economic coordination. A handful of people manipulated the Japanese economy, combining many activities—manufacturing, banking, and commerce—under one management. These conglomerates were called *zaibatsu* and resembled American trusts or European cartels. German neo-mercantilism—featuring a strict governmental control of the economy—served somewhat as the prototype. Matsukata Masayoshi, a former samurai from Satsuma who became finance minister in 1881, created the Bank of Japan the following year and achieved financial solvency for the country five years later.

Japanese industrial success was not solely due to government direction. Much credit must be given to privately operated industries and to the dedicated and hard-working labor force, conditioned by feudal traditions to respect authority. Regardless of one's level in society, the interests of the emperor and the nation came first.

everyone is calling it the stupere
I started it.

Law and Education; Cultural Continuity

The Meiji reforms sought Japanese "equality" among other nations as a major goal. The Japanese chose the French Napoleonic Code for their legal system but changed to the German model after 1896, hoping to eliminate the despised extraterritoriality. Western concepts of individual land ownership supplanted family possession of property. Legal rights, rather than traditional social obligations, inspired the new laws. Individual liability somewhat replaced group responsibility, and such practices as government-sanctioned torture became unlawful. Gradually, the great powers revised the treaties. The British finally withdrew their last extraterritorial rights in 1899. Other countries followed, and by 1911, all had withdrawn their "unequal treaties." Japan had gained complete sovereignty over its own land—a significant achievement for the Meiji era.

Education played a decisive part in modernizing society. Many Japanese students went to college in Europe and the United States and returned to take government positions. Universities trained Japanese in European languages, philosophy, law, and science, providing these studies as a practical benefit to the country. The French educational system, later modified by the American, became the Japanese model. Dr. David Murray of Rutgers University served as adviser to the Ministry of Education for six years after 1873. Missionary schools dominated much of lower education for girls. Tokyo University, founded in 1877, was the first of several imperial universities, while Sophia University was a notable private institution established by the Jesuits. This highly centralized educational system developed almost 100 percent literacy in Japan.

Japan's security demanded modernization, yet it held firmly to essential historic ideals and institutions. Business and industrial organization, although established on the German model, actually preserved the values of the old feudal system. The new imperial army and navy, although German and British in organization, still honored their samurai traditions behind its Western facade. The educational system, although French and American on the surface, instilled loyalty and devotion to the emperor. Renewed stress upon the emperor's historical divinity stimulated popular support for the various Meiji reforms (and later for the rise of the military in the 1930s). Modernization meant the imposition of European institutions onto Japanese traditions, but with the latter always predominant.

I think you have a floor meeting right now... you should come back when it's done.

The Constitution of 1889

The best example of Japanese adaptation of Western institutions was the Constitution of 1889. Intended to form the basis of a modern government, it also preserved Japan's traditional political authoritarianism. After the suppression of feudal protest in the Satsuma Rebellion of 1877, liberal agitators attacked the government, demanding full popular participation. They pointed out that the emperor's Charter Oath (1868) had promised that important questions "would be decided by public opinion," which they understood to mean the institution of representative assemblies. Two political parties, the Jiyuto and the Kaishinto, were organized in 1881, and although both were fairly moderate, they accused the genro oligarchy of monopolizing power. Liberals demanded a representative assembly, a universal franchise, and a national constitution. Newspapers used Western political slogans to criticize the government. Much of this, how-

Samurai who were modernizing Japan in the emperor's name

ever, was only clan protest against the Satsuma-Choshu domination, showing the still smoldering enmity of the majority of samurai and the tenuous Japanese grasp of European political processes.

Ito Hirobumi, most prominent of the genro, went to Europe in 1882 and selected the German imperial constitution as Japan's model. Like Japan, Germany was a new national state that revered the military profession and had a long historical tradition of political authoritarianism. Proclaimed in 1889, the Japanese constitution met the minimum demands of the liberals for a two-house legislature, the *Diet*, yet preserved the central position of the genro by making the imperial cabinet dependent only on the emperor's appointment. The elder statesmen thus retained their rule through the emperor, in many ways continuing the authoritarian tradition of the Tokugawa in Western guise. Likewise, the constitution ensured the preeminence of the military by placing the cabinet posts of war and navy ministers beyond civilian control. Minister of War Yamagata instituted a regulation in 1900 requiring that these positions be filled only by officers of the two highest ranks. The army and navy, therefore, could block the formation of any cabinet simply by refusing to name someone to these offices. The Diet consisted of two bodies: a House of Peers, selected by imperial appointment and numbering some 363 members; and a House of Representatives, whose 463 delegates were elected by a very restricted franchise, barely 2 percent of the population. The Constitution of 1889 was as democratic as most documents in the West, however, and represented the principal Japanese response to Western pressures as well as to their own internal situation.

Japanese Foreign Expansion, 1890-1902

Beginning in the 1890s, Japan sought to recover its commercial position in East and Southeast Asia, forfeited during the seclusion era. By the time Perry "opened" Japan, European interests had already staked out most of the region. Only portions of northern China and Korea remained unclaimed, and Japan coveted these as population outlets and sources of raw materials. The era of Japanese expansionism had begun. Just as modernization after 1868 had accelerated Japan's internal development, compensating for time lost during seclusion, so expansionism after 1894 promised to enhance Japan's diminished international position. Japanese expansion, therefore, was the foreign political counterpart to Meiji domestic reforms. Most immediately, it concerned Korea and the abrogation of the unequal treaties. In the long range, it sought to reinforce national security and achieve the economic well-being of the state.

Expansion, moreover, acted as a shield against further Western imperialism. The Japanese regarded East Asia as a vacuum still attractive to the world's great powers. Hoping to protect the approaches to its island empire, Japan sought what influence it could in south Manchuria and the acquisition of Korea and Formosa (known today as Taiwan) as a "defense perimeter." At the same time, an aggressive foreign policy tended to quiet the domestic scene in Japan. The political parties, resenting their exclusion from effective power by the controlling genro, protested continuously in the Diet, and the government, in turn, used foreign policy to promote national unity. Advocates of expansionism also hoped to terminate the last of Japan's hated unequal treaties especially those which

regulated the collection of customs, limiting the national income. Thus, the ruling genro saw the opportunity to obtain full control of Japan's trade, free from
treaty restrictions.

A direct threat to Japan, however, came from Russia when Count Sergius
Witte became the tsar's finance minister in 1892 and led a new Russian policy of
slow economic penetration of northern China. Witte inspired the construction of
the Trans-Siberian Railway, connecting St. Petersburg, the Russian capital, with
the port of Vladivostok on the Sea of Japan. The Russians stirred Japanese
concern for Korea and ultimately for Japan itself. Korea attracted Russia because its long, indented coastline provided ideal ports to serve as the eastern
terminus of the new railway.

When a nationalist revolt erupted in Korea, Japan clashed with China over
suppression of the rebellion. Korea long had been a dependency of China, but
the relationship was tenuous—one that Russia could exploit—and Japan attacked
China to forestall a Russian advance. In this Sino-Japanese War (1894–1895)
Japan astonished the world with its victories on land and sea. China had undertaken a program of modernization similar to Japan's, and most observers expected China to overwhelm the island empire. Instead, Japanese armies invaded
Korea, while the Japanese navy defeated the Chinese in the battle of the Yalu.
The victorious Japanese could have gone on to capture Peking, and suddenly
the world's powers greatly feared the disintegration of the "Celestial Empire."
China's defeat proved to be its greatest humiliation of the nineteenth century,
since Japan once had been a dependency of China. The Treaty of Shimonoseki
(April 1895) awarded the victor an indemnity, the Pescadores Islands, the island
of Formosa, and the strategic Port Arthur, which controlled the sea lanes to Peking. However, Russia saw its position in northern China endangered and persuaded Germany and France to join with it to stop Japan. Germany was eager
for a Chinese port of its own, while France had tied itself to Russia by the Dual
Alliance of 1891–1894. This Triple Intervention demanded that Japan revise its
treaty with China by returning Port Arthur, because of its proximity to the Chinese capital.

Japan was powerless to resist the Triple Intervention; the European powers
could have used their navies to blockade its home islands, cutting off its armies
still on the continent. Nor had Japan an ally to assist it. Great Britain remained
neutral upon Japan's pledge not to disrupt British concessions in the Shanghai
area. Yet the British were deeply disturbed at Russia's actions, which they felt
posed a threat to British domination of Far Eastern trade. Britain had supported
China as protection for the Indian frontier against possible Russian penetration,
but even Britain's vast sea power could not prevent the Russian exploitation of
China by land (via the Trans-Siberian Railway). Therefore, British diplomats now
began to look to Japan as the best check against tsarist imperialism.

Abandoned by Britain, China turned to Russia for protection in a treaty of
alliance in 1896. Peking gave permission for Russia's construction of a branch
of the Trans-Siberian Railway across Manchuria. At the same time, the French
concluded railway agreements to run lines from Southeast Asia to southern China.
The Dual Alliance thus exploited China, north and south. With the collapse of the
"Celestial Empire" apparently imminent, the powers seized its ports, hurrying to

grab slices of the "Chinese melon." The Germans, angered at their exclusion by the French and Russians, took the city of Tsingtao, which controlled the entry to the Yellow River valley, one of the richest areas of China. Then Russia infuriated Japan by leasing Port Arthur, which Japan had relinquished only three years earlier.

The United States stepped in to proclaim the "open door," which guaranteed commercial access to China for all nations. While the American doctrine halted further partition of China, the outbreak of the Boxer Rebellion (1900) spread havoc throughout that country, threatening all foreign holdings in a furious burst of Chinese nationalism. The Boxers besieged the British legation in Peking, where most of the Westerners had taken refuge. Japan, eager to make a good impression on the West, furnished half of the international force that smashed the rebellion and rescued the Western hostages. The Russians, however, took the opportunity to occupy Manchuria, a direct threat to Western interests in northern China and to Japan as well.

Japan had a serious decision to make. It could conclude an alliance with Russia or with Great Britain. Count Ito favored Russia and proposed the "Exchange Policy," whereby Japan would accept Russia's position in Manchuria if Russia would assent to Japan's domination of Korea. On the other hand, Premier Katsura wanted the British alliance, regarding war with Russia as inevitable. The Japanese conducted simultaneous talks with both countries—Ito in the Russian capital of St. Petersburg, and Baron Hayashi, Japan's minister, in London. The Russians, however, refused to cede Korea, because the tsar's military advisers failed to recognize Japan's power potential. When Ito was unable to get Russian acceptance of the "Exchange Policy," Tokyo concluded the Anglo-Japanese Alliance on February 11, 1902. Japan thus dispelled its perilous isolation of 1895. In effect, this alliance promised Britain's benevolent neutrality in case Japan went to war with Russia. Should another power (France) come to Russia's assistance, then Britain would actively join in the hostilities. The Anglo-Japanese Alliance remained the cornerstone of Japanese foreign policy for the next twenty years. The prestige of an alliance with the world's greatest sea power indicated Japan's full acceptance as an equal by the nations of the world—one of the primary goals of Meiji policy.

The Russo-Japanese War, 1904–1905

Both Britain and Japan hoped their alliance would persuade Russia to evacuate Manchuria peacefully. The Russians, however, remained confident that neither Britain's sea power nor Japan's untested army could dislodge their position in northern China. The Russian military attaché in Tokyo described the Japanese troops as an "infant force," unable to challenge the weakest European army for at least another hundred years. Realizing the hopelessness of negotiation, Japan attacked the Russian fleet at Port Arthur in February 1904, without a declaration of war. The Japanese army invaded Korea, eventually defeating the tsar's main army at Mukden (Shenyang), Manchuria—the greatest battle in history for sheer manpower up to that time. In the meantime, General Nogi Maresuke commanded the Japanese capture of Port Arthur on January 1, 1905, a furious campaign in which his two sons died in the final assault. During the fighting the

Russians found the problem of supply tremendously difficult over the still incomplete Trans-Siberian Railway.

The British forced the Turks to close the Bosporus, bottling up the tsar's Black Sea fleet, while London refused use of the Suez Canal to the Russians. In a last desperate thrust for victory, the Russian Baltic fleet make a tortuous six-month voyage from northern Europe around the tip of southern Africa, heading for the eastern port of Vladivostok on the Sea of Japan. There Admiral Heihachiro Togo mobilized the Japanese imperial navy. Utilizing British intelligence via the newly invented radio, Togo had been tracking the Russian fleet, which he intercepted in the Straits of Tsushima. The Japanese administered a crushing defeat to the Russians, destroying thirty-two of their thirty-eight ships and capturing their commander. For the first time, an Asian nation had defeated a major European power, sending a thrill through the hearts of those subject peoples, burdened with Western imperialism (notably the Chinese), who now looked to Japan with admiration.

The Japanese asked President Theodore Roosevelt to mediate the peace settlement at Portsmouth, New Hampshire, in August–September 1905. Despite the victory, the war had financially drained Japan, and Russia's refusal to pay an indemnity seriously divided the conference. Count Witte, representing the tsar, gained the support of the American press, although Roosevelt sought to create "balanced antagonisms" to neutralize Russia and Japan in East Asia. In the final treaty, Japan obtained Port Arthur, the southern portion of Sakhalin Island, and unquestioned predominance in Korea. Their failure to recover war costs through a Russian indemnity, however, prompted their unmet demands for the annexation of Manchuria, where most of the war had been fought.

Bitter over the outcome of the conference, the Japanese accused the United States of depriving them of their full benefits of victory. Following the conference, a massive anti-American riot resounded from Tokyo's Hibaya Park in September 1905. The ruling oligarchy had so controlled the press during the war that the people did not realize their country's total exhaustion. Although victorious, Japan was militarily and financially depleted. There was no alternative to peace. The American-Japanese estrangement, eventually climaxing at Pearl Harbor, began here. However, Japan's victories over China and Russia had confirmed the success of modernization and allowed it to dominate the western Pacific, now virtually "a Japanese lake."

Militarism

3

to the "Economic Miracle," to Recession, 1905 to 1995

The Meiji leaders achieved Japan's security and status as a world power by mastering Western technology, yet they managed to hold fast to their own cultural heritage. Japan continued to grow in the twentieth century, becoming a great industrial nation, making the words "Made in Japan" a universal slogan. Its people succeeded admirably despite social problems induced by a growing population and labor difficulties, as well as a crisis of cultural priorities forced by rapid modernization. Japan's surplus population and growing industrialism demanded more and more raw materials. Choosing to follow its military leadership, Japan continued in its quest for empire in East and Southeast Asia. Almost simultaneously, the United States sought an imperial position in the same areas. The two expansion efforts eventually collided. For Japan the emperor, once again, acted as the national symbol; this time his leadership ultimately resulted in defeat in World War II.

Japanese Foreign Expansion, 1905–1922

The threat of rising German military power preoccupied the European nations after 1905. As a result, Japan had East Asia virtually to itself. Theodore Roosevelt's "balanced antagonisms" proved a myth when Japan and Russia reached agreements in 1907 and 1910, in which they defined their spheres of influence in northern China. Japan annexed Korea in 1910, and as a British ally during World War I, captured Germany's possessions in China and the southwest Pacific. China now lay at the mercy of Japan, and the United States and Britain feared Japan's free hand. The Japanese government did not ignore the opportunity, and in January 1915, they formally confronted President Yüan Shih-k'ai of China with the "Twenty-one Demands," transferring important iron and coal mines, extending concession leases, and forcing Yüan to accept Japanese advisers into his government. Such a move would have transformed China into a puppet state. The abrupt tone of the ultimatum—presented on war department stationery with watermarks of artillery, rifles, and other weapons—branded Japan as an imperialist to the Chinese. Many Chinese students like Sun Yat-sen (the "father of the Chinese revolution") became disillusioned with Japan as a model for the new China. At China's secret request, the United States intervened to moderate some of the demands, although Yüan gave in and signed a weakened version in May 1915. Most of the Twenty-one Demands, however, were never enacted, again leaving Japan bitter against the United States, essentially for what many Japanese regarded as Washington's much-too-rigid adherence to the open door policy.

Japanese expansion found another area in 1918 when the army participated in a joint allied occupation of eastern Siberia with the United States. When the allies withdrew at the end of World War I, Japan remained in the area, increasing its force to seventy thousand men, installing its own regime in eastern Siberia, and occupying northern Sakhalin Island as a bulwark against Bolshevism. Simultaneously, Japan's ruthless suppression of the Korean revolt (April 1919), in which the Koreans sought freedom from a brutal Japanese colonial rule, shocked the Versailles Conference in Europe. Some Westerners talked of war, but neither Britain nor the United States was prepared to take this step.

At the same time, Japanese business interests desired reconciliation with Europe and the United States and the restoration of normal trade, which had been damaged by strained relations with the West. Consequently, in the 1920s Japan embarked on a course of international cooperation and peaceful economic expansion, especially in China. These policies won almost universal acceptance in the liberal, economically interdependent post–World War I world. In the meantime, the Siberian occupation had lasted for four years and had discredited the military. All the while, some of the dominions in the British Empire wanted to drop the Anglo-Japanese Alliance, fearing their possible involvement in the event of a Japanese-American conflict. The United States, Japan, and the European powers also sought to avert a ruinous naval race during the postwar depression.

At the Washington Conference (1921–1922) the United States, Great Britain, and Japan agreed to limit the building of capital ships (i.e., warships of 10,000 tons and larger) and promised to construct no new fortifications on their island possessions. Each of the Pacific powers now thought it was relatively secure in East Asia, and the conference temporarily resolved many regional problems. Japan felt content that it had secured its naval supremacy in the Western Pacific. Its acquiescence in the Washington agreements proved Japan's resolution to work with the Western maritime powers, especially on the China question. This policy, however, proved severely disappointing to Japan over the next ten years. Winston Churchill observed, moreover, that in the overall "the annulment of the alliance caused a profound impression and was viewed as the spurning of an Asiatic power by the Western World"—still another road to World War II had opened.

Politics under the Meiji Constitution, to 1921

As mentioned, government under the Meiji constitution of 1889 carried over many aspects of traditional Tokugawa absolutism. Although democratic in appearance, the constitution emphasized the emperor's divinity, retained the old class structure, and extolled the military. It provided for a very restrictive franchise, allowing only 1 percent of the adult population to vote. Actually, the various "elites" ran the government: the army and navy; the governmental bureaucracy; the immediate advisers of the emperor (especially the Imperial Council); the zaibatsu (the clique of business giants); and the leading politicians of the Diet. All of these groups were almost completely above popular control. Critics have called the constitution ultra-conservative and considered its favoritism toward the military and its glorification of the emperor at least partly responsible for Japanese military expansionism through World War II.

Ito had formulated the constitution to preserve genro domination of the government. In the strict separation of powers, the executive was made independent of the majority in the Diet. The political parties thus were barred from the imperial cabinet. The Jiyuto and Kaishinto groups resented their exclusion; but through control of state finances they could defeat appropriation bills brought up before the Diet, so that yearly budgets proved inadequate for the increasing costs of national economic expansion. The parties were thus able to wield more power than the framers of the constitution had intended, and politicians soon demanded representation in the cabinet.

Continuing the Satsuma-Choshu monopoly of executive offices, Ito and Yamagata alternated as premiers between 1890 and 1898, with genro party contention quiet only during the Sino-Japanese War. A few party leaders entered the cabinet in these years, but Yamagata fought to keep the cabinet free of party direction. Popular support increased party strength, however, inspiring Ito to form his own group in 1900. The effective organization of this Seiyukai party won bureaucratic support and attracted many defectors from other political factions. The Seiyukai dominated the Diet for the next twelve years, and while Ito was premier (1900–1903), the Diet and cabinet put aside their struggles. Ito's resignation, however, concluded the genro domination of the premiership, although their waning influence continued through the Seiyukai. Baron Saionji, a genro protegé and heir of the old imperial court aristocracy, then held the office, often alternating with Katsura, a front for Yamagata. They represented a new generation of elder statesmen. The real power of government gradually passed to the rank and file of the parties after Hara Kei, a former samurai from northeastern Japan (thus removed from Satsuma-Choshu domination), became Home Minister in 1905. As organizational leader of the Seiyukai, Hara Kei skillfully manipulated his party, becoming Japan's most esteemed parliamentarian of the twentieth century. Appointed premier in 1918, Hara began the era of postwar democracy.

Although not a democratic document, the Meiji constitution proved a successful political foundation for the Japanese. It presided over the era of Japan's industrial expansion and its rise to great-power status. It even made possible the peaceful deposition of the insane Taisho emperor in 1921 and the institution of a regency under his son, Hirohito. Probably, the enormous technological, economic, and social changes undertaken by the Japanese in the early twentieth century required an authoritarian governmental system. At the same time, however, the Meiji constitution made possible a gradual political liberalization upon which Japanese democracy is built today, although the original framers of that document did not intend it that way.

Social and Economic Problems, to 1931

One of the tragedies of Japan's modernization was its failure to share benefits equally with the majority of its people. While the population increased from 30 million in the mid-nineteenth century to 64 million in 1931 and to 73 million by World War II, the zaibatsu managers of industry poured their huge profits back into more economic expansion. The rural and urban sectors of society paid for technological advancement with hard labor, receiving few material benefits in return.

In the countryside, after the overthrow of the shoguns and their feudal system, the peasants, theoretically, were freed from tenant farming. Many poor peasants, however, sought the protection of great lords once again because of a shortage of arable land. At the time of the Meiji Restoration, tenant farmers tilled about 25 to 30 percent of the rural areas. Most farm families (about 35 percent) were both owners and tenants; only about 20 percent owned no land whatsoever. Most Japanese lords were small landowners, with little more than they could cultivate themselves. Peasant wages remained low because of the combination of overpopulation and scarcity of fertile soil. Many engaged in the processing of silk. With the exception of the great estates, most holdings did not exceed two and one-half acres. Most peasants lived in small, single-room cottages made of wood, with tiled roofs, and they cultivated mostly rice and tea with simple hand tools.

In the cities an abundant labor supply meant low wages and substandard living conditions. There were no restrictions on hours of work until the mid-1920s. Many workers suffered from tuberculosis, and children often toiled fourteen hours a day. For most of the urban poor, a bland diet centered around rice. Wretched housing in sprawling slums, mostly tenements, jammed families together in miserable, crowded conditions. Commonly, three generations of a family lived in one unit, consisting usually of two rooms.

Undoubtedly, Japan's greatest natural catastrophe occurred September 1–3, 1923, when the gargantuan Tokyo Earthquake and the resultant fires jolted the capital. More than 140,000 Japanese perished due to that quake of an 8.2 magnitude. Historian Edward Seidensticker's descrption is classic. He laments especially the destruction of much of the "Low City" of Tokyo, the home of merchants and artisans, and the heart of old Edo. More persons died in the fires than from the initial shock, and still more drowned while seeking refuge in the Sumida River than were crushed by collapsing walls. It was the most destructive natural disaster ever to strike an urban area. With their nation situated on the restless Pacific Rim, Japanese know first-hand the unpredictability of nature, the most recent example of which was the January 1995 earthquake that devastated the port city of Kobe, killing some five thousand people and causing somewhere between $30–$80 billion in damage.

Rural dwellers had their problems as well. Farming parents often sold their daughters to work long hours in the urban factories. The typical factory workforce consisted of young girls in their late teens, between graduation and marriage, who comprised a huge, pliable, and surprisingly skilled labor force. The peculiar "double structure" of Japanese industry, however, created oppressive working conditions for these girls. A few large firms controlled thousands of small shops, some with only ten workers, engaged in the preliminary stages of manufacture. Larger industries were heavily dependent upon these exploitative "sweat shops" for some of the simpler, but essential, tasks of production.

After the Russo-Japanese War, about six hundred thousand workers made up the labor force (many of whom worked in small enterprises employing 5–10 persons). Spurred by World War I's industrial expansion, the working body numbered almost 1,700,000 by 1920, when labor unions finally gained legal recognition. At that time there were eighty-six recognized unions, plus many illegal ones associated with Marxian socialism, which attracted many worker-followers when the Japanese Communist party was established in 1922. By the 1930s, there were over three hundred labor unions, but working conditions showed little improvement. In the 1920s, especially, there were always too many workers for too few jobs. As the military rose after 1931, government regulations ensured union cooperation as the industrial worker now labored to feed a ravenous war machine. By this time, 45 percent of the Japanese lived in large cities of over ten thousand, as even more workers migrated to the urban areas from the farms.

In spite of its social problems, Japan's literacy rate remained high, since state schools in urban and rural communities provided education for everyone. Japan was the first Asian country to require education through the first six grades. The curriculum consisted of Chinese literature, Confucian philosophy, Western science, Japanese history, and some foreign languages. Through so-called "morals classes," students were indoctrinated in loyalty to the emperor and national patriotism. The system sought to cultivate a dutiful, cooperative individual, willing to take his or her rightful place in a firmly fixed pattern of society.

Democracy and Intellectualism in the 1920s

During the 1920s, Japanese cities dazzled the public with new crazes: jazz, zesty novels, flappers, noisy bars, movies, phonographs, sexy magazines, flashing advertising signs, and radios. Almost everything Western became the rage. The old three-generation household was being replaced by the one-generation family. Young men and women dated freely, a breach of old social customs, and they drank, smoked, read newspapers, listened endlessly to phonograph records, and kept late hours. Young people also frequented the Ginza, the great entertainment district of Tokyo with its theaters and restaurants, and shopped on Sundays in its great stores. These times saw the emergence of the one-piece bathing suit, the permanent wave, the dance hall and cabaret, and the bare-legged chorus line. All this witnessed Japan's evolution to an urban-centered society. Tokyo, with a population over six million, had become the world's third-largest city, behind only London and New York.

The 1920s saw the decade of so-called "democracy," seemingly the wave of the future because of the allied victory in World War I. Political parties attained their greatest influence, especially the Seiyukai, as Premier Hara Kei established the first genuine party government in 1918. Agitation for universal manhood suffrage, women's rights, and legislation to improve the lot of the worker became popular issues. Extension of the franchise, achieved in 1925, increased the size of the electorate from three to twelve million. The cabinet of Kato Komei, a professional Meiji bureaucrat, also enacted a National Health Insurance Law and a Labor Disputes Law, which strengthened the moderate trade unions. From 1924 to 1932, the more influential parties controlled the imperial cabinet. The practice of selecting the premier from the majority in the legislature might have become permanently established, but it was stopped after 1932. The era of democracy did not greatly alleviate the distress of the laboring and peasant classes, so the support for the political parties was critically weakened.

The United States had barred the immigration of Chinese since 1882; and when Japanese immigration to the United States substantially increased after 1918, American workers demanded the same restrictions against them. Congress expressly excluded Japanese from emigrating to the United States in 1924 (and did not rectify the situation until 1953). Japan's deepest sensibilities—the desire to be "equal" in the family of nations—were injured by this action. In 1930, U.S. restrictions on trade with Japan through the Smoot-Hawley Tariff Bill struck at another sensitive area. These recent U.S. actions, along with the earlier termination of the Anglo-Japanese Alliance at the Washington Conference, angered many Japanese and gravely weakened the position of the liberal parties in Japan, since both the United States and Great Britain had been held up by them as the great parliamentary democracies of the world.

Intellectualism in twentieth-century Japan reflected the tremendous uncertainties stirred by modernization. The conflict involved those who defended the paths of change against many who charged that modernization repudiated Japanese heritage. Defenders of Meiji reforms supported the constitution as the rightful preserver of *kokutai*—the concept that the emperor is the state. The emperor derived from an unbroken imperial lineage and presided over his people as a family, while preserving their unique racial unity, according to Hozumi Yatsuka, a noted professor of public law. Ito Hirobumi had espoused this ideal in defense of absolute authority for the emperor. Minobe Tatsukichi, professor of constitutional law at Tokyo University, also defended the constitution but maintained that the emperor was merely an "organ of the state," hence subject to its laws. Others supported imperial absolutism because of the emperor's descent from the Sun Goddess. This stand was taken by another professor at Tokyo University, Uesugi Shinkichi, to justify imperial rule after 1931.

Disillusionment in the midst of modernization pervaded many areas of Japan's culture. Popular novelists spent much time searching for Japan's true national identity, concluding that the individual was virtually helpless in the face of rapid change. Philosophy, too, reflected this alienation from a society transformed. Marxism invaded the labor unions and student organizations, sloganizing the abuses of capitalism. Christianity made a surprising comeback by identifying with social welfare. Working among the poor and sheltering the outcast, Christians sought to alleviate some of the sufferings of a too-rapid industrialization. Yoshino Sakuzo, a distinguished Christian scholar, attempted to reconcile the "emperor system" with representative government by means of universal suffrage. He advocated a gradual evolution to socialism through parliamentary means, offering still another answer to many Japanese bewildered by their times.

Rural Discontent: Rise of the Military, 1920s

The countryside harbored the deepest resentment against the cities, business interests, political parties, and the era of "democracy." Although the leaders of industry within the cities enjoyed immense profits, the rural areas suffered extensive privation. Virtual collapse of the silk market occurred when the United States developed rayon as a substitute for the natural fiber, and this along with land scarcity and increasing taxation drove many peasants deeply into poverty. In addition, rice production declined as the city dwellers demanded more sophisticated Western foods.

The rural areas also feared the effect the cities exerted on cherished institutions. Even the crown prince had fallen victim to the Western craze. Hirohito toured Europe in 1921 and returned with new interests and ideals—commissioning the construction of a nine-hole golf course outside the imperial palace, ordering bacon and eggs for breakfast, and engaging in more public informality. Many rural poor began to feel that democracy served only the cities and big business. Many in the countryside desired to return to a more harmonious, unitary society—something more Japanese and less Western. The villages especially regarded the individualism of the democratic era as a rank betrayal of Japan's historic "collectivist ethic"—society's transcendent loyalty to the group or family concept, especially the father image of the emperor.

Much of this rural discontent centered in the army. As mentioned, conscription, introduced in 1872, drew heavily upon the peasant classes, and for several generations peasant-born recruits had gradually supplanted the samurai class in the lower ranks of officers (below the rank of captain). These officers blamed the misery of their families on politicians and urban industrialists. Moreover, they resented the eclipse of military prestige since the Washington Conference, when business interests had pushed international disarmament in order to further trade. During the 1920s, Japanese society held the military in such low esteem that most officers felt compelled to wear civilian dress on the streets. Girls of prominent families frequently spurned army men in favor of those from the business world.

Junior officers formed organizations such as the Black Dragon and Cherry societies, which advocated a military takeover of the government and the institution of "National Socialism"—the coordination of all Japanese resources for conquest of East Asia. A great campaign against China and, if necessary, war against the United States and the USSR would achieve Japan's historic destiny—to rule the entire Far East. By their doctrine of the "imperial way," the military as a bloc would recreate the historic role of the shogun and rule in the emperor's name. Many of these young officers belonged to the Kwantung Army of Manchuria, where Japan had controlled 75 percent of the foreign concessions since the Russo-Japanese War. These enterprises, consisting of railway lines, port facilities, timber resources, and some iron and coal mines, were vital to Japan in its critical need for raw materials and became a major concern to its military leaders.

In 1926–1927, the Chinese Nationalists' march northward to retake foreign holdings imperiled Japanese interests in northern China, and clashes occurred between Japanese forces and those of the Chinese leader Chiang Kai-shek. A Chinese economic boycott against all international commerce quickly crippled

Japanese trade with China by 68 percent: fully one-third of Japan's commerce was with the Chinese. By 1931, as the full impact of the worldwide depression struck Japan, the ultranationalist groups in the army rebelled. Fearing Japan would be strangled by its growing population and alarmed at the threat to Japanese interests in northeastern China (with its important trade routes), the militarists began the seizure of political power in Tokyo. Almost at once they deluged the intimidated democratic elements in a tidal wave of chauvinistic propaganda. Terrorist assassinations eliminated prominent liberal statesmen. Simultaneously, the Japanese Kwantung Army of Manchuria capitalized upon a small explosion on the South Manchurian Railway (the "Mukden Incident" of September 18, 1931) to claim Chinese sabotage to their holdings. Launching a full-scale invasion of China's richest province under the pretense of restoring order, the Japanese army conquered all Manchuria. Never officially informed of the army's decision, the government in Tokyo could do nothing. Thus Japan took the path of military conquest that led to World War II.

Military Expansionism, 1931–1941

With the invasion of Manchuria, Japan had repudiated the peaceful economic expansion and international cooperation of the 1920s for the military expansionism that would dominate the nation through 1945. By outright conquest of "vital areas," the military sought to guard against an international boycott that might deny Japan its essential raw materials and rightful place in the world.

The military capitalized on the loss of faith in democracy by almost all classes; the liberal politicians had neither fulfilled the people's needs nor coped with problems of the depression. In 1928, the Japanese per capita income declined to barely one-eighth that of the United States. Peasants saw their meager wages fall by 25 percent as the silk market declined. Workers in the little industries barely survived. When Japan's particular constitutional model, Germany, repudiated democracy for Nazism, Japan followed the example with its own brand of militant nationalism—probably best described as "ultra-Japanism."

After the London Naval Conference of 1930 had reaffirmed and even extended the limitations upon the Japanese navy, the army feared its turn had come. Dismay over the London Conference had been a factor in the Manchurian invasion, since the military held that Japan, as a great power, must have direct access to the natural resources on which its economy relied. Ultra-patriotic organizations in the armed services and many civilian groups favored the armed conquest of northeastern China to seize needed iron and coal mines, as well as oil-producing regions. The area then would be defined as an exclusively Japanese sphere—established by a "Monroe Doctrine" for East Asia.

In 1932, the Japanese designated China's Henry Pu Yi as emperor of the satellite state of Manchukuo, the Japanese name for Manchuria. Pu Yi, the last Manchu emperor of China, had been deposed in 1912. The reason for this subterfuge of setting up an obvious puppet state was not clear, but some scholars have seen it as another example of the traditional Japanese practice of "government from behind the scenes," with the Kwantung Army wielding the real power in the area. China protested to the League of Nations, but this international body took no effective steps against Japan. Although the United States requested sanctions by the League, Great Britain feared that weakening Japan would open China to the Soviet Union. Distracted by Hitler and Mussolini in Europe, Britain and France left the Japanese situation to the Americans. The Japanese military felt confident that the United States would not intervene militarily and expected that it eventually might accept Japan's domination of northern China so long as U.S. interests were respected. Professor Akira Iriye points out that the Japanese officers believed that their country's national survival was at stake. They saw that many international treaties still restricted Japan.

President Herbert Hoover's secretary of state, Henry L. Stimson, however, set the pattern of U.S. policy toward Japan after 1931. Refusing to recognize Japan's territorial conquests, the United States tried to turn democratic elements in Japan against the military. Chiang Kai-shek's preoccupation with fighting the Chinese Communists prevented his taking action against Japan, and the Japanese army continued to press south of Manchukuo until they controlled the strategic mountain passes once used by barbarians in ancient times to invade northern China proper. In May 1933, Japan withdrew from the League of Nations.

At home, the militarists used political assassination to suppress the opposition. Ultra-nationalist radicals systematically eliminated liberal statesmen, including two premiers, along with conservatives among the older officers in the army and navy. On February 26, 1936, a group of young officers attempted to seize the emperor himself. Although the coup failed, radical patriotism so inflamed public opinion that the older (more moderate, but still expansionist) elements of the military took control of the government.

In July 1937, Japan began the full-scale invasion of northeast China with the backing of Nazi Germany, through the Anti-Comintern Pact of 1936. The United States' commitment to "moral persuasion" only, Stalin's army purges in the USSR, as well as recent British and French appeasement of the dictators in Europe provided Japan's opportunity. The Japanese military intended only the erection of another satellite state to control the natural resources of northeastern China, but Chiang Kai-shek, now in alliance with the Chinese Communists, refused to surrender, fearing deposition by his own followers. After overrunning China's east coast, the Japanese were sucked deeper and deeper into the limitless spaces of China's interior. Retreating from the coastal areas, Chiang found refuge on the upper Yangtze River—in the mountainous terrain around Chungking.

Since 1931, the possibility of a Soviet attack from the north had been a paramount Japanese concern. To test Russian resolution, the Japanese deliberately precipitated a series of clashes on the Manchurian and Mongolian frontiers starting in 1934. In a number of engagements in 1938–1939, Russian troops dealt the Japanese several serious defeats, once driving them back across the border. Marshal Gregory K. Zhukov, the USSR's most famous commander of World War II, directed Soviet operations. After the unexpected Nazi-Soviet Pact (August 1939) had made the USSR a German ally, the Japanese turned in another direction, looking toward Southeast Asia and the British, French, Dutch, and U.S. possessions there. They were confident that the control of the region's resources would help offset the growing Anglo-American naval power in the western Pacific.

After the fall of France to Germany, the imperial army occupied northern Indochina in September 1940 and severed the railway lines that supplied Chiang.

Earlier, in an attempt to starve Chiang's forces out, Japan had forced the British, who were by now preoccupied with the war in Europe, to close the Burma Road, the only supply route. Ironically, the United States, hoping to keep the war confined to China, had appeased Japan's search for resources by providing it with essential gasoline and scrap metal. Periodically, however, the Americans withheld portions of these supplies to hinder the Japanese. U.S. Ambassador Joseph C. Grew tried unsuccessfully to arrange talks between the Premier, Prince Fumimaro Konoye, and President Franklin D. Roosevelt. In June 1941, immediately following Hitler's invasion of the USSR, Japan occupied southern Indochina as it continued its drive for resources to reduce its dependence on U.S. supplies. Japan was now poised for a complete takeover of Southeast Asia with its abundant oil, tin, and rubber, and within striking distance of the Philippines. In September 1941, when Japan joined the Axis powers of Germany and Italy, the United States halted all shipments to Japan, leaving it with only a two-years' supply of oil. War became inevitable.

The Pacific War, 1941–1945

During the critical autumn of 1941, economic strangulation imperiled Japan, and its military leaders debated the advisability of striking at the Soviet Union in the north—as Hitler urged—or at the European and U.S. possessions to the south. Southeast Asia's greater natural resources, along with the preponderant role the imperial navy could play, eventually influenced Japan to launch its attack southward. The disastrous skirmishes with the Russians in the late 1930s also played a part in the Japanese decision. Japan's strategists planned for a short war—one that would last no more than one and one half years. In the interim, its Axis partners would win the war in Europe, defeating Britain and the Soviet Union, at which point, a discouraged United States would surely concede Southeast Asia. The Soviet agent in Tokyo, Richard Sorge, revealed these Japanese plans to Moscow.

The Commander in Chief of the Combined Fleet, Japanese Admiral Isoroku Yamamoto, a moderate naval officer, had opposed the radicals' mad rush to war; they once had marked him for assassination. Nevertheless, when Yamamoto saw that war was inevitable, he planned a surprise attack on Pearl Harbor to make a quick victory possible. The assault was intended to immobilize the U.S. Pacific fleet long enough for Japan to achieve and consolidate its conquest of the Southwest Pacific. The surprise strike at the docked U.S. fleet was a daring but overwhelming success. Thirty-two U.S. ships of all descriptions, including eight battleships, suffered severe damage. This crippling of the U.S. Navy, combined with a remarkable twenty-two separate military operations on various islands in the Southwest Pacific within a few days after Pearl Harbor, made possible the Japanese occupation of Southeast Asia within three months. Historian Gordon W. Prange held that the Pearl Harbor attack succeeded because the United States considered it a strategic impossibility. New books and countless television presentations honoring the fiftieth anniversary of the attack (1991) still left the question of (U.S.) responsibility open.

With the attack underway, however, Yamamoto had warned, "I am afraid we have awakened a sleeping giant and filled him with a terrible resolve." The United States recovered from Pearl Harbor sooner than the Japanese had expected, for the impact of the attack unified the American people against the Axis powers. U.S. submarines and aircraft carriers, spared damage at Pearl Harbor, hit Japanese supply lines, carrying critically needed oil from the East Indies. The Japanese tried to erect a "defense perimeter" of fortified islands in order to make the homeland unassailable, but in April 1942, Colonel James H. Doolittle's surprise air raid on Tokyo revealed Japan's vulnerability. Hoping to secure the northern anchor of the Japanese perimeter, the bulk of the imperial navy struck at Midway Island, the western-most island of the Hawaiian chain, where they sought to annihilate the U.S. "flat tops," or aircraft carriers. The U.S. air force's chance discovery of the approaching Japanese armada resulted in a decisive U.S. victory and the loss of four Japanese aircraft carriers and countless planes and pilots—a major setback in the war. The imperial navy had reached its crest; the battle of Midway was a turning point of the war on the sea.

On land, Japan's armies advanced southward as far as Guadalcanal in the Solomons, but a year later, in the spring of 1943, the Allied counteroffensive drove them from the island. All chances for a rapid victory faded, and as Hitler's fortunes in Europe also took an adverse turn, the Japanese, with dwindling resources, were thrown onto the defensive. The U.S. strategy of "island hopping" across the central Pacific utilized U.S. carrier superiority, and the capture of the Gilbert, Marshall, and Mariana islands brought Allied forces to Japan's threshold on the Ryukyus by April 1945. In the furious defense of Okinawa, the desperate Japanese employed the Kamikaze or suicide plane, which had a devastating (physical and psychological) effect on the U.S. forces.

At this point, the U.S. military command feared that the invasion of the Japanese home islands would cost a tremendous expenditure of life; General George C. Marshall, the U.S. Army chief of staff, calculated that it would take three hundred thousand Allied casualties to subdue Japan, whose resistance actually had stiffened the closer the Allies got to the home islands. Okinawa, now site of the nearest Allied base, was four hundred miles from Kyushu. The "Big Three" leaders—Churchill, Roosevelt, and Stalin—meeting at Yalta in February 1945, agreed that Russia should enter the Pacific war after the surrender of Germany. When Germany capitulated in May 1945, its Allied conquerors demanded the "unconditional surrender" of Japan. During prolonged negotiations, the Allies failed to recognize the full significance of Japan's request to retain the emperor after surrender. Therefore, when Japan continued to hold out following the Potsdam Declaration of July 1945, which threatened Japan with total destruction if its demands were not met, President Harry S Truman ordered the atomic bombing of Hiroshima in early August. Along with the Russian entry into the conflict, the use of the atomic bomb was intended to obviate the necessity of a direct invasion. But an unfortunate misunderstanding occurred over the Japanese reply and its use of the term "mokusatsu," which was intended to mean "wait a moment please." Here the Japanese hoped for Russian mediation. The Allies, however, took the term to indicate another defiant rejection; thus a second atomic bomb was dropped, this time on the city of Nagasaki. At this point, Chiang Kai-shek urged the Allies to let the Japanese retain the emperor, and, ironically, the Allies then accepted this condition in Japan's "unconditional surrender." An earlier willingness to mollify the Japanese might have prevented use of the atomic bomb; in addition, the Japanese desire for peace was far greater than U.S. strategists had realized. Facing Japan's certain destruction, the emperor himself stepped forward to sue for peace. Invoking his divine authority, he silenced the "die-hards" among the military who demanded a last-ditch defense in a national Seppuku. For the first time in its history, Japan became subject to a foreign conqueror, and the people braced themselves (in the emperor's words) to "bear the unbearable."

Was the atomic bombing of Japan justified? Those responsible regarded it as an instrument of mercy, which ended the war and saved both American and Japanese lives by preventing an invasion of Japan itself. Critics have judged instead that it was a U.S. instrument to intimidate the Soviet Union into abiding by the Yalta agreement, and they vehemently questioned the morality of its use on populated areas. The debate is endless. Professor Langdon Warner's intercession with President Truman in the summer of 1945 saved the old imperial capitals of Nara and Kyoto from both fire-bombing and the atomic bomb. Warner, one of Harvard University's most eminent authorities on Japanese art, convinced the president that Nara and Kyoto, both cultural centers, should be spared. Hiroshima, however, suffered the total devastation of a four-square-mile area, with over fifty thousand casualties. Those who survived the blast experienced horrible burns, and many of the victims later developed cancer or leukemia. The terrible concussion killed many doctors and nurses, scattered their equipment, and destroyed hospital facilities. Those doctors who survived were untrained in the treatment of "atomic sickness," as it was first called. Today, Hiroshima's Peace Park Memorial preserves wristwatches and clocks whose scorched hands read 8:15 A.M., bits of charred clothing, bottles melted together, twisted lanterns that once lighted walkways, and a large panorama of the city as it looked soon after the cataclysm. A monument to the city's victims stands outside. In front of this cenotaph are engraved the words: "Please rest in peace. For the mistake shall not be repeated."

For the fiftieth anniversary (1995) of the war's end, a proposed Smithsonian Institution exhibit in Washington, D.C., featuring the *Enola Gay* (the U.S. B-29 that dropped the first atomic bomb ever used, on Hiroshima) was considerably curtailed from its original format. The American Legion and several members of Congress protested that the original texts that were to accompany the display had unfairly indicted the United States for its decision to use nuclear weapons.

Japan under the Occupation, 1945–1952

With over two million casualties, four-fifths of its empire gone, and its cities in ashes, Japan lay in crushing defeat. Seven million men, scattered from the home islands to the Southwest Pacific on the emperor's order, laid down their arms. The Japanese formally surrendered in ceremonies aboard the U.S. battleship *Missouri* in Tokyo Bay on September 2, 1945.

In what has been called the "second opening" of Japan, the American occupation in 1945 engendered many reforms in an atmosphere reminiscent of the Meiji era. The Japanese expected the occupation to be vengeful and vindictive; they found it instead positive and constructive. General Douglas MacArthur, Supreme Commander of the Allied Forces in the Far East, headed the occupation

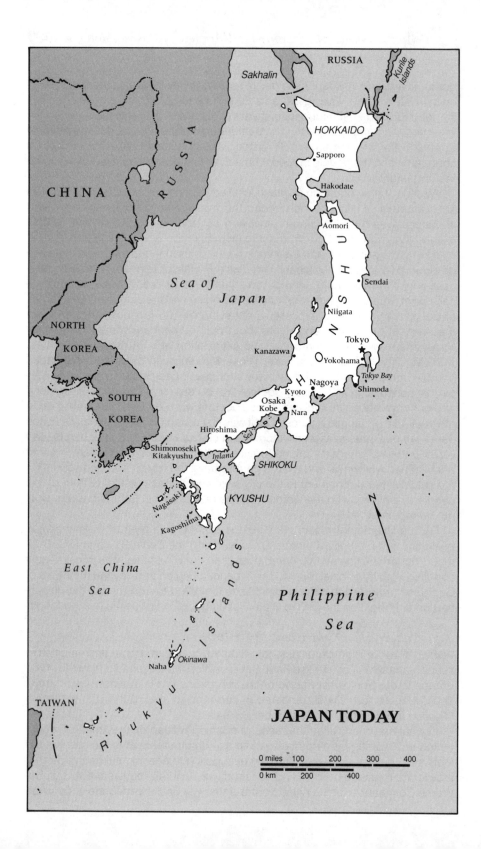

RUSSIA

Sakhalin

Kurile Islands

CHINA

R U S S I A

HOKKAIDO

Sapporo

Hakodate

Aomori

S e a   o f

J a p a n

Sendai

Niigata

NORTH

KOREA

Kanazawa

Tokyo

Yokohama

Tokyo Bay

Nagoya

Shimoda

SOUTH

KOREA

Kyoto

Osaka

Kobe

Nara

Hiroshima

Sea

Shimonoseki

Kitakyushu

Inland

SHIKOKU

Nagasaki

KYUSHU

Kagoshima

East   China

Sea

R y u k y u   I s l a n d s

Philippine

Sea

N

Naha *Okinawa*

TAIWAN

JAPAN TODAY

0 miles   100   200   300   400

0 km   200   400

government. After graduating from West Point in 1903, MacArthur saw extensive service in the Far East in his early career. Following his dramatic escape from the Japanese invasion of the Philippines in 1942, he directed the reconquest of those islands and final victory over Japan. MacArthur announced that he came as "a protector, not as a conqueror," and for the first three years, his military government, designated Supreme Commander Allied Powers (SCAP), sought to disarm and democratize Japan, thus securing the future stability of East Asia. Because of the Cold War, however, by 1948 he reversed this policy in favor of Japan's industrial recovery, rehabilitation, and partial rearmament.

From his years in the Far East, MacArthur knew something of the Japanese mentality. When he first arrived in Japan, accompanied only by his aides, he landed amidst a still heavily armed enemy. He counted on the traditions of Bushido, which regarded the conquered as the special charge of the victor, to ensure his own safety and that of his staff. The Japanese accepted the occupation as inevitable and, with admirable realism, bore it as the price of their defeat in the spirit of their traditional saying: "Seven times fall down, get up eight." They had long believed that nature brought either fortune or misfortune, but, in either case, all things eventually passed. This was the philosophy of Taoism, part of the Chinese heritage. Even more significantly, the individual discipline from Zen Buddhism combined with Confucianism's stress on group obligations to motivate the Japanese to undertake the arduous task of reconstruction.

Although Japan learned democracy from an American five-star general between 1945 and 1948, MacArthur established it on the tradition of the liberal parties, some functions of the Meiji constitution, and finally the achievements of the democratic era of the 1920s. Directives attacked the fundamental inequities of the social and political system. Occupation authorities took the land from the great lords and redistributed it to tenant farmers, who were now free of landlord obligations. It gave legal equality to women and provided for universal suffrage. Other decrees disestablished state-mandated Shinto and stripped education of its emperor worship, while on January 1, 1946, Emperor Hirohito publicly disavowed his divinity, becoming a constitutional monarch the following year. Further regulations disbanded the powerful industrial clique, the zaibatsu.

A new constitution, proclaimed in 1947, terminated the old separation of executive and legislature. Under the new document, popular opinion more directly controlled both branches of government—the House of Representatives and the House of Councillors—both of which became completely elective through universal suffrage. Elections returned to office many of the liberal statesmen of the 1930s. Article IX of the new constitution excluded war as an instrument of national policy and prohibited the maintenance of armed forces. Tribunals imprisoned or executed convicted war criminals. The new pacifism of the Japanese people made Article IX enormously popular.

Wisely, MacArthur, mindful of the notion of "face," refused to try Emperor Hirohito as a war criminal and instead ruled through him and the former imperial administration. Because of his use of what the Japanese saw as the traditional conduct of "government from behind the scenes," MacArthur was what historian William Manchester termed the "Yankee shogun," and his distant and reserved personality enhanced this image for the Japanese, who were grateful for his respect toward the emperor.

In 1948, the occupation shifted from the disarmament of Japan to economic rehabilitation and partial rearmament. Europe's Berlin blockade and the imminent loss of China to Mao Tse-tung's (Mao Zedong) Communists made a strong Japan an indispensable balance on the side of the West in the Cold War. Its industrial support of the United Nations (U.N.) forces in the Korean conflict attested to the success of the occupation. At that time, Japan established "self-defense" forces—small military, naval, and air units, sufficient for the security of the homeland. In September 1951, the United States and other allied nations concluded a formal peace treaty with Japan, which became the showcase of democracy to an East Asia threatened by communism. The Security Treaty, signed the same day, began a U.S.-Japanese cooperation that exists to this day, a tribute to the occupation—one of the outstanding success stories of postwar U.S. foreign policy. Paradoxically, the occupation began with one policy (disarmament) and ended with its opposite (rearmament and economic recovery).

Japanese Society, 1945-1980

One of the significant developments in Japanese society after World War II had been the sharp decline in the population growth rate. At the time of surrender, Japan's populace numbered about 72 million. This figure had more than doubled in less than a century, the increases averaging about 3 percent annually. In 1948, a Eugenics Protection Law, which legalized abortions, rapidly decreased this rate to 1 percent a year. Family planning clinics, usually located at factories, instructed couples to consider two children the ideal number to have. This regulation, therefore, partially solved one of modern Japan's aggravations that endangered the living standard. By the early 1970s, however, Japan faced a serious shortage of young people. In 1970, some one million young Japanese men turned eighteen. By 1975 this figure declined to approximately seven hundred and fifty thousand. For a time industry suffered from a lack of university graduates to occupy skilled jobs, and many good positions remained vacant. From 1948 to the early 1970s, the Japanese may have reduced their projected population growth by 50 million children. As Japan's population totaled over 111 million by 1976—ranking sixth-largest in the world—this represented almost half that figure.

Along with the relatively declining population, workers moving from farms to cities and seeking jobs in new industries had greatly changed Japanese social patterns. At the end of World War II, Japan was 50 percent urban, but by 1970, 80 percent of the Japanese lived in cities, leaving the farms in the hands of the older people. A shortage of rural labor caused the government to collectivize some land and encourage a return to the farms by granting more liberal agricultural subsidies. New government programs paid the farmer for raising things such as chickens and vegetables instead of rice, which was grown in an overabundance. Japanese agricultural techniques utilized almost all available land and produced the highest yield per acre in the world. Since the average Japanese farm measures only about two and one-half acres, comparatively little mechanization was necessary. Central and southern Honshu presented meticulously cultivated, rectangular rice fields, carefully separated by narrow irrigation ditches. Hilly regions employed terrace farming for rice and tea, the plots again carefully partitioned and tended. Japan is self-sufficient in some foods. Fortunately, the government had stopped the manpower drainage from the land by means of the new farm programs.

Industrial expansion brought new social problems. During the "economic miracle" of the 1960s (that remarkable advance in production, climaxing Japan's postwar recovery) Japan still had the lowest standard of living of any of the developed countries. Even as late as 1973, it ranked seventh in personal income, just ahead of Britain, France, and Italy. However, rapid inflation—about a 25 percent rise in consumer prices for 1973–1974—due to a price jump in Mideast oil, resulted in new labor contracts calling for a 30 percent wage increase, and then 1975 saw another 13 percent gain in wages. Because personal incomes had risen, Japan no longer had the commercial advantage of cheap labor. Its industrial system preserved many of the old feudal traditions, and employers gave their workers many fringe benefits. These benefits included insurance of all kinds, as well as company housing, stores, restaurants, resorts for vacations, nurseries for children, marriage counseling, and even computer matchmaking, all of which helped ensure the loyal service of the employee to the company.

At the Matsushita Electric Company's plant in Osaka, employees began each workday with a group singing of the company song, followed by recitation of the firm's creed. During breaks, all employees performed brisk calisthenics to recorded music. Matsushita's slogan, "Seek progress through hard work," inspired production. Employees practiced judo in company facilities after hours, while Saturday classes offered subjects such as flower arranging and Buddhist meditation for the worker and his or her family. In a sense, loyalty to one's employer had replaced the traditional devotion to the emperor. Promotions were based on seniority and life-time employment was the rule. During the economic recession of 1974–1975, however, companies began to furlough employees periodically in order to avoid wholesale dismissals. Quickly, unemployment became a major social problem. By 1976, the jobless totaled over one million. With inflation depleting reserve funds, many companies were forced to discharge workers, threatening Japan's tradition of permanent employment.

Housing was still in short supply, as were good sewage and drainage systems. Commuter trains were packed at rush hours as Tokyo moved three million persons daily. Professional "pushers" jammed passengers tightly into the cars to ensure that the trains were filled to capacity. The tremendous number of automobiles in the country coupled with poor roads created mammoth traffic jams, and consequently Japan suffered one of the highest automobile accident rates in the world. Improvement in living standards had created greater consumer demands. Japan boasted of a larger percentage of households with color television sets than the United States. Baseball was the most popular spectator sport, vying with Sumo wrestling, while golf and bowling provided exercise and diversion for thousands of hard-working Japanese. Travel had boomed, with Hawaii and Europe being the most popular overseas destinations. Despite inflation, 1975 saw a 6 percent rise over the previous year in Japanese travel abroad.

Economic recession, however, had considerably reduced tourism in Japan itself, with average prices for choice hotel rooms and restaurants doubling in just three years by 1976.

Pollution, urban glut, and inflation created the greatest problems of industrialization. The environment ranked with inflation as one of the principal domestic issues. Pollution enveloped Tokyo, then the world's largest city (its population over twelve million) and one of the dirtiest. The beloved Mount Fuji no longer could be seen from the capital because of the smog, and every other industrial city also was choked with auto exhaust and factory waste. (After directing traffic for two hours in the crowded Ginza area, it would not be uncommon for a policeman to retire to a special box in which he could breathe from an oxygen tank.) Political campaigns calling for "blue sky and white clouds" elected a majority of Socialist mayors who campaigned effectively on the environmental issue in the larger cities. In Minamata, a small industrial town, citizens suffered the paralyzing effects of mercury poisoning. Meanwhile, the inflationary spiral that had begun in 1973, terminated the optimistic view of the economic future so prevalent in the 1960s, putting Japanese living standards in jeopardy.

Student Unrest

Military defeat in World War II meant the end of emperor worship. For nearly twenty years after 1945, the Japanese seldom displayed the "Rising Sun" flag in public. Old-time nationalism had died. Among intellectuals, the Western philosophies of existentialism and Marxism gained favor. Many students, frustrated by the "examination hell" they had to endure in order to gain admission to colleges, poor student housing, huge classes, rote-learning, and little social activity, joined Marxist organizations. The *Zengakuren* (All Students Union) became the Japanese equivalent of the American Students for a Democratic Society.

Japanese university students protested numerous times over Japan's tie to the United States in the Security Treaty. In the fall of 1960, one hundred thousand students, professors, laborers, and housewives joined in a massive demonstration against Premier Kishi's manipulating the renewal of the treaty, causing the cancellation of President Dwight D. Eisenhower's visit to Japan. Student unrest continued through the 1960s over the U.S. military bases in Japan, the Okinawa issue (demanding the island's return to Japan), atomic weapon storage, and the Vietnam War. However, Japan's economic resurgence, along with the split between Russia and China, had shattered many Marxist student organizations. While the demonstrations represented students' demands for more freedom from the old restraints of family and group obligations, it was interesting to see that once graduated to regular jobs, many former student protesters accepted and adjusted to traditional society. Company loyalty and new family obligations often replaced student militancy.

Politics

During the occupation, political parties re-emerged. The former Seiyukai appeared as the Liberal party, along with the Progressives (Minseito), later called the Democratic party, and the Socialists and the Communists. Liberals and Democrats, both moderate, dominated the elections. Yoshida Shigeru, a known conservative and opponent of the military before the war, was premier for the great majority of the time from 1946 to 1954. These "Yoshida Years" saw the occupation, the final peace agreement, and the Security Treaty successfully concluded.

The Socialists gained some intellectual, labor, and white-collar votes by capitalizing on a prevalent hostility toward the United States, economic privation, and student and labor unrest. Their success forced the coalition of Liberals and Democrats into the Liberal-Democratic party (LDP) in 1955. Moderately conservative, the LDP controlled the central government since that time with the backing of the bureaucracy, banking, big business, and agrarian interests. Although the Socialists won substantial support in the cities, their participation in student and labor demonstrations, especially the massive turnout against the Security Treaty and Eisenhower's visit in 1960, proved unpopular.

The "economic miracle" of the 1960s left the Socialists with few campaign issues, and the party's more moderate wing, which favored the retention of the Security Treaty, formed the Democratic-Socialist party. However, many young organized workers, as well as recent university graduates, formerly in support of the Socialists, now swung to the LDP. In November 1964, the Liberal-Democratic party named Sato Eisaku, former vice-minister of transportation and a moderate conservative, as premier. Sato retained this position for nine and one-half years— a parliamentary record. Yet the LDP's strength in both houses gradually waned after 1960, primarily because of a population shift to the cities. In 1972, with Tanaka Kakuei as premier, continuing economic prosperity ensured LDP control of government, but their position became shaky in 1973–1974 due to the 25 percent rise in inflation. Elections in July 1974 reduced their majority in the upper house to an extremely thin margin. Big business's open support for LDP candidates definitely weakened Tanaka's government. When the news media identified him with serious financial scandals, he resigned in November 1974. His compromise successor, Miki Takeo, presided over a party with a steadily diminishing majority. Then the revelation, in February 1976, of the Lockheed Company's payment of over $12 million (between 1958 and 1975) to members of Miki's party thoroughly rocked his administration. The climax of this, "Japan's Watergate," came with former Premier Tanaka's indictment for direct implication in the affair. These flagrant attempts to influence aircraft sales in Japan had once again identified the Liberal-Democrats with "money power" politics.

International Affairs
Japan's immediate postwar foreign policy embraced international neutralism. Cold War politics tied Japan closely to the United States, especially after China became Communist in 1949. This American connection made Japan's relationship with the Soviet Union difficult, aggravating the issues of the southern Kurile Islands (taken from Japan by the Soviet Union as part of the Yalta agreement in 1945) and a final treaty to end the war. Japan and Russia concluded the first of a series of economic agreements in 1966, whereby the Japanese would assist Russia in the exploration for oil and other resources in Siberia and for natural gas on Sakhalin Island. Japan would benefit greatly by having these vital resources relatively near at hand, while to Russia a developed Siberia would present a formidable barrier against Chinese expansion.

Meanwhile, Japan's relations with Communist China pursued a tortuous path, complicated by Japan's close ties to the United States. After the Communists defeated the Chinese Nationalists, Chiang Kai-shek's government fled to the island of Taiwan (formerly Formosa), off the southeast coast of China, and both the United States and Japan assisted the island's industrial development through extensive investment. Japanese factories established branches in Taiwan, where labor costs ran 25 percent of those at home. The People's Republic of China (PRC) refused to open trade fully to the Japanese unless it severed its Nationalist Chinese connections. Finally, in September 1972, Tokyo recognized the Beijing (Peking) government officially, withdrawing recognition from Taiwan in order to keep step with U.S. policy. However, most Japanese investment in Taiwan apparently remained intact, while trade with mainland China opened slowly. Only after some time would Japan gain access to those vital resources of northeastern China, so coveted by its military in the 1930s.

A proposed final peace treaty faltered over the Chinese insistence that Japan pledge cooperation against the future "hegemony" of any power—obviously referring to Russia—in East Asia. Japan temporarily refused this stipulation, not wishing to take a side in the Sino-Soviet dispute.

Between 1945 and 1971, the United States enjoyed relatively cordial relations with Japan. In 1972, the United States returned Okinawa and the Bonin Islands to Japan. Despite the good will between President Richard M. Nixon's administration and Premier Sato's government in the early 1970s, many barriers to true cordiality persisted. Economic problems first emerged when U.S. textile manufacturers complained that the Japanese were "dumping" (selling below cost) goods on the American markets, and U.S. businessmen demanded that Japan lower its domestic tariffs to permit more American goods to enter Japan. Americans also protested Japanese investments in Hawaii. On the other hand, the Japanese resented their inferior role in the Security Treaty, wanting instead a full partnership based on Japan's own foreign interests. U.S. military bases in Japan, provided in the Security Treaty, were unpopular, and the Japanese feared the United States might drag Japan into the Vietnam conflict. Furthermore, many Japanese deplored the Americanization of Japanese culture and felt that the United States regarded Japan as an inferior entity—not on the same plane as the European states. Three "Nixon shocks" in 1971 confirmed this view: (1) a new U.S.-China policy on July 15 was announced without prior notice given to Japan; (2) economic restrictions primarily directed at Japan were issued with a callous insensitivity on the anniversary of "VJ" day (August 15); and (3) admission of the (Communist) PRC to the United Nations on October 25 left Japan holding the dead "two Chinas" policy, threatening its isolation as the only non-Communist great power in East Asia. Further strains occurred because of the cancellation of the emperor's trip to the United States and the omission of Japan as a member of the Vietnam peace commission in early 1973.

But the two nations needed each other diplomatically. A meeting in Hawaii in August 1973, saw President Nixon and Premier Tanaka agree to cooperate in several international ventures. In November 1974, just before Tanaka's resignation as premier, President Gerald R. Ford visited Japan as a gesture of reconciliation. Emperor Hirohito and Empress Nagako returned this visit with a fifteen-day tour of the United States in September–October 1975. The imperial couple's first trip to the United States accented the mutual need for Japanese-American cooperation.

When the United States witnessed the collapse of South Vietnam in the spring of 1975, the Japanese began to talk openly of rearming. The situation in Korea also concerned Japan, especially when North Korean Premier Kim Il Sung visited Beijing and demanded "a final, decisive blow" against the U.S. position in East Asia. With the phase-out of American troops in Thailand, the Philippines, and Taiwan, some Japanese considered closer ties to either the USSR or the PRC in the face of the weakening U.S. commitment, but the vast majority still favored an unarmed neutrality.

Immediate Cost of the "Economic Miracle"

The economic surge of the 1960s advanced Japan to the third-greatest industrial power in the world. The gross national product (GNP) increased four times, with an average real growth of 13 percent a year. By 1970, Japan had achieved a production level twice that of China, three times that of Africa, and twice that of Latin America, increasing production twenty times. Projections estimated that by 1975 Japan would have a trillion-dollar economy and out-produce all the rest of Asia combined, while the twenty-first century would become "the Japanese century."

This extraordinary success story began in the ashes and despair of defeat. In 1945, Japan's war-shocked economy amounted to only $1.5 billion. Two years later it reached only 37 percent of its prewar production. The Korean conflict was the turning point, when Japan produced armaments for the U.N. forces. By 1955, output finally matched the level of 1941, and from then on Japanese production soared. In 1972, the GNP totaled $290 billion. Japan's growth was due to a variety of factors: (1) a highly skilled and disciplined labor force, imbued with the ideals of the old feudal system; (2) an enormous advantage over competitors through advanced technology, made possible when U.S. foreign aid replaced war-wrecked machinery; (3) security for Japan with minimum defense expenditures because of its inclusion under the U.S. "nuclear umbrella" (in 1970, Japan spent only 1 percent of its GNP on arms, as opposed to 8 percent spent by the United States and 20 percent spent by the USSR); and (4) a partnership between government and private industry. The Ministry of International Trade and Industry (MITI) acted as the coordinating agency for government, industry, commerce, and banking—an arrangement irate foreign competitors often referred to as "Japan, Inc."

Japan realized its "economic miracle," but at a price. By 1972, pollution of the nation's air and water became a national issue, and environmental concern threatened industrial growth as the premier national goal. While Japan flooded foreign markets with its exports—autos, transistor radios, tape recorders, and television sets—its high tariff walls protected its domestic industries. Many foreign countries thought this unfair. U.S. firms began to pressure Japan to "liberalize" its protectionist policies and to permit U.S. companies to compete in the Japanese domestic market and invest in Japanese concerns. Embarrassed by its $16 billion overall trade surplus for 1971–1972, Japan yielded somewhat by twice revaluing the yen (reducing it by 33.33 percent), regulating exports, and permitting foreign investment in some vital industries.

Meanwhile, other Southeast Asian countries had feared that Japanese economic penetration might be a prelude to its military and political domination of the entire region. To offset such terms as "economic animal", "ugly Japanese," and "yellow yankee," Japan carried out a foreign aid program to Southeast Asian nations but made such aid dependent on commercial agreements.

At home, many Japanese critics of the Sato and Tanaka governments accused them of "kowtow diplomacy"—overaccommodation to Japan's commercial compatriots overseas—but Japan's dependence on foreign sources for raw materials had prompted a conciliatory policy. The oil crisis of 1973–1974 made Japan's vulnerability quite clear. In November 1973, the Arab and other Mideast, oil-producing nations, as part of a worldwide oil boycott, announced a one-quarter cut in oil shipments unless Japan severed relations with Israel. At that time Japan obtained 80 percent of its oil from the Mideast, and this vital fuel accounted for about three quarters of Japanese energy requirements. Toward the end of November, the Tanaka government adopted a pro-Arab stance in the Mideast conflict; the Arab oil shipments were resumed, but at triple their original cost.

As mentioned, the Arab deal contributed to an inflationary surge of 25 percent in 1973–1974 (some called it "oilflation") just as land values were skyrocketing from the government's "remodeling" plans for dispersing industry and resettling the population. Japanese consumer prices rose by one-fourth and labor costs over 30 percent in one year. The trade balance reversed from the great surplus of 1971 to a deficit of over $16.5 billion for the initial half of 1974, causing Japan's first postwar decline in that fiscal year. Japan's inflation rate suddenly far exceeded that of any other developed country. The Miki government faced the most serious economic recession after 1945, highlighted by the declared bankruptcy of Kohjin Co., Ltd. (August 1975), the largest single corporate failure of postwar Japan.

Japan's policy of "friends with everyone" seemed rooted in necessity. The 1974 example of its total dependence on raw material imports recalled the pressures that impelled it to choose a course of military expansionism in 1931. But now Japanese resource vulnerability seemed to preclude militarism, and rearmament would cause hostile reactions by its immediate neighbors and further jeopardize its critical supply lines. Clearly, Japan's disarmament policies, universal economic cooperation, and vigorous promotion of the current spirit of international détente seemed to be in its best interest.

By the close of the 1970s, Japan ranked first in shipbuilding, second in automobile manufacture, and third in steel production. Japanese-made watches outsold those of the Swiss in Switzerland itself; their cameras competed with German photo equipment in Germany; and Japanese automobile sales soared in a gasoline-short United States. After 1945 the Japanese had learned that "the yen was mightier than the sword."

Japan's "Bubble Economy" of the 1980s

By the early 1980s, Japan's economy had surpassed that of Britain, France, West Germany, and, finally, the Soviet Union to challenge the United States. Japan's technology, moreover, already surpassed that of the United States in quality (of both automobiles and electronics). In fact, Japan soon controlled one-third of the domestic U.S. automobile market, and by 1990 the Japanese-made Honda Accord became the best-selling car in the country that had invented the automobile. The Nikkei Index of the Tokyo Stock Market overtook Wall Street as the pulse of international finance. The Japanese yen burgeoned in relation to every other currency. The fact that Japan firmly refused to import any industrial product that it exported, regardless of price, however, proved an international irritant.

The United States talked about, while Western Europe resorted to, a rigid protectionist policy to keep out many Japanese exports, especially automobiles. But other items, such as watches and computers, penetrated European and American markets. Both Europe and the United States put pressure on the Japanese to spend more on internal improvements, especially their own infrastructure. To appease outsiders Prime Minister Toshiki Kaifu replied in 1990 that his country would spend approximately $2.9 trillion in the public sector by the year 2000, but the Japanese deeply resented this Western intrusion into their internal affairs, as the noisy parliamentary debates over the issue clearly showed.

What factors might explain this enormous Japanese success after 1960? Ezra Vogel, an American scholar, attributed it to the way in which Japanese businesses treated their employees, who experienced a family atmosphere within their work places. In his work *Japan as Number 1* (1979), Vogel urged U.S. foremen to learn from their Japanese counterparts and consult their workers for suggestions as to production, and he advised management to take a personal interest in their employees' well-being. Frank Gibney, the American journalist, termed the Japanese system "people-centered capitalism." Whereas the West's business society was founded on the Renaissance ethic that stressed the importance of the individual, Japan's work ethic had developed from the Confucian ideal of group loyalty. While Western capitalism was seen in terms of money, plant, material, and technology, the Japanese had invested in people, training, educating, and developing them within a company. The company became a village, or family, giving the worker a sense of belonging. A spirit of *wa* or "harmony" prevailed from which outsiders were excluded by countless unstated governmental rules. The worker was motivated to do the best job possible, for the good of the employer and fellow laborers.

Beginning in 1989, however, the picture decidedly changed for the Japanese economy, largely because the stock market badly overheated due to intensive "insider trading" and other shady proceedings. Between 1990 and 1992 the Nikkei Index slid some 42 percent. After an initial decline the market seemed to stabilize in December 1990, but it then fell some 26 percent by March 1991, before recovery. A year later a further fall of 15 percent jolted the stocks. By midyear 1992, the economy had suffered a shattering setback, while the United States and Europe anxiously awaited the consequences they would suffer in the world market as a result of Japan's tumble. This formed the background for several rounds of decidedly hostile rhetoric between the United States and Japan. Also, American-made cars were rapidly closing the quality gap with the Japanese, as the Ford Taurus passed the Honda Accord in the fall of 1992 in U.S. sales. Several U.S. companies accused the Japanese of "dumping" (selling below cost) minivans on the U.S. market. Chrysler, whose minivan sales would be hit most directly if the allegations were true, tried to get these latest Japanese imports classified as "trucks," which would incur much higher tariffs.

Meanwhile Japan sought the cheap labor of the other Pacific Rim countries (Korea, Taiwan, Malaysia, Thailand, and Vietnam). Vietnam, a Communist-dominated country, shared in the economic decline of Russia, Eastern Europe, North Korea, and Cuba, which until recently comprised the Marxist world. Vietnam offered an abundant supply of hard-working laborers, earning wages of about $1 a day, and some middle-class consumers, who were ruled by a government seeking the reform of its infrastructure. Japan soon emerged as the largest donor of foreign aid, having surpassed the United States.

It was Japan's domestic economy, however, that drew the most attention. The recession produced harder times. By 1992 the Nikkei Index showed a gargantuan drop of 60 percent for a $3.1 trillion loss in value of shares traded. Many businesses failed, forcing the dismissal of part-time workers, a group that included a high number of women. This, despite the tradition of lifetime employment, under the rubric of "attrition." Most alarming was the weakening of the "real economy," i.e. production and overseas sales. The steady appreciation of the yen made Japanese exports abroad more expensive, causing a drop in foreign sales. Popular consumption also fell off as the home market was "not in a buying mood." Someone observed that Japan's financial system had "imploded," while slowing to its poorest rate of annual growth since the oil embargo of 1974—just 2 percent.

This Japanese downturn nullified any U.S. notions of Japanese infallibility in things economic. Several U.S. plants had introduced Japanese practices in production, especially more worker participation in decision making and more automation. These innovations, however, produced no miracles. Robots, introduced on the assembly lines, delayed quick, necessary changes in production, while U.S. workers found their meetings with administration frequently "lacked focus." Due to "cultural differences" among Japanese and Americans, the changes failed to improve production substantially in the United States.

The resourceful Japanese, however, were always quick to react by undertaking necessary change—witness the Meiji Reforms after 1868 to protect themselves from further Western intrusion. From 1989 they adopted a pace of slower growth, projecting later expansion, perhaps by 1995. Since the U.S. automakers were catching up in "quality" of product, the Japanese responded by introducing "flexibility"—different cars with varying features on the same production line—to speed delivery. At the same time their assembly lines slowed to meet the reduced demand, and offering fewer models and decreasing feature variation slashed production costs and simplified installation. Most notably, Toyota slowed its production line at Marysville, Ohio, as the Japanese sought to adjust to the U.S. recession. Yet at the same time Japanese technology did make a significant breakthrough in communications with high definition television, which was impressively displayed at the 1992 Summer Olympic Games in Barcelona. Interestingly, the Japanese had used the 1964 Tokyo Olympics to introduce their color television to the world.

Many jobless Japanese workers (there was a 7 percent unemployment rate by 1993) blamed the banks for the economic downturn. During the "bubble economy" Japan owned 7 of the 10 largest banks in the world, but many faltered when they made reckless loans to developers. The government made the solvent institutions bail out those that had failed. Many workers also criticized stockbrokers, especially Nomura, for not warning investors of the risks involved in their ventures. Some litigation ensued, a rarity in Japan, where "harmony" was stressed over individual rights and "trust" still prevailed.

Despite the heightened fears, the United States and the rest of the world felt little of Japan's economic slide. Likely, the gradual nature of the decline, spread over two years, along with continued Japanese overseas investment, although on a reduced scale, prevented a sudden impact. Americans, however, did see real estate prices decline at home, which gave the Japanese the opportunity to purchase Rockefeller Center, for $1.7 billion, and Columbia Pictures in 1989, and Pebble Beach golf facility, for $841 million, in 1990; three failing enterprises. American tempers flared again. Lee Iacocca warned "that there is an insidious Japanese economic and political power in the United States."

Had Japan hit its peak? Whatever the answer, business projections forecast that the Pacific Rim nations (Japan included) could well be the world's growth center in the twenty-first century. Fully 40 percent of world trade centered in that region by 1994. Although U.S. foreign policy had "contained" communism, the true winners of the Cold War were the East Asian capitalists. Projections held that the region collectively would outproduce the United States by the year 2000. Japan's position in the future world economy would be central, while the U.S. role might be merely peripheral. One auto executive gave little comfort to the United States when he said, "We are sorry to see America in this trouble."

But the early 1990s brought "trouble" to Japan as well. The Japanese economy had been built on rapid expansion, but this was slowing decidedly. Paradoxically, their trade surplus continued to increase as their stock market declined. The fact that their GNP reached the unprecedented figure of $3,140,948,000,000 for 1990 offered some encouragement for their efforts.

Despite this, however, Japan's GNP grew an anemic 0.8 percent in real terms for fiscal 1992–1993, the lowest rate since 1974. Thus, the Miyazawa government pushed a budget of $603 billion for fiscal 1993–1994 with 5 percent of expenditures earmarked for public works to stimulate the economy. But exports continued to decline due to the appreciation of the yen. Japan's eleven major commercial banks all posted declines in pretax profits as they struggled with problem loans. The Hosokawa cabinet took measures to reduce economic regulations and to pass along the benefits of the appreciated yen to Japan's customers overseas. Nevertheless, the outcome of Japan's worst economic slump since World War II still remained undetermined by the spring of 1994.

Japanese Society, 1980–1995

The 1980s saw Japan become the second-greatest economy in the world, producing about 10 percent of the world's GNP, with their own at almost $2 trillion by 1989. The Japanese seemed to be a living justification of the fundamental virtues of hard work, lifetime dedication to the place of employment, and loyalty to family, country, and emperor. Also, because of the structure of Japanese society, workers felt that they were contributing personally to the tremendous economic success Japan had gained by the 1980s. Teamwork paid off.

Like most Western societies, Japan's social structure continued to mirror the generational conflict of historical traditions versus the relentless pressure for change, especially from the young people, products of the modern industrial city. They still resented the social restrictions that bridled their individualism, for which they looked to the West with its rock music, drugs, and fast-food chains such as McDonald's and Kentucky Fried Chicken. This represented rebellion by the young against family obligations, or group orientation versus the dignity of the individual. With Japan 80 percent urban by the 1980s, the nuclear family (father, mother, and children) lived in a crowded apartment as a rule.

Mothers were central to the family, to a greater degree than in the West. They nursed their babies longer, fondled them more, and supervised their children more strictly during their husbands' long working hours. Having entered school, the children were closely supervised at home by "education moms," who insisted that homework be completed on time. Maternal pressure on the young gave the Japanese an acute sense of obligation. "Women's liberation," popular in the West, had not made great progress in Japan, where women gave greater priority to family obligations apparently. Yet many women were entering the workforce as "office ladies," whose main task seemingly was to serve afternoon tea to their supervisors. One effective example of the aspiring modern Japanese woman was Ms. Doi Takako, long head of the Socialist party after 1986. Another such example is Masako Owada, a graduate of three universities, who wedded Crown Prince Naruhito in June 1993.

The work place continued its essential position in Japanese society, an object of continuous fascination to the West. But during the 1980s, Japan began taking more and more factories outside of the country, to Thailand, Malaysia, Vietnam, and North Korea, to enjoy cheap labor, which tended to further undermine the nation's traditional business ideals. Although factory administration remained in cities such as Tokyo and Nagoya, the impact on the Japanese work ethic weakened as businesses became more international.

The five-and-one-half-day workweek prevailed for both blue- and white-collar workers, leaving little time for one to spend with family. This practice remained despite advice to Japanese workers to take more time off for leisure. Rising at five A.M., riding for an hour on the commuter train, then reporting to work at seven, the employee found little time for family life. A tour through a Japanese factory might reveal some glassy eyes on the assembly line, but no wholesale "goofing-off" by workers. They were mobilized by the rousing company song in the morning, encouraged by their supervisor's personal interest, and urged to make suggestions to improve production. Women were found in the factories in increasing numbers.

Social ethics stressed principally harmony, deference, and courtesy, which governed Japan's personal relations. Its society reflected hierarchies rather than social classes, i.e., students from the same university, employees from the same company, individuals within the same age range, or sportsmen pursuing the same pastimes. In the familiar environment of their own country, Japanese were governed by a "spider web" of social obligations and restraints, but in foreign countries they could become disoriented, as with Japanese troops serving in East and Southeast Asia during World War II, when many "atrocities," especially against prisoners-of-war, were committed. They were bound by "situational ethics" rather than absolute moral principles as in the West, determined often by the status of the person addressed. The virtues of *on* and *giri* were central. *On* is the benevolence extended by one of a superior station to one of lesser status, while *giri* is the reciprocal sense of loyalty and duty from the inferior party. These interacted. One's greatest fear was loss of "face" in individual confrontation or within the group. The individual Japanese was most concerned with the attitudes of others towards him personally. This was really "relativism" as opposed to the absolute moral truth of the West. Likewise, the Japanese disdained the simplified axioms born of Western logic in the Greek tradition; rather they sought answers in a wider spectrum of human perception, including the emotions.

Although Japan was almost completely homogeneous, there were several alien minority groups in the society: these were regarded definitely as social inferiors. The *burakumin*, those engaged in unclean professions such as butchery or leather tanning, were held at arm's length; likewise, Koreans, who had originally been brought over to Japan as laborers after Korea was annexed in 1910, were not accepted as full citizens. The Koreans were made to carry identification cards at all times, and for a long period they had to be fingerprinted every two years. Another excluded minority were the Ainu, those people living in northern Japan, related to the Eskimo. Japanese treatment of minorities was hardly democratic, to say the least.

Education has always occupied a central position in Japanese society, and, as mentioned, one of its notable accomplishments has been a national literacy rating of 99 percent. The Ministry of Education was established in 1871 during the Meiji Era, and by 1907 virtually every Japanese youngster attended school. Six years of grade school, three on the middle echelon, three of high school, and finally four on the university level comprise the educational structure. To this day, the only break in a rigid schedule is a short vacation during the summertime. "Cram schools" often take up even late afternoon hours. Too much time on rote memory is a general criticism against Japanese education. Another is the emphasis on the entrance examinations for the universities, for admission to the prestigious institutions, such as Tokyo University, is the ultimate goal for the student. A degree from one of the top three or four universities virtually ensures a good job for one's lifetime. Pressure on the young people intensifies during "examination hell." Families often accompany their offspring to examination sessions, for suicides among the failures are too common. Those who do not make it to the top-echelon institutions enroll at private schools at a higher tuition and ultimately occupy a lower station in their careers.

Western classical music has long engaged the Japanese. In the early 1980s Tokyo had eleven symphony orchestras. New York's Metropolitan Opera on tour in Japan sold out virtually every performance, as Japanese music students saved for months to purchase the $60 tickets. The name Seiji Ozawa, the eminent conductor, who for years directed both the Boston and San Francisco symphony orchestras, stands as a household word in his country. One Japanese innovation in musical instruction, the Suzuki Method, has been adopted worldwide, often with dramatically good results. The Suzuki Method teaches the stringed instruments (violin, viola, and cello) to groups of students (who are often quite young). Emphasis at first centers on technique rather than music theory, and parents are encouraged to participate in their children's musical experience.

Religion, on the other hand, occupied a peripheral position in the lives of many Japanese, who were too busy making money. Most adhered to a synthesis of Shinto and Buddhism, the first for daily life, the second for the hereafter. Christianity embraced a mere 2 percent of the population but did exert some social influence. Religious holidays, like the feastday of Bon (a sort of Buddhist All-Saints' Day in August), as well as the emperor's birthday were observed out of custom. Like most of those in the West, Japan's society had been steadily secularized within the previous two centuries. Asakusa Kannon Temple was Tokyo's most popular house of worship, as well as a definite tourist attraction.

Sports fascinate the Japanese much as they do the people of the West. Baseball is the great spectator sport, introduced in the early 1870s by American missionaries. Sadaharu Oh, known as "the Babe Ruth of Japan," hit over eight hundred home runs. Japan has two major leagues: the Central League and the Pacific League. Teams represent companies rather than cities. Playing fields are smaller than they are in the United States, because the ball is deader. Crowds attending the games often number over one hundred thousand. American players frequently sign with Japanese teams, to provide them more home-run power, but, unaccustomed to the lifestyle in Japan, these players usually leave after two or three years; nevertheless, they often collect fabulous salaries. Sumo wrestling is the most popular televised spectator sport, but golf and bowling are perhaps the most popular participatory sports. Golf, as in the United States, attracts many businesspeople as a status symbol, for only the most-successful can afford the outrageous entrance fees of the prestigious country clubs. Strange-looking, green, wooden structures, several stories high and covered with netting, can be seen from the windows of the Bullet Train as it glides through the Japanese countryside; these are stacked driving ranges from which golfers, teeing off at different levels, can sharpen their games. Skiing and ice skating are among the popular winter sports, recalling the 1972 Winter Olympics at Sapporo in Hokkaido. Japan also had hosted the Summer Olympics in 1964, in which the Japanese athletes distinguished themselves, especially in swimming.

The negative factors of urban life are many, as pollution still represented the principal cost of industrial expansion. Tokyo now rivaled Los Angeles and Mexico City as the most-polluted community. The rate of traffic-related deaths in Japan remained the highest in the world. Traffic in the big cities is perpetual congestion, and the pedestrian is strictly on his own among a deluge of cars, trucks, taxies, and busses, where seemingly everyone is out for himself. In personal contacts the Japanese are the essence of refined courtesy, but behind the wheel of a car that consideration seems to give way to "a survival of the fittest" struggle.

With the advent of the great stock market decline, beginning in 1989, the "Bubble Economy" burst, producing many aftershocks within Japanese society. Urban violence and street crime increased, as did illegal handgun possession. In the 1990s Japan had 1.1 homicides for every 100,000 persons; this, however, compared favorably with the U.S. rate of 8.7 persons murdered per 100,000. The U.S. example, purported by its violent television shows so popular in Japan, was partially blamed for the upsurge in crime. And the Los Angeles riots of the spring of 1992 left an ugly impression of the United States on most Japanese viewers. On the other hand, much of Japan's crime was attributed to an increasingly large foreign element, consisting of laborers from Southeast Asia, as well as Pakistan, Bangladesh, and Iran, many having entered the country illegally. These *gaijin* purportedly increased crime some 60 percent in 1992 alone. They numbered some 300,000, often avoiding registration, fingerprinting, and the reporting of job changes within two weeks, as was required by law. Far greater as a factor in crime, however, was the *Yakuza*, often termed the "Japanese Mafia." Here was a well-organized underworld, rife with terrorism and planned assassinations, that often intimidated even government officials with threats of violence.

After 1989, as lifetime employment grew increasingly burdensome for Japanese corporations with declining profit margins, some companies resorted to placing their 55-year-old or older workers in "window seats"—jobs that carried no duties but kept the employee on the payroll. "No one likes to be ignored" became the most consistent complaint of the elderly workers, who felt pressured to quit because the workday gave them virtually nothing to do and no sense of accomplishment.

Another historic tradition came under attack as families produced fewer and fewer children, while the number of elderly increased. Between 1985 and 1990, elderly persons (65 years old or more) came to comprise some 38 percent of the total population, whereas the young fell to only 16 percent of the total. Thus, a survey in 1990 referred to the "continued greying of Japanese society." Hence, a diminishing number of young workers would have to support an increasing number of retirees. Much of this was attributed to cramped housing, high land prices, many people choosing to marry later in life, and, finally, the higher costs of education. Admittedly, Japan had severe social problems within economic recession, especially since 1989.

Politics and Imperial Affairs, 1980–1995

Japan's ostensibly democratic government was structured during the occupation on the foundation of the Constitution of 1947. Afterwards, as long as Japan's economic prosperity flourished, democracy was secure. But over time political scandals, largely revealed by the media, plagued the government and undermined public confidence in its integrity. Increasingly, politicians were beheld as a privileged class serving their own self-interest and that of their elite supporters. As was often the case in the United States, Japanese political scandals usually involved private interests purchasing political influence.

The situation intensified in 1989 with the uncovering of the Recruit Scandal. This involved "insider trading" of unlisted stocks by government officials in an aggressive new company in which many profited. This revelation overthrew the government of Noburo Takeshita. These scandals revealed divisions within the dominant Liberal-Democratic party, in power since 1955 and usually controlling both houses of the Diet. With a solid base of support in the rural areas as well as industry, the party had successfully presided over Japan's Economic Miracle. Political favoritism, however, is often the result of virtually unchallenged political supremacy. Hitherto the public blamed individuals within a scandal rather than their government. But in 1992 another revelation, centered on a certain Shin Kanemaru, vice-president of the LDP, termed by one news publication "the god-father of Japanese politics" and by another the "most fearsome political shogun." He accepted a $4 million campaign contribution, substantially beyond the legal limit. He had connections within the party, with certain influential banks, and with the Yakuza, itself. Indicted, Shin Kanemaru was found guilty but paid only a nominal fine. Foreign Minister Michio Watanabe, who earlier had made racist remarks about American blacks, resigned because of his part in the scandal in April 1993. The popular effect appeared in midyear elections (1992), when only 50 percent of eligible voters participated. The following fall voters returned only a 14 percent public approval rating for the government of Prime Minister Kiichi Miyazawa, a negative record for Japanese politics. Political scandals plus the economic downturn after 1989 threatened the LDP's domination of politics.

Imperial affairs also grasped Japanese popular attention in the 1980s. On January 7, 1989, Emperor Hirohito, whose rule of sixty-three years was the long-est in recorded Japanese history, died of cancer at the age of eighty-seven. He had witnessed the rise of the military after 1931, Japan's imperium against China, World War II—with its atomic bombs and "unconditional surrender," the occupa-tion, and finally the Economic Miracle. He had been the 124th emperor and his reign name, "Showa," meant "bright peace." He was the first emperor to travel abroad, to Europe in 1971 and, four years later, to the United States. Having renounced his divinity (in 1946), he had drawn closer to his people, permitting his photograph to be taken and newspapers to print stories about him and the imperial family. His funeral on February 24, 1989, was attended by 163 represen-tatives of foreign countries, including U.S. President George Bush. His actual role in the rise of the military after 1931 likely will remain controversial.

Hirohito's successor was the fifty-five-year-old Crown Prince Akihito, whose marriage to a commoner, the eventual Empress Michiko, was unprecedented. His reign name, "Heisei," was translated "peace and achievement." The new emperor visited China, beginning October 23, 1992, the first time in history a Japanese ruler had journeyed to the "Middle Kingdom."

Popular attention was directed also to the new Crown Prince Naruhito, age 33. He announced his engagement to a 29-year-old woman of the world, Masako Owada, who had lived much of her life in Europe and the United States and graduated from Harvard, Oxford, and finally Tokyo University. Master of five lan-guages, she was a diplomat's daughter, who herself became an official in the Ministry of Foreign Affairs, attached to the U.S. division. After six years' acquain-tance with the prince, during which time they had met on several public occa-sions, she finally consented to marry him. She had heard of the ancient, rigid traditions of the imperial household, but she reluctantly agreed to abide by them. Formal announcement of the engagement came on December 12, 1992. How this "thoroughly modern woman" would bear up under the rules and regulations attendant to the *tenno* ("Son of Heaven") and his Chrysanthemum Throne as a future empress was a matter of intensive popular speculation. The media re-ferred to her as "Japan's Hillary," after the U.S. First Lady. Their wedding on June 9, 1993, gave much joy to the Japanese people.

His majesty, Emperor Hirohito, who reigned from 1926 to 1989, was the 124th emperor of Japan. Consulate General of Japan, Kansas City.

Emperor Akihito opens the 114th regular session of the Diet, Japanese parliament on February 10, 1989. This was Akihito's first appearance at the Diet since ascending the imperial throne. AP/Wide World Photos.

The wedding indeed proved a welcome relief to a Japanese public increasingly disgusted with government scandal and corruption. Japan's last four prime ministers, beginning with Norboru Takeshita in 1989, had fallen, usually as a result of some financial scandal involving unlisted stocks, real estate, or large cash payments from vested interests to politicians.

Public indignation intensified causing an implosion in the dominant LDP with the fall of Kiichi Miyazawa's government in July 1993. Some eight separate factions bolted the party, calling for a vote of no-confidence against their old allegiance. It approached a political revolution. For the first time in thirty-eight years the Liberal Democrats lost their majority. Demand for reform was deafening and Morihiro Hosokawa, former reformist governor of Kumamoto prefecture in Kyushu, assumed the premiership. He headed the Japan New Party (JNP) in partnership with seven other groups, a shaky coalition at best, united only by their opposition to the LDP. He referred to his "historic mission" to reform the country, especially to end political favoritism and corruption and restore public confidence. Perhaps this was not quite a political revolution, but much political turmoil followed the LDP eclipse.

Hosokawa did place curbs on political donations, achieved a new election system for parliament's lower house, and officially opened Japan to a few rice imports, hoping to pave the way for a future world trade agreement. He called for "a third opening" of the country, recalling Perry's visits in 1853–1854 and General MacArthur's occupation government after World War II. But wholesale reform creates enemies among vested interests, and they struck back at Hosokawa with the revelation that he had accepted $970,000 from a scandal-tainted trucking magnate. Reform became a different matter once he was on the inside looking out, and Prime Minister Hosokawa resigned on April 9, 1994. Foreign Minister Tsutomu Hata succeeded Hosokawa, but again with an unsteady coalition, from which the Socialists immediately bolted.

U.S.-Japanese Relations

The decade of the 1980s saw Japan continue its policies of international neutrality alongside an energetic economic expansion, to the increasing chagrin of its trading partners in the United States and Europe. Although dwelling in a consistently contracting world, wherein nations drew closer to one another, Japan fixed on an insular concept that caused others to accuse it of pursuing a protectionist policy in a free-trading international market.

Americans especially feared the effects of a steady Japanese penetration of their domestic markets. Further aggravating factors were the purchase by Japanese of real estate in California, Hawaii, and other states, the acquisition of several U.S. companies, and the outright theft of trade secrets—in 1982 the FBI arrested several Japanese agents who had paid $648,000 for computer data stolen from IBM. In addition, a mounting U.S. trade deficit with Japan of $12.2 billion for 1983, soared to $52 billion by 1989. The dollar fell consistently in relation to the yen, from ¥360 to the dollar in 1969 to ¥129.5 by 1991, and ¥110 two years later. Relentlessly the Japanese pushed into the U.S. market. In the mid-1980s Japan achieved an international trade balance of over $100 billion to become the world's largest creditor nation, while the United States became its greatest debtor.

Automobile sales commanded the most popular attention, because Japan exported more than two million cars annually to the United States after 1985. The names Toyota, Nissan, Honda, and Mazda became American household words. U.S. manufacturers demanded substantial import duties, most notably Lee Iacocca of Chrysler. Japanese competition hit just when U.S. quality was down due to Detroit's new policy in the early 1980s of "built-in obsolescence" or the "throw away car," especially during the presidency of Howard Smith at General Motors. Electronics saw the television market dominated by Sony, Panasonic, and National, and Nintendo led in the sales of the video games that were becoming increasingly popular among young Americans. U.S. political cartoons, depicting a ponderous, overfed Sumo wrestler, gave an ominous image to the Japanese threat. To avoid the enactment of protective tariffs by Congress, Japanese firms established plants in the United States, for example Toyota, which founded factories in California and Marysville, Ohio. As a counter, "Buy American" was a slogan urged on the U.S. public by its manufacturers.

Compounding the strain in U.S.-Japanese economic relations was the exchange of blunt, strident, and decidedly hostile rhetoric, all too reminiscent of the years 1940–1941. Prime Minister Yasuhiro Nakasone charged (1986) that the presence of blacks and Hispanics in the U.S. population lowered that country's intellectual level. Yet that same Nakasone indicated that the U.S. connection was the "cornerstone" of Japanese foreign policy, pointing to the paradox in U.S.-Japanese relations; namely, economic rivals yet diplomatic and military allies. However, the abrasive words continued. A later Prime Minister, Kiichi Miyazawa, complained that U.S. laborers had lost their work ethic. Then, former trade minister Kabun Muto asserted that U.S. workers actually toiled only in midweek, for three days; Fridays were spent in anticipation, while Mondays were wasted recuperating from overly indulgent weekends. House Speaker Yoshio Sararauchi intensified the invective by asserting that the U.S. workforce was lazy and 30 percent illiterate. Later apologies did little to lessen the tension. More positively the Japanese suggested that Americans increase savings, seek long-range goals in investment, as opposed to the quick profit, limit their use of credit cards, and cut drastically the inflated salaries of the top echelon of U.S. management.

This stridency reached a raucous climax by 1988 with the publication of the book *The Japan That Can Say No* by industrialists Akio Morita (president of Sony Corporation) and Shintaro Ishihara. The book's original version accused the United States of racial prejudice against the Japanese and urged the latter to stand up to that country and not give in to "American bluster." It was also suggested that Japan's mastery of the "semiconductor" should be used against the Americans, because being deprived of that device would disrupt the U.S. defense system. If the United States refused to cooperate, then Japan could sell semiconductors to the USSR. It further asserted that industry in the United States was hopelessly short-sighted, looking "only ten minutes ahead to the immediate profit," while Japanese business projected for the coming ten years. Also,

U.S. business too often tried to earn money quickly through manipulation of the stock market.

This book and other, even more irritating Japanese rhetoric inspired "Japan bashing" in the West. The United States in particular pressed Japan to: increase its own supply of armaments; increase its level of domestic spending on its own infrastructure; open its markets to more rice and beef imports; and purchase more American-made automobiles. Several new publications dramatized the American view, notably Michael Crichton's fictional *Rising Sun*. In this best-selling novel, the mysterious murder of an American girl at a party in Los Angeles in celebration of the opening of a new Japanese office building dramatizes the penetration of that city's economic life, for "business is war." Nonfiction works on the conflict included Pat Choate's *Agents of Influence* (1990), which takes a paranoid stance, warning of Tokyo's payoffs to influential Americans to achieve Japanese political domination over the United States. Then Clyde V. Prestowitz, in *Trading Places* (1988), asserted that the Japanese challenge would vitally weaken the international position of the United States. Finally, Karel van Wolferen, a Dutch journalist, accused Japan of being a rudderless, amoral society with no absolute values, in which social conformity to "the will of the collectivity" was the only way to survive: his book was entitled *The Enigma of Japanese Power* (1989). In a television debate with Edwin O. Reischauer, long an apologist for Japan, van Wolferen so vehemently disagreed with the Harvard University professor that the taped show could not be aired.

To many Americans, trade with Japan was "unfair," because it did not take place on a "level playing field." Nintendo's purchase of the Seattle Mariners, the American League baseball club, in June 1992 shocked the sports world. A public opinion poll at that time revealed a substantial 25 percent American disfavor toward Japan. The fiftieth anniversary of Pearl Harbor in December 1991 stirred still more distrust. Many television presentations emphasized that the raid had been a "sneak attack" against a United States at peace. Cooler heads on both sides in 1990, however, set up the Structural Impediments Initiative (SII), a series of talks in which the two countries would discuss what they wished changed in their respective economies. But not much progress resulted. Japanese reminded Americans that Britain owned more of their country than did Japan, while Japan, itself, purchased more U.S. goods than Germany, France, and Italy combined. Indeed, Japan absorbed more U.S. imports than any other country except Canada.

The Mideast crisis in 1990 opened still another area of disagreement. "Operation Desert Storm," in 1991, was a U.N. effort to free Kuwait from Iraqi invasion. That international organization requested that Japan contribute armed forces to the intervention, but Tokyo refused, pointing to their constitutional amendment forbidding use of its Self-Defense Forces outside Japan. Instead, Japan contributed some $12 billion to the operation, an amount regarded by activist countries as totally inadequate. U.S. Ambassador to Japan Michael Armacost commented, "A conscientious objector is not relieved of responsibility to play a part." Japan's contribution came to be called mere "checkbook diplomacy." Japan's innocuous stance here likely did not help in its efforts to secure a U.N. Security Council seat and thus to be accorded great-power status. Yet status and international responsibility to keep world peace ran hand in hand to many observers.

U.S. President George Bush intervened directly in U.S.-Japanese relations by way of an official visit to Tokyo (January 1992), in which he was accompanied by several American auto executives. The trip proved disappointing. Chrysler's Lee Iacocca lectured the Japanese on trade liberalization, which they found most offensive. The local media said he spoke "like a gangster," causing the executive's sullen, early departure. Mr. Bush's hosts, however, seemingly promised to purchase 20,000 U.S.-made cars and $19 billion in auto parts by 1995, but Ford executive Harold Poling charged that this realistically was "no agreement." However, much Japanese solicitude was expressed for the auto executives. "America is tired," mused Naohiro Amaya, a trade negotiator, as Premier Miyazawa expressed his sympathy for the U.S. businessmen. Someone observed that the American executives had reminded them of the "Four Black Ships" of Commodore Perry's fleet that opened Japan a century and a half before. Another Japanese wondered how an American CEO, living on $2 million a year, could complain of things at home. The unfortunate meeting climaxed embarrassingly at the farewell dinner when President Bush became ill and vomited in the lap of the premier. Press reaction was predictably negative: "less than a success;" "a fiasco;" "I think it demeans the presidency for him (Bush) to act like a car salesman," complained one observer. Then, a few days later, Premier Miyazawa emphasized that the concluded agreements were more "a target, rather than a firm promise." Professor Chalmers Johnson of the University of California at San Diego accused the administration of lacking a fundamental policy. Calling the meetings "a flop," he asserted that the different economic structures of Japan and the United States had not been addressed. Senator John Danforth, Republican from Missouri, accused the president of "begging for concessions" and called the accompanying executives "whining, crying, sobbing cry babies who always want to blame somebody else." A paradox presented itself: How could one reconcile the 60 percent decline in the Japanese stock market since 1989 with the country's increasing trade surplus that reached a whopping $133 billion worldwide for 1991–1993? Here was a question that defied American and European explanation.

Yet there were some positive signs in U.S.-Japanese relations. The much maligned American-made car was closing the quality gap by the early 1990s. Someone observed that "rivalry is the mother of invention" in what was apparently the beginning of a successful comeback. Also, the two countries needed each other diplomatically in face of the Communist collapse in Russia, Mao's successors' struggle to survive in China, and the nuclear threat from North Korea. Both the United States and Japan occupied critical places in the East Asian balance of power that had preserved the peace of that region since the end of the Korean War. Americans could not forget that U.S. relations with the two other Far Eastern giants would be far more difficult without the Japanese "keystone."

But all this still left the trade problems unresolved. The new U.S. president, Bill Clinton, had done some "Japan bashing" of his own in his 1992 campaign. To Prime Minister Miyazawa, in an April 1993 conference at the White House, the president emphasized that problems would not be solved simply by Japan's purchase of foreign rice, exporting fewer cars, or importing super computers. Rather Japan must terminate its "multifaceted resistance to foreign goods," as Robert Keatley of *The Wall Street Journal* put it, or face "swift and sure trade punishment." Clinton urged the increasing appreciation of the yen (¥110 to the dollar in 1993) to make U.S. exports to Japan cheaper and Japanese exports more expensive. The new chief executive advised the Japanese to spend excess capital at home in order to stimulate the domestic market's purchasing power of U.S. products and increase the yen value, and to set firm targets for imports of particular U.S. goods. A hopeful note appeared from Akio Morita, Sony's president, in an article in *The Atlantic* (April 1993), calling for the end of commercial restrictions in the new free-trading world of the future, a decidedly encouraging statement coming from him. "In my view, the right prescription for restarting global growth on a new sustenance basis . . . must involve an intensification of efforts to harmonize the inner workings of major economies and business systems."

In the overall, the previous five years (1989–1994) had seen Japan suffering the shocks of a stock market collapse, export contraction, plummeting corporate profits, a credit crunch, and finally the overturn of the political order with the LDP's defeat of July 1993. All this stood alongside U.S. economic pressure to liberalize its trading practices in order to offset a record $59.3 billion trade imbalance between the two countries in 1993–1994. Despite numerous agreements among government heads, it was apparent that Japan's bureaucracy, not its elected officials, really determined policy. As Clyde Prestowitz, who often negotiated for the Reagan administration explained: "It doesn't matter who is prime minister. The power in Japan remains in the hands of the bureaucratic mandarins and their allies in the big Japanese corporations." The United States was learning the hard way about "the men who really ran fortress Japan," namely the bureaucrats.

The United States pressured Japan to set guarantee-oriented trade, threatening to single out that nation and others for retaliation against unfair trade practices. Should negotiations fail within eighteen months, tariffs could be imposed. Thus, U.S.-Japanese economic relations continued to be strained.

Foreign Policy in East Asia

Japan's historic relationship with the Soviet Union had been one of apprehension and distrust, largely because of the proximity of its geographical position. Russia was too big and too close. The Kurile Islands (the Northern Territories), some sixteen in number, jutting northeastward from Hokkaido, continued to be a source of irritation. Ceded to Russia at the Yalta Conference (February 1945) the Kuriles hindered a formal Russo-Japanese treaty closing World War II. Covering some 1,939 square miles (about the size of the state of Delaware) they contained several Russian missile bases, while they sheltered the Soviet coastline from hostile submarines. The main issue involved four of the southernmost islands. The massive neighboring island of Sakhalin provided the Soviets several military airfields, while the shoreline of the Sea of Okhotsk housed a series of submarine bases. The Soviet military buildup to the north clearly menaced Japan. Likely, that was one of the principal reasons why the Russians adamantly refused re-cession of the southern Kuriles.

The threatening nature of the Soviet northern position briefly saw public exposure on September 1, 1983, when Russian interceptor planes shot down a

Boeing 747 passenger craft belonging to Korean Airlines, killing all 269 people aboard. The pilot had flown over sensitive territory on Sakhalin enroute from Alaska to Seoul, South Korea. Only a Soviet veto canceled a U.N. resolution condemning the act. Two weeks later, however, Moscow admitted the misidentification of the plane and expressed official regret. Then years later (fall of 1992), in another gesture of reconciliation, they sent the recovered voice recorder to Tokyo.

Soviet efforts to appease Japan likely were rooted in their need for investment capital in various Siberian ventures, especially in the search for and the refining of oil. Mikhail Gorbachev, Soviet premier, visited Tokyo in April 1991, but he refused to talk about the Northern Territorial issue. Instead, surprisingly, he presented a list of the sixty thousand Japanese prisoners taken in the last week of World War II together with permission to their relatives to visit their graves in Siberia. Repeatedly, the Russians had denied any knowledge of this question after 1945 and also of the Japanese POWs used as slave labor.

Talks continued, however, during the term of Boris Yeltsin as Russian president. Speculation that the Russians might cede the southern Kuriles in return for a Japanese $24 billion aid package was never confirmed. Yeltsin scheduled a conference in Tokyo (fall 1992) but then canceled it on only three-days' notice. Angrily, the Japanese refused a deal for two of the islands. Thus, Russo-Japanese relations continued to be hostile.

Japan's relationship with the People's Republic of China moved in a family context—alternating between periods of storm and calm. After the foundation of the PRC, in 1949, the two nations had stood on opposite sides of the "Bamboo Curtain." Then in 1972 Tokyo and Beijing exchanged diplomatic recognition, at which time Premier Kakuei Tanaka stated that his country "deeply reproaches itself" for some thirteen million Chinese killed during the Japanese imperium against China (1931–1945). At that time China made no claim to an indemnity for war damages. For the next twenty years, Japan invested some $20 billion in the PRC, especially in minerals, yet went no further, largely because of the PRC's chronic political instability, while China held back from too much economic dependency on the Japanese. Mutually distrustful, Japan, though it possessed technology and wealth, suffered a cultural identity crisis from adopting Western ways, while China, although poor, felt culturally secure in being Chinese. Thus, each felt superior to the other in different ways. Recalling especially the "Rape of Nanking (Nanjing)" (1937), the PRC always quailed at any sign of Japanese militarism. When the Chinese proclaimed the "Four Modernizations" in 1978, calling for reforms in agriculture, industry, science and technology, and national defense, Japan contributed substantially. Japan proved to be China's biggest trading partner, with the level reaching $19,330,000,000 by 1989.

An irritating issue arose in 1982 when Japan's Ministry of Education changed the textbook terminology of Japan's imperium against China, referring to it as an "advance." The Korean revolt (1919) against Japan's occupation was now termed a "riot." China protested, and demanded a more realistic coverage. Japanese educators backed down and made changes. But when Prime Minister Nakasone referred to his country as an "unsinkable aircraft carrier," pertaining to his country's military potential, the PRC's *People's Daily* bitterly attacked him at the time of his

China visit in 1983. The Chinese had long memories of Japan's ravenous appetite for the oil, coal, and iron of northeastern China, which, of course, had led to the Manchurian occupation of 1931 and the "China Incident" of 1937.

An unprecedented historical event in Sino-Japanese relations occurred in October 1992, when Emperor Akihito and Empress Michiko traveled to China. Never before had the *tenno* visited the "Middle Kingdom." Their one-week stay honored the twentieth anniversary of the restoration of diplomatic relations. The imperial couple saw Beijing, Shanghai, Xian, and the Great Wall. Many in Japan had opposed the trip for fear the emperor would apologize for the destruction of the past and inspire a Chinese demand for war reparations. The figure of $200 billion was rumored, but the emperor merely expressed his "deep sorrow" for his country's depredations against China, stopping short of an official apology. Both Chinese and Japanese seemed satisfied, but it was a tense situation. Ultimately the visitation proved advantageous to both sides. Japanese businesspeople saw it as a public relations move for improved commercial ties, while PRC leaders viewed it as a sorely needed diplomatic success in the face of Tiananmen Square, in which the world watched (via television) as Chinese students protesting for democracy were shot down by the military in June 1989.

Both North and South Korea's relationship to Japan was one of national resentment over some thirty-five years (1910–1945) of ruthless military rule. Those years witnessed the brutal martial law of the Japanese army in the arrogant domination over the "Hermit Kingdom," guarding against Russian expansion primarily. Situated as it was, Korea always was a strategic concern to Japan.

When South Korean President Chun Doo-hwan visited Tokyo in 1984, Emperor Hirohito referred to Japan's colonial rule as Korea's "unfortunate past." Premier Takashita visited Seoul in 1989 and expressed "remorse and regret" for "serious damage and pain" inflicted during those years. When South Korean President Roh Tae-woo presented himself to the new Emperor Akihito (1990), the latter expressed his "deepest regret" for "serious damage and pain" suffered by Koreans at the hands of Japan. On the occasion of Premier Miyazawa's coming to Seoul in 1992 an old, festering grievance from the past rose to confront him. A group of elderly Korean women informed the world that they had been "comfort girls" for Japanese soldiers during Japan's occupation of their country. Forced into prostitution and to live in fixed "stations in China and elsewhere," these women were made to engage in sexual relations many times a day. Though the majority of these roughly two hundred thousand unfortunate young women were Korean, the total number of "comfort girls" included women of other nationalities as well—Chinese, Japanese, Indonesians, Filipinos, and others also slaved. Records showed that the Japanese soldiers typically paid ¥1 for a Chinese girl, ¥1.5 for a Korean girl, and ¥2 for a Japanese girl. The Japanese premier declared his "remorse at these deeds," and offered "an apology" to the Korean people. Japanese reparations were promised. Official explanation, however, tried to say that the whole issue had been privately sponsored. After some forty-seven years, however, the truth about this wrenching tragedy revealed itself. Now many Koreans asked: If reparations were owed to the "comfort girls" should not the same be offered to all East Asians compelled to endure Japan's (wartime) exploitive "Greater East Asia Co-Prosperity Sphere"? But then in August 1993, Japan's chief cabinet secretary admitted officially that the military itself had been in full control of the entire program from the start.

North Korea's relationship with Japan was minimal after 1948, when Kim II Sung's Communist regime was implanted by a withdrawing Soviet army. By the early 1990s the general worldwide failure of communism played a vital part in opening new North Korean contacts. No diplomatic ties existed, however. North Korea's isolation forced its regime to seek outside assistance, especially when both China and Russia demanded monetary exchange for the oil that they sent to the nation. This created an economic crisis in the North. In 1990 a Japanese Socialist party delegation traveled to Pyongyang and returned to say that Kim would welcome an official delegation from Tokyo preliminary to establishment of diplomatic relations. The Japanese pondered the suggestion, attracted by the prospect of hiring the cheap labor of North Korea. In addition, Tokyo watched the development of Kim's nuclear project at Yongbyon warily, joining with the U.N. in demanding its international inspection. Pyongyang's withdrawal from the Nuclear Non-proliferation Treaty in February 1993, caused Prime Minister Miyazawa to term the situation "a great security threat." Such a prospect could inspire an East Asian arms race that would rekindle memories of the Japanese imperium after 1931, since Japan might then be forced to fully rearm. In addition, the prospect of Korean unification made the Japanese somewhat apprehensive, for it would create a neighboring giant that might eventually rival Japan economically.

Meanwhile other Southeast Asian countries, especially Thailand and Malaysia, attracted much Japanese investment in the late 1980s, again primarily because of an interest in finding inexpensive labor. Vietnam also proved inviting to Japanese businesses. But Southeast Asia inspired a sharp dispute in the Imperial Diet regarding the subject of Japan's military involvement in international peacekeeping operations. U.S. insistence on the subject of Japan's overseas participation had long pressured Tokyo, but the Japanese always pointed to Constitutional Article IX that prohibited military operations outside Japan. One U.S. official commented that it was "inappropriate for Japan to be an economic giant and a political dwarf." Japan's "muzzled" Self-Defense Forces (SDF) had always been given little public exposure. They were seldom photographed, wore civilian clothes in public, did not have a representative in the Imperial Cabinet, and were under strict civil control. Even their maneuvers took place beyond media coverage. The government of Premier Kiichi Miyazawa persuaded the Diet to vote for military participation in the U.N. peacekeeping force in Cambodia in the spring of 1992. In the face of severe opposition by the left, troops landed in that country the following September. Miyazawa explained that the operation was "commensurate with our economic power." His country was now offering something beyond mere "checkbook diplomacy." Miyazawa referred to the "call of the international community" in light of Japan's desire for a place on the U.N.'s Security Council. Yet North Korea made an uneasy reference to the "sugar-coated way" in which Japan was being "remilitarized," while Singapore's former prime minister, Lee Kuan Hew, apprehensively observed that this was like offering liquor candies to a former alcoholic.

Some six-hundred Japanese troops landed in Cambodia, most long-serving officers, who looked "gray and overweight" in the words of the media. For the first time in forty-seven years Japanese troops had been sent abroad. They were military advisers, not combat troops. But in the spring of 1993, armed ambushes by the Cambodian Khmer Rouge killed some Japanese troops near the Thai border. Their comrades were asking: "Who dispatched us to this hell anyway?," as parliamentary clamor in Tokyo increasingly demanded recall of their troops.

Withdrawal did actually take place on September 12, 1993, after some twelve hundred members of the SDF had served. Yet the previous May another SDF group had landed in Mozambique to help the U.N. supervise elections in that Southeast African state. Again, Japan clearly was working hard to land a permanent seat on the Security Council. In 1993, Prime Minister Hosokawa promised "to participate constructively" as he addressed the U.N. on the subject, but he discreetly avoided making a direct request. There the issue remained, awaiting future resolution.

Summary

It is undeniable that Japan has prospered and gained great-power status virtually by economic achievement alone, especially since the Korean War. Whether individual Japanese work harder than other peoples is debatable, but that they work quite effectively with one another is unquestionable. This trait, along with other Japanese cultural characteristics, especially their ability to adapt to change, has contributed to their successes.

Yet problems abounded in the 1990s. Domestically, the economic recession that began in 1989 has threatened the long-established tradition of lifetime employment for Japanese workers. That same economic downturn has ended the LDP's domination of government, which has contributed even more to instability. Internationally, the United States and Europe have continued to object strenuously to Japan's protectionist policies in a free-trading world. Also, many of Japan's foreign investments, especially some in the United States, have failed to respond profitably. Some observers have said that Japan already has hit its peak. Perhaps, but the traditional Japanese dedication to hard work, the strong sense of family responsibility, and what Professor Reischauer has termed a "national energy" has seen Japan through many difficulties in the past.

Suggestions for Further Reading

Beasley, W. G., *The Modern History of Japan* (1981).
Behr, Edward, *Hirohito: Behind the Myth* (1989).
Benedict, Ruth, *The Chrysanthemum and the Sword* (1946).
Berry, William A., *Prisoner of the Rising Sun* (1993).
Bowring, Richard and Peter Kornicki, eds., *Cambridge Encyclopedia of Japan* (1993).
Boxer, C. R., *The Christian Century in Japan, 1549–1650* (1951).
Brackman, Arnold C., *The Other Nuremberg: The Untold Story of the Tokyo War Crimes Trials* (1987).
Choate, Pat, *Agents of Influence* (1990).
Christopher, Robert C., *The Japanese Mind* (1983).
Clausen, Henry C. and Bruce Lee, *Pearl Harbor: Final Judgment* (1992).
Clavell, James, *Shogun: A Novel of Japan* (1975).
———, *Gaijin* (1994).

Coox, Alvin, *Nomanhan: Japan Against Russia* (1985).

Costello, John, *The Pacific War* (1991).

Crichton, Michael, *Rising Sun* (1992).

Emmerson, John K., *The Eagle and the Rising Sun: America and Japan in the Twentieth Century* (1989).

Ensign, Margee, *Doing Good or Doing Well? Japan's Foreign Aid Program* (1992).

Fairbank, John K., *China: A New History* (1992).

———, Reischauer, Edwin O., and Albert M. Craig, *East Asia: Tradition and Transformation* (1989).

Fallows, James, *Looking at the Sun: The Rise of the New East Asian Economic and Political System* (1994).

Feiffer, George, *Tennozan: The Battle of Okinawa and the Atomic Bomb* (1992).

Hall, John H. ed., *The Cambridge History of Japan*, 6 vols (date not set).

Hall, John Whitney and Toyoda Takeshi, eds., *Japan in the Muromachi Age* (1977).

Harries, Meirion, and Susie Harries, *Soldiers of the Sun* (1991).

Hersey, John, *Hiroshima* (1946).

Hideo Ibe, *Japan Thrice Opened: An Analysis of Relations Between Japan and the United States* (1992).

Iriye, Akira, *Pacific Estrangement* (1972).

———, *Power and Culture: The Japanese-American War, 1941–1945* (1981).

Johnson, Chalmers, *MITI and the Japanese Miracle* (1982).

Kidder, J. Edward, *Japan Before Buddhism* (1966).

Mass, Jeffry P., *The Kamakura Bakufu: A Study in Documents* (1976).

MacArthur, General Douglas, *Reminiscences* (1964).

Manchester, William, *American Caesar: General Douglas MacArthur* (1978).

Michener, James A., *The Floating World* (1983).

Mitchell, Richard H., *Janus-faced Justice: Political Criminals in Imperial Japan* (1992).

Morison, Samuel Eliot, *Old Bruin: Commodore Matthew C. Perry* (1967).

Morita Akio and Shintaro Ishihara, *The Japan that Can Say No* (1988).

Orr, Robert M., *The Emergence of Japan's Foreign Aid Power* (1992).

Prange, Gordon W., *At Dawn We Slept* (1981).

———, *Pearl Harbor: The Verdict of History* (1986).

———, *Target Tokyo* (1984).

Prestowitz, Clyde V. *Trading Places* (1988).

Pyle, Kenneth B., *The Japanese Question* (1992).

Reischauer, Edwin O., *The Japanese Today* (1988).

———, *Japan: The Story of a Nation*, 4th ed. (1990).

Ryusaku Tsunoda, et al, eds., *Sources of Japanese Tradition*, 2 vols. (1964).

Sadler, A. L., *The Maker of Modern Japan: The Life of Tokugawa Ieyasu* (1937).

Sansom, G. B., *Japan: A Short Cultural History* (1962).

———, *The Western World and Japan* (1970).

Schaller, Michael, *Douglas MacArthur: The Far Eastern General* (1989).

Seidensticker, Edward, *Low City, High City: Tokyo From Edo to the Earthquake* (1983).

Spector, Ronald H., *Eagle Against the Sun* (1985).

Statler, Oliver, *Japanese Inn* (1984).

———, *Shimoda Story* (1969).

Tasker, Peter, *The Japanese: A Major Exploration of Modern Japan* (1987).

Totman, Conrad, *Politics in the Tokugawa Bakufu, 1600–1843* (1967).

———, *The Collapse of the Tokugawa Bakufu, 1862–1868* (1980).

Turnbull, S. R., *The Samurai: A Military History.* (1977)

van der Vat, Dan, *The Pacific Campaign* (1991).

van Wolferen, Karel, *The Enigma of Japanese Power* (1989).

———, "Japan's Non-Revolution," *Foreign Affairs* (September–October, 1993).

Vogel, Ezra F., *Japan as Number 1: Lessons for America* (1979).

Warner, Langdon, *The Enduring Art of Japan* (1952).

Whiting, Robert, *The Chrysanthemum and the Bat* (1977).
Wilson, Dick, *When Tigers Fight: The Story of the Sino-Japanese War, 1937–1945* (1982).
Wyden, Peter, *Day One: Before Hiroshima and After* (1984).

Glossary

Bakufu: "Camp Government." The shogun's military administration (1192–1867).

be: Occupational groups. Hereditary subgroups of the uji (clans) in early Japan.

biwa: A stringed instrument used primarily in puppet plays.

"Bubble Economy": Japan's burgeoning economy of the 1980s, wherein it exported over 2 million cars to the United States per year after 1985, achieving an international trade surplus of $133 billion by 1994.

Buddhism: Religion of Buddha, originating in India. Passed to Japan after A.D. 552.

Bunraku: Traditional puppet theater of Japan.

burakumin: Literally "hamlet people," who by Buddhist moral standards practice unclean professions, i.e. butchers, those who work with leather, and those who deal with the dead. Social outcasts, who live in six thousand segregated communities. Largest minority group in Japan.

Bushido: "The Way of the Warrior." Traditional samurai code of honor in the Tokugawa Period (1603–1867)

Chonin: The townspeople. Significant during the rise of towns and cities during the seclusion period (1639–1853)

Confucius: "Great Sage" and philosopher of China whose ideals were part of Chinese heritage to Japan.

Daibutsu: "Great Buddha": notably the figures at Nara and Kamakura.

daimyo: "Great Names." Feudal lords under the shoguns.

détente: An easing of strained relations, usually on the international level.

Edo: The capital of the Tokugawa shoguns (1603–1867). Site of modern Tokyo.

Fudai: "Inside Lords." Allies of Tokugawa Ieyasu who profited by his redistribution of lands after his victory of 1600.

gaijin: Literally "outsider," foreigner, or alien. Applies to all foreigners in Japan, especially Koreans, Chinese, and the Ainu, all of whom are denied full citizenship. Today Western teachers, students, businesspeople, and diplomats, as well as temporary, unskilled laborers from Taiwan, the Philippines, and other Asian countries are included.

geisha: "Art person." A professional entertainer. Significant in rise of towns during era of seclusion (1639–1853).

genro: Elder statesmen. Leaders of the Meiji Restoration and modernization after 1868. Dominated the Privy Council after 1889.

giri: Duty or obligation in Japanese society.

haiku: Three-line, seventeen-syllable poem.

han: The estates of feudal lords.

hanamichi: Runway into the audience. Used for entrances and exits of actors in Kabuki plays.

Hara Kiri: Suicide by disembowelment. Popular term for Seppuku.

Heisei: "Peace and Concord." Reign name for the Emperor Akihito (1989–).

Joruri: The puppet theater.

Kabuki: Traditional Japanese theater, featuring stylized singing and dancing, utilizing male actors exclusively.

Kamikaze: "Divine Wind." Protected Japan from Mongol invasions (1274 and 1281). Also, name for Japanese suicide planes in World War II.

kampaku: A regent appointed to rule in the emperor's name. Prominent especially in Fujiwara Period (866–1160).

kimono: Loose outer garment, held in place by a sash.

Kojiki: Record of Ancient Things. One of two histories written in the eighth century (in classical Chinese) substantiating the divine origin of the Japanese rulers and empire.

kokutai: Concept that the emperor is the state and rules as a father over his family. Used to justify absolute imperial rule in the rise of the military (1931ff.)

koto: a stringed horizontal harp.

kowtow: Ceremonial, acknowledging superiority of Chinese emperor or any person in authority, literally "head knocking." Confucian concept.

Kyoto: Imperial capital (794–1868).

Meiji: "Enlightened Rule." Restoration of imperial authority (1868–1912): reign of Emperor Mutsuhito.

metsuke: The shogun's official informers in the Tokugawa period.

miyabi: Courtly refinement. Under Chinese influence, the Japanese imperial court during the Heian Period (794–1185).

Nihongi: Chronicles of Japan. One of two eighth-century histories (written in classical Chinese) asserting the divine origin of the Japanese ruler and empire.

ninjo: Passion or natural inclination.

No: A stylized dance drama.

"Northern Territorial Issue": Refers to the Kurile Islands, S. Sakhalin, and other lands north of Japan, awarded to Russia by its Western allies at the Yalta Conference (February 1945). Japan sought the return of the southern Kuriles, but the USSR refused, likely because of the Soviet missile bases, airfields, and other military installations in those areas. The issue has prevented a formal treaty between Russia and Japan that would officially close World War II.

obi: An elaborate sash, used primarily with a kimono.

Rangaku: "Dutch learning." Japanese study of Western books during the seclusion period (1639–1853).

ronin: Masterless samurai whose lords were casualties of Japan's feudal wars. A roving, discontented element during the Tokugawa Period.

sake: A fermented rice wine, most often served warm.

Sakoku: "Closed Country Policy." The shoguns' rule during the seclusion period.

samisen: A stringed musical instrument.

samurai: "One who serves." The traditional warrior class of Japan during feudal era.

Seppuku: Method of suicide by disembowelment.

seri: The revolving stage used for Kabuki plays.

Shimpan: "Related Lords." Trusted relatives to whom Tokugawa Ieyasu awarded the estates immediately around his capital, Edo.

Shinto: "Way of the Gods." Chinese name given to Japanese native religion stressing the worship of nature.

shoen: Manor controlled by a court aristocrat in feudal Japan.

shogun: "Barbarian Subduing Generalissimo." The head of the military government of Japan (1192–1867).

Showa: "Enlightened Peace." Reign name for Emperor Hirohito (1926–1989), whose reign was the longest in recorded Japanese history.

Suzuki Method: A musical instructional technique developed by Suzuki Shin'ichi, famous teacher and the son of a violin maker. The musical talent of very young children achieved quick development by working in groups, learning the violin and other string instruments by rote. The Suzuki Method achieved astounding results with about 300,000 students internationally.

torii: Gateway to a Shinto shrine or a garden. Signifies a place of reverence.

Tozama: "Outside Lords." Those opposed to Tokugawa Ieyasu before 1600. Generally these lords controlled the most powerful estates.

uji: Clan. Basic political, social unit of early Japan. Ruled by a priest-chieftain and protected by a deity.

ukiyo: "Floating world." A term used to describe town life during the seclusion period.

ukiyo-zoshi: Literature dealing with town life during seclusion period.

wako: Japanese pirates during period of Dark Ages (1333–1571).

Yakuza: "Good for Nothing." Japanese underworld (or "Mafia"), connected with prostitution, blackmail, extortion, and loan-sharking. Active since the eighteenth century, it is closely associated with gambling and garners much popular resentment because it mocks Japanese social conventions of hard work and obedience to the law. The political influence wielded by the Yakuza is substantial.

zaibatsu: Japanese business trusts or cartels, emanating from modernization (1868ff). Usually controlled by small groups of families with preponderant influence on the national economy.

Zengakuren: All Students Union. Predominant student organization in Japanese universities today.

The
World
of

KOREA

Introduction

Korea today, like China, is a divided country. The Communist Democratic People's Republic (or North Korea) confronts the Republic of Korea (South Korea) across a heavily fortified demarcation line. Since both seek the unification of their country, their implacable hostility makes that nation, in the words of one observer, "a smoldering volcano." Both regimes are well-armed dictatorships, but their internal political unrest and economic disparity further divide them. South Korea showed a 10 percent Gross National Product (GNP) growth annually from 1962 to 1976, while North Korea is debt-ridden; this coupled with the fact that North Korea is a potential nuclear power seriously aggravates a dangerous situation.

Throughout its history, Korea has known privation and conflicts because of its geographical location. Seldom a regional threat itself, Korea is surrounded, unfortunately, by neighbors—China, Russia, and Japan—who have over the centuries vied for domination of this critical area. Jutting southward like a thumb from the northeastern coast of China, the Korean peninsula has acted as a two-way bridge for invasion routes between China and Japan. In more peaceful times, however, Korea acted as a corridor through which Chinese culture passed to the Japanese. Koreans have earned the epithet "the Irish of the Far East" because of their frequent subjugation by greater powers seeking to gain the advantage of their country's strategic position.

Ironically, throughout its history Korea has been termed "the land of the morning calm," from *Chosŏn*, its traditional designation. The name "Korea" derives from the Koryŏ dynasty that ruled the country from the tenth to the fourteenth centuries, peacefully absorbing so many ideals and institutions from the great "Middle Kingdom" of China, while separated from the rest of the world. As a Chinese "outlying dependency" for almost two thousand years, Korea preserved its political independence and national identity despite internal factionalism and barbarian attacks. Today, the flag of South Korea honors this Chinese heritage by its representation of the *yin* and *yang*, the two interacting forces of nature. Nineteenth-century imperialism finally overwhelmed Korea, which fell victim to the harsh military, colonial rule of the Japanese for thirty-five years after 1910.

Today, so many Koreans desire unification; yet neither North nor South will submit to the other, and the entire situation threatens war. Undoubtedly, all of these distraught people would welcome the return of a portion of that peace that once made their country "the hermit kingdom."

Early History

to Western Imperialism, 2333 B.C. to A.D. 1860

Shaped somewhat like Florida, Korea is not large by American standards, comparable in size to Utah or Montana. Yet its area of 85,000 square miles exceeds that of many European countries, approximating England, Scotland, and Wales combined. The peninsula extends 670 miles north to south, and about 320 miles east to west at its widest point. Mountains cover most of its area, with the northern sectors and the east coast possessing the tallest ranges. The Yalu and T'umen rivers delimit the northern boundary with Manchuria, while the Naktong flows in the southeast. Seoul, capital of South Korea, is located on the Han, which traverses the center of the country, while Pyongyang, North Korea's capital, lies on the Taedong River.

Climatically, the country is temperate, midway between the continental and marine types, comparable to the U.S. Atlantic coast from Maine to Georgia. The rainy season begins in late June and ends in August, providing about half of the annual precipitation. Agricultural areas comprise only one-fifth of the land and lie chiefly along the western and southern coasts, producing rice, barley, wheat, potatoes, corn, and beans. South Korea's population is about 44,436,000, yet occupies a smaller area than the North, which has 23,067,000 people.

Lying in the heart of the Far East, Korea (meaning "high and lovely land") is separated from China proper by the Yellow Sea on the west and from Japan by the Strait of Tsushima to the south and the Sea of Japan on the east. Korea adjoins the former Soviet Union for only twelve miles in the northeast. About three thousand small islands cluster along its coasts, and its southern and western shorelines especially are well-suited for harbors, such as Pusan and Inchon, South Korea's main ports. North Korea's chief seaport, Wonson, lies on the east coast.

Origins and Early Society

Korean origins are shrouded in legends, as are those of most early peoples. These myths recall the beneficent deeds of culture-heroes or sage rulers. According to these sources, Hwanung, Lord of Heaven, descended to earth to rule mankind. There in a pine forest he found a beautiful young girl, just transformed from a bear. He married her, and she gave birth to Tan'gun, the first king of Korea, in the year 2333 B.C., the beginning of the Korean calendar. Tan'gun ruled for fifteen hundred years thereafter. Anthropologists indicate, however, that the Koreans derive from the Altaic peoples of northern Asia, ancestors of the Mongols, Manchus, and Siberian tribes. Certain pottery artifacts found in northern Korea suggest that these original groups migrated by way of the great plain that stretches across northern Eurasia from the Volga River to the Manchurian highlands. The Korean language is related to Turkish, Mongol, and Japanese. Probably humans first came to the peninsula about thirty thousand years ago, subsisting by hunting and fishing and eating the fruits, nuts, and shellfish they found as they moved from place to place. From the beginning, the family held an honored position, and clans were formed. When an agrarian society had evolved by the second millennium B.C., the inhabitants organized tribes with patriarchs, respected for their wisdom and age, that led the first settled communities. At this time the typical dwellings, often located in small pits, consisted of a wooden framework supporting a thatched roof, with walls of clay and a stone floor. Religion stressed nature worship and addressed the spirits within all objects. Officially designated shamans (usually women) conducted rituals, and the sorceress remains a part of Korean religion today. About 1000 B.C., the Bronze Age saw the development of new implements for war and agriculture, which necessitated the building of new and larger settlements. Arrowheads, axes, and fishhooks, however, continued to be made from bone, while such tools as picks, knives, and scrapers were fashioned from horns or shells. Later, when the Iron Age dawned (ca. 300 B.C.), early Korean society was threatened by barbarians who invaded from the north. This danger resulted in the intrusion of the neighboring Chinese, who in ca. 194 B.C. founded the frontier garrison of Ancient Chosŏn in southern Manchuria and northern Korea for protection, especially against the feared Huns. In turn, Ancient Chosŏn fell in 108 B.C. to the "Marshal Emperor," Han Wu-ti, who established four Chinese prefectures in northern Korea administered by military commanders, again to secure the frontiers against barbarian tribes.

The Three Kingdoms Period. A.D. 313–668

The Chinese fortified areas did not endure, because the Korean people, resenting this alien domination, rose and conquered them, so that after seventy-five years only one last Chinese holding survived. Yet the Chinese presence had had a unifying effect on the area. Native Korean states emerged, based on old tribal foundations but borrowing much from China. The state of Koguryŏ rose in the north in 57 B.C., and later the states of Paekche and Silla achieved domination of the area south of the Han River, which the Chinese had never subdued.

Warfare between Koguryŏ and the northern barbarians overran the last Chinese foothold by A.D. 313. Koguryŏ and Paekche clearly saw the advantage, however, of immediately adopting administrations based on the Chinese model, to strengthen their situations. The scholar bureaucracy (the Chinese civil service, entrance to which was based on competitive examinations) became their central governmental institution, and Confucianism (the philosophy that holds that social harmony derives from respect for authority) the foundation of their educational system. Officials and intellectuals adopted Chinese as the language of administration and literature, while aristocratic landowners took Buddhism, which entered in the fourth–fifth centuries, as their religion, having been attracted to this new religion by its inherent prayers for the protection of the state and its promise of life after death. The aristocrats used Chinese institutions to ensure their supremacy in the state, departing somewhat from Chinese practice, however, since they rigorously trained their sons for war and made sure that the privileged classes alone stood eligible for the scholar examinations. The Chinese themselves, on the other hand, disdained the military profession, while their official examinations represented "a career open to talents," theoretically cutting across class lines.

Silla, the state in the southeast, absorbed Chinese institutions somewhat later and, by preserving much of its old tribal structure, managed to keep its social base intact. Koguryŏ, Paekche, and Silla waged constant war for control of the fertile plain of the valleys of the Han and Imjin rivers. When the great Chinese T'ang Empire allied with Silla in order to secure their Korean flank against the Hsiung-nu (Huns), barbarians who were again threatening the northern frontiers, they overran the other states. Then Silla turned against T'ang and once again drove the Chinese from Korea, by 668 uniting the peninsula for the first time in its history. In its march to conquest, Silla also subdued Kaya, a small Japanese subject state in the south, through which Paekche was passing much of the Chinese heritage to Japan. Japan's armies had participated in these struggles in the interests of its imperial Yamato clan.

The Rise and Fall of Silla. 668–935

After Silla had united Korea south of the Taedong River, the new state continued to look to the T'ang Empire (618–907) as a cultural and administrative model, undoubtedly the most prestigious in China's long history. Consenting to become a tributary state but remaining politically separate as befitted an outlying dependency, Silla dispatched missions annually to the T'ang emperor, who allowed it to trade and send students to China. Silla incorporated the Chinese military organization, land system, and administrative structure (with its "six boards"), established Buddhism as the state religion, and copied imperial court decorum. Truly, the kingdom had become a "little T'ang." Silla was never a slavish imitator, however, rather it adapted certain Chinese institutions to its environment, changing some elements to suit its own purposes.

For example, the scholar bureaucracy did not operate in Silla as it did in China, because the aristocracy (or "bone rank" system) refused to yield their positions to the lower classes. Then the Chinese "well-field" system, which called for the redistribution of land every six years to those who cultivated it, fell victim in Silla to the entrenched estates, and miserable conditions for the farmer resulted. Many farm laborers, often prisoners of war, were virtual slaves to the overbearing landlords. Since the Chinese had introduced rice, a crop requiring intensive cultivation, into Korea in the first century B.C., the majority of Korean peasants were bound forever to the lands they tilled. Riots erupted in the countryside only to be mercilessly crushed. The poor Korean peasants, victims of their country's aristocratic society, totally lacked the necessary resources to gain their freedom, a tragic theme throughout their history.

Once unity was established, however, the power of the Silla court began to diminish. Rivalries among the provincial lords produced factionalism and local separatism, one quarrel resulting in the assassination of the king in the later eighth century. A series of struggles for the throne reduced executive power to a plaything of the aristocrats. Buddhist temples, after acquiring much land, soon became virtually autonomous. Unfortunately, the Korean kings could make no claim to divine authority, subjecting the throne to continuous political manipulation, in vivid contrast to the sanctified positions of the emperors of China and Japan. Silla reached its pinnacle, then the kingdom fragmented. By the year 935, Silla had succumbed to a new power in the north—a state known as Later Koguryŏ or Koryŏ. Silla, interestingly, expired less than thirty years after its mentor, the T'ang Empire.

Society and Culture, to 935
The northern origin of the Korean people is substantiated by neolithic pottery artifacts found chiefly along the Yalu and T'umen river basins. These thin-walled vases, basins, jars, and bowls feature a significant comb-like decor, or stippled surface, similar to those found in Japan and Siberia and typical of a nomadic society. Dolmens (or rock tombs, as tall as seven feet) formed by huge flat stones and resembling a house of cards, that is, four sections forming the sides with one larger, overlapping slab on top, abound in northern Korea. Similar dolmens may also be found in Shantung and Manchuria, further supporting the supposition of the Koreans' northern origins. Finally, the existence of shellmounds, actually refuse heaps of fishing communities, found along the Korean coastline and the banks of major rivers, which are also found northward, makes the northern derivation of the Koreans almost certain.

The Yalu area contains many tomb caves, the walls of which bear paintings that portray life in the settled communities of the Bronze Age. This cave art reflects a remarkably productive civilization, which used metal principally for coins, belt buckles, arrowheads, sickles, and knives. Thousands of mound tombs in the T'ung-kou Plain also contain interior chambers whose walls present a graphic picture of a social life that included religious rituals, dances, and organized hunts. Finally, cave murals of Ancient Chosŏn reflect the nature worship of the Iron Age tribal societies and represent the first extensive Chinese influence in Korean art.

Precisely when the Chinese philosophies of Confucianism and Taoism entered Korea is unknown, but they brought significant civilizing forces to the country. Taoism preached adaptability to nature and conformity to its patterns, while advising withdrawal from society. Confucianism taught respect for the family and the moral improvement of the individual and society through study, virtue, and deference to superiors. The position of the father as the head of the family was analogous to that of the ruler, who was head of the state. Taoism possessed the wider appeal because of its easy accessibility to agricultural peoples and its emphasis on hermitage, while Confucianism largely attracted intellectuals and government officials. Entering Korea between A.D. 372 and 424, Buddhism won adherents among the literate and affluent because of its esoteric creed, promise of an afterlife, and its support of the state. This religion, which had originated in India in the 6th century B.C., passed to China about the time of the birth of Christ. Chinese culture traveled on the popularity of these philosophies. Like the Chinese and the Japanese, the Koreans embraced various beliefs, selecting from each those ideals suitable to their particular needs.

Buddhism inspired many art treasures designed for the veneration of the Buddha. Paekche's greatest creation was the Kudara Kannon, displayed today in Japan. A painted wood Bodhisattva (a mortal who had attained perfection but who, out of compassion for others, decided not to pass to Nirvana immediately), the Kudara Kannon either originated in Korea or was carved by a Korean craftsman who had been brought over to Japan. The Silla Period, however, witnessed the pinnacle of Chinese Buddhism. Built to appear detached from the world, temples of striking beauty, containing Buddha figures with the beatific smile and graceful pose, dotted the Korean landscape. The ruins of Pulguksa Monastery (near the capital city of Kyŏngju) and the cave-temple of Sokkuram (home of an exquisite eleven-foot Buddha of solid granite) on the hillside behind it present splendid examples of Korea's Buddhist art; the most prominent, perhaps, is the temple complex at the foot of Mount Sokni, completed in the eighth century. Korea became a "Land of Pagodas," Buddhist tower-like structures, usually five- or seven-tiered, erected on the tomb of a king or holy man. The casting of magnificent monastery bells, another aesthetic achievement, produced the Pongdoksa Temple Bell in Kyŏngju, which stands eleven feet tall and weighs 158,000 pounds. The recent discovery of the "Tomb of the Flying Horse" in a cave outside Kyŏngju revealed a mural (of the flying horse) that is probably the finest example of Silla painting discovered to date.

Students returning from China founded new educational institutions in Korea, especially the National Academy, established in 651 and dedicated to Confucian studies. These intellectuals also imported calligraphy or the art of brush writing, utilizing the Chinese language. Historians employed this Chinese script to record Korea's past. Another Chinese import was the T'ang court music played for Silla kings on flutes, zithers, and other instruments from China, which, ironically, eventually lost this art form. Buddhist festivals offered the occasion to play folk songs and perform dances on religious themes. Finally, Silla erected the first observatory at Kyŏngju in 682, the study of astronomy having been inspired by early Chinese science.

The Rise and Fall of Koryŏ, 935–1392

Silla surrendered without a fight to Koryŏ, a new, rising state in the north, from which, as mentioned, the modern name "Korea" is derived. A rebel leader, Won Kon, had founded the state of Koryŏ in 918 and, after his conquest, invited the former Silla ruler to become his chief minister, permitting the Silla aristocracy to keep their estates. Won Kon (later called King T'aeju), however, compelled landowners to live in the new capital (Kaesong), enter government service, submit to a fixed income from their estates, and surrender their sons to him as hostages. Thus, he incorporated Silla's administrative structure into Koryŏ, temporarily ensuring the stability of the new state. The king declared Buddhism the official religion but carefully regulated the number of temples constructed. T'aeju also tried to reinstitute the scholar bureaucracy within the T'ang and Sung administrative framework. He designed Kaesong on the gridiron pattern, with streets at right angles, mimicking the layout of the T'ang capital at Ch'ang-an and the Japanese imperial cities of Nara and Kyoto.

Koryŏ relied on its tightly regulated aristocracy to control the country. Gradually, however, the executive weakened as the powerful estates became more independent and quarrels erupted among the various lords. Won Kon's policy of frequent intermarriage between the successive kings and members of the privileged classes, precipitating violent succession disputes, eventually reduced the monarchs merely to the first among equals. The tax structure eventually failed because new estates (created to support public officials) escaped the levy, imposing the financial burden on the poor peasant. Rural rebellions exploded after the first century of the regime. Meanwhile, the landed classes reveled in a pleasure-mad world at the capital. Buddhism, saturated with alien beliefs, lost prestige as rivalries between Buddhist priests and Confucian scholar officials divided the court.

As the regime decayed, its frontier defenses inevitably weakened. The military classes, regarded with social disdain by prominent Confucianists, overthrew the government in 1170 to establish themselves as the Ch'oe "dictators." Then northern barbarians threatened again. The warlike Khitans ravaged parts of Koryŏ and the Chinese Sung Empire, but an effectively coordinated Korean defense defeated these invaders. Next the Jürchids, another northern people, established the hostile state of Chin in the northeast, successfully overrunning China as far as the Yangtze River. Then even this threat gave way to a far greater one. The fierce Mongols, conquerors from East Asia to Central Europe, turned their eyes toward the rich lands and wealth of China and its dependencies. To secure their flanks for attack on the "Celestial Empire," the Mongols invaded Korea in 1231. Their highly mobile mounted warriors easily prevailed over the inept Korean foot soldiers. A desperate king withdrew to Kanghwa Island, abandoning his helpless country to the conquerors. Three thousand royal concubines flung themselves into the sea to escape the marauders. In a despicable act of appeasement, the ruler agreed to pay a monstrous tribute to the invader, who carted off two hundred thousand captives in one year. To climax Korea's humiliation, the country was forced to build nine hundred ships and supply thousands of workers, soldiers, and seamen for the Mongols as they attempted to invade Japan in 1274 and 1281. Not until the Chinese people finally overthrew the hated, alien Mongol (Yüan) dynasty in 1368 was an exhausted Korea liberated.

The Mongol experience so weakened Koryŏ that Japanese pirates (*wako*) regularly preyed on the coastal cities and raided far upstream, practically unopposed. The peasantry, bound to the estates and with little protection, suffered still another scourge. A powerful military clan, the Yi, finally overthrew the weak government in Kaesong, which had ordered General Yi Song-gye northward to attack the forces of the new Ming dynasty of China, which was opposed by the Korean aristocrats whose station depended upon their old tributary relationship to the Yüan. Courageously, General Yi countermanded his instructions, reversed his field, and marched his army on the capital, overthrowing the government. Thus the new Yi dynasty, destined to rule some 518 years (1392–1910)—twice as long as any imperial Chinese dynasty—assumed the throne of troubled Korea.

Koryŏ Culture

Koryŏ cultural achievements compare favorably with those of their contemporaries, Sung China and the Kamakura shogunate in Japan. The most spectacular example of Buddhist art originated as a prayer for protection from the Mongol threat. Faced with imminent peril to the country, the king commissioned the carving of Buddhist scripture on 81,258 wooden panels, which eventually printed over six thousand volumes of the sutras (the sermons of Buddha), also stimulating the development of papermaking. The completion of this exquisite example of block printing took sixteen years to complete. Entitled the *Tripitaka Koreana*, the reverential project, however, failed to protect Korea from the invaders. Also, when many of the temple communities fraternized with the hated Mongols, Buddhism declined in Korea, gradually losing out to a revived Confucianism, Neo-Confucianism, from Sung China, resplendent in the succeeding Yi dynasty.

Other technological advances of Koryŏ consisted of the development of movable type (inspired perhaps by a similar experiment in Sung China) in 1234, more than two hundred years before Johannes Gutenberg's achievement in Europe. Astronomy advanced, and a calendar was formulated, while substantial knowledge of meteorology accumulated. The Confucian tradition of a literary, moralistic education as well as the spiritual otherworldliness of Buddhism, however, militated against further scientific penetration of nature's secrets, leaving these accomplishments relatively isolated, a decided handicap when Korea faced the West in the nineteenth century.

The achievements of Koryŏ had derived from the new emphasis on education. Primarily, schools instructed candidates for government administration, Taehak (founded in 372) having been the first such state-supported institution. During the Silla Period a unique method of training, known as Hwarang-do ("Way of the Flower Knights"), educated young aristocrats in the arts of war and literature. Koryŏ established Kukchagam (992), another government-sponsored school, in Kaesong, in conjunction with private schools, called *Sahak*. Attendance was limited to the privileged, however. These academies did produce two outstanding literary works: *History of the Three Kingdoms* and *Memorabilia of the Three Kingdoms*, the latter accurately portraying the life of the people. Since Korea did not possess its own native script, these works were written in Chinese, still the language of scholarship.

But an indigenous Korean art did flourish, most notably in ceramics. The beauty and quality of Koryŏ celadons (porcelains of grey-green color) often surpassed those of Sung China. Vases, teapots, water bowls, ewers, wine cups, and incense burners with embossed birds, flowers, plants, trees, and clouds, reflected an age of exquisite taste. Tea drinking, popularized by Buddhist monks, acted as an incentive for the creation of celadon tea sets. By 1150–ca.1300, Korean ceramics featured many combinations in white, grey, and black, besides the

Black inlay celadon bowl, Koryŏ dynasty, ca. 1300 A.D. Photograph courtesy of the Saint Louis Art Museum, Purchase Friends Fund.

Celebration in thanksgiving for a bountiful harvest. Called Choo Suk, it takes place in autumn, when farmers express gratitude for a plentiful crop, especially rice. Y. H. Bäng.

lovely green. Furthermore, the discovery of the inlay method in the thirteenth century resulted in the creation of even more superb designs in plain, inlaid, and painted celadon. The Mongol devastation, plus the failure of the Korean authorities to appreciate the accomplishments of Koryŏ potters, caused this class of artisans to expire, and their secrets died with them. As an added misfortune, many of their creations were lost to the country due to their wholesale removal during the Japanese occupation (1910–1945).

Foundation of the Yi dynasty, 1392–1636

Yi Song-gye ruled from 1392 to 1398 and molded Korea into a model Confucian state. He made his submission to the Ming emperor of China, who again selected the name Chosŏn for the kingdom. Neo-Confucianism, the new state philosophy, had formulated a metaphysical explanation of human beings' place in the universe within this traditional code of social ethics, displacing Buddhism, which continued to decline in both China and Korea. An increasing shortage of land likewise contributed to an official desire to liquidate the vast holdings of many Buddhist monasteries.

Scholar examinations again selected government officials, who for the first time received land—property taken from the old aristocracy—as "merit subjects." Villages established primary schools, while the government founded district institutions for the training of officials. New military examinations chose officers for the armed forces, and the combined privileged classes (*Yangban* or "Two Groups") comprised the new aristocracy. Middle classes (*Chungin*) consisted of lower government officials and also traders, while *Yangmin* or commoners, who worked the land, made up the rest of the social structure.

The new regime established its capital at Hanyang (modern Seoul), where it remains to this day, to escape the influence of the Buddhist clergy and the old aristocratic elite at Kaesong. The Yi reigned for over five centuries because their elaborate bureaucracy, composed of local governments of scholar magistrates and provincial governors, ensured an effective political order. Several successful reigns, especially that of King Sejong (1418–1450), also contributed to the period's stability. But over time the dispersal of political authority gradually weakened the Yi, whose kings lacked the stature of the Chinese emperors. Also, factionalism enervated the administration, still rigidly dominated by the aristocracy, who could pass their official positions on to their sons. Quarrels created two contentious parties—"Easterners" versus "Westerners." In time these two large groups splintered into smaller ones, all contesting for domination of the throne. Much political strife centered in the *sŏwŏn*, private estate academies, established for the education of government officials. At the same time, Confucian disdain for the merchant class prevented any effective economic growth, seriously weakening the state's financial structure.

To its credit, the Yi accomplished much in the cultural realm. Emphasis on education, coinciding with continued development of movable-type printing, produced writings on medicine, astronomy, geography, history, and architecture. In 1420 the Yi founded Chiphyonjon, a kind of royal research institute. Under its program calligraphy made further strides. Chiphyonjon's outstanding achievement, however, proved to be *Han'gul,* "Korean letters," a new written language based on twenty-eight simple phonetic symbols (although it incorporated some Chinese characters later), formulated in the reign of King Sejong in 1446. One of the most successful writing systems in the world, it eliminated illiteracy for all time as a national problem. Nevertheless, many scholars opposed Han'gul because they thought that it betrayed the Chinese heritage. So grateful were his people to the memory of the revered monarch, however, that Sejong's proclamation of Han'gul has made October 9 a national holiday in Korea even to this day.

During a dark era known as the "fifty bloody years," foreign invasion plagued the Yi. Although the threat of Japanese pirates gradually waned, a crisis arose with Korea's island neighbor when Hideyoshi, the "Napoleon of Japan," united his country (by 1585). That great soldier then challenged the Ming Empire of China, demanding that Korea give him passage and assistance. Landing on the southern coast, the Japanese army overran most of the country, but the Yi monarch requested the help of the Chinese, who soon invaded to check the Japanese advance. Meanwhile, Korea's Admiral Yi Sun-sin's ironclad "turtle ships" (outfitted with metal plates and an iron ram shaped like a turtle's head), forced the Japanese to withdraw altogether by severing their supply lines at sea. Then, when the Chinese emperor insisted that Hideyoshi acknowledge him as overlord, the Japanese launched another campaign through Korea in 1597, but the death of their leader once again forced their retirement. Korea, however, had been left a broken country.

Once more Korea had provided the battlefield for its more-powerful neighbors. Schools, shrines, art objects, libraries, landed estates, and the capital itself lay in ruins. The administrative structure was destroyed, making tax collection impossible. Perhaps one-third of the Korean people were casualties of the conflict. Hideyoshi's armies had forcibly taken many potters, printers, and scholars back to Japan with them, depriving the country of needed skills. While slowly recovering, Korea was harassed by a second marauder, the Manchus from the north. Preparing to overthrow the reigning dynasty of China, the Manchus sought to compel the Korean kings to abandon their allegiance to the Ming emperors. Invasions followed in 1626 and 1637. These barbarians captured and pillaged the capital, forcing the king to acknowledge the new Manchu (Ch'ing) dynasty as overlord before they began their conquest of China in 1644. Detesting the Japanese and Manchus for their intrusions, the Koreans would experience increasingly strained relations with both from then on. In disdain, Korea closed its borders to virtually all foreigners and became the "hermit kingdom" until imperialist pressures forced it to reopen in the nineteenth century.

New Forces for Change and the Coming of the Westerners

Korea never recovered completely from the invasions that had left the country devastated. The weakened government absorbed some of the ownerless land but let most of it fall into the hand of lords with no ties to the capital. Destruction of their tax base dealt the Yi a telling blow, starting a precipitate decline to their demise in 1910. The military gained in the process, however, especially by the establishment of the "Five Camp System," a series of fortified areas on the northern frontier and in the capital. Many slaves escaped bondage through enlistment in the army. In contrast, the Yangban diminished as a class. Deprived of much of its land, the majority sank into commoner status, as many had already done in the factional disputes. The Yangban decline in turn deprived the peasants of what little security they had left. The tradition of his lord's paternalism, his sole guarantee of protection, had become inoperative. Starvation enveloped the land, the famine of 1671 being especially severe. Hungry farmers dug up graves to devour corpses, and other instances of cannibalism were reported. Infants were abandoned on roadways or thrown into irrigation ditches, and the government allowed those who helped the orphans to take them into their families or to enslave them. Trade stagnated for lack of farm produce.

Protest groups arose. Intellectuals organized a movement called *Sirhak* or "Practical Learning." Insisting on a new, more realistic and less theoretical approach to their country's problems, they repudiated empty Confucian philosophizing about the perfect society or the ideal virtuous man in favor of effective governmental administration. Urging reform through a more practical format for the scholar examinations, subsidization of commerce and industry, and a renewed cultivation of the humanistic spirit of Confucianism, this group gave voice to popular grievances through its paintings, novels, dramas, and even operas. They used Han'gul in their written works, and their efforts helped prepare for the emergence of modern Korea by creating a popular culture.

New scientific ideas, inspired by further Sirhak efforts, derived from China as well as from contact with Westerners. Tribute missions to Peking (Beijing) brought those presenting homage to the Manchu emperor into contact with the Jesuits who were staying at the imperial court. Fathers Matteo Ricci, Adam Schaal, and others had taught the Chinese new ideas about cartography, clockmaking, and astronomy and had formulated a new calendar for them. Thus, the first modern science (called "Western Learning") came to Korea and was absorbed by the "Practical Learners," who urged use of inductive reasoning to solve problems, following their adage: "To clarify truth, seek evidence." The Sirhaks also advocated land reform, change in the governmental system, direct aid to the poverty stricken, and the utilization of European mathematics and technology.

Simultaneously, many of the miserably poor embraced Christianity, which had also come to Korea via China. Chou Wen-mu, a Chinese missionary, entered Korea in 1795 but was martyred in 1801. Korean authorities persecuted the new religion because of its prohibition of ancestor worship and other Confucian rituals. Despite severe repressions in 1839 and 1866, Christianity continued to spread among the common people. Of all East Asians, Koreans have been among the most receptive to Christianity, because it championed the oppressed. Today, Christians compose about 10 percent of South Korea's population.

Western traders, however, applied the greatest pressures for change in Korea. The Portuguese first came to India in 1498, to Japan in 1542–1543, and then established the port of Macao (1557) on the southern Chinese coast. Europeans arrived in Korea in 1656, when a Dutch ship went aground off the southern shore of Cheju Island; the thirty-six men who survived the wreck were imprisoned in

Seoul. After several years, one of the prisoners, Hendrick Hamel, escaped to write of his experience in the first book on Korea published in the West. In the meantime, one peasant uprising followed another, while the rest of the nation seethed with revolt and resentment against the old order. The discontent of so many social classes showed the depth of the unrest. Korea was ripe for change, and the Western powers would supply the impetus.

Western Imperialism 2
through the Korean War, 1860 to 1953

The First Opium War (1839–1842) had forcibly opened China to Westerners, before Commodore Matthew C. Perry's two visits terminated Japanese seclusion in 1853–1854. This was a time in which almost all of the developed Western nations sought foreign markets for the products of the Industrial Revolution. Korea offered little commercially; nevertheless, during the Second Opium War (1856–1860), the Westerners gradually turned towards it as they neared Beijing, the capital of the Chinese empire. Any power dominating Korea would gain control of the sea approaches to the heart of the Middle Kingdom, a significant strategic advantage.

In addition, Korea's geographical situation placed it at the focal point, where the empires of China, Japan, and Russia converged and clashed. Thus, great power rivalries threatened Korean independence.

Korea's military weakness and internal factionalism also invited foreign intervention. King Kojong ascended the Korean throne in 1864, having been chosen from an obscure collateral branch of the royal line. Since he was only twelve years old at the time of his ascension, his father, Taiwon-gun, an orthodox Confucianist, acted as regent. Paternalistically, Taiwon-gun pushed governmental and social reforms to better the lot of the people and adhered to the policy of seclusion. He dismissed corrupt officials, deprived many aristocrats of their land, and made direct loans to farmers. Taking a vigilant antiforeign stance, he persecuted Christians and refused all international commercial negotiations. Korean guns drove away French ships in 1866, as Taiwon-gun resolutely kept the country closed, successfully repelling a sizable U.S. squadron five years later. But his internal enemies ousted him in 1873, when the king came of age, ostensibly because the reforms Taiwon-gun advocated were too costly. True control of the government, however, passed to the monarch's wife, Queen Min, who hated Taiwon-gun and worked to enhance her own family's influence.

Sino-Japanese Rivalry in Korea. 1860-1885

The Japanese could hardly permit any Western power to absorb a country which a Japanese statesman had described as "the arrow pointed at the heart of Japan," because of its proximity to the island empire. Korea's isolation and antiquated arms represented a power vacuum that was especially tempting to Russia. Chinese and Russian land contacts gave them better access to the peninsula; whereas Japan was separated by the 120-mile Strait of Tsushima. Japan, therefore, sought the initial foothold in Korea, but the latter disdained cooperation. Tokyo considered war, but its ruling samurai decided on a calm but determined approach (such as Perry had used on Japan) to terminate Korean isolation. A Japanese naval expedition forced Korea to accept the Treaty of Kanghwa (1876), which opened three ports and stationed a permanent Japanese representative in Seoul. The Western "unequal treaties," which had been imposed on Japan itself, now served as the Japanese model for the subjugation of Korea, an indication of Japan's "progress" in modernization. Thus began a bitter Japanese-Chinese rivalry over the country, as numerous Japanese merchants, the vanguard of an energetic economic penetration, moved into Korean ports.

Now China invoked its historic role as Korea's protector to stand with the nation against Japan. Playing "barbarians against barbarians," Li Hung-chang, China's elder statesman, negotiated a series of commercial treaties between the Western powers and Korea, starting with the United States in 1882. In addition, Li dispatched Yüan Shih-k'ai, a Chinese military man, to Seoul as China's resident-general, to introduce China's "self-strengthening" program of reform. When Taiwon-gun attempted to return to power, Yüan had him transported to China. In addition, Yüan won the support of Queen Min to his cause. At this time, Britain backed the Chinese program to block Russia's penetration into Korea. Counter to this, however, Kim Ok-kuyn, an energetic student, led a group of young progressives, who actually favored reform on the Japanese model. They cooperated with a pro-Japanese element in the Korean army that was secretly supported by Tokyo.

This pro-Japanese military faction suddenly kidnapped the king and queen in the *Kapsin* coup of 1884. Yüan Shih-k'ai's large Chinese force, however, quickly rescued the royal couple. Once again the Japanese considered war, but Count Ito, Japan's most eminent statesman, advised negotiations until his country's internal modernization had been completed. Therefore, by the Li-Ito Agreement (1885), China and Japan promised to withdraw all of their forces and not to send troops to Korea again without consulting one another.

Russo-Japanese Rivalry in Korea. 1885-1905

Foreign intervention overwhelmed Korea, but no one had reckoned with its nationalist reaction. Imperialist penetration had deepened the misery of the peasant. Japan's opening of the country had guaranteed large shipments of rice and soy beans from Korea, and eventually Japan dominated 90 percent of Korean trade. Often poor farmers pledged their entire crop in return for usurious loans from Japanese merchants. Foreclosures then passed much land directly into Japanese hands, while Japanese fishermen moved into Korean coastal areas. This economic penetration sought to transform Korea into a nation of food raisers, a market for Japanese textiles, a source of raw materials, and an outlet for Japan's surplus population, all in preparation for an eventual annexation. Devastating droughts in 1876–1877 and again in 1888–1889 impoverished the peasants and the Yangban, the latter sinking even lower on the social scale. These new burdens further aggravated the endemic rural grievances against local bureaucratic corruption and landlord tyranny.

Consequently, a new religious-nationalist movement arose in the countryside, which denounced foreign exploitation and official malfeasance and promised a heaven on earth to the poor. This *Tonghak* (or "Eastern Learning") challenged the "Western Learning" of the urban officials. The Tonghak leader, Ch'oe Che-u, was an intellectual, impoverished aristocrat who modeled his movement on China's Taiping Rebellion. He sought to synthesize Confucianism, Buddhism, and Taoism with elements of Christianity. Although the authorities beheaded Ch'oe Ch'u in 1864, his Tonghak movement continued to grow in the rural areas.

After 1885, the Li-Ito Agreement inspired a whole series of "unequal treaties" with the Western powers, causing a new wave of popular unrest. The Tonghaks marched to Seoul with a demand for the end of the ruinous rice exports and a posthumous reprieve for their fallen leader. Foreign legations girded for violence, as Taiwon-gun re-emerged to assume the leadership of the insurgents. China and Japan infiltrated agents who encouraged the Tonghaks, because revolt would provide an excuse for armed intervention. The Tonghak Rebellion represented Korea's first nationalist outbreak. Marxist historians today view this upheaval as one harbinger of the great peasant insurrections of the twentieth century.

The Tonghak Rebellion seriously divided the court at Seoul. Many advisers favored Russian assistance, offered by their resourceful minister, Karl Waeber, as a counterweight to Japanese penetration. Instead, the king called upon China, who dispatched imperial armies to help its last remaining dependency on the eastern seaboard. Japan immediately mobilized, landing its armies on Korea's west coast to block the Chinese advance southward. A Japanese attack on an enemy troopship then triggered the Sino-Japanese conflict of 1894–1895, which subjected Korea to Japanese military occupation. Martial law demanded Western dress, in order to benefit the Japanese textile industry, and decreed educational and monetary reforms, wholesale land redistribution, and the construction of a rail system. The Tonghaks rose again, but the Japanese army suppressed them easily.

When Japan's victory over China expelled the latter from Korea, the helpless court at Seoul turned to the Russians. Quick to respond, a Japanese force invaded the imperial palace (October 1895) stabbed Queen Min, and burned her body in the courtyard. When the Japanese "dwarf bastards" abolished the wearing of the Korean farmer's traditional topknot, the outraged peasants rebelled again. In 1896, So Chae-p'il, an enthusiastic Korean patriot, known as Philip Jaisohn in the United States, founded the "Independence Association" and a Korean-English newspaper dedicated to national sovereignty and individual rights. Syngman Rhee, a revolutionary student, belonged to this group and was shortly thereafter imprisoned for his activities.

Meanwhile, after King Kojong had fled to the Russian embassy, So Chae-p'il persuaded him to proclaim himself "emperor" in 1897. Because of this action, many Japanese favored war against the Russians, but the majority of the military cautioned delay. Therefore, the Nishi-Rosen Agreement of 1898 again neutralized Korea, disguising its helplessness in diplomatic euphemisms.

The Russians' interest in Korea increased in proportion to their relentless penetration of northern China. When construction of the Trans-Siberian Railway began in 1891, Russia sought a Korean port for the railway's eastern terminus. Britain saw the Russian threat to their commercial position, and when the Russians occupied Manchuria in the confusion during China's Boxer Rebellion (1900), Britain concluded the Anglo-Japanese Alliance (1902) against the common enemy. The Russians, in turn, utilized the Yalu Timber Project as a façade to slip infiltrators into Korea. When St. Petersburg refused to concede Korea to Japan as within the latter's sphere of control, even in return for Manchuria, the Japanese attacked the Russian fleet at Port Arthur in 1904, defeating them decisively in the war that followed. Korea now faced the victorious Empire of Japan alone. Japan did not wait long to move in.

Last Years of Independence, 1905-1910

The Portsmouth Treaty (September 1905), which had concluded the Russo-Japanese War, internationally recognized Japan's predominance in Korea. Marquis Ito hastened to the imperial palace at Seoul, forced his way into the emperor's apartments, and compelled the hapless ruler to accept a Japanese protectorate over his country. Japanese "advisers" then took over the ministries of finance and foreign affairs. Korea surrendered all treaties with other nations, who recalled their representatives from Seoul, while Japan's agreements with Korea were extended. Ito assumed the office of resident-general.

A desperate Syngman Rhee, having escaped to Hawaii and then to the United States, pleaded for President Theodore Roosevelt's support on the basis of the U.S.-Korean Treaty of 1882. The American executive refused, however, as he was committed to the Portsmouth agreement, which he had mediated. Besides, Roosevelt favored an East Asian balance of power between Japan and Russia, consigning Korea to Japan, thus earning the everlasting resentment of the Koreans. No possibility of British support existed either, as London had just renewed the Anglo-Japanese Alliance the previous August 1905.

Japan proceeded to systematically reduce Korea to a colony, as officials seized control of the army, police, and customs. Schools seldom taught Korean, which was now preempted by the study of the Japanese language. Thousands of Japanese, invariably the dregs of their own country, came to Korea to buy land. Obsequious Korean collaborators were awarded government positions. Submissive farmers labored as food raisers and water carriers. Due to their systematic penetration, dating all the way back to their opening of Korea in 1876, the Japanese controlled all railways, mines, banks, and important businesses.

The pitiful Korean ruler tried to make an international appeal for assistance and dispatched three delegates to the Hague Peace Conference in 1907. Led by Yi Chun, one of his loyal officials, these envoys sought to obtain admittance, but the assembly refused. The International Press Club extended much sympathy but little else. Bitterly frustrated, Yi Chun committed suicide by starving himself. The Japanese, however, responded to the emperor's appeal by forcing Korea into even greater bondage. Its army was demobilized, and its helpless ruler compelled to abdicate. He was carried off to Japan and his retarded son was placed on the throne, but the Korean people still refused to submit.

Insurrection erupted throughout the peninsula. Degraded Yangban led many rebel groups in the rural areas, where discharged army officers trained them in guerrilla warfare. Teachers organized militant student groups, newspapers encouraged revolt, and foreign missionaries steadily supported resistance. But the Japanese army ruthlessly suppressed these "riots." Young Korean girls were stripped, tied by their hair to telegraph poles, sadistically whipped, then left on public display. Helpless farmers and their families were crucified or strangled by the hangman's rope. Japanese soldiers bayonetted Koreans they met on the roadways. Twelve thousand persons were killed in one year; those imprisoned and tortured totaled twice that number. Missionaries suspected of complicity in the revolts were detained but seldom punished, out of concern for Western opinion. Korea once again lay helpless, a ravaged, bleeding land, brutalized by Japanese "discipline."

The worst still lay ahead. Patriotic fanatics assassinated D. W. Stevens, a Japanese-appointed American adviser on foreign affairs, in San Francisco in 1908. In October of the following year, in a Mukden (Shenyang) railroad station, An Chunggun, a young, impetuous Korean, shot the resident-general, Ito Hirobumi, regarded as the personification of Japanese oppression. Two months later Premier Yi Wanyong, head of the puppet government in Korea, was fatally stabbed.

The imperial army again reacted quickly. An official proclamation of August 22, 1910, officially incorporated Korea into the Japanese empire. Chŏsen, the Japanese form of the traditional name for Korea, became the unhappy nation's new designation. Many Koreans left the country and formed patriotic organizations abroad, as their homeland bowed unwillingly to the conqueror.

Korea Under Japanese Rule, 1910-1945

Japan ruled Korea as a police state for the next thirty-five years. The emperor regularly selected the governor-general from the active lists of the armed forces. This meant almost perpetual martial law.

Koreans were constantly reminded of their lower status, deprived of their freedom of assembly, association, press, and speech. The educational system indoctrinated them in Japanese values to transform Korean students into Japanese subjects. The Japanese authorities closed as many missionary schools as they could. In 1910, a land registry required all farmers to designate the legal owner, exact location, and the productivity of their plots. Many did not understand these regulations and lost their holdings when they failed to comply with the directive by the specified date. These unfortunates became tenants, took to the highways to beg, or emigrated to China or Japan, where they constituted a lowly and despised class. Still more Japanese entered the country to take over the ownerless lands, often amassing large estates.

Korea provided Japan with markets for its products and supplied much of its needed food and natural resources, enabling the Japanese to concentrate on their burgeoning industrialization. Northern mines yielded iron, coal, magnesium, gold, and graphite in some quantity, while forests provided timber. Farmers were forced to convert their land almost exclusively to the cultivation of rice, which was destined primarily for Japanese markets. Koreans had little to eat as their own rice consumption fell by 50 percent, and meat was in very short supply. Cheap millet from Manchuria became the main staple in the Korean diet. The people blamed their wretched lives directly on the cupidity of Japanese rule.

Despite repression, Korean resistance to the Japanese occupation intensified. Missionary schools, the only institutions in Korea to oppose the Japanese, continued to encourage resistance, instructing their charges in Western ideals of freedom and individual rights. Many revolutionaries graduated from missionary academies, most notably Syngman Rhee, who was the product of a Methodist school. Also, a rural movement, known as Ch'ondo-gyo, grew from the old Tonghaks and encouraged nationalistic agitation by organizing guerrilla units.

March 1, 1919, however, crowned all resistance on the occasion of King Kojong's funeral. Disparate groups organized a huge nationalist demonstration, using students to coordinate urban and rural groups with organizations outside the country. After leaders had read a public proclamation of independence, an immense throng gathered in Seoul's Pagoda Park to shout *"Manse"* ("Long Live Korea"), a cheer pronounced like *"Bansei"* in Japanese. Simultaneous risings throughout the entire country caught authorities by surprise. Demonstrators marched unarmed, the leaders offering to discuss national independence calmly with the Japanese. Bloodshed resulted when troops fired into the crowds, now totaling two million—a national revolt.

Organizers hoped to arouse world opinion to the cause of Korean independence. They sent envoys to the Versailles Conference, which was formulating the peace treaty terminating World War I, ostensibly on the basis of national self-determination, as enunciated in President Woodrow Wilson's Fourteen Points. Koreans wanted a share in the freedoms being granted to other oppressed peoples, but their entreaties received little response. Japan had served the allied cause well during the war, making its membership in the new League of Nations most essential, but Korea was forsaken and the revolt suppressed. The March 1 Movement lasted two months and resulted in five thousand dead, seven thousand wounded, and over forty-seven thousand imprisoned. Other than establishing that date later as a national holiday, the upheaval accomplished little of substance.

Disheartened revolutionaries now turned to a new quarter. The Russian Revolution had attracted many Korean intellectuals to Bolshevik achievements. More Koreans attended the Congress of the Peoples of the East (1922) than did any other Asians. There the Soviets pledged their support to subject peoples oppressed by Western imperialism. Koreans founded Communist cells in Manchuria, the Maritime Province, and Japan, after training in the Soviet Union. Kim Il Sung, until 1994 the president of the Democratic Peoples's Republic of Korea (North Korea), headed a Manchurian cell as a young man. By 1925, cadres secretly established a Korean Communist party in Seoul. Communism, more than any other ideology, patronized Korean nationalism after 1919. In Shanghai, China, that same year, however, Syngman Rhee founded a provisional government-in-exile, based on a liberal republican constitution.

Following 1919, the Japanese adopted more subtle methods for the government of Korea. An ordinary constabulary force replaced the army, a retired admiral assumed the post of governor-general, while some freedom was granted to the press. The situation improved marginally, but Japan still administered Korea as an inferior nation. Other factors, however, produced more significant changes. The postwar Japanese boom encouraged their businesses to look to Korea as an industrial subsidiary. Considerable planning and investment established a small factory system. Development of hydroelectricity in northern Korea and a highway network, plus the expansion of mining and railway facilities, were important developments of the 1920s.

Starting with the Manchurian invasion (1931), Japanese military expansionism liquidated the exclusively agricultural basis of the Korean economy and its one-crop (rice) dependence. Japan's resultant departure from the League of Nations (1933), coinciding with the Great Depression, intensified the danger of an international boycott against it. Pressures on Japan pushed the development of Korean chemicals, iron, steel, and textiles. The Japanese invasion of China (1937) made use of Korea as a staging area and supply base. When World War II began, however, Korea was again compelled to supply substantial food shipments to the Japanese and to manufacture many of its arms.

During the war, about two and one-half million Koreans were forced laborers on farms, in factories, and in mines, while over seven hundred thousand were sent abroad (also as laborers). After 1942, conscription drafted Korean men into the Japanese armed forces. The steady erosion of Japan's military position, however, filled the hearts of Koreans with increasing hope, as their day of deliverance neared. On the other hand, the Japanese investment in Korean industry, combined with their training of some Koreans in modern technology, laid the foundation for South Korean economic resurgence after 1965.

Korea between the Wars, 1945-1950

The defeat of Japan in 1945 left the Korean people in a state of happy confusion. The oppressor who had tried to obliterate Korea's very identity had been brought low. The Cairo (November 1943) and Potsdam (July 1945) conferences had promised Korean independence, after a joint Soviet-American occupation. Russian entry into the Pacific War had come August 8. Soviet armies entered Korea from the north the following day, but U.S. forces did not arrive in the south until a month later, with the thirty-eighth parallel separating the two zones. The Americans had insisted on this division, not only in order to receive the Japanese surrender, but more probably to prevent the entire peninsula from falling to the Soviets and, by extension, communism, for the Cold War had begun.

The Americans found a hastily formed provisional People's Republic of Korea already entrenched at Seoul. It proved to be a makeshift affair, however, and the U.S. military commander, General John R. Hodge, refused to recognize it. Now that liberation had come, this incident demonstrated the deficiency of Korean political experience, a result of the autocratic nature of Japanese rule. The departure of the Japanese left an administrative vacuum, a tragic barrier to Korea's unification.

When Soviet armies rolled into the north, they were much better prepared to institute an efficient and sympathetic government than had been the Americans in the south. Following Russian occupation policies, like those they had used in

Eastern Europe, Communist cadres accompanied Soviet and North Korean forces and immediately assumed posts in the military government. Kim Il Sung, received as a national hero, wore a Red Army major's uniform. The Americans, on the other hand, had difficulties accommodating exiled Korean nationalists (notably Syngman Rhee) and refugees from the North and overseas. Rhee was temporarily appeased by the formation of his group into an advisory commission, despite his constant agitation for "a march north." Seemingly, however, all these arrangements would be temporary, pending the formation of a unified government.

A big-power conference at Moscow (December 1945) established a trusteeship for Korea to be administered jointly by the United States, the USSR, Great Britain, and China. But virtually all Koreans denounced its stipulation of a five-year preparation period before unification. Moreover, the Cold War had split the powers, who could not agree on which Korean factions should participate. The Russians disdained rightist groups; the Americans refused the leftists. Washington then approached the United Nations (U.N.), which appointed a temporary commission to hold elections for a national government. In the south, this body organized elections to a national assembly in June 1948, which intentionally held about one hundred seats vacant for northern delegates. The Soviets, however, refused to admit the U.N. commission to the North. As a result, in the South, Syngman Rhee assumed the presidency of the new Republic of Korea (ROK) on August 15. The North established the Democratic People's Republic of Korea the following month with Kim Il Sung as premier. The Korean situation had polarized along a "totally unnatural" political boundary.

The Soviet Union withdrew its occupation army in December 1948, but some twelve hundred advisers stayed behind to guide a well-equipped North Korean army of 135,000, supported by a full tank battalion. (During World War II, North Korean officers had trained in Russia, especially in mechanized warfare.) The Americans departed in June 1949, leaving South Korea with a mere constabulary force, equipped only with defensive weapons that were barely adequate for border patrol and police action. Fearful that the nationalistic Rhee might undertake to attack the North, the Americans intentionally left him virtually disarmed.

The North immediately seized this opportunity. Communist terrorists exploded bombs in the cities, attempted assassinations of southern leaders, and propagandized against the Americans to undermine southern confidence. Skirmishes erupted along the thirty-eighth parallel. The North Korean assembly called for national unification on June 6, 1950, but insisted on the imprisonment of South Korean leaders. Seoul scornfully refused. Three weeks later the North struck.

The Korean War

The Soviet Phase, June–October 1950

Without warning, seven North Korean infantry divisions and an armored brigade, supported by Soviet advisers, surged across the thirty-eighth parallel on the morning of June 25, 1950. Unprepared and woefully ill-equipped, the South Koreans retreated rapidly when Seoul fell after just three days. They could do nothing but appeal for assistance.

Though evidence at the time pointed to Soviet participation in both the preparation and execution of the invasion, to this day their motive remains obscure. Likely, the Russians were reacting to the U.S. occupational government of Japan, which had completely excluded Soviet participation and had partially re-armed the recent enemy. Perhaps they sought to surround Japan with Communist power. Overrunning Japan's close neighbor, Korea, might someday force Japan into the Communist orbit, thus weakening the U.S. position in East Asia.

Recent scholarship, especially in the enlightening work, *Uncertain Partners* by Sergei N. Goncharov et al., utilizes newly discovered Communist documents, only available since the end of the Cold War, that tell us much about Communist preparations for the Korean War. It was actually Kim Il Sung who inspired the North Korean attack in an attempt to re-unite the peninsula, obtaining Soviet assistance from Stalin himself. In a critical series of conferences (March–April 1950) Kim promised Stalin a victory in three weeks on the basis of a well-trained North Korean force, the South's unpreparedness, and the previously established guerilla forces in the South's mountains. Kim assured the Soviet leader that the United States would not intervene due to the rapidity of the conflict. Stalin, on the other hand, seeing Communist expansion in Europe blocked by the Marshall Plan and the formation of NATO, realized that the greater opportunity for success was in East Asia, which had already been prepared by the Communist victory in China in 1949. The Soviet dictator, however, had made a critical mistake by having withdrawn the Soviet delegation from the U.N. (the previous January), thus enabling the remaining members of the Security Council to vote for U.N. intervention in the Korean conflict.

The United States had been caught unawares. Secretary of State Dean Acheson had made a defense of the recent U.S.-China policy when he addressed the Washington National Press Club on January 12, 1950. He had declared the U.S. defense perimeter in the new East Asian containment policy as running from the Aleutian Islands down to include Japan, the Ryukyu Islands, and the Philippines, unintentionally omitting Korea. Probably the Soviets now assumed that Korea had been abandoned by U.S. policy.

But it was Acheson who asked for a meeting of the U.N. Security Council on that critical Sunday morning of June 25. By a 9-0 count, it authorized a U.N. fighting force to defend South Korea and branded the North Koreans as the aggressors. The USSR could not veto the action, since, as mentioned, the Soviet delegates had bolted the U.N. the previous January (angry over the U.N.'s refusal to seat Communist China). Since the U.S. occupation army in Japan was the only available military force, this host entered the war under the command of General Douglas MacArthur and finally halted the North Korean advance in the extreme southeast, in the Naktong River perimeter around Pusan. The Americans composed one-half and the South Koreans two-fifths of the defending force, while sixteen other U.N. allies, especially the British and the Turks, gave substantial assistance. MacArthur then dramatically reversed the tide of the war by his daring "end run," the seaborne landing at Inchon (in the face of uncertain tides and an impending typhoon) on September 15, shattering the entire front. Within two weeks the victorious U.N. army had recaptured Seoul, and MacArthur had achieved the first turning point of the war.

Top: One of the many statues of General MacArthur, this one in a park in Inchon. Y. H. Bäng.

Bottom: Sept. 9, 1950, Seoul is returned to South Korea. In the center are General Douglas MacArthur and Sygman Rhee, President of South Korea. Wide World Photos.

The Chinese Phase, 1950–1953

The Inchon invasion made possible MacArthur's crossing of the thirty-eighth parallel in the first week of October. But, concerned that MacArthur's actions might draw the Chinese into the conflict, U.S. President Harry S Truman ordered MacArthur to meet him on Wake Island (October 15). There the general apparently assured the president that there was "little chance" of the Chinese entering the war, although the two men's respective accounts of that fateful conversation differ.

Paradoxically, as the two men conferred, the first Chinese "volunteers" had entered the war. The U.N. force, buoyed by their commander's promise of being "home by Christmas," were forced to broaden their front by the greater geographical expanse of North Korea, as they approached the Yalu and T'umen rivers, separating North Korea from Manchuria. About November 25, a massive force of three hundred thousand Chinese, led by Generals Peng Dehuai and Chen Yi, crossed the river at eleven points, colliding with the dismayed U.N. troops. MacArthur described the situation as an "entirely new war."

Precise Chinese motivation is impossible to ascertain. Allen S. Whiting, the American historian, offered an explanation. Possibly the Communist Chinese, whose leader, Chairman Mao Tse-tung (Mao Zedong) had proclaimed the People's Republic of China (PRC) on October 1, 1949, sought to prove their ability to defend China's frontiers, an historic obligation assumed by every new dynasty that claimed the "Mandate of Heaven." Perhaps also, Mao's policy of "lean to one side" obligated him to assist the Soviet Union (by the Treaty of February 1950) in the Communists' war against capitalism. Finally, the Chinese Communists probably sought retribution against the United States, because the Americans had supported Mao's Nationalist enemies in the recent civil war. In addition, the student should also observe that MacArthur had unwittingly followed the old Japanese invasion route, the Korean "bridge" to northeastern China, a move bound to provoke a Chinese reaction.

Yet more-recent scholarship tells us that Mao really had preferred a Communist attack on Taiwan, the island refuge of the defeated Chinese Nationalists in the recent Chinese civil war. But when the U.S. Seventh Fleet occupied the Taiwan Strait (to neutralize the area) in late June 1950, he saw that he was blocked. Although Mao had done nothing to aid Kim at the beginning of the Korean War, his anger and frustration against the United States (over Taiwan), eventually caused the Chinese leader to regard the U.S. actions as an assault against the PRC. This explains Mao's late decision to enter the Korean War in mid-October 1950. The Soviet Union, however, not wanting to involve themselves directly with the United States, denied the Chinese previously promised air support at the very last moment.

Chinese intervention triggered a bitter debate on the U.N. coalition's war strategy. Truman's administration favored a "limited war" and intended to persuade the Communists to forego military conquest for a negotiated peace, leaving South Korea a free nation. Such a policy denounced the intended use of nuclear weapons, in an effort to avoid an escalation of the conflict, which was geographically confined to Korea alone. This strategy was at variance with MacArthur's belief, which held victory "to be the only objective in war." He favored the bombing of the Chinese staging areas in Manchuria and the bridges over the Yalu, a naval blockade of the Chinese coast, use of the Chinese Nationalists both in Korea and for an invasion of the mainland from Taiwan, and, finally, the laying of a nuclear cobalt belt or screen across Korea's northern frontier to prevent retreat or further re-enforcement of the Red Chinese forces. The general lightly discounted the possibility of direct Soviet intervention, since their only supply line in the event of their entry was the single-track Trans-Siberian Railway, which could be bombed easily. When the disagreement broke into the open, Truman recalled MacArthur on April 11, 1951. (South Koreans, however, honor the general today with a lifesize bronze statue in Inchon's Liberty Park.)

General Matthew B. Ridgway, a commander more amenable to a U.S. strategy of limited war, replaced MacArthur. He drove to a line roughly equivalent to the thirty-eighth parallel and dug in for a war of attrition, killing hundreds of thousands of Chinese. Meanwhile, talks began at Kaesong in July 1951. Subsequently transferred to Panmunjom, these sessions provided grist for the Communists' propaganda mills, as they tried to attain their objectives at the conference table. They accused the Americans of employing germ warfare and enticed a few "brainwashed" prisoners to remain with the Chinese. Talks did not produce a truce until July 27, 1953, establishing the present demarcation line, or Demilitarized Zone (DMZ). A final peace treaty still has not been forthcoming. Since that time, talks continue, and small-scale skirmishes along the DMZ are almost an everyday occurrence. The latest of these episodes concerned U.S. helicopter pilot Bobby Hall, who, while inadvertently in North Korean airspace, was shot down over the DMZ in December 1994. The North Koreans, insisting that Hall had been spying, held him for thirteen days before releasing him (the remains of his dead copilot had been returned soon after the crash), attesting once again to the prevailing tension in the area.

South Korean independence had been preserved at the cost of 163,000 American casualties, including 54,000 dead, and $20 billion in expenditure. Fifty-eight thousand South Korean, about 520,000 North Korean, and over 900,000 Chinese lives were sacrificed. Limited war had temporarily preserved the U.S. containment policy in East Asia, though it was soon shattered later by the Vietnam War.

North and South Korea, 1953 to 1995

When the Potsdam Conference partitioned Korea along the thirty-eighth parallel, it left the South with most of the nation's people, agricultural land, and light industry, whereas the North had the bulk of heavy industry, railways, mines, and hydroelectric capacity. The Korean War destroyed most of these facilities, but the period from 1953 to 1958 witnessed significant postwar reconstruction and rehabilitation in both areas, especially in South Korea.

South Korean Economy, Society, and Culture, 1953–1979

The South Korean economy lay shattered from the war, with a large labor surplus the only surviving asset. Because their country lacked minerals, especially coal, and also other power resources, leaders at first created an economy based on agriculture and light-industry consumer goods, primarily for export.

Relying chiefly on U.S. foreign aid and private loans, new industries initially emphasized the production of such goods as textiles, garments, footwear, wigs, electronics, and plywood, goods having the advantage of very low capital-output ratios. After 1962, however, the First Five-Year Economic Development Plan, followed by a Second and a Third, inspired a truly remarkable growth. Up to 1976, South Korea achieved a GNP expansion of 10 percent yearly, from $5.5 billion to $21 billion. Commodity exports rose from only $50 million to $7.8 billion, a rate of 43 percent per annum and a thirty-six-fold increase overall. In the interim, manufacturers shifted dramatically to the production of commodities demanding sophisticated production techniques, including automobiles, ships, industrial machinery, precision instruments, metal products, and chemicals. Simultaneously, shoe production was up one hundred and forty-four times, electronics two hundred and twenty-four times, and synthetic-fiber products two hundred and thirty times. This amazing success compares to Japan's industrial development from 1880 to 1920. The United States and Japan were South Korea's principal customers, purchasing about 56 percent of its total exports in 1975, although South Korea traded with any country, regardless of ideology. Since an active domestic market has kept imports from rising unduly, expanding exports have consistently improved South Korea's balance of payments.

Unemployment declined from 8 to 4 percent, despite an increase in the population from 1962 to 1978. The dedicated labor force then punched out 50.7 work hours weekly—"the worst workaholics in the world"—as compared to 39.4 in the United States. The Confucian tradition of paternalism created favorable employer-employee relationships. Labor accounted for only 10 percent of the cost of production, whereas the U.S. figure was about 40 percent.

Goals of the new Fourth Five-Year Plan (1976–1981) projected continuation of GNP growth by 9.2 percent annually through the expanded production of heavy machinery, ships, and electronics. The initial year of the Plan (1977) boasted an 11 percent GNP growth with a 32 percent jump in commodity exports. Automobile manufacture increased, while oil production and nuclear power advanced. Future profits promised to expand social services, including health and sanitation, education, housing, and electricity, while creating two million more jobs. After 1960, South Korean and Taiwanese industrial growth were the wonders of the underdeveloped or "Third World." President Park Chung-hee's supervision of South Korea's development was reminiscent of the samurai oligarchy's direction of Japan's modernization during the Meiji period after 1868.

Industrialization and the wholesale reshuffling of people during the war spurred the growth of cities in South Korea after 1953. Seoul, with seven million people, doubled its population between 1965 and 1975. Pusan and Taedong, the steel center, like Seoul assumed the appearance of Western cities in their business districts. Myong-dong was the theater, restaurant, and department-store area of Seoul, much like Tokyo's Ginza. Industry burgeoned in many other cities as well. Changwon was the center for machinery and arms manufacture, made possible by POSCO, South Korea's largest steel mill. The new steel complex at Pohang produced more profit per ton than any other mill in Asia. Hyundai Construction Company produced the largest single one-company shipyard at Ulsan (described as South Korea's Pittsburgh or Osaka), specializing in the production of the 270,000-ton supertanker.

Urban environments have drastically altered Korean lifestyles. The old one-story, wooden houses with sliding doors and rice-paper windows, whose inhabitants sat and slept on mats rather than using chairs or beds, disappeared in the cities. Modern apartment houses replaced them. University and business life intermixed the sexes, who now freely associated. The extended family became less important, as only the father, mother, and children dwelt under one roof. Dating became almost an accepted urban custom, and marriage for love was becoming the new rule. Dress was predominantly Western, but traditional Korean garb appeared occasionally on city streets and was still worn regularly at home.

Modern education advanced with urbanization. A country sharing the Confucian tradition, Korea always stressed education. Following liberation, an Education Law (1949) made six years of elementary school compulsory, with the option of three years of middle school, three years of high school, and four years of undergraduate college. A board of education supervised each province. Be-

Park Chung-hee, a former president of the Republic of Korea. Embassy of the Republic of Korea.

Metropolitan Seoul. The capital of the Republic of Korea attained a population of seven million by the late 1970s.
Y. H. Bäng.

cause of the war, full implementation of the educational system could hardly be attained, however, until long after 1953. Indeed, not until 1968 did the Charter of National Education make primary education possible for five and one-half million pupils in the middle of the next decade. By 1981, compulsory education was extended through middle school, for a total of nine years. South Korea raised its literacy rate to 92 percent in 1977. A state examination restricted the number of college students, who had to take an entrance examination administered by the university. Commensurate with the emphasis on national industrialization, higher education stressed law, engineering, medicine, electronics, and aeronautics.

Modernization from 1962 to 1978 had resulted in the remarkable growth of urbanization, industrialization, and education, but the rural sector had not shown the same progress. Factory development caused many farm workers to move to the cities to find jobs, leaving the old folk behind to tend the fields. Fully 70 percent of the Korean people lived in the countryside in the late 1950s, but only 46 percent did so by 1971. Consequently, agriculture grew only 2.5 percent annually after 1967, whereas industry enjoyed an increase four times greater. The imbalance of the two economies had widened the income gap between farm households and urban dwellers, hastening the labor drain from the countryside. By 1970, the farmer earned only 61 percent of the wage of the average urban worker.

For some time the farmer clung to traditional customs and methods. The typical Korean farmer lived in poverty, in a house built of mud or clay, rocks, and wooden beams, with a thatched roof. Consisting usually of two rooms, this typical farm house often had floors of flat stone heated by rock-lined flues under the house, carrying hot air from the kitchen, the world's earliest form of radiant heating, called *ondol*. Furniture was sparse. The farm family had no electricity, running water, or bathtubs, and seldom ate meat. The principal crop was rice, and it is interesting to note that the Korean word for food means rice. The farmer used night soil (human waste) for fertilizer, and his dependence on rainfall was complete, since there was little irrigation. Because three-quarters of the land is mountainous, farmers often had to resort to terracing and water storage in order to produce rice. Finally, as they had for hundreds of years, oxen pulled the farmer's wooden plow.

Peasant clothing also had seen little change. Men wore a loose jacket and wide, baggy trousers, made of white cotton or linen. Their hats were often the odd-shaped, stove-pipe kind with a narrow brim and high crown, loosely woven of coarse, black, lacquered horsehair, called "bird-cage hats." Women's dress included a very short blouse, tied in the front, with long sleeves, and a full, high-waisted skirt. They wore their hair long but swept back, knotted with large decorative pins, often wrapping cloths around their heads.

Confucian and native religious beliefs predominated in the countryside, still a family-centered society. When referring to family members, the typical rural dweller would say *our* father, *our* mother, *our* sister, never *my*. The father was the central figure, and sons were revered more than daughters. Since courtesy was stressed, a younger person always greeted an older one first, using honorifics. Grandparents were held in high esteem. A young wife was strictly subject to her husband, who often addressed her as "Yobo," the equivalent of "Hey you!" Her mother-in-law often tyrannized her in her new home.

The rural areas had many multidwelling houses for the extended family, in which Confucian ceremonies still honored the deceased members, and filial piety was a cardinal virtue taught all children. Their family-centered lives were reflected in Korean names, which consist of three Chinese characters, with the surname coming first. (When written in the Western alphabet, the order of names is often reversed.) Some families still preselected mates for their children, using a go-between to preserve harmony among all concerned. Most families signally honored the first birthday of a son, as well as his sixtieth (*Hwangap*), the age of retirement. Both were occasions for elaborate gatherings and festivities. Finally, death was the occasion for much ceremonial, such as placing the deceased's coat on the roof of the house to invoke the spirit of the dead. Participants in the elaborate funeral ceremonies customarily wore white as the color of mourning. The mound-like grave was the permanent charge of the family.

The tradition-bound rural areas fell further and further behind the progressive cities, and South Korea's government strove to rectify the imbalance in the two economies, which threatened the country's food resources. President Park, raised in the countryside himself, announced *Saemaul Undong* (The New Community Movement) on April 22, 1970, intended to update agriculture by liberating it from antiquated methods. This nationwide program stressed individual self-help. Specially trained officials organized local cooperative projects on the village level to raise rural living standards. Construction of new roads, bridges, houses (made now of brick and cement and roofed with tiles), water pipes, irrigation canals, electric generators, and medical clinics revitalized the farm areas. In addition, wasteland was reclaimed, fruit trees were planted, more livestock was raised, Suwon (a new high-yield rice) was introduced, and factories were established near villages to utilize seasonally idle labor (thereby increasing off-farm income). By 1976 the Saemaul Undong program had raised rural household income above that of the urban worker, increasing rice production by 55 percent and that of barley by 54 percent over 1962, making South Korea self-sufficient in these essential grains. Observers reported a remarkable transformation in rural lifestyles as a result of the success of the New Community Movement.

Occupying an area about the size of the state of Indiana, South Korea faced the modern problems of city growth and burgeoning materialism. As with so much of the Third World, it saw cherished traditions fading in the face of Western-type industrialization and urban life.

North Korean Politics, Economy, and Society, 1953–1979

In 1945 the Soviet army installed Kim Il Sung as leader of North Korea, largely because his military service in the USSR and his Manchurian revolutionary activities had made him well known to Russian officials. Hence, he prevailed over prominent nationalists and Chinese-backed Communists to quickly found a personality-cult—"our father" to his people. The proclamation of the Democratic People's Republic of Korea (September 1948) established a president (Kim), a presidium of leading party members, a Supreme People's Assembly, and a Supreme Court. Virtually all power, however, fell to the ruling Korean Worker's (or Communist) party, which consisted of about 12 percent of the total population.

Land reform began in 1946, ostensibly passing the lords' estates to peasant ownership, with partial completion (1953–1958) in the establishment of some

16,000 collectives, later consolidated into 3,100 of about 1,000 acres each. The government regulated workers' lives, consisting mostly of toil and political indoctrination, through mass meetings, slogans, posters, and patriotic songs. Propaganda inculcated dedication to the state and sought to eliminate all religious and family loyalties and preached hatred of U.S. "imperialists" as the chief enemy of national unification. Workers earned small wages and tilled private plots on their own time. Collectivization moved slowly, however, due to the difficult adjustment and the scarcity of arable land in the North. Chongson-ri became a model collective farm on which 650 families cultivated 3,000 acres. Families lived in brick and cement dormitories, and all social activities took place in group organizations. Marriage before the age of twenty-five was forbidden. All children were tended in nurseries or "baby palaces," as women composed 37 percent of the workforce. Education required a six-day week, and nine years of schooling was compulsory. After three or four years of military service, the capable students attended college or technical schools. Kim Il Sung University at Pyongyang had 15,000 students in the mid-1970s.

Most attention centered on industry, and many workers were pushed into factories. Soviet technologists assisted North Korean industry after 1953, and Moscow injected it with a $500 million loan. Pyongyang (with one million people by 1974) became an important iron and steel as well as textile center. Kangson boasted the Kum Sung tractor factory, with a yearly output of thirty thousand units. Songnim steel mill, restored after the destruction it had suffered in two wars, and the Hamhung-Hungnam industrial complex, producing small ships, bulldozers, locomotives, and presses, operated successfully. Results on the whole, however, were disappointing. Industrialization was hampered by the looting of North Korean factories by Soviet armies in 1945–1946, the Korean War, and then by the general failure of several preliminary "plans."

The Sino-Soviet dispute, however, had the key role in limiting North Korea's industrial progress after 1956. Kim switched from a pro-Soviet, to a neutral, to a Chinese alignment, adopting an "independent" stance after 1966. The failure of the Six-Year Plan (1971–1976), intended to achieve economic autonomy, can be attributed to Soviet reluctance to help substantially, because of Kim's refusal to give a definite commitment to Moscow, as well as to an unwise acceleration in 1973 in a desperate effort to keep up with the South. Workers labored in eight-hour days for six days a week, earning about $37–$100 a month and living in large apartment complexes, the rent for which cost them about 30 percent of their total income. Again, women made up about one-third of the labor force, and military service was required of all: a hard existence, indeed. Essentials such as pig iron, steel, and cement were in short supply, while sufficient quantities of petroleum were also lacking. Despite possession of 80 percent of Korea's mineral wealth, ample timber resources, and capable hydroelectric facilities (inherited from the Japanese), Kim was "under stress" with his promise of *juche* ("self-reliance") far from realization.

The languid state of the economy forced North Korea to turn to the non-Communist world after 1972. This move coincided with efforts to reduce tensions with the South. Japan, emerging as North Korea's second-largest trading partner, and several Western European countries responded with trade agreements for electronics and machine tools especially. But this policy, too, presented difficulties. Apparently, some North Korean overseas representatives involved themselves in illicit trade, as witnessed by the Danish, Norwegian, and Finnish expulsion of North Korean officials in October 1976, for trafficking in liquor, cigarettes, and drugs to obtain foreign exchange. Also, North Korean indebtedness climbed to over $2 billion by 1976, as its GNP amounted to only $4 billion (with just $522 million in exports), amounting to only one-sixth of the South's GNP in this Korean "GNP war." This economic disparity seriously threatened the stability of the peninsula.

Mid-1977 saw North Korea suspend interest payments on its trade debts to Japan, which totaled $220 million. Kim admitted "temporary strains" in the economy for early 1978 and called for a "year of readjustment." At that time, he indicated a definite willingness (perhaps out of anxiety) to talk to the United States, possibly to seek economic assistance for a new Seven-Year Plan.

Many of Pyongyang's economic difficulties stemmed from its huge expenditure on its armed forces. In the decade after 1965, the North spent 13.6 percent of its income annually on arms, as opposed to just 4.8 percent of income spent in the South. North Korea ranked second in the world in the ratio of men under arms to population. By 1976, Kim could boast of a 495,000-man standing army with a reserve of 1.5 million, an air force of 588 combat planes, and a sizable navy. After 1970, he tripled the number of tanks and increased his air force by a third. Meanwhile, daily skirmishes along the DMZ strained the situation. The North Korean buildup in tanks, trucks, and high-speed boats suggested plans for a lightning strike at Seoul, only three-minutes' flying time from North Korean territory and well within artillery range. The world had not forgotten that Kim had sworn to destroy the rival regime, reunite the peninsula, and achieve "one Korea soon."

Several provocative incidents with the South, which involved the latter's ally, the United States, had occurred. North Korean commandoes attempted to assassinate President Park in January 1968, and were stopped only three hundred yards from the Blue House, the presidential palace. Two days later, the U.S. spy ship *Pueblo* was seized in North Korean waters and taken to the port of Wonson. Although it refused to return the ship and its monitoring equipment, North Korea freed the *Pueblo's* crew the following December. This led to a temporary easing of tensions, exemplified by the Red Cross discussions for the exchange of displaced members of Korean families and the possibility of unification talks by July 1972. But just at that time, apparently, Kim began the construction of several tunnels beneath the DMZ, which would enable whole armies to infiltrate the South in just a few hours. The discovery of these passageways some time later terminated the temporary rapprochement.

Another crisis occurred in August 1976, when U.S. guards, trimming a tree at the Panmunjom joint security area, were hacked to death by their North Korean counterparts. The following July, a U.S. helicopter was shot down, and three Americans were killed and one was injured. By this time, however, Kim was eager to establish U.S. contacts, not only for foreign aid, but to hasten U.S. troop withdrawal from South Korea. The North promptly returned the one survivor and the three dead airmen, suddenly displaying a considerable change of attitude.

Finally, factionalism and the succession problem in North Korea added a dimension of political instability. Apparently, in 1971, Kim designated his son, Kim Chong Il, a relatively minor official, to succeed him. Newspapers, posters, movies, and portraits attempted to create a favorable family image, and included Kim Il Sung's father, uncle, and grandfather. "We will be loyal from generation to generation" went the new song in North Korea. All had been dedicated revolutionaries, and Kim's father had helped to organize the March 1 Movement. Yet the younger Kim (thirty-seven years old in 1978, with a playboy reputation) seldom made public appearances. Rumors circulated that the president (sixty-six years old that year) had a large growth on his neck, possibly a malignant tumor. Opposition to the succession, however, came from the elder Kim's wife (the son's stepmother) and leading party officials dissatisfied with economic failures. Some attributed the "accidental death" of Nam Il, former chief of staff to the North Korean army, as well as the ouster of several high government officials in 1976 to their opposition to the younger Kim. His enemies somehow blamed him for the American "ax murders" at Panmunjom, and he was demoted. However, the succession crisis continued. Added to Kim Il Sung's other difficulties, this issue further contributed to making Korea one of the world's most incendiary "hot spots."

South Korean Politics, 1953-1979

The constitution of 1948 established a presidential system for the First Republic of Korea. Its executive served a four-year term, was chosen by a popularly elected National Assembly, and was supported by a Supreme Court. Conflict between the volatile and politically adroit President Syngman Rhee and the National Assembly raged, even during the Korean War, over the latter's desire to make the executive more responsible to the majority party. Rhee, therefore, was barely elected in 1952 by that body sitting at Pusan. Two years later, however, Rhee successfully pushed through a constitutional amendment providing for popular election of the president, which returned him to that office in 1956, despite evident corruption. Barely a month after he won an obviously rigged election in March 1960, the army deserted Rhee, and demonstrations drove him from office. The eighty-five-year-old politician-patriot sullenly retired to Hawaii. The Second Republic followed, featuring a parliamentary-cabinet system, with a prime minister responsible to the National Assembly, but this failed to restore order. A military junta, headed by General Park Chung-hee, overthrew the republic in favor of martial law in July 1961. In the face of more demonstrations, however, General Park retired from the army to head a civilian government. Elections returned him and his Democratic-Republican party in 1963.

Resurgence of the economy strengthened President Park's government, assisted by the generous foreign aid of the United States. A Normalization Treaty with Japan in June 1965 led to mutual recognition, $800 million in economic assistance, commercial agreements, and an influx of Japanese investments. Then, U.S. President Richard M. Nixon's withdrawal of the Seventh Division from the U.S. forces in South Korea in 1970, which increased the military threat from the North, turned South Korean politics more authoritarian.

After gaining another four years from his victory over the New Democratic candidate, Kim Dae Jung, in August 1971, President Park pushed through a major revision of the constitution. The "Revitalizing Reforms" (*Yushin*) in October 1972, suspended almost all political functions of the National Assembly and gave preponderant power to the executive, whose term was extended to six years with no limit on candidacy. The president banned several newspapers and censured others for their antigovernmental views. More decrees forbade even vocal criticism, especially in the National Assembly. Although his measures were highly controversial, President Park justified his actions by stressing the vulnerability of South Korea's democracy to Communist infiltration from the North, by sea or across the DMZ by agents bent on espionage and subversion. A united national effort, he felt, would thwart any such efforts. Park's decrees also put him in complete control of his country, on a par with Kim Il Sung, as the North-South talks on unification began in July 1972.

Popular resistance to Park's government stiffened, however, when arrests and imprisonments resulted from his new policies. President Park's presidential opponent in 1971, Kim Dae Jung, who received 47 percent of the vote, was seized in a Tokyo hotel, placed under house arrest in Seoul, and eventually given a jail sentence. When missionaries were indicted for governmental criticism, Stephen Cardinal Kim spoke out for "human rights and justice." Riot police used tear gas and clubs to suppress all demonstrations. Park's methods made his opponents recall the suppression of largely the same groups by the Japanese, from whom he had obtained his military training.

Now, liberal opinion throughout the world, especially in the United States, protested U.S. support of an apparently oppressive dictator. Edwin O. Reischauer, renowned scholar and former U.S. ambassador to Japan, suggested a systematic phaseout of U.S. occupation troops and a steady reduction of military assistance, until Park's government restored civil rights. U.S. President Gerald R. Ford warned Park of his injury to U.S. relations during his visit in December 1974. Seoul responded by the periodic release of political prisoners; nevertheless, much of the world still regarded Park's government as a "garrison state."

A Korean citizen of Japan, attempting to assassinate the president on August 15, 1974, instead killed Mrs. Park, who was seated on the speakers' platform as her husband delivered an address. The government responded by further tightening security, making South Korea vulnerable to U.S. President Jimmy Carter's stress on "human rights" in U.S. foreign policy. A compensating factor existed in U.S. businesses' support of the Park regime, however, as investments steadily increased despite the criticism and military dangers. Apparently, U.S. businesspeople did not overly concern themselves with "human rights" in South Korea.

That the Korean peninsula might be losing its military importance in U.S. global strategic thinking seemed to be confirmed by Carter's announcement on June 23, 1976, during the U.S. primary elections, that he would gradually withdraw the remaining thirty-three thousand U.S. troops from South Korea. After his inauguration, Carter pledged to terminate this last U.S. military presence on the Asian mainland by 1982, to remove the troops from a danger area. This "Carter shock" jolted the Park government, who resolutely announced that South Korea would depend on "a self-reliant defense."

Simultaneously, a major scandal erupted in the United States involving South Korean payments to numerous members of Congress. This "Koreagate" issue concerned Tongsun Park, a prominent lobbyist in Washington, who paid some $2 million to influence legislation favorable to Seoul between 1971 and 1975, mostly to deter the U.S. troop evacuation. A former head of the Korean Central Intelligence Agency (KCIA) gave damaging testimony. After much maneuvering, Park made *in camera* statements before a congressional committee in return for immunity from prosecution. Washington attempted to secure the testimony of former South Korean Ambassador Kim Dong Jo (1967–1973), by threatening to curtail U.S. aid. After preliminary refusal, Seoul finally agreed to allow Kim to reply in writing to questions submitted by Congress. The scandal and Carter's withdrawal plan brought the validity of U.S. support of Seoul into considerable question.

But the jolting assassination of President Park Chung-hee, at a formal banquet given for him by the KCIA on the evening of October 26, 1979, bludgeoned the country. Prosecution of the KCIA head, Kim Jae Kyu, for the act revealed a conspiracy among the late president's closest advisers. Fortunately, anarchy was avoided as Choi Kyu Hah, sworn in as acting president, began a liberalization program.

Korea and the Great Powers, through 1979

The possibility that Kim Il Sung might launch a blitzkrieg against the South could draw the great powers into another Korean war. Fortunately, China, the Soviet Union, Japan, and the United States all opposed such a war, for each had an interest in preserving the general balance and stability of East Asia. A reduction of tensions on the peninsula, while achieving a general agreement between North and South, would work to the interest of all. Nevertheless, the two antagonistic Korean regimes vis à vis the four powers represented "one of the most complex tinder boxes in the world," Professor A. Doak Barnett, an American Far Eastern specialist with the Brookings Institution, correctly asserted. International equilibrium kept the general peace, but precariously. Certainly, in this situation, Korea was the "linchpin" for a stable East Asian balance of power.

China wanted no involvement in another Korean war, because a Soviet army of one and one-half million men remained fully mobilized on its northern frontiers after 1969, a year in which China itself was deluged by the Cultural Revolution. The moderates, eventually victorious in this Chinese power struggle, reconciled with the United States to counter Russian moves and facilitate economic reform and military modernization. After the Vietnam War, when Kim Il Sung begged for "one more blow" against the United States in April 1975, Beijing gave him a cool reception. China realized that the U.S. presence in South Korea acted as a shield against Russia, especially after expanding Soviet naval power moved into East Asian waters. Moreover, a Russian-dominated Korea would endanger China's Manchurian industrial complex. Yet the Sino-Soviet split compelled Beijing to publicly back Kim's pledge to unite the peninsula, as the North Korean leader played on the rift to compel support. Chinese Premier Hua Kuofeng's visit to Pyongyang reiterated this equivocal pledge in late May 1978.

The Soviets provided the bulk of Kim's armaments, vying with Chinese advisers at Pyongyang. Moscow, however, also restrained Kim, because a war would create Sino-Soviet competition over military assistance to a smaller Communist state. Besides, a united Korea might, at some time, veer towards China. Détente (a cautious relaxation of tensions) with the United States provided Russia far greater advantages in technological aid and wheat shipments, stemming from the Vietnam settlement in 1973. At the same time, the Russians advocated a policy of containment against the Chinese, fearing a possible future spillover into Siberia, as Beijing's population pressures mounted. The Soviets realized that the U.S. presence in Korea balanced the Chinese, ensuring preservation of the status quo in East Asia.

Korea's situation and the great-power equilibrium most directly affected Japan. The distance separating the two neighbors (120 miles across the Strait of Tsushima) barely equals that between New York and Philadelphia. Japan's relative disarmament made it favor the continued existence of a South Korea supported by U.S. troops. Therefore, Japan worked for a general agreement and favored seating both Koreas in the U.N. Concern for Korea had forced war on Japan in 1894 and 1904 against China and Russia. Given the inadequacy of Japan's small "Self-Defense Forces," it has resorted to a specialized form of protection. By means of its 1965 treaty with the Park government and through agreements with Kim Il Sung after 1972, Japan intruded economically into both Koreas. The lure of cheap labor, investment opportunities, and lucrative markets attracted Japanese electronics, textile, and automobile firms, even in the face of traditional Korean hostility toward its encroachments. These agreements, however, served Japan's interests, because they enabled it to act as a mediator between North and South Korea, and between North Korea and the United States, thus contributing to East Asian stability. Finally, all of these various protective factors shielded Japan against Communist threats. If the North had succeeded in overrunning the South, Japan would have been compelled to rearm, possibly throwing off any U.S. pleas for restraint. No one in East and Southeast Asia could forget Japan's ravenous imperial expansion from 1894 through World War II. Certainly, Japanese rearmament would provoke a hostile reaction from all of its neighbors, especially the Chinese, shattering the quadrilateral balance of power that preserved the peace. Thus Korea's strategic geographical position played its part in international politics once again.

Naturally, then, the proposed withdrawal of U.S. troops from South Korea deeply disturbed the Japanese, who protested President Carter's decision. But many Americans pointed to the supposed "lesson" of the Vietnam War—never again to become embroiled in "nonessential" areas. The $37 billion U.S. expenditure in Korea from 1945 to 1975, more than the total sum for the Marshall Plan and the Apollo Program combined, had returned little. From 1950 to 1979 more than one million Americans served in Korea, and more than fifty-four thousand had died there. Opponents, however, repudiated the presidential view as an open invitation for North Korea to invade the South. General John K. Singlaub, chief of staff of the U.S. forces in Korea, publicly argued this point in May 1977 and was immediately relieved of duty. But General Richard G. Stilwell, his former commander, sustained Singlaub's case. Many observers had long supported America's role of peacemaker or "referee" on the Korean peninsula, keeping the Asian powers from coming to blows. Resolutions by both houses of Congress condemned withdrawal, while the House refused to vote the $800 million appro-

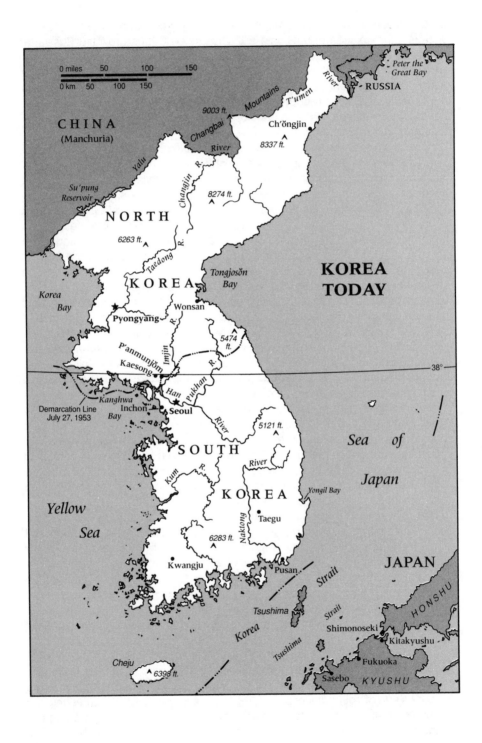

KOREA
TODAY

priation for additional armaments for South Korea, part of the president's plan. In April 1978, the White House, possibly conceding to criticism, announced that two of the three brigades of the U.S. Second Division would not be withdrawn when scheduled. When presidential national security adviser Zbigniew Brzezinski stopped off at Seoul (May 1978) following talks in Tokyo and Beijing, he assured President Park of the continued U.S. commitment to South Korea. Nevertheless, critics questioned why withdrawal could not have been part of a deal in return for the much-needed settlement—a permanent treaty for mutual recognition of North and South Korea with China, the USSR, Japan, and the United States as signatories.

Although the United States, like the three other powers, profited from the general peace and stability of East Asia, dangers abounded. Many observers like Professor Barnett foresaw "no sudden drastic change" in the four-power equilibrium in the foreseeable future, because none of the four would have a realistic basis for trying to achieve regional hegemony. Nevertheless, much depended on the great powers' ability to check Kim Il Sung, whose reckless "miscalculation" could destroy everything.

President Carter, therefore, acted to reduce Korean tension—what one adviser had termed an "anachronism of the Cold War"— when he visited Seoul following the Economic Summit Conference in Japan in late June 1979. With President Park, Carter invited North Korea to participate in three-party discussions to lessen hostilities in preparation for possible unification. Pyongyang's answer was a firm "No." Some days later Mr. Carter announced that withdrawal of the thirty-thousand-man U.S. force would be halted as of July 20, pending restudy of the situation in 1981. The Joint Chiefs of Staff reported that the North Korean army had reached seven hundred thousand men with a decided superiority also in tanks and artillery, which, in their view imperilled the South. The Pentagon and many members of Congress welcomed the announcement.

Despite increasing vocal support for South Korea, however, during his visit Mr. Carter once again criticized Seoul for its poor record on "human rights." Although Park pledged the release of hundreds of political prisoners, the U.S. president advised him to match his record in political liberalization with that in economic modernization. Seoul replied that the continued threat from the North made extension of civil freedoms inadvisable.

Although the Korean situation witnessed some movement toward permanent peace in 1979, the peninsula still presented the world with one of its most incendiary potentials for future war. President Park's tragic assassination (October 1979) brought another military government under General Chun Doo-hwan, increasing tension on the peninsula.

South Korea

Politics, Society, Economy, 1979–1995

The admittedly autocratic, authoritarian, and undoubtedly controversial regime of President Park Chung-hee came to a devastating conclusion on October 26, 1979, when he was assassinated by the head of the KCIA at a dinner in his honor. It marked a shattering climax to South Korea's search for political consensus, which was seemingly unattainable. Martial law reigned immediately afterward, and the military took full control. General Chun Doo-hwan, a classmate of the murdered president at the Korean Military Academy, took charge; and his crackdown proved severe, including a national alert to meet possible attack from the North. Students and factory workers demonstrating against military rule met tear gas and clubs in the streets. Chun continued Park's policies, retaining martial law until 1981, when a new, even more restrictive constitution gave still more authority to the new government. Student and worker demands did achieve some lessening of governmental suppression after 1981, which only intensified their dissatisfaction. Workers clamored for increased wages; students shouted for immediate unification with the North—at one time (1985) organizing a march to the DMZ, which was quickly dispersed. Young people demanded also a more representative government and hence personal freedoms. The general's government prevailed, however, because its prompt actions dealt effectively with any disorder.

A steady economic gain all through the 1980s, however, proved Chun's best political asset. Indeed, from 1960, South Korea averaged a 9.5 percent yearly increase in its GNP, substantially assisted by U.S. aid, vaulting from the 1960 figure of $33 million to $147 billion by 1987. By 1980 the ROK had moved from the production of small, low-cost items for export, largely textiles, to more heavy-industrial products—ships, electronics, and automobiles. Indeed, the automobile began to be a standard possession of Korean families. The name Hyundai entered the U.S. automobile market in the mid-1980s, proving a surprisingly successful import. The relatively low cost of Korean labor continued to attract foreign investment, especially Japanese. South Korea profited from the industrial base that had been developed by the Japanese during their colonial administration. The ROK was now the sixth-best U.S. customer, ahead of France, Italy, and all of Scandinavia. By the mid-1980s South Korea was running a trade surplus of some $7 billion with the United States, which was somewhat discomforting to the Americans who demanded more commercial liberalization from the ROK along with uninterrupted progress to an effective rule of law.

Political unrest continued as intensified student-worker discontent now demanded direct election of the president. The National Assembly was thoroughly dominated by President Chun's Democratic Victory party, even after he promised to step down in 1987. Speculation ran that his retirement was influenced by Philippine President Ferdinand Marcos's overthrow the previous year.

Chun, therefore, bowed out of the December 1987 elections, which saw much hostile agitation, especially when another former general, Roh Tae-woo, won the executive's seat. Roh owed his victory largely to the fact that his opposition was divided. Indeed, he had garnered only 33.9 percent of the vote, whereas the combined opposition won 52 percent. Previously Roh's greatest achievement occurred in 1982, when he was appointed minister of sports in Chun's cabinet. Roh persuaded the International Olympic Committee (IOC) to hold the twenty-fourth summer games (1988) in Seoul, a magnificent spectacle that was enjoyed by athletes and spectators (including a worldwide television audience) alike. Some 13,000 athletes from 160 countries took part. "Conspicuous by their presence" were teams from the PRC and the USSR. The games generated notable prestige for the South and increased the isolation of the North, which was warned by the IOC not to attempt to interfere with the games. The North had demanded that it be allowed to participate in the competition but set so many conditions that an agreement could not be reached, so they were left out entirely. A few unfortunate incidents during the games stood out as indicators of South Korean irritation against the United States. "Blame America," became a frequent saying of the home crowd, especially after a disputed decision in a boxing match between an American and a South Korean athlete. Nevertheless, the success of the summer 1988 Olympic Games earned the ROK the admiration of the world. The "Seoul shock," stemming from the favorable television coverage of the games and the thriving city, helped stir communism's overthrow in Eastern Europe in President Roh's opinion.

Nevertheless, The Republic of Korea found the transition to democracy a difficult one. Roh's group combined with two other parties in 1990 to form the Democratic-Liberal party, in order to secure a majority, while he pledged to stand by his "Declaration of Liberal Reforms." Despite Roh's sincere efforts at pacification, he could not deal with the animosity between business and government. This inspired Chung Ju Yung, founder and president of Hyundai, to accuse the government of placing unfair restrictions on business and to establish his own National Unification party. In addition, more opposition came from the leftist Democratic party. The contentious elections of February 1992 witnessed the loss of the Democratic Liberal party's majority in parliament, a notable jolt for the leading group. Therefore, they nominated their old political opponent, Kim Young Sam, for the presidential elections set for December 1992, which he won. For South Korea the route to democracy proved a troubled political road, although Kim promised to be "a generous president" if elected. Despite the difficult transition, South Korea's movement somewhat mollified the United States and most liberal opinions generally, which had opposed the perpetuation of military rule.

South Korea's society reflected its disturbed political picture, despite considerable national prosperity in the overall. By the early 1990s, South Korea was some 80 percent urban. Labor unrest was recurrent and marked by a demand for higher wages. Witness the mammoth Hyundai strike at Ulsan (fall 1992), which was settled only when the army threatened to storm the gates. Student violence continued to be troublesome, as many students continued to demand unification with the North, but police using tear gas dispersed demonstrations successfully.

"Koreans are discouraged," observed President Kim Young Sam, but why? Despite continued economic advances nationally, there remained areas of sharp discontent. Overall growth had fallen from about 10 percent annually in the 1980s to about 7.5 percent by the early 1990s. Interest rates ran from 18 to 20 percent. A gnawing inflation of 10 percent only increased labor's demands for wage increases, especially with salaries averaging only $3.82 per hour. As wages rose, however, foreign companies began pulling out of the ROK in favor of other countries with cheaper wage scales, in Southeast Asia and Latin America especially. Banks often suffered from too much liberalization, which permitted insolvent institutions to keep operating. Yet the reverse side of the coin revealed that the ROK ranked fifteenth internationally in GNP and was the thirteenth-largest trading nation. It placed second internationally in shipbuilding, while POSCO, its largest steel company, stood third worldwide. True, the ROK had difficulties with the United States over the trade surplus. U.S. President George Bush on his January 1992 tour of East Asia urged South Korea to allow more U.S. imports. Too often U.S. goods would lie for weeks on the docks at Pusan waiting for customs inspection. Then, too, South Korea had its own trade deficit with Japan.

President Kim Young Sam was inaugurated on February 25, 1993. True to his political pledges he set about reform with unparalleled vigor. He dismissed thousands of bureaucrats, military leaders, and businessmen. Those left were ordered in many cases to publicly proclaim their assets—the president himself admitting to having amassed $2.1 million. When other officials followed suit, public indignation forced more of them to resign. But the military proved the main target of the new reforms, as both the chief-of-staff and the head of army intelligence were discharged. Also, the new regime sought to open the South Korean economy to more foreign access, for instance by permitting some foreign rice imports. Another significant measure decreed that anonymous or fabricated names transactions (a convenient tax evasion and stock market manipulation practice of the very wealthy) would henceforth be illegal. President Kim Young Sam's new nonmilitary, democratic regime meant reform to the limit.

In summary, the ROK did represent one of the great success stories of economic advance in the Third World. Parallel with this was the social dislocation spurred by its transition from military dictatorship to democracy and a rule of law. Admittedly, it had not been exactly the "quiet revolution" that former President Roh had envisioned. Nevertheless, South Korea's economic achievements and the elevation in its popular living standard had earned that country much international admiration.

North Korea

Politics, Society, and Economy, 1979–1995
North Korea presented an arresting contrast to the South in the 1980s and early 1990s especially, for the Communist state suffered economic recession and increasing diplomatic isolation as Kim Il Sung's regime stood alone in the general collapse of the Communist world. One institution, however, did not experience decline, namely, the military, because the army burgeoned to an estimated 1.2 million by 1992—the fifth- or sixth-largest force in the world. The armed forces absorbed one-third of the nation's GNP. Even with greater natural resources, more square miles, and only one-half of the South's population (about 22 million people), North Korea's exports for one year (1991–1992 at $1 billion) would equal only five-days' exports from South Korea. The Pyongyang government witnessed the fall of its Eastern European market, which had accepted its coal, iron, and tungsten in exchange for oil, when in 1989 the USSR demanded cash payments for that commodity. Previously, the Warsaw Pact nations accounted for one-half of North Korea's trade. Now, North Korea's oil supplies fell to only 10 percent of need. Infrequent visitors to North Korea told of smokeless factory chimneys, strangely empty roads, and dark cities at night. Factories fell to one-half of production capacity. In addition, the North lacked hard currency with which to pay

its foreign debts. It defaulted on international loans, often having to barter for goods on the world market. Then, in 1990, China also demanded hard currency for its oil. The new Ryu Gyong Hotel in Pyongyang, with its twenty-five stories, stood nakedly unfinished for all to see. A substantial agricultural decline report-edly left some people starving. The government's only response to the crisis was to suggest that the people limit their meals to two a day. Internationally, most of the world knew that Kim Il Sung's regime supported much of the terror-ism and drug smuggling taking place worldwide.

More and more, North Korea needed the outside world. Juche (self-reliance) had failed for a regime that perhaps was the most-isolated internationally. David E. Sanger, correspondent for the *New York Times,* called North Korea the "world's most hermetically sealed nation." Billy Graham, the evangelist, traveled the coun-try for five days in 1992 and described it hopefully as "a closed country, but about to open to the outside world." The late 1980s witnessed North Korea mak-ing strenuous overtures, seeking investment from nations it despised with the lure of cheap labor. Workers' salaries averaged about $45 a month. Kim espe-cially invited the Japanese, whose ruthless martial law had not been forgotten, as well as most Western powers. North Korea's abundance of cheap labor did attract much outside interest—no fear of strikes, for laborers were harshly sup-pressed—as did its abundant mineral resources. Special economic zones, on the Chinese model, were established along the northern frontier, close to the PRC and Russia on the T'umen River, offering special tax incentives.

Upon reaching his eightieth birthday, April 15, 1992, for which there was much formal celebration—a huge rally displayed a sign: "We envy nobody in the world"—Kim Il Sung remained in power, resisting the urge to retire, despite the general decline of the Communist world. At the time of his death, in 1994, Kim was the longest-serving world leader—some 46 years. Most likely, he feared leaving the state in inexperienced hands with the international situation as it was. Nevertheless, as mentioned, he succeeded in preparing the political scene for his son, Kim Chong Il, despite both military and family opposition. Likely, the voluntary overthrow of communism in North Korea can be ruled out in the imme-diate future, for its current system sustains too many governmental personnel in their positions. Kim feared reforms, since he put the blame for the collapse of communism in Eastern Europe on its economic liberalization. Kim Chong Il had his detractors, who regarded him as "a spoiled playboy" with a weakness for liquor and women. He definitely lacked his father's charisma, had never traveled outside of China or North Korea, and was feared by neighboring nations who knew he had inspired several terrorist acts, all despite his pseudonym of "Dear Leader." Kim Il Sung's Democratic People's Republic was probably the one place in which George Orwell's *1984* (with its totalitarian "cult of personality" in "Big Brother") had been realized, an environment that Josef Stalin likely would have found congenial. The recognition of the rival Republic of Korea to the south by Russia in 1990 and by the PRC in 1992 left Kim, the "Great Leader," quite alone.

Western intelligence reports told often of the danger from the Kungang Dam, just north of the DMZ and Seoul. Release of the dam's waters by the North could inundate the ROK's capital. But of even greater significance was intelligence in the later 1980s of a sizable nuclear installation under construction about ninety

Kim Il Sung, President of North Korea, who died July 8, 1994. Wide World Photos.

Kim Chong Il, son of Kim Il Sung, sitting on his luxury yacht. With the death of his father, he is the first communist leader to inherit the mantle of power. AP Photo/Kyodo.

miles from Pyongyang, at Yongbyon. Given enough time this facility could create an atomic bomb, possibly the strength of that which had destroyed Nagasaki in 1945. During World War II the Japanese had established a nuclear experimental facility in North Korea, utilizing the area's uranium deposits. International inquiries directed at North Korea received the reply that this structure produced only electricity (there were, however, no power lines running from the facility). Already, many knew that Kim Il Sung's government was selling military hardware to nations of the Middle East in exchange for oil, especially its Russian-made Scud C missiles to Libya, Syria, Iran, and Iraq. If North Korea had indeed managed to assemble a nuclear warhead, this would put enormously destructive forces in Kim's hands and perhaps, by extension, those of Saddham Hussein of Iraq or Libya's Mu'ammar al-Qadhdhafi, among other internationally-known terrorists.

The United States stood in the vanguard of the Western nations that demanded international inspection of Kim's nuclear facility. North Korea did agree in principle (in January 1992) to inspection by the International Atomic Energy Association (IAEA), but then asked that the inspection be postponed. Many in the West regarded this as a possible stall on Kim's part, until sufficient weapons-grade plutonium could be extracted from the facility and then sufficiently concealed from inspectors. U.S. Ambassador to South Korea Donald Gregg explained the U.S. position: Kim needed the outside world to bolster his nation's faltering economy, but only at the price of agreeing to the international inspection. A May 1992 inspection by an IAEA team found nothing incriminating—the processor was less than half-completed—and were told that the facility was only for "civilian purposes." The existence of what was possibly a primary facility, constructed earlier, left a lingering doubt in Western minds. Neighboring nations feared that North Korea's possession of an atomic bomb would trigger an East Asian chain reaction, with South Korea and Japan feeling compelled to arm themselves accordingly. In April 1992, the North Korean parliament amended its constitution to allow for private property and foreign investment, that government's first step towards capitalism since the inception of the Democratic People's Republic in 1948. In return Kim demanded that all nuclear equipment (first brought there by the United States nine years before) be removed from South Korea—which the United States did in fact do in October 1992. Clearly the ball was in Kim's court and the world awaited his reply to its demands. In the overall, however, North Korea's future looked decidedly "bleak."

The crisis over the possible existence of North Korean nuclear weapons reached a climax in November 1993, with the reports of North Korean troop movements toward the DMZ. The movement continued until fully 75 percent of their forces were in the fortified zones, seemingly poised for a strike against South Korea. At this point the North offered to hold discussions and allow full IAEA inspections, and the U.N. Secretary-General, Butros-Butros Ghali, entered the country. In another conciliatory gesture, the North also turned over the remains of thirty-one U.S. troops killed forty years before in the Korean War. Yet later in December, the U.S. CIA reported candidly that North Korea already had one, perhaps two, nuclear bombs along with sufficient missiles to deliver its warheads to Japan. The situation challenged U.S. President Clinton's promise that "North Korea will not be permitted the bomb." At worst the situation threatened war, at best an East Asian regional arms race. Economic sanctions against North Korea were a possibility, but that step was opposed by South Korea as apt to provoke a North Korean attack. Projections stated that a North Korean assault on the South now might be defeated in three months, due to their shortage of oil, but at the cost of much devastation to the South, given Seoul's proximity to the DMZ. Further intelligence revealed that North Korea continued to exchange nuclear information with Iran and Syria in return for oil. North Korea, however, was only one of several areas in the Third World that might have the bomb, all of critical concern to the United States.

South and North Korea

Foreign Relations, 1980–1995

In the 1980s antagonism between North and South Korea presented perhaps the greatest potential for World War III outside of the situation in the Middle East. A "real flashpoint," the area provided the "final chapter of the Cold War" in the words of historian Nicholas Eberstadt. Two bitterly hostile military dictatorships continued to stand face to face across the DMZ "in a divided, heavily-armed Korean peninsula." Former U.S. Ambassador to Japan Michael J. Mansfield had described the situation as "a smoldering volcano." But by the later part of the decade the relationship had evolved to exist on two almost contradictory levels: intensified hostility alongside an increasing spirit of reconciliation, especially after 1988 and President Roh Tae-woo's efforts at propitiation. Unification perhaps was coming some day, but it still faced herculean obstacles.

The DMZ represented one of the most closely guarded frontiers in the world. In the early 1990s the North Korean army numbered perhaps 1.2 million; that of South Korea about 600,000, aided by a U.S. army of around 35,000 and a supporting air force. The Americans stood as the main deterrent to war. By that time the two Koreas had given some indications of a reconciliation, but only after a decade of disheartening setbacks. In 1982 President Chun Doo-hwan of South Korea initiated talks, but a shattering incident in Rangoon, Burma (Myanmar), interrupted the proceedings. A North Korean bomb had exploded and killed four members of Chun's cabinet and fifty others at a wreath-laying ceremony on October 9, 1983. The president himself was spared only because his limousine was late to the gathering. Then, in 1984, North Korea offered to send relief aid to victims of a South Korean flood, an offer that was accepted and fulfilled at face value. Talks recommenced. The South suggested an agreement on a joint constitution; the North put forward their plan for a confederation. Nothing substantial came of this exchange, yet family ties across the two states could not be denied. Some ten million Koreans on both sides had been separated from their relatives for the past forty years. On a few occasions a handful of civilians, assisted by the International Red Cross, had been allowed to cross the DMZ. Then once again a terrorist incident broke off the talks, when a Korean airliner exploded (January 1987) in midair off the Burmese coast; an investigation established North Korean involvement in the incident.

With the advent of Roh Tae-woo as president of the ROK in 1988, reconciliation efforts commenced yet again as he sought eventual "harmony" with the enemy to the North. Roh's approach had probably restrained the North from taking any hostile actions against the Olympic Games in Seoul. Holding that "unification in this century" was his goal, Roh sought a step-by-step approach as the decline of the Communist world continued to further isolate the North. In October 1990, the two presidents talked for four days at Seoul. By December 1991, the two sides signed an agreement for mutual "inspection" of nuclear facilities, while the South also agreed to cancel the "Team Spirit" joint military exercises with the U.S. forces. In the next month, however, the North Koreans had requested a "delay" in the inspection proceedings.

Nevertheless, both regimes entered the United Nations at last in September 1991. When China finally withheld its veto on the entry of South Korea, the North, too, had requested admission. Soviet and Chinese vetoes had black-balled South Korea on eight previous occasions. Then joint ping-pong teams competed in Japan, while a dual-sponsored soccer club played in Portugal that year. Observers were reminded of the 1971 occasion when China invited the U.S. table-tennis team to the PRC, which had helped lead to détente between the two nations during the Vietnam War.

Regarding the nuclear issue, however, South Korean intelligence had projected the completion of the North's weapon in 1993. Some at the time worried that if unification should supersede, the ROK would have to shoulder a $400 billion burden to rehabilitate the North. The South Korean "Chaebol" (a trust of big industrialists), which included Hyundai, Daewoo, and Samsung, therefore, insisted on making immediate investments to improve the North's economy as much as possible, hoping to lighten the financial impact of an actual unification. Official permission to several firms to proceed was forthcoming. Seoul watched the progress of German unification after October 1990, although the two Germanies did not have the burden of antagonism that hampered Korea. President Roh, nevertheless, liked to compare his policy of "Northern Diplomacy" with Willi Brandt's "Ostpolitik" as examples of gradual but progressive preparation for unification.

Relations with the USSR proved pivotal for both Koreas. Soviet Russia had been South Korea's most consistent enemy, with its military and economic support of the North since 1945, and especially during and after the Korean War (1950–1953). An international tragedy jolted everyone on September 1, 1983, when the Soviet air force shot down a passenger airliner (Korean Airlines Flight 007), supposedly because it had overflown Soviet military installations on Sakhalin Island on its way to Seoul. All 269 passengers perished. Following that incident, the Soviets reportedly provided the necessary data and technicians for North Korea's nuclear power plant in 1986, and the USSR continued as Pyongyang's greatest trading partner.

The political scene changed markedly in 1988 with the entrance of Roh and his Northern Diplomacy—efforts to reconcile South Korea with the North, the PRC, and the USSR in the face of a collapsing Communist world. The ROK now could offer the Soviets capital and advanced technology, primarily for neighboring Siberia. Mikhail Gorbachev, Soviet president, met with Roh in San Francisco (June 1990), ending four decades of relations frozen in animosity. Full diplomatic relations were established the following September 30, and commercial offices opened in Seoul and Moscow. In addition, Moscow released twelve secret documents on the KAL 007 tragedy, along with the plane's flight recorder, to President Roh in November 1992. Yet there still remained the Soviet military buildup—submarine bases, airfields, and missile installations—partially revealed by the KAL 007 incident. This threat, centered in extreme eastern Siberia and the Kurile Islands, as well as on Sakhalin Island, directly menaced Japan but also endangered South Korea, representing a dangerous factor in the general picture of regional reconciliation.

Soviet relations with North Korea exposed the other side of the coin. After 1988, Kim Il Sung witnessed, as mentioned, the alarming collapse of his Eastern European market for North Korean minerals, especially coal, which had been exchanged for critically needed oil. True, the early 1980s saw Kim successfully playing the Sino-Soviet dispute to his advantage, but in the years after 1988, Kim suffered increasing isolation from Russia and its Eastern European allies. In 1990 the Russians, as mentioned, demanded hard cash for their oil, soon forcing an enormous international debt on Kim.

North Korea's mounting difficulties were displayed to the world when it went ahead with its plans to host an eight-day World Youth and Student Festival in July 1989, at a cost of $4–5 million. Here was a spectacle in which the spotlight was cast on new stadiums, hotels, and theaters that had been left unfinished, and in which lighting and air conditioning faltered due to severe power shortages. Kim found that his much proclaimed juche could not dispel his increasing international isolation.

Both Koreas witnessed substantial changes (1980s) in their relations with the PRC. For some time China had supported staunchly its small North Korean ally, especially after October 1950, when it entered the Korean War. Kim's cult of personality modeled itself greatly on that of Chairman Mao, especially as espoused during China's Cultural Revolution from 1966 to 1976. But after the Tiananmen Square massacre in June 1989 precipitated much international discredit to China's government, Kim's strongest remaining Communist ally had been disgraced in the world's eyes. Despite many journeys to Beijing and Moscow, Kim received diminishing support from his major allies, especially Eastern Europe, which now felt that strong ties to Kim might hamper their own commercial assistance from the West, leaving North Korea to its own shriveling resources.

South Korea's experience with China presented a considerable contrast. As mentioned, part of President Roh's Northern Diplomacy was aimed directly at bettering relations with the PRC. Park Chul Un, representing Seoul, visited China in 1990 for the first high-level meeting since 1953. In turn Teng Zhifang, businessman son of China's head of state, visited South Korea in 1991. China sought South Korean investment for its northeastern sector, especially in the neighboring province of Shantung, much as Hong Kong had invested in the Kwantung province in the south, while Taiwan was tied financially to Fukien, across the Taiwan Strait from it. Many Koreans who had emigrated to northeastern China now fled communism by going, as laborers, to South Korea. Both China and Russia participated in the Olympic Games at Seoul in 1988 to Pyongyang's chagrin. Official diplomatic recognition came in late August 1992, but at something of a cost to Seoul, which had to break ties with Taiwan (Republic of China) because of the "one China" policy insisted on by Beijing. Newspapers everywhere pictured a Taiwanese protester—"Korea you have betrayed our trust"—trampling the South Korean flag outside the embassy in Taipei. Companies such as Hyundai and Daewoo immediately moved into China, tripling the trade volume between the two countries in just one year. In the *New York Times,* David E. Sanger expressed the situation well: "Moscow and Beijing pragmatically prefer South Korea's steel plants and car foundries to the North's Stalinist rhetoric."

Japan represented perhaps the sole subject on which the two Koreas could agree, at least in part. Both recalled the brutal colonial subjugation with which Japan ruled Korea from 1910 to 1945. The Japanese, however, had laid Korea's original industrial base, especially its infrastructure, during those years. Relations between Seoul and Tokyo were never cordial, even after diplomatic recognition in 1965. Since then each has sought to exclude the other's products as far as possible because of the competition factor. Japanese tariffs virtually barred South Korean textiles, shoes, and clothing, while Seoul restricted Japanese automobiles and electronics. Japanese investment in South Korea, somewhat extensive after 1965, was regarded as a mixed blessing, all too reminiscent of the ruthless Japanese economic penetration of Korea after it was first opened in 1876. The ROK's irritation centered painfully on its $9 billion trade deficit with Japan, accumulated largely by the extensive importation of Japanese industrial machinery.

Another issue, however, concerned Japanese atrocities committed during its colonial rule through World War II. During the war especially, the Japanese military sent thousands of Korean workers to labor in Japan. In the 1980s some six hundred thousand of them remained in Japan, still suppressed into an inferior status socially, which denied their right to vote and compelled them to be fingerprinted every two years and to carry an identification card at all times. In addition, many Koreans and other wartime victims had been subjected to biological experiments by the Japanese at a special camp in Manchuria. In December 1991, a Korean woman filed suit in a Tokyo court because she was one of thousands of "comfort girls" (*inanfu*) who were compelled to provide sexual satisfaction to Japanese soldiers in World War II. They were forced to "offer their services" to as many as thirty or fifty military personnel per day, were beaten if they refused, and shot if they contracted a venereal disease. Taken forcibly from villages, they were told they would work in factories, but instead were usually taken to one of six "comfort stations" in China, where they lived in filthy barracks. Women were brought to the stations also from China, Taiwan, the Philippines, and Japan. Japanese Prime Minister Kiichi Miyazawa confronted the issue when he made a three-day visit to Seoul in January 1992, where he was met by a hostile demonstration demanding an explanation for the Japanese actions. He tried to say that the stations were privately run, but he then admitted to the true nature of the state-run operation. The prime minister then tried to assert that the women had performed voluntarily, but this statement, too, was received skeptically.

Japanese historian Yoshiaki Yoshimi first uncovered the issue from documents in the library of the Self-Defense Forces. These papers revealed that between 100,000 and 200,000 women had been involved. Finally, on July 6, 1992, the Tokyo government admitted its full culpability, expressing apologies to those "who underwent indescribable pain . . . as comfort women." But many of Japan's neighbors, especially the Koreans, felt that Japan had not yet been fully candid in regard to its wartime atrocities, likely in an effort to avoid demands for reparations.

North Korea, too, had its memories of Japanese rule, but this was another day. Increasingly its inexpensive labor wooed Japanese industrialists. As for North Korea, its new special economic zones on its northern frontier notably angered the South Koreans, who felt that Japan purposely sought to keep the peninsula divided, fearing the economic competition which might arise from a unified Korea.

North Korea would have liked to send students abroad to Japan and the West to learn industrial technology, but it feared inviting the influence of liberal Western ideals on its young people, recalling the incident at Tiananmen Square in China. As mentioned, Kim expressly blamed the fall of communism on the liberal economic measures taken in Eastern Europe. North Korea remained a tightly regimented state, accumulating a foreign debt of $8 billion. One Japanese observer accused North Korea of being "flat broke." Defaulting on international loans, while restricting much private outside capital, North Korea was reduced often to merely bartering for goods in the world outside.

The United States stood as South Korea's "engine of growth," in the words of President Roh, for U.S. aid since 1953 had completely renewed his nation's industrial base; but several differences divided the two countries, especially the $7 billion trade surplus in favor of the ROK, while U.S. automobile interests found yet another foreign competitor in Hyundai. Textiles and electronics represented other areas of competition. In addition, during the 1980s Washington pressed hard the issue of "human rights" on the ROK's military leaders, resulting in President Roh Tae-woo's movement toward democracy.

The protracted presence of a forty-three-thousand-man U.S. army had become an increasing irritant to South Korean students, who continued their demands for unification. North Korea, of course, repeatedly denounced the U.S. presence. In 1991 the Americans temporarily evacuated the DMZ preliminary to North-South talks, but they remained nearby because of the potential nuclear threat at Yongbyon. The year 1992 witnessed the initial withdrawal of three thousand Americans. By January 1993, the level had dropped to thirty-five thousand. Congressmen in Washington frequently argued over the issue of withdrawal, but the danger to the Far Eastern balance of power persisted. Hence, the U.S. army remained posted on the DMZ. Many Koreans overlooked the fact that this force's presence acted as a pledge of immediate U.S. assistance to the ROK, a decided deterrence against war and prevention of an assault from the North.

In the main, U.S.–North Korean relations remained sullen and uncommunicative except for a few informal talks in Beijing, starting in 1989. Commercial relations remained nonexistent due to U.S. "trading with the enemy" restrictions. North Korea in many ways symbolized the old Cold War between the Communist world and the West, otherwise, seemingly, a thing of the past. Yet the Yongbyon facility reminded observers that Kim Il Sung might have a nuclear bomb within two years and the temptation to use it should his situation become desperate enough. Foreign statesmen knew well of the danger of backing Kim into a corner. Some spoke of the feasibility of a U.S. air strike similar to those used in the recent Gulf War against Saddam Hussein's facilities in Iraq, but the vulnerability of Seoul, so close to the DMZ and within three minutes of a North Korean Scud missile attack, could not be forgotten. More rumors filled the air that perhaps as many as 125 American POW's from the Korean War had been taken to North Korea and then to China, while having been reported as casualties to their families. Still more reports told of North Korean ships carrying arms to the Middle East. Did the future hold peace or war for Korea? There was ample evidence for both views. In either case the United States, as the principal deterrent to such a conflict, stood as the party most nearly concerned.

Nevertheless, Pyongyang announced sharply in March 1993 that it intended to withdraw from the Nuclear Non-proliferation Treaty effective the following June 12. Yet it withdrew that threat on the day before the deadline, asking that diplomatic talks be resumed. Then on April 9 the North Korean government took an ominous step by appointing Kim Chong Il Chairman of the National Defense Commission, the nation's top military post, indicating that he might be manipulating the whole nuclear confrontation. Then Western intelligence revealed that North Korea was testing a new missile (the Rodong 1), whose six-hundred-mile range threatened Japanese cities. Also, there was much support for information that many Koreans in Japan were financially supporting the North with perhaps $1 billion annually. Thus, the North Korean crisis mounted as Kim Il Sung tried to maneuver it to his best advantage.

Flagrantly threatening war, which would turn Seoul into "a sea of fire," North Korea intensified its pressure on the South in the spring of 1994. In March of that year the IAEA inspected six of the Yongbyon complexes but were denied access to a seventh. U.S. Defense Secretary William Perry warned that North Korea was close to producing ten nuclear bombs.

President Clinton's administration in Washington was severely tested, faced with simultaneous threats elsewhere in Bosnia, Rwanda, and Haiti. Former U.S. Ambassador to South Korea and China, James Lilly, stressed that his country must "send a clear and unmistakable message to Pyongyang that any resort to force by North Korea will result in its ultimate destruction." In view of strained U.S. relations with China over "human rights" and with Japan over its trade surplus, Washington, needing those nations' support, faced a North Korean situation that severely challenged its East Asian policy. In addition, continued North Korean export of nuclear and missile technology to the Middle East aggravated the West. The U.S. sent (Scud-killing) Patriot missiles to the Seoul government, while reactivating the "Team Spirit" military exercises between U.S. and South Korean forces as the crisis seemingly moved toward a climax. Several key U.S. senators urged economic sanctions despite North Korea's threat to attack in retaliation. U.S. Senator Robert Dole indicated that of all world problems in the spring of 1994 the Korean situation was "the most serious."

Conclusion: The Death of Kim Il Sung

David E. Sanger wrote the obituary for Kim Il Sung in the New York Times, following his death on July 8, 1994. He spoke of that leader's three images during his long public career of forty-six years, making him the longest-serving Communist leader of the Cold War period. There was first his image as the Stalinist dictator whose regime was one of the most-entrenched "cult of personality" systems and rigid police states in history. Then there was his image to his own people, who called him the "sun of the country," and who honored him by erecting some thirty thousand statues of him in Pyongyang alone. Finally there was the image he often projected to visitors of the smiling, genial, grandfatherly host. A prime example of this occurred when former U.S. President Jimmy Carter visited North Korea in mid-June 1994, when that country stood on the brink of war with the United States due to the nuclear issue. Kim had held open a standing invitation to Mr. Carter since 1991. Now, in the midst of threatened U.S. sanctions against North Korea, Carter, a born-again Christian, sincerely sought the role of peacemaker.

The former president perhaps exceeded his instructions from Washington when he informed Kim that the United States would withhold sanctions if talks could be resumed and a definite agreement concluded. The "Great Leader" immediately agreed, and ironically discussions commenced in Geneva the day on which Kim suffered his fatal heart attack. A diplomatic breakthrough, however, had apparently been achieved.

The ensuing treaty of October 21, 1994, absolved the North Koreans of IAEA inspections for five years if their progress on nuclear weapons manufacture could be frozen. In return, Pyongyang would receive $4 billion in aid and two light nuclear reactors (for use in energy production). Trade with the United States and the rest of the outside world would be resumed, preparatory to establishment of diplomatic relations. The agreement could be regarded as Kim's final legacy to his country.

The treaty earned the disfavor of many Americans. Nicholas Eberstadt, Harvard University professor, said the Americans were "outmaneuvered" at the cost of "a few billion dollars," thoroughly indicting the Clinton administration. Then James Schlesinger, former chairman of the Atomic Energy Commission, called it "if not an unconditional surrender, then a negotiated surrender." Its defenders reiterated that war had been prevented.

To the outsider, it was difficult to see the deceased Kim Il Sung as a man of peace. His unfulfilled life's work had aimed to reunite Korea, for which he had unleashed the war in 1950 that had seen the devastation of his country. Someone observed that North Korea was not a country but more a military camp, thoroughly isolated from the rest of the world. Predictably no outside guests were invited to attend Kim's funeral held on July 19, 1994. South Korea sent no condolences.

Former U.S. Congressman Stephan J. Solarz, who had met Kim on two occasions, described his regime as "the most ruthless and tyrannical anywhere in the world . . . . He had the blood of millions on his hands." Yet to his people, he truly possessed "god-like qualities." As for the durability of the October 1994 agreement, history will have to decide whether another Korean war truly has been averted.

Suggestions for Further Reading

Aikman, Robert A., *Major Power Relations in Northeast Asia* (1987).
Bandow, Doug, and Ted Galen Carpenter, eds., *The U.S.–South Korean Alliance: Time for a Change* (1992).
Chong-Sik Lee, *Korea Briefing, 1990* (1991).
Clough, Ralph N., *Embattled Korea: The Rivalry for International Support* (1987).
Council on Foreign Relations, *Korea At The Crossroads* (1987).
Eberstadt, Nicholas, "Can the Two Koreas Be One?" *Foreign Affairs* (Winter, 1992–1993).
Fairbank, John K., Edwin O. Reischauer, and Albert M. Craig, *East Asia: Tradition and Transformation* (1989).
Gibney, Frank, *Korea's Quiet Revolution: From Garrison State to Democracy* (1992).
Goncharov, Sergei N., John W. Lewis, and Xue Litai, *Uncertain Partners: Stalin, Mao, and the Korean War* (1993).
Kang, T. W., *Is Korea the Next Japan?* (1989).
MacDonald, Donald Stone, *U.S.-Korean Relations From Liberation to Self-Reliance: The Twenty Year Record* (1992).
Matray, Frederick C., ed., *Historical Dictionary of the Korean War* (1991).
McGlothen, Ronald L., *Controlling the Waves: Dean Acheson and U.S. Foreign Policy in Asia* (1993).
Olsen, Edward A., *U.S. Policy and the Two Koreas* (1988).
Sanger, David E., "Journey to Isolation," *The New York Times Magazine* (November 15, 1992).
Scalapino, Robert A., *Major Power Relations in Northeast Asia* (1987).
———, and Hongkou Lee, *Korean-U.S. Relations: The Politics of Trade and Security* (1989).
Summers, Harry G., ed., *Korean War Almanac* (1990).
Sutter, Robert G., *East Asia and the Pacific: Challenges for U.S. Policy* (1992).
Vogel, Ezra, *The Four Little Dragons: The Spread of Industrialization in East Asia* (1991).
Wells, Kenneth M., *New God, New Nation, Protestants and Self-reconstruction: Nationalism in Korea, 1896–1937* (1991).
Young Whan Kihl, *Politics and Policies in Divided Korea: Regimes in Contest* (1987).
Yur-Bok Lee, *West Goes East: Paul Georg von Möllendorf and Great Power Imperium in Late Yi Korea* (1988).

Glossary

Chosŏn: "Land of the morning calm." The historical name for Korea.

"Comfort Girls": Young women (mostly Korean, but also other East Asians) pressed into granting sexual favors to Japanese soldiers ca. 1937–1945. The tragedy did not become public until 1992–1993.

Democratic People's Republic of Korea, the: North Korea's Communistic regime established September 9, 1948, with Kim Il Sung as premier. Institutions modeled after the Soviet Union.

DMZ: "De-militarized Zone." Buffer zone separating North and South Korea after the Korean War (1950–1953). One of the world's most heavily fortified areas, it straddled the 38th parallel.

Han'gul: "Korean letters." The present name of the script devised in the reign of King Sejong in 1446. Originally consisted of twenty-eight letters: seventeen vowels, and eleven consonants. Was modified later.

Hwangap: The occasion of a man's sixtieth birthday. The completion of the zodiacal cycle, it is celebrated by the entire family with much feasting among invited friends.

juche: "Self-sufficiency." Economic policy followed by North Korea's "Great Leader," Kim Il Sung, during the Cold War with dependence on the Communist world (USSR, PRC, and Eastern Europe).

March 1 Movement: Great nationalist Korean revolt in 1919 against Japanese rule. Over two million unarmed marchers participated. Uprising suppressed when it failed to arouse support abroad.

"Northern Diplomacy": Policy pursued by South Korean President Roh Tae-woo to reach accommodation with the North. Mutual antagonisms nullified much of this effort.

ondol: The traditional Korean heating system, utilized extensively in rural homes. Floors are warmed by stone-lined flues underneath, which carry steam from the kitchen.

Republic of Korea, the (ROK): South Korea's government established August 15, 1948, with Syngman Rhee as president. Regime had the backing of the United States.

Saemaul Undong: "New Community Movement." The program, enunciated by President Park Chung-hee of South Korea in April 1970, to revitalize the rural areas and bring them economically abreast of the industrialized cities. Increased agricultural production remarkably.

sŏwŏn: Private estate academies, established (in the Confucian tradition) for the education of government officials in the the early years of the Yi dynasty (1392ff.). Centers of much political strife.

Tonghak: "Eastern Learning." A socioreligious movement, originating in the rural areas in 1861. Followers included the poor peasantry, discharged local officials, and degraded aristocrats. Opposed governmental corruption and foreign intervention. The movement's revolt precipitated the Sino-Japanese War (1894–1895).

Yangban: "Two Groups." Civil and military officials in the Yi dynasty (1392–1910). Collectively composed the aristocracy.

Yushin: "Revitalizing Reforms." President Park Chung-hee of South Korea suspended virtually all political functions of the National Assembly in October 1972, to increase the power of the executive. Intended to deal with the increased threat from the north, Park's repressive measures offended much foreign (especially U.S.) opinion.

The World
of

Southeast

ASIA

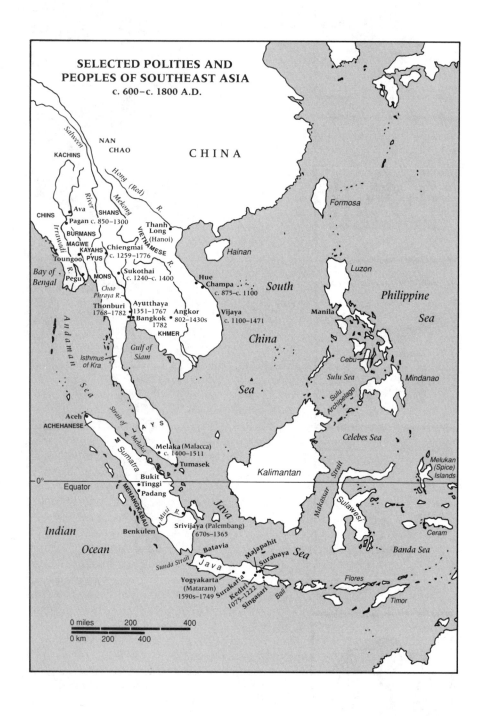

SELECTED POLITIES AND
PEOPLES OF SOUTHEAST ASIA
c. 600–c. 1800 A.D.

NAN
CHAO

KACHINS

CHINA

Salween

Hong (Red)

CHINS

Ava
BURMANS
Pagan c. 850–1300
SHANS
Mekong

Thanh
Long
(Hanoi)

VIETNAMESE

River

Irrawadi

MAGWE
KAYAHS
PYUS
Chiengmai
c. 1259–1776

Toungoo

Formosa

Hainan

Luzon

Bay of
Bengal

Pegu
MONS

Sukothai
c. 1240–c. 1400

Chao
Phraya R.

Hue
Champa
c. 875–c. 1100

South

Philippine

Thonburi
1768–1782

Ayutthaya
1351–1767
Bangkok
1782

Angkor
802–1430s

Vijaya
c. 1100–1471

China

Manila

Sea

KHMER

Andaman

Isthmus
of Kra

Gulf of
Siam

Sea

Cebu

Sea

Mindanao

Sulu Sea

Sulu Archipelago

Celebes Sea

Aceh
ACHEHANESE

Strait of Malaka

M A L A Y S

Melaka (Malacca)
c. 1400–1511

Tumasek

Melukan
(Spice)
Islands

Sumatra

Bukit
Tinggi
Padang

Kalimantan

Makassar Strait

Sulawesi

Ceram

0°
Equator

MENANGKABAU

Musi R.

Java

Srivijaya (Palembang)
670s–1365

Banda Sea

Indian

Ocean

Benkulen

Batavia

Java

Sunda Strait

Majapahit
Surabaya

Sea

Flores

Yogyakarta
(Mataram)
1590s–1749

Surakarta

Kediri
1075–1222
Singasari

Bali

Timor

0 miles   200   400

0 km   200   400

Introduction

Southeast Asia is the land and sea bordered by China to the north, India to the west, the Indian Ocean and Australia to the south, and the Pacific Ocean to the east. Ten countries share this region of the world. On the mainland are Burma (now the Union of Myanmar), Thailand, Laos, Cambodia (known in the 1970s and '80s as Kampuchea), and Vietnam. The island countries are the Philippines, Indonesia, Brunei, and Singapore. Malaysia is divided by the South China Sea, with West or Peninsular Malaysia on the mainland and East Malaysia on the island of Kalimantan (formerly Borneo). Thailand, Malaysia, Brunei, and Cambodia are monarchies; the rest, republics. The region has been the home of several civilizations.

Southeast Asian cultural and political institutions are unlike any in the rest of the world. Southeast Asians did borrow from other civilizations. Living on or near the sea and astride one of the world's oldest trade routes—running between China and Japan on one side and India, Africa, and Europe on the other—Southeast Asians did not find borrowing difficult. But that which was borrowed was adapted and modified to produce unique forms, styles, and institutions. Only in the last decades of the nineteenth century did modern western civilization—borne by imperialism—begin widely and significantly to impact Southeast Asian institutions.

Historians of the region have not yet agreed on a scheme of periods for the many hundreds of years before the late nineteenth century. There are, for example, no ancient or medieval periods as in European history. The use of these terms with regard to Southeast Asia would be misleading. But Southeast Asia's long history has not been without important changes. Some major, "watershed," developments were the attempted Mongol land and sea invasions of much of the region in the thirteenth century; changes in religious beliefs and practices from the thirteenth through the seventeenth centuries; and the arrival of European traders in the sixteenth century.

Between about 1870 and 1914, the Dutch, British, French, and Americans mostly by military means established hegemony over the region, appointing their own governors in place of monarchs or providing the rulers with advisors, which often made the rulers figureheads. The Europeans and Americans had superior military force, in large part because of knowledge gained from the scientific and industrial revolutions. Southeast Asians did not have that experience, and were militarily weak and politically divided. Of the major states, only Thailand managed by wise leadership (and good luck) to remain free of western rule.

Vegetable sellers in Singapore's Chinatown, Singapore Embassy.

Southeast Asia   1
Before the Nineteenth Century

The Peoples of Southeast Asia

Most of the numerous ancestors of today's Southeast Asians came from central and eastern Asia over many centuries, moving southward along the sea coasts and down the valleys of the great rivers—the Irrawaddy, the Salween, the Chao Phraya, the Mekong, and the Hong or Red River. Three of the most important peoples were the Pyus, the Mons, and the Khmers. The Pyus occupied parts of what is today Burma or Myanmar as late as the ninth century. The Mons were found in what is now Thailand and in southern Burma east of the Irrawaddy as late as the sixteenth century. The Mons were related to the Khmers who followed the Mekong River southward into Cambodia, where their descendants are found today. The achievements of these people are evident from existing irrigation works, arts, religion, and languages. For example, the Mons were the transmitters of Theravada Buddhism and the Burmese script is derived from Mon writing. The script in use in Thailand today was adapted from Khmer writing.

The indigenous peoples of Southeast Asia can be classified in terms of race and language into two broad groups—the people of the islands and the people of the mainland. The people of the islands are mostly Malay or Indonesian. They have black hair and brown skin and speak Malayo-Polynesian languages. They make up the principal populations of Indonesia, the Philippines, Brunei, and Malaysia but are found as far east as Hawaii and as far west as South Africa. Scholars recognize two major divisions among them: proto-Malays and deutero-Malays. Proto-Malays have more pronounced features, are darker, and live in the interior of major islands. They include the Bataks in Sumatra and the Torajas in Sulawesi. The deutero-Malays have finer features, are lighter in color, and live in coastal areas. The Javanese people are an example of the deutero-Malay.

The mainland peoples are more diverse, but they also have black hair and most are similar to the Chinese and Japanese in color. Many of them speak languages in which the meaning of a word depends on the tone given to it.

Standard Thai, the language of the Thai people, for example, has five tones; Vietnamese has six tones. Many of the mainland people are recent arrivals, and indeed movement is still occurring. The southward movement of the Thai people from southwestern China was probably given impetus by the conquest of their Nanchao Kingdom in 1253 by Kublai Khan.

Most Southeast Asian countries have important minorities, the largest of whom are Chinese and Indian peoples. Chinese and Indians have lived in Southeast Asia for centuries in small numbers. Today's large minority populations are mostly descendants of immigrants who came or were brought to Southeast Asia by the hundreds of thousands in the late nineteenth and early twentieth centuries. They were "coolie" laborers recruited by European and Chinese employers to work tin mines and rubber estates and by colonial governments to build roads, docks, drainage systems, and public buildings. Racially and culturally distinct from the indigenous peoples of Southeast Asia, the extent to which they have been assimilated varies by country. These minorities are themselves rarely united but rather are divided by education, wealth, language, and the district of origin in their homelands. The Indians are further divided by caste.

When a country has two or more ethnically distinct peoples who differ from each other in religion, language, culture, history, and the food they eat, and who rarely intermarry, the country is said to have a plural society. Several Southeast Asian countries have such societies. The population of Malaysia, for example, is about 50 percent Malay, 35 percent Chinese, and 9 percent Indian. The pluralistic nature of these societies has caused many problems for the postcolonial governments of Southeast Asia as they seek to create national institutions.

For centuries, Southeast Asia has been sparsely populated, generally speaking. This remains true today even though Southeast Asia has some of the most densely populated places in the world. Kings of Southeast Asia rarely fought wars for land and territory; instead they fought for revenge, booty, and people. An historical exception was Vietnam where wars were fought for cultivable land, which was in short supply.

The ethnic and linguistic distinctions among Southeast Asian peoples sometimes combine with differences in education, religion, occupation, income, and social status to produce prejudices and popular stereotypes. For example, enmity still exists between highland and lowland people. People living in lowland and coastal areas regard themselves as smarter and more sophisticated than people who live in the interior and mountainous areas. Lowland people regard the highlanders as rude, backward. The highlanders, in turn, think lowland people are tricky, untrustworthy. Another example is that many Muslim Indonesians regard their Chinese fellow-citizens as self-centered, materialistic, and godless. Many Chinese Indonesians in turn say their Indonesian neighbors are imprudent in financial matters, less than hard-working, and much too fatalistic.

Among Southeast Asians, social hierarchy in the past as well as today is important. Class, social status, and even one's position in the family are often reflected in the use of language. Personal pronouns are used to indicate status. For example, a farmer addressing his king—an infrequent event—would use a form of "I" in "I am pleased. . . ." that clearly indicated the farmer's inferior status. In responding, the king would use pronouns reflecting his superior status. The incorrect use of pronouns gives offense and in times past could have resulted in severe punishment. In Thailand, Malaysia, and Indonesia, whole vocabularies were reserved for use by royalty. Although royalty has disappeared from much of Southeast Asia, the use of language to reflect status is still very much in vogue in parts of the region. A child addressing his or her father or other older person will use words reflecting the older person's senior status. Similarly, certain words are used by adults only when addressing children and young people.

Southeast Asians have long used proverbs as a customary part of their conversation. The proverbs are used to explain social behavior and to teach children differences between right and wrong. For example, about a corrupt policeman, a Malay might say, "Pagar makan padi," which means "the fence devours the rice crop." While the use of proverbs is declining, especially in the modern and urban sectors of Southeast Asian societies, many proverbs are still found in folk literature.

Social mobility, or changing one's social status, was rare, even unthinkable, in Southeast Asia until recently. Most families farmed or fished and had neither educational nor economic opportunity by which to change their status. The village was their focal point. Some individuals by their kinship connections, personality, age, experience, or relative affluence might become village headmen or members of the village council, but they remained farmers or fishermen. On rare occasion, a man might distinguish himself, say as a skillful soldier, and come to the attention of the king, who might then reward him with a job and a title.

Business classes in centuries past were very small or composed of foreigners. Kings often controlled or monopolized surpluses and the largest and most lucrative business activities, both domestic and foreign. The king's subjects who were involved in business seldom did so privately but as royal employees; independent economic power and wealth was rarely permitted. Foreigners, usually persons already familiar with a particular kind of trade or business, were also commonly employed by the king. It was easier and perhaps politically safer for a ruler to engage Indians, Chinese, and others to conduct the royal trade rather than to allow many of one's own subjects to undertake it.

The kings of Southeast Asia employed advisors, administrators, and clerical staff. The most important positions—those of treasurer, provincial governor, harbormaster, head of the armed forces—were held by members of the king's family and families close to the king. There were religious persons—Brahman priests from India in the distant past—who advised on rituals and served as astrologers to determine the most propitious days for royal actions or ceremonies. They often provided royal genealogies. Prosperous rulers made their courts centers for the arts, employing musicians, dancers, poets, painters, and playwrights. Kings also commissioned such buildings as temples, shrines, mosques, and palaces.

Slavery was practiced in most of Southeast Asia through the end of the nineteenth century. Slaves included prisoners taken in war, highland people captured in raids, and persons being punished for crimes. Today in the Chao Phraya valley of central Thailand are villagers whose ancestors were captured in Cambodia and brought to Thailand as slaves of the Thai king. They worked for him as farmers or artisans. Debt slavery or bondage, in which a person unable to repay a debt became a slave of his or her creditor, was also common. Whether king or not, the slave owner had obligations to his slaves. Debt was often the result of gambling losses in long-popular betting on fighting cocks and buffalo, and other contests. The European rulers of Southeast Asia formally prohibited slavery in the late nineteenth and early twentieth centuries, but conditions that were close to slavery often prevailed.

Western rule in the twentieth century altered significantly the class structure of Southeast Asian societies, but it did little to change the values of most indigenous people or to enhance their social mobility. With political independence from the 1950s onwards, opportunities for individuals to improve their economic and social status expanded. Educational opportunity, economic growth, the ending of large-scale immigration, and policies aimed to help the disadvantaged have all contributed to social mobility. Today in several countries large, indigenous middle classes exist and are growing.

Although ethnically and linguistically different from one another, Southeast Asians have shared certain values, practices, and forms of social organization. These have included respect for elders and teachers; love of children; a responsibility for family members and often for village members; a nuclear family (a family composed of father, mother and children); arranged marriages; a division of labor between husband and wife; more freedom for women than found in most premodern societies; decision-making by concensus; a respect for the land; and loyalty to the monarch. In addition, commonly found among Southeast Asians is the patron-client relationship. When persons who are better off materially, patrons, help persons who are less fortunate, clients, the clients reciprocate by helping their patrons, often by contributing their labor at harvest time. All of these values and practices are still found but are weakening or changing as market economics spread, contemporary technologies are adopted, education—especially of women—grows, and urban life develops.

Economic Life

For many centuries, people settled where economic livelihood—farming, fishing, and trading—was most easily done and most amply rewarded. For farmers that meant the rich soils of river basins and deltas and volcanic lands. The great mainland river valleys and the volcanic lands of Java have supported large populations, major kingdoms, and important cultural activities.

Rice, the most commonly grown crop, is cultivated by the "wet-rice" method, which involves the intensive use of land, permitting two or three crops each year. Growing wet rice requires hard work, skill, and organization, especially in the management of water. Farmers developed irrigation systems and sometimes, as in Bali, associations to oversee the distribution of water. Wet rice is grown on flat lands nearly everywhere and on terraces in hilly lands as in west Java and on Luzon in the northern Philippines.

Trading centers grew up at river mouths and at other places of passage. The persons who controlled these points of transit and taxed the trade were usually assured of political and economic power. The Isthmus of Kra and the Straits of

Melaka (or Malacca) and Sunda were places where trade passed or occurred on a large scale, giving rise to major states.

Southeast Asians whatever their livelihood have been especially influenced by the pattern of trade winds, called monsoons in the Eastern Hemisphere. The southwest monsoon blows from the southwest from May through September. It sweeps out of the Indian Ocean across the Bay of Bengal onto the Arakan and Tenasserim coasts of Burma and the Sumatran coast of Indonesia. The northeast monsoon blows out of the northeast from October through March, striking the Philippines and deep into the South China Sea on to the coasts of Vietnam, Malaysia, and Kalimantan.

Monsoons of varying intensity bring heavy rains to Southeast Asia. Mountain ranges often block the monsoons, causing the rains to fall unevenly. In Arakan and Tenasserim, most of the rain falls between the coasts and the mountains paralleling the coasts. Inland, the rain can be sparse. Two relatively dry areas are the "dry zone" in central Burma and the Korat Plateau in northeastern Thailand. In some areas, the monsoon winds become typhoons, roughly equivalent to hurricanes in the Western Hemisphere. They regularly wreck havoc in the northern Philippines, on the coast of Vietnam, and in the Bay of Bengal. Nearly everywhere, the collection, diversion, distribution, and measurement of water have always been essential to life.

The equator runs through Indonesia, but all of Southeast Asia lies in the tropics. Heavy rainfall combined with abundant sunshine, warm temperatures, and high humidity have powerfully influenced where and how people live, dress, work, and think. The climate generally has not been good for the soil, although it has nurtured thousands of different species of plant and animal life. The rain forest, often majestic, provides a protective, green canopy for the soil below. Once the rain forest is cut, the rain and sun can quickly destroy the soil's nutrients. The heavy cutting of the Southeast Asian rain forest in recent years has raised economic and environmental concerns.

Trade and travel by sea were determined by the monsoon winds before the application of steampower to ships beginning in the 1830s. Southern Sumatra and the shores of the Straits of Melaka and Sunda were natural places for sea travellers to wait for the monsoon winds to change, for merchants to meet and trade, and for ships to be supplied and repaired. An eminent scholar has called southeastern Sumatra the "favoured coast."

Religion and Culture

All of the world's major religions have flourished in Southeast Asia at one time or another, prompting the region to be described as a "crossroads of religion." Today, Islam is the principal religion in Malaysia, Indonesia, and Brunei. Indonesia, with two hundred million people, is, in fact, the largest Muslim country in the world. Theravada Buddhism is the religion of Burma, Thailand, Cambodia, and Laos, while Vietnam and Singapore are Mahayana Buddhist. The Filipino people are mostly Christian.

Wherever plural societies exist, important religious minorities are usually found as well. Thus in Malaysia, Thailand, and Indonesia in the Chinese communities,

Mahayana Buddhism is practiced. Hinduism is practiced where there are Indian minorities. Muslims form an important minority in the Philippines. Singapore has Muslim, Christian, and Hindu minorities.

Hinduism and Mahayana Buddhism in its Indian form played very important cultural roles. Hinduism entered Southeast Asia from India as early as the second century A.D., probably with Brahman priests invited by Southeast Asian kings who sought them as advisors. Hinduism spread throughout most of the region, obtaining varying degrees of penetration. Associated with Hinduism was Mahayana Buddhism, also brought from India. Both religions were vehicles for the transfer of many aspects of Indian culture to Southeast Asia. Scripts to enable spoken languages to be written; literature; the arts, including architecture, painting, sculpture, dance, drama; political ideas and practices—all and more were acquired via these religions and then adapted and modified by Southeast Asians. This experience has been called the "Indianization" of Southeast Asia.

Major centers of Indian cultural influence were in Cambodia and central and east Java. Angkor Wat, the great temple at Angkor in Cambodia, dates from the twelfth century and is one of the largest and most sophisticated religio-political structures in the world. It and the many temples nearby blend worship of the gods of Hinduism and Indian Mahayana Buddhism. Angkor Wat is an earthly repesentation in stone of Mount Meru, the home of the gods in Hindu mythology. It also stands as a reference to and a symbol of one of the most important Southeast Asian adaptations of the Hindu religion and culture, the god-king or deva-raj concept. The people of Angkor regarded their kings as gods, actually avatars—gods on earth in human form. In central Java is the Borobudur, the world's greatest artistic expression of Mahayana Buddhism. The construction of this monument was completed in the ninth century.

Both Hinduism and Mahayana Buddhism were aristocratic in that their principal practitioners and supporters were the rulers and elites of society. Most farmers and ordinary people shared only in part in the Hindu-Mahayana belief system. Mostly they prostrated themselves before their god-kings; paid taxes; built roads, temples, and granaries; and served in the god-king's armies.

A belief system less exalted and more practical for ordinary folk, animism, built upon the idea that all things—animate and inanimate—have spirits. Among the spirits are ancestors and long-deceased important village persons. Spirits must be respected because an offended spirit can cause one to do badly in school, lose a friend, get sick, or cause a crop to fail. Help is available to cope with offended spirits. A shaman—a generic term for a go-between—can be employed. Shamans are many; they work for fees and even specialize. The shaman seeks to communicate with the offended spirit and to determine the cause of its anger and how best to remedy the matter. The shaman, in contacting the spirit, very probably will enter a trance and perhaps dance as well. The spirit may speak from the mouth of the shaman. Animism borrows from the culture in which it exists, has its own vocabulary in each society, and thus varies from one society to another, from fairly simple beliefs to elaborate and complex belief systems.

Animism has powerfully influenced the arts of Southeast Asia. Today, in Hindu Bali, where animism and the arts are both highly developed, one of the most famous expressions of both is a dance-drama in which a climactic, physical struggle between Rangda and the Boron occurs. Rangda is the quintessential witch and represents evil while Boron is a mythical animal and represents good. The Boron wins but just. Rangda is never completely vanquished and is sure to appear again. Struggle between good and evil continues for all eternity.

Among the sources of animistic belief are the people's respect for nature and the sense that there is or should be a balance in nature and in people's lives. In centuries past and still today, Southeast Asian people seek to adapt to the environment, to live in harmony with it rather than to change it or challenge it. Modern western civilization, in contrast, has challenged the environment. Animism in Southeast Asia flourishes today alongside as well as in Buddhism, Islam, and Christianity.

Beginning in the thirteenth century and gradually over three centuries or more, Hinduism and Indian Mahayana Buddhism were replaced by Theravada Buddhism, Islam, and Christianity. Exactly how Theravada Buddhism and Islam spread is not clear, but several influences were at work. Each of the new faiths required more of an individual commitment than did the old religions, missionaries were active in spreading each of them, and, with respect to Islam, commercial advantages accrued to kings who became Muslims. Christianity in the Philippines had the strong backing of Spanish rulers.

The new religions were not only more personally demanding but actually at odds with the old ones. Theravada Buddhism, the "southern school" and the oldest form of Buddhism, did not teach belief in a multiplicity of gods, and Islam and Christianity were vigorously monotheistic. Salvation in each of the new religions depended on each believer's personal conduct. In Theravada countries, kings continued to be highly revered, but their status came to depend on their personal merit and ability to maintain moral order rather than the belief that they were gods on earth. The building of Hindu-Buddhist temples came to a halt. In their stead appeared Theravada temples and Muslim mosques, places for prayer and worship by ordinary people. Today, the only remnant of early Hindu-Buddhist practices is found among the Balinese people of Indonesia.

Religion changed but the many cultural adaptations of Indian civilization conveyed by Hinduism-Mahayana Buddhism were retained and may be found in much of Southeast Asia today. For example, the great Indian literary epics—the *Mahabharata* and *Ramayana*—are popular in Java and elsewhere and with modifications and additions to the Indian originals are expressed in virtually all forms of drama, poetry and prose, painting, sculpture, and dance. Besides entertainment, they are a source of learning about right and wrong, good and evil.

Islam, the faith of the Prophet Mohammed, entered Southeast Asia probably in the thirteenth century on the north coast of Sumatra. Melaka became a center for the spread of Islam after the conversion of the ruler in the fifteenth century. It spread eastward to the ports and market towns on the north Java coast and then into the interior of Java and into the southern Philippines, where in the late sixteenth century it encountered Christian missionaries from Spain.

The means by which many Malays, Indonesians, and Filipinos became Muslim is uncertain. The Sufis probably played an important role. They are the mystics of Islam who believe that the salvation of one's soul is possible by complete submission to God and that everyone can and should have a personal relationship with God. The Sufis have been teachers, poets, itinerant preachers, saints, and authors. Some of the world's most beautiful and inspiring religious literature has been written by Sufis. They have often practiced aceticism and have rejected formal religious and political organization, believing that the individual's relationship with God should not be obscured by earthly intermediaries. These characteristics, together with the Sufis' frequent disdain for material possessions and the passion with which many express themselves, have often caused them to be distrusted by kings and especially by the ulamas, the religious arbiters of Islam. Sufis, believing they have an obligation to inform the ignorant about God, served as missionaries. In the Malay-Indonesian world of the seventeenth century and earlier, their sincerity, earnestness, eloquence, and perhaps aceticism must have been impressive. Certainly they must have elicited a sympathetic response from a people steeped in animism who had little or no village-level religious orqanization or leadership.

While Sufism has played a role in the spread of Islam in Southeast Asia, the great majority of Muslims do not regard themselves as mystics but as Sunnis, the main, orthodox branch of Islam. The minority Shiah branch with its Persian roots and contemporary Iranian links is not unknown in Southeast Asia, but it commands no large number of adherents.

Theravada Buddhism, Islam, and Christianity brought other significant changes to the people of Southeast Asia. All three religions valued education but in different ways. In Burma, schools were attached to the village Buddhist temples, called pagodas, and the monks served as teachers. The subjects went beyond reading, writing, and religion in some schools to include secular and practical subjects. Only boys were allowed to attend, and among men literacy was high. As for Muslims, the ability to read the Koran, the words of Allah or God, was essential. *Pondok* and *pesantren* schools, or communities of scholars, were common in some Malay states, in Java, and elsewhere. *Pondok,* or hut, schools usually involved a one-on-one system—one teacher and one student per hut, often arranged in clusters of huts. In *Pesantren* schools, one teacher taught many students. In the Philippines, educating children in Christian doctrine was one means of converting whole families.

Another change was the emphasis which Theravada Buddhism placed on monasteries and monastic life. Monasteries were intended to be centers of learning and places for the preservation of knowledge; certain of them fulfilled this role in a major way. They were (and are) places of refuge in troubled times. It was (and is) expected that men enter a monastery for some part of their lives. Monks typically eschew material advantages and dress simply, shaving their heads and wearing saffron robes in Theravada countries. Part of the daily ritual is to go about the village or town every morning with a begging bowl. Begging induces humility in the beggar, while giving provides the giver with merit. On occasion if monks are sufficiently upset about some matter, they can refuse to beg, thereby registering their discontent and depriving laymen of merit.

In addition to their religious and cultural responsibilities, the monasteries played significant political and economic roles in all the mainland countries. In Pagan, today's Burma or Myanmar, for example, contributions of land and money to the *sangha*, the monkhood, was a means by which individuals gained merit and social status. These contributions were at times so substantial as to endanger the financial strength of the monarchy. The *sangha* was not taxed. The *sangha* was often a source of educated persons for royal appointments as advisors, administrators, and diplomats. In all Buddhist countries, the *sangha* was often politically and economically significant.

Both Buddhism and Islam experienced periodic reform efforts. Buddhist reform typically focussed on the monks. From time to time, they were accused of being lazy, corrupt, ignorant, or too worldly. During periods of reform, monks were sometimes tested by being required to read Buddhist texts in the Pali script. A monk who failed the test might be expelled. Other reform efforts aimed at eliminating or at least reducing the popular belief in spirits. Sometimes a Buddhist king would initiate reform as a means of reducing the economic power of the *sangha*.

While each of the major religions made a cultural impact, Southeast Asians have been eclectic in regard to religion, frequently keeping aspects of one religion while adopting features of another. Thus Islam and Christianity, try as they might, did not displace existing animistic beliefs or the remnants of Hindu-Buddhist ideas and practices. From eclecticism it is only a short step to syncretism, or the reconciliation and blending of different religious beliefs. While examples of religious syncretism are found everywhere in Southeast Asia, probably no people carried syncretism farther than did the Javanese. Their blending of animistic, Hindu-Buddhist, and Islamic beliefs and practices has been called the "religion of Java" by an eminent scholar.

A distinction is made among Javanese according to the "purity" of their Islamic practice. *Santri* are Javanese who more strictly observe Islamic principles. They have tended to be merchants and businessmen, mosque officials, Muslim teachers, and scholars. Many of them have supported the modernist *Muhammadiyah* reform movement and the *Nahdatul Ulama* political party. *Abangan* are Javanese who incorporate much animistic and Hindu-Buddhist belief and practice in their Islamic faith. Historically, the *Santri* were found in the coastal areas and commercial centers while the *Abangan* were concentrated in rural areas.

China's contributions to Southeast Asia were geographically more concentrated. In Vietnam, which was part of China for more than a thousand years, the upper classes absorbed much Chinese culture. Confucian doctrines and practices; language; law and administrative system; education; the Chinese form of Mahayana Buddhism; the arts and many values—all took root. Beyond Vietnam, China's Southeast Asian influence was mostly in trade and diplomacy. The shores of the South China Sea were also from time to time havens for Chinese lawbreakers, pirates, and political refugees.

A special feature of Southeast Asian relations with China was the tributary system. China claimed nominal suzerainty over the polities of Southeast Asia. This meant that from time to time Southeast Asian kings sent missions to China to acknowledge the Chinese emperor as overlord and to bring gifts. The Emperor reciprocated with gifts of his own. Sometimes the volume of "gifts" exchanged was so large as to make the tributary mission a form of trade. The Emperor's reception of the mission was a form of political recognition of the king, which sometimes helped to strengthen or legitimize the king's claim to his throne. If tribute missions were not forthcoming—even after many years—it appears that the Chinese took no action. Sometimes a ruler sought support from the Chinese emperor in rejecting the claims or fighting off the aggressive acts of a neighbor. But the support was no more than a letter to the offending party. China almost never sent its soldiers into Southeast Asia except to those countries on its immediate southern periphery.

For two millenia or more, Southeast Asia has received culture from other civilizations. The blended Indian Hinduism-Mahayana Buddhism is ample demonstration of this. However, archeological discoveries at Non Nok Tha, Ban Chiang, and elsewhere in Thailand have raised questions and caused debate in which the boldest claim is that the region may have been a disseminator of culture in prehistoric times. Evidence for this is the discovery of cultivated rice dating from the fourth millenium B.C. as well as brass foundaries allegedly dating from the same time.

Monarchy

Monarchy was the principal form of government in the two thousand years or so before the imposition of European rule beginning in the late nineteenth century. In the Hindu-Buddhist period, the larger kingdoms were collections of lesser ones arranged in more or less hierarchical order. Chieftains or minor kings gave allegiance to a more powerful king, who in turn with others of roughly similar rank gave fealty to the greatest king, one who often had a title that translated "king of kings." These *mandalas* or circles of kings were created by diplomacy, war, or marriage. A king who ruled in his own right over a major source of income, say a large, well-populated agricultural region or a major trade route, was in a position to require lesser kings to recognize him as the paramount or king of kings. If the ruler of a small state had the misfortune of being on the periphery of two king of kings, he was said to be a bird with two heads.

The relationships between greater and lesser kings had a superficial resemblance to feudalism in medieval Europe. But unlike Europe, in Southeast Asia the system was not usually further defined and bolstered by specific, comprehensive military and other obligations and by a careful definition of lands held. Indeed, in Southeast Asian kingdoms territorial boundaries were rarely well-defined. A king's power and authority were believed to radiate outward from his person and from his residence in his royal city, diminishing with distance to weakest at the periphery of his realm.

Lesser kings sometimes modelled their courts after that of the paramount king but usually ruled in their own domain as they wished rather than observing laws or standards set by the king of kings. The latter expected annual tribute, periodic visits, and public declarations of loyalty, peaceful relations, support in war, and rarely more. Within their own realms, kings were all-powerful with only informal constraints on their authority, at best. Virtually all of them declared themselves to be "universal" kings without peer anywhere.

The stability and success of this system depended, like monarchy elsewhere, on the energy, intelligence, and personality of the king. The greatest rulers possessed auras of magical-spiritual power and exercised religio-political responsibilities, as in the deva-raj system in Angkor. In all kingdoms to a greater or lesser degree, power theoretically derived from merit which could be acquired by religious study, meditation, the practice of asceticism, and the exercise of self-discipline. The models for acquiring power in such a manner are described in Hindu epic literature.

After the disappearance of Hindu-Buddhism, something like the *mandala* system continued. But, on the mainland, Burma, Thailand, and Vietnam developed provincial systems of administration with royally appointed governors and often large central bureaucracies. These were governments with laws, courts, taxes, currencies, and civil services. But distance and poor communications limited centralization. Royal power, in practice, usually rested on the support of an intelligentsia and influential families. The intelligentsia was frequently the Buddhist establishment that provided advisors, administrators, and diplomats. The influential families, both sacerdotal and secular, staffed important positions and undertook military duties. Such families usually married their children to the children of other influential families, seeking to perpetuate their influence from one generation to the next. The king rewarded the monkhood with temples and monasteries and both the monkhood and the families with titles, money, land, slaves, and war booty.

Kinship played a very important role in maintaining power. It was not unusual for influential families and provincial governors to be related to the king, and lesser kings to paramount kings. This was achieved by offering daughters in marriage to monarchs or their sons. Kings, often with multiple wives, had many children whose existence helped bind a kingdom together. Kinship could be a problem, too. Succession, as in monarchies elsewhere, was sometimes a difficult problem. Too many heirs for a throne could result in fratricide, a phenomenon not entirely unknown in Europe.

Early Mainland Kingdoms

The Pagan Kingdom, forerunner of Burma, appeared in history in the mid-ninth century and survived until it was invaded by a Mongol army led by the grandson of Kublai Khan in 1287. Like other early Southeast Asian kingdoms, Pagan drew its name from the city in which the king resided. Pagan was on the Irrawaddy River in central Burma and in a fertile agricultural region. It acquired much of its civilization by conquest of the Mon people at Thaton and Pegu in the Irrawaddy delta.

The most able ruler of Pagan was Anawrahta (1044–1077). He united the kingdom politically to approximately the boundaries of today's Burma; imported a much admired Mon culture in the form of teachers, scholars, administrators, and architects; and sought to strengthen Theravada Buddhism—the religion of the Mons—in Pagan by importing monks. Indeed, tradition has it that Anawrahta was converted to Theravada Buddhism by a famous Mon teacher, Shin Arahan. The Pagan kings and later Burmese kings depended on the Theravada Buddhist religious order to sanctify and support their authority. The kings in turn built temples, endowed monasteries, appointed Buddhists to important positions and, ideally, served as symbols of moral authority.

Anawrahta's most important successor, Kyanzittha (1086), was an admirer of Mon culture and an enthusiastic supporter of Theravada Buddhism. He began the temple building at Pagan, the best known of which is the beautiful Ananda temple, named after the Buddha's famous disciple. Kyanzittha's son commissioned the Myazedi inscription, a four-sided stone with the same text carved on each side in the Mon, Pyu, Burman, and Pali languages. Pali was a language of northern India derived from Sanskrit in which the oldest and most authentic surviving texts of Buddhism were written. Other important and able kings succeeded to the throne of Pagan, and the Mon culture was assimilated and adapted, establishing a Burmese cultural tradition. The Pagan Kingdom was Burma's golden age. Except for the Toungoo dynasty, which briefly revived Burman political fortunes in the sixteenth century, Burma after the fall of Pagan rarely experienced long periods of political unity and stability, peace and economic prosperity. One explanation is that some of the successors of Anawrahta and Kyanzittha did not show good judgment. Some had an inflated view of their power and underestimated badly the power of their opponents. Succession to the throne was too often disputed with bloody consequences. Another cause may have been the location of their capitals up the Irrawaddy River, away from the sea and seaborne trade routes. The location may have contributed to poor understanding of the outside world. Wars to unite the country with non-Burman peoples such as the Shans or to conquer the neighboring Thai Kingdom of Ayutthaya were frequent. The Mons who had been forced to share much of their knowledge and culture with the Burmans never accepted Burman rule and from time to time had a rival kingdom at Pegu on the edge of the Irrawaddy delta.

In the eighteenth century, there appeared one Alaungpaya, who, after establishing his hold on the capital, Ava, proceeded to bring most of the country under his rule. His was a new dynasty, the Kobaung, which ruled until 1886 when Burma was conquered by Britain. Alaungpaya's reign was taken up mostly with campaigning. He died in 1760 from wounds suffered in a siege of Ayutthaya.

When Pagan flourished, much of the rest of mainland Southeast Asia was under the rule of Angkor in today's Cambodia. The monarchy was founded in 802 by Jayavarman II (d. 850), who was thought to have spent some earlier years in Java. He built on the worship of the Hindu god Shiva, already well-established, and is credited with introducing the deva-raj concept. About one hundred years later, a successor moved the royal residence to Angkor near the contemporary town of Siem Reap, north of the Tonle Sap, Cambodia's great lake. The city of Angkor embraced sixteen square miles and was surrounded by a moat two hundred meters wide.

There were many noteworthy Angkor kings. Each was an avatar of either Shiva, Vishnu, or Buddha. They enjoyed enormous revenues from the large and fertile rice lands of the Mekong River basin as well as from trade. Most were avid builders. They spent heavily on religious structures—shrines, temples, monasteries, mausoleums—and on roads, granaries, huge reservoirs and artificial lakes, irrigation works, hospitals, and rest houses for travellers. They lavishly supported the arts. The Angkor Wat (see p. 296) was commissioned by Suryavarman II. The greatest of Angkor's rulers was probably Jayavarman VII (1182–c.1220). He was a Mahayana Buddhist, a military leader, and a builder on a vast scale.

In the thirteenth century, Angkor began to decline. The causes are not agreed upon, but clearly war was one cause. Angkor fought Vietnam and Champa to the north and east and the Thais to the northwest and west. The southward-moving Thais were a persistent and skilled enemy who occupied the lands they conquered. Other suggested causes of Angkor's decline were an epidemic of disease, probably malaria; the inability to maintain vast irrigation works needed for rice production; and the economic burden of temple building and public works. Angkor's decline was probably also linked to religious change. Theravada Buddhist missionaries, one of whom may have been a son of Jayavarman VII, won many converts among ordinary Cambodians. That faith did not support the belief in god-kings and taught that salvation depended on one's personal behavior, not on building temples for the king. Hinduism and Mahayana Buddhism declined. The Khmers abandoned Angkor in the fifteenth century, and over the centuries its memory even slipped from the minds of many Khmers. Today, however, the Kingdom of Angkor is Cambodia's great tradition, its golden age.

The Kingdom of Champa occupied the central and southern coasts of today's Vietnam, and its people spoke a Malay language. Its Indian Hindu-Buddhist religion and culture date from the second century A.D. The Chams farmed pockets of land between the mountains and the sea and engaged in trade and other forms of profit from seafaring. The latter included collecting taxes from ships travelling between China and the Straits, especially as they passed near the coast. The Chams were also active slave traders. They built temples and shrines to Hindu deities, and the ruins of many of their brick structures are still seen in Vietnam. Marco Polo wrote about Champa around 1288. Their long political history largely ended in the 1690s when their state was absorbed by the Vietnamese.

The principal and immediate successor monarchy to Angkor was the Thai kingdom of Ayutthaya. It was a city on the lower Chao Phraya River a few miles north of present-day Bangkok. It was founded by the Thai as their royal capital about 1350 A.D. Thai kingdoms in Thailand were somewhat older. Of these kingdoms, two are especially important. Each was the work of an intelligent, ambitious individual. Mangrai (d. 1327) through war, marriage, and diplomacy established a kingdom with its capital at Chiengmai, today an important and historic city in northern Thailand. He fought off the Mongols, married a Mon princess, sought to gain from the Mongol destruction of Pagan, and issued a book of laws.

The other individual, Ramkamhaeng (d. 1298), became king of Sukothai in 1279. Well to the south of Mangrai's kingdom, Sukothai, on the central plain of the Chao Phraya River, had been an Angkor-fortified town until captured by Thais in the 1240s. A skillful military and political leader, Ramkamhaeng greatly expanded his kingdom to include most of central and southern Thailand to the shores of the Gulf of Siam. More important were his cultural innovations. Under his rule, Theravada Buddhism as well as much of the Khmer culture of Angkor were adopted. Ramkamhaeng sought legitimacy by sending tribute missions to the Chinese emperor and in return receiving imperial recognition for himself and his kingdom.

Thai political unity was precarious for a number of years: lesser kings and political chiefs sought their own destinies, the heirs to Mangrai and Ramkamhaeng fought, and rebellions were common. Nevertheless Ayutthaya survived and grew.

The Thai kingdom was known as Siam, a name of unknown origin, from the fourteenth century or earlier. In 1939, the Thais officially adopted Thailand as the name of their country.

The greatest Ayutthayan monarch was probably King Trailok (1448–1488), who codified many laws and undertook an administrative reorganization of the kingdom. He introduced the concept of making officials responsible for specific functions of government. The result was to reduce the importance of personal relationships and increase the importance of bureaucracy in the conduct of government. Trailok also took steps to define the rights and obligations of each of his subjects, from slave to nobleman. He endeavored to insure a smooth succession. These and other reforms gave direction to the monarchy for many years to come.

Trailok's changes also positioned Ayutthaya well to participate in growing trade, and he is credited with the considerable prosperity experienced by the Thai in the fifty years or so after his death. Among the many interesting skills the Thais developed during this time was the manufacture of pistols and other firearms and gunpowder of varying strengths. Ayutthaya exported both; customers included the rulers of Japan. Thai historians regard the late fifteenth and much of the sixteenth century as a golden age.

Ayutthaya made a striking appearance by virtue of its many gold-roofed Buddhist temples, its royal palace, fine homes of the elite, and its flower-lined canals and water ways. Close to the sea, it was a cosmopolitan city with visitors from China, Japan, the Middle East, and Europe. Some Europeans called it the "Venice of the East." It was a center of Theravada Buddhist learning with royal subsidies for monasteries, some of which had large libraries. Thai kings took pride in making their courts the center of cultural life.

The city was destroyed in April 1767 by invading Burmese. Credit for driving the Burmese out of Siam goes to one Taksin, a former provincial governor and an astute military leader who became king of Siam at the end of 1767. He spent most of the 1770s in military campaigns, reestablishing the kingdom as it had been before the fall of Ayutthaya. He built a new capital at Thonburi (which is today part of greater Bangkok), on the west bank of the Chao Phraya River and closer to the sea than Ayutthaya. Taksin proved to be a poor ruler, alienating the monks and the great families. A rebellion in 1782 forced him to surrender the throne. The rebels named Chaophraya Mahakasatsuk, Taksin's leading general, to the throne. He had not taken part in Taksin's overthrow, but he accepted the monarchy and began to rule as Rama I of the new Chakri dynasty in April 1782, choosing Bangkok on the east bank of the Chao Phraya, opposite Thonburi, for his palace. In 1995, the ninth king of the Chakri dynasty ruled in Bangkok.

The oldest Southeast Asian state is Vietnam, which in the third century B.C. was centered in the lower part of the Red River valley. It was annexed in 111 B.C. by the Chinese, who occupied it until 939 A.D. During the centuries of occupation, the Chinese endeavored with some success to impose their culture on the Vietnamese upper classes.

After Chinese rule ended, some time passed before a united and stable Vietnamese monarchy appeared. The Buddhist monkhood played important roles in the tenth and eleventh centuries and later by assisting in the emergence of a stable government and providing cultural orientation and continuity. In the eleventh century, the monarchical system was sufficiently established that kings began to take on imperial trappings—making use of Chinese imperial ceremony, dress, court titles, and ranks. In the thirteenth century, an examination system for the selection of civil servants modelled on that of China was introduced. Invading Mongol armies in the 1280s were defeated. In these years, Vietnam was known as Dai Viet. The capital was Thang-long, today's Hanoi, which had first appeared in the eighth century as a political and administrative center.

The most notable period in the history of the independent Vietnamese monarchy was probably the fifteenth century. The Le dynasty was founded in 1428. The founder, Le Loi, was a wealthy landowner who became a national hero by successfully leading a guerrilla war that brought an end to two decades of Chinese occupation. China had not given up its intention of recovering Vietnam. The Ming dynasty, taking advantage of political divisions in Dai Viet, had occupied the country in 1406 and sought to make it a Chinese province. Steps to this end included destruction of Buddhist temples and much of the country's literary heritage. The experience was traumatic. Much of the old elite was swept away. The power of the new Le rulers rested on families with military capabilities from south of the Red River and on an intelligentsia independent of the Buddhists and devoted to Confucian values and ethics.

The greatest ruler of the Le dynasty and perhaps the greatest of all Vietnamese emperors was Le Thanh Ton (1460–1497). Under his rule, reorganization and reform produced a well-organized, bureaucratic government that became the model for subsequent rulers. The Le dynasty reclaimed and redistributed land and built canals. The period was one of major cultural achievement, too, especially in literature.

Having made peace with the Chinese, the Vietnamese resumed southward expansion begun earlier into the Indonesian kingdom of Champa and the Khmer empire of Angkor. By 1471, much of Cham territory was brought under Vietnamese administration which then sought to impose Vietnamese culture on the Cham people. A tiny and separate Cham polity recognizing the Vietnamese emperor as overlord remained until 1832.

An apparent flaw in the Le system of government was its dependence on influential families. A strong ruler was needed to manage and control them, but unfortunately Le Thanh Ton's successors were weak. Court intrigues and power struggles between families followed. The rulers became by-standers. In the seventeenth century, two familes divided the country between them. The Trinh controlled the north from Thang-long, and the Nguyen, the south from Hue. The two families periodically fought for control of the throne and the country. Neither the Trinh nor the Nguyen seemed able in the eighteenth century to collect taxes and conduct government effectively, and extreme poverty—such as that in the Red River delta—led to rebellions.

In spite of these problems or perhaps because of them, the Nguyen resumed the Vietnamese drive to the south in the seventeenth century. They had need for cultivable land, and the lands to the south were sparsely settled. Occasionally, expansion occurred by Nguyen recognition of Chinese political refugees who had settled on near-empty lands in or near the Mekong River delta. Cambodia, already long in a weakened condition, gave up Saigon, now Ho Chi Minh City, and other territories in the Mekong delta by the mid-eighteenth century.

In 1771, three brothers from the village of Tayson mounted a successful rebellion against both the Trinh and Nguyen. By the end of the 1780s, the Tayson rebels had killed nearly all the Nguyens and driven the Trinhs from power. The Le dynasty finally came to an end, and one of the Tayson brothers became king. It seemed that at long last Vietnam was united and at peace.

Pierre Pigneau, better known in history as Pigneau de Béhaine, was a French priest and missionary of the *Société des Missions Étrangeres*. He had come to Vietnam in the late 1760s and had become a friend of Prince Nguyen Anh, heir to the Nguyen lands, whom the Tayson had been unable to capture. In 1787, Pigneau, now a bishop, campaigned in France for money, ships, and men to help Prince Anh gain the throne of all Vietnam. If the prince was successful, France would be rewarded with commercial advantages and the right to make Christian converts. Several hundred French volunteers landed in Vietnam in 1788. Over the next several years they trained and organized an army and a navy. Other foreign volunteers included Thais, Khmer, and Chinese. Nguyen Anh reconquered the country, and on June 1, 1802, he was declared king of Vietnam with the reign name of Gia Long, the first of the Nguyen dynasty. Chinese recognition followed. The last Nguyen emperor, Bao Dai, abdicated his throne on August 22, 1945.

Early Island Kingdoms

The first historically known island kingdom of significance was Srivijaya. Politically, it was a loosely knit Malay power based on control of commercial traffic between India and China through the Melaka and Sunda straits. Ships passing through the straits were taxed on the number of passengers and the value of cargoes carried. Srivijaya, the harbor-city and royal residence, was on the Musi River on or near the site of the present Indonesian city of Palembang in southeast Sumatra.

Srivijaya spanned nearly seven centuries from 672 to c. 1365. At its zenith in the ninth and tenth centuries, Srivijaya's authority probably extended over Sumatra, parts of Peninsular Malaysia, and Kalimantan. The absence thus far of major archeological evidence in the form of temples and shrines on a scale like those of Angkor in Cambodia or central Java has caused scholars to question the importance of Srivijaya. But archeological work undertaken in the 1980s has yielded abundant evidence that Srivijaya was a large, world-class commercial harbor-city. Hinduism and Mahayana Buddhism were practiced, including Buddhist tantric rites, which developed in northeast India in the ninth century or earlier. Chinese pilgrims stopping at Srivijaya on the voyage to and from Buddhist holy places in India commented favorably on the city. Of several unresolved questions about Srivijaya, the most tantalizing is its relationships with kingdoms on the adjacent island of Java. At different times, Srivijaya appeared to rule Java; to be at war with Javanese kings; or to be linked to these kings by diplomacy or marriage.

Srivijaya probably was at its peak of prosperity and influence when it suffered a stunning defeat by the Chola kingdom in 1025. The Cholas were Tamil-speaking people of South India and Sri Lanka. The Cholas conducted other raids on Malay ports in the straits and had considerable influence in the Strait of Melaka during the middle decades of the eleventh century. After Srivijaya's defeat by the Cholas, the city was unable to sustain control of shipping in the straits. In the twelfth century many Chinese ships used other Malay ports, by-passing Srivijaya with impunity. In the thirteenth century, east Javanese kingdoms challenged Srivijaya for shares of trade, and in the fourteenth century, the Siamese of Ayutthaya reached the shores of the Strait of Melaka.

Paramesvara, a prince of Javanese origins, fled Sumatra in 1365, going first to Singapore—then called Temasek—and about 1400 to Melaka, a fishing village on the Melaka strait of Peninsular Malaysia. He is credited with founding the prosperous Malay port-city and trading empire of Melaka. In 1405, he successfully sought recognition by China for his kingdom as well as China's support against Ayutthaya, which claimed the peninsula.

Central and East Java

Historical evidence in the form of epigraphical data show the existence of a kingdom on Java c. 410 A.D. The next data of historical significance report a kingdom in central Java in the early eighth century. Called Mataram, its ruler was Sanjaya, a worshipper of the Hindu god Shiva. By the eighth century and probably much earlier, the Javanese had become builders of sophisticated and beautiful structures. Sanjaya and his successors left a large number of Hindu temples and shrines in central Java. Unfortunately, little is known of the political history or of the social and economic conditions in Mataram.

Sanjaya was soon followed by a line of Buddhist kings known as the Sailendras, sometimes called kings of the mountain. Because historical data about the Sailendras are fragmentary, the kings are in many respects a mystery; but they are credited with the creation of numerous Buddhist monuments in the late eighth and ninth centuries. The greatest of these is the Borobudur, "the Mountain of the Accumulation of Virtue in the Ten Stages of the Bodhisattva." Not far from the great cultural center and royal city of Yogyakarta, the Borobudur is an immense stone monument in the shape of a stupa, the South Asian burial mound, rising 150 feet in the air. The Buddhist way to salvation is symbolized by the Borobudur's rising terraces, six square and three upper round ones, crowned by a stupa. The lower terraces have some three miles of open-air stone galleries with scenes from the life of the Buddha and from Buddhist texts carved in bas-relief. The scenes depict human beings, caught up in their earthly existence and gripped by desire, the cause of suffering. The higher levels are without bas-relief. They represent the shedding of earthly desires, the denial of self, and attainment of a formless state. Many thousands of pilgrims from Buddhist countries visit the Borobudur each year.

In the tenth century, the center of Javanese power shifted to East Java and remained there for the next five centuries. As in Central Java, Hinduism and Buddhism provided religious and cultural inspiration. One of Java's most revered kings, Airlangga, ruled at the beginning of the eleventh century. His capital was near today's Surabaya. He reigned from central Java to Bali over an economy that combined fertile rice lands with sea-borne trade. Because he encouraged the arts, the eleventh century was a period of major literary achievement. Airlangga worshipped the Hindu god Vishnu and, after his death in 1049, came to be regarded as an incarnation of Vishnu.

There followed in succession the kingdoms of Kadiri, Singhasari, and Majapahit. King Kertanagara (1268–1292) of Singhasari embarked on a successful campaign of expansion. Singhasari came to control the Spice Islands and, at the expense of Srivijaya, the whole length of the Java Sea. Singhasari prospered from trade and conducted diplomatic and cultural relations with India. Kertanagara's son-in-law defeated a Mongol attempt to conquer Java in 1293 and founded the royal town of Majapahit, the successor state to Singhasari.

Majapahit's most famous personality was not a king but a chief minister, Gaja Mada. He was the real ruler of East Java from 1330 until his death in 1364. In 1331, he announced the resumption of Kertanagara's expansionist policy. The fourteenth-century epic poem *Negarakertagama,* by the Buddhist monk and poet Prapanca, provides a long list of places ruled by Majapahit—roughly the equivalent of all of today's Indonesia and part of Malaysia. How far Majapahit's rule actually extended beyond East Java and Bali has been questioned. The rise of Singhasari/Majapahit no doubt contributed to the decline of Srivijaya.

Majapahit is notable as the last great Indonesian kingdom whose rulers practiced Hinduism. At the same time, however, Javanese indigenous religious beliefs and practices—spirits and ancestor worship—experienced a rise in popularity, blending with Hinduism and producing a rise in cultism. Majapahit disappears from history after about 1520. By then, Islam had already gained many converts in the Indonesian islands. Ibn Batuta, the peripatetic Muslim scholar and geographer, visited northern Sumatra in 1345 and noted that Islam had been established there for nearly a hundred years.

After the disappearance of Majapahit, power shifted to coastal north Java where a commercial economy based on the spice trade flourished. In the fifteenth century, Javanese rulers there became Muslims, adopting the title of sultan. In the early seventeenth century, a devout Muslim, Sultan Agung (d. 1645) of Mataram, conquered all Java. During his reign, the Islam of the coast became rooted in central Java.

Mataram had no formal boundaries. It may be perceived as a series of concentric circles. At the center was the king's palace or *kraton*, a large complex of buildings enclosed by walls and moats. The homes and shops of craftsmen, merchants, and laborers were outside the walls and together with the *kraton* constituted the capital or *negara*. Outside the *negara* was a circle or core domain that constituted much of central Java with its fertile rice lands. The ruler administered this circle closely. Beyond this circle was another of provinces that in the seventeenth century included most of the island of Java. Still another circle was made up of states most distant from the *negara* and *kraton*.

The sultans of Mataram ruled with a class of officials called *priyayi*. The different classes of the hierarchical Javanese society were distinguished by dress, language, and manners. The *priyayi* had an elaborate code of etiquette. Proper behavior was more than good manners; it was an outward sign of self-control and spiritual merit. Their culture was shared with the royal families and the elite generally. *Priyayi* were *halus*, meaning fine, polished, and sophisticated, while peasants were *kasar*, rough and crude. *Priyayi* were loyal to their lords and possessed of a strong sense of honor. Models for *priyayi* behavior could be found in the characters of the *Mahabhrata* and *Ramayana*.

Melaka

The city of Melaka after Paramesvara settled there about 1400 became the true successor to Srivijaya in that its power was dependent on control over commercial shipping that had to pass through the strait. It also became a collection point for products from all of East and Southeast Asia for shipment to India and beyond to the Middle East and Europe. Early in the fifteenth century Melaka's ruler became a Muslim, taking the title of sultan. He was perhaps encouraged to do so by his Arab and Indian Muslim trading partners. Thereafter, Melaka became a center for propagation of the Islamic faith. Melaka's independent history was, however, short. The Portuguese visited the city in 1509; returning in 1511, they took it by force. Melaka passed to the Dutch in 1641 and in 1795 to the British, who ruled it until Malaysia became independent in 1957. The city retains tangible evidence of each of its rulers and is today one of Malaysia's premier historical sites. Two of Melaka's leaders, Tun Perak and Hang Tuah, are heroes to school children in Malaysia today.

The Arrival of European Traders

Between the fifteenth and late eighteenth centuries, much of Europe made the transition from medieval to modern, shaking off the values and institutions of the Middle Ages. In large part this transformation was due to the phenomenon known as the "Age of Discovery." The discoveries increased the supply of Asian and American products in Europe and, together with a large increase in the money supply, resulted in most of Western Europe replacing its feudal political institutions with nation-states and its agricultural economies with ones based on trade and manufacturing. The increased uses of money led to capitalism becoming the dominant economic system and to the decline of the nobility—the rural, landed aristocracy—in favor of an urban middle class made up of business people, entrepreneurs, and professionals.

In the fifteenth century, finding and gaining access to the fabled "Spice Islands"—the Malukan or Moluccan Islands in eastern Indonesia—was the goal of the Europeans. Spices—especially cloves, nutmeg, mace, pepper, and cinnamon—had many uses in food preservation and consumption, in fragrances, and in medicines. Small amounts had come to Europe for centuries by sea and land. Italians, especially Venetians, had dominated the European end of this trade. Their ships loaded Asian goods in eastern Mediterranean ports. Profits from this trade had helped to pay commissions to Leonardo da Vinci and Michelangelo and other Renaissance artists. Leading the way to the Malukan Islands with a carefully planned and researched effort were the Portuguese. Close behind came the Spanish. Columbus, sailing for Spain, was looking for the Malukan Islands when he discovered America instead. At the end of the sixteenth century came the Dutch, followed by the British and French.

In these first three centuries of contact between Europeans and Southeast Asians, the Europeans were motivated by a desire for material gain, principally through trade. The Portuguese, Spanish, and French were in varying degrees also motivated by religion, seeking to make converts to Christianity. Indeed the effort to Christianize was undertaken by some famous churchmen. The most famous was Francis Xavier, one of the founding members of the Society of Jesus or Jesuits, who preached in India, Melaka, the Spice Islands, and elsewhere. His tomb, in Goa in India, is today a major destination for Christian pilgrims.

Technology played an important role. The Europeans often defeated Southeast Asians in battle because of superior weapons and such ships as the caravel and the *fluit*. France mounted the least sustained effort at trade and missionary work in part because as a large European land power it was often preoccupied with European politics.

The Portuguese and Spanish

Vasco da Gama, sailing for the Portuguese Crown, pushed around the Cape of Good Hope and entered the Indian Ocean in 1498. Then with the help of a Muslim pilot, he crossed the Indian Ocean to India. The opening of a European sea route to Asia is one of the major events in world history, and it had profound effects then and through the centuries to the present.

Alfonso d'Albuquerque (d. 1515) gave leadership and direction to the Portuguese trading empire in Asia. He seized Goa on the Malabar coast of India in 1510 from its Muslim rulers and made it Portuguese headquarters for all Asia. Seeking to monopolize the seaborne commerce of South Asia, he sought control of the points of entry and exit to the Indian Ocean. Melaka, one of those points, was essential to his plan as well as necessary for access to the Spice Islands and East Asia. Albuquerque led the bloody conquest of Melaka in 1511. For years, the victors fought to keep Melaka, beating off Malay attacks to retake the city. Part of their defense was diplomatic—allying with first one then another Malay power to keep the Malays divided. Soon after the conquest of Melaka, the Portuguese succeeded in establishing permanent outposts in the Spice Islands.

Melaka then became Portugal's principal port for spices, silks, porcelains, cotton cloth, tin, fragrant woods and many other trade products. The Portuguese attempted to run Melaka as the Malays had—by controlling the strait and serving as an entrepot, collecting and shipping products and goods from both west and east. During most of the sixteenth century, the Portuguese were the only Europeans engaged in this trade, and they prospered mightily. Lisbon succeeded Venice as Europe's market for Asian goods. The century also witnessed many Portuguese individuals, adventurers mostly, seeking their fortunes in Southeast Asia, often as mercenaries in the service of Southeast Asian kings.

Toward the end of the sixteenth century, Portugal's naval and trading empire began to fail. The Portuguese were too few in number to maintain such a far-flung empire, and royal monopoly was an increasingly poor way to administer the empire. Also too little reinvestment was undertaken; corruption went unpunished and grew; and knowledge of routes, winds, currents and related information which the Portuguese had jealousy guarded was obtained by a Dutchman, Jan Huyghen van Linschoten. He published this information in two books in 1595 and 1596; they became sixteenth-century best sellers.

The Spanish first arrived in Southeast Asia when Ferdinand Magellan, seeking the Spice Islands by crossing first the Atlantic and then the Pacific, landed on Cebu Island in the Philippines in 1521. He was killed there in a fight with Filipinos, but the next year one of his ships sailed south to the Spice Islands. The

Portuguese, who had been in the Islands for nearly ten years, were upset by the Spanish arrival. The Spanish, they said, had violated the Treaty of Tordesillas, signed by Spain and Portugal in 1494. This Treaty was based on a decree by the Pope in Rome aimed at defining the Catholic powers' areas of exploration, Christian activity, and influence. A line was drawn on a map of the Atlantic Ocean from the north pole to the south pole. The Spanish were to stay to the west of the line, the Portuguese to the east. But where the line fell on the far side of the globe was disputed. For a time, fighting ensued in the Islands with local rulers allied with either the Portuguese or the Spanish. The Spanish lost this struggle when Hernando Cortez, Viceroy of Mexico, failed to get needed reinforcements to his compatriots across the Pacific. Thereafter, the Spanish occasionally visited the Spice Islands, but mostly they confined their efforts to the Philippines, which they named after Prince Philip. In the second half of the sixteenth century, he ruled Spain and the Spanish Empire as Philip II.

A Spanish expedition commanded by Miguel Lopez de Legaspi landed on Cebu Island in April 1565, establishing a permanent post there. From Cebu, Legaspi, with no major Filipino kingdom to offer resistance and encountering only local opposition, established control of the coastal regions of most of the Philippine Islands. In 1571, Manila was founded on Luzon Island as the Spanish capital. A few years later, the Spanish administration in the Philippines was placed under the government of New Spain, that is, the government of the Spanish colonies in the Americas. Spanish policies and practices in the Americas were in general applied in the Philippines as well. The Spanish were disappointed not to find gold and silver as in the Americas. But Manila developed as a trading center with China and Japan whose merchants brought goods to the Philippines in exchange for silver dollars mined and minted in Mexico and Peru.

Several religious orders—Augustinians, Franciscans, Jesuits, Dominicans, and others—entered the Philippines. They preached and baptized and founded churches, monasteries, and schools. Collectively known as "friars," they influenced Spanish rule of the islands and dominated village affairs. Like other Spanish residents in the Philippines, they regarded themselves as superior to the Filipinos. Filipino rebellions from the sixteenth through the nineteenth centuries were frequently directed at the friars.

Exceptions to Spanish control were Mindanao, the large island in the south, and the Sulu Archipelago, which were better organized for political resistance and whose populations were (and are) largely Muslims. The Spanish called Muslims "Moros" in Spain and applied the name to these populations as well, a name which has continued to the present. The Moros were respected by the Spanish for their fierce conduct in war.

The Dutch and the English

Both the English and the Dutch voyaged to Southeast Asia at the end of the sixteenth century, not as royally owned and operated enterprises but as chartered companies with private citizens owning shares in each. The Dutch company was the Vereenigde Oostindische Compagnie (V.O.C.), and the English company was the East India Company. Both enterprises were secular; that is, they sought profits, not conversions to Christianity. Each company operated according to mercantilism, the economic philosophy of western Europe from the sixteenth through the eighteenth centuries. Monopoly was a goal and wherever possible an operating principle. Each company sought to exclude all other Europeans and to control Asian traders in the countries or regions in which they operated.

The V.O.C. formed in 1602 was far-better financed, equipped, and staffed than was the English company. The Dutch empire-builder in Southeast Asia was Jan Pieterzoon Coen, governor-general. He founded Batavia (today, Jakarta) on the northwest coast of Java as the V.O.C.'s Asian headquarters in 1619. To the monopoly of spices and of other Asian products, Coen sought to add control of the trade between India and Southeast Asia. Much of the clothing worn in Southeast Asia was made of Indian cotton and it had been imported into Southeast Asia for many centuries. Coen saw no reason why the V.O.C. should not profit from this business.

While the Dutch sought to trade, they had difficulty separating the buying and selling of spices from their production. In an effort to control production, they conquered the Spice Islands, at a great loss of Indonesian lives, and appointed a governor. Later, beginning c. 1680, the V.O.C. indirectly took control of much of Java by successfully supporting the ruler of Mataram against rebels. The result was the ceding to the Dutch of numerous economic and political advantages. Although Mataram's laws, courts, and administration remained intact, the kingdom had in effect become a dependency of the V.O.C. In the eighteenth century, the V.O.C. was so powerful as to be able to direct the growing of certain quantities of commercially advantageous crops to be delivered to it at company-determined prices. This system of forced deliveries made Mataram's rulers junior partners of the Dutch. The Javanese aristocracy was rewarded with titles, honors, and shares of the profits.

From Batavia the Dutch sailed to Taiwan, China, and Japan for trade and to Australia and Tasmania for discovery. New crops, sugar and coffee, were introduced in Java. Coffee became so closely identified with the island that "Java" became a slang word for it. The V.O.C. prospered mightily in the seventeenth century, helping to make Amsterdam perhaps the greatest port in the world and indeed to make the Netherlands the leading country in Europe in most of the seventeenth century. By the 1770s, however, the company was in serious financial trouble, which was exaccerbated by French conquest of the Netherlands in 1794. The V.O.C. was formally terminated in 1799.

The British, unable to compete with the Dutch in Southeast Asia in the seventeenth century, withdrew to the shores of India and slowly built up trading posts at Madras, Bombay, and Calcutta. From Madras and Calcutta, the East India Company licensed "country ships" to trade with Southeast Asia and China. Superbly built in Indian shipyards, heavily gunned, carrying the flags of several nations, and crewed by Malays and others chosen for their ability to fight as well as sail, the country ships were a means of breaking into the Dutch monopoly. The Dutch, not surprisingly, regarded the British captains of these ships as pirates. The most famous ships were those belonging to William Jardine and James Matheson, partners and Scotsmen, who carried opium from Calcutta through the Strait of Melaka and South China Sea to Canton in the early nineteenth century.

The French

The French began several east India companies, most of them shortlived. The French obtained a special and unusual relationship at Ayutthaya for a few years in the seventeenth century. The central figures in this relationship were the Thai king, Narai (1657–1688), and a young and ambitious Greek adventurer, Constantine Phaulkon. Phaulkon arrived in Ayutthaya in 1678, as an employee of the English East India Company. The English goal, shared by King Narai, was to break the Dutch domination of Ayutthaya's trade. The Dutch had first opened for business in Ayutthaya in 1608 and by 1630 had a near monopoly of foreign trade. The plan was for Phaulkon to work from inside the Thai government. He became an interpreter and soon rose to be the king's superintendent of foreign trade and chief advisor on foreign policy.

Earlier, French Catholic missionaries of the *Société des Missions Étrangeres* had built a church and a seminary in Ayutthaya and had begun to proselytize. As Christian missionaries have often been, they were enthusiastic about the prospects for converting the Thai people to Christianity. King Narai showed interest in the faith which led the missionaries to the extravagant opinion that he and his court were likely to become Christians. King Narai was less interested in Christianity, however, than in finding alternatives to the Dutch. France was then ruled by Louis XIV, the "Sun King" of Versailles fame. Louis, intrigued with the idea of helping to establish a Christian kingdom in Asia for which he might obtain the credit, decided to support efforts to that end. Jesuits and others in Ayutthaya sought to recruit Phaulkon to the French cause.

The English company, at the moment when success seemed at hand, took a dislike to Phaulkon, withdrawing their support for him. Reluctantly, still with commercial goals in mind, Phaulkon switched his allegiance to the French. This in turn led to an exchange of ambassadors between Paris and Ayutthaya. The French ambassador arrived in Ayutthaya in 1685. He had recently become a Catholic convert from protestantism. A religious fanatic, he cared little for business and saw his sole mission to be the conversion of King Narai to Christianity.

In spite of the French ambassador, Phaulkon managed to get signed a Thai-French treaty that gave French traders and missionaries privileges in the kingdom. Five French warships and more than six hundred troops as well as a number of Jesuit missionaries arrived in 1687. Much to the alarm of the Thais and Phaulkon, the French insisted on permanently basing soldiers in the kingdom, most of them near Ayutthaya. The soldiers began to build fortifications. The Jesuits and the missionaries of the Société began to quarrel, and Phaulkon was blamed for the now unwelcome French connection. After King Narai took ill and left for the countryside, a Thai general, backed by influential families, arrested Phaulkon and had him executed in June 1688. Narai died soon thereafter. The French troops, confronted by vastly superior Siamese forces, chose to withdraw from the country. For a century or more, Ayutthaya was wary of Europeans and rejected various proposals to open trade and other relations. The V.O.C., however, was allowed to return to Ayutthaya at the end of 1688.

In 1624, Alexandre de Rhodes and several other French Jesuits, expelled from Japan, began mission work in Vietnam, claiming several thousand converts after a few years. In 1651, Alexandre, a scholar like many Jesuits, published a history of Tonkin, the Red River delta region of Vietnam. More important, he devised a roman alphabet for the Vietnamese language. Called *quoc-ngu,* it is very much in use today. The Jesuits were joined in Vietnam by members of the Société at the end of the seventeenth century. They soon began to quarrel—the Jesuits were accused of being too tolerant of the Vietnamese belief in spirits. The Pope decided to put the Jesuits to work in Trinh lands and the Société members in Nguyen territories.

In the eighteenth century, the French made several unsuccessful efforts to begin or expand trade in Vietnam, partly motivated by rivalry with the British. That French-British rivalry extended to warfare in India and the Indian Ocean, which in turn limited the resources of the French available for work in Vietnam. Not until Pigneau de Béhaine in the 1790s materially assisted Nguyen Anh to gain the throne of Vietnam did these efforts attain any success.

At the end of the eighteenth century, there were no great kingdoms or empires in Southeast Asia as in earlier centuries—no Pagan, Srivijaya, Angkor, Ayutthaya. The major mainland states had suffered disastrous wars. The Indonesia islands were politically divided into many kingdoms. The Javanese kingdom of Mataram, which might have evolved into an empire, had fallen under Dutch control. The once great Malay port city of Melaka was ruled by the British East India Company. The Europeans with their chartered companies had become important participants in the trade of the region. But with the exception of the Philippines, where the Spanish ruled, the Europeans had had little or no impact on political, social, and cultural values and institutions of Southeast Asia. That would begin to change, however, in the next century. The industrial and scientific revolutions, the appearance of the nation-state and nationalism, the emergence of capitalism as the dominant world economic system, the development of weapons of mass destruction, and a new imperialism—all and more would profoundly impact Southeast Asia and indeed the world beginning in the late nineteenth century.

Southeast Asia, 2
1800 to 1941

Into the Nineteenth Century

At the beginning of the fateful nineteenth century, the polities of Southeast Asia were mostly preoccupied with their own affairs. Siam, under a new dynasty, the Chakri, had recovered from disastrous wars with Burma. Vietnam, too, had a new dynasty of rulers, the Nguyen, after a protracted civil war between powerful families. The King of Burma, a member of the Konbaung dynasty, sought to expand his authority over neighboring peoples. To the south, on the Peninsula, were a number of small Malay sultanates, some of which were vassals of the Siamese or Thai king. One of them, the Sultan of Kedah, handed over the island of Penang in August 1786 to Francis Light (captain of a country ship who was acting for the British East India Company) to obtain Light's help in maintaining the sultan's independence from the Thai king. At the tip of the Peninsula lay Temasek, an island under Malay rule and an old trading outpost, on which in 1819, Thomas Raffles founded the settlement of Singapore for the British East India Company. The "eastern islands" that would become the Netherlands East Indies and eventually Indonesia were divided among many independent states, some of which had long and illustrious histories. The Dutch remained in control of Javanese kingdoms and the Maluku islands. The Spanish continued to occupy the Philippines. Monarchy was the accepted form of government everywhere, and each had its own administration, laws, and revenue system, as well as social, religious, and cultural institutions with attendant values.

Europe in the first years of the century was preoccupied with Napoleon and the wars of the French Revolution. The peace made in Paris in 1814 and in Vienna in 1815 ended the "French menace." British power, demonstrated in its eighteenth-century triumphs in wars for empire in India and North America, was confirmed by Britain's leadership in the defeat of Napoleon. Britain began the nineteenth century as the world's greatest sea power. At the same time, many British and other Europeans were less concerned about empire-building. Some were disillusioned; some were hostile to it. The British had lost their colonies in North America and the Spanish were losing theirs in Latin America. It was a time of increasing attention to developments in Europe such as the growth of nationalism and the spread of the industrial revolution. Although for several decades empire ceased to be of major interest, there were some imperial developments. Britain consolidated its rule in India and worried about Russian designs on South Asia, the French acquired Algeria, the Crimean War was fought, and speculation began on the spoils to be gained from the break-up of the Ottoman Empire. But for the most part, imperial ambitions subsided, not to be earnestly revived until the last decades of the nineteenth century.

The Mainland States

Burma's King Bodawpaya (1782–1819) was the son of Alaungpaya, the Konbaung dynasty's illustrious founder. As was true for earlier kings, his greatest power lay in the north, away from the sea in the vicinity of Ava. Here were rich agricultural lands settled by Burmans, people most loyal to the crown.

Essential to the working of his government was the *hlutdaw*, a council of four to seven members, who met daily and dealt with executive, legislative, and judicial matters. Each member had a principal assistant who provided background information on issues being considered, made recommendations, and with the other principal assistants set the daily agenda. Each assistant had numerous secretaries. Although *hlutdaw* members tended to specialize, there were no departments of government. Outside the royal city, the country was divided into provinces with a *myowun* or governor in charge of each. No official at the capital dealt with foreign affairs. These were the responsibility of border *myowun*. Local officals—headmen of townships—were *myothugyi*.

Essential to good government and social stability was the Buddhist organization that paralleled the secular administration. At the head was the *thathanabaing*, a very prestigious office, whose incumbent was appointed by the king from the most senior persons in the *sangha*. His residence rivalled that of the king's for size and beauty. The *thathanabaing* was assisted by a commission which maintained property and ordination records, disciplined monks, and advised on moral and religious questions.

Bodawpaya's most important responsibilities were to serve as symbol of Burma's unity and to support Buddhism to help maintain moral order. In theory at least, he was a model Buddhist king in an ideal Buddhist state, displaying the characteristics of a universal ruler. In fact, Bodawpaya was active in Buddhist affairs. He sent missionaries among non-Buddhists, banned gambling and alcohol consumption. He built pagodas and set courses of study for the monks, but overall he did not get along well with the *sangha*, or monkhood. He tried to limit the growth of their wealth and failed to reduce factionalism among them.

Beyond his religious responsibilities, Bodawpaya built irrigation works essential to maintaining his core economic base. As was the practice of Burmese kings, he moved his capital from Ava and built a new one nearby at Amarapura, the site being regarded as more suitable for the exercise of the king's religio-magical powers. He received revenues sent to him from the provinces, collected taxes from ships on the Irrawaddy River, took precious gems from mines, and taxed foreign trade.

Bodawpaya was reputedly a person of intelligence and ability, but he had major flaws. One was arrogance and another was an ignorance of the world. The latter may have been the result of the manner in which Burmese kings lived—isolated in their palaces—and of Bodawpaya's dependence on advisors who were perhaps too intimidated by him to be candid. He made war frequently. In 1784, he sent an army into Arakan and after a quick victory annexed the territory. In 1785–1786, he led one hundred thousand men against Siam but with disastrous results. Then he encountered the British East India Company. Burmese troops crossed into India in pursuit of Arakanese refugees, and later, Bodawpaya's general threatened Assam in India. These acts alarmed the British, who were disinclined to suffer arrogance and imprudence on the part of "native rulers." Bodawpaya, on the other hand, did not regard the British in India as his equal. An uneasy relationship existed between the British and Bodawpaya until his death. At his death, he left Burma impoverished and depleted of needed population, especially in the south. He had set Burma on a path to destruction.

Bodawpaya's successor invaded and occupied Assam and other Indian border lands, and the first Anglo-Burmese war followed in 1824–1826. The British won, but it was a costly affair. Some fifteen thousand East India Company soldiers died mostly from disease in the Irrawaddy delta. The Burmese commander, Maha Bandula, was killed, ending his reputation for personal invulnerability. A second war and another British victory followed in 1852–1853. In 1852, Mindon, the ninth and penultimate king of the Konbaung dynasty, came to the throne. Intelligent and conciliatory, he exchanged diplomats and made commercial treaties. He sent missions to Europe, America, and Russia, trying to develop relationships with several western powers. Mindon's successor endeavored to make an alliance with France as well as to import arms. France was slow to reply when Britain asked it to agree that Burma was part of Britain's sphere of influence. In the meantime, more and more French showed up in Burma. Late in 1885, Britain again made war, now risking the enmity of China, which regarded Burma as a tributary state. With each victory, the British had taken Burmese territory until all of Burma was annexed. The last king of Burma was sent into exile.

Rama I (1782–1809), the first Chakri king of Siam, firmly established his dynasty and brought about a remarkable recovery for the country. He was convinced that the fall of Ayutthaya had been the result of society's abandonment of the laws of righteousness and morality. He set about restoring religion to a central place in Siamese life. He convened a council of Buddhist monks in 1788 and commissioned a revision of the *Tripitaka*, the Buddhist scripture, as well as new editions of other Buddhist texts. He required monks to register and made them show proof of ordination. Monks found to be corrupt, immoral, or ignorant were put to hard labor. He regarded wandering "holy men" as a source of the peoples' ignorance and curtailed their activities. He informed everyone that performance of religious obligations was expected. He advised his officials not to ignore the spirits but never to place them above Buddhism. Rama sought not only to reestablish Buddhism but also to reform it by encouraging the use of critical thinking and the application of reason. In the tradition of great Thai kings, he composed a monumental work of literature, the *Ramakian*, a version of the Hindu *Ramayana*.

The king's authority was in theory absolute. In fact, his power depended on his ability to manage powerful families. He had to balance one against another.

If he did it badly, he would become a figurehead at best. His authority to appoint and to reward were two means of manipulating. Another was marriage. The king could and often did establish a family relationship with his key officials. It was not uncommon for high officials to give the king a daughter in marriage. The king usually had many wives.

The central government was organized into six ministries. Beyond the capital the country was divided into *muang* or provinces ranked according to their population and their distance from, and degree of control by, Bangkok. Members of influential families held ministerial positions and some provincial governorships. Typically, their power was based on control of manpower, which was in very short supply, and their relationship to the king. Villages ran their own affairs, providing police and other services.

The Siamese or Thai economy was relatively prosperous; most farmers had enough land and were able to produce two rice crops each year. People were largely self-sufficient, and their living standards good. Taxes, at least in theory, were not heavy. The size and value of crops determined the tax on land. More onerous was a *corvée* by which every free male—not a member of the royal family, the noble families, and the *sangha*—provided three months of labor for the government. The government conducted frequent censuses of people and their property in order to collect taxes effectively. Taxes on the land could be paid in kind—that is, with the products of the land—but as the years passed the government increasingly wanted cash. Trade with other countries was good and growing, and the monarchy urged its high officials to take part in business. Indeed, the king himself, through his agents, controlled much of the foreign trade.

The Chinese figured importantly in the Thai economy. They grew, refined, and exported sugar. Tobacco cultivation and iron-smelting were largely Chinese enterprises. In the 1830s, the Siamese Crown resorted to tax farming, a system by which taxes are collected not by government officials but rather by private persons who pay the government for the right to collect taxes. Districts were auctioned; the highest bidders were Chinese. Some Chinese, long in the Siam or Thailand area, married Siamese women and assimilated into Thai culture. In the mid-nineteenth century, Chinese immigration was even encouraged.

The British attack on Burma in 1824, coupled with a rumor that the British planned the conquest of the Malay state of Kedah, alarmed the Thai. They strengthened their defenses, one of which was the construction in 1825 of an iron chain that could be drawn across the Chao Phraya River. With the British victory in Burma as background, a treaty was signed in June 1826 in which the Thai made trade concessions but obtained some enhancement of their political security. The latter included British recognition of their claim to suzerainty over four Malay states. Overall it was satisfactory to the Thai in that they gained experience in dealing with westerners and trade actually increased substantially.

Thailand, alone among the major traditional states of Southeast Asia, was able to avoid western imperial rule. This was the result of the country's physical location, a willingness to give up border lands to preserve the country as a whole, a stand-off in the rivalry between France and Britain, and most of all the intelligence of Thai leadership. King Mongkut, who ruled between 1851 and 1868, and his son, Chulalongkorn, who succeeded him and ruled until 1890, were each remarkable individuals.

Mongkut, subject of books, plays, and the motion picture, *The King and I,* had not expected to become king. A member of the *sangha,* he had devoted his life to Buddhism, founding a reform order and acquiring a knowledge of the *Pali* scriptures. He also studied Latin, mathematics, astronomy, and science generally. He spoke English and travelled much. He was keenly aware of the British presence in India and Burma, of the Dutch in Java, and of European designs on China. He, more than most of his contemporaries, recognized that the Europeans were potentially a threat. He concluded that the best way for Thailand to keep its independence was to reform the country's institutions by adopting, in varying degrees, European ideas and practices.

As a first step, he negotiated a treaty with Great Britain's Sir John Bowring. The Bowring treaty and others like it granted foreigners rights to residence, travel, trade, investment, ownership of property, and extraterritoriality, meaning exemption from prosecution under Siamese laws. These treaties, like ones written with China, were called "unequal" because they gave advantages to the foreigner not reciprocated. Mongkut invited Europeans to advise him and his ministers on the reform of his government. He moved cautiously, appreciating that changes were threatening to his officials. He held on to his royal prerogatives and often acted in more traditional than modern ways. One of the most interesting persons in Thai and Southeast Asian history, Mongkut died in 1868 from complications of a cold caught while studying an eclipse of the sun.

The ruler of adjacent Vietnam, Gia Long (the reign name of Prince Anh), ruled the three parts of his country, Tonkin, Annam, and Cochin China, from his capital at Hue, beginning in 1802. He obtained recognition from the Chinese emperor. He and his successors chose to be called emperor after the Chinese model, but his subjects referred to him as king. He established a highly centralized government, vigorously restoring the Confucian administrative system. Motivated in part by the fact that Tonkin and Cochin China remained, during the early years of his reign, under semiautonomous warlords, Gia Long probably also needed to establish his own legitimacy after so many years of civil war. His was a rigid and doctrinaire Confucianism, ignoring changes in Confucian practices in Japan and even in China itself. The Vietnamese leadership was aware of changes elsewhere, being so bold in later years as to suggest to the Chinese that their problems stemmed from having strayed from the orthodox Confucianism that they, the Vietnamese, practiced. The Vietnamese believed that the closer they could approximate the theoretical Chinese model the more effective their government would be.

Vietnam's central government was composed of six boards or ministries: Appointments, Finance, War, Rites, Justice, and Public Works. Each was administered by a president and a number of deputies. Outside the capital, the country was organized into provinces, in turn divided into districts and subdistricts. The bureaucracy was large, partly as a result of the king's insistence that all matters must be written out and carefully recorded. Internal rules aimed at quick action on correspondence, and a horse-powered postal system sought to deliver mail in timely fashion. Civil servants belonged to one of three services: civil, military, or censorate. The last were inspectors who evaluated the performance of the members of the other two and checked on their honesty. The bureaucrats were classified into eighteen grades, each distinguished by dress, salary, perquisites, and access to the emperor. These men called mandarins came from the scholar-gentry class, after the style of their Chinese counterparts. Entry into the civil service was by examination, also modelled on the Chinese examination system. Examinations were based on Confucian literary classics and a knowledge of written Chinese.

While the Vietnamese ruling elite, thoroughly Sinicized, followed the Chinese model as closely as possible, there were in fact differences. Unlike the Chinese emperor, for example, the Vietnamese ruler usually participated in interviewing, appointing, promoting, and transferring of civil servants. At the provincial level, there were departures from the Chinese model, especially in Cochin China where there were cultural legacies of the Cham and Khmer people. Ordinary people were not so deeply immersed in the ruling elite's Confucian culture, but they respected it and many held social values and engaged in practices which had their origins in China.

The Vietnamese leadership were also pleased that their Chinese acculturation gave them links not only with China but with Korea and Japan, both of which also enjoyed Chinese cultural heritages. They were eager to receive the latest books from China. Vietnamese diplomats sent to China were among the country's brightest, because they were expected to compete in periodic Chinese poetry and literary events. The Vietnamese regarded themselves as culturally superior to their Southeast Asian neighbors. That they had learned and borrowed from the Chinese was not regarded as demeaning or as compromising Vietnamese independence. Some Vietnamese in the early nineteenth century were in fact ready to borrow from other cultures only as long as it did not conflict with their all-important Chinese system.

The Vietnamese economy was overwhelmingly agricultural. Rice, produced in two crops a year, was supplemented by a variety of fruits, vegetables, and other farm produce. Internal trade was substantial but not so well developed as in other parts of Southeast Asia. The Chinese were active in domestic trade. The court at Hue controlled and taxed foreign trade. Vietnamese crafts were family- and village-based and usually did not compete well with imported, mainly Chinese products.

While the Vietnamese government had numerous problems in the first half of the nineteenth century, the most serious problem—one which it failed to solve—was its relations with the West, principally France. The problem was not trade. Some of the Vietnamese elite were knowledgeable about the West and were interested in trade. In the 1830s the government bought one of the first steamships, clearly seeing its advantages. It was disassembled in Hue, and a factory was built to replicate it. But copying the engine parts was beyond Vietnamese ability, and there was a reluctance to import western help.

The problem was religious and cultural. Christianity had gained a foothold in Vietnam. French Catholic missionaries had helped Nguyen Anh to the throne, and he employed four of them at his court as civil servants. Other missionaries, French and Spanish, were allowed to proselytize. Gia Long died in February 1820. His successors regarded the missionaries and their Vietnamese converts, who numbered perhaps one in twenty Vietnamese, as subversive to government and society. Christianity embraced ideas and engaged in practices which fundamentally challenged the Confucian basis of the Vietnamese state. The missionaries, for example, inveighed against ancestor worship, an essential part of Confucian practice.

The Island States

Trade with the eastern islands (see p. 315) did not cease with the French occupation of Holland or the termination of the V.O.C. in 1799. Most Dutch stayed on in Java, hoping that France would not try to extend its rule to the Dutch overseas empire. Ships of different countries, including those of the newly formed United States, called at Batavia and elsewhere. Then, in 1808, a French-appointed governor-general, Herman Willem Daendels, arrived in Java. Daendels's appearance prompted a British conquest and occupation of Java under Thomas Raffles in 1811.

After the conclusion of the Napoleonic Wars, a British diplomat remarked to a Dutch official that Britain wished Holland to become rich again. Thus, faithful to maintaining a balance of power in Europe, Britain returned most of the Dutch colonies it had seized during the wars. The colonies were believed to be a means of strengthening Holland against a possible revival of French expansionism. In 1824, a treaty addressing British-Dutch relations in Southeast Asia and elsewhere ceded Malacca and Singapore to Britain while Britain gave up such interests as it had in Sumatra.

When the British handed Java back to the Dutch, it was made a ward of the Dutch Crown. The Crown had difficulty governing it, in part because of the Daendels and Raffles administrations, which had made less use of the Javanese *priyayi*. Raffles especially was steeped in the ideas of the Enlightenment—the European intellectual revolution of the eighteenth century. He regarded the Javanese aristocracy as an exploiting "ancien regime" and made sweeping reforms in the revenue, judicial, and administrative systems which undercut their privileged positions. The Java War between 1825 and 1830 was a partial consequence. Dipanagara, a Javanese prince who had been passed over by the Dutch for the throne of Yogyakarta, led the war. Parallels between his life and that of eleventh-century King Airlangga contributed to his popularity. The Dutch won the war, but it was costly in lives as well as money. Nevertheless, the prince of Yogyakarta is today a hero and is remembered in many ways, including what is known in the Indonesian army as the Dipanagara Division. In Sumatra, until 1837, the Dutch were also caught up in the Padri Wars involving an Islamic reform movement.

The Dutch had economic difficulties, too. The colonial treasury was empty, and the Netherlands itself was broke. In trying to recover, application of the popular idea of free trade meant that the British dominated the trade of Java. Governor Johannes Van Den Bosch rejected free trade and in 1830 reverted to eighteenth-century mercantilistic policies, settling on the "Cultivation System." Under this system, Javanese farmers were required to devote one-fifth of their land to a crop such as coffee, sugar, tobacco, or indigo designated by the government. An alternative for some was to give sixty-six days of labor each year to cultivating crops on government land. The crops produced were handed over to the government in lieu of taxes. The Cultivation System was a return to the forced deliv-

ery practices of the V.O.C. Collections were made through indigenous administrative channels. *Priyayi* and Dutch officials, who had oversight and took percentages as their compensation, reestablished their former close relationship.

The Cultivation System aimed initially at filling the colonial government's cof-
fers but quickly became a means of restoring economic prosperity to the Netherlands as well. Java was closed to everyone except the Dutch Crown. The products were shipped to Holland where they were sold to the world at prices far
above their cost in Java. Only Dutch ships were allowed in this trade, and soon
the Netherlands had one of the world's largest merchant fleets. The Netherlands
prospered mightily and became again—as in the halcyon days of the V.O.C—
the major world supplier of many tropical agricultural products.

Rules aimed at protecting the farmers from abuse were often not enforced,
resulting in hardship and deprivation. The Cultivation System came to symbol-
ize for many people imperial exploitation at its worst. But it may also be noted
that rice production and cotton cloth imports rose, suggesting that the Cultivation system was not uniformly bad. Criticisms of the Cultivation System were
raised in the 1840s and 1850s and some minor ameliorating actions were taken.
In 1860, Edward Douwes Dekker, a subordinate official in the coffee culture of
West Java, wrote *Max Havelaar*, a novel, under the pseudonym of Multatuli. A
very popular book, it described the abuses in the Cultivation System. It and
other publications helped bring remedial action. Several crops were abandoned
in the 1860s, thereafter sugar in 1890 and coffee in 1917. An accompanying
belief was that the Crown should get out of the cultivation business and permit
Dutch private capital investment. Large, private investment in the production of
export agricultural crops followed.

The Spanish in the Philippines at the beginning of the nineteenth century
were also experiencing pressures to change. The colonial government was desperately in need of money. The British occupation and sack of Manila during the
Seven Years' War had been a shock and a humiliation. The ideas of the Enlightenment had begun to find expression in the Philippines, in spite of the bitter
opposition of most Spanish residents. The successful rebellions of the Spanish
colonies in the New World and the independence from Spain won by Mexico in
1821 cut the Philippines' indirect link to Spain. This and the use of the steamship, the opening of the Suez canal in 1869, and other nineteenth-century developments resulted in a somewhat closer and more direct Spanish administration
of the Philippines. The social and political effects were profound.

The Philippines emerged from relative economic isolation in the nineteenth
century. The mercantilism of earlier years with its emphasis on monopoly had
kept other Europeans away. But the Spanish had made little effort to establish
trade routes or to develop the islands themselves. Consequently, the colony
had depended heavily on Chinese merchants who brought goods from China to
Manila and on the galleon trade with Mexico. Galleons were sailing ships of up
to two thousand tons, many of them built by Filipino workmen of Philippine hard-
woods and crewed by Filipinos. They carried Chinese and other Asian goods to
Acapulco, Mexico, for transport on to Spain and brought millions of freshly minted
silver dollars from Mexican mines on the return voyage to Manila. The galleon
merchants in Manila jealously controlled this lucrative re-export business. But

their grip began to loosen by the end of the eighteenth century. Free trade was declared by Spanish royal proclamation in 1834. The British, then, became the leading businessmen in Manila. Indeed, efforts were made to emulate the prosperous entrepot of Singapore.

Experimentation with a number of new crops in the late eighteenth century resulted in success with tobacco. It became a major export and was very profitable for owners and the government but hard on the Filipino farmers because of the use of forced deliveries similar to the Dutch practice in Java. The result was Filipino unrest and sporadic rebellion. In the second half of the century, sugar growing and refining began on a large scale. One result of sugar as a major export was that the owners of rice land shifted to more profitable export crops. Previously an exporter of rice, the Philippines began to import rice about 1870. Other agricultural exports included abaca (for hemp) and coffee. Construction of roads and harbor facilities and the establishment of major banks followed. Increasingly, the Philippines became linked to world markets.

The anticlericalism and social reform ideas of the Enlightenment spilled over to the Philippines. Spanish governors took on the powerful "friarocracy." One governor argued that the religious orders should return to their original purposes and get out of secular affairs altogether. The orders possessed large tracts of land which were worked by Filipino farmers as tenants. This governor proposed that they sell these lands—some of which he said had been improperly acquired—and shed their wealth. The Church itself was an ally of the governors' efforts to shrink the power of the religious orders.

Bishops appointed Filipino diocesan priests to friar-served parishes when they became vacant. Not so well-educated, some of the Filipino priests did badly and were severely criticized by the friars and Spanish residents. Morals in the Philippines allegedly declined because of the use of native priests. The struggle, which extended over several decades, ended in a victory for the friars when most parishes were returned to them in 1826.

But it was a costly victory. Filipino priests were allowed only minor religious roles and were in various ways discriminated against by their Spanish brothers. Their grievances became part of a rising tide of criticism of Spanish rule. In 1888, public demonstrations unsuccessfully sought the removal of the religious orders entirely from the country.

The composition of society changed during the century. First, many Spanish left their homes in Latin America for the Philippines because they found life without Spanish rule less congenial. Many new friars came to the islands from Spain when liberal governments there banned their activities. In short, the conservative element among the Spanish in the Philippines increased during the century.

The nineteenth-century shift to commercial agriculture, a rise in population, and the growing scarcity of land speeded up a long-established trend: the concentration of land in fewer hands and the growth of landlordism and tenant farming. When the Spanish came to the Phillippines, land was plentiful and farmers held their land by right of occupancy and tradition. The Spanish introduced the concept of legal property rights, which meant that land ownership had to be registered. Land thereafter could be used as collateral for loans. Village or *barangay* chiefs, *datus* or *caciques*, whom the Spanish used to collect taxes and carry out official tasks, also served as agents for lenders who made loans to farmers against their land. The lenders were often urban-dwelling Chinese mestizos. If the farmer defaulted, the land became the property of the lender. The farming family usually continued to work the land but now as tenants.

All land that was not registered when the system was introduced became government land. The Spanish crown thus acquired many millions of acres. Much of this land was given as royal grants or sold in large tracts beginning in the eighteenth century. Some of the owners built large haciendas, as in Spanish America, and worked the land with tenant farmers.

The nineteenth century produced a new class of Filipinos. They were well-educated and well-to-do—mostly Chinese mestizos—oriented toward nation, interested in Filipino culture, and often idealistic. Some had wanted to become priests and did, but others were put off by the friars. They were called *illustrados*, the enlightened ones, and were the first Filipino intelligentsia. An articulate class by the 1870s, they were Southeast Asia's first nationalists.

The New Imperialism

The empires which the Europeans created in Africa and Asia at the end of the nineteenth century differed from those of the sixteenth through the eighteenth. The earlier empires were commercial, based on ports, factors, merchant ships, trade agreements, and relationships more or less between equals. The empires of the late nineteenth century were based on the physical possession of land, the investment of large amounts of capital in fixed assets, and the extraction on a large scale of raw materials for factories at home and production of food for the world in general. The new imperialism destroyed Asian monarchies, substituting western governments for Asian ones. The Europeans introduced, usually in spite of themselves, western ideas and modern values which undermined Asian institutions and contributed to imperialism's ultimate downfall.

What motivated the new imperialism of the Europeans and Americans? A number of explanations have been offered. Economic ones to be sure: The industrial revolution that dominated western Europe in the second half of the nineteenth century was both a cause of and a means to undertake the new imperialism. As a cause, large volumes of cheap raw materials were wanted. Markets, ones from which competitors could be excluded, were wanted too. A third economic motivation was based on the idea that a colony was a safe place to invest capital that would yield premium returns, better than those attainable at home. These economic motives, taken together, were reminiscent of mercantilism, the policies prevalent earlier in Europe and Southeast Asia. The industrial revolution was the means to imperialism in that it produced technologies in the form of warships, superior weapons, and improved communications. It also produced new forms of organization and management as well as an abundance of managers and administrators. The steamship and the opening of the Suez Canal in 1869 greatly reduced the time and the cost of transit between Europe and Southeast Asia.

Economic motives were real enough although the goals often were not achieved. The captive markets, for example, were often the colonial administrations themselves rather than large numbers of native peoples. Even if they had a taste for European products, the people lacked the purchasing power to acquire them. Capital invested did sometimes bring high yields, especially when the colonial government guaranteed a minimum return, but a good deal of capital was also lost in poor schemes.

Christianity, which partly motivated the earlier empires, inspired the new imperialism, too. The American Baptists were at work early in Burma among the Karen people. American Methodists were busy in Malaya, Singapore, and elsewhere. Catholics, already well established in the Philippines, renewed or extended their work in Vietnam and throughout much of the region. The Lutherans and the Seventh Day Adventists and others participated. Much Christian work was done in education and in health and medicine. Most missionaries were sent into remote areas or permitted to work only among minorities such as the Chinese. To permit them to work among the principal populations could undermine traditional values and might lead to political unrest.

The work of religious organizations was frequently complemented by humanitarian efforts undertaken by secular organizations. These groups saw imperialism as an opportunity to undertake campaigns against the evils of prostitution, slavery, opium, and the consumption of alcohol. The Women's Christian Temperance Union sent young American women into bars and brothels in Rangoon and Singapore to lecture the denizens of such places in English on the evils of their ways.

Politicians, bureaucrats, and military and naval establishments in the imperial countries often supported imperialism. Politicians saw imperialism as a means to distract people's attention from problems at home. For bureaucrats and army and navy officers, imperialism was a means to get more and better jobs, promotions, and larger budgets. The growth of literacy among Europeans and the appearance of cheap newspapers in the nineteenth century helped to popularize imperialism among ordinary people. It was exciting to read of the exploits of people from one's country in far distant lands. Books by the American naval officer Alfred Thayer Mahan, the first of which was published in 1890, argued that a nation's political power and the rise and fall of empires generally resulted from naval strength. His work was supportive of advocates of empire and big navies.

Some imperialists viewed what they were doing as a civilizing effort. Ignorant of Southeast Asians, many Europeans and Americans assumed they were without laws and institutions and only a step, if that, above barbarism. Western civilization in the late nineteenth century was unusually self-confident and certain that its institutions, living standards, and technologies were the best that the world had ever experienced. Why not share, why not lift up the poor souls who still lived in darkness? Probably no Europeans better conceptualized this *raison d'etre* for imperialism than the French. They spoke often of their *mission civilatrice*. A large proimperialist literature developed. Rudyard Kipling's novels, short stories, and poems popularized imperialism. He spoke of the "white man's burden" of civilizing the "heathen" in the remote corners of the globe. He and Teddy Roosevelt hit it off very well.

The new imperialism was shot through with racist feelings and practices. Europeans believed themselves to be superior. Charles Darwin's principle of evolution was applied to political and social organization by Herbert Spencer. The resultant phenomenon called Social Darwinism argued that among the different peoples of the world, those who were most fit would not only survive but dominate the rest. The "fittest" in the late nineteenth century were the white, temperate climate people, and many of them believed they were destined to rule the world.

The Europeans resident in the colonies regarded the indigenous people as their inferiors, and made this opinion clear to the "natives" explicitly and implicitly in many ways. A paternalistic attitude was not uncommon, the natives being treated as children. Although practice varied from colony to colony, color bars were found in hotels, railway trains, and clubs. Romantic liaisons between Europeans and Asians whether solemnized by marriage or not usually resulted in ostracization. In Malaya, the British colonial official who appeared in public with an Asian woman was sacked and sent home. A British doctor in the medical service found to have a non-European ancestor was not promoted and serious consideration was given to his termination and return to Britain out of fear that his "racial impurity" might be discovered by the natives.

The Europeans who participated in the earlier commercial empires usually did not exhibit such racial feelings so obviously. They frequently dressed, ate, and married Asian, and lived like their Asian counterparts. They were often no more than equals at best with the Asians with whom they had to deal for their livelihoods. The advances in technology and communications which made the new imperialism possible also enabled Europeans to bring wives, food, and other features of European life to Southeast Asia. As the years passed, the Europeans increasingly lived in each other's company, becoming more closely knit, and ignoring Asian life around them.

Now and then, Europeans in the new imperialism romanticized native life. Mostly blind to realities, these Europeans saw the natives as simple, uncomplicated souls leading an idyllic, serene existence free of the evils and frustrations of modern western civilization. Now and then, a European "went native."

Colonial rule took different forms and made use of an array of terms to describe the imperial power's relationship to the colony. There were two basic kinds of rule, direct and indirect. In the first, the western power placed its own people in charge and introduced its own laws and institutions. It got rid of the existing government and scrapped indigenous institutions. The changes were usually abrupt. In indirect rule, the native government, officials, and institutions were left intact, and changes came only slowly. But one or more European advisors were provided, usually at the highest level. The advisor looked after European interests; his advice had to be accepted in areas of concern to the imperial power. Failure to do so risked military action. Another frequently used term, "protectorate," meant that the imperial power undertook to protect the native state against its enemies. A "sphere of influence" meant that the imperial power exercised influence, if not control, over an area, to the exclusion of other imperial powers.

Direct and indirect rule are easily understood as concepts. Rarely, however, did they work as described. Imperial rule in Southeast Asia was a mixture of both. But, over time, the trend everywhere was to centralize and concentrate authority in the hands of the colonial administrations; movement was in the direction of direct rule. The forces driving this trend were mainly the requirements of the large, capital-intensive enterprises. Indigenous governments seemed incapable, for example, of dealing with tens of thousands of Indian laborers employed in the rubber plantation industry.

The forms of rule were the subject of a good deal of discussion among Europeans. Indirect rule seemed to have the most advantages. In theory at least it was less expensive to leave local administrators in place. It was less trouble too as long as the people believed their rulers were still in charge. Direct rule where it had been attempted as in Burma had led to conditions described by such phrases as "social disintegration."

World War I was a watershed in thinking about this subject. The terrible loss of lives had shaken the confidence of many Europeans in their superiority and cooled the ardor of some for imperialism. Lord Frederick Lugard, a senior British colonial administrator with experience both in Africa and in Asia, published an important book, *The Dual Mandate in British Tropical Africa* (1923). In it he argued that the imperial powers had two responsibilities. One was to develop a colony's resources to make them available to the world. The other was to educate, reform, adapt, and otherwise prepare the colonial people for their participation in the modern world. For this purpose, indirect rule under which gradual change might be effected seemed preferable. While discussion of the dual mandate was fashionable in ministerial circles, its impact in the colonies was expressed mostly in the form of improvements in education and health. Nationalists tended to denounce indirect rule as a device of the imperialists to delay self-rule and independence.

The effects of European rule were many. On native monarchies, where they were not simply discarded, the usual effect was to halt their further evolution and their possible transition and adaptation to modern systems. The rulers were used for ceremonial show, to discourage proposals for change from the rulers' indigenous subjects, and to fend off occasional demands by minorities for rights and opportunities to participate. Rarely was there any serious attempt by an imperial power to help the native system adapt and grow. In some instances, rulers relieved of many previous responsibilities took up those activities still open to them. In Malaya, for example, some of the sultans devoted more time to Islam and religious affairs.

The Europeans showered their native rulers with material benefits—so much so that some had larger incomes and lived better than had their ancestors. With European help and encouragement, the ceremonial functions were usually staged in a more elaborate and impressive manner than ever before. The net result, however, in most states was ultimately a popular appreciation that the monarch was powerless and little more than an agent of the colonial regime. At the village level, village heads who previously had been chosen and had governed by popular concensus, became permanent salaried employees responsible to the colonial government.

Another major result of imperialism was the drawing of boundaries—the application of the European "territorial imperative"—where often none had existed before. Fixed and certain boundaries were somewhat alien to Southeast Asian political theory. The boundaries were drawn with European interests in mind and often without appreciation for history or culture. The independent states of Southeast Asia have inherited those imperially drawn borders.

The competition—the scramble—to acquire colonies between the European powers took place in Africa, the Middle East, China, and Southeast Asia between about 1870 and 1914. The intense rivalry among the powers contributed to naval and military arms races and was a cause of World War I. In Southeast Asia, the imperial powers at the end of the nineteenth century were Great Britain in Burma, the Malay states, and Singapore; the Netherlands in Indonesia; France in Cambodia, Laos, and Vietnam; and the United States in the Philippines.

Southeast Asian Responses

Western rule was not accepted. Resistance, often in the form of armed violence, occurred everywhere. Initially, opposition was local, sporadic, and unplanned. The difficulties in making common cause that had helped make European hegemony possible also doomed efforts to get rid of the imperialists.

Agrarian unrest is a modern term for a centuries-old phenomenon in Southeast Asia. It means that people in rural areas—virtually the whole of the region—took action to try to correct a perceived injustice or to oppose external interference with local practices and values. Often the actions taken were in a context of ingrained religious and social values, legend, and mysticism. Sometimes they harkened back to an ideal time, a golden age, when all was thought to have been right and proper. Millenarian movements occurred. Leaders were usually charismatic and sometimes messianic. In Java the leader could be a *ratu adil* or just prince, come to deliver the people from injustice. Other leaders were kings or sons of kings long deceased but now returned. Some were religious figures.

Agrarian unrest continued in the late nineteenth and early twentieth centuries under imperial rule. Now, the perpetrators of injustices and interferers with established ways, directly or indirectly, were the colonial powers. The colonial policy usually sought to avoid trouble by trying not to disturb local affairs. But economic and administrative policies did disturb and sometimes led to rebellion. Also, the old reliefs from injustice—evasion or moving—became more difficult as colonial administrations more closely supervised their subjects and as land became less available. An example, one from hundreds of agrarian revolts, was the Saya San rebellion in Burma.

In southern Burma in 1930, small farmers suffering from several years of declining rice prices and the loss of their land to Indian money lenders rose up in protest. Beyond resolving their immediate grievances, they hoped to recreate an earlier ideal time. Saya San, their leader and a former monk, practiced sorcery, magic, and healing. He proclaimed himself a *min-laung*, or embryo king, putting on royal regalia and adopting a forest-residence from which his power would radiate. All of this fit well with Burmese belief that British rule would end with the appearance of an ideal Buddhist king and a new age of justice. The Saya San rebels attacked police stations and government offices. The British put them down with machine guns and aircraft.

Nationalism, Socialism, Communism

The concepts of nation and nationalism are products of western civilization. Nationalism, with its roots in the Enlightenment, flowered in the French Revolution and began to spread throughout Europe with the Napoleonic wars. Nationalism held that people with a common history, language, and culture—and usually of a common race and religion—could identify with each other and make common cause. Nationalism swept western and central Europe in the early and middle years of the nineteenth century. It first found expression in Southeast Asia at the end of the nineteenth century in response to imperialism; it spread and grew in the twentieth century until it embraced virtually all the peoples of the region.

In the early twentieth century, Southeast Asian nationalists included civil servants, schoolteachers, scholars, students, journalists, poets, novelists, labor leaders, doctors, technicians, religious reformers, sons and daughters of aristocrats, and a few workers. Persons with capital and economic power were rare in nationalist ranks; economic power was held by the Europeans and by nonindigenious Asians. Peasant farmers were represented almost not at all before World War II. Most nationalists were urban-based and were among the intelligentsia.

Indigenous intelligentsia were essential to the development of each Southeast Asian nationalism. They acquired western educations and became literate in the language of the colonial government. They had access to the ideas of nation and nationalism. They learned about the French and American Revolutions, the *Social Contract,* the *Declaration of the Rights of Man*, the Glorious Revolution, the *Bill of Rights,* and such democratic principles as personal liberty, equality before the law, freedom of expression, and *habeas corpus.* There were many Asian sources of inspiration as well. These included the Meiji reformers in Japan who had created a modern state capable of defeating the Russians in 1905; Chinese reformers and revolutionaries; the Congress Party in India and individuals such as Mahatma Gandhi and Rabindranath Tagore. The colonial schools attended by the future intelligentsia had students from all over the colony. The unintended result was to give them a previously unappreciated sense of identity with each other and with a larger polity. It was not a large step to the sense of community as a nation.

Nationalism in Southeast Asia passed through stages in most countries. The first occurred when individuals gathered to explore their history, language and literature or to discuss social concerns. At the next stage, discussion was no longer enough. Efforts were made to obtain reforms, to correct abuses, and to solve problems. If reforms failed, some frustrated reformers turned to revolution. Repressive measures sometimes created martyrs and more violent responses. In the actual politics of nationalism, one political party usually emerged as dominant because early on it gained a monopoly of the independence issue. Attempts by competing parties and individuals to gain popularity by exploiting other issues—education, economic problems, sanitation—usually failed. Such issues were real enough but paled beside the issue of political freedom. In any event, these other issues might be divisive so they were better dealt with after independence had been attained. Politically ambitious persons usually found the path to power lay within the dominant party rather than by forming a separate, competing party. Women were prominent in some movements but were rarely in the topmost ranks.

Many Southeast Asians found socialism, both democratic and revolutionary, interesting and attractive. Socialism opposed capitalism, and capitalism in Southeast Asia seemed to them to be inextricably linked with imperialism. Indeed, colonial regimes appeared to exist to facilitate the investment of foreign capital. Few nationalists had ever known an indigenous capitalist. The capitalists they knew were mostly unwanted aliens—Europeans, Americans, Chinese, or Indians. Socialism was also attractive because it was western and modern.

The socialist ideas of Karl Marx and Friedrich Engels were not of primary interest to Southeast Asians. Rather it was the ideas of the Russian revolutionary socialist or communist V.I. Lenin that intrigued them. Lenin, in his *Imperialism, The Highest Stage of Capitalism* (1939), explained why late nineteenth century imperialism had occurred—why the Europeans and Americans had occupied Southeast Asia. Capitalism in the West, he said, had not collapsed as Marx had predicted, because imperialism had given it a respite, a means of postponing its certain demise. Conquered and subject peoples should take heart; imperialism would not last, it was doomed.

Lenin's work was of interest to Southeast Asians in another way. He and his followers had in 1917 conducted a successful revolution in imperial Russia in circumstances which resembled those in Southeast Asia, namely, a small group of leaders, mostly intelligentsia; a very large population of poorly educated rural people; vast distances and poor communications; and a hostile, repressive government. Lenin, standing Marx on his head, contended that revolutions were won by the unity and dedication of small groups of people, operating secretly and believing that ends justified means.

Revolutionary socialism had come to power in Russia, but nowhere else. To make Russia safe from counterrevolution and to propagate communist revolution worldwide, the Third or Communist International, called the Comintern, was founded in Moscow in 1919. Among its tasks were the training of revolutionaries, dissemination of propaganda, and dispatch of agent advisors to fledgling movements.

Asians were given special advice. Revolutionary socialists in Asia should not concentrate only on forming communist parties but also on joining with nationalist parties to rid Asia of colonial regimes. Communist governments would come later, after the Europeans and Americans had been ousted. Lenin, like the imperialists, was in his way exploiting Asians. He believed that the sooner the captalists lost their Asian colonies the sooner capitalism would end in the West, where his primary interests lay. This two-stage plan by which communists would first unite with people whom they regarded as bourgeois and feudal was rejected by the followers of Leon Trotsky, one of Lenin's colleagues and a foe of Stalin. He favored "permanent revolution," or revolution now. Trotskyites were few in Southeast Asia, but occasionally, as in Vietnam, they did create problems for authorities.

Only in Vietnam did communists capture the nationalist movement. In Indonesia, a major interest of the Comintern, Islamic-oriented nationalist leaders quickly understood what the communists were attempting and ousted them from the nationalist mainstream. In retrospect, it is remarkable that so few nationalists succumbed to communism. Many, however, were to greater or lesser degrees attracted to socialist ideas.

Britain in Burma

The British decision in 1886 to abolish the Burmese monarchy, get rid of the *hlutdaw* and rule directly resulted in a country-wide revolt requiring five years and more than forty thousand soldiers to put down. Another immediate problem was the Buddhist organization. For centuries, Burma's kings had supported it as essential to the moral order of the kingdom. The *thathanabaing* appealed for such support from the new British rulers, even offering to have the monks preach acceptance of British rule. The British administration concluded it could not give support because subsequent to the 1857 Mutiny in India, attributed by many to British interference with religious practices, the British Crown had forbidden such interference in its colonies. Without government support, overall monastic discipline and Buddhism's role as moral arbiter declined; the politicization of the *sangha* occurred. The effect of British rule on the Buddhist organization was disastrous.

Burma's new rulers also decided early to make changes in local government. Many of the *myothugyi* were leaders in the fight against the British. They had to go. In their place beginning in 1888, each of Burma's more than seventeen thousand villages received a *thugyi* or headman, as in India. He was appointed by and made responsible to the British officer in charge of the district in which the village was located. The headman's duties were many, including village defense, policing, serving as a judge, and maintenance of burial grounds, roads, and paths. Previously the *myothugyis* were local residents who had inherited their jobs. While they had to carry out the royal will, they also served as buffers between higher authority and the people. The *thugyis*, on the other hand, were agents of the new British government. Many of them lacked the background and skills for their jobs and were simply not up to the many tasks set for them. Indeed, because it was believed that there were too few capable Burmese, the British appointed some Indians to be *thugyis*.

Burma's judicial system was changed, too. Before British rule, many civil disputes were settled in the village before an arbiter according to well known customary laws, the parties representing themselves. Decisions were based on precedent and equity and sealed by the disputants taking tea together. Now, disputes were taken to courts modelled on those of British India using a British Indian code of laws. Burmese farmers found the new courts confusing and alien. Most concluded that the new courts were mainly for the benefit of lawyers and should be avoided.

Britain's most fundamental error in what proved to be a series of mistakes was to make Burma a province of British India. That the Burmese were different from Indians in terms of race, culture, religion, history, customs, and institutions was ignored for administrative convenience. It meant that British administrators on transfer from India had little incentive to learn a Burmese language, to acquire knowledge of Burmese history, customs, and values. The link to India also opened Burma to Indians, who became junior partners with the British in the exploitation of Burma. They came by the tens of thousands to work as laborers, railway workers, soldiers and policemen, bureaucrats, shopkeepers, lawyers, and moneylenders. As the plural society grew, Indians became hated symbols of British rule. Britain's actions in Burma may be better understood if it is remembered that at the end of the nineteenth century, Britain was the most powerful country in the world and most British colonial administrators were supremely confident in the correctness of their actions.

Specialist departments began to be established in the administration of Burma from 1899 onwards. These included departments for forests, agriculture, and justice. Specialists took over some of the functions previously performed by the British district officers. From the Burmese point of view, government became more distant and bureaucratic. While the colonial regime became more specialized and provided more services, its knowledge of the Burmese people and of Burmese society got no better. Society at large was becoming more lawless. By 1900, crime was rampant.

The beginnings of modern Burmese nationalism are found in the first years of the twentieth century in cultural and historical activities. Pride was taken in new editions of chronicles compiled by Burmese kings. A Buddhist revival occurred, and the Young Men's Buddhist Association (YMBA) was founded in 1906. At the end of World War I, nationalism became strident and demanding with the introduction of the Government of India Act of 1919. The Act was intended to advance India toward self-government. Earlier Burmese representations that Burma was different and should be separated from India were accepted. The Act did not apply to Burma, and alternative proposals for Burma were not nearly so favorable. British officials justified them by claiming that Burma was a generation behind India in political experience and sophistication.

The alternative proposals were rejected as an attempt to give Burma a "second-class constitution," and demands were made to be included in the Act of 1919. The YMBA, seeking to broaden its support, changed its name in 1921 to the General Council of Burmese Associations (GCBA). Boycotts and strikes were organized, partly inspired by events in India. Some members of the *sangha* preached revolution, and student actions played a central and vital role. Adding to Burmese anger and frustration were efforts by the government to control and depress rice prices in the midst of worldwide soaring demand.

Britain yielded, agreeing to apply the India Act of 1919 to Burma. The Act provided for dyarchy, that is, a division of ministerial reponsibilities into reserved (British) and transferred (Burmese) subjects. Transferred were education, agriculture, forests, health, public works, and excise taxes. All other matters were reserved. The government of India, acting through its governor in Rangoon, retained firm control even of the transferred subjects by virtue of the governor's fiscal and veto powers. Local and district councils were given more self-rule with election of members. Dyarchy was not well received; some 93 percent of eligible voters boycotted the first elections. The subjects of greatest popular interest— taxes, police, the courts—were reserved.

The Government of Burma Act, passed by the British Parliament in 1935, separated Burma from India and gave Burma almost complete internal self-rule beginning in 1937. The British governor retained power over defence and for-

Squatters' housing on outskirts of Manila (1970s). Wide World.

Ploughing the rice field, Central Java. Department of Information, Republic of Indonesia.

Top left: Vietnam's Ho Chi Minh and Vo Nguyen Gap (1945).

Top right: Ho at age 79, shortly before his death in 1969.

Bottom: President Achmed Sukarno of Indonesia, his wife, Hartini, and at right, Sanusi Hardjadinata (1966). All photos, Wide World.

eign relations, monetary policy and currency, as well as the Shan, Karen and Tribal Hills areas. All other government functions were the responsibility of a Burmese premier and a Burmese Cabinet responsible to a House of Representatives of 132 members of whom 92 were chosen by popular election. Seats were designated for minorities, business groups, and labor. The vote was given to men upon reaching twenty-one years of age and women at the same age who could pass a literacy test. The first Burmese premier was Dr. Ba Maw.

A strike of university students in February 1936 brought national attention to the *Dobama Asiayone*, "We Burmans Association," whose members were popularly known as *"Thakins." Thakin* is the Burmese word for "master," and it had become a term mostly reserved for the British. *Dobama* members used the term in addressing each other as a means of defying the British. Students in politics dated from the events of 1920-1921. In the 1920s, a student union building was built on the campus of the University of Rangoon where freedom of discussion was permitted. The building became a center for politics for all of Burma. University graduates in the 1930s found jobs scarce. Employers tended to avoid those who had shown an interest in politics. The 1936 Thakin-led student strike—aimed at changes in the governance of the university—led to the expulsion of a number of students, including Thakin Nu, and to the disciplining of Thakin Aung San.

Thirty young Burmese men received Japanese military training on Hainan Island and returned to Burma in 1942 with Japanese invasion troops. They organized and led the Burmese Independence Army, initially allied to the Japanese. Stories of their exploits circulated in Burma, and they became known as the "Thirty Comrades." The best known and most popular of them was Aung San. Another was Ne Win.

The final British conquest of Burma in 1886 raised questions in regard to the Burma-China border in two areas, the far north (occupied by the Kachin people), where China, India, Tibet and Burma meet, and the northern Shan states. China recognized British rule of Burma and agreed to a commission to delineate the borders. Because of various delays, the border in the Shan states was not fixed until 1941. The border in the Kachin area was not resolved before the Japanese conquest in 1942.

France in Vietnam. Cambodia. and Laos

Louis Napoleon, Napoleon III, ruler of France between 1852 and 1870 and nephew of the first Napoleon, hungered for military glory and pursued it in Mexico, Italy, China, and Vietnam. Although he was not very successful in emulating his uncle, other Frenchmen followed him in the pursuit of empire. Jules Ferry, sometimes called the builder of the modern French Empire, was convinced of the superiority of French culture and of France's obligation to pursue its *mission civilatrice*. As premier in the early 1880s, he advanced French imperial interests in Vietnam, North Africa, the Congo, and elsewhere. Officers of the French Navy were vigorous advocates and skillful opportunists of empire.

The conquest of Vietnam began in August 1858 when a French naval force, initially sent to China, attacked the Vietnamese port city of Danang. The aim was to obtain religious liberty for Christians and force the acceptance of French trade and diplomatic representatives. The attack shifted to Saigon, which was captured in February 1859. In June 1862, Vietnam made concessions, ceding Saigon and much of Cochin China to France. In 1867, France took control of the remainder of Cochin China.

France regarded itself in a race with Britain for access to the trade of western China. A young naval officer, Francis Garnier, seeking such access, led a mission up the Mekong River in 1866. He had a hatred of Britain. In a two-volume book in 1873, he argued that France must have an empire in order to avoid national decline, to harness the energy of the French people, and to halt the advance of Anglo-Saxon civilization. Garnier found the Mekong impassable. Thereafter, French interest shifted to the Red River in Tonkin as a passage to China. Garnier was subsequently killed there. In France he became a martyr for the imperialist cause.

The Vietnamese king presiding over these events was Tu Duc (1848–1883). An intelligent and scholarly person who loved literature, he worried about the inroads made by Christianity in his country. He feared for the Confucian ideology and institutions of his government. If Christianity succeeded in gaining many adherents, then the state and indeed the society would profoundly change. Unfortunately, the Vietnamese political system had no good way of dealing with dissent. Conflicts in Vietnamese society were not so much resolved as regulated by repressing differences in deference to a higher authority, ultimately the king. If that was not possible, then rebellion occurred.

The reign of Tu Duc was filled with dissent and rebellion. Some mandarins were so upset by his ceding a part of Cochin China to the French in 1862 that they tried to topple him. Christian Vietnamese joined in some of these efforts and launched rebellions of their own. Some of the mandarins understood what was happening and proposed reforms. One who had become a Christian, Nguyen Trung To (d. 1871), urged numerous changes, citing Thailand as a model. He even proposed the unthinkable—the abandonment of written Chinese. While Tu Duc seemed to understand the need for reforms, he was unable to bring them about because they would probably have ended the Confucian system to which he and the mandarins were so firmly committed.

The French moved against Tonkin again, taking Hanoi in April 1882. Tu Duc died in 1883, precipitating a succession struggle. The dispute helped France, in August 1883, make Annam and Tonkin protectorates. France gave itself numerous privileges, including control of Vietnamese customs and the opening of the Red River to trade. China objected to the French presence in Vietnam, and war between France and China followed until 1885. At the same time, a guerrilla war against the French broke out in Tonkin. Matters did not go well for France; Tonkin was not pacified until 1897.

The conquest of Cochin China brought France into conflict with Thailand over Cambodia and Laos. In July 1863, a French naval officer with pistol in hand made the Cambodian king accept French protection. The Thai gave up claims to Cambodia in 1867 in exchange for two Cambodian provinces. A French *Resident Superieur* was assigned to the Cambodian king and took responsibility for all financial, judicial, and administrative matters. But the king was uncooperative. French control was not very effective until the late 1880s. Even then Buddhist education and village administration were little disturbed.

Laos was divided into different principalities in the 1860s. The small kingdom of Luang Prabang in the north had long been one of the peripheral states under the Thai monarchy. Other parts of Laos were nominally under Thai suzereignty, too, but were in turmoil in the 1870s and 1880s. This was due to the arrival of armed bands of Chinese who were known by the color of the flag they flew. An important person in the events that followed was Auguste Pavie, a colonial civil servant of many talents and a scholar of Khmer civilization and the Mekong valley as well. He was French consul to the Luang Prabang kingdom in the late 1880s when France claimed all of Laos east of the Mekong. The territory, it was said, had once been part of Vietnam, and as Vietnam was now under France's protection, France claimed the territory. The Thais were ordered to leave Laos, and French troops were sent to enforce the order. In July 1893, two French warships shelled the Siamese forts at Paknam at the entrance of the Chao Phraya River and then moved up the river to Bangkok where they levelled their guns on the royal palace. The Thais capitulated, handing Laos east of the Mekong over to France. Britain, which had been a silent advisor to the Siamese, was France's real nemesis. British and French imperial rivalry was settled by the *Entente Cordial* signed in 1904. France successfully pressured Thailand, however, for the return of the two Cambodian provinces taken in 1867.

The *Union Indochinoise*, a French administrative creation, was established in 1887. It consisted of Tonkin, Annam, Cochin China, and Cambodia. Laos was added in 1893. Cochin China was directly ruled by a French governor. Some semblance of indirect rule prevailed in the other four territories. Tonkin and Annam were in fact directly ruled, although there were dual administrative systems— one Vietnamese and the other French. The king in Hue exercised nominal rule over Annam. Ruling the *Union* was a French governor-general. Terms were usually short and appointees were frequently politicians rather than persons with knowledge of and a long-term interest in Indochina. Administrative policy varied between centralization and decentralization.

At the end of the nineteenth century, French policy in the Indochinese states was "assimilationist," that is, the aim was to make the Vietnamese like the French in politics, society, and culture. The key was believed to be the French language. If Vietnamese learned French, it was argued, they would be introduced to the glories of French civilization and gladly embrace it. The policy, while much discussed among the French, had little impact. The French grossly underestimated the strength of Vietnamese culture while overestimating the appeal of their own. The French also recoiled from the expense. About 1908, with serious unrest manifest, "association" replaced assimilation as policy. This meant that the Vietnamese would be permitted to keep their culture and only gradually be introduced to modern, French ways.

French rule was bureaucratic. Two-thirds of all Frenchmen in Indochina worked for the colonial regime. Salaries were better than in France, servants were cheap, and life was very good. Saigon became an attractive French tropical city with wide boulevards, a cathedral, modern apartments and office buildings, restaurants and cafes. *La mission* had its compensations.

French economic policies were mercantilistic in that Indochina was reserved for French investors and for French products. But while Vietnam was reasonably well-endowed with natural resources such as coal, tin, and iron, French private investment capital came slowly until after World War I. When investment did quicken, much of it was in production of consumer-goods, damaging to Vietnamese cottage industries. To improve rice production for export, the French built canals and irrigation works, as did the Vietnamese kings before them. Under French rule, thousands of miles of all-weather roads were constructed and river transport was improved. Partly to unite the territories as well as to enhance their own security, the French began building railways in 1881. The most famous, the *Transindochinois*, between Hanoi and Saigon, was extremely costly in money and lives. Built in sections, it was not completed until 1936. A railroad line northwest from Hanoi to the Chinese province of Yunnan, completed in 1910, realized the French ambition of an entry into southwestern China.

Vietnam's population grew substantially. Tonkin in particular became very densely populated, with an attendant growth of rural indebtedness and landlessness. Many Tonkinese farmers migrated southward to Cochin China as they had before French rule. They crowded out many earlier Cambodian residents. Others sought relief from overcrowding by becoming contract laborers on French Pacific islands. The growing Chinese population of Vietnam concentrated in Cochin China; Cholon, sister city to Saigon, was virtually a Chinese city. The resident Chinese controlled the trade in rice and fish, among other products, and dominated river transportation. Chinese were fewer in Tonkin where Vietnamese enmity discouraged their presence. In the 1930s, most Chinese living in Vietnam were unassimilated but appeared to be increasingly permanent.

Social services were minimal, the authorities being more concerned about costs and political security than eager to spread French civilization. Education policy succeeded in creating a small number of Vietnamese who were thoroughly French in culture. These Vietnamese became friends and supporters of France and held important positions in the government and society. The French also aimed to wean Lao and Cambodian students away from Thai influence and Vietnamese students away from Chinese ideas and values. They encouraged the use of *Quoc ngu* to break the hold which the Chinese language had over the scholar-gentry. They limited elementary education, giving only a few boys access and even fewer girls. Secondary schools were rare. The *Ecole Francais de l'Extreme Orient* was founded in Hanoi in 1898 principally as a center for the study of Southeast Asia by Europeans. The University of Hanoi, founded in 1907, was quickly closed (but later reopened) when its students began to study the French Revolution diligently.

The French conquest of Indochina had been prolonged and often bloody. After the conquest, nearly everywhere the French continued to meet resistance, frequently violent. Until 1914, most efforts were aimed at "restoring" the monarchy; elements of the scholar-gentry provided leadership. The late 1880s and early 1890s were dominated by an "aid the King" armed movement. It failed due to lack of coordination and superior French weaponry, among other reasons.

The French triumph was traumatic for the mandarins; they blamed themselves. Many felt they had not only lost their country but had perhaps brought an end to Vietnamese society and culture. While some mandarins led opposition efforts, many, however, collaborated with the French. Those in opposition divided into reformers and activists. Reformers advocated specific changes in policies and institutions and the formation of educational and agricultural societies. Activists were prepared physically to fight the French. A further division was between those who favored restoration of the monarchy and those who favored a western form of government.

Two very influential leaders, both from the scholar-gentry class, were Phan Boi Chau (d. 1940) and Phan Chu Trinh (d. 1926). Phan Boi Chau was an activist who sought to restore the monarchy. Although some Vietnamese faulted China for not effectively helping Vietnam fight the French conquest, Phan Boi Chau had early made contact with Chinese reformers and revolutionaries and was influenced by them. He admired Japanese reformers, too, for they had retained their monarchy while acquiring modern skills. His many literary works have inspired several generations of Vietnamese. A major contribution was the *History of the Loss of Vietnam* which appeared about 1905. In it he called on Vietnamese to form a united front to oppose French rule. In contrast to Phan Boi Chau, Phan Chu Trinh was a reformer who broke sharply with the scholar-gentry and the Confucian system. He advocated a western-style republic. Whatever their differences, both men spent time in French prisons and were heroes to the people. Phan Chu Trinh's funeral in Saigon in 1926 was the occasion for a huge demonstration against French rule.

Major confrontations with the French occurred in 1908. In the years preceding, anti-French poetry and songs had spread through the country. Some mandarins toured villages, advocating self-reliance, the launching of local industries, opposition to the French, and the boycotting of French products. Taxes and a *corvée* bore heavily on peasant farmers. Protesting, farmers in central Vietnam began in March 1908 to demonstrate at the offices of French officials. Some mandarins, collaborating with the French, were badly beaten. Eventually, clashes with troops resulted in deaths, injuries, and arrests. In June, an elaborate coup was attempted in Hanoi, a key feature of which was the planned assassination of the French garrison by poisoning. Unfortunately for the plotters, the French soldiers only became ill. The significance of these uncoordinated efforts was that the majority of the Vietnamese Confucian intelligentsia opposed to the French was imprisoned; leadership in due course passed to a new generation of largely western-educated leaders. In the meantime, however, peasants in the Mekong delta led by charismatic religious figures mounted other attacks against the French in Saigon and elsewhere. In 1915 and 1916, further attacks were made against the French in central and northern Vietnam.

Education—pragmatic, secular, and divorced from Confucian ideology—was an important vehicle for the development of a modern Vietnamese nationalism. In 1907, the private *Dong Kinh* free school opened in Hanoi. It taught modern subjects, promoted the use of romanized Vietnamese instead of Chinese characters, attacked the examination system as perpetuating an anachronistic Confucian culture, and encouraged western-style dress. French authorities soon closed the school, sending the most outspoken teachers to Poulo Condore, a prison island. But Dong Kinh students influenced thinking about politics and society for years to come and other schools were founded on the Dong Kinh model.

France recruited some 140,000 Vietnamese to serve as soldiers and laborers in Europe in World War I. The colony also loaned money to France to help pay for the war. A grateful France promised to give the Vietnamese more education and political power after the war, but these promises were not well remembered. In the 1920s, moderate Vietnamese opinion called for greater representation in colonial councils and relaxation of mercantilistic economic policies. The French responded with modest reforms which failed to satisfy. French residents in Vietnam were an obstacle. Like most resident colonialists elsewhere, they opposed almost any change. Large, syncretic religious movements such as the *Cao Dai* and *Hao Hao* actively began to oppose the French in the 1920s.

In December 1927, the *Quoc dan dang* or Vietnamese Nationalist Party (VNQDD) was formed in Hanoi, inspired by and modelled on the successful *Kuomintang* or Nationalist Party of China. The VNQDD was handicapped by its leaders' idealism and inexperience. It also lacked clear ideas of what kind of independent Vietnam it wanted. The VNQDD's strength was mostly in the North, where in 1929 party members assassinated a French labor recruiter. The French responded swiftly, executing many of the party's leaders. The VNQDD then organized an uprising at Yen Bay among Vietnamese troops. Most of the remaining VNQDD leaders were captured and executed. The French effectively cleared the field for more radical politicians.

The Indochina Communist Party (ICP) was founded in 1930. Its leader was Nguyen Ai Quoc, better known by the pseudonym Ho Chi Minh. Born in 1890 in Nghe An province, he went to Europe as a young man, imbibing Marxism and Leninism in Paris. He was part of a group seeking to represent colonial peoples at the Paris peace conference in 1918. In 1922, he was in Moscow from where he was sent in 1925 to China as a representative of the Comintern. It is unknown whether Vietnamese peasant uprisings in northern Vietnam in 1930–1931 were instigated by the ICP or rather, as is more likely, the Party associated itself with the rebellions after they had begun. The ICP published clandestine newspapers, organized demonstrations, and set up Russian-style "soviets" among northern peasants in the late 1930s. The French with the help of a colonial secret police successfully suppressed the Party.

Britain in the Straits Settlements and Malay States

In 1819, Thomas Stamford Raffles, the East India Company official who had briefly ruled Java during the Napoleonic Wars, established the Company's presence on Singapore Island over Dutch objections. Raffles applied the principle of free trade that was gaining popularity in Britain, and Singapore quickly prospered. In a few years, it became the greatest commercial entrepot in Southeast Asia. It attracted traders from all over Asia and was a mecca for Chinese, becoming a Chinese city. The large capital investments in neighboring states at the end of the nineteenth century which accompanied western imperialism benefitted Singapore enormously. Virtually the whole of Southeast Asia became Singapore's hinterland with tremendous growth in ship repair and support services, banking, insurance, warehousing, processing, distribution, oil storage, and transhipping of western and Asian products. During the last third of the nineteenth century and well into the twentieth century, Singapore was the world's largest labor market. Chinese coolies, or *sinkhehs*, were brought to Singapore on formal and informal indenture contracts by the hundreds of thousands where they were "sold" to employers in Sumatra, Burma, Siam, the Malay states, and elsewhere.

The Sultan of Kedah in 1786 leased the island of Penang at the northern end of the Strait of Malacca to Francis Light who was acting for the British East India Company. Light leased the island for a modest sum and a subsequently unfulfilled promise to help the sultan in the event of a Siamese attack. The company built the port and settlement of Georgetown, intending it to be a haven for British naval and merchant ships.

Although no longer the great port that it had been in the fifteenth and sixteenth centuries, Malacca was acquired from the Dutch by Britain in 1795. Singapore, Penang, and Malacca were administered from British India as the Straits Settlements. In 1867, they were made a Crown Colony, which they remained until the Japanese conquest in 1942. The colony was ruled by a governor assisted by ex officio and appointed executive and legislative councils.

British authorities had a love-hate relationship with the Chinese. "John Chinaman" was absolutely essential to the prosperity of the colony and the Malay states. British officials and businessmen waxed poetic about his self-reliance, hard work, and thriftiness. They also railed against his pig-headedness, secretiveness, and stupidity. On occasion he was suspected of being subversive. The immigrant Chinese were indeed difficult to govern. They spoke different South China dialects which almost no British person understood, belonged to secret societies which periodically fought each other in the streets, and went to great lengths to shun contact with government. A British "Protector" of Chinese was appointed for the Straits Settlements and later for the Malay states who kept in touch with the Chinese community through their own headmen. The latter were often labor contractors and secret society chiefs who in varying degrees exploited the coolies. As long as the Chinese continued to work and did not disrupt the public peace, the colonial government allowed them to go their own way.

Singapore did not experience nationalist demands for independence before 1941. But its vast unassimilated Chinese population did experience the politics, antiimperialist and anti-British, of twentieth-century China. The Nationalist and Communist parties of China maintained agents and branches, mostly illegal and clandestine, among Chinese communities in Southeast Asia. Singapore celebrated politically important anniversaries by flying Chinese flags and sometimes holding public parades. The Chinese were also an important source of funds for political causes in China. Singapore was, from time to time, a haven for many Chinese political figures.

At the beginning of the nineteenth century, Malay sultans ruled the Malay states or *negeri*. The states were small, forested, and sparsely populated. Malay people lived along river banks and made their livelihood by farming, fishing, or trading at river mouths. Malay aristocrats owned tin mines on the west coast of the Peninsula, which were usually worked by Chinese labor. The Sultan of Perak claimed descent from the rulers of Melaka. The Sultans of Patani, Kedah, Kelantan, and Trengganu recognized, if reluctantly, the Siamese monarch as overlord. Negri Sembilan was populated with industrious and resourceful *Menangkabau* people from Sumatra. At the southern tip of the Peninsula opposite Singapore, the rulers of Johore would come to prosper mightily from their links with Raffles's creation.

Still important to the destiny of several of the *negeri* were the Bugis people. Traders and seafarers as well as capable fighters and organizers, they had established themselves in Johore and on both coasts of the Strait in the eighteenth century. In the Riau islands, Bugis operated a very successful port and entrepot in the 1770s, foreshadowing the later British success of Singapore. Malay resistance to Bugis power together with political pressures of the Siamese monarchy on the states had produced much concern and some political confusion.

In the first half of the nineteenth century, British administrators in the Straits Settlements were keenly interested in the *negeri* and jealous of any interest shown in them by other powers. Agreements with the Dutch (1824) and with the Thai (1826) defined the limits of these powers in the Peninsula while articulating British interest there. In the meantime, British and Chinese businessmen in the Straits Settlements were encouraged to invest in the *negeri*. They did, principally in Kedah, Perak, and Johore. Sugar, pepper, and gambier estates were opened and later coffee was cultivated and tin mining expanded.

Tin mining became especially attractive as demand for the metal rose dramatically from the 1850s. Malay chiefs in Perak and Selangor struck deals with Chinese entrepreneurs to mine lands they possessed. Ipoh and Kuala Lumpur emerged as boom towns, and the districts of Larut, Kinta, and Ampang exhibited frontier conditions. Many of the *sinkhehs* who worked the mines spent their wages on opium and prostitutes and, as secret society members, fought rival society gangs and served as enforcers for extortion and protection rackets. Malay chiefs with Chinese allies disputed with each other over valuable pieces of mining land. The frequent violence allegedly threatened the investments of the Straits entrepreneurs, and they asked for British protection. Amidst rumors that Germany or some other European power might try to enter the *negeri*, the newly arrived governor of the Straits Settlements, Sir Andrew Clarke, in 1874, met with Malay chiefs and Chinese secret society heads at Pangkor Island. The governor recognized a contender to the Perak throne as sultan who then agreed to the "Pangkor Engagement." The freshly made sultan agreed to receive a British advisor, called a Resident, whose advice the sultan had to accept on all matters except Malay religion and custom. Not all the sultan's subjects were pleased, and the first Resident whose personality contributed to the stressful situation was murdered. A British punitive expedition made clear who was in charge.

Similar agreements with the states of Selangor, Negri Sembilan, and Pahang followed. Except for Pahang, the states prospered. The Chinese had a monopoly of tin mining until capital-intensive dredge mining by British companies began about 1900. About the same time, coffee, only modestly successful at best, gave way to rubber planting. In the first decade of the twentieth century, the demand for rubber in the United States and Europe boomed in response to the growing automobile industry. In the 1920s, the Malay states were the world's largest producer of rubber.

In 1896, British authorities created the Federated Malay States (FMS), bringing the four states of Perak, Selangor, Negri Sembilan, and Pahang under a single all-British administration in Kuala Lumpur. The aim was to create a larger entity to facilitate investment and economic growth. In 1909 Siam gave up its claim on the states of Kedah, Perlis, Kelantan, and Trengganu and each accepted a British Advisor. In 1914, Johore accepted an Advisor. These five states remained separate from the FMS and were administered as the Unfederated Malay States. All of these administrative divisions together with the Straits Settlements colony were the responsibility of the British governor in Singapore and together were referred to as British Malaya.

The FMS was a roaring economic success, but it provoked a debate mostly within the British community and among some of the sultans on the role of the Malays. Should not the Malays be participating in decision-making and the economic progress of their country? The debate was conducted in terms of decentralization versus centralization. Decentralization or "devolution," as it was called, meant transferring some authority from the FMS back to the states, where Malays were once thought to have had power. It was an attempt to return to an indirect rule that in truth had never existed. Decentralization implied a hampering of business and a slowing of investment and economic growth. Centralization meant continued British administration in Kuala Lumpur with little or no Malay participation and continued provision of services in support of the large mining and estate companies. Some colonial administrators believed in Lugard's *Dual Mandate,* and a few decentralization measures were taken in the 1930s, but the major corporations were not willing to see the dismantling of a structure that served them so well.

A second issue which became full blown in the 1930s were requests by the Straits-born and English-educated Chinese as well as some Indians to be allowed to share in decisions affecting them. Most regarded the Straits Settlements and the Malay states as their only home. They wanted to participate in the administration, to serve in the military forces, and to have English-medium education for all children. Although the British made some modest concessions in the Straits Settlements, which was, afterall, a British colony, they said they could do nothing in the states because these were sovereign Malay countries in which they, the British, and everyone else were guests. The Straits-born Chinese regarded this response as thoroughly dishonest and angrily charged that the government was playing them, the non-Malays, against the Malays in order to divide and rule.

Most of the Malay people themselves remained quiet on political issues. They were poor; their educations, meager. They were loyal to their sultans, too, and to the conservative Islamic State religious establishments. Many Malays had not yet imagined a political community larger than the *negeri* in which they resided. British officials worked diligently to keep Malay political horizons limited. They showed much deference to the rulers, arranged ceremonial public displays of them, rewarded them financially, and hushed up their occasional peccadillos. They used the rulers to deny ordinary Malays those benefits which they, the British, did not want to give. When Malay parents asked for admission of their sons into English-medium schools, British officials told them that it was the policy of the rulers to permit English education only after elementary school, a thorough grounding in the *Koran*, and acquisition of a good knowledge of English.

British officials and the rulers were in fact allies in keeping the majority of the Malay people set in their traditional ways.

A Malay intelligentsia began to form early in the twentieth century. First, there were Malays often of Arab or other non-Peninsular ancestry who had visited the Middle East and imbibed ideas of Islamic reform. They wished to reform Islam among the Malays, shedding non-Islamic beliefs and practices. They were frustrated by the opposition of the religious and secular establishments in each of the states. Next were Malay teachers and journalists, products of schools—notably the Sultan Idris Training College set up in 1922—to train teachers for Malay primary schools and to train technical assistants for government departments. In the late 1920s, these members of the Malay intelligentsia were critical of the Malay ruling elite and influenced by Indonesian nationalism; they hoped for a union with Indonesia. Such radical positions were not well received by most Malay people.

Third, English-educated Malay aristocrats, members of the ruling elite, began to be concerned about the growing numbers of Chinese and Indians. In the early 1930s, unemployed Chinese and Indian workers had settled on the land and become farmers. The British had not objected to this violation of a Malay preserve. Moreover, the immigration of Chinese females in the 1930s, with veiled British approval, gave a permanency to the Chinese population that disturbed the Malays. They were concerned, too, about Straits-born Chinese and Indian demands for a share of power. With the blessings of the Malay rulers, Malay Associations were formed in several states in the late 1930s. The Associations wanted policy changes but remained pro-British. Indeed, their members undertook to raise funds to buy one or more fighter planes for Britain for the war in Europe. Efforts to unite them into a single national organization on the eve of the Japanese invasion were unable to overcome *negeri* loyalties. But the Associations and their leaders provided the organizational foundation for post-Japanese occupation expressions of Malay nationalism.

The Malay intelligentsia before 1940 were mostly concerned with intellectual matters rather than articulated, overt political issues. Focussing on education and religion, they divided into two groups, *Kaum Muda* (the young group), and *Kaum Tua* (the older group). *Kaum Muda*, making use of reform ideas current in the Middle East, sought to rid Islam in the Malay states of its accretions. *Kaum Tua* were members of the Malay aristocracy and religious establishments who opposed change.

The Netherlands in Indonesia

The government of the Netherlands East Indies (NEI) began to get seriously involved in the Indonesian states outside Java and the Malukus (Moluccas) in the middle of the nineteenth century. The Englishman James Brooke's successful personal adventure in Sarawak in western Borneo in the 1840s troubled the Dutch. They occupied Billiton Island in 1851 to acquire rich tin deposits; intervened in the gold fields of Sambas and Pontianak in Borneo in 1854–1855; and annexed the east Borneo sultanate of Bandjermasin in 1863 in a dispute over coal mines. Then, another British adventurer appeared in East Sumatra in the 1850s. After expelling him, the Dutch caused the reigning sultan in 1858 to cede the East Sumatran districts of Deli, Serdang, Langat, and Asahan. The importance of this action can hardly be exaggerated. These lands soon became the home of the world's largest concentration of capitalist, export agriculture.

The Dutch next turned their attention to the Sultanate of Acheh. The opening of the Suez Canal in 1869 to European imperialists searching for new territory and the growing competition to acquire colonies made Acheh on the north coast of Sumatra strategically and economically attractive. In an action typical of the resourceful Achehanese, the sultan in 1869 unsuccessfully sought assistance from Ottoman Turkey. Acheh's attractiveness as well as its history of fierce independence worried the Dutch. They began a war to conquer Acheh in 1873. It was the longest and costliest war in Dutch imperial history. Effective control was not achieved until 1904, while armed resistance lasted until 1908.

The military tactic—lightly armed, fast-moving units combined with sustained attack—developed in the Acheh wars was applied elsewhere in the islands with success. The officer who devised this tactic, J. B. van Heutz, was made governor-general of the NEI. By the end of his administration in 1909, more than two hundred rulers of Indonesian states had signed "the Short Declaration" by which they recognized Dutch rule.

The Dutch Crown had yielded responsibility for the NEI to the Netherlands Parliament in 1867. The subsequent in-pouring of investment capital transformed the NEI. The colonial government assisted and promoted private investment in numerous ways. It built an excellent network of railways in Java and supported research on export crops. Millions of acres of land were brought under cultivation for production of tobacco, rubber, coconut, chinchona, tea, sugar, and vegetable oil. Mineral production included tin, coal, gold, diamonds, bauxite for aluminum, and petroleum. Indonesia became the world's largest producer of rubber and tin. Indonesian farmers who were in a position to do so began the cultivation of export crops, notably rubber. Much criticized by the large foreign-owned estate managers, these smallholders had by the 1920s become responsible for a significant percentage of the total rubber exported. A very large share of investment occurred outside Java, especially in Sumatra.

Large scale western capital investment in the NEI was accompanied by the importation of hundreds of thousands of Chinese laborers. Chinese, especially Hokkien-speaking Chinese, had long been in Indonesia. Many had taken Indonesian wives and acquired some Indonesian culture. These Chinese, called *Peranakan*, had developed their own distinctive culture. *Peranakans* were most numerous on Java where they were mostly middlemen. The new arrivals, called *Totoks*, remained unassimilated. They were most numerous outside Java where they worked on mines and estates. They usually had a Dutch-appointed Chinese leader whom the Dutch called *kapitan*. Most *Totoks* were members of Chinese secret societies.

At the end of the nineteenth century, elements of public opinion in the Netherlands became increasingly critical of Indonesian affairs. Indonesian peasants first abused in the Cultivation System were now seen as helpless against the exploitation of large corporations. The Dutch, it was said, had a moral responsibility to the Indonesian people. These sentiments were the origin of the Ethical Policy announced by the Dutch monarch in 1901. The Netherlands government declared it would no longer take any revenue surpluses generated by the colony and cancelled debt the colony owed to it. A spate of legislation followed, addressing many genuine problems.

Many Dutch were proud of the Ethical Policy, but it encountered much resistance in Indonesia. For example, decentralizing the administration and placing limited power in the hands of the villages was not well received. Protecting indigenous industries and workers, permitting agricultural colonization, controlling abuses in labor recruitment, and providing credit alternatives to money lenders and pawnbrokers—all features of the Ethical Policy—were only partly successful. Other measures aimed at improving housing and expanding irrigation met with mixed success. There were development programs for villages, but funds were sparse and the villagers themselves did not always respond. Elementary education expanded to seven thousand schools by 1913 with 227,000 students.

At the end of the nineteenth century, the Dutch colonial administration was changing. The colony was becoming more modern, requiring special skills. In terms of its excellent roads, railways, inter-island shipping, and medical services, the NEI was a model colony. Dutch rule became increasingly direct; the *priyayi* were no longer so useful. They had clung to their aristocratic ways as changes occurred all about them; they had difficulty adjusting to an age which placed a premium on accountants and technicians. By the 1920s, they had declined in prestige and indeed were disintegrating as a class. Nationalist criticism of the Dutch was directed at the *priyayi* as well. A few *priyayi* at the highest levels retained their positions. Many of the lower-ranking ones moved into politics, joining the nationalist movement. Some became communists. The Dutch themselves became an increasingly closed community. The steamship and the Suez Canal made it possible to go home more often, for wives to join husbands in Indonesia, to eat European food and to live in a European manner.

The history of twentieth century Indonesian nationalism begins with a Javanese woman, Raden Adjeng Kartini, daughter of the *priyayi* regent of Japara. Her letters published in 1911 reveal her keen interest in the modern world and in western education, especially for women. A friend of hers, Dr. Waidin Sudira Usada, founded *Budi Utomo* (Glorious Endeavor) in 1908. Its members included Dutch-trained administrators and doctors who sought to establish schools on a national basis.

Sarekat Islam was founded in 1911 by Javanese merchants, initially in response to challenges by Chinese competitors and by Christian missionary activity. Its aims were to support Muslim commercial activity and to serve various Islamic purposes. While nonpolitical at first, in 1916 its leaders called for self-government in a political union with the Netherlands. It became a mass movement. Its charismatic leader, Umar Sayed Tjokroaminoto, was eventually arrested by the Dutch. His successor, Agus Salim, while emphasizing Islam, modernism, and democratic ideas, stressed intellectual and moral development of the people as prerequisite for their participation in politics.

The Dutch, in an attempt to permit some representation of local Dutch as well as Indonesian opinion and to bring some of its critics into government, established the *Volksraad* or People's Council which first met in May 1918. Members were appointed and indirectly elected. It had only advisory powers and did not provide a forum for political debate. In the 1920s, nationalists became more confrontational, even revolutionary.

Revolutionary socialism or communism came to the NEI with the founding in 1914 of the *Indische Sociaal-Demokratische Vereeniging* (ISDV) or Indies Social Democratic Association. Its founder was Hendricus Sneevliet, a Dutchman. As the party was not popular, Sneevliet sought, successfully, to link up with *Sarekat Islam* to obtain a mass membership. Consequently, ISDV people in *Sarekat Islam* grew in numbers and became more extreme, calling for revolution. Dutch authorities responded with arrests in 1918. Agus Salim and others representing conservative and religious interests passed a resolution in 1921 forbidding members of *Sarekat Islam* to belong to other organizations. In the meantime, the ISDV adopted the name, *Perserikatan Komunis di India* (PKI), the Indonesian Communist Party. The PKI split, one faction plotting revolution. Beginning in November 1926 and for the next few months, uprisings occurred in Java and Sumatra. But Dutch suppression was so effective that the communists did not reappear again in any strength until 1945.

Sarekat Islam was left as the principal nationalist party but its emphasis on religion, education, and amelioration of economic conditions did not satisfy a new generation of mostly western-educated Indonesians. Some of these had been politically active in the early 1920s while students in the Netherlands. They were members of the *Perhimpunan Indonesia* or Indonesian Association. Some, such as Mohammad Hatta and Sutan Sjahrir, later became national leaders. Another important development was the formation of Study Clubs. The most important one was founded in Bandung in 1925. It was there in 1927 that the *Perserikatan Nasional Indonesia* (PNI), the Indonesian National Association, was formed in order to promote unity among Indonesians and work toward independence. A national flag, a national anthem, and other national symbols were divised and adopted by the nationalist movement. A national language, Indonesian, based on the *lingua franca,* Malay, and new names—Indonesia for NEI and Jakarta for Batavia—were proposed. Sukarno, an engineering student and member of the Bandung Study Club, was a member of the PNI's executive committee. He quickly showed himself to be an extraordinary speaker. As the PNI grew increasingly bold, the watchful Dutch detained and in some cases exiled a number of its leaders in December 1929, including Sukarno. As a result, the 1930s was a period when nationalists devoted themselves to educational and cultural reform activities.

Indonesians have long had a cultural, educational, religious, and nonpolitical stream of social-reform activities supportive of nationalism. For example, the *Muhammadiyah,* an Islamic reform movement with roots in the Middle East, was founded in Yogyakarta in 1912 and grew rapidly. It attacked belief in spirits, *adat,* religious syncretism, the *priyayi,* and Westernization. It advocated social reform and education, including the teaching of modern science and mathematics. Nonrevolutionary and not overtly political until the late 1930s, the *Muhammadiyah* has remained strong in independent Indonesia where it operates schools and hospitals. Another example is the *Taman Siswa* (Garden of Students) founded in 1922. It operated schools which combined Javanese culture with a modern curriculum.

The United States in the Philippines

Peasant uprisings and other rebellions seemed endemic to the Philippines. In 1872, the Filipino garrison at Cavite Arsenal, across the bay from Manila, mutinied. The new Spanish governor had sworn to rule "with a cross in one hand and a sword in the other." His swift and bloody response was to execute many Filipinos, including three priests. Many thousands attended their executions and heard their cries for justice. The martyrdom of the priests gave birth to Filipino nationalism. Many *ilustrados* were deported, and others fled the country. One of those who fled was José Rizal, a wealthy fifth-generation Chinese mestizo.

The emigre *ilustrados* in Europe organized the "Propaganda Movement." It was reformist rather than revolutionary, advocating freedom of speech, Filipino representation in the Spanish legislature in Spain, the replacement of friars with Filipino clergy, fair taxes, and a number of actions relating to Filipino language and culture. Rizal and Marcelo H. del Pilar were the two most prominent Propagandists. They wrote for the Movement's newspaper, *La Solidaridad.* Rizal, who obtained M.D. and Ph.D. degrees at the University of Madrid and did further studies in France and Germany, had considerable talent as a writer. In Berlin in 1886, he published his first novel, *Noli Me Tangere (Touch Me Not).* It was a vigorous attack on the religious orders in the Philippines and is today regarded as the greatest work of modern Filipino literature.

Spain continued to govern the Philippines in a repressive manner. The reformers, making little impact, became frustrated and some began to talk of revolution. They also drifted home. Rizal arrived in Manila in 1892. He created a new organization, *La Liga Filipina*, with educational and economic reforms as goals. He was quickly arrested and deported to Mindanao. In August 1896, a revolution was launched and had hardly got beyond Manila when it was crushed. The revolutionaries had wanted *ilustrado* support; when it was not forthcoming, they forged implicating documents. The Spanish wrongly declared Rizal to have masterminded the effort and publicly executed him in 1896. A reign of terror followed. The martyrdom of Rizal united the *ilustrados* and the revolutionaries, and José Rizal is today hailed as the "father of Filipino nationalism."

The organization which attempted the failed revolution of 1896 was the *Katipunan* (Sons of the People), led by Andres Bonifacio, a poor Manila clerk. Bonifacio sought the help of the *ilustrados* because he appreciated his own lack of education and other limitations. Indeed, he was soon challenged for leadership of the *Katipunan* by Emilio Aguinaldo. In 1897, Bonifacio was falsely accused of betraying the revolution and was shot. Aguinaldo became the undisputed leader. From a mountain retreat, Aguinaldo issued a constitution for an independent Philippine republic. The revolutionaries were, however, in deep trouble. Spain, despite also fighting to suppress the Cuban war for independence, was able to get the upper hand militarily in the Philippines. Aguinaldo compromised and made peace with the Spanish, the latter yielding very little more than a cash payment to the revolutionaries and safe conduct out of the country. The Spanish celebrated.

But it was not over. The United States intervened in the Cuban struggle for independence, declaring war on Spain in April 1898. On May 1, Commodore George Dewey sailed the U.S. Navy's Pacific Squadron into Manila Bay and destroyed the Spanish naval ships there. But the Spanish retained control of Manila. Aguinaldo returned to the Philippines with the help of the American Navy, and the revolution resumed. Aguinaldo handed over its direction to the *ilustrados*. The independence of the Philippine Republic was declared on June 12, 1898, a capital was established at Malolos, and the revolutionaries quickly took charge of the countryside. Apolinario Mabina, an *ilustrado*, played key roles in all of these activities. On August 13, 1898, Manila and the Spanish colonial government surrendered.

The Spanish-American War of 1898 provided the opportunity for Filipinos to rid themselves of Spanish rule. But now Americans asked if they should not take over the Philippines. The virus of imperialism had infected many Americans who wanted to get into the European race for colonies. Theodore Roosevelt, the Under Secretary of the Navy and an enthusiastic proponent of imperialism, on his own initiative had ordered Admiral Dewey to Manila. If the United States did not take over the Philippines, maybe the islands would be seized by another power.

President William McKinley said that he had agonized over the question until finally God had told him—in answer to his prayers—that the United States should keep the islands. The United States had the responsibility, he said, to Christianize and educate the poor Filipinos! (Apparently he was unaware that most Filipinos were Catholic Christians.) But antiimperialist voices were raised, too, and the vote in the U.S. Senate ratifying the Peace treaty by which the Philippines was handed over to the United States passed by only one vote. The Filipino revolutionaries cried foul and resumed fighting, now against the American troops that were occupying the country. The Filipino reaction caught most Americans by surprise, and, even worse, the Filipinos using guerrilla tactics were difficult to defeat. The Republican party, which had advocated Philippine annexation, became worried as the Democrats sought to make the Philippines and antiimperialism an election issue.

The United States made peace by offering the *ilustrados* all they could possibly want. The United States promised to end the religious orders, guarantee private property, limit the franchise to the educated, place *ilustrados* in key positions, hold early elections, and make America's stay in the Philippines brief. The Philippines, declared the chief American negotiator, would be a "daughter republic" and a "beacon of hope" to Asia's oppressed millions. The effect was to split the Filipinos. Filipino peasant soldiers kept up the struggle but eventually capitulated.

From about 1907, the *Nacionalista* party dominated politics into the 1940s. The older *ilustrados* moved to the background and a new generation of leaders emerged. The principal figures were Sergio Osmena and Manuel Quezon. Americans periodically debated when to grant independence to the Philippines. Democrats were willing to move quickly; the Republicans, more slowly. At the end of World War I, a war fought for democracy and self-determination, the prospects seemed good for early action. But Republican administrations in the 1920s decided otherwise. General Leonard Wood was made governor-general in 1921. He doubted Filipino capacity for self-rule, dismissed or ignored Filipino institutions, took personal charge and surrounded himself with U.S. military officers as advisors. Filipinos became very hostile. Quezon, a superb politician, led the nationalist opposition to Wood, consolidating his position as the Philippine national leader. In March 1934, the Tydings-McDuffie Act was enacted by the U.S. Congress. It provided for independence for the Philippines after a ten year Commonwealth period.

The American record in the Philippines contrasts favorably with that of other European imperial powers in Southeast Asia in regard to education, sanitation, health, Filipinization of the civil service, and steps toward self-rule. A major failing of U.S. rule in the opinion of some was that the United States did little to reduce Filipino poverty. To do so would probably have required the breaking-up of large concentrations of land and other forms of wealth in the hands of relatively few Filipinos who were the United States' closest friends. The eagerness of the United States to end the Philippine revolution resulted in making an informal alliance with a class of people who, ultimately, in an independent Philippines, would monopolize power. William Howard Taft, who set up the U.S. administration in 1900 and was the first governor, perceived this in 1908. He observed that the United States had turned power over to a social class that could become an aristocracy or an oligarchy.

Thailand

Chulalongkorn, Mongkut's son, ruled for forty-two years (1868–1910), the second longest reign in Thai history. He continued the modernization efforts of his father. He took the first steps toward abolishing slavery and in 1905 began to abolish *corvée*. He ended the custom of prostration by subjects whenever they were in the royal presence. Fiscal reform was difficult, but the first budget was published in 1901. He sent his sons and nephews to Europe to study and required many court officials to send their sons for western educations.

He chose as his models the European colonial regimes in Southeast Asia. To the consequent centralization of royal power, he encountered strong opposition from families which currently and historically held lucrative positions. Provincial governors also resisted changes which shifted authority to Bangkok. In some instances, Chulalongkorn simply waited for incumbents to die before acting. He faced a shortage of the right people. Chulalongkorn believed that the only persons he could trust and who had the necessary education to bring about changes were the royal princes, his brothers and half-brothers. One of the half-brothers, Prince Damrong, took charge of the interior ministry in 1892. A superb administrator, he created an almost wholly new system of provincial and local government. The king also employed Europeans in government ministries and departments. They were brought from different countries in the hope that no one country could claim an advantage or undue influence. In due course, most of the old families lost control over parts of the government and the princes came to occupy many major positions.

Educational reform came slowly. Buddhist village schools were retained but with some curricular changes. Two kinds of secondary schools were established— some taught in Thai, others in English. These efforts were guided mainly by British educators. Major educational developments came after Chulalongkorn's death.

Economic growth was handicapped by a shortage of labor and capital. Government revenue was insufficient to undertake large development projects. The unequal treaties negotiated by Mongkut, while opening the country to Europeans, limited taxes and duties that might be collected. In addition, the fiscally conservative British financial advisors counselled the maintenance of large reserves and the avoidance of debt. Railway construction finally got started late in the century, with Chinese immigrant laborers helping to fill labor requirements. In the 1920s major revisions were made in the treaties, which were finally ended altogether in the late 1930s.

Although Chulalongkorn's modernization efforts were comprehensive and very important, his major achievement in his own time was maintenance of the country's independence. Thailand's eastern neighbors, the states of Laos and Cambodia, had long been areas of contention with Vietnam. Both Thailand and Vietnam had tried to exercise hegemony over these states. France beginning in the late 1860s assumed Vietnam's claims over these states and thus became Thailand's adversary. Similarly, Thailand had claimed suzereignty over certain of the Malay states in the peninsula. The British extension of indirect rule over these states beginning in 1874 put Thailand in potential conflict with that imperial power. Indeed, there had been problems even earlier. In the race for empire in the last years of the nineteenth century, both France and Britain seemed ready to seize on almost any incident to advance their interests.

Caught between these two great imperial powers, Chulalongkorn wisely chose not to try a military solution. As his military reforms had not yet gained momentum, he required a diplomatic solution. He was advised by both Prince Damrong and the first Thai foreign minister to speak European languages, Prince Devawongse. Devawongse was an intimate companion of the king. Chulalongkorn traded peripheral lands and claims to those lands, and made other concessions for Siam's survival as an independent state. In 1893, French warships entered the Chao Phraya and levelled their guns at the royal palace. Devawongse, putting a good face on a bad situation, went down to the water's edge, welcomed the French commander and congratulated him on his success in getting past Thai guns at the river's mouth.

Chulalongkorn's successor, a son, was Vajiravudh or Rama VI (1910–1925). He was the first Thai king to be educated abroad. He was fluent in English, well travelled, a voracious reader, the author of many plays and other literary pieces, and an actor. His lack of romantic interest in women and his lifestyle upset his mother and members of the royal family. His batchelor status was declared a "national calamity."

Vajiravudh is remembered for his vigorous efforts to stimulate nationalism among his subjects. He wanted them to become more patriotic, united, loyal, and willing to make sacrifices. So many countries—neighbors once independent—had fallen under European rule. Thailand was still free but was in danger, he said, because its people were soft and complacent. His nationalism has been described as "elitist" and "cultural," the first because the people's loyalties ran upward to the king more than sideways to other Thais; the second because he stressed Thai buddhism and ethnicity as essential elements. In the conduct of affairs, he stressed loyalty and hierarchy and surrounded himself with personal favorites rather than good administrators. He criticized ideas of self-rule as inappropriate for Asians.

As a means of promoting his ideas, he formed several organizations, the most notable of which was the paramilitary *Wild Tiger Corps*. Members were to strengthen their bodies and commit their minds to the nation. The king took a keen personal interest in the *Tigers*. He set goals; coined mottos; designed uniforms; wrote rules, drills, exercises, and songs; and conducted parades. Some of its members became an elite, personal guard. Regular Army officers resented the *Tigers*. The officers believed the king did not appreciate them. Vajiravudh alienated many people, and one or more coups were planned against him. Only timely arrests forestalled their execution.

Another major aspect of Vajiravudh's efforts toward nationalism was an attack on the Chinese whom his predecessors had encouraged to come to the country. He worried about them, in part because of the overthrow of the Chinese monarchy in 1911. He compared them to European Jews, especially in terms of their business acumen, in an essay entitled *The Jews of the Orient*. It is worthy of note that, genetically speaking, the king was more Chinese than Thai due to his ancestors having taken Chinese wives and concubines.

Vajiravudh died on November 26, 1925, at the age of 44. He left the kingdom in trouble. The prestige of the monarchy had declined, the government's finances were in chaos, the bureaucracy was leaderless and engaged in internecine fighting. He is credited with having bequeathed to his country martial values and the patriotic phrase "King, Nation, Religion." He left no male heir. The throne passed to his brother, Prajadiphok, a young man who had not anticipated the throne and was not prepared for it. But Prajadiphok worked conscientiously to deal with the problems he had inherited. One of his first acts was to disband the *Wild Tigers*. The most fundamental problem Prajadiphok faced was the future of the monarchy and the kind of government the country should have. Royal absolutism seemed increasingly inappropriate.

Another, and related problem, was deep resentment of the royal family's monopolization of the highest positions in government. Once so essential to change, the princes now seemed like so much deadwood. Bangkok's newspapers, relatively unfettered by government, printed articles on the prince's corruption and incompetence and the need for democratic reforms. Public opinion appeared for the first time in Thai history, and an intelligentsia not dependent on the monarchy emerged. Many people wondered if the government was capable of undertaking its own reform.

Prajadiphok was not unsympathetic. He wondered if Thailand should have a western style parliamentary government. If so, he believed steps should be taken to prepare the people for it, perhaps by starting with municipal elections. Like his brother, he worried about the Chinese whose assimilation into Thai society had slowed. They were more important than their numbers suggested because of their economic power. The Chinese, thought the king, might dominate representative politics with their money. Assimilation had slowed because of the arrival of Chinese women immigrants, establishment of Chinese schools and the growing politicization of the Chinese by the spread of Chinese nationalism and communism.

The worldwide Great Depression was devastating to Thailand, and it brought political change. Rice and land prices were in a free fall. Farmers could not sell their rice for enough money to pay taxes. Urban middle-class people watched their assets dwindle. Many bureaucrats were dismissed, and salaries were cut. The king worried about popular discontent but freely admitted he did not know what to do. Many were persuaded that the king and princes were no longer able to lead.

At dawn on June 24, 1932, forty-nine military and naval officers and sixty-five middle-ranking civil servants, collectively known as the "promoters," seized power. The coup was not aimed at establishing democracy, and it had not been demanded by the majority of the people. Prajadiphok, vacationing, was invited to return to Bangkok as a constitutional monarch. He agreed, saying he had been thinking about a similar change. The king's politeness, respect for others, and candor were taken as weakness; but in fact he was strong, hard-working, and intellectually able. His failures were to underestimate the desire for change among the Bangkok elite and his unwillingness to rid the upper echelons of government of many of his kin.

The new government was led initially by Pridi Phanomyang, who had studied law in Paris, had been a student leader there, and had acquired socialist ideas. He proposed setting up a single-party Soviet-style constitution and introducing a planned economy. The constitution that was actually introduced was far more conservative—one half of the legislature being indirectly elected and the other half being appointed. It was intended to prepare the way for a more democratic government. But the 1930s was a decade of growing nationalism and increasing political power by the Thai Army. In 1937, the Army, led by Colonel Phibun Songkhram, assumed control of the government. An ardent nationalist and an incipient fascist, the colonel changed the name of the country from Siam to Thailand in 1939 and sought to regain former Thai lands in Cambodia, Laos, and Malaysia. Friendly toward the Japanese, he took Thailand into the war by signing an alliance with them in 1941. His principal opponent was Pridi, who, angry over Phibun's friendliness with the Japanese, resigned from the Cabinet in 1941.

The events of the 1930s and later were free of the prominent presence of the king. Prajadiphok abdicated in 1935 and died in exile in 1941. His successor was a boy studying in Switzerland who did not return to Thailand until 1946.

In the seventy years or so before 1941, Southeast Asia experienced profound, if uneven and unbalanced, political and economic changes from which there could be no turning back. These changes were brought about by European and American imperialism. Now, at the end of the third decade of the twentieth century, the world would again become enveloped in war. Southeast Asia would inevitably be caught up in that war and indeed experience another imperialism, that of Japan.

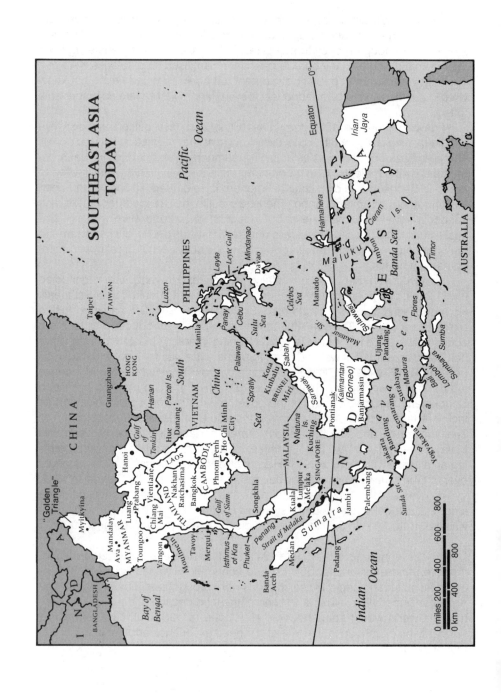

SOUTHEAST ASIA
TODAY

Southeast Asia, 3
1941 to 1995

The Japanese Conquest and Occupation

That the Japanese intended to conquer Southeast Asia seemed clear enough to informed observers in the late 1930s. Yet when the war came the European powers were unprepared. With minor exceptions, they had not armed their Southeast Asian subjects, nor indeed had they otherwise prepared them for war. Believing their own forces were superior, the imperial powers doubted that the Japanese or any Asian force was a real match for them. They placed great confidence in their bases, the Americans at Clark air base and Subic Bay naval base in the Philippines and the British at the great naval and air base complex in Singapore. They had not counted on having to fight in Europe and Asia at the same time. Also, the great economic depression of the early 1930s had reduced their military spending.

Encouraged by Britain's appeasement of Adolf Hitler's Germany and the subsequent outbreak of war in Europe, Japan gambled that the Europeans would be unwilling or unable to fight for their colonies in Southeast Asia. Shortly after Germany defeated France in June 1940, Japan joined fascist Germany and Italy in an alliance. Japan used Indochina as an advanced staging area. Only the United States with its formidable naval forces in the Pacific gave Japan's military leaders pause.

Acting with boldness, Japanese naval and air forces almost totally destroyed the U.S. fleet at Pearl Harbor in Hawaii in a surprise attack on December 7, 1941. Japan's consequent naval superiority was further assured by the sinking of two large and powerful British warships near Singapore and the defeat of a mostly Dutch naval force in the "Battle of the Java Sea." Invasion of the Philippines and Malaysia began on December 8, followed by invasions of Burma and the Netherlands East Indies. The Japanese were successful everywhere. Winston Churchill had ordered Singapore defended until the last man, but General Arthur Percival surrendered tens of thousands of his soldiers to General Yamashita Tomoyuki, who led a much smaller force, on February 15, 1942. The British abandoned Rangoon in early March 1942 and withdrew from Burma, employing a scorched-earth policy. The Japanese occupied Java in the same month. An heroic stand on Corregidor Island in the Philippines ended in May. Thailand avoided Japanese conquest by signing a friendship treaty with Japan and later entering World War II as its ally. Thailand profited by regaining parts of Laos and Cambodia earlier taken by the French.

The Japanese had talked of freeing Southeast Asia from imperialism, but nowhere were the Japanese received by any large number of people as liberators. In effect, European and American rule was replaced by Japanese rule. The Japanese proclamation of a "co-prosperity sphere" soon lost whatever meaning it may have had for some Southeast Asians. The Japanese granted nominal independence to Burma in August 1943 and to the Philippines in October 1943.

Japan's intention of acquiring large supplies of Southeast Asian raw materials, especially oil from the Netherlands East Indies, for its factories and armed forces was not realized due to effective U.S. submarine warfare. At the same time, Japan was unable to supply machinery and spare parts, previously imported from Europe and America, to keep mines and estates, railways, cars and trucks, and communications operating. The modern and export-oriented sectors of the region's economies came to a halt. Shortages of medicines, food, clothing, and cooking oil developed. By 1944 in most Southeast Asian countries serious deprivation occurred. In Malaysia and Singapore, heavily dependent on imported rice, many people suffered dietary deficiencies. Preventive health measures broke down, and there was a resurgence of malaria, cholera, hook worm, and other diseases. Shortages of just about everything coupled with the Japanese practice of printing money as they needed it produced black markets and severe inflation. The Japanese from time to time forced European prisoners and Southeast Asians into labor gangs. Some of these were used to build the Thailand-Burma rail line, which was commemorated in many books as the "death railway" and the motion picture, *Bridge on the River Kwai* (1957, based on the novel by Pierre Boulle).

The Japanese treated different ethnic communities differently. They treated the Chinese badly. Unknown thousands were executed because of Japanese hatred or distrust, as a means of communal punishment, or as a result of individual or communal extortion attempts. Mass graves of persons executed were still being discovered in the 1980s. Indians generally fared better, as the Japanese hoped to recruit them into the Indian National Army for a Japanese-led invasion of British India. Indigenous Southeast Asians were often treated best because the Japanese hoped to establish long-term favorable relationships with them. Overall, though, Japanese rule exacerbated racial feelings. The Japanese themselves often exhibited a sense of racial superiority. A half-century later, Japanese were still debating the war and their own culpability. A strongly held point of view among Japanese was that they had been liberators and therefore had nothing for which to apologize.

The retaking of Southeast Asia and the ultimate defeat of Japan was planned and organized in 1943. A special Southeast Asia Command was formed at Colombo in Ceylon, today Sri Lanka. Britain's Lord Louis Mountbatten was made supreme commander and America's General Joseph Stillwell, deputy commander. Forces under these officers would attack from the west, especially concentrating on Burma, through which it was possible to supply China. Another drive, essentially American, was mounted from the Pacific and Australia. The Japanese navy suffered major defeats at Midway Island in June 1942 and then in the Leyte Gulf in the Philippines in October 1944, removing it as a serious force in the defense of Japan. In the same year, Japan lost important battles in Burma and in the Pacific islands. The war in Europe ended in May 1945. Full attention then focussed on the defeat of Japan, and preparations were made for the invasion of Japan's home islands. The first atom bomb was dropped on Hiroshima, Japan, on August 6; the second, on Nagasaki on August 9, 1945. On August 8, Russia declared war on Japan. On August 10, Japan unconditionally surrendered.

The collapse of Japan and the abrupt end of the war caught nearly everyone by surprise. In Malaysia and elsewhere the Japanese simply stacked their arms in advance of the actual arrival of Allied troops. When the first Allied troops did arrive, they were everywhere too few in number to guard surrendered Japanese and maintain law and order.

Among the effects of the Japanese conquest and occupation was that the war everywhere destroyed the idea that Europeans were invincible and infallible. Another effect was that many Asians were given larger responsibilities, mainly because the Japanese were too few to fill all the important positions. Indonesians, for example, found they could do technical and administrative jobs which formerly had been reserved for the Dutch on the ground that Indonesians were supposedly not capable enough. Such persons were not very keen about handing their jobs back to the Dutch on the latter's return. A third effect of Japanese occupation was that Nationalist political leaders found it generally easier to carry on their work, and the opportunity was taken to build or improve national political organizations. In short, the political effect of the Japanese occupation was to speed up the coming of independence.

Indeed, although the Europeans returned to Southeast Asia in 1945 intending to reestablish their rule, Burma, Vietnam, and Indonesia had each declared independence before their former imperial masters had arrived. Independence was actually attained by the Philippines in July 1946; by Burma, January 1948; by Indonesia, December 1949. Full independence for the whole of Vietnam was delayed until 1976, first by eight years of warfare with the French, followed by nearly a decade of warfare with the United States. The newly independent states of Southeast Asia had a number of common problems.

Problems of Independence

The first task was to establish governments. Nearly everywhere, colonial rule had destroyed or reduced to ineffectiveness existing indigenous governments, while the Japanese occupation had ended colonial administrations. Most Southeast Asians had had little experience at governing. National institutions were generally lacking, public opinion was little developed, and the media—press and radio—had been under the influence or control of the colonial governments.

Nationalist leaders had called for freedom and democracy. To the extent they had discussed what these terms meant, they sometimes disagreed. Because they feared that differences among themselves would be exploited by the colonial rulers, debate as to the kind and form of government waited mostly until after independence was won. So, what was meant by democracy? Southeast Asia had never experienced democracy except perhaps in its villages where democratic practices such as consultation and consensus were common. But the villages operated with small numbers and with persons of like race, language, and religion, in communities of long residence, well-known to each other. Village practices were not necessarily adaptable to national governments. Probably most Southeast Asian ordinary people did not dwell on interpretations of democracy. They were less concerned with political rights and more interested in economic and social issues, such as improved land tenure and retention of a larger share of the fruits of their labor and better education for their children.

Among the elites the fundamental question was what form of government should be established? The principal choices seemed to be the British parliamentary system or one of its variants with its dependence on well-organized political parties; the U.S. presidential system which provided a stable executive; or the Soviet Russian single-party dominant system where a good deal of power was exercised outside the formal structures of government.

Then, who should have the rights of citizenship? Most Southeast Asian countries were plural societies. Colonial regimes had not sought to assimilate immigrant minorities into local cultures but rather had encouraged differences between communities, practicing divide and rule. In a plural society, who should be a citizen, who should have the right to vote and stand for office? Who should be members of administrative and technical services and of the police and armed forces? Under colonial rule, these essential services had mostly been performed by the Europeans, Chinese, and Indians. How should people now be chosen and trained for these jobs?

Some indigenous persons who had worked in the colonial administrations were carried into the workforce of the new independent governments. Many low-ranking staff were not well educated and were poorly paid. They, as well as better-educated civil servants, having no other models, sometimes mimicked the ways of their former colonial bosses. These holdovers lacked a public service orientation and were not sympathetic to change. Colonial regimes were notably not free of corruption. In the immediate postcolonial years, with dire shortages of qualified people and poor pay, corruption was commonplace.

Internal security was another problem everywhere. In Burma, ethnic minorities as well as communists did not accept Burmese policies and even challenged the new government's right to rule them. In the Philippines and Malaysia, communist terrorists were active. The Philippines were also confronted with a Moro Muslim revolt. In eastern Indonesia, a Dutch adventurer led an armed rebellion. Solutions were as much or more political as they were military. In the meantime, the lack of internal security was an obstacle to economic reconstruction.

Social problems of many kinds were widespread. In colonial times, to the extent schools existed, they were mostly elementary schools, teaching horticulture and homemaking and avoiding those subjects which would prepare young people for jobs and citizenship responsibilities in an independent society. In Malaysia, only four elementary grades were offered and then mostly to Malay boys, many of whom dropped out after one or two years. Education for Malay girls was regarded as unnecessary. There were few schools at the secondary level, and these were often private and missionary-run or founded and operated by minority communities, mostly Chinese. Schools such as the Victoria Institution in Kuala Lumpur and the Jean Jacques Rousseau high school in Ho Chi Minh City taught the curriculum of the home country in the language of the imperial ruler. Chinese high schools founded and maintained by Chinese benefactors taught in Chinese and provided a curriculum steeped in Chinese history and culture and sometimes in Chinese nationalism and politics. Universities were few. A few technical schools trained persons to work under European direction.

The independent countries of Southeast Asia needed schools both to prepare administrators, managers, engineers, doctors, and other professionals and to teach national identity and loyalty. Education was also intended to be more widely available than in colonial times, and thus hundreds of new school buildings and thousands of new teachers were needed. The expense was a problem, but even more difficult were fundamental questions regarding curriculum and teachers. In plural societies, whose history is taught? Whose language is used for instruction? How were teachers to be trained? How were existing private schools to be integrated into a national education system and their teachers retrained? What professional schools should be created, and who was to be admitted? The struggle to answer these questions sometimes made education a bitterly fought political battleground.

Despite the gravity of such problems, economic questions were even more pressing. Apart from the need to rebuild destroyed infrastructure and businesses, legacies of colonial rule had to be addressed. For example, colonial economies were often dual. One economy was that of large capital investments employing thousands of wage-workers whose products such as tin, rubber, coffee, and sugar were exported to foreign markets where their prices were determined. Banks, agency houses, and equipment suppliers served these export industries and had little else to do with the economy and people of the country in which they operated. The other economy consisted of the people who practiced farming, fishing, crafts, and small trade, many of whom lived on a subsistence level and were deeply in debt or had lost their land to moneylenders. Most of them were inexperienced with an economy based on the intensive use of money. They lacked facilities for saving, for obtaining credit, and support. They had little or no knowledge of the markets for their labor. The challenge was to convert the dual colonial economies to a single national economy.

Many nationalist leaders in Southeast Asia favored socialist economies. The hated imperialism seemed to them to be an extension of capitalism. Socialism also appeared to be more fair, and economic justice had been a nationalist goal. The temptation to expropriate foreign-owned mines, estates, and factories was great. In some newly independent countries, the regimes that were created were declared by critics to be "neocolonial," meaning that little real change had occurred and that the new indigenous rulers had simply succeeded to the powers and perquisites once enjoyed by the imperial rulers.

Burma

The undisputed leader of Burma at the end of the Japanese occupation was Aung San, student activist in the 1930s, a member of the Thakin group and the Thirty Comrades, initially a supporter of the Japanese, and commander of the

Burma Independence Army, which he turned against the Japanese in the last months of the war. Louis Mountbatten chose to regard him as an ally rather than a collaborator. Aung San became the leader of the Antifascist Peoples' Freedom League (AFPFL), the principal political party and champion of independence.

British plans for Burma called for restoration of peace and order and rehabilitation of the economy before reinstituting the constitution of 1935 and taking further steps toward self-rule. Aung San and the AFPFL rejected these plans and called for independence. Sir Hubert Rance, British governor from August 1946, was well regarded by Aung San. Rance gave Burma's leaders cabinet responsibilities, including control of the budget and the armed forces. These progressive acts culminated in a conference in London in January 1947 at which Britain's labor government agreed to abide by the results of a popular election. The AFPFL won the election and a constituent assembly unanimously adopted a constitution for an independent Burma in September. Burma suffered a severe blow to its political future when in July Aung San and six of his provisional cabinet members were assassinated. No one in Burma equalled Aung San in leadership skills and popular support. More bloodshed followed. Britain nevertheless proceeded with the transfer of power to the Union of Burma on January 4, 1948. Burma was led by U Nu, a superb orator, a well-intentioned person, and a devout Buddhist.

Burma suffered more seriously than most other countries from the problems of independence. It was, and is, a multiethnic society in which such minority peoples as the Kachins, Chins, Kayahs, Karens, and others lack a strong sense of identity with the culture of the dominant Burman population and with the country of Burma. The constitution of 1947 was nominally a federal system, permitting minorities some voice in their affairs. But the minorities wanted more autonomy or even independence. In 1948 a communist rebellion began while a part of the Burmese Army mutinied. The next year, the Karens began an armed revolt. Remnants of the Chinese Nationalist Army fleeing from Chinese communist armies occupied part of northern Burma in the same year and later allied with Shan rebels. The *sangha* was rebellious and undisciplined. The government had difficulty maintaining basic services. The new Union of Burma was, to say the least, in dire circumstances.

U Nu, besides being an ardent Buddhist, was, like virtually all of Burma's elite, a socialist. He regarded Buddhism and socialism as complementary. Conciliation, an important Buddhist principle, was a major theme of Nu's government. He worked hard to accommodate the minorities and believed that Buddha's teachings could heal divisions in Burmese society. He sponsored a Buddhist religious revival, which included the hosting of a two-year-long Theravada Buddhist Great Council. It ended in 1956 on the 2,500th anniversary of the death of the Buddha. In 1961, Buddhism was made the state religion, an action which angered the minorities. U Nu's preoccupation with religion and his efforts to make it a unifying force in Burma's society were politically and economically costly.

Nu's economic policies emphasized state planning and controls, but major private companies were allowed to operate. A land nationalization act was hastily drawn up in 1948 but only slowly implemented because of lack of data and personnel. The intended use of profits from the state's marketing of rice was to develop manufacturing industries. Policies did not work for several reasons. The people appointed to oversee government economic activities had little or no experience. Some key program directors were chosen on the basis of their devotion to Buddism. Inefficiency and corruption, as well as insecurity in the countryside, all reigned at once. Major blunders were admitted in 1957 and a new start made. But again, there was little progress. Rice production and exports revived, but overall the economy did poorly. Burma's war-damaged industries found it difficult to rebuild.

U Nu resigned from the prime minister's position in June 1956 to undertake the reform of the AFPFL, of which he was president. He returned to the office on March 1, 1957, a date said to be astrologically propitious. In 1958 personal rivalries among AFPFL leaders became intense and a power struggle split the Party. U Nu was at the center of this struggle. There was much dissatisfaction with him for his lack of administrative efficiency and decisiveness. In October 1958, he asked General Ne Win to assume temporary power as a "caretaker" government. Ne Win, born in 1911, was the first son of a civil servant and prosperous farmer. He entered the university in Rangoon in 1929. The name his parents gave him was She Maung, meaning "apple of one's eye." But as one of the Thirty Comrades, he took another name, Ne Win, which means "brilliant as the sun." He retained the name after the war ended. General Ne Win ruled with vigor, cleaning up slum areas and putting the Army in charge of a number of state enterprises. Army rule lasted for eighteen months. New elections early in 1960 made U Nu prime minister again, but in increasingly chaotic political conditions, Ne Win deposed U Nu in March 1962.

Ne Win and the Army justified their coup as necessary to "save" the unity of the country. Under the constitution, separate states had been created for the Shan, Kachin, Karen, and Kayah peoples. Ne Win feared the possible secession of one or more of these states and believed that loss of unity would lead to foreign intervention, citing Vietnam as an example. Ne Win suspended the constitution, dissolved state councils, and centralized authority. He was determined to wipe out ethnic representation in political and administrative affairs, and to emphasize national unity. At the same time, several efforts to end insurgencies and to conciliate minorities were unsuccessful. Ne Win sought to force the assimilation of the minority peoples into a common culture and loyalty. Insurgency continued through the 1970s and 1980s.

Ne Win was also unhappy with the ineptness and corruption of the political parties and parliamentary government, which, he said, were controlled by capitalists and landlords. He abolished parliament and ruled with the assistance of a Revolutionary Council of Army officers. Only one political party, a government party, was permitted—the Burma Socialist Programme Party (BSPP). It began as a "cadre" party but after 1971 sought to acquire ancillary mass organizations. Like U Nu, Ne Win was a socialist, but unlike him, he opposed mixing religion and politics. The *sangha*, he said, had misused religion by involving itself in politics. Like the kings of old, he endeavored to get control over the *sangha* by undertaking reforms in the 1960s and again in the 1980s. In an effort to establish a state ideology around which various political factions and ethnic groups could rally, Ne Win published *The Burmese Way to Socialism* (1962). The cumulative result of all this was that Burmese middle class and professional people left the country in large numbers.

The Burmese Way to Socialism set out the military regime's social and economic intentions: to create a "new society for all, economically secure and morally better, to live in peace and prosperity." In January 1963, Ne Win announced a new economic policy—state control and management of production, marketing, and foreign trade. Nationalization of existing enterprises proceeded rapidly. Cooperatives and state corporations were created, and a program of industrialization begun. The Army had had administrative experience and was confident that it could run these enterprises. But the need for good managers was underestimated or not understood, and there were too few for the responsibilities undertaken. Severe dislocations, shortages, black markets, unemployment, corruption, and inflation resulted. Other actions to aid farmers were taken, more cautiously and slowly. But these social and economic intentions of the military did not work well, and matters were made worse by natural disasters such as drought. Exports and foreign exchange earnings declined. Conditions improved somewhat in the late 1960s, but conditions turned bad again in the early 1970s. Ne Win's efforts to apply socialist ideas in the social and economic circumstances of Burma were disastrous.

Ne Win had his opponents. He was determined to end student political activity and in 1962 sought to regulate closely the University of Rangoon. Protesting students were shot down by soldiers and the famous student union building, a symbol of freedom, was dynamited in July. Anti-Chinese rioting occurred in 1967, initially over the wearing of "red badges" by some Chinese. The badges represented support for China's cultural revolution. Because the principal black-marketers were Chinese, townspeople and students attacked Chinese shops and restaurants and even the Chinese embassy. These attacks on the Chinese deflected some popular anger away from the Ne Win government. In December 1974, the "U Thant Affair" occurred. Ne Win and U Thant had long been hostile to each other, and Ne Win refused to provide honors for the deceased U.N. secretary general on the return of his body to Burma. Outraged students seized the casket of Burma's world-famous citizen and placed it on the site of the razed student union. Troops burst through the campus gate, killed many students, and removed the casket. The monks, who had been politically quiet since the mid-1960s, reentered politics by joining student protests.

A new constitution was approved by referendum in December 1973 and made effective on January 4, 1974. Elections were held shortly afterwards for a national one-house Peoples' Assembly and for three levels of Peoples' Councils. The Army's Revolutionary Council disbanded, many high-ranking military officers retired, and the government at least nominally became civilian. But the constitution, in no sense democratic, was designed to keep the military in power. Political peace and stability did not come to Burma. Ne Win and a few others continued to exercise real power. Ne Win repeatedly cloaked his actions in the mantle of Aung San, saying that had the dead hero lived, he would act as Ne Win acted. He also conducted himself in a manner reminiscent of Burmese kings. Ultimately, of course, Ne Win relied for his power on the Army's loyalty to him.

An economic policy paper presented at the BSPP first congress in 1971 became the basis of economic action in the rest of the decade. It reversed industrialization aims and played to Burma's strengths, concentrating on improvement of agriculture and fisheries and the extraction of Burma's mineral resources. It called for administrative reforms and invited private and foreign investors. To some degree, pragmatism was substituted for doctrinaire socialism.

In the late 1970s, the economy improved and Burmese became cautiously optimistic. In large part, improvement was the result of rising rice production, which had been spurred by the introduction in Burma and elsewhere in Southeast Asia of high-yielding, hybrid rice. The new rice was developed at the International Rice Research Institute (supported by the Rockefeller Foundation) in the Philippines. Unfortunately, fundamental economic and political problems were not addressed, and by the mid-1980s the economy was in decline again. The black market based on smuggled goods became the real economy. Inflation revived. Economic chaos and ultimately economic paralysis occurred.

In foreign relations, Ne Win believed Burma to be self-reliant. In 1962, he terminated U.S. and Russian technical assistance programs. Fearing that Burma might be drawn into a major war, he adhered to a policy of nonalignment and limited Burma's contacts with the world. Foreign diplomats were restricted in their movements in Burma; journalists and visitors were frequently denied entry to the country. Because of his association with Japan during the days of the Thirty Comrades, and because Japan gave Burma economic assistance as well as a gift of a center for the study of spirits and the occult (a subject of keen interest to Ne Win), Ne Win maintained relations with Japan. But otherwise, over the next two decades, Burma became increasingly isolated.

In September 1987, Ne Win took two actions which served to make the economy more chaotic in the short run. He deregulated grain markets and demonetized the currency. At the end of the year, the United Nations confirmed that Burma had become one of the world's poorest and most backward countries by declaring it to be a "least developed nation." This classification is given to countries with low levels of literacy, per capita incomes of under U.S. $200 per year, and in which economic conditions are so bad as to almost preclude the possibility of economic development. The Japanese government also told Burma, in April 1988, that if it did not undertake economic reforms, Japanese assistance would be reconsidered.

In the meantime, in March 1988, a dispute between students and a teashop owner in Rangoon led to a riot that was put down with excessive force. The brutality sparked a series of explosive demonstrations. A tired and impoverished people rose up, seeking to end years of mismanagement and oppression. The protests spread from Bangkok to Mandalay and other cities. A series of "letters to Ne Win," highly critical of the regime, circulated. Ne Win, who had the title of president, resigned on July 25. His choice to succeed him, an Army general much detested by the people, provoked further demonstrations by arresting prominent critics. In late August and September, the government made concessions, but it had lost control. Chaos reigned.

For several days, soldiers reportedly fired their weapons more or less indiscriminately into crowds of civilians. But the people refused to be cowed. In the countryside, local governments were replaced by prodemocracy monks and townspeople. A revolution was under way, and many Burmese were optimistic that political and economic change for the better was at hand.

But this was not to be. On September 18, 1988, a group of military officers seized power. They called themselves the State Law and Order Restoration Council (SLORC). Ten of its eighteen members had no more than a primary education. The BSPP was disbanded, the law banning political parties lifted, and democratic elections promised. At the same time, SLORC ruthlessly suppressed public demonstrations. Thousands of young people fled to the border regions, especially to the Thai border, there to take up arms. General Khin Nyunt, chief of military intelligence, emerged as the most powerful leader of SLORC. University educated, he was reputed to be Ne Win's protégé. In 1989, Burma was renamed Myanmar, an ancient and literary term for the country; Rangoon became Yangon.

The promised elections were held in May 1990. Campaign conditions were repressive, but to everyone's amazement, the National League for Democracy (NLD) won 80 percent of the seats. The leader of the NLD was Aung San Suu Kyi, the daughter of national hero Aung San, wife of an Oxford University professor. Under house arrest since 1989, she later won the Nobel Peace Prize (1991). SLORC was stunned by the election because they had believed that with many parties contesting there would be no clear result and continued military rule would be necessary. SLORC simply refused to transfer power and, in July 1990, declared it would continue to rule. There were many arrests of NLD and other party leaders.

Opposition did not cease. In September 1990, several thousand members of the *sangha* met in Mandalay to commemorate the 1988 prodemocracy uprisings. Army troops attacked the gathering; monks retaliated with a ritual boycott of the military (refusing to offer spiritual merit-making opportunities to officers and soldiers). Some shopkeepers refused to sell to soldiers. In 1991 and 1992, first the U.N. General Assembly and then the U.N. Human Rights Commission rejected SLORC's explanation of its domestic acts. SLORC argued that the popular revolution of 1988 was in reality a communist plot and that only its quick action saved the nation.

Concerned about the economy and probably about Burma's pariah status among nations, SLORC in 1992 began to relax its grip but only a little. It released some political prisoners, ended martial law, lifted a daily curfew, reopened colleges and universities, allowed a few foreign reporters entry into the country, and invited foreign investment. It lifted economic controls and permitted more market freedom. Bumper rice crops were reported. The development of large deposits of offshore natural gas was agreed upon. Efforts were made to fix up Rangoon, Mandalay, and other long-neglected cities. New buildings were erected and large numbers of people were forcibly moved out of cities into new satellite towns. A commission began in January 1993 to draw up principles on which a new constitution would be written. Commission members were told that they must provide a central role for the military.

In the meantime, students, politicians, monks and members of the minorities assembled in Karen-held territory on the Thai-Burma border and formed the Democratic Alliance of Burma (DAB) and a government in exile. Aung San Suu Kyi remained under house arrest in Rangoon. SLORC repeatedly urged her to leave the country; she agreed to do so but on conditions which were unacceptable to SLORC.

After repeated earlier failures of SLORC military campaigns against the DAB early in 1995, the SLORC was reportedly successful, with many DAB killed, their bases captured. Their survival was in doubt. SLORC campaigns spilled over into Thailand, resulting in the destruction of Thai villages and the killing of Thai civilians.

SLORC had come to rely on the People's Republic of China (PRC) as its principal trading partner and ally. In September 1988, SLORC agreed to open its border with China to trade. Many other agreements followed. Besides consumer goods, Chinese people by the tens of thousands have moved into northern Burma, transforming Mandalay. Burma and China have also cooperated on road- and bridge-building projects along their border. The PRC has provided more than a billion U.S. dollars worth of arms to a much enlarged Burmese army. The PRC was rumored to want SLORC to agree to a Chinese naval base on the Bay of Bengal. The rapid growth of a large Chinese presence in Burma has been a cause of concern to India and to Southeast Asian governments. At the same time, SLORC efforts began to end civil war with ethnic minorities in the name of "national conciliation" by offering them some autonomy in trade and education. Unfortunately, these efforts have aided the increased production of opium and heroin, of which Burma in the "golden triangle" is the world's largest producer. While the SLORC has taken U.N. money for antidrug programs, it and Burmese Army officers in the border areas have shared handsomely in profits from this business.

SLORC's efforts to attract foreign investment were succeeding, at least on a modest scale. Neighboring Southeast Asian countries, rejecting U.S. appeals to act, have largely avoided criticizing SLORC. Instead, Singapore and other countries have invested in Burma, calling their actions "constructive engagement" and the "Asian Way." Police-state conditions notwithstanding, western cruise ships began calling at Rangoon, and tours to ancient Pagan were becoming popular.

Indonesia

On the conclusion of World War II, the Netherlands was determined to resume its rule over the Netherlands East Indies (NEI). But, on August 17, 1945, six weeks before Allied forces were able to land in Indonesia, Indonesia's nationalist leaders declared the country an independent republic.

Revolution followed until December 1949, when the Netherlands finally transferred sovereignty to Indonesia. West New Guinea, a part of the NEI, remained in dispute until it became a part of Indonesia as Irian Jaya in 1963. In 1976, Indonesia annexed Portuguese Timor, a controversial action, which as late as 1995 was yet to be recognized by the United Nations.

The revolution was the single greatest event in modern Indonesian history. It was accompanied by large and mostly spontaneous expressions of popular patriotism and nationalism. Young people joined the *pemuda* movement. *Pemuda* means youth, but in the revolution it came to mean revolutionary, patriotic youth. The *pemuda* consisted of mostly local groups, often with charismatic leaders. They advanced the Revolution by undertaking many deeds, some peaceful but many violent. In the name of *merdeka*, or freedom, traditional rulers who had served the Dutch were overthrown. Many Chinese and Eurasians who were thought to be part of the old colonial order were killed. British troops, who had preceded Dutch troops, were attacked and held in coastal enclaves. The Revolution substituted new meanings for old terms, introduced new ideas, and created many heroes, a national army, and an outpouring of art and literature.

Independent Indonesia was ruled by Sukarno as president and Mohammad Hatta as vice-president, a Supreme Advisory Council and a People's Deliberative Assembly. Batavia became Jakarta; a national motto, "Unity in Diversity," and a national creed, the *Pancasila*, were adopted. The *Pancasila* consisted of five principles: belief in the one and only God; a just and civilized society; Indonesian unity; democracy guided by the inner wisdom of representatives' deliberations; and social justice. The hastily written constitution of 1945 gave power primarily to the president. Another provisional constitution written in 1950 established a unitary state (as compared to a federal one) and a parliamentary democracy on the European model. The first elections were held in 1955 with some thirty parties contesting. Four parties divided about equally some 80 percent of the votes. These were the Indonesian Nationalist Party (PNI), the Masjumi (Federation of Muslim Organizations), the Nahdatul Ulama (Federation of Muslim Scholars), and the Indonesian Communist Party (PKI). The PKI showing was remarkable in that, in 1948 at Madiun in Java during the fight against the Dutch, the communists had failed at an attempted coup against the nationalists. No party had anything near a majority.

Politics were fragmented, and this period of "liberal democracy," as it was called, did not function well. The Army became impatient, and commanders in Sumatra and Sulawesi seized power from local governments. In part their action was motivated by an older resentment by "Outer Island" people of the domination of Java. The economy did poorly, the communists grew in strength, and the government in Jakarta had little authority. Efforts to write a permanent constitution failed.

In mid-1959, President Sukarno reintroduced the 1945 constitution and announced "Guided Democracy." He had for several years expressed dissatisfaction with the principal of majority rule, saying that it was not an Asian or Indonesian principal. Political parties had not served the people well. Elections had been exploited by various groups to grab wealth. The spirit of the Indonesian Revolution, he said, had almost disappeared. He wanted a system like the traditional village way of making decisions—consultation, discussion, and consensus. He, Sukarno, understood the Indonesian people, and his voice was their voice. Now he would guide the country. Subsequently, certain political parties were made illegal, political leaders were arrested, the press curtailed.

This period of Guided Democracy has been described as a descent into chaos. Sukarno ruled by decree and slogan, drawing support from the armed forces—namely, *Angkatan Bersenjata Republik Indonesia* (ABRI), which controlled much of the country's administrative machinery—and from the PKI with its many labor unions, women's, and youth organizations. Many new words and acronyms were added to the then current political jargon for new ideas and organizations, most of which seemed to accomplish little. Sukarno also began the construction of a number of costly buildings and monuments, "show" projects, in Jakarta. In the early 1960s, Indonesia's armed forces were reorganized, modernized, and expanded with large quantities of weapons supplied by the Soviet Union.

In 1963, Sukarno opposed the formation of Malaysia, contending that it was a British creation, an imperialist, neocolonial plot. Indonesia protested in sessions of the United Nations and temporarily resigned from that body when the U.N. recognized Malaysia. Sukarno then made war against Malaysia. In international affairs, Indonesia had established its neutralist credentials by hosting the 1955 "Bandung Conference" of twenty-nine African and Asian nations. These countries sought peace and ways to avoid big power and cold war politics. Sukarno now modified Indonesia's nonaligned foreign policy not only by declaring war on Malaysia, but also by denouncing the United States and other western nations as imperialist and developing close relationships with the PRC.

The economy declined further and by 1965 inflation was out of control. Sensing the loss of ABRI support, Sukarno relied increasingly on the PKI, which had become the largest communist party in Asia after that of the PRC. Sukarno's turn to the communists disturbed many Indonesians and especially Army officers. Now old and tired, Sukarno lost some of his charisma and spent much of his time in the company of beautiful young women.

A coup, attempted on October 1, 1965, was suppressed by General Suharto. While the coup's origins and purposes are debated, it was officially attributed to the communists. In the weeks that followed, hundreds of thousands of communists were killed, mostly by civilians but with the encouragement and support of the Army. The opportunity was also taken to settle old ethnic scores, and many Chinese died. A fictionalized account of these events was provided in the motion picture, *The Year of Living Dangerously*.

Early in 1967, Sukarno was persuaded to transfer his authority to Suharto. Suharto, seeking to play down what was in effect military rule, donned civilian clothes and was elected president in 1968. To help legitimize his rule, he brought Sultan Hamengku Buwoni IX of Yogyakarta into his government as vice president. The sultan was a highly respected national figure; unlike most of his aristocratic colleagues, he had opposed the Dutch. Suharto called his government the New Order.

The New Order had a passion for political stability and economic growth. Politically, it placed reliance on ABRI and on *Golongan Karya,* or Golkar, an organization of functional groups such as the Army, civil servants, women's organizations, and youth groups. Golkar was, and is, a state political party. Because existing political parties—advocates of ideologies—were considered divisive, they were severely curtailed and then made to consolidate. Suharto sought to keep Indonesia a secular state and keep religion out of politics. Since 1983, the Indonesian parliament has required all political parties to adopt the *Pancasila* as the basis for their political philosophy.

Initially cautious and conciliatory, Suharto became more confident and authoritarian as time passed. Parliament passed few laws; the president ruled by decree. Elections were managed; the press, censored; and opponents, imprisoned. At the same time, economic gains were impressive, and a growing urban middle and professional class tended to be supportive of the New Order. But by the end of the 1980s, they became critical and their desire for more political freedom became obvious. In response, Suharto occasionally relaxed his grip a bit and encouraged discussion, saying that differences of opinion were desirable and legitimate. There was much talk in the early 1990s of *keterbukaan*, or openness, in politics. Golkar won 68 percent of the popular vote in parliamentary elections in June 1992, and Suharto was elected for a sixth five-year-term in March 1993. Thereafter, openness came to an end and the regime tightened its control of the media, closing *Tempo*, Indonesia's most popular weekly news magazine, and other journals.

Economically, Suharto inherited a mess. A pragmatist, he quickly turned to the industrialized countries and Indonesia's wealthy Chinese, successfully promoting investment. On the initiative of the United States, the Intergovernmental Group on Indonesia (IGGI) was founded in 1967. Composed of western powers and Japan, the IGGI provided advice and capital essential to the expansion of the Indonesian economy. The IGGI was disbanded in 1992 when Indonesia objected to an effort to link continued assistance to the improvement of human rights in Indonesia. It was replaced, however, with the Consultative Group on Indonesia (CGI), which performed essentially the same role.

Suharto made use of Indonesian "technocrats," western-educated economists, and other professionals to study, plan, and direct economic development. To the exploitation of Indonesia's rich natural resources—oil, natural gas, coal, copper, nickel, tin, timber, rubber—were added major manufacturing enterprises, including steel, chemicals, weapons, and passenger aircraft. Banking, shipping, and tourism developed into major industries as well. Indonesia became self-sufficient in rice. The increased use of mechanical power on rice lands made landowners richer and contributed to rural unemployment. The patron-client system disappeared or was weakened. A further result was massive migration to the cities where some country people got jobs in newly built factories but many became "squatters," living in shantytowns on the edges of cities. By the mid-1990s, Indonesia had experienced more than a quarter century of economic growth. Many ordinary Indonesians as well as the growing professional classes had benefited. Suharto was called "Father of Development."

The Indonesian economic growth has been driven by the large part played by the government in the economy. Under the constitution it must control those parts of the economy important to the welfare of the people. It has created, planned, set priorities, invested public funds, and managed enterprises. It continues to own shares in many companies. Government participation in the economy has also been accompanied by waste, poor management, corruption, and political patronage. In 1974, Pertamina, the government oil company, was rocked by scandal involving billions of dollars. Suharto and his family have reportedly grown very rich by using his position for personal gain. Army officers were taken more fully into government as governors and ambassadors and into the economy as businessmen. Army officers became silent partners of Indonesian-Chinese businessmen to the financial benefit of both.

In the mid-1990s, Indonesians pondered some major questions. Who might succeed Suharto, now in his '70s, and would the succession be peaceful? Was there likely to be more individual liberty and freedom of expression? Would the growing concentration of wealth and the widening gap between rich and poor be halted and perhaps even reduced? What roles might Indonesia play in Asian and world affairs?

The Philippines

The Japanese conquest and occupation of the Philippines, followed by U.S. reconquest, left the country in an economic shambles. Nevertheless, many Filipinos were pleased to be rid of Japanese rule and there was general pleasure at the return of the United States. Disappointment quickly followed for many Filipinos. General Douglas MacArthur embraced the wealthy landowners and businessmen, some of whom had collaborated with the Japanese. At the same time, he rebuffed the guerrillas who had fought the Japanese. He disbanded the *Hukbalahaps,* or Huks, the People's Anti-Japanese Army, and arrested its leader, Luis Taruc. Taruc was later released and elected to the Philippine legislature but was denied his seat. The Huks, bitter over their treatment and capitalizing on official corruption and rural poverty, launched a rebellion in 1948. Taruc declared himself a communist. The Huks soon controlled most of central Luzon and began collecting taxes and performing government functions.

In the meantime, the United States fulfilled its promise of independence, transferring power on July 4, 1946. Many Filipinos were unhappy over conditions the United States attached to the transfer of power. U.S. payments for war damages, for example, were conditioned on U.S. investors having access equal to that of Filipinos to the development of Philippine natural resources through 1974. Equal access required an amendment to the Philippine constitution. It barely passed. Legislators who probably would have voted no were barred from taking their seat. Filipinos believed the constitutional amendment compromised Philippine sovereignty. Another condition was that there be free trade between the United States and the Philippines for eight years. Free trade was important to Filipino sugar producers because it gave them duty-free access to the United States. The effect was to tie much of the country's economy to the U.S. American naval and air bases at Subic Bay and Clark Field, and many smaller military installations were retained.

Political power in the Philippine Republic has been exercised by wealthy families known as oligarchs. Politics has been, essentially, a struggle between the oligarch families, well-educated, conservative, and Christian. The basis of their wealth is the ownership and control of large tracts of land on which live tenants from whom they receive rents. The oligarchs were supporters of the U.S. colonial administration. Then and now, they have held important positions that they have used to gain entry into many other businesses and increase their wealth. Their ownership of land is also a basis for their political power. A hierarchy of patron-client relationships running from these families down to the smallest villages delivers the vote in elections.

The oligarchs have usually held the presidency. One exception was Ramon Magsaysay. Of humble origins, Magsaysay was a guerrilla fighter during the Japanese occupation. He won election for president in 1953 with the help of U.S. officials who wanted to work through him to fight the Huks. Magsaysay did deal the Huks a setback by offering amnesty and land to those who surrendered and promising strong military action against those who did not. He endeavored to introduce land reform, eliminate corruption in government, and introduce other positive measures. He died in an airplane crash in 1957.

In the 1960s, lawlessness grew and the rich created private armies. Society was disintegrating. Communism revived in the form of the Communist Party of the Philippines (CPP) and its auxiliary, the New Peoples Army (NPA). In 1962, the Philippine government objected to the proposed formation of Malaysia, not on the same neocolonial ground of Indonesia's objection but rather that Sabah, formerly North Borneo, was a part of the domain of the rulers of the Sulu Archipelago which was a part of the Philippines. In 1967, the Muslim Nationalist League, later the Moro National Liberation Front (MNLF), was organized among Muslims in Mindanao and Sulu partly in response to their sense that Manila treated them as colonial subjects. The MNLF was supported by Libya and Tun Mustapha, Malaysian chief minister of Sabah, who had Filipino connections.

Ferdinand Marcos became president in 1965, campaigning against corruption and portraying himself as savior of the country. In his second term in 1972, he proclaimed martial law, justifying his action by declaring that communists were plotting to seize power. Marcos introduced the "New Society," an attempt to address Filipino problems. Too much emphasis, said Marcos, had been placed on the individual and individual rights. The result was selfishness and greed and a breakdown of society. Like Sukarno and Ne Win in the early 1960s, Marcos argued that democracy was wasteful, promoted corruption, and yielded little progress. The answer was a more authoritarian government. He urged people to put community needs ahead of personal interests.

To this end, Marcos vigorously restored order, made thousands of arrests, and crushed critics and opponents. He curtailed the freedom of the press, disbanded private armies, confiscated hundreds of thousands of guns, and greatly enlarged the regular Army. He ended the nonpolitical tradition of the Army by bringing its officers into public affairs and giving them positions in which they could make themselves wealthy. He began a land reform program in 1973 that, however, exempted the sugar and coconut properties of the oligarchs. He introduced a new constitution that gave himself supreme power and created a political organization reaching from his office down to the smallest village. By 1976, both the NPA and the MNLF had been beaten back. In foreign policy, Marcos sought less intimacy with the United States and closer links to third world countries.

Law and order attracted investments and tourists. The oligarchs and Marcos's "cronies" grew richer. Big industrial projects were begun because Marcos wanted them, whether they made business sense or not. Debt to foreign banks and external lending agencies soared. Marcos gained personally from contracts let to major corporations. His personal wealth in New York City real estate, Swiss banks, and elsewhere was allegedly in excess of U.S. $1 billion. Marcos's attractive wife, Imelda, shared power and the spoils. She headed many government agencies and was governor of Manila. In the meantime, millions of Filipinos suffered unemployment, landlessness, homelessness, and malnutrition. Concerned about foreign criticism of his rule, Marcos ended martial law in January 1981 and stood for election. President Bush praised Marcos for his support for democracy. But Marcos's actions were for show; his power hardly diminished.

In the 1980s it became apparent that Marcos was seriously ill, and political maneuvering began among possible successors. The leading candidate and a sharp critic of Marcos was Benigno Aquino, popularly known as "Ninoy." In August 1983, Aquino returned to the Philippines from exile in the United States, risking danger to himself. He was shot and killed leaving the plane in Manila by one of the guards sent to protect him. The deed was ascribed to Marcos. It was the beginning of the end for the Marcos regime. Rich Filipinos began to move their money out of the country; many Filipino professionals left for the United States and elsewhere. Foreign creditors sought repayment of loans. The banking system and the economy virtually collapsed.

The martyrdom of Aquino turned the rich and influential Catholic Church against Marcos. The Church was conservative and generally supported the oligarchs, although it had a small number of "radical clergy" siding with the CCP on social and economic issues. Led by Cardinal Jaime Sin, the people rallied around Aquino's widow, Corazon, or "Cory." A member of a wealthy oligarch family, she was shy and unassuming and was drawn reluctantly into politics. With the help of the Church, a "People Power" movement was organized to make her president. Marcos, confident his political machine would win for him, allowed the press considerable freedom and even invited foreign observers. Marcos did win, but amidst charges of fraud. A popular revolution followed with hundreds of thousands of Filipinos in Manila's streets, converging on the Presidential Palace. Soldiers defending the palace refused to shoot. Helicopters rescued Marcos, his family, and a few friends, flying them all to Clark Field. Marcos accepted asylum in Hawaii. Cory Aquino became president on February 25, 1986. A more democratic constitution was introduced. She successfully stood for election in 1987 to confirm that she was the people's choice.

Well-intentioned, she attempted to dismantle the New Society while fighting off several coup attempts. During her administration, the question of U.S. military bases, long a sore issue for many Filipinos, was finally resolved, partly by the Philippine Senate voting the Americans out.

In elections held in May 1992, General Fidel Ramos, Aquino's defense secretary, won the presidency by a slim margin in a field of seven candidates. A West Point graduate, experienced, articulate and with a reputation for honesty, Ramos gave people hope for better government. Indeed, he assumed office as a reformer and sought to reorganize the bureaucracy, the police, the central bank, and other government operations as well as to improve the climate for foreign investment. Referring to the oligarchs and "crony capitalism," Ramos implied that they had to go, declaring that Philippine national survival was at stake. The country could not survive, he said, if the masses of poor people saw their opportunities dwindling while an elite few steadily increased their wealth and control of the economy. Ramos forced the Cojuangco family to relinquish its control over two of the Philippines' largest corporations, including the Philippine Long-Distance Telephone Company. More "de-monopolization" steps were promised. Although critics were impatient and called him indecisive, early returns in national elections in May 1995 appeared to give Ramos a fresh mandate as well as control of both houses of the Philippine Congress. Such a decisive victory would enable him to renew his efforts at economic reform.

Filipinos suffer from extreme poverty, unemployment, underemployment, low wages, indebtedness, landlessness, tenancy, serious malnutrition, and a high rate of population increase. Poverty drives many abroad to low-paying jobs as laborers and domestic servants in countries from Singapore to Saudi Arabia. More than two million Filipinos worked overseas at the end of 1994. They were often badly treated in the countries in which they worked. Flora Contemplacion, working as a maid in Singapore in 1994, was convicted of murder—unfairly in Filipino popular opinion. Her execution made her name a rallying cry for the Filipino poor. The case has also strained Philippine-Singapore relations.

Vietnam

Ho Chi Minh declared the independent Democratic Republic of Vietnam (DRV) on September 2, 1945, before the return of French troops. In the ceremony, he referred to the U.S. Declaration of Independence and the French Declaration of the Rights of Man. Ho was bright, clever, and popular. A communist, he was also a pragmatist. The Indochina Communist Party was small and its socialist program of limited appeal. In an attempt to appeal to nationalists as well as socialists and to broaden his political base, Ho had founded in 1941 the Vietnamese Independence Brotherhood League, better known as the Vietminh. Its objective was first to establish a middle class democratic republic and later a socialist society.

France did not agree to an independent Vietnam and in December 1946 began a military effort to reimpose its rule. The DRV, on its side, aimed to force France out of Indochina (Vietnam, Cambodia, and Laos). After three years of fighting with little to show, France, with the urging of the United States, granted Vietnam "independence" on June 14, 1949. Bao Dai, former emperor of Vietnam, was made head of state. The "nightclub emperor" had little power and was not much respected by the Vietnamese. The war continued.

Events in 1949 and 1950 external to Vietnam powerfully influenced the subsequent course of the war. In China, the Communists defeated the Nationalists and on October 1, 1949, established the People's Republic of China. A treaty between the PRC and Russia followed. The Korean War began in 1950, and the PRC joined the side of North Korea. In the United States, the "loss" of China became an angry domestic political issue and Congress vowed its intention of stopping the global spread of communism. Later U.S. officials and politicians would fear being charged with responsibility for further losses of territory to communism. Early in 1950, the PRC and the Soviet Union recognized the DRV while the United States and Britain recognized the Bao Dai government. The Vietnamese struggle for independence was thus caught up in the "cold war."

In spite of massive U.S. assistance, the war went badly for France, and, by 1954, many French were ready to end it. Negotiations began in Geneva in late April. The major powers were present. In the meantime, a battle had begun for the village of Din Binh Phu, northwest of Hanoi. The French had made the place a fortress and staked their prestige and future in Indochina on winning. The DRV forces were led by General Vo Nguyen Giap, a former schoolteacher, later hailed by some western analysts as one of the great generals of the twentieth century. The French arrogantly underestimated the abilities of their enemy. Giap made deadly use of American artillery supplied by the PRC which it had captured in the war with the Nationalists. A French call for U.S. military intervention at Din Binh Phu was rejected. The village fell on May 7, 1954.

The Geneva Conference ended in late July. It made peace and provided for: temporary military regroupment zones, the Vietminh to the north and the French to the south of the 17th parallel; national elections reunifying the country in two years; and an International Control Commission to supervise arrangements. For a limited period, civilian movements were not restricted and many thousands of Vietnamese Catholics and anticommunists in the north moved south. Although the Geneva Agreements gave the DRV less than its military achievements seemed to warrant, Ho Chi Minh appeared to take consolation in the promised national elections. The United States did not give its official assent to the Geneva Agreements because the results were unlikely to produce the kind of Vietnam the U.S. policy planners had in mind. There was also a concern about political reaction in the United States to giving up more Asian territory to communists.

At the end of June, a month before the Geneva Conference ended, Ngo Dinh Diem arrived in Saigon with Vietnamese and American aides. Diem, a Catholic, a bona fide nationalist, and a vigorous anticommunist, came from a mandarin family. He had earlier left Vietnam and taken refuge with the Maryknoll religious order in New Jersey. The U.S. Central Intelligence Agency (CIA) and the U.S. military establishment seemed to think highly of him, while the U.S. State Department had doubts. With the help of bribes, Ngo Dinh Diem was appointed prime minister in the Bao Dai government. A year later, in a rigged referendum, Diem got rid of Bao Dai. On October 26, 1955, he declared the Republic of Vietnam (RVN) and made himself president. He initiated sweeping arrests of suspected communists and refused to proceed with the Geneva-prescribed national elections.

The installation of Diem in Saigon was part of a larger U.S. policy of containing the spread of communism throughout the world. Containment, backed by the North Atlantic Treaty Organization (NATO), had blocked Russian expansion in Europe. Now Southeast Asia with its newly independent states looked vulnerable, especially with communists in power in China. The U.S. feared that if Vietnam became communist, other states in Southeast Asia would fall one by one, like dominoes, to communism. The United States had successfully intervened in other countries such as Greece, Iran, and the Philippines to stop communism. Why not now in Vietnam? Some argued that the earlier interventions were different in that none had directly confronted a war for national independence as appeared to be the case in Vietnam. But the American decision makers saw only communism and were confident that the United States could succeed where the French had failed.

The goal of U.S. involvement then, at least initially, was to establish in the south the Republic of Vietnam (RVN), noncommunist and linked to the United States. In due course, the United States hoped that the RVN would be able to absorb the DRV, thus reunifying the country under anticommunist leadership. The creation of a separate, sovereign state in the south violated the Geneva Agreements but was justified by its proponents because the alternative was believed to be a single communist Vietnam. The premise of U.S. policy was that Ho and the Vietminh were communists and part of an expanding global movement rather than patriots engaged in a struggle for national independence. As a legal means to permit possible armed intervention, the United States formed a regional defense organization, the Southeast Asia Treaty Organization (SEATO), in September 1954. Only three Asian countries joined: Thailand, the Philippines, and Pakistan. The Indochina states were precluded from joining by the Geneva Agreements, but in a protocol to the SEATO treaty, the United States declared that the treaty's provisions extended to the three states.

Diem was not without his own goals. He regarded Vietnam's problems and the rise of the communists as the result of the breakdown of morals and a weakening of values. Thus, he mounted campaigns against alcoholism, prostitution, gambling, and opium smoking. Confucian virtues were emphasized, temples built, and the birthday of Confucius made a national holiday. This contrasted sharply with the DRV, which sought to eradicate Confucianism. Diem mixed traditional Vietnamese ideas with modern, western ones. Madame Nhu, the wife of Ngo Dinh Nhu, the most powerful of Diem's brothers, induced Diem to introduce a family law which gave some rights to women but also made divorce almost impossible.

The United States soon encountered problems with their protégé. While the United States promoted economic and social reforms and encouraged Diem to broaden his political base, Diem undercut these efforts. He did not believe in representative government and sought to monopolize political power in himself and his family. Indeed, he acted as if he wanted to establish a new imperial dynasty. He created his own covert political apparatus to identify, spy on, and get rid of his enemies. Diem could not tolerate criticism and responded to it with arbitrary arrests. He provoked widespread discontent in the rural areas. Urban discontent was attenuated by the growing prosperity of the middle class, who profited from the war and from U.S. financial support for the RVN. Diem was distrustful, stubborn, and politically inept. A coup attempted in 1960 failed.

Diem initially paid little attention to the Buddhists, while they came to resent him and rule by a Christian minority. In 1963, Diem enforced a law which forbid the display of religious banners on the occasion of the celebration of the Buddha's birthday. But some days earlier, Catholics had displayed banners at a ceremony honoring the Catholic archbishop of Hue, another of Diem's brothers. Buddhists flew their banners anyway, and Diem's troops opened fire, killing and wounding a number of people. The act radicalized the Buddhists and they began protests, including acts of self-immolation by monks. Madame Nhu callously referred to these acts as "barbecues." Diem responded with a violent campaign, raiding Buddhist temples and arresting hundreds of monks, some of whom were killed. The shock waves were felt all the way to Washington, D.C. Diem believed he was indispensable to the United States, but now his days were numbered. In November, Army officers led by General Duong Van Minh with the help of the U.S. State Department conducted a successful coup in which Diem and his brother, Nhu, were killed. Minh, like his successors, had fought for the French in the years 1946–1954.

North of the 17th parallel, the DRV was slow to react to the creation of the RVN and to Diem's actions for several reasons, including their own preoccupation with governing. They had undertaken land reform measures in 1954. Larger landowners were made to give up some of their land to those without land.

Mistakes in identification of landowners were made, and steps were taken in 1956 to rectify those mistakes. Irrigation works were built, rice production rose, and optimism prevailed among farmers. In 1958 collectivization of agriculture was begun through the creation of cooperatives. Genuine gains were made in spreading literacy and improving peoples' health. The status of women was improved in law but only partially in practice. Intellectual and other criticisms were suppressed, and the Communist Party was purged.

The Geneva peace began to crumble in 1957 with the assassination of a number of Diem's local officials. The first major military action occurred in January 1960 when insurgents, led by a woman named Nguyen Thi Dinh, took control of three districts in the Mekong Delta. Then, in December 1960, the National Front for the Liberation of South Vietnam (NLF) or Vietcong was formed. The NLF was an alternative southern government with a set of goals designed to appeal to communist and noncommunist alike, including the ultimate reunification of the country. The relationship between the NLF and the DRV was unclear, but it appears the NLF was formed more quickly than the DRV wished. The NLF also appeared to have much autonomy in the early 1960s. By the end of 1962, two-thirds of the countryside was reported to be under NLF control. Nguyen Thi Dinh later became deputy chief of all NLF forces in South Vietnam.

Minh proved to be popular and able as well as somewhat independent. U.S. agencies in the RVN were badly divided. The military, which had favored Diem and reportedly had not been consulted in his overthrow, was angry with the State Department and displeased with Minh's unwillingness to follow some of its advice. Alleging that Minh sought a political rather than a military solution and that he was "neutralist leaning," the U.S. military encouraged and helped organize a successful coup against him on January 30, 1964, a little more than a year after the overthrow of Diem.

By the end of 1964, U.S. officials were unhappy with Minh's successor and some began to consider another coup. From the U.S. point of view, the situation in the RVN was deteriorating rapidly. Vietnamese public opinion was against continued war. Popular poems, stories, and songs told of the tragedies of war, a longing for peace, love of country, and the hope for reunification of north and south. RVN government officials talked of negotiating with the DRV. Buddhists pressed for a negotiated peace. Officers of the ARVN fought with each other. South Vietnam was on the brink of political chaos.

Over the winter months of 1964–1965, discouraged U.S. policymakers admitted to themselves that they had failed and that the United States was on a course of defeat. They talked about how the humiliation of defeat would be disastrous for U.S. policies elsewhere in the world. Their reputations and places in history were also of concern to them. Options presented to President Lyndon Johnson were few; negotiating a settlement was not one of them. It was decided to make the cost of continued war extremely high—so high that the NLF and DRV would be convinced that they could not win, cease military actions, and accept the RVN. The legal basis for U.S. military escalation lay in the SEATO treaty as well as in the Tonkin Gulf Resolution passed by the U.S. Congress in August 1964. It authorized the president to take all necessary steps to repel armed attack and aggression in Southeast Asia. Congress acted on the basis of a report that two

U.S. destroyers in international waters had been attacked by a North Vietnamese torpedo boat. The report, which originated with the U.S. Navy or U.S. intelligence authorities, was later shown to be spurious.

An effort systematically to destroy North Vietnam by bombing began early in 1965. On the ground in South Vietnam, the U.S. Army pushed the ARVN aside and took over responsibility for the war. Search and destroy missions and napalm bombing began. The CIA launched "Operation Phoenix" which aimed at killing village-level communist officials. Giant B-52 bombers began missions on targets in South Vietnam. The result of these and other programs was the destruction in the south of thousands of homes and crops and the deaths of tens of thousands of people. Refugees poured into the cities from rural areas. By the end of 1967, more than a half million American soldiers were fighting in South Vietnam. U.S. forces were augmented by troops from South Korea, Australia, New Zealand, the Philippines, and Thailand. In that year, the forces of the DRV came south and took over the conduct of the war from the NLF. U.S. officers marvelled at the tenacity of their enemy and its ability to recruit replacements and maintain fighting morale. Many found this tenacity inexplicable, not understanding or not accepting that, communist or not, the Vietnamese were patriots, fighting for their national independence. The U.S. military, like the French before them, continued to underestimate their enemy and continued to have confidence that U.S. technically superior weapons would win the war.

The United States did change in one respect. It no longer told itself that it was fighting in support of a popular, viable RVN against the aggression of the DRV. A military junta took power in 1965 whose members were cooperative with the United States but represented no one but themselves. In June 1967, under a new, American-style constitution, General Nguyen Van Thieu became chief of state of the Republic of Vietnam. His prime minister was air force chief, Nguyen Cao Ky, an unabashed advocate of a larger, more vigorously fought war by the United States. In the meantime, the ARVN suffered numerous defeats at the hands of the Vietcong and was deemed by U.S. military authorities to be ineffective.

The success of tremendous U.S. military efforts were called into question when Vietcong and DRV troops launched a coordinated attack throughout the RVN on January 30, 1968, the beginning of the Vietnamese lunar new year or "Tet." The attacks were nearly everywhere successful, the communists holding several cities for a week or more. The U.S. Embassy in Saigon was captured and held for a number of hours. The bloody horrors of Tet, watched on television in the United States, gave a tremendous fillip to mounting American opinion against the war. Later in 1968, the United States began negotiations with the DRV in Paris.

Finally in 1973, Richard Nixon's secretary of state, Henry Kissinger, agreed to a peace treaty. While providing for the withdrawal of U.S. forces, it allowed the Viet Minh to keep its armed forces in South Vietnam. The ARVN, now over a million strong but dispirited, would henceforth have to fight by itself. In the spring of 1975, the DRV mounted a major offensive. The ARVN collapsed and Saigon fell on April 30, bringing an end to the RVN and a hasty departure of remaining Americans. The country was reunited in 1976 under the name, Socialist Republic of Vietnam (SRV). Saigon was renamed Ho Chi Minh City.

The Second Indochina War, or the "American War" as the Vietnamese call it, was the longest continuous war ever fought by the United States. It was also one of the most costly. Millions of Vietnamese and fifty-eight thousand Americans died. The cost in money to the U.S. taxpayer was staggering. The war which was never declared by Congress did not have the united support of the American people and in the mid-1990s remained a matter of controversy and divisiveness in American society.

The SRV government sought to destroy what it regarded as the vestiges of neocolonialism and American culture in the south. Hundreds of thousands of southerners were sent to reeducation camps. Many more thousands, including many Chinese long-resident in the south, fled to the United States and to neighboring countries as "boat people." The SRV replaced the south's capitalist economy with a socialist one.

The economy of Vietnam did poorly. Reductions in foreign assistance and increased military expenditures due to the war with Cambodia in 1977–1979 and to the Chinese invasion of northern Vietnam in February and March 1979 added to other difficulties. In 1978–1980, Vietnam experienced a severe food shortage. By 1980, the economy seemed to be grinding to a halt, popular dissatisfaction was widespread, and SRV leaders realized that their socialist system was not working. Steps were taken to begin dismantling collective farming by restoring the farmers' incentives to produce. Other actions in the early 1980s experimented with a market-oriented economy.

Admitting that Vietnam had become one of the poorest countries in the world, the SRV government in 1986 began to introduce changes aimed at the creation of a "market socialism," said to be a euphemism for capitalism. New laws encouraged foreign investment. State enterprises were merged into private conglomerates. Managers were permitted to make their own decisions. The government monopoly of banking and foreign trade ended. Private commercial banks were begun while the state bank moved toward central banking functions. A foreign investment law was drafted modelled on the "best" foreign investment laws of other countries. These reforms were called *Doi Moi*, or "renovation." A major architect of these changes was Nguyen Yuan Oanh, a Harvard-educated economist with years of experience in international finance agencies. He had worked for the RVN in the 1960s but remained in Vietnam when the RVN collapsed and was under house arrest for a time. The economy improved with agricultural production rising and rice once again becoming a major export.

In 1992, a new constitution was adopted which formalized free market economic reforms while reaffirming Communist Party rule. It provided for a more powerful president as well as for a prime minister and a cabinet. A new national assembly, elected in September 1992, chose Le Duc Anh as president. Vo Van Kiet, a pragmatist and an advocate of capitalist style economic reform, became prime minister.

While constitutional and legal changes helped in the development of a market-oriented economy, the development was slowed by poor transportation and communications facilities, a desperate lack of capital, and by a trade and investment embargo imposed by the U.S. government. In the early 1990s, many American business people were eager to have the embargo lifted. They found Vietnam's literate, industrious, low paid, and growing population attractive. But the MIA question, the issue of American servicemen missing in action, made it politically difficult to lift the embargo. In the meantime, investors from Japan, Singapore, Hong Kong, Malaysia, and other countries were active in Vietnam. President Bill Clinton lifted the United States' embargo in February 1994. At the end of that year, investors in more than forty countries had announced plans to invest U.S. $10.2 billion in Vietnam. Taiwan, Hong Kong, and Singapore led the list with the United States ranked thirteenth. Substantial amounts of investment capital were also expected from some two million Vietnamese living abroad.

In the mid-1990s, American products filled Vietnamese markets and the SRV government wanted U.S. contacts. Many people were eager to learn English, the study of which earlier had been forbidden. At the same time, Vietnamese were very proud of their victory over the United States. The capture of Saigon was regarded as a victory comparable to the American defeat of the British at York Town.

The SRV encountered scattered, domestic opposition, the most serious being that posed by the Buddhists. The SRV banned the established Buddhist organization, the Unified Buddhist Church of Vietnam, in 1981, and arrested a number of its leaders. The government sought to coopt Buddhists with a state-sponsored organization. But most supported the banned organization, one stronghold of which was the Linh Mu pagoda in Hue. There a citizen in 1993 set himself afire and died in political protest. In December, Thich (Reverend) Huyen Quang, leader of the banned organization, called for an end to the single-party system and for free elections.

Vietnam's leaders remained communists, and arbitrary arrests and political trials still occurred. Yet they were reported to believe, unlike Singapore's leaders, that successful economic growth would require a politically more open, liberal, and democratic government. Indeed, the limits of political opinion and of intellectual and literary expression seemed to be growing ever wider in the mid-1990s, but actually enlarging the scope for political expression would likely be a tricky matter for some time to come.

Cambodia

The French returned to Cambodia in October 1945 and set aside an earlier declaration of independence by Cambodian nationalists. Cambodian nationalists traced their roots to the Buddhist Institute founded in 1930. They were mostly an intelligentsia and in varying degrees were anti-French and anti-monarchy. Their leader, Son Ngoc Thanh, was born of a Cambodian father and a Vietnamese mother. He had been librarian of the Institute and founder of an influential newspaper in 1936. As head of the *Khmer Issarak,* or Khmer Freedom Party, and prime minister of independent Cambodia, he was arrested by the French and exiled.

Because the French felt it necessary to make some modest move in the direction of Cambodian self-rule, Cambodia became a constitutional monarchy in 1947. After the elections held in 1951, France yielded to demands that Son Ngoc Thanh be permitted to return to Cambodia. Politics, however, were not to center on Thanh but on Norodom Sihanouk, king of Cambodia.

Sihanouk was eighteen when he became king in 1941. He was French educated, keenly interest in literature and drama, and shy. He grew into a loqua-

Top: Angkor Wat, Cambodia. © National Geographic Society.
Bottom: Singapore financial district. Singapore Embassy.

cious, charming, witty, opportunistic, adroit, and enduring politician. He claimed Jayavarman VII of the Angkor empire to be his inspiration. He skillfully coopted opponents and ideas. At home he was anticommunist; abroad, he made friends with communist powers. Sometimes dissembling and procrastinating, he spoke clearly and moved quickly when the occasion warranted. Sihanouk frustrated foreign diplomats, some of whom said he was unstable and untrustworthy. His admirers said that he was constant to a single purpose: the survival of Cambodia as an independent state. Keenly aware of history, he distrusted Vietnam and Thailand which since the fall of Angkor had taken turns reducing Cambodia to dependency. He called on China to make the balance of power. He has always been popular with the Cambodian people.

In the early 1950s, Sihanouk became a vigorous nationalist leader, calling for full independence. The Geneva Conference ended French rule over Cambodia and Laos. Sihanouk abdicated the throne in March 1955, saying that as monarch he was too isolated from the people whom he wished to know and lead. He founded the *Sangkum Reastre Niyum,* the People's Socialist Community (PSC), which won national elections in that and later years. During the late 1950s and early 1960s, Cambodia was relatively peaceful and prosperous. Some Cambodians profited from the war in Vietnam. Farmers sold their rice to the Vietnamese communists while Cambodian Army officers sold them weapons. The Vietnamese communists made use of Cambodian territory for their troops. The Sihanouk government became increasingly corrupt.

Political opposition in the 1960s came from the Cambodian Communist Party (CCP) formed in 1951 with the help of the Vietnamese Communist Party. The CCP was at a low ebb when Saloth Sar became secretary of the Party's central committee in 1962. He was a schoolteacher who had studied in France. A Sihanouk campaign against leftists in 1963 sent Saloth Sar and his colleagues underground, where they remained until 1975.

The CCP led by Saloth Sar had begun vigorous insurgency activity in 1967 after the government crushed a peasant uprising with great loss of life. The Communists had considerable success. Sihanouk travelled to Russia and China to try to obtain support against Vietnamese communist use of Cambodian territory. Upset by Sihanouk's behavior, the Army, with the encouragement of the United States, overthrew him in March 1970. As Sihanouk took up residence in Beijing, General Lon Nol became head of state. In May, U.S. and ARVN forces invaded eastern Cambodia to attack Vietnamese "sanctuary," withdrawing after about a month of operations. In October, Cambodia's name was changed to the Khmer Republic.

The Lon Nol government had little success fighting the Communist insurgency but at the same time became ever more repressive. By the end of 1972, the Communists controlled two-thirds of the country. The United States sought to aid Lon Nol in 1973 by sending B-52s to bomb areas held by the Communists. Many thousands of people fled from the bombed areas into Phnom Penh, adding to the government's problems and damaging the economy.

The CCP, called the Khmer Rouge by Sihanouk, seized Phnom Penh early in 1975. Lon Nol fled. Saloth Sar began calling himself Pol Pot and introduced "reforms." Doctrinaire and without practical experience, the Khmer Rouge attempted to apply socialist theories. Its actions were arbitrary, harsh, puritanical, and rural-oriented. The economy was ordered collectivized with production targets set unrealistically high. People were made to leave the city by foot and find work in the countryside. More orders followed dealing with social behavior, language, marriage, and dress. An attempt was made to root out western ideas and institutions. Western medicine, for example, was replaced with traditional medical practices. Executions of the "exploiting classes" began. These included teachers, civil servants, merchants and business people, and army officers. Soon after these killings had subsided, a purge of the Communist Party was undertaken. Thousands of Party members were made to confess to various crimes, including working for the United States. The Khmer Republic became Democratic Kampuchea.

The Pol Pot government attacked Vietnam in 1977 to regain lands which had once been Cambodian and which still had Khmer populations. Vietnam responded by invading Cambodia. By mid-1978, Pol Pot and the Khmer Rouge were fighting an internal rebellion as well as a well-equipped and experienced Vietnamese Army. Apparently suffering from a new bout of paranoia, Pol Pot began a new round of executions. Many hundreds of thousands of Cambodians were killed, so many that the Pol Pot government was accused of genocide and comparisons were made with the holocaust in Europe. The motion picture *The Killing Fields* (1984) vividly portrayed these events and the emotional and political climate of the country at the time.

Phnom Penh was captured in January 1979 by Vietnamese forces. A pro-Vietnamese government was promptly installed, and the People's Republic of Kampuchea was declared. By the end of the year, the Vietnamese controlled most of Cambodia. The Khmer Rouge took refuge in the northwestern forests along the Thai border. Cambodian antipathy for the Vietnamese led two other groups, anti-communist ones, to join with the Khmer Rouge in 1982 to form a coalition government in exile with Sihanouk as president. The Khmer Rouge was only one, albeit militarily the largest, of the groups conducting guerrilla warfare against the Vietnamese-backed government in Phnom Penh. China, the United States, Thailand, and Singapore gave assistance to the coalition, although the United States later ceased to provide support because of its antipathy to the Khmer Rouge. Although seldom seen, Pol Pot was regarded still to be the Khmer Rouge's leader. In April 1989, the name of the country was changed to the State of Cambodia. Vietnam began to withdraw its troops and completed this in September, leaving its Phnom Penh government to fight the coalition forces. Guerrilla warfare continued.

The United Nations, long concerned with the civil war in Cambodia, drafted a peace plan. The four contending parties—the government, the Khmer Rouge, and the two anti-communist groups—agreed to the plan in a treaty signed in 1991. Khmer Rouge acquiescence was the result of pressure from its long-time ally, the People's Republic of China. A force of twenty-two thousand—the largest ever assembled by the United Nations—led by a Japanese diplomat, entered Cambodia. The Khmer Rouge subsequently changed its mind and resumed guerrilla attacks in an attempt to disrupt the elections which it boycotted. The elections held for the National Assembly in May 1993 saw a 90 percent voter turn out. *Funcinpec*, a French acronym for a political party led by Sihanouk's son, Prince Ranariddh, won a plurality of seats and proceeded to form a coalition government with the next largest winner, the Cambodian People's Party (CPP). Led by Hun Sen, the CPP was the creation of the government installed by Vietnam in 1979. The U.N. force withdrew from Cambodia in November 1993.

The first task of the new National Assembly was to draft a constitution. It was announced in August 1993 that the monarchy would be restored and that Sihanouk should become King again. Ranariddh, would become First President and Hun Sen, Second President. The coronation ceremony in September embodied elements some ten-centuries old. Shortly afterwards, Sihanouk, now 70 years of age, had a malignant tumor removed in China. It was reported as not life-threatening. The Khmer Rouge continued its guerrilla war against the elected government. The government's new national army acquitted itself well fighting the guerrillas, and there were reports of numerous defections from the Khmer Rouge.

Be that as it may, by 1995 many Cambodians regarded the government that came to power in 1993 as incompetent and corrupt. Civil servants with tiny salaries drove luxury sedans and took vacations abroad. While Cambodians feared the Khmer Rouge, some also had a grudging admiration for it. The Khmer Rouge, they say, is not corrupt. Also, Khmer Rouge clandestine radio broadcasts repeatedly state that Vietnam is the enemy. Most Cambodians agree with this patriotic sentiment.

In November 1994, Vietnam, Cambodia, Laos, and Thailand signed an agreement to develop, manage, and conserve the resources of the lower Mekong River for such purposes as irrigation, hydroelectric power production, fishing, flood control, tourism, and navigation. Burma and China have been invited to join. An earlier scheme in the 1950s, modelled in part after the U.S. Tennessee Valley Authority, had been scrapped because of enmity between the participants.

Indeed, enmity had not disappeared. Cambodian-Thai border problems, for instance, are very old. In recent years, Cambodia has accused the Thai of supplying arms to the Khmer Rouge. Many thousands of Cambodian refugees, unwanted supporters of the Khmer Rouge, were being sent back to Cambodia by the Thais in early 1994.

In the mid-1990s, Cambodia continued struggling to rebuild its economy and society, terribly handicapped by the loss of thousands of educated people, lack of capital, and on-going insecurity in some rural areas.

Laos

The French made Laos a constitutional monarchy in 1947 under King Sisavong Vong. Independence came in 1953. There followed twenty-two years of civil war in which the Pathet Lao, an organization backed by the Vietnamese communists and Russia, fought the royal government backed by the United States and other western powers. The Pathet Lao emerged victorious in 1975. The king abdicated and the Lao People's Democratic Republic (LPDR) was proclaimed.

The LPDR maintained close relations with the Socialist Republic of Vietnam and applied socialist policies through the mid-1980s. These policies did not work very well, and Laos, already very poor, became poorer. Following the path of Vietnam, Laos introduced market-oriented reforms in 1986. Since then, the economy has improved. Timber, opium, and hydroelectric power were Laos's principal exports in the early 1990s. Roads and internal communications remained poor.

A new constitution was introduced in 1991. Elections to the National Assembly were held in December 1992. The Lao People's Revolutionary Party (LPRP) was the only legal political party. The president was Nouhak Phonmsavan; the prime minister, General Khamtai Siphandone.

Laos is a plural society, with thirty-eight officially recognized ethnic communities, none of which has a majority. They are roughly divided into lowland, midland, and highland peoples. The lowland peoples have been and continue to be economically and politically dominant. Official policy seeks to integrate these different people into one—to Laoize them, so to speak, into a society modelled on the culture of the lowland peoples. Education is a major means to this end. Poverty, however, thwarts the attainment of this goal as it does nearly every other official effort. Malnutrition, too, is a serious problem affecting no less than 40 percent of the people.

Malaysia

The reestablishment of British authority in Malaya in September 1945 ended strife brought about by the earlier Japanese surrender and communist assumption of control of parts of the country. The Malayan Communist Party (MCP), which had conducted armed resistance during the occupation through the Malayan People's Anti-Japanese Army (MPAJA), sought to take revenge on those whom the Party regarded as collaborators. Physical clashes between Malays and Chinese occurred. Early in 1946, Britain introduced the Malayan Union constitution. It rationalized the pre-1941 collection of colonial administrations, transferred sovereignty from the Malay rulers to the British Crown, and gave non-Malays equal status with Malays. Singapore was separated from the Malay states and made a separate crown colony.

The Malayan Union satisfied no one. Malays were angry. In their view, Britain had usurped Malay sovereignty. Equal status for non-Malays was a betrayal of trust that meant handing the country over to the Chinese. The United Malays National Organization (UMNO) was formed to lead Malay nationalist opposition. The Chinese and Indians failed to rally to the support of the Union in any appreciable numbers. Numerous middle-class persons and intellectuals opposed the Union on different grounds, namely, that it did not provide for self-rule. Britain replaced the Union with the Federation of Malaya in February 1948. It kept a single administration headed by a British high commissioner but restored sovereignty to the Malay rulers and the primary position in society to the Malays. Britain had concluded that the Malays were the largest and most politically articulate community in Malaya.

The first years of the Federation were taken up with a bloody communist rebellion, called the "Emergency." The MCP, composed mostly of Chinese, had operated legally until early 1948 when its leaders decided on armed rebellion using guerrilla, terrorist tactics. The MCP failed to gain popular support and often made mistakes. But the struggle still went badly for the British, and when the British High Commissioner was killed, in November 1951, an MCP victory seemed possible. Early in 1952, General Sir Gerald Templer took command and commenced draconian actions, which ultimately reduced the communists to a nuisance. The MCP was unable to attract Malays in significant numbers; its class appeal could not overcome ethnic loyalty. British propaganda depicted the communists as Chinese and godless. For many Malays, by extension, all Chinese were communists and godless. Godlessness was a detestable condition to Muslim Malays. The Emergency worsened ethnic relations.

In Malaya and in Britain individuals argued that the best way to fight communism would be to allow self-rule. The first elections were local contests in 1951–1952. These went well. Britain wanted to transfer power to a Malayan government that would be friendly to its economic interests and strong enough to govern effectively. These strengths appeared in the Alliance, a partnership of communal political parties, which overwhelmingly won the first national elections in July 1955. Parties making multiethnic or class appeals did poorly.

The dominant party in the Alliance representing the Malays was UMNO, led by Abdul Rahman, a Cambridge-educated member of the Kedah royal family. Later called the father of his country, the Tunku (Prince) as he was affectionately known, was a gregarious, modern, politically conservative, and pragmatic individual with a passion for horse racing and golf. He joined UMNO with the Malayan Chinese Association (MCA) and later the Malayan Indian Congress (MIC) to form the Alliance. Leaders of each party appealed for political unity within their ethnic community and represented themselves as defenders of their race and culture against the other races. Critics argued that such appeals made race relations worse, but Alliance leaders argued that ethnic political unity combined with cooperation between communal parties was the only politics possible.

Malaya, in contrast to some of its neighbors, obtained *merdeka* (freedom) peacefully. It became an independent monarchy with a democratic, parliamentary, and federal system of government on August 31, 1957. The monarch, with the title of *Yang di-pertuan Agung,* Supreme Head of State or King, was chosen by and from among the nine hereditary Malay state rulers and held office for five years. The Tunku became prime minister. The constitution of independent Malaya gave citizenship and political power preponderantly to the Malay people. They were also given privileges to enable them to enter business and the professions and participate in the modern and developing sectors of the economy. The British and the Malay rulers in colonial times had largely excluded the Malay people from the modern economy. UMNO leaders believed that Malaya could not succeed as a nation if Malays continued as a social and economic underclass. But non-Malay property owners were protected from having their interests expropriated. The constitution also carried over from British rule the power to arrest and detain persons without trial.

In the 1960s the Alliance government made great strides in economic development, education, and public health. The person driving most of these activities was Abdul Razak, deputy prime minister. Economic policy emphasized government planning and the pragmatic use of public and private capital. A national economy began to replace the colonial one, new primary industries and manufacturing enterprises were begun, incomes and living standards rose, and the middle and professional classes grew. Special attention was given to rural peoples who were mostly Malays.

Social goals, mainly improving the status of the Malay people, took precedence over economic ones, and very large social gains were made in the 1960s. A system of universal and free education was established from primary through high school. The achievement was truly remarkable given the crazy-quilt of Chinese and Indian, English-medium, Christian missionary, and Malay elementary schools inherited from the time of British rule. Education was a politically explosive subject, too. Many Chinese parents, students, and teachers strongly objected to adapting to a Malay-medium, national school system. But patience and compromise and a strong economy attenuated education issues. The accomplishment in public education was matched by the creation of a public health care system within physical and financial reach of all. These achievements were almost entirely domestically financed. There was some modest Colombo Plan assistance. The only U.S. aid was in the form of Peace Corps Volunteers, mostly as teachers and medical workers.

In September 1963, the Federation of Malaya was joined by the British dependencies, Sabah (formerly British North Borneo), Sarawak (formerly ruled by the British Brooke family), and by Singapore. The enlarged Malaya became Malaysia. The inclusion of Singapore was especially controversial because of its very large Chinese population. The main concern, however, was that Singapore might become communist. The Tunku said he did not want to see a "second Cuba" on Malaya's doorstep. In August 1965, Singapore separated (see p. 390), leaving Malaysia with thirteen states. The Philippines and Indonesia objected to the formation of Malaysia, and Sukarno took Indonesia to war against Malaysia in a conflict called "Konfrontasi" or Confrontation. His successors made peace in 1967.

On May 13, 1969, racial rioting—a rare occurrence—took place in the aftermath of national elections. In response, Parliament was suspended and interim executive and consultative bodies created. Communal problems and remedies were discussed. One result was to outlaw public and parliamentary discussion of certain potentially inflammatory issues relating to race. Parliamentary government resumed in 1971. The Alliance was replaced with a new political coalition, the *Barisan Nasional,* or National Front. It consisted of the UMNO and the communal parties of the old Alliance together with several small parties which had previously been in opposition.

UMNO remained the most powerful party. In the late 1950s it was the best organized and the only party that was national in scope. It became stronger in the 1960s. UMNO supporters were rewarded with jobs, government contracts, a new village market or mosque, and other benefits that a party in power can provide. The party also became wealthy. By the mid-1980s, it owned the largest newspaper publisher, a television network, banking and insurance properties, and other businesses. UMNO virtually monopolized Malay political representation so that most Malays found it preferable to pursue political careers inside rather than outside UMNO. UMNO was, however, rarely united. A wide range of views on social and economic questions existed, although in elections, the appeal of Malay communal unity was paramount, and the party would be united. In the 1980s, party and communal unity were challenged by a break-away group, the *Semangat 46.* Its founders and supporters were Malays who resented and opposed Prime Minister Mahathir's style and actions. Its success at the polls was limited, but it survived into the mid-1990s.

The fundamental cause of the May 1969 race riots was ascribed to the disparities of wealth between Malays and non-Malays, in turn due to occupational specialization by race. To address these problems, efforts to restructure society were redoubled under the New Economic Policy (NEP) introduced in 1971. About two-thirds of Malaysia's commerce and industry was owned by foreign corporations and nearly all the rest by non-Malays, mostly Chinese. A goal of 30 percent Bumiputra ownership and Bumiputra staff and management by the year 1990 was set. The word Bumiputra was now frequently used instead of Malay. It means "sons of the soil" and embraces Malays and other indigenous people principally in East Malaysia.

Under the NEP, the government began to intervene massively in the economy. Tax revenues were used to subsidize fledgling Malay entrepreneurs, to launch Malay businesses, and to buy up shares for Malays in existing companies. Government licenses were reserved for Bumiputras, and government gave contracts to Bumiputra companies. By the late 1980s, the government reportedly owned all or part of more than nine hundred companies and statutory boards at a cost of many billions of Malaysian ringgits. Among the largest were *Petronas*, an oil company; *Bank Bumiputra;* and *Pernas*, a trading company. University, professional, and postsecondary technical education were hugely expanded, with places reserved for Bumiputra students. Many tens of thousands of Bumiputras were sent abroad to study, especially to the United States, Britain, and Australia.

The NEP appears to have been a success in that there are now many Bumiputra entrepreneurs, managers, and professional people. But the results have been uneven. Malay political leaders and civil servants were in the best position to seize the opportunities created for Bumiputras. They often had the requisite knowledge, skill, and sophistication. The rulers, too, were well-placed to benefit. As a consequence, a kind of bureaucratic capitalism emerged with a large concentration of wealth—and power—in the hands of a relatively few Malay people. Concerns have been raised as to whom they are accountable. The NEP was also costly in terms of failed businesses, waste, and corruption. Another cost was the alienation of many non-Malays, primarily young people. There also remain many poor Bumiputras.

Beginning in the mid-1970s, the Malay people experienced an Islamic revival. Its origins lay in similar movements in other Muslim countries as well as in the challenge to traditional values by secular and material influences accompanying rapid economic growth. It was led by the *dakwah* movement, a loose and diverse collection of individuals and organizations voluntarily seeking to revive Islam and purify religious practices among the Malay people. Although observers tended to think of *dakwah* as fundamentalist, that was not necessarily so. Many in the *dakwah* sought and still seek continued economic growth and modernization but want it done consistent with Islamic principles and without the evils which they believe exist in the United States and other western countries. UMNO, which had been mostly modernist and secular, regarded Islamic revival as a political challenge. Indeed, *Partai Islam se-Malaysia* (PAS), an opposition party, used Islamic revival to its advantage. UMNO responded by coopting the movement and its leaders with some success.

Mahathir Mohamad became prime minister in July 1981. He was the first commoner and first second-generation political figure to hold the post. A medical doctor, he entered politics as an UMNO "back-bencher," often critical of the Tunku and older leaders. He authored a controversial book, *The Malay Dilemma* (1970), in which he addressed the problems of the Malay people with dire conclusions about their future. Unlike the stereotype of the Malay, Mahathir is impatient, often outspoken and brusque. He has taken the Malaysian economy beyond light manufacturing into heavy industry. The latter includes the production of steel and chemicals and, in 1985, the first Malaysian automobile, the *Proton*. Mahathir was at first cautious in regard to Islam, but in the 1990s he has sought to encourage a moderate and modern Islamic theology.

The nine hereditary Malay rulers and the *Agung* are the subject of controversy. They have been regarded as a defense against demands by the Chinese, but as the Malay middle class has grown and the Malay community generally has become more self-confident, that role has seemed less needed. It is also argued that UMNO has replaced the rulers as protectors of the Malays. Malays have increasingly questioned the powers and the activities of the rulers. In 1983, Mahathir successfully challenged the *Agung's* right to withhold assent to laws passed by Parliament, thus effectively vetoing them. In the early 1990s, objections were raised to business activities of the rulers, especially to deals done with Chinese partners to the detriment of Malay businessmen. Efforts have been made to end their immunity from legal actions. In the mid-1990s, some middle class Malays believed the rulers were anachronisms, too numerous and too costly to keep, but defended the idea of a single monarch, that is, the *Agung*.

The economy has continued to do well. Indeed, Malaysia in the early 1990s had one of the fastest growing economies in the world. In part this was due to very large investments by Japanese since the late 1980s. Mahathir has encouraged Japanese investment and has urged Malaysians to "Look East" and emulate the Japanese in regard to hard work, discipline, and placing the community before the individual. The Japanese are not so well accepted by some Malaysians, however. Older Malaysians remember the Japanese occupation, while some who now work in Japanese factories claim poor working conditions, arrogant manners, union-busting practices, and a reluctance to share technology. The Japanese are, however, politically well connected in Malaysia, having, for example, contracted with UMNO-owned Malaysian companies.

In February 1991, Mahathir outlined a new set of national goals called "Vision 2020." Malaysia, he said, will become a fully developed country by the year 2020 and will do this in its own way without following any other country. Fully developed means not only economically but also politically, socially, spiritually, psychologically, and culturally. Malaysians, he said, will be united, confident, democratic, tolerant, progressive, and outward looking and possess well-rooted moral and ethical values. Everyone will have a place and take pride in being a Malaysian. To attain these goals, the government continued to rely on official planning, industrial expansion, and capital accumulation. Saving was encouraged and wasteful consumer spending was discouraged. If Vision 2020 was to succeed, Malaysia would have to overcome its most serious economic problem, a shortage of labor.

Another goal set in the 1990s for the Malay people complemented Vision 2020. It was a new ideal called *Melayu Baru,* or the "New Malay." The new Malay was one who is independent, resourceful, educated, successful, capable of meeting challenges but keeps his or her Malay cultural identity and Islamic faith. It was a bold effort to convey to Malays that they must be prepared to compete with non-Malays without help. To what extent Malays may still require assistance in the future is debated. UMNO critics have defined *Melayu Baru* as meaning a westernized, materialistic, individual alienated from his or her Malay culture and religion.

Malaysia's foreign policy has been conditioned by the need for trade, foreign capital and technology, the country's small size, and its ethnic composition. In the 1970s, a bias toward western powers was modified somewhat by trade overtures to Russia, China, and Eastern Europe. Malaysia established diplomatic relations with the People's Republic of China in 1974.

Since 1981, Mahathir has determined foreign policy. He has been a vigorous critic of Britain, the United States, and Australia. The United States is "racist," he says, and democracy in the United States means that anyone can carry a gun and publicly flaunt his or her homosexuality. The United States is hypocritical because it advocates democracy but props up dictators, urges free trade but has its own protectionist policies. The West's criticism of Asia's disappearing rain forest, he says, is a means to shift attention from its failure to do much about its carbon-monoxide poisoned cities. He has linked environmental issues to development, saying that if the West wants Southeast Asians to protect the environment then it must provide investment capital and technology on a sustained basis. As for human rights, he argues that given the West's record, it has no business preaching to Asians on the subject. Moreover, the western definition of human rights is too narrow, he says, and does not take into account Asian values.

Mahathir is very popular in Japan because of his "Look East" policy and because he says it is time to stop blaming Japan for its wartime excesses. On the other hand, his blunt, confrontational style has upset some of his ASEAN colleagues and made him enemies. He is regarded by many Malaysians as the most successful prime minister since Malaysia's independence. He has been hailed as a new spokesperson for the "Third World."

Brunei

The Malay state of Brunei on the northeast coast of Kalimantan returned to British protection at the end of the Japanese interregnum. Small in area and in population but possessed of very large oil revenues, it was, and is, ruled by an absolute and hereditary Muslim sultanate. In 1959, a new constitution was drafted that continued British responsibility for defense, foreign affairs, and internal security. The sultan's absolute power was modified by the creation of executive and legislative councils and elected district councils. Sultan Omar, the twenty-eighth ruler, sought by this constitution to control the direction of nascent Brunei nationalism. He was opposed by the *Parti Rakyat Brunei* (PRB), or Brunei People's

Party, led by Ahmad Azahari, which sought immediate independence in a federation with Sarawak and North Borneo (later Sabah). The PRB handily won district elections in 1962. Azahari forfeited the PRB's strong position in December 1962 by launching an armed rebellion against the sultan which was quickly put down by British troops. The sultan thereupon suspended the constitution and ruled by decree.

The rebellion caused Sultan Omar to give serious consideration to joining the proposed Malaysian federation. He later chose not to join for several reasons, the principle one of which was loss of control over oil revenues. Malaysia was upset by the sultan's decision not to join the federation and became critical of the lack of representative institutions in Brunei. Kuala Lumpur gave asylum to some PRB leaders, and relations between Brunei and Malaysia were strained for many years.

Sultan Omar surrendered his throne in 1967 to his son, Hassanal Bolkiah, then 21 years old and a student at Sandhurst, the elite military college in Britain. Brunei and Singapore developed close ties from the late 1960s, making use of financial advisors and others from the island republic. A Malaysian-sponsored United Nations resolution in 1977 called on Brunei to liberalize its government. The sultan, however, preferred to keep his link with Britain, concerned in part that his larger and physically stronger neighbors might seek to take over his very wealthy state. At the end of 1983, British protection was formally ended and Brunei became an independent, fully sovereign state. However, British Gurkha troops continued to be stationed in Brunei. Brunei subsequently joined the United Nations and other international organizations, including the Association of Southeast Asian Nations (ASEAN) in 1984, signalling an improvement in relations with Malaysia and Indonesia.

Brunei continued to be a prosperous country with new oil and gas wells being developed and added to existing ones. Under Sultan Hassanal, Brunei's wealth has been shared with the people, muting demands for political reforms. Scholarships for study abroad and a university in Brunei have improved education. The sultan engages in personal rule, visiting each of the country's districts to hear and rule on grievances. He personally holds several ministries while his brothers hold others. Governing Brunei is a family affair. The sultan's personal wealth was assessed in 1992 at U.S. $37 billion.

Singapore

After Britain separated Singapore from the Malayan Union and made it a crown colony in 1946, the first significant steps toward self-rule came in 1955. The second half of the decade witnessed demands for more self-rule against a background of bitter and sometimes bloody confrontations between students, teachers, and workers, on the one hand, and the government, on the other, over economic and educational issues that were political as well. The basic divisions were militant versus moderate socialists and Chinese-educated versus English-educated people. The People's Action Party (PAP), founded in 1954, vigorously championed socialist views. Led by Lee Kuan Yew, a Cambridge-educated lawyer, it won forty-three of fifty-one seats in elections for the legislature in 1959. Lee later attributed the Party's victory to his and his English-educated colleague's ability to make common cause with the militants and the Chinese-educated. The

PAP government exercised considerable self-rule, but Britain kept responsibility for defense and foreign relations while internal security was the joint responsibility of Singapore, Britain, and Malaya.

The partnership of militants and moderates in the PAP was an uneasy one, and in 1961 the Party split, in part over Lee's proposal that Singapore merge with Malaysia. The militants saw the merger as neocolonialist and left the PAP to form the *Barisan Sosialis,* or Socialist Front. Accused of being communist and with some of its key leaders imprisoned under internal security legislation, the *Barisan* soon withdrew from political activity. The PAP moderates survived, and Singapore became a one-party state with the PAP having little tolerance for political opposition.

Singapore merged with Malaysia, becoming its fourteenth state in 1963, but it did not go well. Lee's slogan of "Malaysia for Malaysians" sounded to many Malays like a prelude to a Chinese takeover. Racial tensions rose. Lee's style and ambitions were incompatible with Malaysian politics, and in August 1965, Singapore was forced out of Malaysia, becoming an independent republic. The event was traumatic for many Singaporeans who believed that tiny Singapore could not survive alone. Lee, addressing the people on television, said that their survival was at stake. Survival would depend on Singaporeans working hard, saving and sacrificing, being disciplined and lawabiding. He spoke of a "tight society," one that was tough, determined, and highly trained. Such a Singapore could, he said, survive thousands of years. Survival remained the fundamental motivator of Singaporeans through the mid-1990s.

The people did not disappoint Lee. The closing of the British naval base at Singapore announced in 1968 and the consequent unemployment of many thousands of civilian workers was overcome. In due course, Singapore prospered mightily and in the early 1970s had one of the fastest-growing economies in the world. Multinational corporations found Singapore a superb place to locate, while tax revenues were used when deemed necessary to start new companies and new industries or to buy into existing ones. This was done without creating excessive foreign or domestic debt while maintaining relatively stable consumer prices. The government, in fact, accumulated large capital surpluses. This was partly the result of compulsory savings through the Central Provident Fund (CPF), a social security scheme. It helped make Singaporeans among the most saving people in the world. In the mid-1990s, Singapore had a mixed economy of state- and privately owned enterprises. Small local and private firms did not always do well and were squeezed to some degree between large wealthy multinational corporations and the many powerful state-owned companies.

Accompanying the economic successes were social ones as well. Good schools, housing, medical care, and public services were provided for all. Education was and remains a very high priority on the premise that without mineral and agricultural resources the island republic must invest in its most important resource, people. There has been a large and continuing expansion of universities, colleges, and technical schools. English has been the predominant language of instruction in schools, making Singapore a multilingual, English-speaking society. Singapore's accomplishments with respect to housing are probably without parallel. When the PAP came to power, few Singaporeans owned the places in which they lived and the majority lived in poor conditions. By the early 1990s, more than 90 percent of Singaporeans owned their own homes, mostly in high-rise apartment buildings. Initially rehoused in modern government-subsidized apartments, citizens were encouraged to buy an apartment by borrowing from their CPF accumulations. Similar borrowing has been permitted to buy certain conservative common stocks listed on the Singapore stock exchange. A result of the government's policy of creating property owners has been to make Singaporeans politically conservative. Poverty, homelessness, and unemployment have been virtually eliminated. Indeed, since the late 1980s, Singapore has imported labor from neighboring countries to cope with a chronic labor shortage. Singaporeans by the early 1990s enjoyed one of the highest living standards in the world.

As the policy of making Singaporeans property owners might imply, the PAP government engages in massive social-engineering, believing it has a responsibility to determine peoples' behavior. The means have been legislation, the schools, rewards and often severe punishments, public praise as well as public humiliation, and exhortation. The social-engineering affects everything from family size to urination in public, cleanliness of toilets to the use of chewing gum. The government has had a good deal of success. A very-high birth rate has been curbed, middle-class values have been inculcated, a Chinese tradition of low esteem for those in military careers has been blunted, professional people have been urged to marry and have children at a younger age, and the city has been made much cleaner. Crime, too, has been curtailed, making Singapore possibly the safest large city in the world. A public campaign to modify some aspect of people's behavior is nearly always in progress.

On what is perhaps a more fundamental level, Singapore's leaders have been concerned about the peoples' values. On the one hand, they want Singapore to be a modern and secular society. But, on the other hand, appreciating that Singaporeans are Asians who must live in Asia, they worry that economic success will make their citizens too western and too materialistic. The spread of Christianity among the Chinese population has been viewed with concern. An important step for Singaporean society was taken in 1991 with the formal adoption of five "shared values," namely, society above one's self and nation above community, a strong and viable family as the fundamental social unit, respect and community support for the individual, consensus above conflict, and ethnic and religious harmony. To promote the last, religious leaders have been forbidden to engage in politics.

The PAP's economic and social policies have required a strong organizational and political base. In the early 1960s, with the loss of its leftwing, PAP moderates keenly felt this need. Having little in common with most Chinese-educated businessmen, they turned to the bureaucrats. Western-educated and English-speaking like the PAP moderates, they were natural allies. But they had the attitudes and values of colonial bureaucrats. PAP reorganized and reeducated them, giving them new values and directions. Civil servants became development oriented and selected members became entrepreneurs and chief executive officers of state-owned businesses. Merit became the basis for advancement. Salaries and perquisites were very good—in the late 1980s cabinet-level civil servants earned upwards of U.S. $300 thousand per year; these were raised to more than U.S. $1 million in 1994. A high standard of integrity was maintained, and the most intelligent persons were recruited into the Civil Service. The result has been called a mandarinate—a class of modern scholar-bureaucrats.

The alliance between PAP and the mandarinate has worked well and has been a key factor in the emergence of the "administrative state," a name sometimes given to Singapore. It means a rational, efficient, goal-oriented government in which decisions are made by a few. The rationale is that decisions about investment and economic expansion are best made by experts free of politics.

Another major move by the PAP in the 1960s to shore up its power base as well as to promote economic growth was to gain control of workers' unions. The National Trades Union Congress (NTUC) was formed by Devan Nair, a teacher, trade unionist, and co-founder of the PAP. Moderate and conservative unions joined the NTUC. Left-wing unions were suppressed. The NTUC became the means by which the PAP controlled and disciplined workers. Work stoppages declined dramatically. The National Wages Council, formed in 1972, brought together representatives of government, employers, and the NTUC annually to set wage rates.

To strengthen relationships with the people, the PAP established "grass-roots" organizations. In 1960, the Party launched People's Associations (PAs) which used community centers to build support for the PAP and to explain government policies. The PAs were later supplemented by other organizations including Residence Committees formed in 1978 and 1979. These organizations have not always worked well, probably in part because the growing middle class has acquired larger and more diverse political interests. In the mid-1980s, letters to the controlled press accused the government of arrogance, elitism, and insensitivity. The PAP took remedial measures, one of which was to assert better control over the bureaucracy. In the late 1980s, the PAP began to privatize some government enterprises as a means of reducing the power of the bureaucracy. The PAP continued, however, to rely heavily on its mandarin allies.

The PAP government has not hesitated to amend the constitution to achieve its objectives. Lee, in part concerned that the government's large reserves of cash and equities not be squandered by future politicians, proposed changes in the powers of the president in 1984. Previously ceremonial, the position acquired substantial executive powers in 1991 by constitutional amendment. Assisted by a council, the president guards against the irresponsible drawdown of the government's reserves—about U.S. $58 billion in 1994. Previously appointed, the position was made elective but candidates must be approved by a screening committee. The committee is guided by criteria so stringent that most Singaporeans are excluded from candidacy. Critics argued that the powers given to the president are so large that it means the end of parliamentary government. The first presidential elections were held in August 1993; Ong Teng Cheong was the successful candidate.

Singapore's strict society with severe limitations on individual behavior has been justified on the basis of past political turmoil, the smallness of Singapore, and the island state's economic and military vulnerability. Critics have argued that history suggests that authoritarian rule is incompatible with the development of middle and professional classes and a market economy. Singapore's leaders reply that the critics are wrongly applying western historical experience to Singapore. Singapore, indeed Asia, is different, they say. In Singapore, community and consensus are all-important. In the West, the individual is first, but in Asia the individual is subordinate to the family and group. Lee Kuan Yew has questioned the worth of human rights and free speech. In the United States, he says, individualism has been allowed to run rampant at the expense of society. Singapore's leaders often cite violence and crime in the United States, indeed specifically in Washington, D.C., as what Singapore must avoid.

While Singaporeans respected Lee for his past leadership and remained supportive of him in 1994, there were many and probably a growing number who were critical of him and of Singapore's government. Those few persons who had publicly spoken critically were punished in one manner or another. One who, late in 1993, had not was David Marshall, prime minister in the 1950s and former ambassador. Called the "conscience of the nation" by supporters, he said that the PAP had a computer brain and a plastic heart and ruled by fear.

Singapore had become a role-model beginning in the early 1980s for China, Vietnam, and other countries who admired its combination of a dynamic, expanding economy and authoritarian government. Whether and how well Singapore's economic successes and political practices can be applied in other countries remained unanswered questions in the mid-1990s. Indeed, questions which remain unanswered for Singapore itself were whether the role of government in business could be successfully sustained over the long run and whether growing political pluralism would be accommodated or suppressed.

In November 1991, after twenty-five years as prime minister, Lee, "the father of modern Singapore," handed over his post to Goh Chok Tong. Lee remained in government as senior minister. A year later, Goh became general-secretary of the PAP. The most powerful position in the Party, it had been held for thirty-eight years by Lee. Earlier there had been popular speculation that Lee's son, Lee Hsien Loong, a retired brigadier-general and deputy prime minister, would become prime minister, perhaps succeeding Goh. But late in 1992, the younger Lee was found to have cancer. Although treatment resulted in an encouraging prognosis, the illness cast doubt as to his political future.

Goh and his colleagues—a new generation but very much like the old one—embarked on economic plans and policies which would more closely link government and business. Singapore's intended future is set forth in *The Strategic Development Plan* (1991). The island republic's economy will be based not primarily on the production of goods but rather on innovation and information. A significant part of Singapore economic plans include the Bantam "growth triangle" in which areas of nearby Malaysia and Indonesia join with Singapore to provide a low-cost, tariff-free zone for manufacturing and trade. Several multinational companies had located there by early 1994, and the concept was being emulated elsewhere in Southeast Asia. In the early 1990s, Singaporeans were encouraged by tax and other incentives to invest overseas. China, Vietnam, Burma, Malaysia, and India were among the countries in which Singaporeans invested capital.

Singapore's pragmatic foreign policy in the mid-1990s derived from its dependence on trade, its location and size, and its Chinese population. All three required Singapore to be friendly to all. Good relations with Indonesia and Malaysia were a high priority. Both countries remained essential economic hinterlands for Singapore. Singapore's considerable wealth was a cause of jealousy, resentment, and grudging admiration. Singapore continued to maintain army, navy, and air forces which were among the largest, best trained, and best equipped in the region.

Thailand

In 1945, the United States took the position that Thailand had been forced to become an ally of the Japanese and that Thailand's declaration of war did not represent the true sympathies of the Thai monarch and people. In fact, a Thai resistance movement had operated against the Japanese during the war. Pridi Phanomyong and Thailand's ambassador to the United States had formed the Free Thai Movement, made broadcasts to Thailand, and worked clandestinely to help the U.S. Office of Strategic Services get agents into Thailand. A quick peace with Thailand freed up stocks of rice for shipment to hungry people elsewhere in Southeast Asia. The United States sponsored Thailand's entry into the United Nations.

Constitutional changes in 1946 provided for a parliamentary democracy in civilian hands. But it did not work well because of voter apathy, candidates' inexperience, office-holders' pursuit of personal gain, and weak leadership. The shocking death of the young king, Ananda, in June 1946, by a bullet from his own pistol was a cause of political controversy. Political opponents of Pridi Phanomyong, now prime minister, blamed him for the king's death, and he was branded as a communist for his socialist views. Pridi was forced to resign. Bhumibol Adulyadej became king in 1946, and is still Thailand's reigning monarch! (See p. 397.)

The government drifted until 1947 when the military seized power. Thereafter, authoritarian regimes led by Army officers ruled most years until the early 1990s. The officers used their positions to acquire privileges and large financial assets. The military was itself divided so that the generals formed cliques that competed for power. They created their own political parties and allied with existing parties composed of civilians and bureaucrats, many of whom were eager to share in the spoils. Throughout there have been individuals and groups who have genuinely sought democratic government. Broadly speaking, the recent political history of Thailand has been one of a struggle between the Thai armed forces who have sought to keep their privileges and a growing middle class seeking more freedom and a larger role in the conduct of the nation's affairs.

The dominance of the military in Thai politics may be better understood if it is appreciated that, for many years, it enjoyed popular prestige. It is a social institution and a bureaucracy as well as a military organization. It has been better organized and more united than any other group in Thai society. It has had a sense of mission, believing that it was the protector of the nation. And only the military has had the physical force that could, if necessary, be used to resolve issues. In office, the military perpetuated its power by sharing the spoils with career bureaucrats and by coopting or jailing its opponents. The Bangkok demonstrations in October 1973 (see p. 395) marked the beginning of decline in the military's prestige and popular support.

Certain major figures deserve mention. Marshall Phibun Songkhram who ruled in the late 1930s and during much of World War II, emerged again to rule between 1948 and 1957. He promoted state enterprises, making use of the capital and management expertise of Thai-Chinese businessmen. More than one hundred state businesses were established by the mid-1950s. He worked well with the United States, sending Thai troops to fight with the U.S. and U.N. forces in Korea. He readily brought Thailand into the Southeast Asia Treaty Organization (SEATO) in 1954.

Phibun was followed by Sarit Thanarat, who ruled from 1958 until his death in 1963. Sarit established a dictatorship in order, he said, to save the country from communism. His regime was ruthless, critics were arrested, and suspected communists were executed. At the same time, Sarit embarked on economic, health, and educational development programs with the advice of the World Bank and the International Monetary Fund. He created a Ministry of National Development and encouraged private investment. Industrialization was undertaken to reduce Thai dependence on agricultural exports. Special development efforts were made in the northeast where poverty was widespread and communist sympathies strong. Sarit's economic expansion policies brought prosperity and the growth of the urban middle class.

While Phibun had often harassed Chinese businessmen, Sarit made them partners. Army officers became company directors, were given large blocks of stock, and obtained lucrative positions with Thai-Chinese companies in return for profitable government licenses and contracts. The expanded U.S. military involvement in Vietnam from about 1965 served as an additional spur to the Thai economy with numerous U.S. air bases and thousands of U.S. troops in Thailand.

Sarit's successor in 1963 was Marshall Thanom Kittikachorn. He rejected democratic institutions as too unwieldy and time-consuming. But the Thai urban middle class was becoming increasingly politically sophisticated, and complaints about the military multiplied. There was also some desire to broaden the base of government. Thanom promulgated a new constitution in 1968 and elections were held in February 1969. Thanom and several Army officers seized power at the end of 1971. They were motivated by domestic and international concerns, some of which were potentially threatening to their privileges. Formally, the officers explained that they seized power to protect the king and defend the country against communist plots, student riots, workers' strikes, and a miscellany of threats, including terrorism, subversion, parliamentary obstructionism, and abuse of democratic privileges.

Tensions built until in October 1973 students and many thousands of people demonstrated in Bangkok. Thanom, his hand partially stayed by the king, was defeated and left the country. The most political freedom Thailand had ever experienced followed during the next three years. Everyone with an opinion seemed to speak at once. Many political parties were formed, grievances were aired, strikes occurred, public debates were many, and elections were held. It was often chaotic, providing an excuse to reestablish Army rule in October 1976.

Many people acquiesced in the return of Army rule and relative stability. Civilian rule had been exciting but unnerving; it was often inept and it failed to put an end to corruption. Also, the Army seemed likely to deal more effectively with external concerns such as the first oil price hike in 1973 and the communist reunification of Vietnam in 1975. Prem Tinsulanond, an Army chief described as incorruptible, became prime minister in 1980 and held power until 1988. In office, he relaxed control somewhat, becoming a bit more tolerant of critics and allowing more freedom of expression. Elections in 1988 brought a civilian, Chatichai Choonaven, to the prime minister's office.

In the 1960s and 1970s, the Thai economy changed dramatically. In the early 1960s, 70 percent of Thai exports consisted of rice, tin, teak, and rubber. About 80 percent of the population was engaged in producing these primary products. But in 1980, manufacturing accounted for more than 30 percent of exports and primary products were declining as a percentage of exports. Banks experienced tremendous growth as well as increased concentration of ownership. Families or groups of families were the owners of larger Thai businesses. These families were almost all descendants of ethnic Chinese, although they were regarded as Thai because they had assimilated the Thai language, culture, and society. Virtually all had acquired their wealth initially by having the monarchy as patron before 1941 and the military clique in power as patron after 1947. A second source of their wealth was foreign Chinese and European capitalists.

The Thai economy boomed in the second half of the 1980s. Large multinational corporations found Thailand a good place to invest. The Japanese led the way, the Americans followed. Steel, chemicals, pharmaceuticals, and electronics industries were built. Farmers increasingly became factory workers. The Bangkok Bank became a major regional financial power. Economic growth raised living standards and helped to expand the middle class.

During the '80s, many Thais talked about the need for political reform. The growing middle class was tired of government by coup and rule by generals. The military, on the other hand, feared that civilian rule would end their business activities. Besides officers serving as company directors and owning company shares, they had lucrative positions with state enterprises that operated the country's telecommunications, sea and airports, and railways. Some officers were allegedly involved in the golden triangle drug trade and in stripping the country's hardwood forests. Other officers, linked to gem and timber companies, allegedly provide money and guns to the Khmer Rouge for the privilege of mining and logging in Cambodian border areas held by the Khmer Rouge.

A military junta, the National Peace Keeping Council (NPKC), overthrew the civilian government of Chatichai Choonavan in February 1991. The NPKC promised to return power to the people in one year, appointed a caretaker prime minister, and began writing a new constitution which was structured to perpetuate military rule. Elections under the new charter were held in March 1992, the parties and candidates dividing into promilitary and prodemocracy forces. The promilitary parties won but had trouble getting approval for their prime minister because of his alleged link to drug trafficking.

General Suchinda Kraprayoon became prime minister. Not only was he not a member of parliament, he was popularly believed to have directed the 1991 coup. Public anger built in the days following Suchinda's appointment, climaxing in May 1992. Hundreds of thousands of people poured into the streets of Bangkok and other cities. Army troops broke up meetings and fired on demonstrators. Chamlong Srimuang, a Buddhist ascetic and principal leader of the prodemocracy movement, was arrested. Hundreds were injured or wounded; an unknown number were killed. But people refused to be intimidated. Groups of young people set fire to government buildings; protestors on motorcycles attacked police stations. Older persons participated, too. Doctors and nurses volunteered medical treatment for the wounded, while businessmen used their cellular phones to relay information about troop movements to groups of demonstrators. Finally, the king intervened, and Suchinda resigned on May 24. A caretaker government was soon appointed.

Thailand held general elections in September 1992. A prodemocracy coalition won a thin majority in the 360-member House of Representatives and formed a government with Chuan Leekpai, leader of the Democrat Party, as prime minister. Fifty-six in 1994 and educated in the law, Chuan was a career politician genuinely committed to democratic government. A major goal of Chuan's government was to break the powerful interior ministry's hold over local government by introducing elections for all local offices. Another was land reform to help landless farmers as well as to stop their encroachment on forest reserves. In December 1994, the prodemocracy coalition seemed on the verge of collapse when one of its members, the New Aspirations Party with much of its power based in the interior ministry, defected. The Chuan government also won praise from the United States for the arrest of ten golden triangle "drug lords," and has done more than any other Thai government to curtail the illicit trade in gems, timber, and guns with the Khmer Rouge although the trade still flourished in early 1995.

King Bhumibol Adulyadej, the world's longest-reigning monarch, was 68 years old in April 1995. While maintaining the traditional roles of symbol of Thai unity and upholder of the moral order, he takes a keen interest in contemporary issues, especially the problems of farmers, whom he often visits. Intelligent and enlightened, he has selectively sought to influence events. In 1973, he stopped military efforts to suppress student demonstrations against the regime of Thanom Kittikachorn. Again in 1992, he appeared on national television with Suchinda and Chamlong and told them to make peace. Such actions have enhanced his already considerable popularity. His avocations include playing the clarinet, composing Dixieland jazz, and operating a ham radio.

Who will succeed Bhumibol is a popular topic in Thailand. It is assumed that his son, Vajiralongkorn, will succeed him, but he does not have much popular esteem. One of the king's daughters, Sirindhorn, is universally loved. He flies an F-16 fighter plane; she plays the cello and goes into the villages with her father.

Regional Associations

Some form of regional cooperation was first brought up for discussion as early as the 1950s. The Southeast Asia Treaty Organization (SEATO) was not what most Southeast Asians had in mind because it was U.S.-initiated and clearly intended for political and military purposes. The Columbo Plan was aimed at economic development but was British in origins and included countries outside the region. But some kind of linkage was clearly desirable because Southeast Asians' ignorance of each other was large. The imperial powers had encouraged communication with the imperial centers rather than between Southeast Asian states.

Malaysia, the Philippines, and Thailand formed the Association of Southeast Asia (ASA) in 1961. The founders were motivated by a desire to combat communist subversion and promote economic development. The Philippine claim to Sabah and Sukarno's hostility toward Malaysia made ASA virtually still-born. The Association of Southeast Asian Nations (ASEAN) was established in Bangkok in 1967. The original members were Malaysia, the Philippines, Thailand, Singapore, and Indonesia. Brunei joined in January 1984. The emphasis from the first was on regional economic, social, and cultural cooperation. Members were reluctant to take political positions in the early years and have remained throughout adamantly opposed to becoming a military alliance. Policy is made at an annual meeting of foreign ministers. Numerous other meetings occur between like ministries.

Early prognostications about ASEAN were not optimistic. It was difficult to see how economic cooperation might occur when ASEAN members had similar economies and were competitors for markets, capital, and technology. Indeed the social and cultural achievements have been more numerous than its economic ones.

ASEAN members did engage in joint political and diplomatic activity in the 1970s. The Association opposed the Vietnamese invasion of Cambodia as a violation of the latter's sovereignty, and successfully opposed U.N. recognition of the Vietnam-backed Cambodian government while supporting those groups fighting the Vietnamese regime. Vietnam in the late 1970s bitterly opposed ASEAN, calling it a U.S. neocolonialist creation intended to replace SEATO. The United States did indeed encourage and support ASEAN, especially in its fledgling years, believing that regional cooperation could only be beneficial. Early in 1995, it was anticipated that Vietnam would soon become a member of ASEAN.

ASEAN celebrated its 25th anniversary in 1992. Some internal strains were evident. One was ASEAN policy toward the PRC. China has long been a serious concern to ASEAN governments, and thus they have been slow to establish formal relations. Malaysia was the first to accord diplomatic recognition in 1974, followed by Thailand and the Philippines in 1975. Indonesia, with the most reservations, only exchanged diplomats in 1990. Singapore in 1992 appeared to want closer ASEAN-PRC relations. Indonesia opposed the idea. ASEAN relations with the PRC have been made more difficult by China's pouring of guns and people into northern Burma and by the PRC's occupation of the Paracel, Spratly, and other islands and reefs deep in the South China Sea, some of which may have oil. These islands are variously claimed by Vietnam, the Philippines, and Malaysia.

At the end of the 1980s, the focus of regional cooperation shifted to trade. Proposals for a trading group were heard, motivated in part by the example of European Economic Cooperation and later by the creation of the North American Free Trade Agreement (NAFTA). Proposals were put forward by Indonesia, Malaysia, and Thailand. The objective was and is to expand trade between members by reducing tariffs and other impediments to trade. The United States insisted on participating, and favored a larger trading group. It helped to sponsor the Asia-Pacific Economic Cooperation forum (APEC). APEC's first meeting was held in Seattle in 1993. A second meeting was held in Jakarta in November 1994. Open to "Pacific Rim" countries, some eighteen governments participated, including Chile. APEC headquarters is in Singapore. It is mainly a consulting group and lacks means to enforce decisions. At the 1994 meeting, the goal of free trade among all its members by the year 2020 was set with an earlier date, 2010, of free trade for Japan, the United States, and other "developed" nations. The General Agreement on Tariffs and Trade (GATT) efforts to reduce trade barriers—the "Uruguay round" completed in December 1993—and the creation of its successor, the World Trade Organization in 1995, are all supportive of APEC. Backing up its economic diplomacy, the United States has repeatedly said it will keep a strong "security presence in Asia."

Conclusions

In the years after the end of the Japanese occupation, many observers doubted that the peoples of Southeast Asia would be able to create and sustain their own independent governments. These doubts were expressed not only by the ousted colonialists—some of whom could not imagine how they could be replaced by natives—but also by political observers, scholars, and even some Southeast Asians. Communism threatened several of the new states in the early years of independence. Ethnic divisions (see table) have caused much strife. The onset of the cold war was also threatening to the new nations of Southeast Asia. There has indeed been much strife and turmoil and not a few deaths. Horrendous social and economic problems remain in at least half of the countries. But in fact after a half century, the countries of the region have survived and a few have done well, bringing important benefits to their citizens.

Population of Southeast Asia, 1955 and 1994

1955 Population (Millions)	Country	1994 Population (Millions)	Life Expectancy (Male)	% Natural Increase (Annual)	Ethnic Composition Majority/Minority
—	Brunei	0.3	69	2.1	Malay/Chinese
4.5	Cambodia	10.3	48	2.9	Khmer/Vietnamese
80.0	Indonesia	200.4	59	1.6	Indonesian/Chinese
2.0	Laos	4.7	50	2.8	Lao/Thai
5.7	Malaysia	19.2	66	2.3	Malay/Chinese
18.0	Myanmar	44.2	58	1.9	Burmese/Shan
21.0	Philippines	69.8	63	2.0	Malay/Chinese
1.12	Singapore	2.9	73	1.1	Chinese/Malay
19.5	Thailand	59.5	65	1.3	Thai/Chinese
21.0	Vietnam	73.1	63	1.9	Vietnamese/Chinese
	Total	484.4			

Notes: Sources are *The World Almanac* (1995) and *Whitaker's Almanac* (1995) and D.G.E. Hall, *A History of Southeast Asia* (1968), p. 869; "Minority" is largest minority.

Answers to questions about kinds of government and the meaning of democracy are still evolving but have been answered in part. Several countries opted for multiparty, parliamentary systems but soon found them too slow, too costly, and too divisive. Social and economic goals seemed unattainable. They were replaced by systems in which the executive possessed considerable power. Hence the appearance of "guided democracy" and what some have called "maximum government." In these regimes, authoritarian in varying degree, the military usually played large roles. Officers were rewarded with participation in the economy in ways that allowed them to acquire rich assets and lucrative incomes. Single, dominant parties became the rule. And these were sometimes created by those in control to bolster their own power.

Of the kinds of economies adopted by the countries of Southeast Asia, socialism was not a good choice. But it may also be said that capitalism, at least like that of the contemporary western model, has only been partly adopted. The governments of the countries with successful economies have eschewed ideology and practiced pragmatism. They have often first determined the social and/or economic goal they wanted to achieve, and then chosen the means to achieve it. This has frequently meant a combination of public and private capital and the use of government bureaucrats as entrepreneurs and managers. Southeast Asian governments have not hesitated to plan, to create, to invest, to own, and to manage state corporations. The economically successful regimes used their best-educated persons to plan, advise, and manage investments. They also made use of their resident capitalists and managers, usually the Chinese, and opened their doors to large multinational corporations. Economic success has been accompanied by waste, inefficiency, and corruption as well as use of development for political purposes, such as patronage. No one term has been agreed upon for these kinds of economies, but some of the names applied to them have been "market oriented," "market socialist," "market Leninist," "developmental authoritarianism," and "bureaucratic capitalism." The consequences of state participation in the economy have been the enrichment of individuals—politicians, Army officers and bureaucrats—and increasing disparities of wealth between social classes. The political consequences are many; the most obvious has been the perpetuation of ruling parties and politicians in power.

Beginning in the 1980s, privatization of state-owned enterprises became fashionable. Governments sold portions—percentages of stock—to private investors whom it was believed could run the businesses more cheaply and efficiently. But privatization has produced its problems. Bureaucrats who operate the state enterprises have often been reluctant to go along with the change; privileged persons have acquired privileged access to the stock. In many cases, governments have retained large ownership positions. Government participation in economic activity appears likely to continue for a long time to come.

The very large, dynamic, and sustained economic growth in certain countries has dramatically increased the number of middle class and professional persons and increased intellectual activity and diversity of political views. The political ramifications of large, growing, and more sophisticated middle classes in several countries together with better-educated populations generally will hold the attention of observers in the years ahead. Authoritarian regimes are under pressure to allow more political freedom. The dismantling of authoritarian rule has everywhere been difficult. What steps to take, how large the steps should be, and when to take them are questions not easily answered even assuming a willingness to move toward political freedom.

Where economic gains have been the largest, there have been worries about values. Some individuals see values as the most important key to the future social, economic, and political well-being of their countries. Governments want modern economies and higher living standards. But they worry about materialism, secularism, and the increasing penetration of western ideas and practices. They know what they do not want—crime, drugs, broken families, moral decline generally—citing the experience of western countries and especially the United States. They seek progress in their own way. Most Southeast Asian governments have, each to a greater or lesser degree, tried to promote and shape values, usually invoking their own history and tradition.

It is too early to know whether and in what ways these efforts will succeed.

Suggestions for Further Reading

Anderson, Benedict, *Java in a Time of Revolution* (1972).

Bellows, Thomas J., *The People's Action Party of Singapore* (1970).

Bresnan, John, *Managing Indonesia: The Modern Political Economy* (1993).

Cady, John F., *A History of Modern Burma* (1958).

Chandler, David P., *A History of Cambodia* (1992).

Chan Heng Chee, *The Sensation of Independence: A Political Biography of David Marshall* (1984).

Chew, Ernest C. T., and Edwin Lee, *Singapore* (1991).

Coedes, G., *Angkor, An Introduction*. Translated and edited by Emily Gardner (1963).

——, *Indianized States of Southeast Asia*. Translated by Susan Brown Cowing and edited by Walter F. Vella (1968).

Duiker, William J., *The Rise of Nationalism in Vietnam, 1900–1941* (1976).

Frederick, William H., *Visions and Heat: The Making of the Indonesian Revolution* (1989).

Friend, Theodore, *Between Two Empires: The Ordeal of the Philippines, 1929–1946* (1965).

Furnivall, John, *Colonial Policy and Practice: A Comparative Study of Burma and the Netherlands India* (1948).

Geertz, Clifford, *The Religion of Java* (1960).

Gullick, John M., *Malaysia: Its Political and Economic Development* (1986).

Halberstam, David, *HO* (1987).

Hirschman, Charles, *Ethnic and Social Stratification in Peninsular Malaysia* (1975).

Holt, Claire, *Art in Indonesia: Continuities and Change* (1967).

Holt, Claire, et al. (eds.), *Culture and Politics in Indonesia* (1972).

Kahin, George McT., *Intervention: How America Became Involved in Vietnam* (1987).

——, *Nationalism and Revolution in Indonesia* (1952).

Keyes, Charles F., *The Golden Peninsula: Culture and Adaptation in Mainland Southeast Asia* (1977).

Legge, J. D., *Sukarno: A Political Biography* (1972).

Leur, J. C. van, *Indonesian Trade and Society*. Translated by James S. Holmes and A. van Marle (1968).

Lev, Daniel, *Islamic Courts in Indonesia: A Study in the Political Bases of Legal Institutions* (1972).

Lim, Linda, *Women Workers in Multinational Corporations: The Case of the Electronics Industry in Malaysia and Singapore* (1978).

Lim, Linda, and Peter Gosling (eds.), *The Chinese in Southeast Asia* (1983). Two volumes.

Mahathir bin Mohamad, *The Malay Dilemma* (1970).

Marr, David G., *Vietnamese Tradition on Trial, 1920–1945* (1981).

Marr, David G., and A. C. Milner (eds.), *Southeast Asia in the Ninth to Fourteenth Centuries* (1986).

McVey, Ruth T., *The Rise of Indonesian Communism* (1965).

Milne, R. S. Mauzy, *Singapore: The Legacy of Lee Kuan Yew* (1990).

Muscat, Robert J., *Thailand and the United States: Development, Security and Foreign Aid* (1990).

Nguyen Thi Dinh, *No Other Road to Take: Memoir.* Translated by Mai Elliott (1976).

Osborne, Milton E., *Sihanouk: Prince of Light, Prince of Darkness* (1994).

Parmer, J. Norman, *Colonial Labor Policy and Practice* (1960).

Purcell, Victor, *Chinese in Southeast Asia* (1980).

Quah, Jon S. T., *Government and Politics of Singapore.* Edited by Chan Heng Chee and Seah Chee Meow (1985).

Reid, Anthony, *Southeast Asia in the Age of Commerce, 1450–1680* (1988–1993). Two volumes.

Reid, Anthony, and David Marr (eds.), *Perceptions of the Past in Southeast Asia* (1979).

Roff, William R., *The Origins of Malay Nationalism* (1967).

Sharom Ahmat, *Tradition and Change in a Malay State: A Study of the Economic and Political Development of Kedah, 1878–1923* (1984).

Silverstein, Josef, *Burmese Politics: The Dilemma of National Unity* (1980).

Skinner, William, *Chinese Society in Thailand: An Analytical History* (1957).

Steinberg, David, *The Future of Burma: Crisis and Choice in Myanmar* (1990).

———, *The Philippines, A Singular and Plural Place* (1990).

Taylor, Keith, *The Birth of Vietnam: Sino-Vietnamese Relations to the Tenth Century and the Origins of Vietnamese Nationhood* (1983).

Taruc, Luis, *Born of the People* (1973).

Van Niel, Robert, *The Emergence of the Modern Indonesia Elite* (1960).

Vella, Walter F., *Chaiyo! King Vajiravudh and the Development of the Thai Nation* (1978).

Wang, Gungwu, *China and the Chinese Overseas* (1991).

Wyatt, David K., *Thailand: A Short History* (1986).

Wickberg, Edgar, *The Chinese in Philippine Life, 1859–1898* (1965).

Wolters, O. W., *The Fall of Srivijaya in Malay History* (1970).

Woodward, Mark R., *Islam in Java: Normative Piety and Mysticism in the Sultanate of Yogyakarta* (1989).

Glossary

Adat: (Malaysia, Indonesia) Customary law.

Abangan: Javanese who incorporate much animism and Hindu-Buddhist belief and practice into their Islamic faith.

Annam: One of three major parts of Vietnam together with Tonkin in the north and Cochin China in the south. For centuries and even today, Chinese refer to Vietnam as Annam.

Avatar: Human form of a god.

Barangay: In pre-Spanish Philippines, a community of families headed by a datu, a chief. Under Spanish rule, a number of families classified as a subdivision of a municipality.

Bupati: In pre-Dutch Java, a chief whose power was based on his control over households or fighting men and who gave his loyalty to a king. Under Dutch, the bupati, now called regent, became an official identified with a specific territory and responsible for mobilizing labor and collecting crops in the Cultivation System.

Corvée: A number of days' labor annually required by king of every man in Thailand and elsewhere, monks and aristocracy excepted. A tax.

Dai Viet: "Great Viet." Official name of Vietnam, 1054–1802.

Dai Nam: "Great South." Official name of Vietnam, 1838–1945.

Dakwah: A movement of the late twentieth century consisting of a loose and diverse collection of individuals and organizations voluntarily seeking to revive Islam and purify religious practices among the Malay people.

Datus, caciques: In the Philippines, local officials, bosses. The datu was head of a barangay (see above). The cacique was and is a local chief or boss; used pejoratively, caciquism or bossism. Both collected taxes for the Spanish and locally carried out official tasks; also served as agents for moneylenders.

Doi Moi: (Vietnam) Term given to political and market-oriented economic reforms from the 1980s.

Dong Kinh Nghia Thuc: Private "free school" opened briefly in Hanoi in 1907. It taught modern subjects, promoted the use of romanized Vietnamese, regarded Confucian culture as anachronistic.

Halus: (Indonesia, Java) Fine, polished, sophisticated behavior typical of the priyayi. Indicative of personal self-control, self-discipline.

Hlutdaw: In the Burmese kingdom, a council of four to seven members, who met daily and dealt with executive, legislative, and judicial affairs.

Ilustrados: "Learned." Spanish term applied to Filipino well-to-do, urban, educated, and mestizo class, about 1870–1920. Many were active in political and economic reform, even revolutionary, efforts under Spanish rule.

Kapitan: Title given to Chinese community chief by colonial authorities in Indonesia and Malaysia in late nineteenth and early twentieth centuries. For authorities, a means of indirect rule of Chinese population.

Kasar: (Indonesia, Java) Rough, crude, undisciplined behavior as might be displayed by a farmer.

Kaum Muda/Kaum Tua: Malay terms for Malay intelligentsia. Kaum Muda, the younger group—influenced by ideas and Muslim religious reform efforts in the Middle East—sought to rid Islam of its non-Islamic accretions. Kaum Tua, the older group, was represented by the aristocracy and state religious authorities who were satisfied with the status quo. Terms also used in Indonesia.

Kraton: A Javanese king's palace, a large complex of pavilions, courtyards enclosed by walls and moats. At the center of the kingdom.

Mandalas: "Circles of kings."

Mataram: Kingdoms in the south of central Java. The first existed from the eighth through early tenth centuries. A later Mataram kingdom existed from the sixteenth to the mid-eighteenth century. Most important ruler of the latter was Sultan Agung (1613–1641), who fought the Dutch in 1628–1629.

Merdeka: (Malay, Indonesia) "Freedom," "political independence."

Min-laung: In Burma, an "embryo king," one who is in process of becoming a king.

Mission civilatrice: French term used to describe one of the major purposes for French imperial expansion in the late nineteenth century: to spread French civilization to non-European peoples.

Muang: (Thailand) "Province."

Muhammadiyah: (Indonesia) Islamic reform movement founded in 1912, based on the modern ideas of Muhammad Abduh of Cairo. Aim was and is to revitalize Islam.

Myothugyi: In pre-British Burma, local officals, headmen of townships.

Myowun: (Burma) "Province."

Negara: Malay word for nation.

Negeri: A large Muslim Malay community lacking precisely defined borders and ruled by a sultan. It was the largest Malay territorial unit. In the twentieth century under British rule, the term gradually came to mean a Malay state.

Pali: Written language derived from the Indian classical language, Sanskrit, in which the oldest extant Buddhist scriptures were written.

Pancasila: Indonesian state philosophy. Five principles: belief in the one God, a just society, unity, democracy, and social justice.

Pemuda: Indonesian term for youth. Revolutionary connotation during Indonesian revolution.

Peranakan: Chinese long resident in Indonesia and Malaysia. Many had taken Indonesian or Malay wives and acquired some Indonesian culture and developed their own distinctive culture.

Pondok/pesantren: Islamic schools or communities of scholars usually found in rural areas in some Malay states, Java, and elsewhere. In the twentieth century, these traditional schools have had to compete with modern religious and secular schools.

Priyayi: Javanese officials of the king, later of the Dutch. Distinguished by dress, language, loyalty, a strong sense of honor, and an elaborate code of etiquette. Their proper, halus, behavior was an outward sign of self-control and spiritual merit.

Quoc-ngu: "National language." Romanized form of written Vietnamese language, in use today. Devised by Alexandre de Rhodes, missionary, in the seventeenth century.

Ratu adil: In Java, the just prince, who will appear and deliver the people from injustice.

Sangha: Buddhist community of enlightened men and women; monks or nuns. The monkhood.

Santri: Javanese who more strictly observe Islamic principles as opposed to Abangan.

Sinkhehs: Chinese term for "coolie" laborers brought to Southeast Asia to work on mines, estates, public works.

Taman Siswa: A "garden of pupils." Local schools in Indonesia begun in 1922 which aim to provide a modern, secular, nonpolitical curriculum while maintaining Javanese culture and instilling self-confidence.

Thathanabaing: Head of Buddhist hierarchy in Burma, prestigious office, appointed by the king from the most senior persons in the sangha.

Thugyi: In Burma, a village headman.

Totoks: Term applied to recent immigrants to Indonesia. Frequently applied to unassimilated Chinese immigrants.

Tributary system: That by which Southeast Asian kings periodically sent missions to China to acknowledge the Chinese emperor as overlord and to present gifts. The emperor reciprocated with gifts of his own. Sometimes a form of trade and a means to help strengthen or legitimize the king's claim to his throne.

Tipitaka: Pali word for Buddhist scripture. Tipitaka is in three parts or collections: **Vinaya** (laws); **Sutra** (Buddha's discourses); and **Ahbidharma** (Buddha's philosophies).

Yang di-pertuan Agung, or **Agung:** Malaysian Supreme Head of State, or King.

Index

for The World of China

Index
for The World of India

Index
for The World of Japan

Index

for The World of Korea

420

Index

for The World of Southeast Asia

The World of Asia, Second Edition, was copyedited and proofread by the team of Maureen Hewitt, Andrew J. Davidson, and Lucy Herz. Text design and production by Lucy Herz. Maps by Jim Bier. Bruce Leckie set the type, and the book was first printed and bound by BookCrafters, Inc.

Cover design by Jay Bensen.

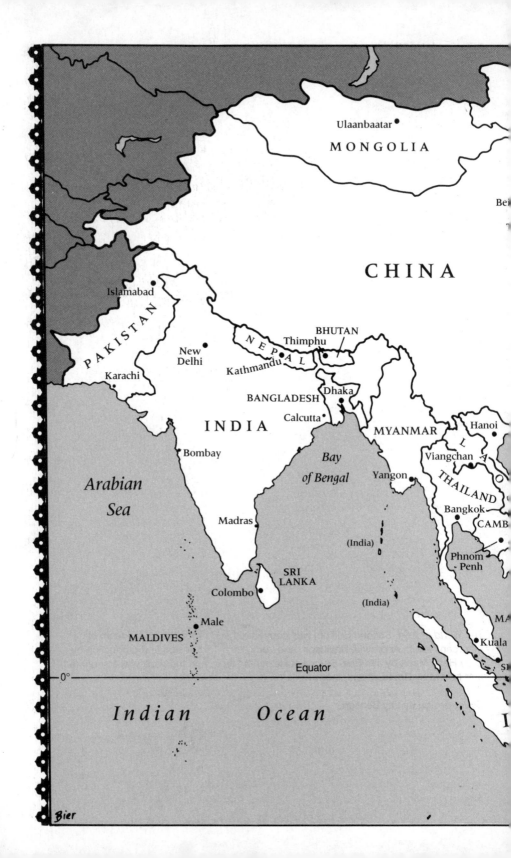